I0199988

ΠΝΕΥΜΑΤΟΛΟΓΙΑ

Pneumatologia

Or, A Discourse Concerning the Holy Spirit

Volume I

By John Owen

This Edition Edited By Anthony Uyl

Ingersoll, Ontario, Canada 2020

ΠΝΕΥΜΑΤΟΛΟΓΙΑ
Pneumatologia
Or, A Discourse Concerning the Holy Spirit
Volume I
By John Owen
This Edition Edited By Anthony Uyl

What kind of philosophies do you have?
Let us know!

Contact us at: devotedpub@hotmail.com
Visit us on Facebook: @DevotedPublishing
See the full catalogue of Devoted Publishing books at:
http://www.lulu.com/spotlight/devotedpublishing

Published in Ingersoll, Ontario, Canada 2020

For bulk educational rates, please contact us at the above email address.

ISBN: 978-1-77356-402-9

Note: This is a revised edition of the original Devoted Publishing edition. The text hasn't changed just some print size, formatting and footnote layouts have been altered.

Wherein an Account is Given of His Name, Nature, Personality, Operations, and Effects; His Whole Work in the Old and New Creation is Explained; the Doctrine Concerning it Vindicated from Oppositions and Reproaches.

The Nature and Necessity of Gospel Holiness; the Differences Between Grace and Morality, or a Spiritual Life Unto God in Evangelical Obedience and a Course of Moral Virtues, are Stated and Declared.

Search the Scriptures, etc. — John v. 39.

Ἐκ τῶν θείων γραφᾶν θεολογοῦμεν, καὶ θέλωσιν οἱ ἐχθροὶ, καὶ μή. — Chrysostom.

London: 1674.

Table of Contents

Prefatory note

The year 1674 saw issuing from the press some of the most elaborate productions of our author. Besides his own share in the Communion controversy, he published in the course of that year the second volume of his Exposition of the Epistle to the Hebrews, and another folio of equal extent and importance, the first part of his work on the Holy Spirit; for what is generally known under the title of "Owen on the Holy Spirit," is but the first half of a treatise on that subject. The treatise was completed in successive publications:— "The Reason of Faith," in 1677; "The Causes, Ways, and Means of Understanding the Mind of God," etc., in 1678; "The Work of the Holy Spirit in Prayer," in 1682; and, in 1693, two posthumous discourses appeared, "On the Work of the Spirit as a Comforter, and as he is the Author of Spiritual Gifts." From the statements of Owen himself, in various parts of these works, as well as on the authority of Nathaniel Mather, who wrote the preface to the last of them, we learn that they were all included in one design, and must be regarded as one entire and uniform work. In Owen's preface to the "Reason of Faith," he expressly states, "About three years since I published a book about the dispensation and operations of the Spirit of God. That book was one part only of what I designed on that subject. The consideration of the work of the Holy Spirit as the Spirit of illumination, of supplication, of consolation, and as the immediate author of all spiritual offices and gifts, extraordinary and ordinary, is designed unto the second part of it." Uncertain, as he advanced in years, whether he should be spared to finish it, Owen was induced to issue separately the treatises belonging to the second part, according as he was able, under the pressure of other duties, to overtake the preparation and completion of them. They are now for the first time collected, and arranged into the order which, it is believed, the author would have made them assume, had he lived to publish an edition comprehending all his treatises on the Holy Spirit in the form and under the title of one work. No other liberty, however, is taken with the treatises than simply to number the four of them which were published separately, and which are contained in the next volume, as so many additional books, continuing and completing the discussion of the subject which had been begun and so far prosecuted in the five previous books embraced in this volume. To all of them the general designation πνευματολογια is equally applicable. Thus arranged and seen in its full proportions, the work amply vindicates the commendation bestowed on it, as the most complete exhibition of the doctrine of Scripture on the person and agency of the Spirit "to be found in any language." As no author had previously attempted to treat "of the whole economy of the Holy Spirit, with all his adjuncts, operations, and effects," Owen urges the circumstance in extenuation of any want of system and lucid order in his work. If such an attempt had never previously been made, it is equally true that no successor has been found in this walk of theology who has ventured to compete with Owen in the fall and systematic discussion of this great theme. Treatises of eminent ability and value have appeared on separate departments of it; but in the wide range embraced in this work of Owen, as well as in the power, depth, and resources conspicuous in every chapter, it is not merely first, but single and alone in all our religious literature.

The work, as we may gather from various allusions in it, was written in opposition to the rationalism of the early Socinians, especially as represented by Crellius; to the mysticism of the Quakers, a sect which had grown into notoriety within thirty years before the publication of this work; and to the irreligion of a time when the derision of all true piety was the passport to royal favour. That, during the religious fervours of the commonwealth, fanaticism of various kinds should appear, is no more strange than that when genuine coin is in circulation, attempts should be made to utter what is counterfeit and base. Against such fanaticism it was natural that a reaction should ensue, and certain divines pandered to the blind prejudice of the times succeeding the Restoration, by sarcastic invective against all that was evangelical in the creed of the Puritans and vital in personal godliness. Samuel Parker, in his infamous subserviency to the malice of the Court against dissent, and even against the common interests of Protestantism, distinguished himself in this assault upon the doctrines of grace and the distinctive principles of the Christian faith. Owen accordingly administers to him a rebuke in terms as severe as the calm dignity of his temper ever allowed him to employ in controversy; but the prominent aim in his whole work is to discriminate the gracious operations of the Spirit in the hearts of believers from the excesses of fanaticism on the one hand, whether as it appeared in the ruder sects of the age, or in the more genial mysticism of the Quaker, elevating his subjective experience of a spiritual light to co-ordinate authority with the objective revelation of God in the word; and, on the other hand, from the morality which, springing from no gracious principle, scarcely brooked an appeal to the only divine code for the regulation of human conduct.

This comprehensive treatise abounds in more than Owen's usual prolixity; — a feature of the work which may, perhaps, be explained by the consciousness under which the author seems always to labour that he is prosecuting an argument with opponents, rather than dealing with the conscience in a treatise on practical religion. He moves heavily, as if he were panoplied for conflict rather than girt for useful work. As he proceeds, however, the interest deepens; weighty questions receive clear elucidation; practical difficulties are judiciously resolved; and momentous distinctions, such as those between gospel holiness and common morality, and between natural and moral inability, are skilfully given. Indeed, many points which he brings out with sufficient precision, when stripped of the wordiness which encumbers them, are found to be identical with certain modes in the presentation of divine truth which have been deemed the discoveries and improvements of a later theology. No work of the author supplies better evidence of his pre-eminent skill in what may be termed spiritual ethics, — in tracing the effect of religious truth on the conscience, and the varied phases of human feeling as modified by divine grace and tested by the divine word; and his reasonings would have been reputed highly philosophical if they had not been so very scriptural.

It is in reference to the following work that Cecil, an acute and rather severe judge of books and authors, has observed, "Owen stands at the head of his class of divines. His scholars will be more profound and enlarged, and better furnished, than those of most other writers. His work on the Spirit has been my treasure-house, and one of my very firstrate books." A good abridgment of it by the Rev. G. Burder has appeared in more than one edition.

In 1678, Dr Clagett, preacher to the Honourable Society of Gray's Inn, and one of his Majesty's chaplains in ordinary, in "A Discourse concerning the Operation of the Holy Spirit," etc., attempted "a confutation of some part of Dr Owen's work on that subject." Mr John Humfrey, in his "Peaceable Disquisitions," having animadverted on the spirit in which Clagett had dealt with Owen, Clagett published another volume, and promised a third on the opinions of the Fathers respecting the points at issue. The manuscript of this last volume was lost in a fire which consumed the house of a friend with whom it had been lodged. Henry Stebbing published, in 1719, an abridgment of the first two volumes. The principles of the work are not evangelical; a tone of cold pedantry pervades it; and the author seems as much influenced by a desire to differ from Owen as to discover the truth in regard to the points on which they differed.

Analysis

The first book of the treatise is devoted to considerations of a general and preliminary nature. The promise of spiritual gifts contained in Scripture is examined; and occasion is hence taken to illustrate the importance of sound views on the doctrine of the Spirit, from the place it holds in Scripture; from the abuses practised under his name; from certain pretences that were urged to inward light, inconsistent with the claims of the Spirit of God; from many dangerous opinions which had become prevalent respecting his work and influence; and from the opposition directly offered to the Spirit and his work in the world, chap. i. The name and titles of the Holy Spirit are next considered, ii. The evidence of his divine nature and personality follows, from the formula of our initiation into the covenant, Matt. xxviii. 19; from the visible sign of his personal existence, Matt. iii. 16; from the personal properties ascribed to him; from the personal acts he performs; and from those acts towards him on the part of men which imply his personality. A short proof of his Godhead, from the divine names he receives, and the divine properties ascribed to him, is appended to the argument in illustration of his personality, iii. The work of the Spirit in the old creation, in reference to the heavens, to the earth, to man, and to the continued sustentation of the universe, is fully explained, iv. The dispensation of the Spirit is illustrated in reference to the Father as giving, sending him, etc., and in reference to his own voluntary and personal agency as proceeding, coming, etc., v.

In the second book, the peculiar operations of the Holy Spirit under the old testament, and in preparation for the new, are considered, such as prophecy, inspiration, miracles, and other gifts, i. The importance of the Holy Spirit in the new creation is proved by the fact that he is the subject of the great promise in sacred Scripture respecting new testament times, ii. His work in reference to Christ is unfolded under a twofold aspect, — 1. As it bore on himself, in framing his human nature, iii.; sanctifying it in the instant of conception, filling it with the needful grace, anointing it with extraordinary gifts, conveying to it miraculous powers, guiding, comforting, and supporting Christ, enabling him to offer himself without spot unto God, preserving his human nature in the state of the dead, raising it from the grave, and finally glorifying it; and, 2. As he secures, throughout successive ages, a sound and explicit testimony to the person and work of Christ, iv. General considerations are urged regarding the work of the Spirit in the new creation, as it relates to the mystical body of Christ, — all believers, v.

The third book is occupied with the subject of regeneration as the especial work of the Spirit; it is shown not to consist in baptism merely, or external reformation, or enthusiastic raptures, i. The operations of the Spirit preparatory to regeneration are exhibited, such as illumination, conviction, etc., ii. Two important chapters of a digressive character follow, in which the condition of man by nature is stated, as spiritually blind and impotent, iii., and as spiritually dead, iv. The true nature of regeneration is next illustrated, — first negatively, under which head it is proved not to consist in any result of moral suasion, moral suasion being defined, and the extent of its efficacy being fixed. No change which it can effect can be viewed as tantamount to regeneration, because, — 1. It leaves the will undetermined; 2. Imparts no supernatural strength; 3. Is not all we pray for when we pray for efficient grace; 4. And does not actually produce regeneration or conversion. Regeneration is then considered positively, as implying all the moral operation which means can effect, and not only a moral but a physical immediate operation of the Spirit, and the irresistibility of this internal efficiency on the minds of men. After explanations to the effect that the Holy Ghost in regeneration acts according to our mental nature, does not act upon us by an influence such as inspiration, and offers no violence to the will, three arguments in support of this view of regeneration are given, — from the collation of faith by the power of God, from the victorious efficacy of internal grace as attested by Scripture, and from the nature of the work itself as described in various terms of Scripture, "quickening," "regeneration," etc., and also from the terms in which the effect of grace on the different faculties of the soul is represented, v. The manner of conversion is then explained in the instance of Augustine, the account by that eminent father of his own conversion being selected to illustrate both the outward means of conversion, and the various degrees and effects of spiritual influence on the human mind, vi.

The fourth book discusses the doctrine of sanctification, which is exhibited as the process completing what the act of regeneration has begun. A general view is then given of the nature of sanctification, as consisting, 1. In external dedication; and, 2. In internal purification, i. Its progressive character is unfolded, ii.; and that it is a gracious process, extending to believers only, is proved, iii. Sanctification, so far as it relates to the removal of spiritual defilement, is illustrated; and that man cannot purge himself from his natural pravity is proved, iv. It is shown how the Spirit and blood of Christ are effectual to the purgation of the heart and conscience, the Spirit efficaciously, the blood of Christ meritoriously, faith as the instrumental cause, and afflictions as a subordinate instrumentality, v. The positive work of sanctification follows, embracing evidence of two propositions: 1. That the Spirit implants a supernatural habit and principle enabling believers to obey the divine will, and differing from all natural habits, intellectual or moral; and, 2. That grace is requisite for every act of acceptable obedience. Under the first proposition four things are considered, — the reality of the principle asserted; its nature in inclining the will; the power as well as the inclination it imparts; and, lastly, its specific difference from all other habits, vi. Under the second proposition the acts and duties of holiness are reviewed, and proof supplied of the necessity of grace for them, vii. The nature of the mortification of sin, as a special part of sanctification, is considered; directions for this spiritual exercise are given; particular means for the mortification of sin are specified; and certain errors respecting this duty corrected, viii.

The fifth book simply contains arguments for the necessity of holiness, — from the nature of God, i.; from eternal election, ii.; from the divine commands, iii.; from the mission of Christ, iv.; and from our condition in this world, v.— Ed.

To the readers

An account in general of the nature and design of the ensuing discourse, with the reasons why it is made public at this time, being given in the first chapter of the treatise itself, I shall not long detain the readers here at the entrance of it. But some few things it is necessary they should be acquainted withal, and that both as to the matter contained in it and as to the manner of its handling. The subject-matter of the whole, as the title and almost every page of the book declare, is, the Holy Spirit of God and his operations. And two things there are which, either of them, are sufficient to render any subject either difficult on the one hand, or unpleasant on the other, to be treated of in this way, both which we have herein to conflict withal: for where the matter itself is abstruse and mysterious, the handling of it cannot be without its difficulties; and where it is fallen, by any means whatever, under public contempt and scorn, there is an abatement of satisfaction in the consideration and defence of it. Now, all the concernments of the Holy Spirit are an eminent part of the "mystery" or "deep things of God;" for as the knowledge of them doth wholly depend on and is regulated by divine revelation, so are they in their own nature divine and heavenly, — distant and remote from all things that the heart of man, in the mere exercise of its own reason or understanding, can rise up unto. But yet, on the other hand, there is nothing in the world that is more generally despised as foolish and contemptible than the things that are spoken of and ascribed unto the Spirit of God. He needs no furtherance in the forfeiture of his reputation with many, as a person fanatical, estranged from the conduct of reason, and all generous principles of conversation, who dares avow an interest in His work, or take upon him the defence thereof. Wherefore, these things must be a little spoken unto, if only to manifest whence relief may be had against the discouragements wherewith they are attended.

For the first thing proposed, it must be granted that the things here treated of are in themselves mysterious and abstruse. But yet, the way whereby we may endeavour an acquaintance with them, "according to the measure of the gift of Christ unto every one," is made plain in the Scriptures of truth. If this way be neglected or despised, all other ways of attempting the same end, be they never so vigorous or promising, will prove ineffectual. What belongs unto it as to the inward frame and disposition of mind in them who search after understanding in these things, what unto the outward use of means, what unto the performance of spiritual duties, what unto conformity in the whole soul unto each discovery of truth that is attained, is not my present work to declare, nor shall I divert thereunto. If God give an opportunity to treat concerning the work of the Holy Spirit, enabling us to understand the Scriptures, or the mind of God in them, the whole of this way will be at large declared.

At present, it may suffice to observe, that God, who in himself is the eternal original spring and fountain of all truth, is also the only sovereign cause and author of its revelation unto us. And whereas that truth, which originally is one in him, is of various sorts and kinds, according to the variety of the things which it respects in its communication unto us, the ways and means of that communication are suited unto the distinct nature of each truth in particular. So the truth of things natural is made known from God by the exercise of reason, or the due application of the understanding that is in man unto their investigation; for "the things of a man knoweth the spirit of a man that is in him." Neither, ordinarily, is there any thing more required unto that degree of certainty of knowledge in things of that nature whereof our minds are capable, but the diligent application of the faculties of our souls, in the due use of proper means, unto the attainment thereof. Yet is there a secret work of the Spirit of God herein, even in the communication of skill and ability in things natural, as also in things civil, moral, political, and artificial; as in our ensuing discourse is fully manifested. But whereas these things belong unto the work of the old creation and the preservation thereof, or the rule and government of mankind in this world merely as rational creatures, there is no use of means, no communication of aids, spiritual or supernatural, absolutely necessary to be exercised or granted about them. Wherefore, knowledge and wisdom in things of this nature are distributed promiscuously among all sorts of persons, according to the foundation of their natural abilities, and a superstruction thereon in their diligent exercise, without any peculiar application to God for especial grace or assistance, reserving still a liberty unto the sovereignty of divine Providence in the disposal of all men and their concerns.

But as to things supernatural, the knowledge and truth of them, the teachings of God are of another nature; and, in like manner, a peculiar application of ourselves unto him for instruction is required of us. In these things also there are degrees, according as they approach, on the one hand, unto the infinite abyss of the divine essence and existence, — as the eternal generation and incarnation of the Son, the procession and mission of the Holy Spirit, — or, on the other, unto those divine effects which are produced in our souls, whereof we have experience. According unto these degrees, as the divine condescension is exerted in their revelation, so ought our attention, in the exercise of faith, humility, and prayer, to be increased in our inquiries into them. For although all that diligence, in the use of outward means, necessary to the attainment of the knowledge of any other useful truth, be indispensably required in the pursuit of an acquaintance with these things also, yet if, moreover, there be not an addition of spiritual ways and means, suited in their own nature, and appointed of God, unto the receiving of supernatural light and the understanding of the deep things of God, our labour about them will in a great measure be but fruitless and unprofitable: for although the letter of the Scripture and the sense of the propositions are equally exposed to the reason of all mankind, yet the real spiritual knowledge of the things themselves is not communicated unto any but by the especial operation of the Holy Spirit. Nor is any considerable degree of insight into the doctrine of the mysteries of them attainable but by a due waiting on Him who alone giveth "the Spirit of wisdom and revelation in the knowledge of them;" for "the things of God knoweth no man but the Spirit of God," and they to whom by him they are revealed. Neither can the Scriptures be interpreted aright but by the aid of that Spirit by which they were indited; as Hierom affirms, and as I shall afterward fully prove. But in the use of the means mentioned we need not despond but that, seeing these things themselves are revealed that we may know God in a due manner and live unto him as we ought, we may attain such a measure of spiritual understanding in them as is useful unto our own and others' edification. They may, I say, do so who are not slothful in hearing or learning, but "by reason of use have their senses exercised to discern both good and evil."

Wherefore, the subject of the ensuing discourses being entirely things of this nature, in their several degrees of access unto God or ourselves, I shall give no account of any particular endeavours in my inquiries into them, but leave the judgment thereof unto the evidence of the effects produced thereby: only, whereas I know not any who ever went before me in this design of representing the whole economy of the Holy Spirit, with all his adjuncts, operations, and effects, whereof this is the first part (the attempt of Crellius in this kind being only to corrupt the truth in some few instances), as the difficulty of my work was increased thereby, so it may plead my excuse if any thing be found not to answer so regular a projection or just a method as the nature of the subject requireth and as was aimed at.

In the first part of the whole work, which concerneth the name, divine nature, personality, and mission of the Holy Spirit, I do but declare and defend the faith of the catholic church against the Socinians; with what advantage, with what contribution of light or evidence, strength or order, unto what hath been pleaded before by others, is left unto the learned readers to judge and determine. And in what concerns the adjuncts and properties of His mission and operation, some may, and I hope do, judge themselves not unbeholden unto me for administering an occasion unto them of deeper and better thoughts about them. The second part of our endeavour concerneth the work of the Holy Spirit in the old creation, both in its production, preservation, and rule. And whereas I had not therein the advantage of any one ancient or modern author to beat out the paths of truth before me, I have confined myself to express testimonies of Scripture, with such expositions of them as sufficiently evidence their own truth; though also they want not such a suffrage from others as may give them the reputation of some authority.

The like may be said of what succeeds in the next place, concerning His work under the New Testament, preparatory for the new creation, in the communication of all sorts of gifts, ordinary and extraordinary, all kind of skill and ability in things spiritual, natural, moral, artificial, and political, with the instances whereby these operations of this are confirmed.

All these things, many whereof are handled by others separately and apart, are here proposed in their order with respect unto their proper end and design.

For what concerns His work on the head of the new creation, or the human nature in the person of our Lord Jesus Christ, I have been careful to keep severely under the bounds of sobriety, and not to indulge unto any curious or unwarrantable speculations. I have, therefore, therein not only diligently attended unto the doctrine of the Scripture, our only infallible rule and guide, but also expressly considered what was taught and believed in the ancient church in this matter, from which I know that I have not departed.

More I shall not add as to the first difficulty wherewith an endeavour of this kind is attended, arising from the nature of the subject treated of. The other, concerning the contempt that is cast by many on all these things, must yet be farther spoken unto.

In all the dispensations of God towards his people under the Old Testament, there was nothing of good communicated unto them, nothing of worth or excellency wrought in them or by them, but it is expressly assigned unto the Holy Spirit as the author and cause of it. But yet, of all the promises given unto them concerning a better and more glorious state of the church to be afterward introduced, next unto that of the coming of the Son of God in the flesh, those are the most eminent which concern an enlargement and more full communication of the Spirit, beyond what they were or could in their imperfect state be made partakers of. Accordingly, we find in the New Testament, that whatever concerns the conversion of the elect, the edification of the church, the sanctification and consolation of believers, the performance of those duties of obedience which we owe unto God, with our conduct in all the ways thereof, is, in general and particular instances, so appropriated unto him, as that it is withal declared that nothing of it in any kind can be enjoyed or performed without his especial operation, aid, and assistance; so careful was God fully to instruct and to secure the faith of the church in this matter, according as he knew its eternal concernments to lie therein. Yet, notwithstanding all the evidence given hereunto, the church of God in most ages hath been exercised with oppositions either to his person, or his work, or the manner of it, contrary unto what is promised and declared concerning them in the word of truth; nor doth it yet cease so to be. Yea, though the contradictions of some in former ages have been fierce and clamorous, yet all that hath fallen out of that kind hath been exceeding short of what is come to pass in the days wherein we live; for, not to mention the Socinians, who have gathered into one head, or rather ulcerous imposthume, all the virulent oppositions made unto His deity or grace by the Photinians, Macedonians, and Pelagians of old, there are others, who, professing no enmity unto his divine person, yea, admitting and owning the doctrine of the church concerning it, are yet ready on all occasions to despise and reproach that whole work for which he was promised under the Old Testament, and which is expressly assigned unto him in the New. Hence is it grown amongst many a matter of reproach and scorn for any one to make mention of his grace, or to profess an interest in that work of his, as his, without which no man shall see God, if the Scripture be a faithful testimony; and some have taken pains to prove that sundry things which are expressly assigned unto him in the gospel as effects of his power and grace are only filthy enthusiasms, or at least weak imaginations of distempered minds. Neither is there any end of calumnious imputations on them by whom his work is avowed and his grace professed. Yea, the deportment of many herein is such as that, if it were not known how effectual the efforts of profaneness are upon the corrupted minds of men, it would rather seem ridiculous and [to] be despised than to deserve any serious notice: for let any avow or plead for the known work of the Spirit of God, and it is immediately apprehended a sufficient ground to charge them with leaving the rule of the word to attend unto revelations and inspirations, as also to forego all thoughts of the necessity of the duties of obedience; whereas no other work of his is pleaded for, but that only without which no man can either attend unto the rule of the Scripture as he ought, or perform any one duty of obedience unto God in a due manner. And there are none of this conspiracy so weak or unlearned but are able to scoff at the mention of him, and to cast the very naming of him on others as a reproach. Yea, it is well if some begin not to deal in like manner with the person of Christ himself; for error and profaneness, if once countenanced, are at all times fruitful and progressive, and will be so whilst, darkness and corruption abiding on the minds of men, the great adversary is able, by his subtle malice, to make impressions on them. But in these things not a few do please themselves, despise others, and would count themselves injured if their Christianity should be called in question. But what value is there in that name or title, where the whole mystery of the gospel is excluded out of our religion? Take away the dispensation of the Spirit, and his effectual operations in all the intercourse that is between God and man; be ashamed to avow or profess the work attributed unto him in the gospel, — and Christianity is plucked up by the roots. Yea, this practical contempt of the work of the Holy Spirit being grown the only plausible defiance of religion, is so also to be the most pernicious, beyond all notional mistakes and errors about the same things, being constantly accompanied with profaneness, and commonly issuing in atheism.

The sense I intend is fully expressed in the ensuing complaint of a learned person, published many years ago: " In seculo hodie tam perverso prorsus immersi vivimus miseri, in quo Spiritus Sanctus omnino ferme pro ludibrio habetur: imo in quo etiam sunt qui non tantum corde toto eum repudient ut factis negent, sed quoque adeo blasphemi in eum exsurgant ut penitus eundem ex orbe expulsum aut exulatum cupiant, quum illi nullam in operationibus suis relinquant efficaciam; ac propriis vanorum habituum suorum viribus, ac rationis profanæ libertati carnalitatique suæ omnem ascribant sapientiam, et fortitudinem in rebus agendis. Unde tanta malignitas externæ proterviæ apud mortales cernitur. Ideoque pernicies nostra nos jam ante fores expectat," etc. Herein lies the rise and spring of that stated apostasy from the power of evangelical truth, wherein the world takes its liberty to immerge itself in all licentiousness of life and conversation; the end whereof many cannot but expect with dread and terror.

To obviate these evils in any measure; to vindicate the truth and reality of divine spiritual operations in the church; to avow what is believed and taught by them concerning the Holy Spirit and his work who are most charged and reflected on for their profession thereof, and thereby to evince the iniquity of those calumnies under the darkness and shades whereof some seek to countenance themselves in their profane scoffing at his whole dispensation; to manifest in all instances that what is ascribed unto him is not only consistent with religion, but also that without which religion cannot consist, nor the power of it be preserved, — is the principal design of the ensuing discourses.

Now, whereas the effectual operation of the blessed Spirit in the regeneration or conversion of sinners is, of all other parts of this work, most violently opposed, and hath of late been virulently traduced, I have the more largely insisted thereon. And because it can neither be well understood nor duly explained without the consideration of the state of lapsed or corrupted nature, I have taken in that also at large, as judging it necessary so to do; for whereas the knowledge of it lies at the bottom of all our obedience unto God by Christ, it hath always been the design of some, and yet continueth so to be, either wholly to deny it, or to extenuate it unto the depression and almost annihilation of the grace of the gospel, whereby alone our nature can be repaired. Designing, therefore, to treat expressly of the reparation of our nature by grace, it was on all accounts necessary that we should treat of its depravation by sin also.

Moreover, what is discoursed on these things is suited unto the edification of them that do believe, and directed unto their furtherance in true spiritual obedience and holiness, or the obedience of faith. Hence, it may be, some will judge that our discourses on these subjects are drawn out into a greater length than was needful or convenient, by that continual intermixture of practical applications which runs along in them all. But if they shall be pleased to consider that my design was, not to handle these things in a way of controversy, but, declaring and confirming the truth concerning them, to accommodate the doctrines treated of unto practice, and that I dare not treat of things of this nature in any other way but such as may promote the edification of the generality of believers, they will either be of my mind, or, it may be, without much difficulty admit of my excuse. However, if these things are neglected or despised by some, yea, be they never so many, there are yet others who will judge their principal concernment to lie in such discourses as may direct and encourage them in the holy practice of their duty. And whereas the way, manner, and method of the Holy Spirit, in his operations as to this work of translating sinners from death unto life, from a state of nature unto that of grace, have been variously handled by some, and severely reflected on with scorn by others, I have endeavoured so to declare and assert what the Scripture manifestly teacheth concerning them, confirming it with the testimonies of some of the ancient writers of the church, as I no way doubt but it is suited unto the experience of them who have in their own souls been made partakers of that blessed work of the Holy Ghost. And whilst, in the substance of what is delivered, I have the plain testimonies of the Scripture, the suffrage of the ancient church, and the experience of them who do sincerely believe, to rest upon, I shall not be greatly moved with the censures and opposition of those who are otherwise minded.

I shall add no more on this head but that, whereas the only inconvenience wherewith our doctrine is pressed is the pretended difficulty in reconciling the nature and necessity of our duty with the efficacy of the grace of the Spirit, I have been so far from waiving the consideration of it, as that I have embraced every opportunity to examine it in all particular instances wherein it may be urged with most appearance of probability. And it is, I hope, at length made to appear, that not only the necessity of our duty is consistent with the efficacy of God's grace, but also, that as, on the one hand, we can perform no duty to God as we ought without its aid and assistance, nor have any encouragement to attempt a course of obedience without a just expectation thereof, so, on the other, that the work of grace itself is no way effectual but in our compliance with it in a way of duty: only, with the leave of some persons, or whether they will or no, we give the pre-eminence in all unto grace, and not unto ourselves. The command of God is the measure and rule of our industry and diligence in a way of duty; and why anyone should be discouraged from the exercise of that industry which God requires of him by the consideration of the aid and assistance which he hath promised unto him, I cannot understand. The work of obedience is difficult and of the highest importance; so that if anyone can be negligent therein because God will help and assist him, it is because he hates it, he likes it not. Let others do what they please, I shall endeavour to comply with the apostle's advice upon the enforcement which he gives unto it: "Work out your own salvation with fear and trembling; for it is God which worketh in you both to will and to do of his own good pleasure."

These things, with sundry of the like nature, falling unavoidably under consideration, have drawn out these discourses unto a length much beyond my first design; which is also the occasion why I have forborne the present adding unto them those other parts of the work of the Holy Spirit, in prayer or supplication, in illumination with respect unto the belief of the Scriptures and right understanding of the mind of God in them, in the communication of gifts unto the church, and in the consolation of believers; which must now wait for another opportunity, if God in his goodness and patience shall be pleased to grant it unto us. Another part of the work of the Holy Spirit consisteth in our sanctification, whereon our evangelical obedience or holiness doth depend. How much all his operations herein also are by some despised, what endeavours there have been to debase the nature of gospel-obedience, yea, to cast it out of the hearts and lives of Christians, and to substitute a heathenish honesty at best in the room thereof, is not unknown to any who think it their duty to inquire into these things. Hence I thought it not unnecessary, on the occasion of treating concerning the work of the Holy Spirit in our sanctification, to make a diligent and full inquiry into the true nature of evangelical holiness, and that spiritual life unto God which all believers are created unto in Christ Jesus. And herein, following the conduct of the Scriptures from first to last, the difference that is between them and that exercise of moral virtue which some plead for in their stead did so evidently manifest itself, as that it needs no great endeavour to represent it unto any impartial judgment. Only, in the handling of these things, I thought meet to pursue my former method and design, and principally to respect the reducing of the doctrines insisted on unto the practice and improvement of holiness; which also hath occasioned the lengthening of these discourses. I doubt not but all these things will be by some despised; they are so in themselves, and their declaration by me will not recommend them unto a better acceptation. But let them please themselves whilst they see good in their own imaginations; whilst the Scripture is admitted to be an infallible declaration of the will of God and the nature of spiritual things, and there are Christians remaining in the world who endeavour to live to God, and to come to the enjoyment of him by Jesus Christ, there will not want sufficient testimony against that putid figment of moral virtue being all our gospel holiness, or that the reparation of our natures and life unto God doth consist therein alone.

In the last place succeeds a discourse concerning the necessity of holiness and obedience.

Some regard, I confess, I had therein, though not much, unto the ridiculous clamours of malevolent and ignorant persons, charging those who plead for the efficacy of the grace of God and the imputation of the righteousness of Christ, as though thereby they took away the necessity of a holy life; for who would much trouble himself about an accusation which is laden with as many convictions of its forgery as there are persons who sincerely believe those doctrines, and which common light gives testimony against in the conversations of them by whom they are received, and by whom they are despised? It was the importance of the thing itself, made peculiarly seasonable by the manifold temptations of the days wherein we live, which occasioned that addition unto what was delivered about the nature of evangelical holiness; seeing "if we know these things, happy are we if we do them." But yet, the principal arguments and demonstrations of that necessity being drawn from those doctrines of the gospel which some traduce as casting no good aspect thereon, the calumnies mentioned are therein also obviated. And thus far have we proceeded in the declaration and vindication of the despised work of the Spirit of God under the New Testament, referring the remaining instances above mentioned unto another occasion.

The oppositions unto all that we believe and maintain herein are of two sorts:— First, Such as consist in particular exceptions against and objections unto each particular work of the Spirit, whether in the communication of gifts or the operation of grace. Secondly, Such as consist in reflections cast on the whole work ascribed unto him in general. Those of the first sort will all of them fall under consideration in their proper places, where we treat of those especial actings of the Spirit whereunto they are opposed. The other sort, at least the principal of them, wherewith some make the greatest noise in the world, may be here briefly spoken unto:—

The first and chief pretence of this nature is, that all those who plead for the effectual operations of the Holy Spirit in the illumination of the minds of men, the reparation of their natures, the sanctification of their persons, and their endowment with spiritual gifts, are therein and thereby enemies to reason, and impugn the use of it in religion, or at least allow it not that place and exercise therein which is its due. Hence, some of those who are otherwise minded affirm that it is cast on them as a reproach that they are rational divines; although, so far as I can discern, if it be so, it is as Hierom was beaten by an angel for being a Ciceronian (in the judgment of some), very undeservedly. But the grounds whereon this charge should be made good have not as yet been made to appear; neither hath it been evinced that any thing is ascribed by us unto the efficacy of God's grace in the least derogatory unto reason, its use, or any duty of man depending thereon. I suppose we are agreed herein, that the reason of man, in the state wherein we are, is not sufficient in itself to find out or frame a religion whereby we may please God and be accepted with him; or if we are not agreed herein, yet I shall not admit it as a part of our present controversy, wherein we suppose a religion proceeding from and resolved into supernatural revelation. Neither is it, that I know of, as yet pleaded by any that reason is able to comprehend all the things in their nature and being, or to search them out unto perfection, which are revealed unto us; for we do not directly deal with them by whom the principal mysteries of the gospel are rejected, because they cannot comprehend them, under a pretence that what is above reason is against it. And it may be it will be granted, moreover, that natural reason cannot enable the mind of a man unto a saving perception of spiritual things, as revealed, without the especial aid of the Spirit of God in illumination. If this be denied by any, as we acknowledge our dissent from them, so we know that we do no injury to reason thereby, and will rather suffer under the imputation of so doing than, by renouncing of the Scripture, to turn infidels, that we may be esteemed rational. But we cannot conceive how reason should be prejudiced by the advancement of the rational faculties of our souls, with respect unto their exercise towards their proper objects, — which is all we assign unto the work of the Holy Spirit in this matter; and there are none in the world more free to grant than we are, that unto us our reason is the only judge of the sense and truth of propositions drawn from the Scripture or proposed therein, and do wish that all men might be left peaceable under that determination, where we know they must abide, whether they will or no.

But the inquiry in this matter is, what reasonableness appears in the mysteries of our religion when revealed unto our reason, and what ability we have to receive, believe, and obey them as such. The latter part of this inquiry is so fully spoken unto in the ensuing discourses as that I shall not here again insist upon it; the former may in a few words be spoken unto. It cannot be, it is not, that I know of, denied by any that Christian religion is highly reasonable; for it is the effect of the infinite reason, understanding, and wisdom of God. But the question is not, what it is in itself? but what it is in relation to our reason, or how it appears thereunto? And there is no doubt but everything in Christian religion appears highly reasonable unto reason enlightened, or the mind of man affected with that work of grace, in its renovation, which is so expressly ascribed unto the Holy Spirit in the Scripture; for as there is a suitableness between an enlightened mind and spiritual mysteries as revealed, so seeing them in their proper light, it finds by experience their necessity, use, goodness, and benefit, with respect unto our chiefest good and supreme end. It remains, therefore, only that we inquire how reasonable the mysteries of Christian religion are unto the minds of men as corrupted; for that they are so by the entrance of sin, as we believe, so we have proved in the ensuing treatise. And it is in vain to dispute with any about the reasonableness of evangelical faith and obedience until the state and condition of our reason be agreed [on]. Wherefore, to speak plainly in the case, as we do acknowledge that reason, in its corrupted state, is all that any man hath in that state whereby to understand and to judge of the sense and truth of doctrines revealed in the Scripture, and, in the use of such aids and means as it is capable to improve, is more and better unto him than any judge or interpreter that should impose a sense upon him not suited thereunto; so, as to the spiritual things themselves of the gospel, in their own nature, it is enmity against them, and they are foolishness unto it. If, therefore, it be a crime, if it be to the impeachment and disadvantage of reason, to affirm that our minds stand in need of the renovation of the Holy Ghost, to enable them to understand spiritual things in a spiritual manner, we do acknowledge ourselves guilty thereof. But otherwise, that by asserting the efficacious operations of the Spirit of God, and the necessity of them unto the discharge of every spiritual duty towards God in an acceptable manner, we do deny that use and exercise of our own reason in things religious and spiritual whereof in any state it is capable, and whereunto of God it is appointed, is unduly charged on us, as will afterward be fully manifested.

But it is moreover pretended, that by the operations we ascribe unto the Holy Spirit, we expose men to be deceived by satanical delusions, [and] open a door to enthusiasms, directing them to the guidance of unaccountable impulses and revelations; so making way unto all folly and villainy. By what means this charge can be fixed on them who professedly avow that nothing is good, nothing duty unto us, nothing acceptable unto God, but what is warranted by the Scripture, directed unto thereby, and suited thereunto, which is the alone perfect rule of all that God requires of us in the way of obedience, but only [by] ungrounded clamours, hath not yet been attempted to be made manifest; for all things of this nature are not only condemned by them, but all things which they teach concerning the Holy Spirit of God are the principal ways and means to secure us from the danger of them. It is true, there have been of old, and haply do still continue among some, satanical delusions, diabolical suggestions, and foul enthusiasms, which have been pretended to proceed from the Spirit of God, and to be of a divine original; for so it is plainly affirmed in the Scripture, both under the Old Testament and the New, directions being therein added for their discovery and disprovement. But if we must therefore reject the true and real operations of the Spirit of God, the principal preservative against our being deceived by them, we may as well reject the owning of God himself, because the devil hath imposed himself on mankind as the object of their worship. Wherefore, as to enthusiasms of any kind, which might possibly give countenance unto any diabolical suggestions, we are so far from affirming any operations of the Holy Ghost to consist in them, or in any thing like unto them, that we allow no pretence of them to be consistent therewithal. And we have a sure rule to try all these things by; which as we are bound in all such cases precisely to attend unto, so hath God promised the assistance of his Spirit, that they be not deceived, unto them who do it in sincerity. What some men intend by impulses, I know not. If it be especial aids, assistances, and inclinations unto duties, acknowledged to be such, and the duties of persons so assisted and inclined, and these peculiarly incumbent on them in their present circumstances, it requires no small caution that, under an invidious name, we reject not those supplies of grace which are promised unto us, and which we are bound to pray for; but if irrational impressions, or violent inclinations unto things or actions which are not acknowledged duties in themselves, evidenced by the word of truth, and so unto the persons so affected in their present condition and circumstances, are thus expressed, as we utterly abandon them, so no pretence is given unto them from any thing which we believe concerning the Holy Spirit and his operations: for the whole work which we assign unto him is nothing but that whereby we are enabled to perform that obedience unto God which is required in the Scripture, in the way and manner wherein it is required; and it is probably more out of enmity unto him than us where the contrary is pretended. The same may be said concerning revelations. They are of two sorts, — objective and subjective. Those of the former sort, whether they contain doctrines contrary unto that of the Scripture, or additional thereunto, or seemingly confirmatory thereof, they are all universally to be rejected, the former being absolutely false, the latter useless. Neither have any of the operations of the Spirit pleaded for the least respect unto them; for he having finished the whole work of external revelation, and closed it in the Scripture, his whole internal spiritual work is suited and commensurate thereunto. By subjective revelations, nothing is intended but that work of spiritual illumination whereby we are enabled to discern and understand the mind of God in the Scripture; which the apostle prays for in the behalf of all believers, Eph. i. 16–19, and whose nature, God assisting, shall be fully explained hereafter. So little pretence, therefore, there is for this charge on them by whom the efficacious operations of the Spirit of God are asserted, as that without them we have no absolute security that we shall be preserved from being imposed on by them or some of them.

But, it may be, it will be said at last that our whole labour, in declaring the work of the Spirit of God in us and towards us, as well as what we have now briefly spoken in the vindication of it from these or the like imputations, is altogether vain, seeing all we do or say herein is nothing but canting with unintelligible expressions. So some affirm, indeed, before they have produced their charter wherein they are constituted the sole judges of what words, what expressions, what way of teaching, are proper in things of this nature. But, by any thing that yet appears, they seem to be as unmeet for the exercise of that dictatorship herein which they pretend unto, as any sort of men that ever undertook the declaration of things sacred and spiritual. Wherefore, unless they come with better authority than as yet they can pretend unto, and give a better example of their own way and manner of teaching such things than as yet they have done, we shall continue to make Scripture phraseology our rule and pattern in the declaration of spiritual things, and endeavour an accommodation of all our expressions thereunto, whether to them intelligible or not, and that for reasons so easy to be conceived as that they need not here be pleaded.

Book I

Chapter I - General principles concerning the Holy Spirit and his work

1 Cor. xii. 1 opened — Πνευματικά, spiritual gifts — Their grant unto, use and abuse in, that church — Jesus, how called "anathema" — Impiety of the Jews — How called "Lord" —The foundation of church order and worship — In what sense we are enabled by the Spirit to call Jesus "Lord" — The Holy Spirit the author of all gifts — why called "God," and "The Lord" — General distribution of spiritual gifts — Proper end of their communication — Nine sorts of gifts — Abuse of them in the church — Their tendency unto peace and order — General design of the ensuing discourse concerning the Spirit and his dispensation — Importance of the doctrine concerning the Spirit of God and his operations — Reasons hereof — Promise of the Spirit to supply the absence of Christ, as to his human nature — Concernment thereof — Work of the Spirit in the ministration of the gospel — All saving good communicated unto us and wrought in us by him — Sin against the Holy Ghost irremissible — False pretences unto the Spirit dangerous — Pretences unto the spirit of prophecy under the Old Testament — Two sorts of false prophets: the first; the second sort — Pretenders under the New Testament — The rule for the trial of such pretenders, 1 John iv. 1–3 — Rules to this purpose under the Old and New Testaments compared — A false spirit, set up against the Spirit of God, examined — False and noxious opinions concerning the Spirit, and how to be obviated —Reproaches of the Spirit and his work — Principles and occasions of the apostasy of churches under the law and gospel — Dispensation of the Spirit not confined to the first ages of the church — The great necessity of a diligent inquiry into the things taught concerning the Spirit of God and his work.

The apostle Paul, in the 12th chapter of his First Epistle to the Corinthians, directs their exercise of spiritual gifts, concerning which, amongst other things and emergencies, they had made inquiry of him. This the fast words wherewith he prefaceth his whole discourse declare: Verse 1, "Now, concerning spiritual gifts," — Περὶ δὲ τῶν πνευματικῶν· that is χαρισμάτων as his ensuing declaration doth evince. And the imagination of some, concerning spiritual persons to be here intended, contrary to the sense of all the ancients, is inconsistent with the context:[1] for as it was about spiritual gifts and their exercise that the church had consulted with him, so the whole series of his ensuing discourse is directive therein; and, therefore, in the close of it, contracting the design of the whole, he doth it in that advice, Ζηλοῦτε δὲ τὰ χαρίσματα τὰ κρείττονα, — "Covet earnestly the best gifts," — namely, among those which he proposed to treat of, and had done so accordingly, verse 31. The τὰ πνευματικὰ of verse 1 are the τὰ χαρίσματα of verse 31; as it is expressed, chap. xiv. 1, Ζηλοῦτε δὲ τὰ πνευματικά — that is, χαρίσματα, — "'Desire spiritual gifts,' whose nature and use you are now instructed in, as it first was proposed." Of these that church had received an abundant measure, especially of those that were extraordinary, and tended to the conviction of unbelievers: for the Lord having "much people in that city," whom he intended to call to the faith, Acts xviii. 9, 10, not only encouraged our apostle, against all fears and dangers, to begin and carry on the work of preaching there, wherein he continued "a year and six months," verse 11, but also furnished the first converts with such eminent, and some of them such miraculous gifts, as might be a prevalent means to the conversion of many others; for he will never be wanting to provide instruments and suitable means for the effectual attaining of any end that he aimeth at. In the use, exercise, and management of these "spiritual gifts," that church, or sundry of the principal members of it, had fallen into manifold disorders, and abused them unto the matter of emulation and ambition, whereon other evils did ensue;[2] as the best of God's gifts may be abused by the lusts of men, and the purest water may be tainted by the earthen vessels whereinto it is poured. Upon the information of some who, loving truth, peace, and order, were troubled at these miscarriages, 1 Cor. i. 11, and in answer unto a letter of the whole church, written unto him about these and other occurrences, chap. vii. 1, he gives them counsel and advice for the rectifying of these abuses. And, first, to prepare them aright with humility and thankfulness, becoming them who were intrusted with such excellent privileges as they had abused, and without which they could not receive the instruction which he intended them, he mindeth them of their former state and condition before their calling and conversion to Christ, chap. xii. 2, "Ye know that ye were Gentiles, carried away with dumb idols, even as ye were led;" ὡς ἂν ἤγεσθε ἀπαγόμενοι, — hurried with violent impressions from the devil into the service of idols. This he mentions not to reproach them, but to let them know what frame of mind and what fruit of life might be justly expected from them who had received such an alteration in their condition.[3] Particularly, as he elsewhere tells them, if they had not made themselves to differ from others, if they had nothing but what they had received, — they should not boast nor exalt themselves above others, as though they had not received, chap. iv. 7; for it is a vain thing for a man to boast in himself of what he hath freely received of another, and never deserved so to receive it, as it is with all who have received either gifts or grace from God.

This alteration of their state and condition he farther declares unto them by the effects and author of it: chap. xii. 3, "Wherefore I give you to understand, that no man speaking by the Spirit of God calleth Jesus accursed: and that no man can say that Jesus is the Lord, but by the Holy Ghost." The great difference which was then in the world was concerning Jesus, who was preached unto them all. Unbelievers, who were still carried with an impetus of mind and affections after "dumb idols," being led and acted therein by the spirit of the devil, blasphemed, and said Jesus was anathema, or one accursed. They looked on him as a person to be detested and abominated as the common odium of their gods and men. Hence, on the mention of him they used to say, "Jesus anathema," "He is," or, "Let him be, accursed," detested, destroyed. And in this blasphemy do the Jews continue to this day, hiding their cursed sentiments under a corrupt pronunciation of his name: for instead of יֵשׁוּעַ, they write and call him יֵשׁוּ, the initial letters of יִמַּח שְׁמוֹ וְזִכְרוֹ, — that is, "Let his name and memory be blotted out;" the same with "Jesus anathema" And this blasphemy of pronouncing Jesus accursed was that wherewith the first persecutors of the church tried the faith of Christians, as Pliny in his epistle to Trajan, and Justin Martyr, with other apologists, agree; and as the apostle says, those who did thus did not so "by the Spirit of God," so he intends that they did it by the acting and instigation of the devil, the unclean spirit, which ruled in those children of disobedience. And this was the condition of those Corinthians themselves to whom he wrote, whilst they also were carried away after "dumb idols" On the other side, those that believed called Jesus "Lord," or professed that he was the Lord; and thereby avowed their faith in him and obedience unto him. Principally, they owned him to be Jehovah, the Lord over all, God blessed forever; for the name יְהוָה is everywhere in the New Testament expressed by Κύριος, here used. He who thus professeth Jesus to be the Lord, in the first place acknowledgeth him to be the true God. And then they professed him therewithal to be their Lord, the Lord of their souls and consciences, unto whom they owed all subjection and performed all obedience; as Thomas did in his great confession, "My Lord and my God," John xx. 28. Now, as he had before intimated that those who disowned him and called him "accursed" did speak by the instinct and instigation of the devil, by whom they were acted, so he lets them know, on the other hand, that no man can thus own and confess Jesus to be the "Lord" but by the Holy Ghost. But it may be said that some acted by the unclean spirit confessed Christ to be the Lord. So did the man in the synagogue, who cried out, "I know thee who thou art, the Holy One of God," Mark i. 23, 24; and verse 34, he "suffered not the devils to speak, because they knew him." And the damsel possessed with a spirit of divination cried after the apostle and his companions, saying, "These men are the servants of the most high God," Acts xvi. 17. So also did the man who abode in the tombs, possessed with an unclean spirit, who cried out unto him, "What have I to do with thee, Jesus, thou Son of the most high God," Mark v. 7. And other testimonies to the like purpose among the heathen, and from their oracles, might be produced. Ans. 1. Our apostle speaks of such a saying of Jesus to be Lord as is accompanied with faith in him and subjection of soul unto him; which is from the Holy Ghost alone. Thus none acted by the unclean spirit can call him Lord. 2. These acknowledgments were either (1.) wrested from the devil, and were no small part of his punishment and torment; or (2.) were designed by him with an intention to prejudice the glory of Christ by his testimony, who was a liar from the beginning; and

> "Malus bonum cum simulat, tunc est pessimus."

These things, therefore, can have here no place.[4] Hereby, then, the apostle informs them wherein the foundation of all church relation, order, and worship, did consist: for whereas they had all respect unto the Lordship of Christ and their acknowledgment thereof, this was not from themselves, but was a pure effect of the operation of the Holy Ghost in them and towards them. And any thing of the like kind which doth not proceed from the same cause and fountain is of no use to the glory of God, nor of any advantage unto the souls of men.

Some think that this saying of Jesus to be the Lord is to be restrained unto the manner of speaking afterward insisted on;[5] for the apostle in the following verses treateth of those extraordinary gifts which many in that church were then endowed withal. None can," saith he, "say 'Jesus is the Lord,' in an extraordinary manner, with divers tongues, and in prophecy, but by the Holy Ghost;" — without his especial assistance, none can eminently and miraculously declare him so to be. And if this be so, it is likely that those before intended, who said Jesus was accursed, were some persons pretending to be acted, or really acted, by an extraordinary spirit, which the apostle declares not to be the Spirit of God; and so Chrysostom interprets those words of them who were visibly and violently acted by the devil. Many such instruments of his malice did Satan stir up in those days, to preserve, if it were possible, his tottering kingdom from ruin. But there is no necessity thus to restrain the words, or to affix this sense unto them; yea, it seems to me to be inconsistent with the design of the apostle and scope of the place: for intending to instruct the Corinthians, as was said, in the nature, use, and exercise of spiritual gifts, he first lays down the spring and fountain of all saving profession of the gospel, which those gifts were designed to the furtherance and improvement of. Hereupon, having minded them of their heathen state and condition before, he lets them know by what means they were brought into the profession of the gospel, and owning of Jesus to be the Lord, in opposition unto the dumb idols whom they had served; and this was by the Author of those gifts, unto whose consideration he was now addressing himself. The great change wrought in them, as to their religion and profession, was by the Holy Ghost; for no man can say that Jesus is the Lord, which is the sum and substance of our Christian profession, but by him, though some think he hath little or no concern at all in this matter. But to say Christ is the Lord includes two things:— First, Faith in him as Lord and Saviour. So was he declared and preached by the angels, Luke ii. 11, "A Saviour, which is Christ the Lord." And this word "Lord" includes, as the dignity of his person, so his investiture with those offices which for our good this Lord did exercise and discharge. Secondly, The profession of that faith. Which two, where they are sincere, do always accompany each other, Rom. x. 10; for as the saying of Jesus to be anathema did comprise an open disclaimer and abrenunciation of him, so the calling of him Lord expresseth the profession of our faith in him, and subjection unto him. And both these are here intended to be sincere and saving: for that faith and profession are intended whereby the church is built upon the rock; the same with that of Peter, "Thou art the Christ, the Son of the living God," Matt. xvi. 16. And that these are the works of the Holy Ghost, which none of themselves are sufficient for, shall, God assisting, be afterward abundantly declared.

Having thus stated the original and foundation of the church, in its faith, profession, order, and worship, he farther acquaints them that the same Spirit is likewise the author of all those gifts whereby it was to be built up and established, and whereby the profession of it might be enlarged: 1 Cor. xii. 4, "Now there are diversities of gifts, but the same Spirit." These are the things which he intendeth to discourse upon, wherein he enlargeth himself in the whole ensuing chapter. Now, became the particulars here insisted on by him in the beginning of his discourse will all of them occur unto us and be called over again in their proper places, I shall only point unto the heads of the discourse in the verses preceding the 11th, which we principally aim at.

Treating, therefore, περὶ τῶν πνευματικῶν, of these spiritual things or gifts in the church, he first declares their author, from whom they come, and by whom they are wrought and bestowed. Him he calls the "Spirit," verse 4; the "Lord," verse 5; "God," verse 6; and to denote the oneness of their author, notwithstanding the diversify of the things themselves, he calls him the same Spirit, the same Lord, the same God. The words may be understood two ways: First, That the whole Trinity, and each person distinctly, should be intended in them; — for consider the immediate operator of these gifts, and it is the "Spirit" or the Holy Ghost, verse 4; consider them as to their procurement and immediate authoritative collation, and so they are from Christ, the Son, the "Lord," verse 5; but as to their first original and fountain, they are from "God," even the Father, verse 6: and all these are one and the same. But rather the Spirit alone is intended, and hath this threefold denomination given unto him; for as he is particularly denoted by the name of the "Spirit," which he useth that we may know whom it is that eminently he intendeth, so he calls him both "Lord" and "God," as to manifest his sovereign authority in all his works and administrations, so to ingenerate a due reverence in their hearts towards him with whom they had to do in this matter. And no more is intended in these three verses but what is summed up, verse 11, "But all these worketh that one and the self-same Spirit, dividing to every man severally as he will."

Secondly, With respect unto their general nature, the apostle distributes them into "gift," χαρίσματα, verse 4; "administrations," διακόνιαι, verse 5; "operations," ἐνεργήματα, verse 6; — which division, with the reasons of it, will in our progress be farther cleared.

Thirdly, He declares the general end of the Spirit of God in the communication of them, and the use of them in the church: Verse 7, "But the manifestation of the Spirit is given to every man to profit withal." Φανέρωσις τοῦ Πνεύματος· Syr., דרוחה גליגא, — "the revelation of the Spirit;" that is, the gifts whereby and in whose exercise he manifests and reveals his own presence, power, and effectual operation. And the Spirit of God hath no other aim in granting these his enlightening gifts, wherein he manifests his care of the church, and declares the things of the gospel unto any man, but that they should be used to the profit, advantage, and edification of others. They are not bestowed on men to make their secular gain or advantage by them, in riches, honour, or reputation, — for which ends Simon the magician would have purchased them with his money, Acts viii. 18, 19, — no, nor yet merely for the good and benefit of the souls of them that do receive them; but for the edification of the church, and the furtherance of faith and profession in others: Πρὸς τὸ συμφέρον· "Ad id quod expedit, prodest;" "For that which is expedient, useful, profitable," — namely, to the church, 1 Cor. vi. 12, x. 23; 2 Cor. viii. 10. Thus was the foundation of the first churches of the gospel laid by the Holy Ghost, and thus was the work of their building unto perfection carried on by him. How far present churches do or ought to stand on the same bottom, how far they are carried on upon the same principles, is worth our inquiry, and will in its proper place fall under our consideration.

Fourthly, The apostle distributes the spiritual gifts then bestowed on the church, or some members of it, into nine particular heads or instances: as, — 1. Wisdom; 2. Knowledge, 1 Cor. xii. 8, or the word of wisdom and the word of knowledge; 3. Faith; 4. Healing, verse 9; 5. Working of miracles; 6. Prophecy; 7. Discerning of spirits; 8. Kinds of tongues; 9. Interpretation of tongues, verse

10. And all these were extraordinary gifts, in the manner of the communication and exercise, which related unto the then present state of the church. What is yet continued analogous unto them, or holding proportion with them, must be farther inquired into, when also their especial nature will be unfolded. But now if there be that great diversity of gifts in the church,[6] if so much difference in their administrations, how can it possibly be prevented but that differences and divisions will arise amongst them on whom they are bestowed and those amongst whom they are exercised? It is true, this may so fall out, and sometimes doth so; and, de facto, it did so in this church of Corinth. One admired one gift, a second another of a different kind, and so the third. Accordingly, among those who had received them, one boasted of this or that particular gift and ability, and would be continually in its exercise, to the exclusion and contempt of others, bestowed no less for the edification of the church than his own. And so far were they transported with vain-glory and a desire of self-advancement, as that they preferred the use of those gifts in the church which tended principally to beget astonishment and admiration in them which heard or beheld them, before those which were peculiarly useful unto the edification of the church itself; which evil, in particular, the apostle rebukes at large, chap. 14. By this means the church came to be divided in itself, and almost to be broken in pieces, chap. i. 11, 12. So foolish ofttimes are the minds of men, so liable to be imposed upon, so common is it for their lusts, seduced and principled by the craft of Satan, to turn judgment into wormwood, and to abuse the most useful effects of divine grace and bounty! To prevent all these evils for the future, and to manifest how perfect a harmony there is in all these divers gifts and different administrations, at what an agreement they are among themselves in their tendency unto the same ends of the union and edification of the church, from what fountain of wisdom they do proceed, and with what care they ought to be used and improved, the apostle declares unto them both the author of them and the rule he proceedeth by in their dispensation, chap. xii. 11. "All these," saith he,[7] "worketh that one and the self-same Spirit, dividing to every man severally as he will."

I shall not at present farther open or insist upon these words. Frequent recourse must be had unto them in our progress, wherein they will be fully explicated as to what concerns the person of the Spirit, his will, and his operations, which are all asserted in them; for my purpose is, through the permission and assistance of God, to treat from hence of the name, nature, existence, and whole work of the Holy Spirit, with the grace of God through Jesus Christ in the communication of him unto the sons of men: a work in itself too great and difficult for me to undertake, and beyond my ability to manage unto the glory of God or the edification of the souls of them that do believe, for "who is sufficient for these things?" but yet I dare not utterly faint in it nor under it, whilst I look unto Him whose work it is, who giveth wisdom to them that lack it, and upbraideth them not, James i. 5. Our eyes, therefore, are unto him alone, who both supplieth seed to the sower, and when he hath done, blesseth it with an increase. The present necessity, importance, and usefulness of this work, are the things which alone have engaged me into the undertaking of it. These, therefore, I shall briefly represent in some general considerations, before I insist on the things themselves whose especial explanation is designed.

First, then, we may consider, That the doctrine of the Spirit of God, his work and grace, is the second great head or principle of those gospel truths wherein the glory of God and the good of the souls of men are most eminently concerned. And such also it is, that without it, — without the knowledge of it in its truth, and the improvement of it in its power, — the other will be useless unto those ends. For when God designed the great and glorious work of recovering fallen man and the saving of sinners, to the praise of the glory of his grace, he appointed, in his infinite wisdom, two great means thereof. The one was the giving of his Son for them, and the other was the giving of his Spirit unto them. And hereby was way made for the manifestation of the glory of the whole blessed Trinity; which is the utmost end of all the works of God. Hereby were the love, grace, and wisdom of the Father, in the design and projection of the whole; the love, grace, and condescension of the Son, in the execution, purchase, and procurement of grace and salvation for sinners; with the love, grace, and power of the Holy Spirit, in the effectual application of all unto the souls of men, — made gloriously conspicuous. Hence, from the first entrance of sin, there were two general heads of the promise of God unto men, concerning the means of their recovery and salvation. The one was that concerning the sending of his Son to be incarnate, to take our nature upon him, and to suffer for us therein; the other, concerning the giving of his Spirit, to make the effects and fruits of the incarnation, obedience, and suffering of his Son, effectual in us and towards us. To these heads may all the promises of God be reduced. Now, because the former was to be the foundation of the latter, that was first to be laid down and most insisted on until it was actually accomplished. Hence, the great promise of the Old Testament, the principal object of the faith, hope, and expectation of believers, was that concerning the coming of the Son of God in the flesh, and the work which he was to perform. Yet was this also, as we shall see in our progress, accompanied with a great intermixture of promises concerning the Holy Spirit, to render his coming and work effectual unto us. But when once that first work was fully accomplished, when the Son of God was come, and had destroyed the works of the devil, the principal remaining promise of the New Testament, the spring of all the rest, concerneth the sending of the Holy Spirit unto the accomplishment of his part of that great work which God had designed. Hence, the Holy Ghost, the doctrine concerning his person, his work, his grace, is the most peculiar and principal subject of the Scriptures of the New Testament, and a most eminent immediate object of the faith of them that do believe; and this must be farther cleared, seeing we have to deal with some who will scarce allow him to be of any consideration in these matters at all. But I shall be brief in these previous testimonies hereunto, because the whole ensuing discourse is designed to the demonstration of the truth of this assertion.

1. It is of great moment, and sufficient of itself to maintain the cause as proposed, that when our Lord Jesus Christ was to leave the world, he promised to send his Holy Spirit unto his disciples to supply his absence. Of what use the presence of Christ was unto his disciples we may in some measure conceive. They knew full well whose hearts were filled with sorrow upon the mention of his leaving of them, John xvi. 5, 6. Designing to relieve them in this great distress, — which drew out the highest expressions of love, tenderness, compassion, and care towards them, — he doth it principally by this promise; which he assures them shall be to their greater advantage than any they could

receive by the continuance of his bodily presence amongst them. And to secure them hereof, as also to inform them of its great importance, he repeats it frequently unto them, and inculcates it upon them. Consider somewhat of what he says to this purpose in his last discourse with them: John xiv. 16–18, "I will pray the Father, and he shall give you another Comforter, that he may abide with you for ever; even the Spirit of truth; whom the world cannot receive, because it seeth him not, neither knoweth him: but ye know him; for he dwelleth with you, and shall be in you. I will not leave you comfortless: I will come to you;" that is, in and by this Holy Spirit. And verses 25–27, "These things have I spoken unto you, being yet present with you. But the Comforter, which is the Holy Ghost, whom the Father will send in my name, he shall teach you all things, and bring all things to your remembrance, whatsoever I have said unto you. Peace I leave with you," etc. And chap. xv. 26, "But when the Comforter is come, whom I will send unto you from the Father, even the Spirit of truth, which proceedeth from the Father, he shall testify of me." And chap. xvi. 5–15, "Now I go my way to him that sent me; and none of you asketh me, Whither goest thou? But because I have said these things unto you, sorrow hath filled your heart. Nevertheless I tell you the truth; It is expedient for you that I go away: for if I go not away, the Comforter will not come unto you; but if I depart, I will send him unto you. And when he is come, he will reprove the world of sin, and of righteousness, and of judgment: of sin, because they believe not on me; of righteousness, because I go to my Father, and ye see me no more; of judgment, because the prince of this world is judged. I have yet many things to say unto you, but ye cannot bear them now. Howbeit when he, the Spirit of truth, is come, he will guide you into all truth: for he shall not speak of himself; but whatsoever he shall hear, that shall he speak: and he will show you things to come. He shall glorify me: for he shall receive of mine, and shall show it unto you. All things that the Father hath are mine: therefore said I, that he shall take of mine, and shall show it unto you."[8] This was the great legacy which our Lord Jesus Christ, departing out of this world, bequeathed unto his sorrowful disciples. This he promiseth unto them as a sufficient relief against all their troubles, and a faithful guide in all their ways. And because of the importance of it unto them, he frequently repeats it, and enlargeth upon the benefits that they should receive thereby, giving them a particular account why it would be more advantageous unto them than his own bodily presence; and, therefore, after his resurrection he minds them again of this promise, commanding them to act nothing towards the building of the church until it was accomplished towards them, Acts i. 4, 5, 8. They would have been again embracing his human nature, and rejoicing in it; but as he said unto Mary, "Touch me not," John xx. 17, to wean her from any carnal consideration of him, so he instructs them all now to look after and trust unto the promise of the Holy Ghost. Hence is that of our apostle, "Though we have known Christ after the flesh, yet now henceforth know we him no more," 2 Cor. v. 16; for although it was a great privilege to have known Christ in this world after the flesh, yet it was much greater to enjoy him in the dispensation of the Spirit. And this was spoken by the apostle, as the ancients judge, to rebuke the boasting of some about their seeing the Lord in the flesh, who were thereon called δεσπόσυνοι, whom he directs unto a more excellent knowledge of him. It is in vain pretended that it was the apostles only, and it may be some of the primitive Christians, who were concerned in this promise, for although the Holy Ghost was bestowed on them in a peculiar manner and for especial ends, yet the promise in general belongs unto all believers unto the end of the world;[9] for as to what concerns his gracious operations, whatever the Lord Christ prayed for them, and so promised unto them (as the Spirit was procured for them on his prayer, John xiv. 16, 17), he "prayed not for it for them alone, but for them also which should believe on him through their word," chap. xvii. 20. And his promise is, to be "with his alway, even unto the end of the world," Matt. xxviii. 20; as also, that "wherever two or three are gathered together in his name, there he would be in the midst of them," chap. xviii. 20; — which he is no otherwise but by his Spirit; for as for his human nature, "the heaven must receive him until the times of restitution of all things, Acts iii. 21. And this one consideration is sufficient to evince the importance of the doctrine and things which concern the Holy Spirit; for is it possible that any Christian should be so supinely negligent and careless, so unconcerned in the things whereon his present comforts and future happiness do absolutely depend, as not to think it his duty to inquire with the greatest care and diligence into what our Lord Jesus Christ hath left unto us, to supply his absence, and at length to bring us unto himself? He by whom these things are despised hath neither part nor lot in Christ himself; for "if any man have not the Spirit of Christ, he is none of his," Rom. viii. 9.

2. The great work of the Holy Ghost in the dispensation and ministration of the gospel, unto all the ends of it, is another evidence unto the same purpose.[10] Hence, the gospel itself is called "The ministration of the Spirit," 2 Cor. iii. 8, in opposition to that of the law, which is called the ministration of the letter and of condemnation. Διακονία τοῦ Πνεῦματος, the "ministry of the Spirit," is either that ministry which the Spirit makes effectual, or that ministry whereby the Spirit in his gifts and graces is communicated unto men. And this is that which gives unto the ministry of the gospel both its glory and its efficacy. Take away the Spirit from the gospel and you render it a dead letter, and leave the New Testament of no more use unto Christians than the Old Testament is of unto the Jews. It is therefore a mischievous imagination, proceeding from ignorance, blindness, and unbelief, that there is no more in the gospel but what is contained under any other doctrine or declaration of truth, — that it is nothing but a book for men to exercise their reason in and upon, and to improve the things of it by the same faculty: for this is to separate the Spirit, or the dispensation of the Spirit, from it, which is in truth to destroy it; and therewith is the covenant of God rejected, which is, that his word and Spirit shall go together, Isa. lix. 21. We shall, therefore, God assisting, manifest in our progress that the whole ministry of the gospel, the whole use and efficacy of it, do depend on that ministration of the Spirit wherewith, according to the promise of God, it is accompanied. If, therefore, we have any concernment in, or have ever received any benefit by, the gospel, or the ministration of it, we have a signal duty lying before us in the matter in hand.

3. There is not any spiritual or saving good from first to last communicated unto us, or that we are from and by the grace of God made partakers of, but it is revealed to us and bestowed on us by the Holy Ghost. He who hath not an immediate and especial work of the Spirit of God upon him and towards him did never receive any especial love, grace, or mercy, from God. For how should he do so? Whatever God works in us and upon us, he doth it by his Spirit; he, therefore, who hath no work of the Spirit of God upon his heart did never

receive either mercy or grace from God, for God giveth them not but by his Spirit. A disclaimer, therefore, of any work of the Spirit of God in us or upon us is a disclaimer of all interest in his grace and mercy; and they may do well to consider it with whom the work of the Spirit of God is a reproach. When they can tell us of any other way whereby a man may be made partaker of mercy and grace, we will attend unto it; in the meantime we shall prove from the Scripture this to be the way of God.

4. There is not any thing done in us or by us that is holy and acceptable unto God, but it is an effect of the Holy Spirit; it is of his operation in us and by us. Without him we can do nothing; for without Christ we cannot, John xv. 5, and by him alone is the grace of Christ communicated unto us and wrought in us. By him we are regenerated;[11] by him we are sanctified; by him we are cleansed; by him are we assisted in and unto every good work. Particular instances to this purpose will be afterward insisted on and proved. And it is our unquestionable concernment to inquire into the cause and spring of all that is good in us, wherein also we shall have a true discovery of the spring and cause of all that is evil, without a competent knowledge of both which we can do nothing as we ought.

5. God lets us know that the only peculiarly remediless sin and way of sinning under the gospel is to sin in an especial manner against the Holy Ghost. And this of itself is sufficient to convince us how needful it is for us to be well instructed in what concerns him; for there is somewhat that doth so, which is accompanied with irrecoverable and eternal ruin; and so is nothing else in the world. So Mark iii. 28, 29, "All sins shall be forgiven unto the sons of men, and blasphemies wherewith soever they shall blaspheme: but he that shall blaspheme against the Holy Ghost hath never forgiveness." Or, "Whosoever speaketh against the Holy Ghost, it shall not be forgiven him, neither in this world, neither in the world to come," Matt. xii. 32. There remains nothing for him who doth despite to the Spirit of grace but a "certain fearful looking for of judgment and fiery indignation, which shall devour the adversaries," Heb. x. 27, 29. This is that "sin unto death" whose remission is not to be prayed for, John v. 16: for he having taken upon him to make effectual unto us the great remedy provided in the blood of Christ for the pardon of our sins, if he in the prosecution of that work be despised, blasphemed, despitefully used, there neither is relief nor can there be pardon for that sin. For whence, in that case, should they arise or spring? As God hath not another Son to offer another sacrifice for sin, — so that he by whom his sacrifice is despised can have none remaining for him, — no more hath he another Spirit to make that sacrifice effectual unto us, if the Holy Ghost in his work be despised and rejected. This, therefore, is a tender place.[12] We cannot use too much holy diligence in our inquiries after what God hath revealed in his word concerning his Spirit and his work, seeing there may be so fatal a miscarriage in an opposition unto him as the nature of man is incapable of in any other instance.

And these considerations belong unto the first head of reasons of the importance, use, and necessity, of the doctrine proposed to be inquired into. They are enough to manifest what is the concernment of all believers herein; for on the account of these things the Scripture plainly declares, as we observed before, that "he who hath not the Spirit of Christ is none of his," — their portion is not in him, they shall have no benefit by his mediation. Men may please themselves with a profession of being Christians and owning the gospel, whilst they despise the Spirit of God, both name and thing. Their condition we shall examine and judge by the Scripture before we come to the end of this discourse. And for the Scripture itself, whoever reads the books of the New Testament, besides the great and precious promises that are given concerning him in the Old, will find and conclude, unless he be prepossessed with prejudice, that the whole of what is declared in those writings turns on this only hinge. Remove from them the consideration of the Spirit of God and his work, and it will be hard to find out what they aim at or tend unto.

Secondly, The great deceit and abuse that hath been, in all ages of the church, under the pretence of the name and work of the Spirit make the thorough consideration of what we are taught concerning them exceeding necessary. Had not these things been excellent in themselves, and so acknowledged by all Christians, they would never have been by so many falsely pretended unto. Men do not seek to adorn themselves with rags, or to boast of what, on its own account, is under just contempt. And according to the worth of things, so are they liable to abuse; and the more excellent any thing is, the more vile and pernicious is an undue pretence unto it. Such have been the false pretences of some in all ages unto the Spirit of God and his work, whose real excellencies in themselves have made those pretences abominable and unspeakably dangerous; for the better the things are which are counterfeited, the worse always are the ends they are employed unto. In the whole world there is nothing so vile as that which pretendeth to be God, and is not; nor is any other thing capable of so pernicious an abuse. Some instances hereof I shall give, both out of the Old Testament and the New.

The most signal gift of the Spirit of God, for the use of the church under the Old Testament, was that of prophecy. This, therefore, was deservedly in honour and reputation, as having a great impression of the authority of God upon it, and in it of his nearness unto man. Besides, those in whom it was had justly the conduct of the minds and consciences of others given up unto them: for they spake in the name of God, and had his warranty for what they proposed; which is the highest security of obedience. And these things caused many to pretend unto this gift who were, indeed, never inspired by the Holy Spirit; but were rather, on the contrary, acted by a spirit of lying and uncleanness: for it is very probable that when men falsely and in mere pretence took upon them to be prophets divinely inspired, without any antecedent diabolical enthusiasm, that the devil made use of them to compass his own designs Being given up, by the righteous judgment of God, unto all delusions, for belying his Spirit and holy inspirations, they were quickly possessed with a spirit of lying and unclean divination. So the false prophets of Ahab, who encouraged him to go up unto Ramoth-gilead, foretelling his prosperous success, 1 Kings xxii. 6, seemed only to have complied deceitfully with the inclinations of their master, and to have out-acted his other courtiers in flattery by gilding it with a pretence of prophecy; but when Micaiah came to lay open the mystery of their iniquity, it appeared that a lying spirit, by the permission of God, had possessed their minds, and gave them impressions, which being supernatural, they were deceived as well as they did deceive, verses 19–23. This they were justly given up unto, pretending falsely unto the inspiration of that Holy Spirit which they had not received. And no otherwise hath it fallen out with some in our days, whom we have seen visibly acted by an extraordinary power. Unduly pretending unto supernatural agitations from God, they were really acted by the devil; a thing they neither desired nor looked after, but, being surprised by it, were pleased with it for a while: as it was with sundry of the Quakers at their first appearance.

Now, these false prophets of old were of two sorts, both mentioned, Deut. xviii. 20:—

First, Such as professedly served other gods, directing all their prophetic actings unto the promotion of their worship. Such were the prophets of Baal, in whose name expressly they prophesied, and whose assistance they invocated: "They called on the name of Baal, saying, O Baal, hear us," 1 Kings xviii. 26–29. Many of these were slain by Elijah, and the whole race of them afterward extirpated by Jehu, 2 Kings x. 18–28. This put an end to his deity, for it is said, "he destroyed Baal out of Israel," false gods having no existence but in the deceived minds of their worshippers. It may be asked why these are called "prophets?" and so, in general, of all the false prophets mentioned in the Scripture. Was it because they merely pretended and counterfeited a spirit of prophecy, or had they really any such? I answer, that I no way doubt but that they were of both sorts. These prophets of Baal were such as worshipped the sun, after the manner of the Tyrians. Herein they invented many hellish mysteries, ceremonies, and sacrifices; these they taught the people by whom they were hired. Being thus engaged in the service of the devil, he actually possessed their minds "as a spirit of divination," and enabled them to declare things unknown unto other men. They, in the meantime, really finding themselves acted by a power superior to them, took and owned that to be the power of their god; and thereby became immediate worshippers of the devil. This our apostle declares, 1 Cor. x. 20. Whatever those who left the true God aimed at to worship, the devil interposed himself between that and them, as the object of their adoration. Hereby he became the "god of this world," 2 Cor. iv. 4, — he whom in all their idols they worshipped and adored. With a spirit of divination from him were many of the false prophets acted, which they thought to be the spirit of their god; for they found themselves acted by a superior power, which they could neither excuse nor resist.[13] Others of them were mere pretenders and counterfeits, that deceived the foolish multitude with vain, false predictions. Of these more will be spoken afterward.

Secondly, Others there were who spake in the name, and, as they falsely professed, by the inspiration of the Spirit, of the holy God. With this sort of men Jeremiah had great contests; for in that apostatizing age of the church, they had got such an interest and reputation among the rulers and people as not only to confront his prophecies with contrary predictions, chap. xxviii. 1–4, but also to traduce him as a false prophet, and to urge his punishment according to the law, chap. xxix. 25–27. And with the like confidence did Zedekiah the son of Chenaanah carry it towards Micaiah, 1 Kings xxii. 24; for he scornfully asks him, "Which way went the Spirit of the Lord from me to speak unto thee?" that is, "Whereas assuredly he speaketh in me, how came he to inspire thee with a contrary revelation?" Ezekiel, at the same time with Jeremiah, was exercised and perplexed with them, chap. xiii. and xiv.; for this sort of persons, — namely, false pretenders unto divine extraordinary revelations, — did of old usually abound in times of danger and approaching desolations. The devil stirred them up to fill men with vain hopes, to keep them in sin and security, that destruction might seize upon them at unawares: and whoever take the same course in the time of deserved, threatened, impendent judgments, though they use not the same means, yet they also do the work of the devil; for whatever encourageth men to be secure in their sins is a false divination, Jer. v. 30, 31. And this sort of men is characterized by the prophet chap. xxiii., from verse 9 to 33; where anyone may read their sin and judgment. And yet this false pretending unto the spirit of prophecy was very far from casting any contempt on the real gift of the Holy Ghost therein; nay, it gave it the greater glory and lustre. God never more honoured his true prophets than when there were most false ones; neither shall ever any false pretence to the Spirit of grace render him less dear unto those that are partakers of him, or his gifts of less use unto the church.

It was thus also under the New Testament, at the first preaching of the gospel. The doctrine of it at first was declared from the immediate revelation of the Spirit, preached by the assistance of the Spirit, made effectual by his work and power, [and] was accompanied in many by outward miraculous works and effects of the Spirit; whence the whole of what peculiarly belonged unto it, in opposition to the law, was called "The ministration of the Spirit." These things being owned and acknowledged by all, those who had any false opinions or dotages of their own to broach, or any other deceit to put upon Christians, could think of no more expedite means for the compassing of their ends than by pretending to immediate revelations of the Spirit; for without some kind of credibility given them from hence, they knew that their fond imaginations would not be taken into the least consideration. Hence the apostle Peter, having treated concerning the revelation of God by his Spirit in prophecy, under the Old Testament and the New, 2 Epist., chap. i. 19–21, adds, as an inference from that discourse, a comparison between the false prophets that were under the Old Testament and the false teachers under the New, chap. ii. 1: "But there were false prophets also among the people, even as there shall be false teachers among you." And the reason of it is, because that as they pretended to the Spirit of the Lord in their prophecies, saying, "Thus saith the Lord," when he sent them not, so these ascribed all their abominable heresies to the inspiration of the Spirit, by whom they were not assisted.

Hence is that blessed caution and rule given us by the apostle John, who lived to see much mischief done in the church by this pretence: 1 Epist. chap. iv. 1–3, "Beloved, believe not every spirit, but try the spirits whether they are of God: because many false prophets are gone out into the world. Hereby know ye the Spirit of God: Every spirit that confesseth that Jesus Christ is come in the flesh is of God: and every spirit that confesseth not that Jesus Christ is come in the flesh is not of God." A twofold direction doth the apostle here give unto all believers; the first by the way of caution, that they would not believe every spirit, — that is, not receive or give credit to every doctrine that was proposed unto them as of immediate revelation and inspiration of the Spirit. He intends the same with the apostle Paul, Eph. iv. 14, who would not have us "carried about with every wind of doctrine," like vessels at sea without anchors or helms, by the "sleight of men, and cunning craftiness, whereby they lie in wait to deceive;" for the crafts and sleights intended are such as men use when they cast a mist, as it were, before the eyes of others whom they intend to cheat and defraud. So dealt false teachers with their disciples, by their pretences of immediate revelations. His next direction informs us how we may observe this caution unto our advantage; and this is, by trying the spirits themselves. This is the duty of all believers on any such pretences. They are to try these spirits, and examine whether they are of God or no. For the observation of this rule and discharge of this duty, the church of Ephesus is commended by our Lord Jesus Christ: Rev. ii. 2, "Thou hast tried them which say they are apostles, and are not, and hast found them liars;" for those who said they were apostles pretended therewithal to apostolical authority and infallibility, on the account of the immediate inspirations which they received by the Holy Ghost. In trying them, they tried the spirits that came unto them; and by this warrant may we try the spirit of the church of Rome, which in like manner pretends unto apostolical authority and infallibility.

Unto these two directions the apostle subjoins the reason of the present watchfulness required unto the discharge of this duty: "Because," saith he, "many false prophets are gone out into the world." It is "false teachers," as Peter calls them, "bringing in damnable heresies," concerning whom he speaks. And he calleth them "false prophets," partly in an allusion unto the false prophets under the Old Testament, with whom they are ranked and compared by Peter, and partly because, as they fathered their prejudices on divine revelation, so these falsely ascribed their doctrines unto immediate divine inspiration. And on this account also he calleth them spirits: "Try the spirits;" for as they pretended unto the Spirit of God, so indeed for the most part they were acted by a spirit of error, lying, and delusion, — that is, the devil himself. And therefore I no way doubt but that mostly those who made use of this plea, that they had their doctrines which they taught by immediate inspiration, did also effect other extraordinary operations or undiscoverable appearances of them, as lying miracles, by the power of that spirit whereby they were acted, as Matt. xxiv. 24. Hence the apostle doth not direct us to try their pretensions unto inspiration by putting them on other extraordinary works for their confirmation, for these also they made a show and appearance of, and that in such a manner as that they were not to be detected by the generality of Christians; but he gives unto all a blessed stable rule, which will never fail them in this case who diligently attend unto it; and this is, to try them by the doctrine that they teach, 1 John iv. 2, 3. Let their doctrine be examined by the Scriptures, and if it be found consonant thereunto, it may be received without danger unto the hearers, whatever corrupt affections the teachers may be influenced by; but if it be not consonant thereunto, if it keep not up a harmony in the analogy of faith, whatever inspiration or revelation be pleaded in its justification, it is to be rejected, as they also are by whom it is declared. This rule the apostle Paul confirms by the highest instance imaginable: Gal. i. 8, "Though we, or an angel from heaven, preach any other gospel unto you than that which we have preached unto you, let him be accursed." And the apostle shows that, for our advantage in this trial we are to make of spirits, it is good to have a clear conviction of, and a constant adherence unto, some fundamental principles, especially such as we have reason to think will be the most cunningly attacked by seducers. Thus, because in those days the principal design of Satan was, to broach strange, false imaginations about the person and mediation of Christ, endeavouring thereby to overthrow both the one and the other, the apostle adviseth believers to try the spirits by this one fundamental principle of truth, namely, that "Jesus Christ is come in the flesh;" which contains a confession both of his person and mediation. This, therefore, believers were to demand of all new teachers and pretenders unto spiritual revelations in the first place, "Do you confess that Jesus Christ is come in the flesh?" and if they immediately made not this confession, they never stood to consider their other pretences, but turned from them, not bidding them God speed,2 John 7, 10, 11. And I could easily manifest how many pernicious heresies were obviated in those days by this short confession of faith. For some of late (as Grotius, following Socinus and Schlichtingius) interpreting this coming of Christ in the flesh of his outward mean estate and condition, and not in the pomp and glory of an earthly king, do openly corrupt the text. His coming in the flesh is the same with the "Word's being made flesh," John i. 14; or "God being manifest in the flesh," 1 Tim. iii. 16, — that is, the Son of God being made "partaker of flesh and blood," Heb. ii. 14; or "taking on him the seed of Abraham," verse 16, — that is, his being "made of a woman," Gal. iv. 4; or his being "made of the seed of David according to the flesh," Rom. i. 3; or his "being of the fathers as to the flesh," Rom. ix. 5. And this was directly opposed unto those heresies which were then risen, whose broachers contended that Jesus Christ was but a fantasy, an appearance, a manifestation of divine love and power, denying that the Son of God was really incarnate, as the ancients generally testify. And well had it been for many in our days had they attended unto such rules as this; but through a neglect of it, accompanied with an ungrounded boldness and curiosity, they have hearkened in other things to deceiving spirits, and have been engaged beyond a recovery before they have considered that by their cogging deceits they have been cheated of all the principal articles of their faith; by which if at first they had steadily tried and examined them, they might have been preserved from their snares.

The Jews say well that there was a double trial of prophets under the Old Testament, — the one by their doctrine, the other by their predictions. That by their doctrine, — namely, whether they seduced men from the worship of the true God unto idolatry, — belonged unto all individual persons of the church. Direction for this is given, Deut. xiii. 1–3, "If there arise among you a prophet, or a dreamer of dreams, and giveth thee a sign or a wonder, and the sign or the wonder come to pass, whereof he spake unto thee" (effect any thing by a seeming presence of an extraordinary power), saying, "Let us go after other gods, which thou hast not known, and let us serve them; thou shalt not hearken unto the words of that prophet, or that dreamer of dreams." Let his signs and wonders be what they would, the people were to try them by what they taught. The judgment upon predictions was left unto the sanhedrim, for which directions are given, Deut. xviii. 20–22; and by virtue hereof they falsely and cruelly endeavoured to take away the life of Jeremiah, because he foretold the ruin of them and their city, chap. xxvi. 11. In the first place, though his sign, wonder, or prediction came to pass, yet the doctrine he sought to confirm by it being false, he was to be rejected. In the latter, the fulfilling of his sign acquitted him, because he taught with it nothing in point of doctrine that was false. The first kind of trial of the spirits of prophets is the duty of all believers under the gospel; and those who would deprive them of this liberty would make brutes of them instead of Christians, — unless to believe a man knows not what, and to obey he knows not why, be the properties of Christians. See Rom. xii. 2; Eph. v. 8–12; Phil. i. 10; 1 Thess. v. 21. The other, so far as was needful to preserve the church in truth and peace, was provided for in those primitive times, whilst there was a real communication of extraordinary gifts of the Spirit (and so more occasion given to the false pretence of them, and more danger in being deceived by them), by a peculiar gift of discerning them, bestowed on some amongst them. 1 Cor. xii. 10, "Discerning of spirits" is reckoned among the gifts of the Spirit. So had the Lord graciously provided for his churches, that some among them should be enabled in an extraordinary manner to discern and judge of them who pretended unto extraordinary actings of the Spirit. And upon the ceasing of extraordinary gifts really given from God, the gift also of discerning spirits ceased, and we are left unto the word alone for the trial of any that shall pretend unto them. Now, this kind of pretence was so common in those days, that the apostle Paul, writing to the Thessalonians to caution them that they suffered not themselves to be deceived in their expectation and computations about the time of the coming of Christ, in the first place warns them not to be moved in it "by spirit," 2 Thess. ii. 2; that is, persons pretending unto spiritual revelations. Something, also, of this nature hath continued, and broken out in succeeding ages, and that in instances abominable and dreadful. And the more eminent in any season are the real effusions of the Holy Spirit upon the ministers of the gospel and disciples of Christ, the more diligence and watchfulness against these delusions are necessary; for on such opportunities it is, when the use and reputation of spiritual gifts is eminent, that Satan doth lay hold to intrude under the colour of them his own deceitful suggestions. In the dark times of the Papacy, all stories are full of satanical delusions, in fantastical apparitions, horrors, spectrums, and the like effects of darkness. It was seldom or never that any falsely pretended to the gifts and graces of the Holy Spirit; for these things were then of little use or request in the world. But when God was pleased to renew really a fresh communication of spiritual gifts and graces unto men, in and upon the Reformation, the old dreads and terrors, nightly appearances, tending unto deeds of darkness, vanished, and everywhere, by Satan's instigation, arose false pretenders to the Spirit of God; in which way of delusion he will still be more active and industrious, as God shall increase the gifts and graces of his Spirit in his churches; though as yet, in these latter ages, he hath not attained what he was arrived unto in the primitive times of the gospel. A full and clear declaration from the Scripture of the nature of the Holy Spirit and his operations may, through the blessing of God, be of use to fortify the minds of professors against satanical delusions counterfeiting his actings and inspirations; for directions unto this purpose are given us by the holy apostle, who lived to see great havoc made in the churches by deluding spirits. Knowledge of the truth, trying of spirits that go abroad by the doctrines of the Scriptures, dependence on the Holy Spirit for his teachings according to the word, are the things which to this purpose he commends unto us.

Thirdly, There is in the days wherein we live an anti-spirit set up and advanced against the Spirit of God, in his being and all his operations, in his whole work and use towards the church of God; for this new spirit takes upon him whatever is promised to be effected by the "good Spirit of God." This is that which some men call "the light within them," though indeed it be nothing but a dark product of Satan upon their own imaginations, or at best the natural light of conscience; which some of the heathens also call "a spirit."[14] But hereunto do they trust, as to that which doth all for them, leaving no room for the "promise of the Spirit of God," nor any thing for him to do. This teacheth them, instructs them, enlightens them; to this they attend as the Samaritans to Simon Magus, and, as they say, yield obedience unto it; and from hence, with the fruits of it, do they expect acceptation with God, justification and blessedness hereafter. And one of these two things these deluded souls must fix upon, — namely, that this light whereof they speak is either the Holy Spirit of God, or it is not. If they say it is the Spirit, it will be easy to demonstrate how by their so saying they utterly destroy the very nature and being of the Holy Ghost, as will evidently appear in our explication of them. And if they say that it is not the Holy Spirit of God which they intend thereby, it will be no less manifest that they utterly exclude him, on the other side, from his whole work, and substitute another, yea, an enemy, in his room: for another God is a false god; another Christ is a false Christ; and another Spirit is a false spirit, — the spirit of antichrist. Now, because this is a growing evil amongst us, many being led away and seduced, our duty unto Jesus Christ and compassion for the souls of men do require that our utmost endeavour, in the ways of Christ's appointment, should be used to obviate this evil, which eateth as doth a canker; which also is propagated by profane and vain babblings, increasing still unto more ungodliness. Some, I confess, do unduly rage against the persons of those who have imbibed these imaginations, falling upon them with violence and fury, as they do also on others; — the Lord lay it not unto their charge! Yet this hinders not but that, by those "weapons of our warfare which are not carnal, but mighty through God to the pulling down of strongholds, casting down such like imaginations, and every high thing that exalteth itself against the knowledge of God, and bringing into captivity every thought unto the obedience of Christ," we ought to attempt the destruction of their errors and the breaking of the snares of Satan, by whom they are taken captive alive at his pleasure. The course, indeed, of opposing errors and false spirits by praying, preaching, and writing, is despised by them in whose furious and haughty minds ure, seca, occide, "burn, cut, and kill," are alone of any signification, — that think, "Arise, Peter, kill and eat," to be a precept of more use and advantage unto them than all the commands of Jesus Christ besides; but the way proposed unto us by the Lord Jesus Christ himself, walked in by his holy apostles, and all the ancient, holy, learned writers of the church, is that which, in these matters, we must and shall attend unto: and that course which is particularly suited to obviate the evil mentioned, is, to give a full, plain, evident declaration from the Scripture of the nature and operations of the Holy Spirit of God. Hence it will be undeniably manifest what a stranger this pretended light is unto the true Spirit of Christ; how far it is from being of any real use to the souls of men; yea, how it is set up in opposition unto him and his work, by whom and by which alone we become accepted with God, and are brought unto the enjoyment of him.

Fourthly, There are, moreover, many hurtful and noxious opinions concerning the Holy Ghost gone abroad in the world, and entertained by many, to the subversion of the faith which they have professed.[15] Such are those whereby his deity and personality are denied.

About these there have been many contests in the world: some endeavouring with diligence and subtlety to promote the perverse opinions mentioned; others "contending," according to their duty, "for the faith once delivered unto the saints." But these disputations are for the most part so managed, that although the truth be in some of them strenuously vindicated, yet the minds of believers generally are but little edified by them; for the most are unacquainted with the ways and terms of arguing, which are suited to convince or "stop the mouths of gainsayers," rather than to direct the faith of others.

Besides, our knowledge of things is more by their operations and proper effects than from their own nature and formal reason.

Especially is it so in divine things, and particularly with respect unto God himself. In his own glorious being he dwelleth in light, whereunto no creature can approach. In the revelation that he hath made of himself by the effects of his will, in his word and works, are we to seek after him. By them are the otherwise invisible things of God made known, his attributes declared, and we come to a better acquaintance with him than any we can attain by our most diligent speculations about his nature itself immediately. So is it with the Holy Ghost and his personality. He is in the Scripture[16] proposed unto us to be known by his properties and works, adjuncts and operations; by our duty towards him and our offences against him. The due consideration of these things is that which will lead us into that assured knowledge of his being and subsistence which is necessary for the guidance of our faith and obedience; which is the end of all these inquiries, Col. ii. 2. Wherefore, although I shall by the way explain, confirm, and vindicate the testimonies that are given in the Scripture, or some of them, unto his deity and personality, yet the principal means that I shall insist on for the establishing of our faith in him is the due and just exposition and declaration of the administrations and operations that are ascribed unto him in the Scriptures; which also will give great light into the whole mystery and economy of God in the work of our salvation by Jesus Christ.

Fifthly, The principal cause and occasion of our present undertaking is, the open and horrible opposition that is made unto the Spirit of God and his work in the world. There is no concernment of his that is not by many derided, exploded, and blasphemed. The very name of the Spirit is grown to be a reproach; nor do some think they can more despitefully expose any to scorn than by ascribing to them a "concern in the Spirit of God." This, indeed, is a thing which I have often wondered at, and do continue still so to do: for whereas in the gospel everything that is good, holy, praiseworthy in any man, is expressly assigned to the Spirit, as the immediate efficient cause and operator of it; and whereas the condition of men without him, not made partakers of him, is described to be reprobate or rejected of God, and foreign unto any interest in Christ; yet many pretending unto the belief and profession of the gospel are so far from owning or desiring a participation of this Spirit in their own persons, as that they deride and contemn them who dare plead or avow any concern in him or his works. Only, I must grant that herein they have had some that have gone before them, — namely, the old scoffing heathens; for so doth Lucian, in his Philopatris [18], speak in imitation of a Christian by way of scorn, Λέγε, παρὰ τοῦ Πνεύματος δύναμιν τοῦ λόγου λαβών· — "Speak out now, receiving power or ability of speaking from the Spirit," or "by the Spirit." Certainly an attendance to the old caution. Si non castè, tamen cautè, had been needful for some in this matter. Could they not bring their own hearts unto a due reverence of the Spirit of God, and an endeavour after the participation of his fruits and effects, yet the things that are spoken concerning him and his work in the whole New Testament, and also in places almost innumerable in the Old, might have put a check to their public contemptuous reproaches and scornful mockings, whilst they owned those writings to be of God; — but such was his entertainment in the world upon his first effusion, Acts ii. 13. Many pretences, I know, will be pleaded to give countenance unto this abomination;

for, first, they will say, "It is not the Spirit of God himself and his works, but the pretence of others unto him and them, which they so reproach and scorn." I fear this plea or excuse will prove too short and narrow to make a covering unto their profaneness. It is dangerous venturing with rudeness and petulancy upon holy things, and then framing of excuses. But in reproaches of the Lord Christ and his Spirit men will not want their pretences, John x. 32, 33. And the things of the Spirit of God, which they thus reproach and scorn in any, are either such as are truly and really ascribed unto him and wrought by him in the disciples of Jesus Christ, or they are not. If they are such as indeed are no effects of the Spirit of grace, such as he is not promised for, nor attested to work in them that do believe, as vain enthusiasms, ecstatical raptures and revelations, certainly it more became Christians, men professing, or at least pretending, a reverence unto God, his Spirit, and his word, to manifest to and convince those of whom they treat that such things are not "fruits of the Spirit," but imaginations of their own, than to deride them under the name of the Spirit, or his gifts and operations. Do men consider with whom and what they make bold in these things? But if they be things that are real effects of the Spirit of Christ in them that believe, or such as are undeniably assigned unto him in the Scripture, which they despise, what remains to give countenance unto this daring profaneness? Yea, but they say, secondly, "It is not the real true operations of the Spirit themselves, but the false pretensions of others unto them, which they traduce and expose." But will this warrant the course which it is manifest they steer in matter and manner? The same persons pretend to believe in Christ and the gospel, and to be made partakers of the benefits of his mediation; and yet, if they have not the Spirit of Christ, they have no saving interest in these things; for "if any man have not the Spirit of Christ, he is none of his." If it be, then, only their false pretending unto the Spirit of God and his works which these persons so revile and scorn, why do they not deal with them in like manner with respect unto Christ and the profession of the gospel? why do they not say unto them, "You believe in Christ, you believe in the gospel," and thereon expose them to derision? So plainly dealt the Jews with our Lord Jesus Christ, Ps. xxii. 7, 8; Matt. xxi. 38, 39. It is, therefore, the things themselves, and not the pretences pretended, that are the objects of this contempt and reproach. Besides, suppose those whom at present on other occasions they hate or despise are not partakers of the Spirit of God, but are really strangers unto the things which hypocritically they profess, — will they grant and allow that any other Christians in the world do so really partake of him as to be led, guided, directed by him; to be quickened, sanctified, purified by him; to be enabled unto communion with God, and all duties of holy obedience by him, with those other effects and operations for which he is promised by Jesus Christ unto his disciples? If they will grant these things to be really effected and accomplished in any, let them not be offended with them who desire that they should be so in themselves, and declare themselves to that purpose; and men would have more charity for them under their petulant scoffing than otherwise they are able to exercise. It will, thirdly, yet be pleaded, "That they grant as fully as any the being of the Holy Ghost, the promise of him and his real operations; only, they differ from others as to the sense and exposition of those phrases and expressions that are used concerning these things in the Scripture, which those others abuse in an unintelligible manner, as making them proper which indeed are metaphorical." But is this the way which they like and choose to express their notions and apprehensions, — namely, openly to revile and scorn the very naming and asserting the work of the Spirit of God, in the words which himself hath taught? A boldness this is, which, as whereof the former ages have not given us a precedent, so we hope the future will not afford an instance of any to follow the example. For their sense and apprehension of these things, they shall afterward be examined, so far as they have dared to discover them. In the meantime, we know that the Socinians acknowledge a Trinity, the sacrifice of Christ, the expiation of sin made thereby, and yet we have some differences with them about these things; and so we have with these men about the Spirit of God and his dispensation under the gospel, though, like them, they would grant the things spoken of them to be true, as metaphorically to be interpreted. But of these things we must treat more fully hereafter.

I say it is so come to pass, amongst many who profess they believe the gospel to be true, that the name or naming of the Spirit of God is become a reproach; so also is his whole work. And the promise of him made by Jesus Christ unto his church is rendered useless and frustrated. It was the main, and upon the matter the only, supportment which he left unto it in his bodily absence, the only means of rendering the work of his mediation effectual in them and among them; for without him all others, as the word, ministry, and ordinances of worship, are lifeless and useless. God is not glorified by them, nor the souls of men advantaged. But it is now uncertain with some of what use he is unto the church; yea, as far as I can discern, whether he be of any or no. Some have not trembled to say and contend, that some things as plainly ascribed unto him in the Scripture as words can make an assignation of any thing, are the cause of all the troubles and confusions in the world! Let them have the word or tradition outwardly revealing the will of God, and what it is that he would have them do (as the Jews have both to this day); these being made use of by their own reason, and improved by their natural abilities, they make up the whole of man, all that is required to render the persons or duties of any accepted with God! Of what use, then, is the Spirit of God in these things? Of none at all, it may be, nor the doctrine concerning him, "but only to fill the world with a buzz and noise, and to trouble the minds of men with unintelligible notions." Had not these things been spoken, they should not have been repeated; for death lieth at the door in them. So, then, men may pray without him, and preach without him, and turn to God without him, and perform all their duties without him well enough; for if anyone shall plead the necessity of his assistance for the due performance of these things, and ascribe unto him all that is good and well done in them, he shall hardly escape from being notably derided. Yet all this while we would be esteemed Christians! And what do such persons think of the prayers of the ancient church and Christians unto him for the working of all good in them, and their ascriptions of every good thing unto him?[17] And wherein have we any advantage of the Jews, or wherein consists the pre-eminence of the gospel? They have the word of God, that part of it which was committed unto their church, and which in its kind is sufficient to direct their faith and obedience; for so is the "sure word of prophecy," if diligently attended unto, 2 Pet. i. 19. And if traditions be of any use, they can outvie all the world. Neither doth this sort of men want their wits and the exercise of them. Those who converse with them in the things of this world do not use to say they are all fools. And for their diligence in the consideration of the letter of the Scripture, and inquiring into it according to the best of their understanding, none will question it but those unto whom they and their concernments are unknown. And yet after all this, they are Jews still. If we have the New Testament no otherwise than they have the Old, — have only the letter of it to philosophize upon, according to the best of our reasons and understandings, without any dispensation of the Spirit of God accompanying it to give us a saving light into the mystery of it, and to make it effectual unto our souls, — I shall not fear to say, but that as they call themselves "Jews and are not, but are the synagogue of Satan," Rev. ii. 9, so we who pretend ourselves to be Christians, as to all the saving ends of the gospel, shall not be found in a better condition.

And yet it were to be wished that even here bounds might be fixed unto the fierceness of some men's spirits. But they will not suffer themselves to be so confined. In many places they are transported with rage and fury, so as to stir up persecution against such as are really anointed with the Spirit of Christ, and that for no other reason but because they are so, Gal. iv. 29. Other things, indeed, are pretended by them, but all the world may see that they are not of such importance as to give countenance unto their wrath. This is the latent cause which stirs it up, and is oftentimes openly expressed.

These things at present are charged only as the miscarriages of private persons. When they are received in churches, they are the cause of and an entrance into a fatal defection and apostasy. From the foundation of the world, the principal revelation that God made of himself was in the oneness of his nature and his monarchy over all. And herein the person of the Father was immediately represented with his power and authority; for he is the fountain and original of the Deity, the other persons as to their subsistence being of him: only, he did withal give out promises concerning the peculiar exhibition of the Son in the flesh in an appointed season, as also of the Holy Spirit, to be given by him in an especial manner. Hereby were their persons to be signally glorified in this world, it being the will of God that all "men should honour the Son as they honoured the Father," and the Holy Spirit in like manner. In this state of things, the only apostasy of the church could be polytheism and idolatry. Accordingly, so it came to pass. The church of Israel was continually prone to these abominations, so that scarcely a generation passed, or very few, wherein the body of the people did not more or less defile themselves with them. To wean and recover them from this sin was the principal end of the preaching of those prophets which God from time to time sent unto them, 2 Kings xvii. 13. And this also was the cause of all the calamities which befell them, and of all the judgments which God inflicted on them, as is testified in all the historical books of the Old Testament, and confirmed by instances innumerable. To put an end hereunto, God at length brought a total desolation upon the whole church, and caused the people to be carried into captivity out of their own land; and hereby it was so far effected that, upon their return, whatever other sins they fell into, yet they kept themselves from idols and idolatry, Ezek. xvi. 41–43, xxiii. 27, 48. And the reason hereof was, because the time was now drawing nigh wherein they were to be tried with another dispensation of God; — the Son of God was to be sent unto them in the flesh. To receive and obey him was now to be the principal instance and trial of their faith and obedience. They were no longer to be tried merely by their faith, whether they would own only the God of Israel, in opposition unto all false gods and idols, for that ground God had now absolutely won upon them; but now all is to turn on this hinge, whether they would receive the Son of God coming in the flesh, according to the promise. Here the generality of that church and people fell by their unbelief, apostatized from God, and became thereby neither church nor people, John viii. 24. They being rejected, the Son of God calls and gathers another church, founding it on his own person with faith, and the profession of it therein, Matt. xvi. 18, 19. In this new church, therefore, this foundation is fixed, and this ground made good, that Jesus Christ, the Son of God, is to be owned and honoured as we honour the Father, 1 Cor. iii. 11; John v. 23. And herein all that are duly called Christians do agree, as the church of Israel did in one God after their return from the captivity of Babylon. But now the Lord Jesus Christ being ascended unto his Father, hath committed his whole affairs in the church and in the world unto the Holy Spirit, John xvi. 7–11. And it is on this design of God that the person of the Spirit may be singularly exalted in the church; unto whom they were so in the dark before, that some (none of the worst of them) professed they had not so much as heard whether there were any Holy Ghost or no, Acts xix. 2, — that is, at least, as unto the peculiar dispensation of him then introduced in the church. Wherefore, the duty of the church now immediately respects the Spirit of God, who acts towards it in the name of the Father and of the Son; and with respect unto him it is that the church in its present state is capable of an apostasy from God. And whatever is found of this nature amongst any, here it hath its beginning; for the sin of despising his person and rejecting his work now is of the same nature with idolatry of old, and the Jews' rejection of the person of the Son. And whereas there was a relief provided against these sins, because there was a new dispensation of the grace of God to ensue, in the evangelical work of the Holy Ghost, if men sin against him and his operations, containing the perfection and complement of God's revelation of himself unto them, their condition is deplorable.

It may be some will say and plead, that whatever is spoken of the Holy Ghost, his graces, gifts, and operations, did entirely belong unto the first times of the gospel, wherein they were manifested by visible and wonderful effects, — to those times they were confined; and, consequently, that we have no other interest or concern in them but as in a recorded testimony given of old unto the truth of the gospel. This is so, indeed, as unto his extraordinary and miraculous operations, but to confine his whole work thereunto is plainly to deny the truth of the promises of Christ, and to overthrow his church; for we shall make it undeniably evident that none can believe in Jesus Christ, or yield obedience unto him, or worship God in him, but by the Holy Ghost. And, therefore, if the whole dispensation of him and his communications unto the souls of men do cease, so doth all faith in Christ and Christianity also.

On these and the like considerations it is that I have thought it necessary for myself, and unto the church of God, that the Scripture should be diligently searched in and concerning this great matter; for none can deny but that the glory of God, the honour of the gospel, the faith and obedience of the church, with the everlasting welfare of our own souls, are deeply concerned herein.

The apostle Peter, treating about the great things of the gospel, taught by himself and the rest of the apostles of our Lord Jesus Christ, tells those to whom he wrote that in what was so preached unto them they had not "followed cunningly-devised fables," 2 Pet. i. 16; for so were the "power and coming of our Lord Jesus Christ" then reported to be in the world. What was preached concerning them was looked on as "cunningly-devised" and artificially-framed "fables," to inveigle and allure the people. This the apostle gives his testimony against, and withal appeals unto the divine assurance which they had of the holy truths delivered unto them, verses 17–21. In like manner, our Lord Jesus Christ himself having preached the doctrine of regeneration unto Nicodemus, he calls it into question, as a thing incredible or unintelligible, John iii. 4; for whose instruction and the rebuke of his ignorance, he lets him know that he spake nothing but what he brought with him from heaven, — from the eternal Fountain of goodness and truth, verses 11–13. It is fallen out not much otherwise in this matter.

The doctrine concerning the Spirit of God, and his work on the souls of men, hath been preached in the world. What he doth in convincing men of sin; what in working godly sorrow and humiliation in them; what is the exceeding greatness of his power, which he puts forth in the regeneration and sanctification of the souls of men; what are the supplies of grace which he bestows on them that do believe; what assistance he gives unto them as the Spirit of grace and supplications, — hath been preached, taught, and pressed on the minds of them that attend unto the dispensation of the word of the gospel. Answerable hereunto, men have been urged to try, search, examine themselves, as to what of this work of the Holy Ghost they have found, observed, or had experience to have been effectually accomplished in or upon their own souls. And hereon they have been taught that the great concernments of their peace, comfort, and assurance, of their communion among themselves as the saints of God, with many other ends of their holy conversation, do depend. Nay, it is, and hath been constantly, taught them that if there be not an effectual work of the Holy Ghost upon their hearts, they "cannot enter into the kingdom of God." Now, these things, and whatever is spoken in the explication of them, are by some called in question, if not utterly rejected; yea, some look on them as "cunningly-devised fables," — things that some not long since invented, and others have propagated for their advantage. Others say that what is delivered concerning them is hardly, if at all, to be understood by rational men, being only empty speculations about things wherein Christian religion is little or not at all concerned. Whereas, therefore, many, very many, have received these things as sacred truths, and are persuaded that they have found them realized in their own souls, so that into their experience of the work of the Holy Spirit of God in them and upon them, according as it is declared in the word, all their consolation and peace with God is for the most part resolved, as that which gives them the best evidence of their interest in him who is their peace; and whereas, for the present, they do believe that unless these things are so in and with them, they have no foundation to build a hope of eternal life upon, — it cannot but be of indispensable necessity unto them to examine and search the Scripture diligently whether these things be so or no. For if there be no such work of the Spirit of God upon the hearts of men, and that indispensably necessary to their salvation; if there are no such assistances and supplies of grace needful unto every good duty as wherein they have been instructed, — then in the whole course of their profession they have only been seduced by "cunningly-devised fables," their deceived hearts have fed upon ashes, and they are yet in their sins. It is, then, of no less consideration and importance than the eternal welfare of their souls immediately concerned therein can render it, that they diligently try, examine, and search into these things, by the safe and infallible touchstone and rule of the word, whereon they may, must, and ought, to venture their eternal condition. I know, indeed, that most believers are so far satisfied in the truth of these things and their own experience of them, that they will not be moved in the least by the oppositions which are made unto them and the scorn that is cast upon them; for "he that believeth on the Son of God hath the witness in himself," 1 John v. 10: but yet, as Luke wrote his Gospel to Theophilus "that he might know the certainty of those things wherein he had been instructed," Luke i. 4, — that is, to confirm him in the truth, by an addition of new degrees of assurance unto him, — so it is our duty to be so far excited by the clamorous oppositions that are made unto the truths which we profess, and in whose being such, we are as much concerned as our souls are worth, to compare them diligently with the Scripture, that we may be the more fully confirmed and established in them. And, upon the examination of the whole matter, I shall leave them to their option, as Elijah did of old: "If Jehovah be God, follow him; but if Baal be God, follow him." If the things which the generality of professors do believe and acknowledge concerning the Spirit of God and his work on their hearts, his gifts and graces in the church, with the manner of their communication, be for the substance of them (wherein they all generally agree) according to the Scripture, taught and revealed therein, on the same terms as by them received, then may they abide in the holy profession of them, and rejoice in the consolations they have received by them; but if these things, with those others which, in the application of them to the souls of men, are directly and necessarily deduced, and to be deduced from them, are all but vain and useless imaginations, it is high time the minds of men were disburdened of them.

Footnotes:

1. Πνευματικὰ τὰ σημεῖα καλῶν, ὅτι ταῦτα ἔργα τοῦ πνεύματος μόνου, οὐδὲν ἀνθρωπίνης ἐπεισφερούσης σπουδῆς, εἰς τὸ τὰ τοιαῦτα θαυματουργεῖν. — Chrysost. in loc. So also Ambros. and Theophylact. in loc.

2. Χαρίσματα δὲ εἶχον, οἱ μὲν ἐλάττονα, οἱ δὲ πλείω· καὶ τοῦτο αἴτιον σχίσματος αὐτοῖς ἐγένετο, οὐ παρὰ τὴν οἰκείαν φύσιν, ἀλλὰ παρὰ ἀγνωμοσύνην τῶν εἰληφότων· οἵτε γὰρ τὰ μείζονα ἔχοντες ἐπήροντο κατὰ τῶν τὰ ἐλάττονα κεκτημένων· οὗτοι δὲ αὖ πάλιν ἤλγουν, καὶ τοῖς τὰ μείζονα ἔχουσιν ἐφθόνουν. — Chrysost. in loc.

3. "Spiritualia illis traditurus, exemplum prioris conversationis memorat; ut sicut simulacrorum fuerunt formâ colentes idola, et ducebantur duce voluntate dæmoniorum; ita et colentes deum sint formâ legis dominicæ." — Ambros. in loc.

4. Τί οὖν οὐδεὶς δαίμων ὀνομάζει τὸν Θεὸν; οὐχὶ οἱ δαιμονιζόμενοι ἔλεγον οἴδαμέν σε τίς εἶ ὁ υἱὸς τοῦ Θεοῦ; οὐχὶ Παύλῳ ἔλεγον, οὗτοι οἱ ἄνθρωποι δοῦλοι τοῦ Θεοῦ τοῦ ὑψίστου εἰσίν; ἀλλὰ μαστιζόμενοι, ἀλλ' ἀναγκαζόμενοι, ἑκόντες δὲ καὶ μὴ μαστιγούμενοι, οὐδαμνοῦ. — Chrysost. in loc.

5. Crel. de Spir. Sanc., Prolegom., pp. 29–31.

6. "Ex hoc capite et proximo licet conjicere quæ fuerint dotes illius veteris ecclesiæ Christianæ, priusquam tot ceremoniis, opibus, imperiis, copiis, bellis aliisque id genus esset onerata. Nunc fere tot præclara munia ad unam Potestatem redacta sunt: h. e., Christi titulo palliatam Tyrannidem. Quid enim aliud est potestas nisi adsit animus apostolicus?" — Erasm. Annot. ad v. 4.

7. Ἀποστέλλεται μὲν οἰκονομικῶς, ἐνεργεῖ δὲ αὐτεξουσίως. — Basil. Homil. xv. de Fide.

8. "Spiritus Sanctus ad hoc missus a Christo, ad hoc postulatus de Patre ut esset doctor veritatis, Christi vicarius." — Tertul. advers. Hæret. cap. xxviii."Quoniam Dominus in cælos esset abiturus, Paracletum discipulis necessario dabat, ne illos quodammodo pupillos, quod minimè decebat, relinqueret; et sine advocato et quodam tutore desereret. Hic est enim qui ipsorum animos mentesque firmavit, qui in ipsis illuminator rerum divinarum fuit; quo

confirmati, pro nomine Domini nec carceres nec vincula timuerunt: quin imo ipsas seculi potestates et tormenta calcaverunt, armati jam scilicet per ipsum atque firmati, habentes in se dona quæ hic idem Spiritus ecclesiæ Christi sponsæ, quasi quædam ornamenta distribuit et dirigit." — Novat. de Trinitat."Totum ex Spiritus Sancti constat ducatu, quod devii diriguntur, quod impii convertuntur, quod debiles contirmantur. Spiritus rectus, Spiritus Sanctus, Spiritus principalis regit, componit, consummat et perficit, nostras inhabitat mentes, et corda quæ possidet; nec errare patitur, nec corrumpi, nec vinci quos docuerit, quos possederit, quos gladio potentissimæ veritatis accinxerit." — Cypr. de Spir. Sanc.

9. "Præsentia spirituali cum eis erat ubique futurus post ascensionem suam, et cum tota ecclesia sua in hoc mundo usque in consummationem seculi: neque enim de solis apostolis potest intelligi, 'sicut dedisti ei potestatem omnis carnis, ut onme quod dedisti ei det eis vitam æternam;' sed ubique de omnibus quibus in eum credentibus vita æterna datur." — Aug. Tractat. 106, in Evangel. Johan."Munus hoc quod in Christo est, — in consummationem seculi nobiscum; hoc expectationis nostræ solatium, hoc in donorum operationibus futuræ spei pignus est; hoc mentium lumen, hic splendour animorum est." — Hilar, lib. ii. 35, de Trinitat.

10. "Hic est qui prophetas in ecclesia constituit, magistros erudit, linguas dirigit, vertutes et sanctitates facit, opera mirabilia gerit, discretiones spirituum porrigit, gubernationes contribuit, consilia suggerit, quæque alia sunt charismatum dona componit et digerit; et ideo ecclesiam Domino undique et in omnibus consummatam et perfectam facit." — Tertul.

11. "Hic est qui operatur ex aquis secundam nativitatem, semen quoddam divini generis, et consecrator cælestis nativitatis; pignus promissæ hæreditatis et quasi chirographum quoddam æternæ salutis; qui nos Dei faciat templum et nos efficiat domum, qui interpellat divinas aures pro nobis gemitibus ineloquacibus, advocationis officia, et defensionis exhibens munera, inhabitator corporibus nostris ductus, et sanctitatis effector; hic est qui inexplebiles cupiditates coercet," etc. — Novat. de Trinitat.

12. "Omnibus quidem quæ divina sunt cum reverentia et vehementi cura opertet intendere, maxime autem his quæ de Spiritus Sancti divinitate dicuntur, præsertim cum blasphemia in eum sine venia sit; ita ut blasphemantis pœna tendatur non solum in omne præsens seculum, sed etiam in futurum. Ait quippe Salvator, blasphemanti in Spiritum Sanctum non esse remissionem, 'neque in isto seculo neque in futuro:' unde magis ac magis intendere oportet quæ Scripturarum de eo relatio sit: ne in aliquem, saltem per ignorantiam, blasphemiæ error obrepat." — Didym, de Spir. Sanc. lib. i., Interpret. Hieron.[Didymus, from whom Owen quotes so copiously in the following pages, was a professor of theology in Alexandria, and died A.D. 396 at the age of eighty-five. He became blind when only four years old, and yet contrived to acquire great distinction for his knowledge of all the sciences of the age, and especially of theology. His treatise on the Holy Spirit was translated by Jerome into Latin, and appears among the works of that father. — Ed.]

13. Ἐπειδὰν γὰρ τελεταῖς τισι καὶ μαγγανείαις κατέδησε δαίμονά τις εἰς ἄνθρωπον, καὶ ἐμαντεύετο ἐκεῖνος, καὶ μαντευόμενος ἐῤῥίπτετο, καὶ ἐσπαράττετο, καὶ ἐνεγκεῖν τοῦ δαίμονος τὴν ὀρνὴν οὐκ ἠδύνατο ἀλλ' ἔμελλε διασπώμενος οὕτως ἀπόλλυσθαι, τοῖς τὰ τοιαῦτα μαγγανεύουσι φησί.Λύσατε λοιπὸν ἄνακτα, βροτὸς Θεὸν οὐκ ἔτι χωρεῖ. — Chrysost. in 1 Cor. xii.

14. "Ita dico, Lucili, sacer intra nos spiritus sedet, malorum bonorumque nostrorum observator et custos: hic prout a nobis tractatus est, ita nos ipse tractat." — Senec. Ep. xli.

15. "Quoniam quidam temeritate potius quam recta via etiam in superna eriguntur, et hæc de Spiritu Sancto jactitant, quæ neque in Scripturis lecta, nec a quoquam ecclesiasticorum veterum usurpata sunt, compulsi sumus creberrimæ exhortationi fratrum cedere, quæque sit nostra de eo opinio etiam Scripturarum testimoniis comprobare; ne imperitiâ tanti dogmatis, hi qui contraria opponunt decipiant eos qui sine discussione sollicita in adversariorum sententiam statim pertrahuntur." — Didym. De Spir. Sanc. lib. i.

16. "Appellatio Spiritus Sancti, et ea quæ monstratur ex ipsa appellatione substantia, penitus ab his ignoratur, qui extra sacram Scripturam philosophantur: solummodo enim in nostratibus literis et notio ejus et vocabulum refertur tam in nobis quam in veteribus." — Didym. de Spir. Sanc. lib. i.

17. "Adesto Sancte Spiritus, et paraclesin tuam expectantibus illabere cælitus, sanctifica templum corporis nostri et consecra in habitaculum tuum; desiderantes te animas tua præsentiâ

lætifica, dignam te habitatore domum compone; adorna thalamum tuum, et quietis tuæ reclinatorium circumda varietatibus virtutum; sterne pavimenta pigmentis; niteat mansio tua carbunculis flammeis, et gemmarum splendoribus; et omnium Chrismatum intrinsecus spirent odoramenta; affatim balsami liquor fragrantiâ sua cubiculum suum imbuat; et abigens inde quicquid tabidum est, quicquid corruptelæ seminarium, stabile et perpetuum hoc facias gaudium nostrum, et creationis tuæ renovationem in decore immarcessibili solides in æternum." — Cypr., de Spir. Sanc.

Chapter II - The name and titles of the Holy Spirit

Of the name of the Holy Spirit — Various uses of the words רוּחַ and πνεῦμα — רוּחַ for the wind or any thing invisible with a sensible agitation, Amos iv. 13 — Mistakes of the ancients rectified by Hierom — רוּחַ metaphorically for vanity, metonymically for the part or quarter of any thing; for our vital breath, the rational soul, the affections, angels good and bad — Ambiguity from the use of the word, how to be removed — Rules concerning the Holy Spirit — The name "Spirit," how peculiar and appropriate unto him — Why he is called the "Holy Spirit" — Whence called the "Good Spirit," the "Spirit of God," the "Spirit of the Son" — Acts ii. 33, 1 Pet. i. 10, 11, explained — 1 John iv. 3, vindicated.

Before we engage into the consideration of the things themselves concerning which we are to treat, it will be necessary to speak something unto the name whereby the third person in the Trinity is commonly known and peculiarly called in the Scripture. This is the "Spirit," or the "Holy Spirit," or the "Holy Ghost," as we usually speak. And this I shall do that we be not deceived with the homonymy of the word, nor be at a loss in the intention of those places of Scripture where it is used unto other purposes: for it is so that the name of the second person, ὁ Λόγος, "the Word," and of the third τὸ Πνεῦμα, "the Spirit," are often applied to signify other things; I mean, those words are so. And some make their advantages of the ambiguous use of them. But the Scripture is able of itself to manifest its own intention and meaning unto humble and diligent inquirers into it.

It is, then, acknowledged that the use of the words רוּחַ and πνεῦμα in the Old Testament and New is very various; yet are they the words whereby alone the Holy Spirit of God is denoted. Their peculiar signification, therefore, in particular places is to be collected and determined from the subject-matter treated of in them, and other especial circumstances of them. This was first attempted by the most learned Didymus of Alexandria, whose words, therefore, I have set down at large, and shall cast his observations into a more perspicuous method, with such additions as are needful for the farther clearing of the whole matter.[18]

First, In general, רוּחַ and πνεῦμα signify a wind or spirit, — that is, any thing which moves and is not seen. So the air in a violent agitation is called רוּחַ: Gen. viii. 1, אֱלֹהִים וַיַּעֲבֵר עַל־הָאָרֶץ רוּחַ; — "And God made a wind," or "spirit," that is, a strong and mighty wind, "to pass over the earth," for the driving and removal of the waters. So πνεῦμα is used, John iii. 8, Τὸ πνεῦμα ὅπου θέλει πνεῖ κ.τ.λ., — "The wind bloweth where it listeth, and thou hearest the sound thereof, but canst not tell whence it cometh, nor whither it goeth;" which is a proper description of this first signification of the word. It is an agitation of the air which is unseen. So Ps. i. 4. And in this sense, sometimes it signifies a "great and strong wind," — that is, 1, וְחָזָק גְּדוֹלָה רוּחַ Kings xix. 11; and sometimes a cool and soft wind, or a light easy agitation of the air, such as often ariseth in the evenings of the spring or summer. So Gen. iii. 8, "God walked in the garden" לְרוּחַ הַיּוֹם, "in the cool of the day;" that is, when the evening air began to breathe gently, and moderate the heat of the day. So in the poet, —

> "Solis ad occasum, quum frigidus aëra vespe Temperat."

Virg. Geor.iii. 336. "At the going down of the sun, when the cold evening tempers the heat of the air." And some think this to be the sense of that place, Ps. civ. 4, "Who maketh his angels רוּחוֹת, spirits," — swift, agile, powerful as mighty winds. But the reader may consult our Exposition on Heb. i. 7. This is one signification of the word רוּחַ, or this is one thing denoted by it in the Scripture. So, among many other places, expressly Amos iv. 13, "For, lo," הָרִים יוֹצֵר רוּחַ וּבֹרֵא, he that formeth the mountains, and createth the spirit," that is, "the wind." The LXX. render this place, Στερεῶν βροντὴν καὶ κτίζων πνεῦμα· — "Who establisheth the thunder, and createth the spirit;" though some copies read, τὰ ὄρη, "the mountains."

And the next words in the text, מַה־שֵּׂיחוֹ לְאָדָם וּמַגִּיד,[19] — "And declareth unto man what is his thought," they render, Καὶ ἀπαγγέλλων εἰς ἀνθρώπους τὸν Χριστὸν αὐτοῦ, — "And declareth unto men his Christ," or his Anointed, or his Messiah; for they took מַה־שֵּׂיחוֹ for מְשִׁיחוֹ by inadvertency, and not for want of points or vowels as some imagine, seeing the mistake consists in the casting out of a letter itself. And thence the old Latin translation renders the words, "Firmans tonitruum, et creans Spiritum, et annuncians in homines Christum suum;" which Hierom rectified into "Formans montes, et creans ventum, et annuntians homini eloquium suum," discovering in his comment the mistake of the LXX. But it is certain that, from the ambiguity of the word רוּחַ in this place, with the corrupt translations making mention of Christ in the next words, some who of old denied the deity of the Holy Spirit mightily insisted on it to prove him a creature; as may be seen in Didymus, Ambrose, Hierom, Hilary, and the ancients generally. But the context determines the signification of the word beyond all just exceptions. It is the power of God in making and disposing of things here below, whether dreadful for their greatness and height, as the mountains; or mighty and effectual in their operations, as the wind; or secret in their conceptions, as the thoughts of men; or stable in their continuance, as the night and day, the evening and morning, without the least respect to Christ or the Spirit, that it treateth of.

And I cannot but observe from hence the great necessity there is of searching the original text in the interpretation of the Scriptures, as it might be evidenced by a thousand other instances; but one we may take from two great and learned men, who were contemporaries in the Latin church, in their thoughts on this place.

The one is Ambrose, who, interpreting these words in his second book, De Spiritu Sancto, lib. ii. cap. 6, being deceived by the corrupt translation mentioned, "Annuncians in homines Christum suum," is forced to give a very strained exposition of that which, in truth, is not in the text, and to relieve himself also with another corruption in the same place, where "forming the mountains" is rendered by "establishing the thunder;" and yet, when he hath done all, he can scarce free himself of the objection about the creation of the Spirit, which he designs to answer. His words are, "Siquis propheticum dictum, ideo derivandum putet ad interpretationem Spiritus Sancti; quia habet, 'annuncians in homines Christum suum,' is ad incarnationis Dominicæ mysteria dictum facilius derivabit. Nam si te movet quia Spiritum dixit, et hoc non putas derivandum ad mysterium assumptionis humanæ; prosequere scripturas et invenies optime congruere de Christo, de quo bene convenit æstimari, quia firmavit tonitrua adventu suo; vim videlicet et sonum cœlestium scripturarum; quarum velut quodam tonitru mentes nostræ redduntur attonitæ, ut timere discamus, et reverntiam cœlestibus deferamus oraculis. Denique, in Evangelio fratres Domini filii tonitru dicebantur. Et cum vox Patris facta esset dicentis ad Filium, 'Et honorificavi te, et iterum honorificabo,' Judæi dicebant, 'Tonitruum factum est illi.' " And hereon, with some observations to the same purpose, he adds, "Ergo tonitrua ad sermones Domini retulit, quorum in omnem terram exivit sonus; Spiritum autem hoc loco animam, quam suscepit rationabilem et perfectam intelligimus." The substance of his discourse is, that treating of Christ (who indeed is neither mentioned nor intended in the text), he speaks of "confirming the thunder" (which nowhere here appears), by which the sound of the Scriptures and preaching of the word is intended; the spirit that was created being the human soul of Jesus Christ. Nor was he alone in this interpretation. Didym. lib. 2 de Spiritu Sancto, Athanas. ad Serapion, Basil. lib. 4. contra Eunom., amongst the Grecians, are in like manner entangled with this corruption of the text; as was also Concil. Sardicen. in Socrat. lib. 2 cap. 20.

The other person intended is Hierom, who, consulting the original, as he was well able to do, first translated the words, "Quia ecce formans montes, et creans ventum, et annuncians homini eloquium suum," declares the mistake of the LXX. and the occasion of it:— "Pro montibus qui Hebraicè dicuntur הָרִים; soli LXX. βροντήν, id est, tontitruum, verterunt. Cur autem illi Spiritum et nos dixerimus ventum, qui Hebraice רוּחַ vocatur, causa manifesta est: quodque sequitur, 'Annuncians homini eloquium suum,' LXX. transtulerunt, Ἀπαγγέλλων εἰς ἀνθρώπους τὸν Χριστὸν αὐτοῦ, verbi similitudine, et ambiguitate decepti." So he shows that it is not מְשִׁיחוֹ in the text, but מַה־שֵּׂיחוֹ; — that is, saith he, "juxta Aquilam, ὁμιλίαν αὐτοῦ· Symmachum, τὸ φώνημα αὐτοῦ· juxta Theodotionem, τὸν λόγον αὐτοῦ· juxta quintam editionem, τὴν ἀδολεσχίαν αὐτοῦ.

And as שִׂיחַ, whence the word is, signifies both to meditate and to speak, so the word itself intends a conceived thought, to be spoken afterward. And that ו here is reciprocal, not relative. And to this purpose is his ensuing exposition, "Qui confirmat montes, ad cujus vocem cœlorum cardines et terræ fundamenta quatiuntur. Ipse qui creat spiritum, quem in hoc loco non Spiritum Sanctum, ut hæretici suspicantur, sed ventum intelligimus, sive spiritum hominis, annuncians homini eloquium ejus, qui cogitationum secreta cognoscit," Hieron. in loc.

Secondly, Because the wind, on the account of its unaccountable variation, inconstancy, and changes, is esteemed vain, not to be observed or trusted unto, — whence the wise man tells us that "he that observeth the wind shall not sow," Eccles. xi. 4, — the word is used metaphorically to signify vanity: Eccles. v. 16, "What profit hath he that hath laboured לָרוּחַ, for the wind?" So Mic. ii. 11, "If a man walk" רוּחַ; וָשֶׁקֶר, "with the windand falsehood;" — that is, in vanity, pretending to a spirit of prophecy; and falsehood, vainly, foolishly, falsely boasting. So Job xv. 2, "Should a wise man utter" רוּחַ דעת "knowledge of wind?" vain words, with a pretence of knowledge and wisdom; and he calls them דִּבְרֵי רוּחַ, "words of wind," chap. xvi. 3. So also Jer. v. 13, "And the prophets shall become לְרוּחַ, wind," or be vain, foolish, uncertain, and false, in their predictions. But πνεῦμα is not used thus metaphorically in the New Testament.

Thirdly, By a metonymy, also, it signifies any part or quarter, as we say, of the world from whence the wind blows; as also a part of any thing divided into four sides or quarters.

So Jer. lii. 23, "There were ninety and six pomegranates רוּחָה, towards a wind;" that is, on the one side of the chapiter that was above the pillars in the temple. Ezek. v. 12, "I will scatter a third part" לְכָל רוּחַ, "into all the winds," or all parts of the earth. Hence, the "four quarters" of a thing lying to the four parts of the world are called its four winds, 1, אַרְבַּע רוּחוֹת Chron. ix. 24; whence are the τέσσαρες ἄνεμοι, "the four winds," in the New Testament, Matt. xxiv. 31. This is the use of the word in general with respect unto things natural and inanimate, and every place where it is so used gives it [a] determinate sense.

Again, [Fourthly], These words are used for any thing that cannot be seen or touched, be it in itself martial and corporeal, or absolutely spiritual and immaterial. So the vital breath which we and other living creatures breathe is called: Everything wherein was נִשְׁמַת־רוּחַ חַיִּים, "the breath of the spirit of life," Gen. vii. 22, — that vital breath which our lives are maintained by in respiration. So Ps. cxxxv. 17; Job xix. 17; which is a thing material or corporeal. But most frequently it denotes things purely spiritual and immaterial, as in finite substances it signifies the rational soul of man: Ps. xxxi. 5, "Into thine hand I commit" רוּחִי, that is, "my spirit." They are the words whereby our Saviour committed his departing soul into the hands of his Father, Luke xxiii. 46, τὸ πνεῦμά μου. So Ps. cxlvi. 4, רוּחוֹ תֵּצֵא, — "His breath," say we, "goeth forth; he returneth to his earth." It is his soul and its departure from the body that is intended. This is רוּחַ בְּנֵי הָאָדָם, that "spirit of the sons of man that goeth upward," when the "spirit of a beast goeth downward to the earth," or turneth to corruption, Eccles. iii. 21: see chap. viii. 8, xii. 7. Hence, —

Fifthly, By a metonymy also, it is taken for the affections of the mind or soul of man, and that whether they be good or evil: Gen. xlv. 27, "The spirit of Jacob revived;" he began to take heart and be of good courage. Ezek. xiii. 3, "The prophets that walk" אַחַר רוּחָם, "after their own spirit" — that is, their own desires and inclinations, — when, indeed, they had no vision, but spake what they had a mind unto. Num. xiv. 24, Caleb is said to have "another spirit" than the murmuring people, — another mind, will, purpose, or resolution. It is taken for prudence, Josh. v. 1; anger, or the irascible faculty, Eccles. vii. 9 fury, Zech. vi. 8. "He shall cut off the spirit of princes" [Ps. lxxvi. 12]; that is, their pride, insolency, and contempt of others. Πνεῦμα in the New Testament frequently intends the intellectual part of the mind or soul, and that as it is active, or in action, Luke i. 47; Rom. i. 9; — and ofttimes is taken for the mind in all its inclinations, in its whole habitual bent and design, 1 Thess. v. 23.

[Sixthly], Angels also are called spirits:— good angels, Ps. civ. 4; (and it may be an angel is intended, 1 Kings xviii. 12;) and evil angels or devils, 1 Kings xxii. 21, 22; for that spirit who appeared before the Lord, and offered himself to be a lying spirit in the mouths of Ahab's prophets, was no other but he who appeared before God, Job i. 6, who is called "Satan." These in the New Testament are called "unclean spirits," Matt. x. 1; and the observation of the ancients, that Satan is not called a spirit absolutely, but with an addition or mark of distinction, holds only in the New Testament.[20] And because evil spirits are wont to torment the minds and bodies of men, therefore evil thoughts, disorders of mind, wicked purposes, disquieting and vexing the soul, arising from or much furthered by melancholy distempers, are called, it may be, sometimes "an evil spirit." The case of Saul shall be afterward considered.

In such variety are these words used and applied in the Scripture, because of some very general notions wherein the things intended do agree. For the most part, there is no great difficulty in discovering the especial meaning of them, or what it is they signify in the several places where they occur. Their design and circumstances as to the subject-matter treated of determine the signification. And notwithstanding the ambiguous use of these words in the Old and New Testament, there are two things clear and evident unto our purpose:— First, That there is in the holy Scriptures a full, distinct revelation or declaration of the Spirit, or the Spirit of God,[21] as one singular, and every way distinct from everything else that is occasionally or constantly signified or denoted by that word "Spirit." And this not only a multitude of particular places gives testimony unto, but also the whole course of the Scripture supposeth, as that without an acknowledgment whereof nothing else contained in it can be understood or is of any use at all; for we shall find this doctrine to be the very life and soul which quickens the whole from first to last. Take away the work and powerful efficacy of the Holy Spirit from the administration of it, and it will prove but a dead letter, of no saving advantage to the souls of men; and take away the doctrine concerning him from the writing of it, and the whole will be unintelligible and useless. Secondly, That whatever is affirmed of this Holy Spirit, the Spirit of God, it all relates either to his person or his operations, and these operations of his being various, are sometimes, by a metonymy, called "spirit;" whereof afterward. I shall not, therefore, need to prove that there is a Holy Spirit distinct from all other spirits whatever, and from everything else that on several occasions is signified by that name; for this is acknowledged by all that acknowledge the Scriptures, yea, it is so by Jews and Mohammedans, as well as all sorts of Christians. And, indeed, all those false apprehensions concerning him which have at this day any countenance given unto them may be referred unto two heads:— 1. That of the modern Jews, who affirm the Holy Ghost to be the influential power of God; which conceit is entertained and diligently promoted by the Socinians. 2. That of the Mohammedans, who make him an eminent angel, and sometimes say it is Gabriel; which, being traduced from the Macedonians of old, hath found some defenders and promoters in our days.

This, then, being the name of him concerning whom we treat, some things concerning it and the use of it, as peculiarly applied unto him, are to be premised:[22] for sometimes he is called the "Spirit" absolutely; sometimes the "Holy Spirit," or, as we speak, the "Holy Ghost;" sometimes the "Spirit of God," the "good Spirit of God," the "Spirit of truth" and "holiness;" sometimes the "Spirit of Christ" or "of the Son." The first absolutely used denotes his person; the additions express his properties and relation unto the other persons.

In the name Spirit two things are included:— First, His nature or essence, — namely, that he is a pure, spiritual, or immaterial substance; for neither the Hebrews nor the Greeks can express such a being in its subsistence but by רוּחַ and πνεῦμα, a spirit. Nor is this name, firstly, given unto the Holy Spirit in allusion unto the wind in its subtlety, agility, and efficacy;[23] for these things have respect only unto his operations, wherein, from some general appearances, his works and effects are likened unto the wind and its effects, John iii. 8. But it is his substance or being which is first intended in this name.[24] So it is said of God, chap. iv. 24, Πνεῦμα ὁ Θεός· — "God is a Spirit;" that is, he is of a pure, spiritual, immaterial nature, not confined unto any place, and so not regarding one more than another in his worship; as is the design of the place to evince. It will therefore be said, that on this account the name of "Spirit" is not peculiar unto the third person, seeing it contains the description of that nature which is the same in them all; for whereas it is said, "God is a Spirit," it is not spoken of this or that person, but of the nature of God abstractedly. I grant that so it is;[25] and therefore the name "Spirit" is not, in the first place, characteristical of the third person in the Trinity, but denotes that nature whereof each person is partaker. But, moreover, as it is peculiarly and constantly ascribed unto him, it declares his especial manner and order of existence; so that wherever there is mention of the "Holy Spirit," his relation unto the Father and Son is included therein; for he is the Spirit of God. And herein there is an allusion to somewhat created, — not, as I said, to the wind in general, unto whose agility and invisibility he is compared in his operations, but unto the breath of man; for as the vital breath of a man hath a continual emanation from him, and yet is never separated utterly from his person or forsaketh him, so doth the Spirit of the Father and the Son proceed from them by a continual divine emanation, still abiding one with them: for all those allusions are weak and imperfect wherein substantial things are compared with accidental, infinite things with finite, and those that are eternal with those that are temporary. Hence, their disagreement is infinitely more than their agreement; yet such allusions doth our weakness need instruction from and by. Thus he is called פְּיו רוּחַ, Ps. xxxiii. 6, "The Spirit" or "breath of the mouth of the Lord," or "of his nostrils;" as Ps. xviii. 15, wherein there is an eminent allusion unto the breath of a man. Of the manner of this proceeding and emanation of the Spirit from the Father and the Son, so far as it is revealed, and as we are capable of a useful apprehension of it, I have treated elsewhere. And from hence, or the subsistence of the Holy Spirit in an eternal emanation from the Father and Son, as the breath of God, did our Saviour signify his communication of his gifts unto his disciples by breathing on them: John xx. 22, Ἐνεφύσησε· and because in our first creation it is said of Adam that God בְּאַפָּיו יִפַּח חַיִּים נִשְׁמַת, "breathed into his nostrils the breath of life," Gen. ii. 7. He hath the same appellation with respect unto God, Ps. xviii. 15. Thus is he called the "Spirit." And because, as we observed before, the word πνεῦμα is variously used, Didymus, de Spiritu Sancto, lib. iii., supposeth that the prefixing of the article τὸ doth distinguish the signification, and confine it to the Holy Ghost in the New Testament. Ofttimes no doubt it doth so, but not always, as is manifest from John iii. 8, where τὸ is joined with πνεῦμα, and yet only signifies "the wind." But the subject treated of, and what is affirmed of him, will sufficiently determine the signification of the word, where he is called absolutely "The Spirit."

Again; He is called, by way of eminency, the Holy Spirit, or the Holy Ghost.[26] This is the most usual appellation of him in the New Testament; and it is derived from the Old: Ps. li., קָדְשְׁךָ רוּחַ, "The Spirit of thy Holiness," or "Thy Holy Spirit" Isa. lxiii. 10, 11, רוּחַ קָדְשׁוֹ, "The Spirit of his Holiness," or "His Holy Spirit." Hence are הַקָּדוֹשׁ רוּחַ and הַקֹּדֶשׁ רוּחַ, "The Holy Spirit," and "The Spirit of Holiness," in common use among the Jews. In the New Testament he is τὸ Πνεῦμα τὸ Ἅγιον, "That Holy Spirit." And we must inquire into the special reasons of this adjunct. Some suppose it is only from his peculiar work of sanctifying us, or making us holy: for this effect of sanctification is his peculiar work, and that of what sort soever it be; whether it consist in a separation from things profane and common, unto holy uses and services, or whether it be the real infusion and operation of holiness in men, it is from him in an especial manner. And this also manifesteth him to be God, for it is God alone who sanctifieth his people: Lev. xx. 8, "I am Jehovah which sanctify you." And God in that work ascribes unto himself the title of Holy in an especial manner, and as such would have us to consider him: chap. xxi. 8, "I the Lord, which sanctify you, am holy." And this may be one reason of the frequent use of this property with reference unto the Spirit.

But this is not the whole reason of this name and appellation: for where he is first so mentioned, he is called "The Spirit of God's Holiness," Ps. li. 11, Isa. lxiii. 10, 11; and in the New Testament absolutely "The Spirit of Holiness," Rom. i. 4 And this respects his nature, in the first place, and not merely his operations.[27] As God, then, absolutely is called "Holy," "The Holy One," and "The Holy One of Israel," being therein described by that glorious property of his nature whereby he is "glorious in holiness," Exod. xv. 11, and whereby he is distinguished from all false gods, ("Who is like unto thee, O Jehovah, among the gods? who is like thee, glorious in holiness?") so is the Spirit called "Holy" to denote the holiness of his nature. And on this account is the opposition made between him and the unholy or unclean spirit: Mark iii. 29, 30, "He that shall blaspheme against the Holy Ghost hath never forgiveness: because they said, He hath an unclean spirit." And herein first his personality is asserted; for the unclean spirit is a person, and if the Spirit of God were only a quality or accident, as some fancy and dream, there could no comparative opposition be made between him and this unclean spirit, — that is, the devil. So also are they opposed with respect unto their natures. His nature is holy, whereas that of the unclean spirit is evil and perverse. This is the foundation of his being called "Holy," even the eternal glorious holiness of his nature.

And on this account he is so styled also with respect unto all his operations; for it is not only with regard unto the particular work of regeneration and sanctification, or making of us holy, but unto all his works and operations, that he is so termed: for he being the immediate operator of all divine works that outwardly are of God, and they being in themselves all holy, be they of what kind soever, he is called the "Holy Spirit." Yea, he is so called to attest and witness that all his works, all the works of God, are holy, although they may be great and terrible, and such as to corrupt reason may have another appearance; in all which we are to acquiesce in this, that the "Holy One in the midst of us will do no iniquity," [Hos. xi. 9], Zeph. iii. 5. The Spirit of God, then, is thus frequently and almost constantly called "Holy," to attest that all the works of God, whereof he is the immediate operator, are holy: for it is the work of the Spirit to harden and blind obstinate sinners, as well as to sanctify the elect; and his acting in the one is no less holy than in the other, although holiness be not the effect of it in the objects. So, when he came to declare his dreadful work of the final hardening and rejection of the Jews, — one of the most tremendous effects of divine Providence, a work which, for the strangeness of it, men "would in no wise believe though it were declared unto them," Acts xiii. 41, — he was signally proclaimed Holy by the seraphims that attended his throne, Isa. vi. 3, 9–12; John xii. 40; Acts xxviii. 25, 26.

There are, indeed, some actions on men and in the world that are wrought, by God's permission and in his righteous judgment, by evil spirits; whose persons and actings are placed in opposition to the Spirit of God. So 1 Sam. xvi. 14, 15, "The Spirit of the Lord departed from Saul, and an evil spirit from the Lord troubled him. And Saul's servants said unto him, Behold now, an evil spirit from God troubleth thee." So also verse 23, "The evil spirit from God was upon Saul." So chap. xviii. 10, xix. 9. This spirit is called, רוּחַ־אֱלֹהִים רָעָה, — an evil spirit of God," chap. xvi. 15; and absolutely רוּחַ־אֱלֹהִים — "a spirit of God," verse 23, where we have supplied "evil" in the translation. But these expressions are to be regulated and explained by verse 14, where he is called רוּחַ־רָעָה מֵאֵת יְהוָה, — "an evil spirit from the Lord;" that is, appointed and commissioned by him for the punishing and terrifying of Saul: for as the Spirit of the Lord departed from him, by withdrawing his assistance and influential operations, whereby he had wrought in him those gifts and abilities of mind which fitted him unto the discharge of his kingly office, upon the first impressions whereof he was "turned into another man" from what he was in his private condition, chap. x. 6–9; so the evil spirit came upon him to excite out of his own adust melancholy, discontents, fears, a sense of guilt, as also to impress terrifying thoughts and apprehensions on his imagination; for so it is said," An evil spirit from the Lord" בִּעֲתַתּוּ, chap. xvi. 14, "terrified him," frightened him with dreadful agitations of mind. And, that we may touch a little on this by the way, the foundation of this trouble and distress of Saul lay in himself: for as I do grant that he was sometimes under an immediate agitation of body and mind from the powerful impressions of the devil upon him, — for under them it is said he "prophesied in the midst of the house," 1 Sam. xviii. 10, which argues an extraordinary and involuntary effect upon him, — yet principally he wrought by the excitation and provocation of his personal distempers, moral and natural; for these have in themselves a great efficacy in cruciating the minds of guilty persons. So Tacitus observes out of Plato, Annal. lib. vi. 6, "Neque frustra præstantissimus sapientiæ firmare solitus est, si recludantur tyrannorum mentes, posse aspici laniatus et ictus; quando, ut corpora verberibus, ita sævitia, libidine, malis consultis, animus dilaceretur;" — "The most eminent wise man was not wont in vain to affirm, that if the minds of tyrants were laid open and discovered, it would be seen how they were cruciated and punished; seeing that as the body is rent and torn by stripes, so is the mind by cruelty, lusts, evil counsels and undertakings." So he, as I suppose from Plato de Repub. lib. ix., where Socrates disputes sundry things to that purpose. And another Roman historian gives us a signal instance hereof in Jugurtha, after he had contracted the guilt of many horrible wickednesses.[28] And yet this work in itself is of the same kind with what God sometimes employs holy angels about, because it is the execution of his righteous judgments. So it was a "watcher and an holy one" that in such a case smote Nebuchadnezzar with a sudden madness and frenzy, Dan. iv. 13–17 To return; As he is called the Holy, so he is the Good Spirit of God: Ps. cxliii. 10, רוּחֲךָ טוֹבָה תַּנְחֵנִי; — "Thy Spirit is good; lead me into the land of uprightness;" so ours:— rather, "Thy good Spirit shall lead me;" or, as Junius, "Spiritu tuo bone deduc me," — "Lead me by thy good Spirit." The Chaldee here adds קוּדְשָׁךְ, — "The good Spirit of thy holiness" or "Thy holy good Spirit." Didymus, lib. ii.

de Spir. Sanc., says that some copies here read τὸ ἅγιον, a remembrance whereof is in the ms. of Thecla, and not elsewhere. So Neh. ix. 20, "Thou gavest them" רוּחֲךָ הַטּוֹבָה, "thy good Spirit to instruct them." And he is called so principally from his nature, which is essentially good, as "there is none good but one, that is, God," Matt. xix. 17; as also from his operations, which are all good as they are holy; and unto them that believe are full of goodness in their effects. Crell. Prolegom., p. 7, distinguisheth between this good Spirit and the Holy Spirit, or the Holy Ghost; for this good Spirit he would confine unto the Old Testament, making it the author or cause of those gifts of wisdom, courage, prudence, and government, that were granted unto many of the people of old. So it is said of Bezaleel, that he was "filled with the Spirit of God, in wisdom, and understanding, and in knowledge," Exod. xxxi. 3; so xxxv. 31; — "That is," saith he, "with this 'good Spirit of God.'" So also, it is pretended, in all those places where the Spirit of God is said to "come on" men to enable them unto some great and extraordinary work, as Judges iii. 10. But this is plainly to contradict the apostle, who tells us that there are, indeed, various operations, but one Spirit; and that the one and self-same Spirit worketh all these things as he pleaseth, 1 Cor. xii. 6, 11. And if from every different or distinct effect of the Spirit of God we must multiply spirits, and assign every one of them to a distinct spirit, no man will know what to make of the Spirit of God at last.[29] Probably, we shall have so many feigned spirits as to lose the only true one. As to this particular instance, David prays that God would "lead him by his good Spirit," Ps. cxliii. 10. Now, certainly, this was no other but that Holy Spirit which he prays in another place that the Lord would not take from him: Ps. li. 11, "Take not thy Holy Spirit from me;" which is confessed to be the Holy Ghost. This he also mentions, 2 Sam. xxiii. 2, "The Spirit of the Lord spake by me, and his word was in my tongue." And what Spirit this was Peter declares, 2 Epist. i. 21, "Holy men of God spake in old time as they were moved by the Holy Ghost." So vain is this pretence.

Again; He is commonly called the Spirit of God, and the Spirit of the Lord; so, in the first mention of him, Gen. i. 2, רוּחַ אֱלֹהִים, "The Spirit of God moved upon the face of the waters." And I doubt not but that the name אֱלֹהִים, "Elohim," which includes a plurality in the same nature, is used in the creation and the whole description of it to intimate the distinction of the divine persons; for presently upon it the name Jehovah is mentioned also, chap. ii. 4, but so as Elohim is joined with it. But that name is not used in the account given us of the work of creation, because it hath respect only unto the unity of the essence of God. Now, the Spirit is called the "Spirit of God" originally and principally, as the Son is called the "Son of God;" for the name of "God" in those enunciations is taken personally for the Father, — that is, God the Father, the Father of Christ, and our Father, John xx. 17. And he is thus termed ὑποστατικῶς, upon the account of the order and nature of personal subsistence and distinction in the holy Trinity. The person of the Father being "fons et origo Trinitatis," the Son is from him by eternal generation, and is therefore his Son, the Son of God; whose denomination as the Father is originally from hence, even the eternal generation of the Son. So is the person of the Holy Spirit from him by eternal procession or emanation. Hence is that relation of his to God even the Father, whence he is called the "Spirit of God." And he is not only called Πνεῦμα τοῦ Θεοῦ, the "Spirit of God," but Πνεῦμα τὸ ἐκ τοῦ Θεοῦ, "the Spirit that is of God," which proceedeth from him as a distinct person.[30] This, therefore, arising from and consisting in his proceeding from him, he is called, metaphorically, "The breath of his mouth," as proceeding from him by an eternal spiration. On this foundation and supposition he is also called, secondly, "The Spirit of God" διακριτικῶς, to difference him from all other spirits whatever; as, thirdly, also, because he is promised, given, and sent of God, for the accomplishment of his whole will and pleasure towards us. The instances hereof will be afterward considered. But these appellations of him have their foundation in his eternal relation unto the Father, before mentioned.

On the same account originally, he is also called the Spirit of the Son: "God hath sent forth the Spirit of the Son into your hearts," Gal. iv. 6; — and the Spirit of Christ: "What time the Spirit of Christ which was in them did signify," 1 Pet. i. 11. So Rom. viii. 9, "But ye are not in the flesh, but in the Spirit, if so be that the Spirit of God dwell in you. Now if any man have not the Spirit of Christ, he is none of his."[31] The Spirit, therefore, of God and the Spirit of Christ are one and the same; for that hypothetical proposition, "If any man have not the Spirit of Christ, he is none of his," is an inference taken from the words foregoing, "If so be that the Spirit of God dwell in you." And this Spirit of Christ, verse 11, is said to be the "Spirit of him that raised up Christ from the dead." Look, then, in what sense he is said to be the Spirit of God, — that is, of the Father, — in the same he is said to be the Spirit of the Son. And this is because he proceedeth from the Son also; and for no other reason can he be so called, at least not without the original and formal reason of that appellation. Secondarily, I confess he is called the "Spirit of Christ" because promised by him, sent by him, and that to make effectual and accomplish his work towards the church. But this he could not be unless he had antecedently been the Spirit of the Son by his proceeding from him also: for the order of the dispensation of the divine persons towards us ariseth from the order of their own subsistence in the same divine essence; and if the Spirit did proceed only from the person of the Father, he could not be promised, sent, or given by the Son. Consider, therefore, the human nature of Christ in itself and abstractedly, and the Spirit cannot be said to be the Spirit of Christ; for it was anointed and endowed with gifts and graces by him, as we shall show. And if from hence he may be said to be the Spirit of Christ, without respect unto his proceeding from him as the Son of God, then he may be also said to be the Spirit of every believer who hath received the unction, of is anointed with his gifts and graces; for although believers are so, as to measure and degree, unspeakably beneath what Christ was, who received not the Spirit by measure, yet as he is the head and they are the members of the same mystical body, their unction by the Spirit is of the same kind. But now the Spirit of God may not be said to be the Spirit of this or that man who hath received of his gifts and graces. David prays, "Take not thy Holy Spirit from me," — not "my Holy Spirit." And he is distinguished from our spirits even as they are sanctified by him: Rom. viii. 16, "The Spirit himself beareth witness with our spirit." No more, then, can he be said to be the Spirit of Christ merely upon the account of his communications unto him, although in a degree above all others inconceivably excellent; for with respect hereunto he is still called the Spirit of God or the Father, who sent him, and anointed the human nature of Christ with him.

It will be said, perhaps, that he is called the "Spirit of Christ" because he is promised, given, and poured out by him. So Peter speaks, Acts ii. 33, "Having received of the Father the promise of the Holy Ghost, he hath shed forth this, which ye now see and hear." But in this regard, namely, as given by Christ the mediator, he is expressly called the Spirit of the Father; he was given as the promise of the Father: for so he is introduced speaking, verse 17, "It shall come to pass in the last days, saith God, I will pour out of my Spirit on all flesh." And so our Saviour tells his disciples that he would "pray the Father, and he should give them another Comforter, even the Spirit of truth," John xiv. 16, 17. Nor is he otherwise the Spirit of Christ, originally and formally, but as he is the Spirit of God, — that is, as Christ is God also. On this supposition I grant, as before, that he may consequently be called the "Spirit of Christ," because promised and sent by him, because doing his work, and communicating his grace, image, and likeness to the elect.

And this is yet more plain, 1 Pet. i. 10, 11, "Of which salvation the prophets have inquired and searched diligently, who prophesied of the grace that should come unto you: searching what, or what manner of time the Spirit of Christ which was in them did signify." And this Spirit is said absolutely to be the "Holy Ghost," 2 Pet. i. 21. So, then, the Spirit that was in the prophets of old, in all ages since the world began, before the incarnation of the Son of God, is called the "Spirit of Christ," — that is, of him who is so. Now, this could not be because he was anointed by that Spirit, or because he gave it afterward to his disciples; for his human nature did not exist in the time of their prophesying. Those, indeed, who receive him after the unction of the human nature of Christ may be said in some sense to receive the Spirit of Christ, because they are made partakers of the same Spirit with him, to the same ends and purposes, according to their measure; but this cannot be so with respect unto them who lived and prophesied by him, and died long before his incarnation. Wherefore, it is pleaded by those who oppose both the deity of Christ and the Spirit, which are undeniably here attested unto, that the Spirit here, whereby they cannot deny the Holy Ghost to be intended, is called the "Spirit of Christ," because the prophets of old, who spake by him, did principally prophesy concerning Christ and his grace, and delivered great mysteries concerning them. So Christ is made in this place the object of the Spirit's teaching, and not the author of his sending! So Crell. Prolegom., pp. 13, 14. But why, then, is he not called the "Spirit of God" also on this reason, because the prophets that spake by him treated wholly of God, the things and the will of God? This they will not say, for they acknowledge him to be the "virtue and power of God, inherent in him and proceeding from him." But, then, whereas God even the Father is a person, and Christ is a person, and the Spirit is said to be the "Spirit of God" and the" Spirit of Christ," whence doth it appear that the same expression must have different interpretations, and that the Spirit is called the "Spirit of God" because he is so, and proceedeth from him, but the "Spirit of Christ" because he is not so, but only treateth of him? The answer is ready, — namely, "Because the Father is God, but Christ is not, and therefore could not give the Spirit when he was not." This is an easy answer, — namely, to deny a fundamental truth, and to set up that denial in an opposition unto a clear testimony given unto it. But the truth is, this pretended sense leaves no sense at all in the words: for if the Spirit which was in the prophets be called the "Spirit of Christ" only because he did beforehand declare the things of Christ, — that is, his "sufferings and the glory that did follow," — and that be the sole reason of that denomination, then the sense or importance of the words is this, "Searching what or what manner of time the Spirit — 'which did signify when it testified beforehand the sufferings of Christ' — which was in them did signify when he testified beforehand the sufferings of Christ;" for according to this interpretation, the Spirit of Christ is nothing but the Spirit as testifying beforehand of him, and thence alone is he so called, — the absurdity whereof is apparent unto all.

But countenance is endeavoured unto this wresting of the Scripture from 1 John iv. 3, "Every spirit that confesseth not that Jesus Christ is come in the flesh is not of God: and this is that of antichrist, whereof ye have heard that it should come; and even now already is it in the world;" — for say some, "The spirit of antichrist is said to be in the world, when antichrist was not as yet come." But the spirit here intended is not called the spirit of antichrist because it declared and foretold the things of antichrist before his coming; on which account alone they allow the Spirit of God in the prophets of old to be called the "Spirit of Christ:" they have, therefore, no countenance from this place, which fails them in the principal thing they would prove by it. Again, supposing these words, "Whereof ye have heard that it should come, and even now already is it in the world," are to be interpreted of the spirit mentioned, and not of antichrist himself, yet no more can be intended but that the false teachers and seducers which were then in the world acted with the same spirit as antichrist should do at his coming; and so there is no conformity between these expressions. Besides, the spirit of antichrist was then in the world, as was antichrist himself. So far as his spirit was then in the world, so far was he so also; for antichrist and his spirit cannot be separated. Both he and it were then in the world in their forerunners, who opposed the truth of the gospel about the incarnation of the Son of God and his sufferings. And, indeed, the spirit of antichrist in this place is no more but his doctrine, — antichristian doctrine, which is to be tried and rejected. Neither is any singular person intended by antichrist, but a mysterious opposition unto Christ and the gospel, signally headed by a series of men in the latter days. He, therefore, and his spirit began to be together in the world in the apostles' days, when the "mystery of iniquity" began to "work," 2 Thess. ii. 7. There is, therefore, no countenance to be taken from these words unto the perverting and wresting of that other expression concerning the Spirit of Christ in the prophets of old. This, therefore, is the formal reason of this appellation: The Holy Spirit is called the "Spirit of the Son," and the "Spirit of Christ," upon the account of his procession or emanation from his person also. Without respect hereunto he could not be called properly the "Spirit of Christ;" but on that supposition he may be. He is so denominated from that various relation and respect that he hath unto him in his work and operations. Thus is the Spirit called in the Scripture, these are the names whereby the essence and subsistence of the third person in the Holy Trinity are declared. How he is called on the account of his offices and operations will be manifested in our progress.

Footnotes:

18. "Quia vero Spiritus vocabulum multa significat, enumerandum est breviter quibus rebus nomen ejus aptetur. Vocatur spiritus et ventus, sicut in Ezechiele cap. v.: Tertiam partem disperges in spiritum; hoc est, in ventum. Quod si volueris secundum historiam illud sentire, quod scriptum est, In spiritu violento conteres naves Tharcis, non aliud ibi spiritus quam ventus accipitur. Nec non Salomon inter multa hoc quoque munus a Deo accepit ut sciret violentias spirituum; non aliud in hoc se accepisse demonstrans, quam scire rapidos ventorum flatus, et quibus causis eorum natura subsistat. Vocatur et anima spiritus, ut in Jacobi epistola, Quomodo corpus tuum sine spiritu

mortuum est. Manifestissime enim spiritus hic nihil aliud nisi anima nuncupatur. Juxta quam intelligentiam Stephanus animam suam spiritum vocans: Domine, inquit, Jesu, suscipe spiritum meum, Acts vii. Illud quoque quod in Ecclesiaste dicitur, Quis scit an spiritus hominis ascendat sursum, et spiritus jumenti descendat deorsum? Eccl. iii. Considerandum utrumnam et pecudum animæ spiritus appellentur. Dicitur etiam excepta anima, et excepto spiritu nostro, spiritus alius quis esse in homine, de quo Paulus scribit: Quis enim scit hominum ea quæ sunt hominis, nisi spiritus hominis qui in eo est? 1 Cor. ii. 11 … Sed et in alio loco idem apostolus a nostro spiritu Spiritum Dei secernens ait, Ipse Spiritus testimonium perhibet spiritui nostro, Rom. viii.; hoc significans, quod Spiritus Dei, id est, Spiritus Sanctus, testimonium spiritui nostro præbeat, quem nunc diximus esse spiritum hominis. Ad Thessalonicenses quoque, Integer, inquit, spiritus vester et anima et corpus, 1 Thess. v.:— Appellantur quoque supernæ rationabilesque virtutes, quas solet Scriptura angelos et fortitudines nominare, vocabulo spiritus ut ibi, Qui facis angelos tuos spiritus; et alibi, Nonne omnes sunt administratores spiritus? Heb. i. … Rationales quoque aliæ creaturæ, et de bono in malum sponte propria profluentes, spiritus pessimi et spiritus appellantur immundi; sicut ibi, Cum autem spiritus immundus exierit ab homine, Matt. xii., et in consequentibus, assumit septem alios spiritus nequiores se. Spiritus quoque dæmones in Evangeliis appellantur: sed et hoc notandum, nunquam simpliciter spiritum sed cum aliquo additamento spiritum significari contrarium, ut spiritus immundus et spiritus dæmonis; hi vero qui sancti sunt spiritus absque ullo additamento spiritus simpliciter appellantur. Sciendum quoque quod nomen spiritus et voluntatem hominis et animi sententiam sonet. Volens quippe apostolus virginem non solum corpore sed et mente sanctam esse, id est, non tantum corpore, sed et motu cordis interno, ait, Ut sit sancta corpore et spiritu, 1 Cor. vii., voluntatem spiritu, et corpore opera, significans. Considera utrum hoc ipsum in Esaia sonet quod scriptum est, Et scient qui spiritu errant intellectum, Isa. xxix. 24 … Et super omnia vocabulum spiritus, altiorem et mysticum in Scripturis sanctis significat intellectum; ut ibi, Litera occidit, spiritus autem vivificat, 2 Cor. iii. — Hæc juxta possibilitatem nostri ingenii, quot res spiritus significet, attigimus. — Nonnunquam autem spiritus et Dominus noster Jesus Christus, id est, Dei Filius, appellatur: Dominus autem spiritus est, ut ante diximus: ubi etiam illud adjunximus, spiritus Deus est, non juxta nominis communionem, sed juxta naturæ substantiæque consortium. — Porro ad hæc necessario devoluti sumus, ut quia frequenter appellatio spiritus, in Scripturis est respersa divinis, non labamur in nomine sed unumquodque secundum locorum varietates et intelligentias accipiamus. Omni itaque studio ac diligentia vocabulum Spiritus, ubi et quomodo appellatum sit contemplantes, sophismata eorum et fraudulentas decipulas conteramus, qui Spiritum Sanctum asserunt creaturam. Legentes enim in propheta, Ego sum firmans tonitruum, et creans spiritum, Amos iv. 13, ignorantia multiplicis in hac parte sermonis putaverunt Spiritum Sanctum ex hoc vocabulo demonstrari; cum in præsentiarum spiritus nomen ventum sonet … Ergo ut prælocuti sumus, quomodo unumquodque dictum sit, consideremus ne forte per ignorantiam in barathrum decidamus erroris." — Didym. de Spir. Sanc. lib. iii.

19. So the word is constantly given by Owen. The י is uniformly elided from modern editions of the Hebrew Scriptures, and the word stands thus מַה־שֵּׂחוֹ. The origin of the mistake to which Owen refers is more apparent from the way in which the word is printed, but the insertion of the י seems without authority. — Ed.

20. "Discant (homines) Scripturæ sanctæ consuetudinem, nunquam spiritum perversum absolute, sed cum additamento aliquo spiritum nuncupari: sicut ibi, Spiritu fornicationis seducti sunt; et in Evangelio, Cum autem spiritus immundus exierit de homine; et cætera his similia." — Hieron. Comment. in Hab. cap. ii.

21. "Qui Spiritum negavit, et Deum Patrem negavit et Filium; quoniam idem est Spiritus Dei, qui Spiritus Christi est," cap. 3. "Unum autem esse Spiritum nemo dubitaverit; etsi de uno Deo plerique dubitaverunt," cap. 4. — Ambros. de Spir. Sanc. lib. i.

22. Ὄνομα αὐτοῦ πνεῦμα ἅγιον, πνεῦμα ἀληθείας, πνεῦμα τοῦ Θεοῦ, πνεῦμα κυρίου, πνεῦμα τοῦ Πατρὸς, πνεῦμα Χριστοῦ, καὶ οὕτω καλεῖ αὐτὸν ἡ γραφή. Μᾶλλον δὲ αὐτὸ ἑαυτὸ καὶ πνεῦμα Θεοῦ, καὶ πνεῦμα τὸ ἐκ τοῦ Θεοῦ. — Chrysost. de Adorand. Spir.

23. Crell. Prolegom.

24. "Sanctificationis bonitatisque vocabulum, et ad Patrem, et ad Filium, et ad Spiritum Sanctum æquè refertur; sicut ipsa quoque appellatio Spiritus. Nam et Pater Spiritus dicitur ut ibi, Spiritus est Deus, Joan. iv. 24. Et Filius Spiritus, Dominus,

inquit, Spiritus ejus, 2 Cor. iii. 17. Spiritus autem Sanctus semper Spiritus Sancti appellatione censetur; non quod ex consortio tantum nominis Spiritus cum Patre ponatur et Filio, sed quod una natura unum possideat et nomen." — Didym. de Spir. Sanc. lib. iii.

25. "Multa sunt testimonia, quibus hoc evidenter ostenditur, et Patris et Filii ipsum esse Spiritum, qui in Trinitate dicitur Spiritus Sanctus. Nec ob aliud existimo ipsum proprie vocari Spiritum, cum etiam si de singulis interrogemur, non possimus non Patrem et Filium Spiritum dicere; quoniam Spiritus est Deus, id est, non Corpus est Deus sed Spiritus; hoc proprie vocari oportuit eum, qui non est unus eorum, sed in quo communitas apparet amborum." — August. Tractat. xcix. in Johan.

26. Ἄνωθεν παρὰ Θεοῦ κατιοῦσα ἐπὶ τοὺς ἄνδρας ἁγίους δωρεὰ, ἣν πνεῦμα ἅγιον ὀνομάζουσιν οἵ ἱεροὶ προφῆται. — Justin Mart.

27. Λέγεται τοίνυν πνεῦμα ἅγιον. Αὕτη γάρ ἐστιν ἡ κυρία καὶ πρώτη προσηγορία ἡ ἐμφαντικώτεραν ἔχουσα τὴν διάνοιαν, καὶ περιστᾶσα τοῦ ἁγίου πνεύματος τὴν φύσιν. — Chrysost. ub. Sup.

28. "Neque post id locorum Jugurthæ dies aut nox ulla quieta fuere: neque loco, neque mortali cuiquam, aut tempori, satis credere: civis, hostis, juxta metuere: circumspectare omnia, et omni strepitu pavescere: alio atque alio loco, sæpe contra decus regium requiescere: interdum, somno excitus arreptis armis tumultum facere: ita formidine, quasi vecordia, agitari." — Bell. Jugur. lxxii.

29. "Nemo suspicetur alium Spiritum Sanctum fuisse in Sanctis, nimirum ante adventum Domini, et alium in apostolis cæterisque discipulis, et quasi homonymum in differentibus esse substantiis; possumus quidem testimonia de divinis literis exhibere, quia idem Spiritus et in apostolis et in prophetis fuerit. Paulus in epistola quam ad Hebræos scribit, de Psalmorum volumine testimonium proferens, a Spiritu Sancto id dictum esse commemorat." — Didym. de Spir. Sanc. lib. i.

30. Ἵνα μήποτε ἀκούσαντες ἡμεῖς πνεῦμα Θεοῦ, νομίσωμεν δὲ οἰκειότητα λέγεσθαι πνεῦμα Θεοῦ, εἰσάγει ἡ γραφὴ τὸ πνεῦμα τὸ ἅγιον, καὶ προστίθησι τοῦ Θεοῦ, τὸ ἐκ Θεου. Ἄλλο δὲ τὸ τοῦ Θεοῦ, καὶ ἄλλο τὸ ἐκ Θεοῦ. Θεοῦ μὲν γὰρ οὐρανὸς καὶ γῆ ὡς πὲρ αὐτῷ πεποιημένα. Ἐκ Θεοῦ δὲ οὐδὲν λέγεται, εἰ μὴ ὅ ἐκ τῆς οὐσίας ἐστί. — Chrysost. de Spir. Sanc.

31. Εἴπερ πνεῦμα Θεοῦ οἰκεῖ ἐν ὑμίν, — ἴδε πνεῦμα Θεοῦ. Εἰ δέ τις πνεῦμα Χριστοῦ οὐκ ἔχει, — καὶ μὲν ἐχρῆν εἰπεῖν, εἰ δέ τις πνεῦμα Θεοῦ οὐκ ἔχει, ἀλλ᾽ εἶπε πνεῦμα Χριστοῦ. Εἶπε Θεοῦ πνεῦμα καὶ, ἐπήγαγε τὸ πνεῦμα τοῦ Χριστοῦ. Εἰ δέ τις πνεῦμα Χριστοῦ οὐκ ἔχει, οὗτος οὐκ ἔστιν αὐτοῦ, ἀλλὰ τοῦτο εἶπεν, ἵνα δείξῃ ὅτι ἓν πνεῦμα, καὶ ἴσον ἐστὶν εἰπεῖν πνεῦμα Θεοῦ, καὶ πνεῦμα Χριστοῦ. — Ibid.

Chapter III - Divine nature and personality of the Holy Spirit proved and vindicated

Ends of our consideration of the dispensation of the Spirit — Principles premised thereunto — The nature of God the foundation of all religion — Divine revelation gives the rule and measure of religious worship — God hath revealed himself as three in one — Distinct actings and operations ascribed unto these distinct person; therefore the Holy Spirit a divine distinct person — Double opposition to the Holy Spirit — By some his personality granted and his deity denied — His personality denied by the Socinians — Proved against them — The open vanity of their pretences — Matt. xxviii. 19, pleaded — Appearance of the Spirit under the shape of a dove explained and improved — His appearance as fire opened — His personal subsistence proved — Personal properties assigned unto him — Understanding — Argument from hence pleaded and vindicated — A will — John iii. 8, James iii. 4, cleared — Exceptions removed — Power — Other personal ascriptions to him, with testimonies of them, vindicated and explained.

We shall now proceed to the matter itself designed unto consideration, — namely, the dispensation of the Spirit of God unto the church; and I shall endeavour to fix what I have to offer upon its proper principles, and from them to educe the whole doctrine concerning it. And this must be so done as to manifest the interest of our faith, obedience, and holy worship, in the whole and each part of it; for these are the immediate ends of all divine revelations, according to that holy maxim of our blessed Saviour, "If ye know these things, happy are ye if ye do them." To this end the ensuing principles are to be observed:—

First, The nature and being of God is the foundation of all true religion and holy religious worship in the world. The great end for which we were made, for which we were brought forth by the power of God into this world, is to worship him and to give glory unto him; for he "made all things for himself," or his own glory, Prov. xvi. 4, to be rendered unto him according to the abilities and capacities that he hath furnished them withal, Rev. iv. 11. And that which makes this worship indispensably necessary unto us, and from whence it is holy or religious, is the nature and being of God himself. There are, indeed, many parts or acts of religious worship which immediately respect (as their reason and motive) what God is unto us, or what he hath done and doth for us; but the principal and adequate reason of all divine worship, and that which makes it such, is what God is in himself. Because he is, — that is, an infinitely glorious, good, wise, holy, powerful, righteous, self-subsisting, self-sufficient, all-sufficient Being, the fountain, cause, and author of life and being to all things, and of all that is good in every kind, the first cause, last end, and absolutely sovereign Lord of all, the rest and all-satisfactory reward of all other beings, — therefore is he by us to be adored and worshipped with divine and religious worship. Hence are we in our hearts, minds, and souls, to admire, adore, and love him; his praises are we to celebrate; him [are we] to trust and fear, and so to resign ourselves and all our concernments unto his will and disposal; to regard him with all the acts of our minds and persons, answerably to the holy properties and excellencies of his nature. This it is to glorify him as God; for seeing "of him, and through him, and to him are all things," to him must be "glory for ever," Rom. xi. 36. "Believing that God thus is, and that he is a rewarder of them that diligently seek him," is the ground of all coming unto God in his worship, Heb. xi. 6. And herein lies the sin of men, that the "invisible things of God being manifest unto them, even his eternal power and Godhead," yet "they glorify him not as God," Rom. i. 19–21. This is to honour, worship, fear God for himself; that is, on the account of what he is himself. Where the divine nature is, there is the true, proper, formal object of religious worship; and where that is not, it is idolatry to ascribe it to or exercise it towards any. And this God instructs us in, in all those places where he proclaims his name and describes his eternal excellencies, and that either absolutely or in comparison with other things. All is, that we may know him to be such a one as is to be worshipped and glorified for himself, or his own sake.

Secondly, The revelation that God is pleased to make of himself unto us gives the rule and measure of all religious worship and obedience. His being, absolutely considered, as comprehending in it all infinite, divine perfections, is the formal reason of our worship; but this worship is to be directed, guided, regulated, by the revelation he makes of that being and of those excellencies unto us. This is the end of divine revelation, — namely, to direct us in paying that homage which is due unto the divine nature. I speak not now only of positive institutions, which are the free effects of the will of God, depending originally and solely on revelation, and which, therefore, have been various and actually changed; but this is that which I intend:— Look, what way soever God manifesteth his being and properties unto us, by his works or his word, our worship consisteth in a due application of our souls unto him according to that manifestation of himself.

Thirdly, God hath revealed or manifested himself as three in one, and, therefore, as such is to be worshipped and glorified by us; — that is, as three distinct persons, subsisting in the same infinitely holy, one, undivided essence. This principle might be, and, had not that labour been obviated, ought to have been, here at large confirmed; it being that which the whole ensuing discourse doth presuppose and lean upon. And, in truth, I fear that the failing of some men's profession begins with their relinquishment of this foundation. It is now evident unto all that here hath been the fatal miscarriage of those poor deluded souls amongst us whom they call Quakers; and it is altogether in vain to deal with them about other particulars, whilst they are carried away with infidelity from this foundation. Convince any of them of the doctrine of the Trinity, and all the rest of their imaginations vanish into smoke. And I wish it were so with them only. There are others, and those not a few, who either reject the doctrine of it as false, or despise it as unintelligible, or neglect it as useless, or of no great importance. I know this ulcer lies hid in the minds of many, and cannot but expect when it will break out, and cover the whole body with its defilements whereof they are members But these things are left to the care of Jesus Christ. The reason why I shall not in this place insist professedly on the confirmation and vindication of this fundamental truth is, because I have done it elsewhere, as having more than once publicly cast my mite into this sanctuary of the Lord; for which and the like services, wherein I stand indebted unto the gospel, I have met with that reward which I did always expect. For the present I shall only say, that on this supposition, that God hath revealed himself as three in one, he is in all our worship of him so to be considered. And, therefore, in our initiation into the profession and practice of the worship of God, according to the gospel, we are in our baptism engaged to it, "In the name of the Father, and of the Son, and of the Holy Ghost," Matt. xxviii. 19. This is the foundation of our doing all the things that Christ commands us, as verse 20. Unto this service we are solemnly dedicated, namely, of God, as Father, Son, and Holy Spirit; as they are each of them equally participant of the same divine nature.

Fourthly, These persons are so distinct in their peculiar subsistence that distinct actings and operations are ascribed unto them. And these actings are of two sorts:— 1. Ad intra, which are those internal acts in one person whereof another person is the object. And these acts ad invicem, or intra, are natural and necessary, inseparable from the being and existence of God. So the Father knows the Son and loveth him, and the Son seeth, knoweth, and loveth the Father. In these mutual actings, one person is the object of the knowledge and love of the other: John iii. 35, "The Father loveth the Son, and hath given all things into his hand." Chap. v. 20, "The Father loveth the Son." Matt. xi. 27, "No man knoweth the Son, but the Father; neither knoweth any man the Father, save the Son." John vi. 46, "None hath seen the Father, save he which is of God, he hath seen the Father." This mutual knowledge and love of Father and Son is expressed at large, Prov. viii. 22–31; which place I have opened and vindicated elsewhere. And they are absolute, infinite, natural, and necessary unto the being and blessedness of God. So the Spirit is the mutual love of the Father and the Son, knowing them as he is known, and "searching the deep things of God." And in these mutual, internal, eternal actings of themselves, consists much of the infinite blessedness of the holy God. Again, 2. There are distinct actings of the several persons ad extra; which are voluntary, or effects of will and choice, and not natural or necessary. And these are of two sorts:— (1.) Such as respect one another; for there are external acts of one person towards another: but then the person that is the object of these actings is not considered absolutely as a divine person, but with respect unto some peculiar dispensation and condescension. So the Father gives, sends, commands the Son, as he had condescended to take our nature upon him, and to be the mediator between God and man. So the Father and the Son do send the Spirit, as he condescends in an especial manner to the office of being the sanctifier and comforter of the church. Now, these are free and voluntary acts, depending upon the sovereign will, counsel, and pleasure of God, and might not have been, without the least diminution of his eternal blessedness. (2.) There are especial acts, ad extra, towards the creatures.[32] This the whole Scripture testifieth unto, so that it is altogether needless to confirm it with particular instances. None who have learned the first principles of the doctrine of Christ, but can tell you what works are ascribed peculiarly to the Father, what to the Son, and what to the Holy Ghost. Besides, this will be manifested afterward in all the distinct actings of the Spirit; which is sufficient for our purpose.

Fifthly, Hence it follows unavoidably that this Spirit of whom we treat is in himself a distinct, living, powerful, intelligent, divine person; for none other can be the author of those internal and external divine acts and operations which are ascribed unto him. But here I must stay a little, and confirm that foundation which we build upon; for we are in the investigation of those things which that one and self-same Spirit distributeth according to his own will. And it is indispensably necessary unto our present design that we inquire who and what that one and selfsame Spirit is, seeing on him and his will all these things do depend. And we do know, likewise, that if men prevail in the opposition they make unto his person, it is to no great purpose to concern ourselves in his operations; for the foundation of any fabric being taken away, the superstructure will be of no use nor abide.

The opposition that is made in the world against the Spirit of God doctrinally may be reduced unto two heads; for some there are who grant his personality, or that he is a distinct self-subsisting person, but they deny his deity, deny him to be a participant of the divine nature, or will not allow him to be God. A created finite spirit they say he is, but the chiefest of all spirits that were created, and the head of all the good angels. Such a spirit they say there is, and that he is called the "Spirit of God," or the "Holy Ghost," upon the account of the work wherein he is employed. This way went the Macedonian heretics of old, and they are now followed by the Mohammedans; and some of late among ourselves have attempted to revive the same frenzy. But we shall not need to trouble ourselves about this notion. The folly of it is so evident that it is almost by all utterly deserted; for such things are affirmed of the Holy Ghost in the Scripture as that to assert his personality and deny his deity is the utmost madness that anyone can fall into in spiritual things. Wherefore, the Socinians, the present great enemies of the doctrine of the holy Trinity, and who would be thought to go soberly about the work of destroying the church of God, do utterly reject this plea and pretence. But that which they advance in the room of it is of no less pernicious nature and consequence: for, granting the things assigned to him to be the effects of divine power, they deny his personality, and assert that what is called by the name of the "Spirit of God," or the "Holy Spirit," is nothing but a quality in the divine nature, or the power that God puts forth for such and such purposes; which yet is no new invention of theirs.[33] I do not design here professedly to contend with them about all the concernments of this difference; for there is nothing of importance in all their pretences or exceptions, but it will in one place or other occur unto consideration in our progress. I shall only at present confirm the divine personality of the Holy Ghost with one argument; which I will not say is such as no man can return the show of an answer unto, — for what is it that the serpentine wits of men will not pretend an answer unto, or an exception against, if their lusts and prejudices require them so to do? — but I will boldly say it is such as that the gates of hell shall never prevail against it in the hearts of true believers, the strengthening of whose faith is all that in it I do aim at. And if it do not unto all unprejudiced persons evince the truth and reality of the divine personality of the Holy Ghost, it must certainly convince all men that nothing which is taught or delivered in the Scripture can possibly be understood.

One consideration, which hath in part been before proposed, I shall premise, to free the subject of our argument from ambiguity; and this is, that this word or name "Spirit" is used sometimes to denote the Spirit of God[34] himself, and sometimes his gifts and graces, the effects of his operations on the souls of men. And this our adversaries in this cause are forced to confess, and thereon in all their writings distinguish between the Holy Spirit and his effects. This alone being supposed, I say, it is impossible to prove the Father to be a person, or the Son to be so (both which are acknowledged), any other way than we may and do prove the Holy Ghost to be so; for he to whom all personal properties, attributes, adjuncts, acts, and operations, are ascribed, and unto whom they do belong, and to whom nothing is or can be truly and properly ascribed but what may and doth belong unto a person, is a person, and him are we taught to believe so to be. So know we the Father to be a person, as also the Son; for our knowledge of things is more by their properties and operations than by their essential forms. Especially is this so with respect to the nature, being, and existence of God, which are in themselves absolutely incomprehensible. Now, I shall not confirm the assumption of this argument with reference unto the Holy Ghost from this or that particular testimony, nor from the assignation of any single personal property unto him, but from the constant, uniform tenor of the Scripture in ascribing all these properties unto him. And we may add hereunto, that things are so ordered, in the wisdom of God, that there is no personal property that may be found in an infinite divine nature but it is in one place or other ascribed unto him.

There is no exception can be laid against the force of this argument, but only that some things, on the one hand, are ascribed unto the Spirit which belong not unto a person, nor can be spoken of him who is so; and, on the other, that sundry things that properly belong to persons are in the Scripture figuratively ascribed unto such things as are not so. Thus, as to the first head of this exception, the Holy Spirit is said to be "poured out," to be "shed abroad," to be "an unction," or the like; of all which expressions we shall treat afterward. What then? shall we say that he is not a person, but only the power of God? Will this render those expressions concerning him proper? How can the virtue of God, or the power of God, be said to be poured out, to be shed abroad, and the like? Wherefore, both they and we acknowledge that these expressions are figurative, as many things are so expressed of God in the Scripture, and that frequently; and what is the meaning of them under their figurative colours we shall afterward declare. This, therefore, doth not in the least impeach our argument, unless this assertion were true generally, that whatever is spoken of figuratively in the Scripture is no person; which would leave no one in heaven or earth. On the other side, it is confessed that there are things peculiar unto rational subsistents or persons, which are ascribed sometimes unto those that are not so. Many things of this nature, as to "hope," to "believe," to "bear," are ascribed unto charity, 1 Cor. xiii. 7. But everyone presently apprehends that this expression is figurative, the abstract being put for the concrete by a metalepsis, and charity is said to do that which a man endued with that grace will do. So the Scripture is said to "see," to "foresee," to "speak," and to "judge," which are personal actings; but who doth not see and grant that a metonymy is and must be allowed in such assignations, that being ascribed unto the effect, the Scripture, which is proper to the cause, the Spirit of God speaking in it? So the heavens and the earth are said to "hear," and the fields, with the trees of the forest, to "sing" and "clap their hands," by a prosopopœia. Now, concerning these things there is no danger of mistake. The light of reason and their own nature therein do give us a sufficient understanding of them; and such figurative expressions as are used concerning them are common in all good authors. Besides, the Scripture itself, in other places innumerable, doth so teach and declare what they are, as that its plain and direct proper assertions do sufficiently expound its own figurative enunciations: for these and such like ascriptions are only occasional; the direct description of the things themselves is given us in other places. But now with respect unto the Spirit of God all things are otherwise. The constant uniform expressions concerning him are such as declare him to be a person endowed with all personal properties, no description being anywhere given of him inconsistent with their proper application to him.

If a sober, wise, and honest man should come and tell you that in such a country, where he hath been, there is one who is the governor of it, that doth well discharge his office, — that he heareth causes, discerneth right, distributes justice, relieves the poor, comforts them that are in distress; supposing you gave him that credit which honesty, wisdom, and sobriety do deserve, would you not believe that he intended a righteous, wise, diligent, intelligent person, discharging the office of a governor? What else could any man living imagine? But now suppose that another unknown person, or, so far as he is known, justly suspected of deceit and forgery, should come unto you and tell you that all which the other informed you and acquainted you withal was indeed true, but that the words which he spake have quite another intention; for it was not a man or any person that he intended, but it was the sun or the wind that he meant by all which he spake of him: for whereas the sun by his benign influences doth make a country fruitful and temperate, suited to the relief and comfort of all that dwell therein, and disposeth the minds of the inhabitants unto mutual kindness and benignity, he described these things figuratively unto you, under the notion of a righteous governor and his actions, although he never gave you the least intimation of any such intention; — must you not now believe that either the first person, whom you know to be a wise, sober, and honest man, was a notorious trifler, and designed your ruin, if you were to order any of your occasions according to his reports, or that your latter informer, whom you have just reason to suspect of falsehood and deceit in other things, hath endeavoured to abuse both him and you, to render his veracity suspected, and to spoil all your designs grounded thereon? One of these you must certainly conclude upon. And it is no otherwise in this case. The Scripture informs us that the Holy Ghost rules in and over the church of God, appointing overseers of it under him; that he discerns and judgeth all things; that he comforteth them that are faint, strengthens them that are weak, is grieved with them and provoked by them who sin; and that in all these, and in other things of the like nature innumerable, he worketh, ordereth, and disposeth all "according to the counsel of his own will." Hereupon it directeth us so to order our conversation towards God that we do not grieve him nor displease him, telling us thereon what great things he will do for us; on which we lay the stress of our obedience and salvation. Can any man possibly, that gives credit to the testimony thus proposed in the Scripture, conceive any otherwise of this Spirit but as of a holy, wise, intelligent person? Now, whilst we are under the power of these apprehensions, there come unto us some men, Socinians or Quakers, whom we have just cause on many other accounts to suspect, at least, of deceit and falsehood; and they confidently tell us that what the Scripture speaks concerning the Holy Spirit is indeed true, but that in and by all the expressions which it useth concerning him, it intendeth no such person as it seems to do, but "an accident, a quality, an effect, or influence of the power of God," which figuratively doth all the things mentioned, — namely, that hath a will figuratively, and understanding figuratively, discerneth and judgeth figuratively, is sinned against figuratively, and so of all that is said of him. Can any man that is not forsaken of all natural reason as well as spiritual light choose now but determine that either the Scripture designed to draw him into errors and mistakes about the principal concernments of his soul, and so to ruin him eternally; or that these persons, who would impose such a sense upon it, are indeed corrupt seducers, that seek to overthrow his faith and comforts? Such will they at last appear to be. I shall now proceed to confirm the argument proposed:—

1. All things necessary to this purpose are comprised in the solemn form of our initiation into covenant with God. Matt. xxviii. 19, our Lord Jesus Christ commands his apostles to "disciple all nations, baptizing them in the name of the Father, and of the Son, and of the Holy Ghost" This is the foundation we lay of all our obedience and profession, which are to be regulated by this initial engagement. Now, no man will or doth deny but that the Father and the Son are distinct persons. Some, indeed, there are who deny the Son to be God; but none are so mad as to deny him to be a person, though they would have him only to be a man; — all grant him, whether God and man, or only man, to be a distinct person from the Father. Now, what confusion must this needs introduce, to add to them, and to join equally with them, as to all the concerns of our faith and obedience, the Holy Ghost, if he be not a divine person even as they! If, as some fancy, he be a person indeed, but not one that is divine, but a creature, then here is openly the same honour assigned unto him who is no more as unto God himself. This elsewhere the Scripture declares to be idolatry to be detested, Gal. iv. 8, Rom. i. 25. And if he be not a person, but a virtue and quality in God, and emanation of power from him, concerning which our adversaries τερατολογοῦσι, speak things portentous and unintelligible, what sense can any man apprehend in the words?

Besides, whatever is ascribed unto the other persons, either with respect unto themselves or our duty towards them, is equally ascribed unto the Holy Ghost; for whatsoever is intended by the "name" of the Father and of the Son, he is equally with them concerned therein. It is not the name "Father," and the name "Son," but the name of "God," that is, of them both, that is intended. It is a name common to them all, and distinctly applied unto them all; but they have not in this sense distinct or diverse names. And by the "name" of God either his being or his authority is signified; for other intention of it none have been able to invent. Take the "name" here in either sense, and it is sufficient as to what we intend: for if it be used in the first way, then the being of the Spirit must be acknowledged to be the same with that of the Father; if in the latter, he hath the same divine authority with him. He who hath the nature and authority of God is God, — is a divine person.

Our argument, then, from hence is not merely from his being joined with the Father and the Son, for so, as to some ends and purposes, any creatures may be joined with them (this our adversaries prove from Acts xx. 32, Eph. vi. 10, Phil. iii. 10, 2 Thess. i. 9, and might do it from other places innumerable, although the first of these will not confirm what it is produced to give countenance unto, — Schlichting. de Trinitat. ad Meisner., p. 605); but it is from the manner and end of his being conjoined with the Father and the Son, wherein their "name," — that is, their divine nature and authority, — is ascribed unto him, that we argue.

Again; We are said to be baptized εἰς τὸ ὄνομα, "into his name." And no sense can be affixed unto these words but what doth unavoidably include his personality; for two things they may and do intend, nor any thing else but what may be reduced unto them:— First, Our religious owning the Father, Son, and Holy Ghost, in all our divine worship, faith, and obedience. Now, as we own and avow the one, so we do the other; for we are alike baptized into their name,[35] equally submitting to their authority, and equally taking the profession of their name upon us. If, then, we avow and own the Father as a distinct person, so we do the Holy Ghost. Again; by being baptized into the name of the Father, and of the Son, and of the Holy Ghost, we are sacredly initiated and consecrated, or dedicated, unto the service and worship of the Father, Son, and Holy Ghost. This we take upon us in our baptism. Herein lies the foundation of all our faith and profession, with that engagement of ourselves unto God which constitutes our Christianity. This is the pledge of our entrance into covenant with God, and of our giving up ourselves unto him in the solemn bond of religion. Herein to conceive that anyone who is not God as the Father is, who is not a person as he is also, and the Son likewise, is joined with them for the ends and in the manner mentioned, without the least note of difference as to deity or personality, is a strange fondness, destructive of all religion, and leading the minds of men towards polytheism. And as we engage into all religious obedience unto the Father and Son herein, to believe in them, trust, fear, honour, and serve them, so we do the same with respect unto the Holy Ghost; which how we can do, if he be not as they are, no man can understand.

We do not, then, in this case, from hence merely plead our being baptized into the "Holy Ghost," as some pretend; nor, indeed, are we said so to be. Men may figuratively be said to be baptized into a doctrine, when their baptism is a pledge and token of their profession of it. So the disciples whom the apostle Paul met with at Ephesus, Acts xix. 3, are said to be baptized εἰς τὸ Ἰωάννου βάπτισμα, "into the baptism of John," — that is, the doctrine of repentance for the forgiveness of sins, whereof his baptism was a pledge. So also the Israelites are said to be baptized εἰς Μωϋσῆν, "into Moses," 1 Cor. x. 2, because he led and conducted them through the sea, when they were sprinkled with the waves of it as a token of their initiation into the rites and ceremonies which he was to deliver unto them. But we are said to be baptized into his "name;" which is the same with that of the Father and Son. And certainly this proposal of God as Father, Son, and Holy Ghost, to be the object of all our faith and worship, and our engagement hereunto required as the foundation of all our present religion and future hopes, being made unto us, and that under one and the same name; if the doctrine of a Trinity of persons, subsisting in the same undivided essence, be not taught and declared in these words, we may justly despair of ever having any divine mystery manifested unto us.

2. His appearance in and under a visible sign argues his personal existence. This is related, Matt. iii. 16; Luke iii. 22; John i. 32. Luke speaks first in general that he descended ἐν εἴδει σωματικῷ, "in a bodily shape" or appearance; and they all agree that it was the shape of a dove under which he appeared. The words in Matthew are, Εἶδε τὸ Πνεῦμα τοῦ Θεοῦ καταβαῖνον ὡσεὶ περιστερὰν καὶ ἐρχόμενον ἐπ' αὐτόν· — "He saw the Spirit of God descending like a dove, and lighting" (or rather coming) "upon him." "He," that is John the Baptist, not Christ himself. The relative, αὐτός, refers in this place to the more remote antecedent; for although "he," that is Christ himself, also

saw the descending of the Holy Spirit, yet I suppose this relates unto that token which was to be given of him unto John, whereby he should know him, John i. 32, 33. The following words are ambiguous: for that expression, "like a dove," may refer to the manner of his descending, — descending (in a bodily shape) as a dove descends; or they may respect the manner of his appearance, — he appeared like a dove descending. And this sense is determined in the other evangelists to the bodily shape wherein he descended. He took the form or shape of a dove to make a visible representation of himself by; for a visible pledge was to be given of the coming of the Holy Ghost on the Messiah, according to the promise, and thereby did God direct his great forerunner to the knowledge of him. Now, this was no real dove. That would not have been a thing so miraculous as this appearance of the Holy Ghost is represented to be. And the text will not bear any such apprehension, though it was entertained by some of the ancients; for it is evident that this shape of a dove came out of heaven. He saw the heavens opened and the dove descending; that is, out of heaven, which was opened to make way, as it were, for him. Moreover, the expression of the opening of the heavens is not used but with respect unto some appearance or manifestation of God himself. And so (or which is the same) the bowing of the heavens is often used: Ps. cxliv. 5, "Bow thy heavens, O Lord, and come down;" 2 Sam. xxii. 10; Isa. lxiv. 1; Ezek. i. 1, "The heavens were opened, and I saw visions of God;" so Acts vii. 56. God used not this sign but in some manifestation of himself; and had not this been an appearance of God, there had been no need of bowing or opening the heavens for it. And it is plainly said that it was not a dove, but the shape or representation of a dove. It was εἶδος σωματικόν, "a bodily shape;" and that περιστερᾶς, "of a dove."

As, then, at the beginning of the old creation, the Spirit of God מְרַחֶפֶת, "incubabat," came and fell on the waters, cherishing the whole, and communicating a prolific and vivific quality unto it, as a fowl or dove in particular gently moves itself upon its eggs, until, with and by its generative warmth, it hath communicated vital heat unto them; so now, at the entrance of the new creation, he comes as a dove upon him who was the immediate author of it, and virtually comprised it in himself, carrying it on by virtue of his presence with him. And so this is applied in the Syriac ritual of baptism, composed by Severinus, in the account ורוחא דקודשא בדמות יונא פרחת נחתת ועל Christ: of baptism the of given רהפת מיא ועל שכנת דברא רישא; — "And the Spirit of Holiness descended, flying in the likeness of a dove, and rested upon him, and moved on the waters." And in the assumption of this form there may be some respect unto the dove that brought tidings to Noah of the ceasing of the flood of waters, and of the ending of the wrath of God, who thereon said that he would curse the earth no more, Gen. viii. 11, 21, for herein also was there a significant representation of him who visited poor, lost mankind in their cursed condition, and proclaimed peace unto them that would return to God by him, the great peace-maker, Eph. ii. 14–17. And this work he immediately engaged into on the resting of this dove upon him. Besides, there is a natural aptness in that creature to represent the Spirit that rested on the Lord Jesus; for the known nature and course of a dove is such as is meet to mind us of purity and harmless innocency. Hence is that direction, "Be harmless as doves," Matt. x. 16. So also the sharpness of its sight or eyes, as Cant. i. 15, iv. 1, is fixed on to represent a quick and discerning understanding, such as was in Christ from the resting of the Spirit upon him, Isa. xi. 2–4.

The shape thereof that appeared was that of a dove, but the substance itself, I judge, was of a fiery nature, an ethereal substance, shaped into the form or resemblance of a dove. It had the shape of a dove, but not the appearance of feathers, colours, or the like. This also rendered the appearance the more visible, conspicuous, heavenly, and glorious. And the Holy Ghost is often compared to fire, because he was of old typified or represented thereby; for on the first solemn offering of sacrifices there came fire from the Lord for the kindling of them. Hence Theodotion of old rendered יְהוָה וַיִּשַׁע, Gen. iv. 4, "The Lord had respect unto Abel, and to his offering," by Ἐνεπύρισεν ὁ Θεός, "God fired the offering of Abel;" sent down fire that kindled his sacrifice as a token of his acceptance. However, it is certain that at the first erection of the altar in the wilderness, upon the first sacrifices, "fire came out from before the Lord, and consumed upon the altar the burnt-offering and the fat; which when all the people saw, they shouted, and fell on their faces," Lev. ix. 24. And the fire kindled hereby was to be perpetuated on the altar, so that none was ever to be used in sacrifice but what was traduced from it. For a neglect of this intimation of the mind of God were Nadab and Abihu consumed, chap. x. 1, 2. So was it also upon the dedication of the altar in the temple of Solomon: "Fire came down from heaven and consumed the burnt-offering and the sacrifices," 2 Chron. vii. 1; and a fire thence kindled was always kept burning on the altar. And in like manner God bare testimony to the ministry of Elijah, 1 Kings xviii. 38, 39. God by all these signified that no sacrifices were accepted with him where faith was not kindled in the heart of the offerer by the Holy Ghost, represented by the fire that kindled the sacrifices on the altar. And in answer hereunto is our Lord Jesus Christ said to offer himself "through the eternal Spirit," Heb. ix. 14. It was, therefore, most probably a fiery appearance that was made. And in the next bodily shape which he assumed it is expressly said that it was fiery: Acts ii. 3, "There appeared unto them cloven tongues like as of fire;" which was the visible token of the coming of the Holy Ghost upon them. And he chose, then, that figure of tongues to denote the assistance which, by the miraculous gift of speaking with divers tongues, together with wisdom and utterance, he furnished them withal for the publication of the gospel. And thus, also, the Lord Christ is said to "baptize with the Holy Ghost and with fire," Matt. iii. 11. Not two things are intended, but the latter words, "and with fire," are added ἐξηγητικῶς, and the expression is ἕν διὰ δυοῖν, — with the Holy Ghost, who is a spiritual, divine, eternal fire. So God absolutely is said to be a "consuming fire," Heb. xii. 29, Deut. iv. 24. And as in these words, "He shall baptize with the Holy Ghost and with fire," there is a prospect unto what came to pass afterward, when the apostles received the Holy Ghost with a visible pledge of fiery tongues, so there seems to be a retrospect, by way of allusion unto what is recorded, Isa. vi. 6, 7; for a living or "fiery coal from the altar," where the fire represented the Holy Ghost, or his work and grace, having touched the lips of his prophet, his sin was taken away, both as to the guilt and filth of it. And this is the work of the Holy Ghost, who not only sanctifieth us, but, by ingenerating faith in us, and the application of the promise unto us, is the cause and means of our justification also, 1 Cor. vi. 11, Tit. iii. 4–7, whereby our sins on both accounts are taken away. So also his efficacy in other places is compared unto fire and burning: Isa. iv. 4, 5, "When the Lord shall have washed away the filth of the daughters of Zion, and shall have purged the blood of Jerusalem from the midst thereof, by the spirit of judgment, and by the spirit of burning." He is compared both to fire and water, with respect unto the same cleansing virtue in both. So also Mal. iii. 2. Hence, as this is expressed by "the Holy Ghost and fire" in two evangelists, Matt. iii. 11, Luke iii. 16; so in the other two there is mention only of the "Holy Ghost," Mark i. 8, John i. 33, the same thing being intended. I have added these things a little to clear the manner of this divine appearance, which also belongs unto the economy of the Spirit.

Now, I say that this appearance of the Holy Ghost in a bodily shape, wherein he was represented by that which is a substance and hath a subsistence of its own, doth manifest that he himself is a substance and hath a subsistence of his own; for if he be no such thing, but a mere influential effect of the power of God, we are not taught right apprehensions of him but mere mistakes by this appearance, for of such an accident there can be no substantial figure or resemblance made but what is monstrous. It is excepted by our adversaries (Crell. de Natur. Spir. Sanc.), "That a dove is no person, because not endued with an understanding, which is essentially required unto the constitution of a person; and therefore," they say, "no argument can thence be taken for the personality of the Holy Ghost" But it is enough that he was represented by a subsisting substance; which if they will grant him to be, we shall quickly evince that he is endued with a divine understanding, and so is completely a person. And whereas they farther object, "That if the Holy Ghost in the appearance intended to manifest himself to be a divine person, he would have appeared as a man, who is a person, for so God, or an angel in his name, appeared under the Old Testament," it is of no more importance than the preceding exception. The Holy Ghost did manifest himself as it seemed good unto him; and some reasons for the instructive use of the shape of a fiery dove we have before declared. Neither did God of old appear only in a human shape. He did so sometimes in a burning fiery bush, Exod. iii. 2, 4; sometimes in a pillar of fire or a cloud, chap. xiv. 24. Moreover, the appearances of God, as I have elsewhere demonstrated, under the Old Testament, were all of them of the second person; and he assumed a human shape as a preludium unto, and a signification of, his future personal assumption of our nature. No such thing being intended by the Holy Ghost, he might represent himself under what shape he pleased. Yea, the representation of himself under a human shape had been dangerous and unsafe for us; for it would have taken off the use of those instructive appearances under the Old Testament teaching the incarnation of the Son of God. And also, that sole reason of such appearances being removed, — namely, that they had all respect unto the incarnation of the second person, — as they would have been by the like appearance of the third, there would have been danger of giving a false idea of the Deity unto the minds of men; for some might from thence have conceived that God had a bodily shape like unto us, when none could ever be so fond as to imagine him to be like a dove. And these, with the like testimonies in general, are given unto the divine personality of the Holy Spirit. I shall next consider those personal properties which are particularly and distinctly ascribed unto him.

First, Understanding or wisdom, which is the first inseparable property of an intelligent subsistence, is so ascribed unto him in the acts and effects of it: 1 Cor. ii. 10, "The Spirit searcheth all things, yea, the deep things of God." What Spirit it is that is intended is declared expressly, verse 12, "Now we have not received τὸ πνεῦμα τοῦ κόσμου, the spirit of the world," are not acted by the evil spirit; ἀλλὰ τὸ Πνεῦμα τὸ ἐκ τοῦ Θεοῦ, "but the Spirit which is of God," — a signal description of the Holy Ghost. So he is called "His Spirit," verse 10, "God hath revealed these things unto us by his Spirit." Now, to search is an act of understanding; and the Spirit is said to search, because he knoweth: Verse 11, "What man knoweth the things of a man, save the spirit of man which is in him?" — which is intimate unto all its own thoughts and counsels; "even so the things of God knoweth no man, but the Spirit of God." And by him are they revealed unto us, for by him "we know the things that are freely given to us of God," verse 12. These things cannot be spoken of any but a person endued with understanding. And he thus "searcheth τὰ βάθη τοῦ Θεοῦ, the deep things of God," — that is, the mysteries of his will, counsel, and grace; — and is, therefore, a divine person that hath an infinite understanding; as it is said of God, אֵין חֵקֶר לִתְבוּנָתוֹ, Isa. xl. 28, There is no end," measure, or investigation, "of his understanding;" Ps. cxlvii. 5, there is "no number of his understanding," — it is endless, boundless, infinite. It is excepted (Schlichting. de Trinitat., p. 605) "That the Spirit is not here taken for the Spirit himself, nor doth the apostle express what the Spirit himself doth, but what by the assistance of the Holy Ghost men are enabled to do. By that believers are helped to search into the deep counsels of God." But as this exception is directly against the words of the text, so the context will by no means admit of it; for the apostle giveth an account how the wisdom, counsels, and deep things of God, which the world could not understand, were now preached and declared unto the church. "God," saith he, "hath revealed them unto us by his Spirit." But how cometh the Spirit himself, the author of these revelations, to be acquainted with these things? This he hath from his own nature, whereby he knoweth or "searcheth all things, yea, the deep things of God." It is, therefore, the revelation made by the Spirit unto the apostles and penmen of the scripture of the New Testament, — who were acted by the Holy Ghost in like manner as were the holy men of old, 2 Pet. i. 21, — which the apostle intendeth, and not the illumination and teaching of believers in the knowledge of the mysteries by them revealed, whereof the apostle treateth in these words. But who is this Spirit? The same apostle tells us that the "judgments of God are unsearchable, and his ways past finding out," Rom. xi. 33; and asketh, "Who hath known the mind of the Lord? or who hath been his counsellor?" verse 34. And yet this Spirit is said to "search all things, yea, the deep things of God;" such as to all creatures are absolutely unsearchable and past finding out. This, then, is the Spirit of God himself, who is God also; for so it is in the prophet from whence these words are taken, "Who hath directed the Spirit of the Lord, or being his counsellor hath taught him?" Isa. xl. 13.

It will not relieve the adversaries of the Holy Ghost, though it be pleaded by them that he is compared with and opposed unto the "spirit of a man," 1 Cor. ii. 11, which, they say, is no person; for no comparisons hold in all circumstances. The spirit of a man is his rational soul, endued with understanding and knowledge. This is an individual intelligent substance, capable of a subsistence in a separate condition. Grant the Spirit of God to be so far a person, and all their pretences fall to the ground. And whereas it is affirmed by one among ourselves, though otherwise asserting "the deity of the Holy Ghost" (Goodwin, p. 175), "That this expression, of 'searching the things of God,' cannot be applied directly to the Spirit, but must intend his enabling us to search into them, because to search includes imperfection, and the use of means to come to the knowledge of any thing," it is not of weight in this matter; for such acts are ascribed unto God with respect unto their effects. And searching being with us the means of attaining the perfect knowledge of any thing, the perfection of the knowledge of God is expressed thereby. So David prays that God would "search him, and know his heart," Ps. cxxxix. 23. And he is often said to "search the hearts of men," whereby his infinite wisdom is intimated, whereunto all things are open and naked. So is his Spirit said to "search the deep things of God," because of his infinite understanding and the perfection of his knowledge, before which they lie open. And as things are here spoken of the Spirit in reference unto God the Father, so are they spoken of him in reference unto the Spirit: Rom. viii. 27, "He that searcheth the hearts knoweth what is the mind of the Spirit." Add hereunto that this Spirit is the author of wisdom and understanding in and unto others, and therefore he must have them in himself; and that not virtually or casually only, but formally also. 1 Cor. xii. 8, wisdom and knowledge are reckoned among the gifts bestowed by him. For those of faith and tongues, it is enough that they are in him virtually; but wisdom and understanding, they cannot be given by any but he that is wise and understandeth what he doth; and hence is he called expressly a "Spirit of wisdom and understanding, of counsel and knowledge," Isa. xi. 2. I might confirm this by other testimonies, where other effects of understanding are ascribed unto him, as 1 Tim. iv. 1; 1 Pet. i. 11; 2 Pet. i. 21; but what hath been spoken is sufficient unto our purpose.

Secondly, A will is ascribed unto him. This is the most eminently distinguishing character and property of a person. Whatever is endued with an intelligent will is a person; and it cannot by any fiction, with any tolerable congruity, be ascribed unto any thing else, unless the reason of the metaphor be plain and obvious. So when our Saviour says of the wind that it bloweth ὅπου θέλει, "as it willeth," or listeth, John iii. 8, the abuse of the word is evident. All intended is, that the wind, as unto us, is ἀνυπεύθυνος, and not at all at our disposal, acts not by our guidance or direction. And no man is so foolish as not to apprehend the meaning of it, or once to inquire whether our Saviour doth properly ascribe a will to the wind or no. So James iii. 4. The words rendered by us, "Turned about with a very small helm, whithersoever the governor listeth," are in the original, Ὅπου ἂν ἡ ὁρμὴ τοῦ εὐθύνοντος βούληται· in which the act of willing is ascribed to the ὁρμή, the impetus or inclination of the governor, which yet hath not a will. But the ὁρμή in that place is not the πρώτη κίνησις of the philosophers, the motus primo-primus, or the first agitation or inclination of the mind; but it is the will itself under an earnest inclination, such as is usual with them who govern ships by the helms in storms. Hereunto the act of willing is properly ascribed, and he in whom it is proved to be is a person. Thus, a will acting with understanding and choice, as the principle and cause of his outward actions, is ascribed unto the Holy Ghost: 1 Cor. xii. 11, "All these worketh that one and the self-same Spirit, dividing to every man severally as he will." He had before asserted that he was the author and donor of all the spiritual gifts which he had been discoursing about, verses 4–6. These gifts he declares to be various, as he manifests in nine instances, and all variously disposed of by him, verses 8–10. If now it be inquired what is the rule of this his distribution of them, he tells us that it is his own will, his choice and pleasure. What can be spoken more fully and plainly to describe an intelligent person, acting voluntarily with freedom and by choice, I know not.

We may consider what is excepted hereunto. They say (Schlichting. p. 610) "That the Holy Ghost is here introduced as a person by a prosopopœia, — that the distribution of the gifts mentioned is ascribed unto him by a metaphor; and by the same or another metaphor he is said to have a will, or to act as he will." But is it not evident that if this course of interpreting, or rather of perverting, Scripture may be allowed, nothing of any certainty will be left unto us therein? It is but saying this or that is a metaphor, and if one will not serve the turn, to bring in two or three, one on the neck of another, and the work is done; — the sense intended is quite changed and lost. Allow this liberty or bold licentiousness, and you may overthrow the being of God himself and the mediation of Christ, as to any testimony given unto them in the Scripture. But the words are plain, "He divideth to every man severally as he will." And for the confirmation of his deity, though that be out of question on the supposition of his personality, I shall only add from this place, that he who hath the sovereign disposal of all spiritual gifts, having only his own will, which is infinitely wise and holy, for his rule, he is "over all, God blessed for ever."

Thirdly, Another property of a living person is power. A power whereby anyone is able to act according to the guidance of his understanding and the determinations of his will, declares him to be a person. It is not the mere ascription of power absolutely, or ability unto any thing, that I intend; for they may signify no more but the efficacy wherewith such things are attended in their proper places, as instruments of the effects whereunto they are applied. In this sense power is ascribed to the word of God, when it is said to be "able to save our souls," James i. 21; and Acts xx. 32, "the word of God's grace" is said to be "able to build us up, and to give us an inheritance among all them which are sanctified," if that place intend the word written or preached (whereinto I have made inquiry elsewhere): but these things are clearly interpreted in other places. The word is said to be "able," yea, to be the "power of God unto salvation," Rom. i. 16, because God is pleased to use it and make it effectual by his grace unto that end. But where power, divine power, is absolutely ascribed unto anyone, and that declared to be put forth and exercised by the understanding and according to the will of him to whom it is so ascribed, it doth undeniably prove him to be a divine person; for when we say the Holy Ghost is so, we intend no more but that he is one who by his own divine understanding puts forth his own divine power. So is it in this case: Job xxxiii. 4, "The Spirit of God hath made me, and the breath of the Almighty hath given me life." Creation is an act of divine power, the highest we are capable to receive any notion of; and it is also an effect of the wisdom and will of him that createth, as being a voluntary act, and designed unto a certain end. All these, therefore, are here ascribed to the Spirit of God. It is excepted (Schlichting. pp. 613–615) "That by the 'Spirit of God' here mentioned no more is intended but our own vital spirits, whereby we are quickened, called the 'Spirit of God' because he gave it." But this is too much confidence. The words are, רוּחַ־אֵל עָשָׂתְנִי וְנִשְׁמַת שַׁדַּי תְּחַיֵּנִי. There were two distinct divine operations in and about the creation of man. The first was the forming of his body out of the dust of the earth; this is expressed by עָשָׂה, and יָצַר; — "he made," "he formed." And secondly, the infusion of a living or quickening soul into him, called נִשְׁמַת חַיִּים, or "the breath of life." Both these are here distinctly mentioned; the first ascribed to the Spirit of God, the other to his breath, — that is, the same Spirit considered in a peculiar way of operation in the infusion of the rational soul.

Such is the sense of these figurative and enigmatical words, "God breathed into man the breath of life," — that is, by his Spirit he effected a principle of life in him; as we shall see afterward. Isa. xi. 2, As he is called a "Spirit of wisdom and understanding," so is he also of "might" or power. And although it may be granted that the things there mentioned are rather effects of his operations than adjuncts of his nature, yet he who affecteth wisdom and power in others must first have them himself. To this purpose also is that demand, Mic. ii. 7, "Is the Spirit of the Lord straitened," or shortened? that is, in his power; that he cannot work and operate in the prophets and his church as in former days; and the same prophet, chap. iii. 8, affirms that he is "full of power, and of judgment, and of might, by the Spirit of the Lord." These things were wrought in him by his power, as the apostle speaks to the same purpose, Eph. iii. 16.

Those by whom this truth is opposed do lay out all their strength and skill in exceptions, I may say cavils, against some of these particular testimonies and some expressions in them; but as to the whole argument, taken from the consideration of the design and scope of the Scripture in them all, they have nothing to except.

To complete this argument, I shall add the consideration of those works and operations of all sorts which are ascribed to the Spirit of God; which we shall find to be such as are not capable of an assignation unto him with the least congruity of speech or design of speaking intelligibly, unless he be a distinct, singular subsistent or person, endued with divine power and understanding. And here what we desired formerly might be observed must be again repeated. It is not from a single instance of every one of the works which we shall mention that we draw and confirm our argument; for some of them, singly considered, may perhaps sometimes be metaphorically ascribed unto other causes, which doth not prove that therefore they are persons also, — which contains the force of all the exceptions of our adversaries against these testimonies; — but as some of them, at least, never are nor can be assigned unto any but a divine person, so we take our argument from their joint consideration, or the uniform, constant assignation of them all unto him in the Scriptures: which renders it irrefragable. For the things themselves, I shall not insist upon them, because their particular nature must be afterward unfolded.

First, He is said to teach us: Luke xii. 12, "The Holy Ghost shall teach you what ye ought to say." John xiv. 26, "The Comforter, which is the Holy Ghost, whom the Father will send in my name, he shall teach you all things, and bring all things to your remembrance." 1 John ii. 27, He is the "anointing which teacheth us all things;" how and whence he is so called shall be afterward declared. He is the great Teacher of the church, unto whom the accomplishment of that great promise is committed, "And they shall be all taught of God," John vi. 45. It is sad with the church of God when her teachers are removed into a corner, and her eyes see them not; but better lose all other teachers, and that utterly, than to lose this great Teacher only: for although he is pleased to make use of them, he can teach effectually and savingly without them where they are removed and taken away; but they cannot teach without him unto the least spiritual advantage. And those who pretend to be teachers of others, and yet despise his teaching assistance, will one day find that they undertook a work which was none of theirs. But as unto our use of this assertion, it is excepted "That the apostle affirms that nature also teaches us: 1 Cor. xi. 14, 'Doth not even nature itself teach you?' now, nature is not a person." This is the way and manner of them with whom we have to do. If any word in a testimony produced by us have been anywhere used metaphorically, though it be never so evident that it is so used in that place, instantly it must have the same figurative application in the testimony excepted against, although they can give no reason why it should so signify! And if this course of excepting be allowed, there will be nothing left intelligible in the Scripture, nor in any other author, nor in common conversation in the world; for there is scarce any word or name of [a] thing but, one where or other, is or hath been abused or used metaphorically. In particular, nature in this place of the apostle is said to teach us objectively, as the heavens and earth teach us in what we learn from them; for it is said to teach us what we may learn from the customs and actings of them who live, proceed, and act, according to the principles, dictates, and inclinations of it. Everyone sees that here is no intimation of an active teaching by instruction, or a real communication of knowledge, but it is said figuratively to do what we do with respect unto it. And not only in several places, but in the same sentence, a word may be used properly with respect unto one thing and abusively with respect unto another; as in that saying of the poet, —

"Disce, puer, virtutem ex me, verumque laborem; Fortunam ex aliis:"

[Æn. xii. 435.] for virtue and industry are to be learned properly, but fortune, as they called it, or prosperous events, are not so. These things, therefore, are very different, and their difference is obvious unto all. But we insist not merely on this or that particular instance. Let any man not absolutely prepossessed with prejudice read over that discourse of our Saviour unto his disciples, wherein he purposely instructs them in the nature and work of the Spirit of God, on whom, as it were, he then devolved the care of them and the gospel, according unto the promise, John xiv., xv., xvi., and he will need no farther instruction or confirmation in this matter. He is there frequently called "The Comforter," the name of a person, and that vested with an office, with respect unto the work that he would do; and "Another Comforter," in answer and conformity unto the Lord Christ, who was one Comforter and a person, as all grant, chap. xiv. 16, 26. If he be not so, the intention of this expression with these circumstances must be to deceive us, and not instruct us. He tells them, moreover, that he is one whom the world neither sees nor knows, but who abideth with and dwelleth in believers, verse 17; one whom the Father would send, and who would come accordingly, and that to teach them, to lead and guide them and to bring things to their remembrance, verse 26; a Comforter that should come and testify or bear witness unto him, chap. xv. 26; one that should be sent of him, "to reprove the world of sin, and of righteousness, and of judgment," chap. xvi. 7, 8, and to abide with his disciples, to supply his own bodily absence. So is he said to "speak," "guide," "teach," "hear," to "receive of Christ's and to show it unto others," chap. xiv. 26, xvi. 13, 14, with sundry other things of the same nature and importance. And these things are not spoken of him occasionally or in transitu, but in a direct continued discourse, designed on purpose by our Lord Jesus Christ to acquaint his disciples who he was, and what he would do for them. And if there were nothing spoken of him in the whole Scripture but what is here declared by our Saviour, all unprejudiced men must and would acknowledge him to be a divine person. And it is a confidence swelling above all bounds of modesty, to suppose that because one or other of these things is or may be metaphorically or metaleptically ascribed unto this or that thing which are not persons, when the figurativeness of such an ascription is plain and open, that therefore they are all of them in like manner so ascribed unto the Holy Ghost in that discourse of our Saviour unto his disciples, wherein he designed the instruction of them, as above declared. Of the same nature is that which we discoursed before concerning his searching of all things, from 1 Cor. ii. 10; which as it proves him to be an understanding agent, so it undeniably denotes a personal action. Such also are the things mentioned, Rom. viii. 16, 26: He "helpeth our infirmities," he "maketh intercession for us," he himself "beareth witness with our spirit;" the particular meaning of all which expressions shall be afterward inquired into. Here the only refuge of our adversaries is to cry up a prosopopœia (Schlichting. p. 627) But how do they prove it? Only by saying that "these things belong properly to a person, which the Spirit is not." Now, this is nothing but to set up their own false hypothesis against our arguments, and, not being able to contend with the premises, to deny the conclusion.

There are two other places of this nature, both to the same purpose, sufficient of themselves to confirm our faith in the truth pleaded for; and these are, Acts xiii. 2, 4, "As they ministered unto the Lord, and fasted, the Holy Ghost said, Separate me Barnabas and Saul for the work whereunto I have called them. So they, being sent forth by the Holy Ghost, departed." The other is chap. xx. 28, "Take heed therefore unto yourselves, and to all the flock, over the which the Holy Ghost hath made you overseers." These places hold a good correspondence; and what is reported in an extraordinary case, as matter of fact, in the first, is doctrinally applied unto ordinary cases in the latter. And two things are remarkable in the first place:— 1. The Holy Ghost's designation of himself as the person unto whom and whose work Barnabas and Saul were to be separated and dedicated. Saith he, Ἀφορίσατε δή μοι, not "Separate me," as in our translation, making the Spirit only the author of the command, but "Separate unto me;" which proposeth him also as the object of the duty required, and the person whose work was to be attended. Who or what, then, is intended by that pronoun "me?" Some person is directed unto and signified thereby; nor can any instance be given where it is so much as figuratively used, unless it be in a professed parable. That remains, therefore, to be inquired into, Who is intended in that word "me?" And the words are the words of the Holy Ghost: "The Holy Ghost said, Separate unto me;" he, therefore, alone is intended. All the answer which the wit and diligence of our adversaries can invent is, that "these words are ascribed unto the Holy Ghost because the prophets that were in the church of Antioch spake therein by his instinct and inspiration." But in this evasion there is no regard unto the force of our argument; for we do not argue merely from his being said to speak, but from what is spoken by him, "Separate unto me," and do inquire whether the prophets be intended by that word or no? If so, which of them? for they were many by whom the Holy Ghost spake the same thing, and some one must be intended in common by them all; and to say that this was any of the prophets is foolish, indeed blasphemous. 2. The close of the second verse confirms this application of the word, "For the work whereunto I have called them." This confessedly is the Holy Ghost. Now, to call men to the ministry is a free act of authority, choice, and wisdom; which are properties of a person, and none other. Nor is either the Father or the Son in the Scripture introduced more directly clothed with personal properties than the Holy Ghost is in these places. And the whole is confirmed, verse 4, "So they, being sent forth by the Holy Ghost, departed." He called them, by furnishing them with ability and authority for their work; he commanded them to be set apart by the church, that they might be blessed and owned in their work; and he sent them forth, by an impression of his authority on their minds, given them by those former acts of his. And if a divine person be not hereby described, I know not how he may so be.

The other text speaks unto the same purpose. Acts xx. 28, it is expressly said that the Holy Ghost made the elders of the church the overseers of it. The same act of wisdom and authority is here again assigned unto him. And here is no room left for the evasion insisted on; for these words were not spoken in a way of prophecy, nor in the name of the Holy Ghost, but concerning him. And they are explicatory of the other; for he must be meant in these expressions, "Separate unto me those whom I have called," by whom they are made ministers. Now, this was the Holy Ghost; for he makes the overseers of the church. And we may do well to take notice, that if he did so then, he doth so now; for they were not persons extraordinarily inspired or called that the apostle intends, but the ordinary officers of the church. And if persons are not called and constituted officers, as at the first, in ordinary cases, the church is not the same as it was. And it is the concernment of those who take this work and office upon them to consider what there is in their whole undertaking that they can ascribe unto the Holy Ghost. Persons furnished with no spiritual gifts or abilities, entering into the ministry in the pursuit of secular advantages, will not easily satisfy themselves in this inquiry when they shall be willing, or be forced, at the last to make it.

There remains yet one sort of testimonies to the same purpose, which must briefly be passed through: and they are those where he is spoken of as the object of such actings and actions of men as none but a person can be; for let them be applied unto any other object, and their inconsistency will quickly appear. Thus he is said to be tempted of them that sin: "How is it that ye have agreed together to tempt the Spirit of the Lord," Acts v. 9. In what sense soever this word is used, — whether in that which is indifferent, to try, as God is said to tempt Abraham, or in that which is evil, to provoke or induce to sin, — it never is, it never can be, used but with respect unto a person. How can a quality, an accident, an emanation of power from God, be tempted? None can possibly be so but he that hath an understanding to consider what is proposed unto him, and a will to determine upon the proposal made. So Satan tempted our first parents; so men are tempted by their own lusts; so are we said to tempt God when we provoke him by our unbelief, or when we unwarrantably make experiments of his power; — so did they "tempt the Holy Ghost" who sinfully ventured on his omniscience, as if he would not or could not discover their sin; or on his holiness, that he would patronize their deceit. In like manner, Ananias is said to "lie to the Holy Ghost," verse 3; and none is capable of lying unto any other but such an one as is capable of hearing and receiving a testimony, for a lie is a false testimony given unto that which is spoken or uttered in it. This he that is lied unto must be capable of judging and determining upon; which without personal properties of will and understanding none can be. And the Holy Ghost is here so declared to be a person as that he is declared to be one that is also divine; for so the apostle Peter declares in the exposition of the words, verse 4, "Thou hast not lied unto men, but unto God." These things are so plain and positive that the faith of believers will not be concerned in the sophistical evasions of our adversaries. In like manner, he is said to be resisted, Acts vii. 51; which is the moral reaction or opposition of one person unto another. So also is he said to he grieved, or we are commanded not to grieve him, Eph. iv. 30; as they of old were said to have "rebelled and vexed the Holy Spirit of God," Isa. lxiii. 10. A figurative expression is allowed in these words. Properly, the Spirit of God cannot be grieved or vexed; for these things include such imperfections as are incompetent unto the divine nature. But as God is said to "repent" and to be "grieved at his heart," Gen. vi. 6, when he would do things correspondent unto those which men will do or judge fit to be done on such provocations, and when he would declare what effects they would produce in a nature capable of such perturbations; so on the same reason is the Spirit of God said to be grieved and vexed. But this can no way be spoken of him if he be not one whose respect unto sin may, from the analogy unto human persons, be represented by this figurative expression. To talk of grieving a virtue or an actual emanation of power, is to speak that which no man can understand the meaning or intention of. Surely he that is thus tempted, resisted, and grieved by sin and sinners, is one that can understand, judge, and determine concerning them; and these things being elsewhere absolutely spoken concerning God, it declares that he is so with respect unto whom they are mentioned in particular.

The whole of the truth contended for is yet more evident in that discourse of our Saviour, Matt. xii. 24. The Pharisees said, "He doth not cast out devils, but by Beelzebub, the prince of devils." And Jesus answered, verse 28, "If I cast out devils by the Spirit of God, then the kingdom of God is come unto you." Verses 31, 32, "Wherefore I say unto you, All manner of sin and blasphemy shall be forgiven unto men: but the blasphemy against the Holy Ghost shall not be forgiven unto men. And whosoever speaketh a word against the Son of man, it shall be forgiven him: but whosoever speaketh against the Holy Ghost, it shall not be forgiven him." To the same purpose, see Luke xii. 8–10. The Spirit is here expressly distinguished from the Son, as one person from another. They are both spoken of with respect unto the same things in the same manner, and the things mentioned are spoken concerning them universally in the same sense. Now, if the Holy Ghost were only the virtue and power of God, then present with Jesus Christ in all that he did, Christ and that power could not be distinctly spoken against, for they were but one and the same. The Pharisees blasphemed, saying, that "he cast out devils by Beelzebub, the prince of devils." A person they intended, and so expressed him by his name, nature, and office. To which our Saviour replies, that he cast them out by the Spirit of God, — a divine person, opposed to him who is diabolical. Hereunto he immediately subjoins his instruction and caution, that they should take heed how they blasphemed that Holy Spirit, by assigning his effects and works to the prince of devils. And blasphemy against him directly manifests both what and who he is, especially such a peculiar blasphemy as carrieth an aggravation of guilt along with it above all that human nature in any other instance is capable of. It is supposed that blasphemy may be against the person of the Father: so was it in him who "blasphemed the name of Jehovah and cursed" by it, Lev. xxiv. 11. The Son, as to his distinct person, may be blasphemed; so it is said here expressly; — and thereon it is added that the Holy Ghost also may be distinctly blasphemed, or be the immediate object of that sin which is declared to be inexpiable. To suppose now that this Holy Ghost is not a divine person is for men to dream whilst they seem to be awake.

I suppose by all these testimonies we have fully confirmed what was designed to be proved by them, — namely, that the Holy Spirit is not a quality, as some speak, residing in the divine nature; not a mere emanation of virtue and power from God; not the acting of the power of God in and unto our sanctification; but a holy intelligent subsistent or person. And in our passage many instances have been given, whence it is undeniably evident that he is a divine, self-sufficient, self-subsisting person, together with the Father and the Son equally participant of the divine nature. Nor is this distinctly much disputed by them with whom we have to do; for they confess that such things are ascribed unto him as none but God can effect: wherefore, denying him so to be, they lay up all their hopes of success in denying him to be a person. But yet, because the subject we are upon doth require it, and it may be useful to the faith of some, I will call over a few testimonies given expressly unto his deity also.

First, he is expressly called God; and having the name of God properly and directly given unto him, with respect unto spiritual things, or things peculiar unto God, he must have the nature of God also. Acts v. 3, Ananias is said to "lie to the Holy Ghost." This is repeated and interpreted, verse 4, "Thou hast not lied unto men, but unto God." The declaration of the person intended by the "Holy Ghost" is added for the aggravation of the sin, for he is "God." The same person, the same object of the sin of Ananias, is expressed in both places; and, therefore, the Holy Ghost is God. The word for lying is the same in both places, ψεύδομαι, only it is used in a various construction. Verse 3, it hath the accusative case joined unto it: Ψεύσασθαί σε τὸ Πνεῦμα τὸ ἅγιον, — that "thou shouldst deceive," or think to deceive, or attempt to deceive, "the Holy Ghost." How? By lying unto him, in making a profession in the church wherein he presides of that which is false. This is explained, verse 4, by ἐψεύσω τῷ Θεῷ, "thou hast lied unto God;" the nature of his sin being principally intended in the first place, and the object in the latter. Wherefore, in the progress of his discourse, the apostle calls the same sin, a "tempting of the Spirit of the Lord," verse 9; it was the Spirit of the Lord that he lied unto, when he lied unto God. These three expressions, "The Holy Ghost," "God," "The Spirit of the Lord," do denote the same thing and person, or there is no coherence in the discourse. It is excepted "That what is done against the Spirit is done against God, because he is sent by God." It is true, as he is sent by the Father, what is done against him is morally and as to the guilt of it done against the Father. And so our Saviour tells us with respect unto what was done against himself; for saith he, He that despiseth me despiseth him that sent me." But directly and immediately, both Christ and the Spirit were sinned against in their own persons. He is God [who is] here provoked. So also he is called "Lord," in a sense appropriate unto God alone: 2 Cor. iii. 17, 18, "Now the Lord is that Spirit;" and, "We are changed from glory to glory," ἀπὸ Κυρίου Πνεύματος, "by the Lord the Spirit," or the Spirit of the Lord; where also divine operations are ascribed unto him. What is affirmed to this purpose, 1 Cor. xii. 6–8, hath been observed in the opening of the beginning of that chapter at the beginning of our discourse. The same, also, is drawn by just consequence from the comparing of Scriptures together, wherein what is spoken of God absolutely in one place is applied directly and immediately unto the Holy Ghost in another. To instance in one or two particulars: Lev. xxvi. 11, 12, "I will," saith God, "set my tabernacle among you; and I will walk among you, and will be your God, and ye shall be my people." The accomplishment of this promise the apostle declares, 2 Cor. vi. 16, "Ye are the temple of the living God; as God hath said, I will dwell in them, and walk in them; and I will be their God, and they shall be my people." How and by whom is this done? 1 Cor. iii. 16, 17, "Know ye not that ye are the temple of God, and that the Spirit of God dwelleth in you? If any man defile the temple of God, him shall God destroy; for the temple of God is holy, which ye are." If it were, then, God who of old promised to dwell in his people, and to make them his temple thereby, then is the Holy Spirit God; for he it is who, according to that promise, thus dwelleth in them. So Deut. xxxii. 12, speaking of the people in the wilderness, he saith, "The Lord alone did lead him;" and yet, speaking of the same people, at the same time, it is said, that "the Spirit of the Lord did lead them, and caused them to rest," Isa. lxiii. 14. "The Spirit of the Lord," therefore, is Jehovah, or Jehovah alone did not lead them. That, also, which is called in the same people their "sinning against God, and provoking the Most High in the wilderness," Ps. lxxviii. 17, 18, is termed their "rebelling against and vexing the Holy Spirit," Isa. lxiii. 10, 11. And many other instances of an alike nature have been pleaded and vindicated by others.

Add hereunto, in the last place, that divine properties are assigned unto him, as eternity, Heb. ix. 14, he is the "eternal Spirit;" — immensity, Ps. cxxxix. 7, "Whither shall I go from thy Spirit?" — omnipotency, Mic. ii. 7, "The Spirit of the Lord is not straitened," compared with Isa. xl. 28; "The power of the Spirit of God," Rom. xv. 19; — prescience, Acts i. 16, This scripture must be fulfilled, "which the Holy Ghost by the mouth of David spake before concerning Judas;" — omniscience, 1 Cor. ii. 10, 11, "The Spirit searcheth all things, yea, the deep things of God;" — sovereign authority over the church, Acts xiii. 2, 4, xx. 28. The divine works, also, which are assigned unto him are usually, and to good purpose, pleaded in the vindication of the same truth; but these in the progress of our discourse I shall have occasion distinctly to consider and inquire into, and, therefore, shall not in this place insist upon them. What hath been proposed, cleared, and confirmed, may suffice as unto our present purpose, that we may know who he is concerning whom, — his works and grace, — we do design to treat.

I have but one thing more to add concerning the being and personality of the Holy Spirit; and this is, that in the order of subsistence, he is the third person in the holy Trinity. So it is expressed in the solemn numeration of them, where their order gives great direction unto gospel worship and obedience: Matt. xxviii. 19, "Baptizing them in the name of the Father, and of the Son, and of the Holy Ghost." This order, I confess, in their numeration, because of the equality of the persons in the same nature, is sometimes varied. So, Rev. i. 4, 5, "Grace be unto you, and peace, from him which is, and which was, and which is to come; and from the seven Spirits which are before his throne; and from Jesus Christ." The Holy Spirit, under the name of the seven Spirits before the throne of God, because of his various and perfect operations in and towards the church, is reckoned up in order before the Son, Jesus Christ. And so in Paul's euctical conclusion unto his epistles, the Son is placed before the Father: 2 Cor. xiii. 14, "The grace of the Lord Jesus Christ, and the love of God, and the communion of the Holy Ghost, be with you all." And some think that the Holy Ghost is mentioned in the first place, Col. ii. 2, "The acknowledgment of the mystery of God, and of the Father, and of Christ." In this expression of them, therefore, we may use our liberty, they being all one, "God over all, blessed for ever." But in their true and natural order of subsistence, and consequently of operation, the Holy Spirit is the third person; for as to his personal subsistence, he "proceedeth from the Father and the Son," being equally the Spirit of them both, as hath been declared. This constitutes the natural order between the persons, which is unalterable. On this depends the order of his operation; for his working is a consequent of the order of his subsistence. Thus the Father is said to send him, and so is the Son also, John xiv. 16, 26, xvi. 7. And he is thus said to be sent by the Father and the Son, because he is the Spirit of the Father and Son, proceeding from both, and is the next cause in the application of the Trinity unto external works. But as he is thus sent, so his own will is equally in and unto the work for which he is sent; as the Father is said to send the Son, and yet it was also his own love and grace to come unto us and to save us. And this ariseth from hence, that in the whole economy of the Trinity, as to the works that outwardly are of God, especially the works of grace, the order of the subsistence of the persons in the same nature is represented unto us, and they have the same dependence on each other in their operations as they have in their subsistence. The Father is the fountain of all, as in being and existence, so in operation. The Son is of the Father, begotten of him, and, therefore, as unto his work, is sent by him; but his own will is in and unto what he is sent about. The Holy Spirit proceedeth from the Father and the Son, and, therefore, is sent and given by them as to all the works which he immediately effecteth; but yet his own will is the direct principle of all that he doth, — he divideth unto every one according to his own will. And thus much may suffice to be spoken about the being of the Holy Spirit, and the order of his subsistence in the blessed Trinity.

Footnotes:

32. "In hac divini magisterii schola, Pater est qui docet et instruit; Filius qui arcana Dei nobis revelat et aperit; Spiritus Sanctus qui nos replet et imbuit. A Patre potentiam, a Filio sapientiam, a Spiritu Sancto accipimus innocentiam. Pater eligit, Filius diligit, Spiritus Sanctus conjungit et unit." — Cypr. de Baptismo Christi.

33. "'Hæc autem omnia operatur unus atque idem Spiritus, dividens singulis prout vult;' unde dicentes operatricem, et ut ita dicam, distributricem naturam Spiritus Sancti, non abducamur ab his qui dicunt, operationem et non substantiam Dei esse Spiritum Sanctum. Et ex aliis quoque plurimis locis subsistens natura demonstratur Spiritus Sancti." — Didym. de Spir. Sanc. lib. ii.

34. Ἐπειδήπερ τὸ δωρούμενον τὸ πνεῦμα τὸ ἅγιόν ἐστι, καλεῖται καὶ τὸ δῶρον ὁμωνύμως τῷ χαρίσματι. — Chrysost."Nec existimare debemus Spiritum Sanctum secundum substantias esse divisum quia multitudo bonorum dicatur, — impassibilis enim et indivisibilis atque immutabilis est, sed juxta differentes efficientias et intellectus multis bonorum vocabulis nuncupatur; quia participes suos, non juxta unam eandemque virtutem communione sui donet, quippe cum ad utilitatem uniuscujusque aptus sit." — Didym. lib. i.

35. "Baptizate gentes in nomine Patris et Filii et Spiritus Sancti. In nomine dixit, non in nominibus. Non ergo aliud nomen Patris, aliud nomen Filii, aliud nomen Spiritus Sancti, quam unus Deus." — Ambros. de Spir. Sanc. lib. i. cap. 4.

Chapter IV - Peculiar works of the Holy Spirit in the first or old creation

Things to be observed in divine operations — The works of God, how ascribed absolutely unto God, and how distinctly to each person — The reason hereof — Perfecting acts in divine works ascribed unto the Holy Spirit, and why — Peculiar works of the Spirit with respect unto the old creation — The parts of the old creation — Heaven and its host — What the host of heaven — The host of the earth — The host of heaven completed by the Spirit — And of the earth — His moving on the old creation, Ps. civ. 30 — The creation of man; the work of the Spirit therein — The work of the Spirit in the preservation of all things when created, natural and moral — Farther instances thereof, in and out of the church — Work of the Spirit of God in the old creation, why sparingly delivered.

Intending to treat of the operations of the Holy Ghost, or those which are peculiar unto him, some things must be premised concerning the operation of the Godhead in general, and the manner thereof; and they are such as are needful to guide us in many passages of the Scripture, and to direct us aright in the things in particular which now lie before us. I say, then, —

1. That all divine operations are usually ascribed unto God absolutely. So it is said God made all things; and so of all other works, whether in nature or in grace. And the reason hereof is, because the several persons are undivided in their operations, acting all by the same will, the same wisdom, the same power. Every person, therefore, is the author of every work of God, because each person is God, and the divine nature is the same undivided principle of all divine operations;[36] and this ariseth from the unity of the persons in the same essence. But as to the manner of subsistence therein, there is distinction, relation, and order between and among them; and hence there is no divine work but is distinctly assigned unto each person, and eminently unto one. So is it in the works of the old creation, and so in the new, and in all particulars of them. Thus, the creation of the world is distinctly ascribed to the Father as his work, Acts iv. 24; and to the Son as his, John i. 3; and also to the Holy Spirit, Job xxxiii. 4; but by the way of eminence to the Father, and absolutely to God, who is Father, Son, and Holy Spirit.

The reason, therefore, why the works of God are thus distinctly ascribed unto each person is because, in the undivided operation of the divine nature, each person doth the same work in the order of their subsistence; not one as the instrument of the other, or merely employed by the other, but as one common principle of authority, wisdom, love, and power. How come they, then, eminently to be assigned one to one person, another to another? as unto the Father are assigned opera naturæ, the works of nature, or the old creation; to the Son, opera gratiæ procuratæ, all divine operations that belong unto the recovery of mankind by grace; and unto the Spirit, opera gratiæ applicatcæ, the works of God whereby grace is made effectual unto us. And this is done, — (1.) When[37] any especial impression is made of the especial property of any person on any work; then is that work assigned peculiarly to that person. So there is of the power and authority of the Father on the old creation, and of the grace and wisdom of the Son on the new. (2.) Where there is a peculiar condescension of any person unto a work, wherein the others have no concurrence but by approbation and consent. Such was the susception of the human nature by the Son, and all that he did therein; and such was the condescension of the Holy Ghost also unto his office, which entitles him peculiarly and by way of eminence unto his own immediate works.

2. Whereas the order[38] of operation among the distinct persons depends on the order of their subsistence in the blessed Trinity, in every great work of God, the concluding, completing, perfecting acts are ascribed unto the Holy Ghost.[39] This we shall find in all the instances of them that will fall under our consideration. Hence, the immediate actings of the Spirit are the most hidden, curious, and mysterious, as those which contain the perfecting part of the works of God. Some seem willing to exclude all thoughts or mention of him from the works of God; but, indeed, without him no part of any work of God is perfect or complete.[40] The beginning of divine operations is assigned unto the Father, as he is fons et origo Deitatis, — "the fountain of the Deity itself:" "Of him, and through him, and to him, are all things," Rom. xi. 36. The subsisting, establishing, and "upholding of all things," is ascribed unto the Son: "He is before all things, and by him all things consist," Col. i. 17. As he made all things with the Father, so he gives them a consistency, a permanency, in a peculiar manner, as he is the power and wisdom of the Father. He "upholdeth all things by the word of his power," Heb. i. 3. And the finishing and perfecting of all these works is ascribed to the Holy Spirit, as we shall see. I say not this as though one person succeeded unto another in their operation, or as though where one ceased and gave over a work, the other took it up and carried it on; for every divine work, and every part of every divine work, is the work of God, that is, of the whole Trinity, inseparably and undividedly: but on those divine works which outwardly are of God there is an especial impression of the order of the operation of each person, with respect unto their natural and necessary subsistence, as also with regard unto their internal characteristical properties, whereby we are distinctly taught to know them and adore them. And the due consideration of this order of things will direct us in the right understanding of the proposals that are made unto our faith concerning God in his works and word.

These things being premised, we proceed to consider what are the peculiar operations of the Holy Spirit, as revealed unto us in the Scripture. Now, all the works of God may be referred unto two heads:— 1. Those of nature; 2. Those of grace; — or the works of the old and new creation. And we must inquire what are the especial operations of the Holy Spirit in and about these works, which shall be distinctly explained.

The work of the old creation had two parts:— 1. That which concerned the inanimate part of it in general, with the influence it had into the production of animated or living but brute creatures. 2. The rational or intelligent part of it, with the law of its obedience unto God, [and] the especial uses and ends for which it was made. In both these sorts we shall inquire after and consider the especial works of the Holy Spirit.

The general parts of the creation are the heavens and the earth: Gen. i. 1, "In the beginning God created the heaven and the earth." And what belongs unto them is called their "host:" chap. ii. 1, "The heavens and the earth were finished, and all the host of them." The host of heaven is the sun, moon, and stars, and the angels themselves. So are they called, 1 Kings xxii. 19, "I saw the Lord sitting on his throne" וְכָל־צְבָא הַשָּׁמַיִם, "and all the host of heaven standing by him, on his right hand and on his left;" — that is, all the holy angels, as Dan. vii. 10; 2 Chron. xviii. 18. And the host of God: Gen. xxxii. 1, 2, "And Jacob went on his way, and the angels of God met him. And when Jacob saw them, he said, This is God's host." מַחֲנֶה, the word he useth, signifieth a host encamped. Στρατιὰ οὐράνιος, Luke ii. 13, "The heavenly host," or army. The sun, moon, and stars, are also called the host of heaven: Deut. iv. 19, "Lest thou lift up thine eyes unto heaven, and when thou seest the sun, and the moon, and the stars, even all the host of heaven." So Isa. xxxiv. 4; Jer. xxxiii. 22. This was that host of heaven which the Jews idolatrously worshipped: chap. viii. 2, "They shall spread them before the sun, and the moon, and all the host of heaven, whom they have loved, and whom they have served, after whom they have walked, and whom they have sought, and whom they have worshipped." The expressions are multiplied, to show that they used all ways of ascribing that divine honour unto them which was due to God alone, whom only they ought to have loved, to have served, to have walked after, to have sought and worshipped. So Jer. xix. 13. This they called מְלֶכֶת הַשָּׁמַיִם, the "queen of heaven," chap. xliv. 17, because of its beauty and adornings. The "host of the earth" is men and beasts, with all other creatures that either grow out of it or live upon it, and are nourished by it. And these things are called the host of heaven and earth upon a double account:— 1. Because of their order and beautiful disposition. A host properly is a number of men put into a certain order, for some certain end or purpose; and all their strength and power, all their terror and beauty, consisteth in and ariseth from that order. Without this they are but a confused multitude. But a host or army with banners is beautiful and terrible, Cant. vi. 10. Before things were cast into this order, the universe was, as it were, full of confusion; it had no beauty nor glory, for the "earth was without form and void," Gen. i. 2. Hence the Vulgar Latin in this place renders the word by "ornatus eorum," all their beauty and adorning; for the creation and beautiful disposal of these hosts gave them beauty and ornament: and thence do the Greeks call the world κόσμος, — that is, an adorned thing. 2. Because all creatures in heaven and earth are God's armies, to accomplish his irresistible will and pleasure. Hence he often styles himself "The Lord of hosts," — of both these hosts, that above, of the heavens, the holy angels and the celestial bodies, and that of all creatures beneath in the earth; for all these he useth and applieth at his pleasure, to do his will and execute his judgments. Thus, one of those angels slew a whole host of men in one night, Isa. xxxvii. 36. And it is said that the "stars in their courses fought against Sisera," Judges v. 20. God overruled the influences of heaven against him, though it may be angels also are here intended. And among the meanest creatures of the earth, he calls locusts and caterpillars, when he sends them to destroy a country for sin, his host or "army," Joel ii. 11. This by the way.

Now, the forming and perfecting of this host of heaven and earth is that which is assigned peculiarly to the Spirit of God; and hereby the work of creation was completed and finished. First, for the heavens: Job xxvi. 13, "By his Spirit he hath garnished the heavens; his hand hath formed the crooked serpent;" — or rather, "his Spirit hath garnished;" for שִׁפְרָה agrees with רוּחַ,[41] the "Spirit," and not with "he;" and the word signifies to "adorn," to make fair, to render beautiful to the eye. Thus the heavens were garnished by the Spirit of God, when, by the creation and disposal of the aspectable host of them, he rendered them so glorious and beautiful as we behold. So the Targum, "His Spirit beautified the face of the heavens," or gave them that comely beauty and order wherein their face appeareth unto us. Hence the heavens, as adorned with the moon and stars, are said to be the "work of God's fingers," Ps. viii. 3, — that is, not only those which were powerfully made, but also curiously wrought and adorned by the Spirit of God; for by the finger or fingers of God the Spirit of God is in an especial manner intended. Hence those words of our Saviour, Luke xi. 20, "But if I with the finger of God cast out devils," are, Matt. xii. 28, "If I cast out devils by the Spirit of God." By him were the heavens, as it were, curiously wrought, adorned, garnished, rendered beautiful and glorious, to show forth the praise of his power and wisdom, Ps. xix.

1. And by the "crooked serpent," which is added to the "garnishing of the heavens," the Hebrews understand the galaxy or milky way; which to the eye represents the moving or writhing of a serpent in the water. This, then, is peculiarly assigned to the Spirit with respect to the heavens and their host: The completing, finishing work is ascribed unto him; which we must understand by the rules before mentioned, and not exclusively to the other persons. And thus was it also in the earth. God first out of nothing created the earth, which comprised the whole inferior globe, which afterward divided itself into seas and dry land, as the heavens contain in that expression of their creation all that is above and over it. The whole material mass of earth and water, wherewith probably the more solid and firm substance was covered, and as it were overwhelmed, is intended by that "earth" which was first created; for immediately there is mention made of the "deep" and the "waters," without any intimation of their production but what is contained in that of the creation of the earth, Gen. i. 2. This mass being thus framed and mixed, the "Spirit of God moved upon the face of the waters;" not taken distinctly, but as containing that radical humour which was the וְרוּחַ אֱלֹהִים מְרַחֶפֶת עַל־פְּנֵי creatures: all unto being and life of principle material הַמָּיִם. The word merachepheth signifies an easy, gentle motion, such as a dove, or other fowl, useth over its nest or young ones, either to communicate vital heat unto its eggs, or to cherish and defend its young. And this will no way consist with that exposition which some would give in this place of אֱלֹהִים רוּחַ. "Ruah, they say, "here signifies 'the wind,' as it doth sometimes; and it is called the 'wind of God,' because it was great and mighty: for this phrase of speech is usual in the sacred language to set out the greatness and singular eminency of any thing. So a great trembling is called a 'trembling of God,' 1 Sam. xiv. 15; great cedars, the 'cedars of God,' Ps. lxxx. 10; and the like." But, — 1. When was this wind created? The meteors were not made before the fourth day, with the firmament, the place of their residence. And whence or what this wind should be is not to be discovered. 2. The word here used signifies such an "easy and gentle motion" as is in birds when they move themselves upon their nests. And it is but three times used in the Scripture, — in this place, and Deut. xxxii. 11, Jer. xxiii. 9. In Deuteronomy it is expressly applied unto the motion of an eagle over her young, for their safety, protection, and growth: כְּנָפָיו יִפְרֹשׂ יְרַחֵף, "As an eagle fluttereth,

spreading her wings over her young." And in the other place we render it "shake:" "All my bones shake," — that is, are in a trembling motion, like the feathers of a fowl over her nest. No such great and violent wind, therefore, as from thence should be called a wind of God, can be intended in this place; but it is the Spirit of God himself and his work that is expressed.

This, therefore, was the work of the Holy Spirit of God in reference unto the earth and the host thereof: The whole matter being created out of which all living creatures were to be educed, and of which they were to be made, he takes upon him the cherishing and preservation of it; that as it had its subsistence by the power of the Word of God, it might be carried on towards that form, order, beauty, and perfection, that it was designed unto. To this purpose he communicated unto it a quickening and prolific virtue, inlaying it with the seeds of animal life unto all kinds of things. Hence, upon the command of God, it brought forth all sorts of creatures in abundance, according to the seeds and principles of life which were communicated unto the rude, inform chaos, by the cherishing motion of the Holy Spirit. Without him all was a dead sea, a confused deep, with darkness upon it, able to bring forth nothing, nor more prepared to bring forth any one thing than another; but by the moving of the Spirit of God upon it, the principles of all those kinds, sorts, and forms of things, which, in an inconceivable variety, make up its host and ornament, were communicated unto it. And this is a better account of the original of all things, in their several kinds, than any [that] is given by ancient or modern philosophers. And hence was the old tradition of all things being formed of water, which the apostle alludes unto, 2 Pet. iii. 5. The whole is declared by Cyprian, whose words I have, therefore, transcribed at large.[42] And as at the first creation, so in the course of providence, this work of cherishing and nourishing the creatures is assigned in an especial manner unto the Spirit: Ps. civ. 30, "Thou sendest forth thy Spirit, they are created; and thou renewest the face of the earth." The making or creation of things here intended is not the first great work of the creation of all, but the daily production of creatures in and according to their kind; for in the verse foregoing the Psalmist treats of the decay of all sorts of creatures in the world, by a providential cutting off and finishing of their lives: Verse 29, "Thou hidest thy face, they are troubled: thou takest away their breath, they die, and return to their dust." That, under this continual decay and dying of all sorts of creatures, the world doth not come to emptiness and desolation, the only reason is, because the Spirit of God, whose office and work it is to uphold and preserve all things continually, produceth by his power a new supply of creatures in the room of them that fall off like leaves from the trees, and return to their dust everyday. And whereas the earth itself, the common nurse of them all, seems in the revolution of every year to be at an end of its use and work, having death brought upon the face of it, and ofttimes entering deep into its bowels, the Spirit of God, by its influential concurrence, renews it again, causing everything afresh to bring forth fruit according unto its kind, whereby its face receiveth a new beauty and adorning. And this is the substance of what the Scripture expressly asserts concerning the work of the Spirit of God towards the inanimate part of the creation. His actings in reference unto man, and that obedience which he owed to God, according to the law and covenant of his creation, is nextly to be considered.

Man in his creation falleth under a twofold notion; for he may be considered either merely naturally, as to the essentially constitutive parts of his being, or morally also, with reference unto his principles of obedience, the law given unto him, and the end proposed as his reward. And these things are distinctly proposed unto our contemplation in the Scripture. The first is expressed, Gen. ii. 7, "And the Lord God formed man of the dust of the ground, and breathed into his nostrils the breath of life; and man became a living soul."

1. There is the matter whereof he was formed; 2. The quickening principle added thereunto; and, 3. The effect of their conjunction and union. For the matter he was made of, it is said he was formed מִן־הָאֲדָמָה עָפָר, [of] "dust of the ground," or dust gathered together on a heap from and upon the ground: תֵּבֵל עַפְרוֹת רֹאשׁ, Prov. viii. 26. So is God, the great δημιουργός, the universal framer of all, represented as an artificer, who first prepares his matter, and then forms it as it seemeth good unto him. And this is mentioned for two ends:— First, To set forth the excellency, power, and wisdom of God, who out of such vile, contemptible matter as a heap of dust, swept as it were together on the ground, could and did make so excellent, curious, and glorious a fabric as is the body of man, or as was the body of Adam before the fall. Secondly, To mind man of his original, that he might be kept humble and in a meet dependence on the wisdom and bounty of his Creator; for thence it was, and not from the original matter whereof he was made, that he became so excellent. Hereof Abraham makes his solemn acknowledgment before the Lord: Gen. xviii. 27, "Behold now, I have taken upon me to speak unto the Lord, which am but dust and ashes." He abaseth himself with the remembrance of his original And this, as it were, God reproacheth Adam withal upon his sin and transgression: Gen. iii. 19, "Thou shalt return unto the ground; for out of it wast thou taken: for dust thou art, and unto dust shalt thou return." He lets him know that he had now, by sin, lost that immortality which he was made in a condition to have enjoyed; and that his body, according to his nature and constitution, should return again into its first principles, or the dust of the earth. Into this formed dust, secondly, God breathed חַיִּים נִשְׁמַת, the "breath of life;" divinæ auræ particulam, "a vital immortal spirit." This God breathed into him, as giving him something of himself, somewhat immediately of his own, not made out of any procreated matter. This is the rational soul, or intelligent spirit. Thus man became a middle creature between the angels above and the sensitive animals below. His body was formed, as the beasts, from the matter made the first day, and digested into dry land on the third day; his soul was an immediate production of and emanation from the divine power, as the angels were. So when, in the works of the new creation, our blessed Saviour bestowed the Holy Ghost on his disciples, he breathed on them, as a sign that he gave them something of his own. This celestial spirit, this heavenly breath, was unto man a quickening principle; for, thirdly, the effect hereof is, that man became לְנֶפֶשׁ חַיָּה, a "living soul." His body was hereby animated, and capable of all vital acts. Hence he could move, eat, see, hear, etc.; for the natural effects of this breath of life are only intended in this expression. Thus the "first man Adam was made a living soul," 1 Cor. xv. 45. This was the creation of man, as unto the essentially constituting principles of his nature.

With respect unto his moral condition and principle of obedience unto God, it is expressed, Gen. i. 26, 27, "And God said, Let us make man in our image, after our likeness: and let them have dominion," etc. "So God created man in his own image, in the image of God created he him." He made him "upright," Eccles. vii. 29, perfect in his condition, every way complete, — fit, disposed, and able to and for the obedience required of him; without weakness, distemper, disease, contrariety of principles, inclinations, or reasonings. A universal rectitude of nature, consisting in light, power, and order, in his understanding, mind, and affections, was the principal part of this image of God wherein he was created. And this appears, as from the nature of the thing itself, so from the description which the apostle giveth us of the renovation of that image in us by the grace of Christ, Eph. iv. 24, Col. iii. 10. And under both these considerations we may weigh the especial operations of the Spirit of God:—

First, As to the essential principles of the nature of man, it is not for nothing that God expresseth his communication of a spirit of life by his breathing into him: "God breathed into his nostrils the breath of life." The Spirit of God and the breath of God are the same, only, the one expression is proper, the other metaphorical; wherefore, this breathing is the especial acting of the Spirit of God. The creation of the human soul, a vital immortal principle and being, is the immediate work of the Spirit of God: Job xxxiii. 4, "The Spirit of God hath made me, and the breath of the Almighty hath given me life." Here, indeed, the creation and production of both the essential parts of human nature, body and soul, are ascribed unto the same author; for the Spirit of God and the breath of God are the same, but several effects being mentioned causeth a repetition of the same cause under several names. This Spirit of God first made man, or formed his body of the dust, and then gave him that breath of life whereby he became a "living soul." So, then, under this first consideration, the creation of man is assigned unto the Holy Spirit, for man was the perfection of the inferior creation; and in order unto the glory of God, by him were all other things created. Here, therefore, are his operations distinctly declared, to whom the perfecting and completing of all divine works is peculiarly committed.

Secondly, We may consider the moral state and condition of man, with the furniture of his mind and soul, in reference unto his obedience to God and his enjoyment of him. This was the principal part of that image of God wherein he was created. Three things were required to render man idoneous, or fit unto that life to God for which he was made:— First, An ability to discern the mind and will of God with respect unto all the duty and obedience that God required of him; as also so far to know the nature and properties of God as to believe him the only proper object of all acts and duties of religious obedience, and an all-sufficient satisfaction and reward in this world and to eternity. Secondly, A free, uncontrolled, unentangled disposition to every duty of the law of his creation, in order unto living unto God. Thirdly, An ability of mind and will, with a readiness of compliance in his affections, for a due regular performance of all duties, and abstinence from all sin. These things belonged unto the integrity of his nature, with the uprightness of the state and condition wherein he was made. And all these things were the peculiar effects of the immediate operation of the Holy Ghost; for although this rectitude of his nature be distinguishable and separable from the faculties of the soul of man, yet in his first creation they were not actually distinguished from them, nor superadded, or infused into them when created, but were concreated with them, — that is, his soul was made meet and able to live to God, as his sovereign lord, chiefest good, and last end. And so they were all from the Holy Ghost, from whom the soul was, as hath been declared. Yea, suppose these abilities to be superadded unto man's natural faculties, as gifts supernatural (which yet is not so), they must be acknowledged in a peculiar manner to be from the Holy Spirit; for in the restoration of these abilities unto our minds, in our renovation unto the image of God in the gospel, it is plainly asserted that the Holy Ghost is the immediate operator of them. And he doth thereby restore his own work, and not take the work of another out of his hand: for in the new creation the Father, in the way of authority, designs it, and brings all things unto a head in Christ, Eph. i. 10, which retrieved his original peculiar work; and the Son gave unto all things a new consistency, which belonged unto him from the beginning, Col. i. 17. So also the Holy Spirit renews in us the image of God, the original implantation whereof was his peculiar work. And thus Adam may be said to have had the Spirit of God in his innocency. He had him in these peculiar effects of his power and goodness; and he had him according to the tenor of that covenant whereby it was possible that he should utterly lose him, as accordingly it came to pass. He had him not by especial inhabitation, for the whole world was then the temple of God. In the covenant of grace, founded in the person and on the mediation of Christ, it is otherwise. On whomsoever the Spirit of God is bestowed for the renovation of the image of God in him, he abides with him forever. But in all men, from first to last, all goodness, righteousness, and truth, are the "fruits of the Spirit," Eph. v. 9.

The works of God being thus finished, and the whole frame of nature set upon its wheels, it is not deserted by the Spirit of God; for as the preservation, continuance, and acting of all things in the universe, according to their especial nature and mutual application of one unto another, are all from the powerful and efficacious influences of divine Providence, so there are particular operations of the Holy Spirit in and about all things, whether merely natural and animal, or also rational and moral. An instance in each kind may suffice. For the first (as we have showed), the propagation of the succeeding generations of creatures and the annual renovation of the face of the earth are ascribed unto him, Ps. civ. 30; for as we would own the due and just powers and operations of second causes, so we abhor that atheism which ascribes unto them an original and independent efficacy and causality, without a previous acting in, by, and upon them of the power of God. And this is here ascribed unto the Spirit, whom God sendeth forth unto that end and purpose. As to rational and moral actions, such as the great affairs of the world do consist in and are disposed of by, he hath in them also a peculiar efficiency. Thus those great virtues of wisdom, courage, and fortitude, which have been used for the producing of great effects in the world, are of his especial operation. So when God stirred up men to rule and govern his people of old, to fight against and to subdue their enemies, it is said the Spirit of God came upon them: Judges iii. 10, "The Spirit of the Lord came upon Othniel, and he judged Israel, and went out to war." The Spirit of God endued him with wisdom for government, and with courage and skill in conduct for war. So chap. vi. 34. And although instances hereof are given us principally among the people of God, yet wherever men in the world have been raised up to do great and wonderful things, whereby God executeth his judgments, [and] fulfilleth any of his promises or his threatenings, even they also have received of the especial gifts and assistances of the Holy Spirit of God. For this reason is Cyrus expressly called "God's anointed," Isa. xlv. 1. Cyrus had, by God's designation, a great and mighty work to effect. He was utterly to ruin and destroyeth great, ancient, Babylonian monarchy. God had a concern herein as to the avenging of the quarrel of his people, and therein the accomplishment of many promises and threatenings. The work itself was great, arduous, and insuperable to ordinary human abilities. Wherefore God "sends his Spirit" to fill Cyrus with wisdom, courage, skill in all military affairs, that he might go through with the work whereunto, in the providence of God, he was designed. Hence is he called "God's anointed," because the unction of kings of old was an instituted sign of the communication of the gifts of the Holy Ghost for government unto them. See verses 1–4; and other instances of the like kind might be given.

Thus, when the church was to have a blessed restoration of the worship of God, after the return of the people from their captivity, Zerubbabel is, in an especial manner, called to begin and carry on this work in the building of the temple. But the difficulties he had to conflict withal were great, and appeared insuperable. The people were few and poor, and the oppositions made unto them and their work great and many, especially what arose from the power of the Persian monarchy, under whose rule and oppression they were; for although they had permission and encouragement from Cyrus for their work, yet immediately upon his death they were oppressed again, and their "work caused to cease." This power they could no way conflict withal; yet God tells them that all this opposition shall be removed and conquered. "Who art thou," saith he, "O great mountain? before Zerubbabel thou shalt become a plain," Zech. iv. 7; — "All the hinderance that arose from that great mountain of the Persian empire shall be removed out of the way, and the progress of Zerubbabel in his work shall be made smooth, plain, and easy." But how shall this be effected and brought about? "Not by an army or 'by might, nor by power, but by my Spirit, saith the Lord of hosts,' " verse 6; — "You would suppose that it must be done by armies and open force, which you are altogether insufficient for; but this is not the way I will take in this matter. My Spirit shall work in their hearts, minds, and counsels, that, contrary to your fears, they shall themselves further that work which hitherto they have impeded; and he shall work in the minds and counsels of others, to oppose them and entangle them where they would hinder it, until they are destroyed, and that great mountain be fully removed;" — as in the event it came to pass. So that the providential alterations that are wrought in the world are effects of his power and efficacy also.

And thus have we taken a short view of the dispensation and works of the Spirit of God in the first creation. But the effect hereof being a state of things that quickly passed away, and being of no advantage to the church after the entrance of sin, what belonged unto it is but sparingly delivered in the Scriptures, the true sense of what is so delivered depending much on the analogy of the following works of God in man's renovation and recovery. But as to the new creation (which falls under our consideration in the next place, as that alone which is directly intended by us), the foundation, building up, and finishing the church of God therein, being the things whereon depends the principal manifestation of the glory of God, and wherein the great concerns of all the elect do lie, they are more fully and directly declared in the Scripture; and in reference unto them we shall find a full, distinct declaration of the whole dispensation and work of the Spirit of God.

Footnotes:

36. Μία ἄρα καὶ ἐκ τούτων, ἡ τῆς Τρίαδος ἐνέργεια δείκνυατι. Οὐ γὰρ ὡς παρ' ἑκάσοτυ διάφορα, καὶ διηρημένα τὰ διδόμενα σημαίνει ὁ ἀπόστολος. Ἀλλ' ὅτι τὰ διδόμενα ἐν Τριάδι δίδοται, καὶ τὰ πάντα ἐξ ἑνὸς Θεοῦ ἐστι. — Athanas. Epistol. [i. 31] ad Serapionem.Μίαν ἐνέργειαν ὁρῶμεν πατρὸς καὶ υἱοῦ, καὶ ἁγίου πνεύματος. Basil. Homil. xvii., in Sanctum Baptisma. Ὧν αἱ αὐται ἐνέργειαι τούτων καὶ οὐσία μία, ἐνέργεια δὲ υἱοῦ καὶ πατρὸς μία ὡς τὸ· ποιήσωμεν ἄνθρωπον. Καὶ πάλιν· ἃ γὰρ ἄν ὁ πατὴρ ποιῇ ταῦτα καὶ ὁ υἱὸς ὁμοίως ποιεῖ. Ἄρα καὶ οὐσία μία πατρὸς καὶ υἱοῦ. — Idem advers. Eunom., lib. iv."Quicquid de Spiritu Sancto diximus hoc similiter de Patre et Filio communiter et indivise volumus intelligi; quia sancta et inseparabilis Trinitas nunquam aliquid se sigillatim operari noverit." — Ambros. in Symbol Apost. cap. ix.

37. Πάντα τὰ θεοπρεπῶς λέγόμενα ἐπὶ τῆς ὑπερουσίου τρίαδος καθ' ἑκάστης τῶν τριῶν ὑποστάσεων ἐξιδιοῦται καὶ ἐναρμόττεται πλὴν ἃ τὴν προαγωγὴν τούτων, ἤγουν τὴν ὑποστασικὴν γνώρισιν ἐμποιοῦνται. — Arethas, in Apocal. Commentar. cap. 1.

38. "Hoc non est inæqualitas substantiæ, sed ordo naturæ; non quod alter esset prior altero, sed quod alter esset ex altero." — Aug. lib. iii. contra Maxentium, cap. 14.

39. Πᾶσα ἐνέργεια ἡ θεόθεν ἐπὶ τὴν κτίσιν διήκουσα, καὶ κατὰ τὰς πολυτρόπους ἐννοίας ὀνομαζομένη ἐκ πατρὸς ἀφορμᾶται, καὶ διὰ τοῦ υἱοῦ πρόεισι, καὶ ἐν τῷ πνεύματι τῷ ἁγίῳ τελειοῦται. — Gregor. Nyssen. ad Ablabium Ἐν δὲ τῇ τούτων (ἀγγέλων) κτίσει, ἐννόησόν μοι τὴν προκαταρκτικὴν αἰτίαν τῶν γενομένων τὸν πατέρα, τὴν δημιουργικὴν τὸν υἱὸν, τὴν τελειωτικὴν τὸ πνεῦμα. — Basil. de Spir. Sanc. cap. xvi.

40. Καὶ γὰρ διὰ μὲν τῆς παλαιᾶς ὡς προκαταρκτικὸν τῶν ὅλων ὁ πατὴρ πρώτως κηρύττεται. Καὶ δευτέρως δὲ ὁ υἱὸς ὡς δημιουργικὸν αἴτιον ἐμφανίζεται. Καὶ τρίτως ὡς τελειωτικὸν τὸ πνεῦμα τὸ ἅγιον. Τὰ τελειωτικὰ γὰρ τῶ τέλει φερωνύμως ἀναφαίνεται, τῆ προκοπῇ καὶ αὐξήσει τῶν πραγμάτων καὶ τῶν χρὸνων οἷα στέφανος ἀναῤῥήσεως ἐπὶ τοῖς ἀθλητικοῖς ἱδρῶσι κατὰ τὸ τέλος ἐναρμοζόμενος. Δὶα καὶ τὸν ἄνθρωπον πλάσας ὁ Θεὸς πρῶτον εἶτα τέλει ἐνεφύσησεν εἰς τὸ πρόσωπον αὐτοῦ πνεῦμα ζωῆς. — Jobius apud Photium, lib. cxxii. cap. 18.

41. This word in the original is בְּרוּחוֹ. To make it agree with שִׁפְרָה, Owen must have adopted the opinion of Aben Ezra, that בְּ in the former word is redundant. Eminent critics demur to this conclusion; Simonis and others rendering the clause, "By his Spirit the heavens [are] beauty." — Ed.

42. "Hic Spiritus Sanctus ab ipso mundi initio aquis legitur superfusus; non materialibus aquis quasi vehiculo egens, quasi potius ipse ferebat, et complectentibus firmamentum dabat congruum motum et limitem præfinitum. Hujus sempiterna virtus et divinitas, cum in propria natura ab inquisitoribus mundi antiquis philosophis proprie investigari non posset, subtilissimis tamen intuiti sunt conjecturis compositionem mundi; compositis et distinctis elementorum affectibus presentem omnibus animam affuisse, quæ secundum genus et ordinem singulorum vitam præberet et motum, et intransgressibiles figeret metas, et stabilitatem assignaret et usum. Hanc vitam, hunc motum, hanc rerum essentiam, animam mundi philosophi vocaverunt, putantes cœlestia corpora, solem dico lunam et stellas ipsumque firmamentum hujus animæ virtute moveri et regi, et aquas, et terram, et aërem hujus semine imprægnari. Qui si spiritum et dominum, et creatorem, et vivificatorem, et nutritorem crederent onmium quæ sub ipso sunt, convenientem haberent ad vitam accessum. Sed abscondita est a sapientibus, et prudentibus tantæ rei majestas; nec potuit humani fastus ingenii secretis interesse cœlestibus, et penetrare ad superessentialis naturæ altitudinem; et licet intelligerent, quod vere esset creatrix et gubernatrix rerum Divinitas, distinguere tamen nullo modo potuerunt quæ esset Deitatis Trinitas, vel quæ unitas vel quæ personarum proprietas. Hic est Spiritus vitæ cujus vivificus calor animat omnia et fovet et provehit et fecundat. Hic omnium viventium anima, ita largitate sua se omnibus abundanter infundit, ut habeant omnia rationabilia et irrationabilia secundum genus suum ex eo quod sunt, et quod in suo ordine suæ naturæ competentia agunt; non quod ipse sit substantialis anima singulis, sed in se singulariter marens, de plenitudine sua distributor magnificus proprias efficientias singulis dividit et largitur; et quasi sol omnia calefaciens subjecta, onmia nutrit, et absque ulla sui diminutione, integritatem suam de inexhausta abundantia quod satis est et sufficit omnibus commodat et impartit." — Cypr. Lib. de Spir. Sanc.

Chapter V - Way and manner of the divine dispensation of the Holy Spirit

Dispensation of the Spirit to be learned from the Scripture only — General adjuncts thereof — The administration of the Spirit and his own application of himself to his work, how expressed — The Spirit, how and in what sense given and received — What is included in the giving of the Spirit — What in receiving of him — Privilege and advantage in receiving the Spirit — How God is said to send the Spirit — What is included in sending — How God ministers the Spirit — How God is said to put his Spirit on us — What is included in that expression — The Spirit, how poured out — What is included and intended herein — The ways of the Spirit's application of himself unto his work — His proceeding from Father and Son explained — How he cometh unto us — His falling on men — His resting — How and in what sense he is said to depart from any person — Of the distributions of the Holy Ghost, Heb. ii. 4 — Exposition of them vindicated.

Before we treat of the especial operations, works, and effects of the Holy Ghost in and on the new creation, the order of things requires that we should first speak somewhat of the general nature of God's dispensation of him, and of his own application of himself unto his actings and workings in this matter; for this is the foundation of all that he doth, and this, for our edification, we are instructed in by the Scriptures. Unto them in this whole discourse we must diligently attend; for we are exercised in such a subject as wherein we have no rule, nor guide, nor any thing to give us assistance but pure revelation. And what I have to offer concerning these things consists upon the matter solely in the explication of those places of Scripture wherein they are revealed. We must, therefore, consider, — 1. What we are taught on the part of God the Father with respect unto the Holy Spirit and his work; and, 2. What relates immediately unto himself.

I. God's disposal of the Spirit unto his work is five ways expressed in the Scripture: for he is said, — 1. To give or bestow him; 2. To send him; 3. To minister him; 4. To pour him out; 5. To put him on us. And his own application of himself unto his work is likewise five ways expressed: for he is said, — 1. To proceed; 2. To come, or come upon; 3. To fall on men; 4. To rest; and, 5. To depart. These things, containing the general manner of his administration and dispensation, must be first spoken unto.

First, He is said to be given of God; that is, of God the Father, who is said to give him in an especial manner: Luke xi. 13, "Your heavenly Father will give the Holy Spirit to them that ask him;" John iii. 34. 1 John iii. 24, "He hath given the Spirit unto us." John xiv. 16, "The Father shall give you another Comforter;" "which is the Holy Ghost," verse 26. And in answer unto this act of God, those on whom he is bestowed are said to receive him: John vii. 39, "This he spake of the Spirit, which they that believe on him should receive." 1 Cor. ii. 12, "We have received the Spirit which is of God." 2 Cor. xi. 4, "If ye receive another Spirit, which ye have not received;" where the receiving of the Spirit is made a matter common unto all believers. So Gal. iii. 2; Acts viii. 15, 19; John xiv. 17, xx. 22. For these two, giving and receiving, are related, the one supposing the other. And this expression of the dispensation of the Holy Ghost is irreconcilable unto the opinion before rejected, — namely, that he is nothing but a transient accident, or an occasional emanation of the power of God; for how or in what sense can an act of the power of God be given by him or be received by us? It can, indeed, in no sense be either the object of God's giving or of our receiving, especially as this is explained in those other expressions of the same thing before laid down, and afterward considered. It must be somewhat that hath a subsistence of its own that is thus given and received. So the Lord Christ is frequently said to be given of God and received by us. It is true, we may be said, in another sense, to "receive the grace of God;" which is the exception of the Socinians unto this consideration, and the constant practice they use to evade plain testimonies of the Scripture: for if they can find any words in them used elsewhere in another sense, they suppose it sufficient to contradict their plain design and proper meaning in another place. Thus we are exhorted "not to receive the grace of God in vain," 2 Cor. vi. 1. I answer, The grace of God may be considered two ways:— 1. Objectively, for the revelation or doctrine of grace; as Tit. ii. 11, 12. So we are said to receive it when we believe and profess it, in opposition unto them by whom it is opposed and rejected. And this is the same with our receiving the word preached, so often mentioned in the Scripture, Acts ii. 41, James i. 21; which is by faith to give it entertainment in our hearts: which is the meaning of the word in this place, 2 Cor. vi. 1. Having taken the profession of the doctrine of grace, that is, of the gospel, upon us, we ought to express its power in holiness and suitable obedience, without which it will be of no use or benefit unto us. And the grace of God is sometimes, — 2. Taken subjectively, for the grace which God is pleased to communicate unto us, or gracious qualities that he works in our souls by his Spirit. In this sense, also, we are sometimes said to receive it: 1 Cor. iv. 7, "Who maketh thee to differ from another? and what hast thou that thou didst not receive?" where the apostle speaketh both of the gifts and graces of the Spirit. And the reason hereof is, because in the communication of internal grace unto us, we contribute nothing to the procurement of it, but are merely capable recipient subjects. And this grace is a quality or spiritual habit, permanent and abiding in the soul: But in neither of these senses can we be said to receive the Spirit of God, nor God to give him, if he be only the power of God making an impression on our minds and spirits, — no more than a man can be said to receive the sunbeams, which cause heat in him by their natural efficacy, falling on him: much less can the giving and receiving of the Spirit be so interpreted, considering what is said of his being sent and his own coming, with the like declarations of God's dispensation of him; whereof afterward.

Now, this giving of the Spirit, as it is the act of him by whom he is given, denotes authority, freedom, and bounty; and, on the part of them that receive him, privilege and advantage.

1. Authority. He that gives any thing hath authority to dispose of it. None can give but of his own, and that which in some sense he hath in his power. Now, the Father is said to give the Spirit, and that upon our request, as Luke xi. 13. This, I acknowledge, wants not some difficulty in its explication; for if the Holy Ghost be God himself, as hath been declared, how can he be said to be

given by the Father, as it were in a way of authority? But keeping ourselves to the sacred rule of truth, we may solve this difficulty without curiosity or danger. Wherefore, — (1.) The order of the subsistence of the three persons in the divine nature is regarded herein; for the Father, as hath been showed, is the fountain and original of the Trinity, the Son being of him, and the Spirit of them both. Hence, he is to be considered as the principal author and cause of all those works which are immediately wrought by either of them; for of whom the Son and Spirit have their essence, as to their personality, from him have they life and power of operation, John v. 19, 26. Therefore, when the Holy Spirit comes unto any, the Father is said to give him, for he is the Spirit of the Father. And this authority of the Father doth immediately respect the work itself, and not the person working; but the person is said to be given for the work's sake. (2.) The economy of the blessed Trinity in the work of our redemption and salvation is respected in this order of things. The fountain hereof lies in the love, wisdom, grace, and counsel of the Father. Whatever is done in the pursuit hereof is originally the gift of the Father, because it is designed unto no other end but to make his grace effectual. Hence is he said to send and give his Son also. And the whole work of the Holy Ghost, as our sanctifier, guide, comforter, and advocate, is to make the love of the Father effectual unto us, John xvi. 13, 14.[43] As this, out of his own love and care, he hath condescended unto, so the fountain of it being in the love and purpose of the Father, and that also, or the making them effectual, being their end, he is rightly said to be given of him. (3.) In the whole communication of the Spirit, respect is had unto his effects, or the ends for which he is given. What they are shall be afterward declared. Now, the authority of this giving respects principally his gifts and graces, which depend on the authority of the Father.

2. This expression denotes freedom. What is given might be withheld. This is the "gift of God" (as he is called, John iv. 10), not the purchase of our endeavours, nor the reward of our desert. Some men delight to talk of their purchasing grace and glory; but the one and the other are to be "bought without money and without price." Even "eternal life" itself, the end of all our obedience, is the "gift of God, through Jesus Christ our Lord," Rom. vi. 23. The Scripture knows of no earnings that men can make of themselves but death; for as Austin says, "Quicquid tuum est peccatum est:" and the wages of sin is death. To what end or purpose soever the Spirit is bestowed upon us, whether it be for the communication of grace or the distribution of gifts, or for consolation and refreshment, it is of the mere gift of God, from his absolute and sovereign freedom.

In answer hereunto they are said to receive him, on whom as a gift he is bestowed; as in the testimonies before mentioned. And in receiving, two things are implied:— 1. That we contribute nothing thereunto which should take off from the thing received as a gift. Receiving answers giving, and that implies freedom in the giver. 2. That it is their privilege and advantage; for what a man receives, he doth it for his own good. First, then, we have him freely as a gift of God; for to receive him in general is to be made partaker of him, as unto those ends for which he is given of God. Be those ends what they will, in respect of them they are said to receive him who are made partakers of him. Two things may be pleaded to take off the freedom of this gift and of our reception, and to cast it on something necessary and required on our part; for, — (1.) Our Saviour tells us "that the world cannot receive him, because it seeth him not, neither knoweth him," John xiv. 17. Now, if the "world" cannot receive him, there is required an ability and preparation in them that do so, that are "not of the world;" and so the gift and communication of the Spirit depends on that qualification in us. But all men are naturally alike the world and of it. No one man by nature hath more ability or strength in spiritual things than another; for all are equally "dead in trespasses and sins," all equally "children of wrath." It must, therefore, be inquired how some come to have this ability and power to receive the Spirit of God, which others have not. Now this, as I shall fully manifest afterward, is merely from the Holy Ghost himself and his grace, respect being had herein only unto the order of his operations in us, some being preparatory for and dispositive unto others, one being instituted as the means of obtaining another, the whole being the effect of the free gift of God; for we do not make ourselves to differ from others, nor have we any thing that we have not received, 1 Cor. iv. 7. Wherefore, the receiving of the Holy Ghost intended in that expression of our Saviour, with respect whereunto some are able to receive him, some are not, is not absolute, but with respect unto some certain work and end; and this, as is plain in the context, is the receiving of him as a comforter and a guide in spiritual truth. Hereunto faith in Christ Jesus, which also is an effect and fruit of the same Spirit, is antecedently required. In this sense, therefore, believers alone can receive him, and are enabled so to do by the grace which they have received from him in their first conversion unto God. But, (2.) It will be said that we are bound to pray for him before we receive him, and therefore the bestowing of him depends on a condition to be by us fulfilled; for the promise is, that "our heavenly Father will give the Holy Spirit to them that ask him," Luke xi. 13. But this doth not prove the bestowing and receiving of him not to be absolutely free. Nay, it proves the contrary. It is gratia indebita, "undeserved grace," that is the proper object of prayer. And God, by these encouraging promises, doth not abridge the liberty of his own will, nor derogate from the freedom of his gifts and grace, but only directs us into the way whereby we may be made partakers of them, unto his glory and our own advantage.

And this also belongs unto the order of the communication of the grace of the Spirit unto us. This very praying for the Spirit is a duty which we cannot perform without his assistance; for "no man can call Jesus Lord, but by the Holy Ghost," 1 Cor. xii. 3. He helps us, as a Spirit of grace and supplication, to pray for him as a Spirit of joy and consolation.

3. This is such a gift as in God proceeds from bounty; for God is said to give him unto us "richly," Tit. iii. 6. This will be spoken unto in the fourth way of his communication: only I say at present, the greatness of a gift, the free mind of the giver, and want of desert or merit in the receiver, are that which declare bounty to be the spring and fountain of it; and all these concur to the height in God's giving of the Holy Ghost.

Again; On the part of them who receive this gift, privilege and advantage are intimated. They receive a gift, and that from God, and that a great and singular gift, from divine bounty. Some, indeed, receive him in a sort, as to some ends and purposes, without any advantage finally unto their own souls. So do they who "prophesy" and "cast out devils" by his power, in the name of Christ, and yet, continuing "workers of iniquity," are rejected at the last day, Matt. vii. 22, 23. Thus it is with all who receive his gifts only, without his grace to sanctify their persons and their gifts; and this whether they be ordinary or extraordinary: but this is only by accident. There is no gift of the Holy Ghost but is good in its own nature, tending to a good end, and is proper for the good and advantage of them by whom it is received. And although the direct end of some of them be not the spiritual good of them on whom they are bestowed, but the edification of others, — for "the manifestation of the Spirit is given unto every man to profit withal," 1 Cor. xii. 7, — yet there is that excellency and worth in them, and that use may be made of them, as to turn greatly to the advantage of them that receive them; for although they are not grace, yet they serve to stir up and give an edge unto grace, and to draw it out unto exercise, whereby it is strengthened and increased. And they have an influence into glory; for it is by the abilities which they give that some are made wise and effectual instruments for the "turning of many to righteousness," who "shall shine as the brightness of the firmament, and as the stars for ever and ever," Dan. xii. 3. But the unbelief, ingratitude, and lusts of men can spoil these, and any other good things whatever. And these things will afterward in particular fall under our consideration. In general, to be made partaker of the Holy Ghost is an inestimable privilege and advantage, and as such is proposed by our Saviour, John xiv. 17.

Secondly, God is said to send him: Ps. civ. 30, "Thou sendest forth thy Spirit;" John xiv. 26, "The Father will send the Holy Ghost in my name." This is also spoken of the Son: "I will send unto you the Comforter from the Father," chap. xv. 26, xvi. 7. And in the accomplishment of that promise, it is said he "shed him forth," Acts ii. 33; Gal. iv. 6, "God hath sent forth the Spirit of his Son into your hearts;" and in other places the same expression is used. Now, this, upon the matter, is the same with the former, of giving him, arguing the same authority, the same freedom, the same bounty. Only, the word naturally includes in its signification a respect unto a local motion. He which is sent removeth from the place where he was, from whence he is sent, unto a place where he was not, whither he was sent. Now, this cannot properly be spoken of the Holy Ghost; for he being God by nature is naturally omnipresent, and an omnipresence is inconsistent with a local mutation. So the Psalmist expressly: Ps. cxxxix. 7, 8, "Whither shall I go from thy Spirit? or whither shall I flee from thy presence? If I ascend up into heaven," etc. There must, therefore, a metaphor be allowed in this expression, but such a one as the Scripture, by the frequent use of it, hath rendered familiar unto us. Thus God is said to "come out of his place," to "bow the heavens and come down;" to "come down and see what is done in the earth," Isa. xxvi. 21; Ps. cxliv. 5; Gen. xviii. 21. That these things are not spoken properly of God, who is immense, all men acknowledge. But when God begins to work in any place, in any kind, where before he did not do so, he is said to come thither; for so must we do, — we must come to a place before we can work in it. Thus, the sending of the Holy Ghost includeth two things as added unto his being given:— 1. That he was not before in or with that person, or amongst those persons, for that especial work and end which he is sent for. He may be in them and with them in one respect, and be afterward said to be sent unto them in another. So our Lord Jesus Christ promiseth to send the Holy Ghost unto his disciples as a comforter, whom they had received before as a sanctifier. "I will," saith he, "send him unto you; and ye know him, for he dwelleth with you," John xiv. 17, xvi. 7. He did so as a sanctifier before he came unto them as a comforter. But in every coming of his, he is sent for one especial work or another; and this sufficiently manifests that in his gifts and graces he is not common unto all. A supposition thereof would leave no place for this especial act of sending him, which is done by choice and distinction of the object. Much less is he a light which is always in all men, and which all men may be in if they please; for this neither is nor can be absent in any sense from anyone at any time. 2. It denotes an especial work there or on them, where and on whom there was none before of that kind. For this cause is he said to be sent of the Father.[44] No local motion, then, is intended in this expression, only there is an allusion thereunto; for as a creature cannot produce any effects where it is not, until it either be sent thither or go thither of its own accord, so the Holy Ghost produceth not the blessed effects of his power and grace but in and towards them unto whom he is given and sent by the Father. How, in answer hereunto, he is said himself to come, shall be afterward declared. And it is the person of the Spirit which is said to be thus sent; for this belongs unto that holy dispensation of the several persons of the Trinity in the work of our salvation. And herein the Spirit, in all his operations, is considered as sent of the Father, for the reasons before often intimated.

Thirdly, God is said to minister the Spirit: Gal. iii. 5, "He that ministereth to you the Spirit." Ὁ οὖν ἐπιχορηγίῶν ὑμῖν τὸ Πνεῦμα· — "He that giveth you continual or abundant supplies of the Spirit." Χορηγέω is "to give a sufficiency of any thing;" and χορηγία and χορήγημα are dimensum, "a sufficiency of provision." An addition thereunto is ἐπιχορηγία, whereby the communication of the Spirit is expressed: Phil. i. 19," For I know that this shall turn to my salvation through your prayers," καὶ ἐπιχορηγίας τοῦ Πνεύματος Ἰησοῦ Χριστοῦ, "and the additional supply of the Spirit of Jesus Christ." That Spirit and its assistance he had before received, but he yet stood in need of a daily farther supply. So is the word used constantly for the adding of one thing to another, or one degree of the same thing unto another: 2 Pet. i. 5, Ἐπιχορηγήσατε ἐν τῇ πίστει ὑμῶν τὴν ἀρετήν· — "Add to your faith virtue;" or, "In your faith make an increase of virtue." When, therefore, God is thus said to "minister the Spirit," it is his continual giving out of additional supplies of his grace by his Spirit which is intended; for the Holy Spirit is a voluntary agent, and distributes unto everyone as he will. When, therefore, he is given and sent unto any, his operations are limited by his own will and the will of him that sends him; and therefore do we stand in need of supplies of him and from him; which are the principal subject-matter of our prayers in this world.

Fourthly, God is said to put his Spirit in or upon men; and this also belongeth unto the manner of his dispensation: Isa. xlii. 1, "Behold my servant, whom I uphold; I have put my Spirit upon him." The word there, indeed, is נָתַתִּי, "I have given my Spirit upon him;" but because עָלָיו, "upon him," is joined to it, it is by ours rendered by "put." As also Ezek. xxxvii. 14, where בָּכֶם, "in you," is added; — "Put my Spirit in you." The same is plainly intended with that, Isa. lxiii. 11, קָדְשׁוֹ אֶת־רוּחַ בְּקִרְבּוֹ הַשָּׂם — "That put his Holy Spirit in the midst of them." Hence, נָתַתִּי, "I have given," or "I will give," Isa. xlii. 1, is rendered by θήσω, Matt. xii. 18: Θήσω τὸ Πνεῦμά μου ἐπ' αὐτόν, — "I will put my Spirit upon him." The word נָתַן, then, used in this sense, doth not denote the granting or donation of any thing, but its actual bestowing, as שׂוּם doth. And it is the effectual acting of God in this matter that is intended. He doth not only give and send his Spirit unto them to whom he designs so great a benefit and privilege, but he actually collates and bestows him upon them.[45] He doth not send him unto them, and leave it in their wills and power whether they will receive him or no, but he so effectually collates and puts him in them or upon them as that they shall be actually made partakers of him. He efficaciously endows their hearts and minds with him, for the work and end which he is designed unto. So Exod. xxxi. 6, "I have put wisdom," is as much as, "I have filled them with wisdom," verse 2. So, then, where God intendeth unto any the benefit of his Spirit, he will actually and effectually collate him upon them. He doth not, indeed, always do this in the same manner. Sometimes he doth it, as it were, by a surprisal, when those who receive him are neither aware of it nor do desire it. So the Spirit of the Lord, as a Spirit of prophecy, came upon Saul, when his mind was remote and estranged from any such thoughts. In like manner, the Spirit of God came upon Eldad and Medad in the camp, when the other elders went forth unto the tabernacle to receive him, Num. xi. 27. And so the Spirit of prophecy came upon most of the prophets of old, without either expectation or preparation on their parts. So Amos giveth an account of his call unto his office, chap. vii. 14, 15. "I was," saith he, "no prophet, neither was I a prophet's son; but I was an herdman, and a gatherer of sycomore fruit: and the Lord took me as I followed the flock, and the Lord said unto me, Go, prophesy." He was not brought up with any expectation of receiving this gift, he had no preparation for it; but God surprised him with his call and gift as he followed the flock. Such, also, was the call of Jeremiah, chap. i. 5–7. So vain is the discourse of Maimonides on this subject, prescribing various natural and moral preparations for the receiving of this gift. But these things were extraordinary. Yet I no way doubt but that God doth yet continue to work grace in many by such unexpected surprisals; the manner whereof shall be afterward inquired into. But sometimes, as to some gifts and graces, God doth bestow his Spirit where there is some preparation and cooperation on our part; but wherever he designs to put or place him, he doth it effectually.

Fifthly, God is said to pour him out, and that frequently: Prov. i. 23, אַבִּיעָה הִנֵּה רוּחִי לָכֶם, — "Behold, I will pour out my Spirit unto you." נָבַע signifies "ebullire more scaturiginis," — "to bubble up as a fountain."[46] Hence, the words are rendered by Theodotion, Ἀναβλύσω ὑμῖν Πνεῦμά μου, — "Scaturire faciam," — "I will cause my Spirit to spring out unto you as a fountain." And it is frequently applied unto speaking, when it signifies "eloqui aut proferre verba more scaturiginis." See Ps. lxxviii. 2, cxlv. 7. And בָּעָה, also, which some take to be the root of, אַבִּיעָה, Prov. i. 23, hath the same signification. And the word hath a double lively metaphor: for the proceeding of the Spirit from the Father is compared to the continual rising of the waters of a living spring; and his communication unto us to the overflowing of those waters, yet guided by the will and wisdom of God: Isa. xxxii. 15, "Until the Spirit be poured upon us from on high, and the wilderness be a fruitful field," — עַד־יֵעָרֶה עָלֵינוּ רוּחַ מִמָּרוֹם. עָרָה is, indeed, sometimes "to pour out," but more properly and more commonly "to uncover," "to make bare," "to reveal;" — "Until the Spirit be revealed from on high." There shall be such a plentiful communication of the Spirit as that he and his work shall be made open, revealed, and plain; or, the Spirit shall be bared, as God is said to make his arm bare when he will work mightily and effectually, chap. lii. 10. Chap. xliv. 3, "I will pour my Spirit upon thy seed, and my blessing upon thine offspring." יָצַק, the word here, is so to pour a thing out as that it cleaveth unto and abideth on that which it is poured out upon; as the Spirit of God abides with them unto whom he is communicated. Ezek. xxxix. 29, "I have poured out my Spirit upon the house of Israel," — שָׁפַכְתִּי,

another word: this is properly to pour out, and that in a plentiful manner, [and is] the same word that is used in that great promise, Joel ii. 28, which is rendered, Acts ii. 17, by ἐκχεῶ, "effundam," — "I will pour out my Spirit;" and the same thing is again expressed by the same word, chap. x. 45, "On the Gentiles also was poured out the gift of the Holy Ghost."

Let us, then, briefly consider the importance of this expression. And one or two things may be observed concerning it in general; as, — 1. Wherever it is used, it hath direct respect unto the times of the gospel. Either it is a part of the promises concerning it, or of the story of their accomplishment under it. But wherever it is mentioned, the time, state, and grace of the gospel are intended in it: for the Lord Christ was "in all things to have the pre-eminence," Col. i. 18; and, therefore, although God gave his Spirit in some measure before, yet he poured him not out until he was first anointed with his fullness. 2. There is a tacit comparison in it with some other time and season, or some other act of God, wherein or whereby God gave his Spirit before, but not in the way and manner that he intended now to bestow him. A larger measure of the Spirit to be now given than was before, or is signified by any other expressions of the same gift, is intended in this word.

Three things are therefore comprised in this expression:— 1. An eminent act of divine bounty. Pouring forth is the way whereby bounty from an all-sufficing fullness is expressed; as "The clouds, filled with a moist vapour, pour down rain," Job xxxvi. 27, until "it water the ridges of the earth abundantly, settling the furrows thereof, and making it soft with showers," as Ps. lxv. 10; which, with the things following in that place, verses 11–13, are spoken allegorically of this pouring out of the Spirit of God from above. Hence, God is said to do this richly: Tit. iii. 6, "The renewing of the Holy Ghost," οὗ ἐξέχεεν ἐφ' ἡμᾶς πλουσίως, "which he hath poured on us richly," — that is, on all believers who are converted unto God; — for the apostle discourseth not of the extraordinary gifts of the Holy Ghost, which were then given forth in a plentiful manner, but of that grace of the Holy Ghost whereby all that believe are regenerated, renewed, and converted unto God; for so were men converted of old by a rich participation of the Holy Ghost, and so they must be still, whatever some pretend, or die in their sins. And by the same word is the bounty of God in other things expressed: "The living God, who giveth us richly all things to enjoy," 1 Tim. vi. 17. 2. This pouring out hath respect unto the gifts and graces of the Spirit, and not unto his person: for where he is given, he is given absolutely, and as to himself not more or less; but his gifts and graces may be more plentifully and abundantly given at one time than at another, to some persons than to others. Wherefore this expression is metonymical, that being spoken of the cause which is proper to the effect; the Spirit being said to be poured forth, because his graces are so. 3. Respect is had herein unto some especial works of the Spirit. Such are the purifying or sanctifying, and the comforting or refreshing [of] them on whom he is poured. With respect unto the first of these effects, he is compared both unto fire and water; for both fire and water have purifying qualities in them, though towards different objects, and working in a different manner. So, by fire are metals purified and purged from their dross and mixtures; and by water are all other unclean and defiled things cleansed and purified. Hence, the Lord Jesus Christ, in his work by his Spirit, is at once compared unto a "refiner's fire" and to "fullers' soap," Mal. iii. 2, 3, because of the purging, purifying qualities that are in fire and water.

And the Holy Ghost is expressly called a "Spirit of burning," Isa. iv. 4; for by him are the vessels of the house of God that are of gold and silver refined and purged, as those that are but of wood and stone are consumed. And when it is said of our Lord Jesus that he should "baptize with the Holy Ghost and with fire," Luke iii. 16, it is but ἓν διὰ δυοῖν, the same thing doubly expressed; and, therefore, mention is made only of the "Holy Ghost," John i. 33. But the Holy Ghost was, in his dispensation, to purify and cleanse them as fire doth gold and silver. And on the same account is he compared to water, Ezek. xxxvi. 25, "I will sprinkle clean water upon you, and ye shall be clean;" which is expounded, verse 26, by "A new spirit will I put within you;" which God calls his Spirit, verse 27. So our Saviour calls him "rivers of water," John vii. 38, 39: see Isa. xliv. 3. And it is with regard unto his purifying, cleansing, and sanctifying our natures that he is thus called. With respect, therefore, in an especial manner, hereunto is he said to be poured out. So our apostle expressly declares, Tit. iii. 4–6. Again, it respects his comforting and refreshing them on whom he is poured.

Hence is he said to be poured down from above as rain that descends on the earth: Isa. xliv. 3, "I will pour water upon him that is thirsty, and floods upon the dry ground," — that is, "I will pour my Spirit on thy seed, and my blessing upon thine offspring; and they shall spring up as among the grass, as willows by the water courses," verse 4; see chap. xxxv. 6, 7. He comes upon the dry, parched, barren ground of the hearts of men, with his refreshing, fructifying virtue and blessing, causing them to spring and bring forth fruits in holiness and righteousness to God, Heb. vi. 7. And in respect unto his communication of his Spirit is the Lord Christ said to "come down like rain upon the mown grass, as showers that water the earth," Ps. lxxii. 6. The good Lord give us always of these waters and refreshing showers!

And these are the ways, in general, whereby the dispensation of the Spirit from God, for what end or purpose soever it be, is expressed.

II. We come nextly to consider what is ascribed unto the Spirit himself in a way of compliance with these acts of God whereby he is given and administered. Now, these are such things or actions as manifest him to be a voluntary agent, and that not only as to what he acts or doth in men, but also as to the manner of his coming forth from God, and his application of himself unto his work. And these we must consider as they are declared unto us in the Scripture.

The first and most general expression hereof is, that he proceedeth from the Father; and being the Spirit of the Son, he proceedeth from him also in like manner: John xv. 26, "The Spirit of truth, which proceedeth from the Father, he shall testify of me." There is a twofold ἐκπόρευσις or "procession" of the Holy Ghost. The one is φυσικὴ or ὑποστατικὴ, "natural" or "personal." This expresseth his eternal relation to the persons of the Father and the Son.

He is of them by an eternal emanation or procession.[47] The manner hereof unto us, in this life, is incomprehensible; therefore it is rejected by some, who will believe no more than they can put their hands into the sides of. And yet are they forced, in things under their eyes, to admit of many things which they cannot perfectly comprehend! But we live by faith, and not by sight.[48] This is enough unto us, that we admit nothing in this great mystery but what is revealed. And nothing is revealed unto us that is inconsistent with the being and subsistence of God; for this procession or emanation includes no separation or division in or of the divine nature, but only expresseth a distinction in subsistence, by a property peculiar to the Holy Spirit. But this is not that which at present I intend. The consideration of it belongeth unto the doctrine of the Trinity in general, and hath been handled elsewhere. Secondly, There is an ἐκπόρευσις or "procession" of the Spirit, which is οἰκονομική or "dispensatory." This is the egress of the Spirit in his application of himself unto his work. A voluntary act it is of his will, and not a necessary property of his person. And he is said thus to proceed from the Father, because he goeth forth or proceedeth in the pursuit of the counsels and purposes of the Father, and, as sent by him, to put them into execution, or to make them effectual. And in like manner he proceedeth from the Son, sent by him for the application of his grace unto the souls of his elect, John xv. 26. It is true, this proves his eternal relation to the Father and the Son, as he proceeds from them, or receives his peculiar personal subsistence from them, for that is the ground of this order of operation; but it is his own personal voluntary acting that is intended in the expression. And this is the general notation of the original of the Spirit's acting in all that he doth:— He proceedeth or cometh forth from the Father. Had it been only said that he was given and sent, it could not have been known that there was any thing of his own will in what he did, whereas he is said to "divide unto every man as he will;" but in that ἐκπορεύεται, he proceedeth of his own accord unto his work, his own will and condescension are also asserted. And this his proceeding from the Father is in compliance with his sending of him to accomplish and make effectual the purposes of his will and the counsels of his grace.

Secondly, To the same purpose he is said to come : John xv. 26, "When the Comforter is come." John xvi. 7, "If I go not away, the Comforter will not come." Verse 8, "And when he is come." So is he said to come upon persons. We so express it, 1 Chron. xii. 18, "The Spirit came upon Amasai," — וְרוּחַ לָבְשָׁה אֶת־עֲמָשַׂי. "And the Spirit clothed Amasai," possessed his mind as a man's clothes cleave unto him. Acts xix. 6, "The Holy Ghost came on them, and they prophesied," ἦλθε. Ἔρχομαι, "to come," is, as it were, the terminus ad quem of ἐκπορεύομαι, "going forth" or "proceeding;" for there is in these expressions an allusion unto a local motion, whereof these two words denote the beginning and the end.

The first intendeth his voluntary application of himself to his work, the other his progress in it; such condescensions doth God make use of in the declaration of his divine actings, to accommodate them unto our understandings, and to give us some kind of apprehension of them. He proceedeth from the Father, as given by him; and cometh unto us, as sent by him. The meaning of both is, that the Holy Ghost, by his own will and consent, worketh, in the pursuit of the will of the Father, there and that, where and what, he did not work before.[49] And as there is no local motion to be thought of in these things, so they can in no tolerable sense be reconciled to the imagination of his being only the inherent virtue or an actual emanation and influence of the power of God. And hereby are our faith and obedience regulated in our dealing with God about him: for we may both pray the Father that he would give and send him unto us, according to his promise; and we may pray to him to come unto us to sanctify and comfort us, according to the work and office that he hath undertaken. This is that which we are taught hereby; for these revelations of God are for our instruction in the obedience of faith.

Thirdly, He is said to fall on men: Acts x. 44, "While Peter yet spake these words, the Holy Ghost fell on all them which heard the word." So chap. xi. 15, where Peter, repeating the same matter, says, "The Holy Ghost fell on them, as on us at the beginning," — that is, Acts ii. 4. A greatness and suddenness in a surprisal is intended in this word; as, when the fire fell down from heaven (which was a type of him) upon the altar and sacrifice of Elijah, the people that saw it were amazed, and falling on their faces, cried out, "The Lord he is the God!" 1 Kings xviii. 38, 39. When men are no way in expectation of such a gift, or when they have an expectation in general, but are suddenly surprised as to the particular season, it is thus declared. But wherever this word is used, some extraordinary effects evidencing his presence and power do immediately ensue, Acts x. 44–46; and so it was at the beginning of his effusion under the New Testament, chap. ii. 4, viii. 16.

Fourthly, Being come, he is said to rest on the persons to whom he is given and sent: Isa. xi. 2, "And the Spirit of the Lord shall rest upon him." This is interpreted by "abiding" and "remaining," John i. 32, 33. Num. xi. 25, 26, "The Spirit of the Lord rested upon the elders." So the "spirit of Elijah rested on Elisha," 2 Kings ii. 15. 1 Pet. iv. 14, "The Spirit of glory and of God resteth on you." Two things are included herein:— 1. Complacency; 2. Permanency. First, He is well pleased in his work wherein he rests. So where God is said to "rest in his love," he doth it with "joy" and "singing," Zeph. iii. 17. So doth the Spirit rejoice where he rests. Secondly, He abides where he rests. Under this notion is this acting of the Spirit promised by our Saviour: "He shall abide with you for ever," John xiv. 16. He came only on some men by a sudden surprisal, to act in them and by them some peculiar work and duty; to this end he only transiently affected their minds with his power; — but where he is said to rest, as in the works of sanctification and consolation, there he abides and continues with complacency and delight.

Fifthly, He is said to depart from some persons. So it is said of Saul, 1 Sam. xvi. 14, "The Spirit of the Lord departed from him." And David prays that God would not "take his Holy Spirit from him," Ps. li. 11. And this is to be understood answerably unto what we have discoursed before about his coming and his being sent. As he is said to come, so is he said to depart; and as he is said to be sent, so is he said to be taken away. His departure from men, therefore, is his ceasing to work in them and on them as formerly; and as far as this is penal, he is said to be taken away. So he departed and was taken away from Saul, when he no more helped him with that ability for kingly government which before he had by his assistance. And this departure of the Holy Ghost from any is either total or partial only. Some on whom he hath been bestowed, for the working of sundry gifts for the good of others, with manifold convictions, by light and general assistance unto the performance of duties, he utterly deserts, and gives them up unto themselves and their own hearts' lusts. Examples hereof are common in the world. Men who have been made partakers of many "gifts of the Holy Ghost," and been in an especial manner enlightened, and, under the power of their convictions, carried out unto the profession of the gospel and the performance of many duties of religion, yet, being entangled by temptations, and overcome by the power of their lusts, relinquish all their beginnings and engagements, and turn wholly unto sin and folly. From such persons the Holy Ghost utterly departs, all their gifts dry up and wither, their light goeth out, and they have darkness instead of a vision. The case of such is deplorable; for "it had been better for them not to have known the way of righteousness, than, after they have known it, to turn from the holy commandment delivered unto them," 2 Pet. ii. 21. And some of these add despite and contempt of that whole work of the Spirit of God, whereof themselves were made partakers, unto their apostasy. And the condition of such profligate sinners is, for the most part, irrecoverable, Heb. vi. 4–6, x. 26–30. From some he withdraweth and departeth partially only, and that mostly but for a season; and this departure respects the grace, light, and consolation which he administers unto believers, as to the degrees of them, and the sense of them in their own souls. On whom he is bestowed to work these things in a saving way, from them he never utterly or totally departs. This our blessed Saviour plainly promiseth and asserteth: John iv. 14, "Whosoever drinketh of the water that I shall give him shall never thirst; but the water that I shall give him shall be in him a well of water springing up into everlasting life." That this well of "living water" is his sanctifying Spirit himself declares, chap. vii. 37–39. He who hath received him shall never have a thirst of total want and indigence anymore. Besides, he is given unto this end by virtue of the covenant of grace; and the promise is express therein that he shall "never depart from them" to whom he is given, Isa. lix. 21; Jer. xxxi. 33, xxxii. 39, 40; Ezek. xi. 19, 20. But now, as to the degrees and sensible effects of these operations, he may depart and withdraw from believers for a season. Hence they may be left unto many spiritual decays and much weakness, the things of grace that remain in them being as it were "ready to die," Rev. iii. 2; and they may apprehend themselves deserted and forsaken of God, — so did Zion, Isa. xl. 27, xlix. 14: for therein doth God "hide himself," or "forsake his people for a small moment," chap. liv. 7, 8. He "hideth himself, and is wroth," chap. lvii. 17. These are the things which David so often and so bitterly complaineth of, and which with so much earnestness he contendeth and wrestleth with God to be delivered from. These are those spiritual desertions which some of late have laden with reproach, contempt, and scorn. All the apprehensions and complaints of the people of God about them, they would represent as nothing but the idle imaginations of distempered brains, or the effects of some disorder in their blood and animal spirits. I could, indeed, easily allow that men should despise and laugh at what is declared as the experience of professors at present, — their prejudice against their persons will not allow them to entertain any thoughts of them but what are suited unto folly and hypocrisy; — but at this I acknowledge I stand amazed, that whereas these things are so plainly, so fully, and frequently declared in the Scriptures, both as to the actings of God and his Holy Spirit in them, and as to the sense of those concerned about them; whereas the whole of God's dealings, and believers' application of themselves to him in this matter, are so graphically exemplified in sundry of the holy saints of old, as Job, David, Heman, and others; and great and plentiful provision is made in the Scripture for the direction, recovery, healing, and consolation of souls in such a condition; yet men professing themselves to be Christians, and to believe the word of God at least not to be a fable, should dare to cast such opprobrious reproaches on the ways and works of God. The end of these attempts can be no other but to decry all real intercourse between God and the souls of men, leaving only an outside form or shape of religion, not one jot better than atheism.

Neither is it only what concerns spiritual desertions, whose nature, causes, and remedies, are professedly and at large handled by all the casuistical divines, even of the Roman church, but the whole work of the Spirit of God upon the hearts of men, with all the effects produced in them with respect unto sin and grace, that some men, by their odious and scurrilous expressions, endeavour to expose to contempt and scorn, S. P.,[50] pp. 339–342. Whatever trouble befalls the minds of men upon the account of a sense of the guilt of sin; whatever darkness and disconsolation they may undergo through the displeasure of God, and his withdrawing of the wonted influences of his grace, love, and favour towards them; whatever peace, comfort, or joy, they may be made partakers of, by a sense of the love of God shed abroad in their hearts by the Holy Ghost, — it is all ascribed, in most opprobrious language, unto melancholy reeks and vapours, whereof a certain and mechanical account may be given by them who understand the anatomy of the brain. To such a height of profane atheism is the daring pride and ignorance of some in our days arrived!

There remaineth yet one general adjunct of the dispensation and work of the Holy Ghost, which gives a farther description of the manner of it, which I have left unto a single consideration. This is that which is mentioned, Heb. ii. 4, "God bearing them witness, both with signs and wonders, and with divers miracles," καὶ Πνεύματος Ἁγίου μερισμοῖς, "and gifts," say we, "of the Holy Ghost." But μερισμοί are "distributions" or "partitions;" and hence advantage is taken by some to argue against his very being. So Crellius contends that the Holy Ghost here is taken passively, or that the expression Πνεύματος Ἁγίου is genetivus materiæ. Wherefore, he supposes that it followeth that the Holy Ghost himself may be divided into parts, so that one may have one part and parcel of him, and another may have another part. How inconsistent this is with the truth of his being and personality is apparent. But yet neither can he give any tolerable account of the division and partition of that power of God which he calls the "Holy Ghost," unless he will make the Holy Spirit to be a quality in us and not in the divine nature, as Justin Martyr affirms Plato to have done, and so to be divided.[51] And the interpretation he useth of the words is wrested, perverse, and foolish; for the contexture of them requires that the Holy Ghost be here taken actively, as the author of the distribution mentioned. He gives out of his gifts and powers unto men in many parts, not all to one, not all at once, not all in one way; but some to one, some to another, some at one time, some at another, and that in great variety. The apostle, therefore, in this place declares that the Holy Spirit gave out various gifts unto the first preachers of the gospel, for the confirmation of their doctrine, according to the promise of our Saviour, John xv. 26, 27. Of these he mentions in particular, first, Σημεῖα, "signs;" that is, miraculous works, wrought to signify the presence of God by his power with them that wrought them, so giving out his approbation of the doctrine which they taught. Secondly, Τέρατα, "prodigies" or "wonders," works beyond the power of nature or energy of natural causes, wrought to fill men with wonder and admiration, manifesting τὸ θεῖον, and surprising men with a sense of the presence of God. Thirdly, Δυνάμεις, "mighty works" of several sorts, such as opening of the eyes of the blind, raising the dead, and the like. These being mentioned, there is added in general μερισμοὶ Πνεύματος Ἁγίου, that is, מַתְּנוֹת הָרוּחַ הַקָּדוֹשׁ, "gifts of the Holy Ghost;" for these and other like things did the Holy Ghost work and effect to the end mentioned. And these distributions are from him as the signs and wonders were, — that is, effects of his power: only there is added an intimation how they are all wrought by him; which is, by giving them a power for their operation, variously dividing them amongst those on whom they were bestowed, and that, as it is added, κατὰ τὴν αὑτοῦ θέλησιν, "according unto his own will." And this place is so directly and fully expounded, 1 Cor. xii. 7–11, that there is no room of exception left unto the most obstinate; and that place having been opened before, in the entrance of this discourse, I shall not here call it over again. These μερισμοί, therefore, are his gifts; which, as parts and parcels of his work, he giveth out in great variety.[52] To the same purpose are his operations described, Isa. xi. 2, 3, "The Spirit of the Lord shall rest upon him, the Spirit of wisdom and understanding, the Spirit of counsel and might, the Spirit of knowledge and of the fear of the Lord." He is first called "The Spirit of the Lord," to express his being and nature; and then he is termed "The Spirit of wisdom and of counsel," etc., — that is, he who is the author of wisdom and counsel, and the rest of the graces mentioned, who divides and distributes them according to his own will. That variety of gifts and graces wherewith believers are endowed and adorned are these μερισμοί, or "distributions," of the Holy Spirit. Hence, the principal respect that we have unto him immediately, in our worship of him under the New Testament, is as he is the author of these various gifts and graces. So John, saluting the churches of Asia, prayeth for grace for them from God the Father, and from "the seven Spirits which are before his throne," Rev. i. 4; that is, from the Holy Spirit of God considered in his care of the church and his yielding supplies unto it, as the author of that perfection of gifts and graces which are, and are to be, bestowed upon it. So doth the number of "seven" denote. And, therefore, whereas our Lord Jesus Christ, as the foundation of his church, was anointed with all the gifts and graces of the Spirit in their perfection, it is said that upon that one stone should be "seven eyes," Zech. iii. 9, — all the gifts of the seven Spirits of God, or of that Holy Spirit which is the author of them all.

All, therefore, that is pleaded for the division of the Holy Ghost from this place is built on the supposition that we have before rejected, — namely, that he is not a divine person, but an arbitrary emanation of divine power. And yet neither so can the division of the Holy Ghost pleaded for be with any tolerable sense maintained. Crellius says, indeed, "That all divine inspirations may be considered as one whole, as many waters make up one sea. In this respect the Holy Ghost is one, — that is, one universal made up of many species;" This is totum logicum. And so he may be divided into his subordinate species! But what ground or colour is there for any such notions in the Scripture? Where is it said that all the gifts of the Holy Ghost do constitute or make up one Holy Ghost? or the Holy Ghost is one in general, because many effects are ascribed unto him? or that the several gifts of the Spirit are so many distinct kinds of it? The contrary unto all these is expressly taught, — namely, that the one Holy Spirit worketh all these things as he pleaseth; so that they are all of them external acts of his will and power. And it is to as little purpose pleaded by the same author, "That he is divided as a natural whole into its parts, because there is mention of a measure and portion of him: so God is said not to give him to Jesus Christ 'by measure,' John iii. 34; and to every one of us is given grace 'according to the measure of the gift of Christ,' Eph. iv. 7;" — as though one measure of him were granted unto one, and another measure to another! But this "measure" is plainly of his gifts and graces. These were bestowed on the Lord Christ in all their fullness, without any limitation, either as to kinds or degrees; they were poured into him according unto the utmost extent and capacity of human nature, and that under an inconceivable advancement by its union unto the Son of God. Others receive his gifts and graces in a limited proportion, both as to their kinds and degrees. To turn this into a division of the Spirit himself is the greatest madness. And casting aside prejudices, there is no difficulty in the understanding of that saying of God to Moses, Num. xi. 17, "I will take of the Spirit which is upon thee, and I will put it upon the elders;" for it is evidently of the gifts of the Spirit, enabling men for rule and government, that God speaketh, and not of the Spirit himself. Without any diminution of that Spirit in him, — that is, of the gifts that he had received, — God gave unto them, as lighting their candle by his. And so, also, the "double portion of the spirit of Elijah," which Elisha requested for himself, was only a large and peculiar measure of prophetical light, above what other prophets which he left behind him had received, 2 Kings ii. 9. He asked פִּי־שְׁנַיִם, "os duorum" or "duplex;" τὸ διπλοῦν μέρος. Or τὰ διπλᾶ This expression is first used, Deut. xxi. 17, where the double portion of the first-born is intended; so that probably it was such a portion among the other prophets as the first-born had among the brethren of the same family which he desired: and so it came to pass; whence, also, he had the rule and government of them.

Footnotes:

43. Ἀποστέλλεται μὲν τὸ πνεῦμα τὸ ἅγιον οἰκονομικῶς, ἐνεργεῖ δὲ αὐτεξουσίως. — Basil. Hom. xv. de Fide.

44. "Etenim si de loco procedit Spiritus et ad locum transit, et ipse Pater in loco invenietur et Filius: si de loco exit quem Pater mittit aut Filius, utique de loco transiens Spiritus et progediens, et Patrem sicut corpus secundum impias interpretationes relinquere videtur et Filium. Hoc secundum eos loquor qui dicunt quod habeat Spiritus descensorium motum … Venit non de loco in locum, sed de dispositione constitutionis in salutem redemptionis." — Ambros. de Spir. Sanc. lib. i. cap. 11.

45. "Quid igitur Spiritus Sancti operatione divinius, cum etiam benedictionum suarum præsulem Spiritum Deus ipse testetur, dicens, Ponam Spiritum meum super semen tuum, et benedictiones meas super filios tuos. Nulla enim potest esse plena benedictio nisi per infusionem Spiritus Sancti." — Ambros. de Spir. Sanc. lib. i. cap. 7.

46. "Significat autem effusionis verbum largam et divitem muneris abundantiam; itaque cum unus quis alicubi aut duo Spiritum Sanctum accipiant non dicitur, 'Effundam de Spiritu meo,' sed tunc quando in universas gentes munus Spiritus Sancti redundaverit." — Didym. de Spir. Sanc. lib. i.

47. "Spiritus Sanctus qui a Patre et Filio procedit, nec ipse cœpit; quia processio ejus continua est, et ab eo qui non cœpit." — Ambros. in Symbol. Apostol., cap. 3."Spiritus quidem Sanctus nec ingenitus est nec genitus alicubi dicitur, ne si ingenitus diceretur sicut Pater, duo Patres in Sancta Trinitate intelligerentur; aut si genitus diceretur sicut Filius, duo itidem Filii in eadem estimarentur esse Sancta Trinitate: sed tantummodo procedere de Patre et Filio salva fide dicendum est. Qui tamen non de Patre procedit in Filium, et de Filio procedit ad sanctificandam creaturam, sicut quidam male intelligentes credendum esse putabant, sed simul de utroque procedit. Quia Pater talem genuit Filium, ut quemadmodum de se, ita et de illo quoque procedat Spiritus Sanctus." — Aug. Serm. xxxviii. de Tempore.

48. Οὐ γὰρ ἐπειδὰν πάμπαν ἀκατάληπτον τὸ Θεῖον διὰ τοῦτο που πάντως μηδόλως ζητεῖν περὶ αὐτοῦ προσῆκεν, ἀλλ᾽ ἐν ῥᾳστώνῃ τὸν τοῦ βίου καταναλίσκειν χρόνον· κατὰ δὲ τὸ μέτρον τὸ μεριθὲν ἑκάστῳ παρὰ τοῦ κυριου, τῆς γνώσεως τὴν ἐξέτασιν φιλοπόνως ποιεῖσθαι· ὅτι μὲν ἀκατάληπτον ἀκριβῶς πεπεισμένους· ἐφ᾽ ὅσον δὲ χωροῦμεν διὰ τῆς θεωρίας, ἑαυτοὺς ἐκείνῳ συνάπτοντας. — Justin. Martyr. Expositio Fidei de rectâ Confess.

49. "Nullus sine Deo, neque ullus non in Deo locus est. In cœlis est, in inferno est, ultra maria est. Inest interior, excedit exterior. Itaque cum habet atque habetur, neque in aliquo ipse, neque non in omnibus est." — Hilar. lib. i. de Trinitat.

50. These initials refer to Samuel Parker, in whose "Defence and Continuation of the Ecclesiastical Polity," 1671, the sentiments to which Owen objects will be found. For an account of Parker, see vol. xiii., p. 344 of Owen's works. — Ed.

51. Ταῦτα, οἶμαι, σαφῶς παρὰ τῶν προφητῶν περὶ τοῦ ἁγίου πνεύματος μεμαθηκὼς Πλάτων εἰς τὸ τῆς ἀρετῆς ὄνομα μεταφέρων φαίνεται. Ὁμοίως γὰρ ὥσπερ οἱ ἱεροὶ προφῆται τὸ ἓν καὶ τὸ αὐτὸ πνεῦμα εἰς ἑπτὰ πνεύματα μερίζεσθαι φασίν, οὕτω καὶ αὐτὸς μίαν καὶ τὴν αὐτὴν ὀνομάζων ἀρετήν, ταύτην εἰς τέσσαρας ἀρετὰς μερίζεσθαι λέγει. — Justin. Martyr. ad Græc. Cohortat., [cap. xxxii.]Aliter statuit Cyprianus seu quisquis fuit author lib. de Spir. Sanc. inter opera Cypriani. "Hic est Spiritus Sanctus quem Magi in Ægypto tertii signi ostensione convicti, cum sua defecisse præstigia faterentur, Dei digitum appellabant, et antiquis philosophis ejus intimarunt præsentiam defuisse. Et licet de Patre et Filio aliqua sensissent Platonici, Spiritus tamen tumidus et humani appetitor favoris santificationem mentis divinæ mereri non potuit, et ubi ad profunditatem sacramentorum deventum est, omnis eorum caligavit subtilitas, nec potuit infidelitas sanctitudini propinquare" — Cypr. de Spir. Sanc.

52. Τῶν τοῦ ἁγίου· πνεύματος ἀξιουμένων ἐστὶ διαφορὰ, πλεῖον ἢ ἔλαττον λαμβανόντων τοῖ ἁγίου πνεύματος τῶν πιστευόντων. — Origen. Comment. in Matthæum.

Book II

Chapter I - Peculiar operations of the Holy Spirit under the Old Testament preparatory for the New

The work of the Spirit of God in the new creation; by some despised — Works under the Old Testament preparatory to the new creation — Distribution of the works of the Spirit — The gift of prophecy; the nature, use, and end of it — The beginning of prophecy — The Holy Spirit the only author of it — The name of a "prophet;" its signification, and his work — Prophecy by inspiration; whence so called — Prophets, how acted by the Holy Ghost — The adjuncts of prophecy, or distinct ways of its communication — Of articulate voices — Dreams — Visions — Accidental adjuncts of prophecy — Symbolical actions — Local mutations — Whether unsanctified persons might have the gift of prophecy — The case of Balaam answered — Of writing the Scriptures — Three things required thereunto — Of miracles — Works of the Spirit of God in the improvement of the natural faculties of the minds of men in things political — In things moral — In things corporeal — In things intellectual and artificial — In preaching of the word.

Having passed through these general things, which are of a necessary previous consideration unto the especial works of the Holy Ghost, I now proceed unto that which is the principal subject of our present design; and this is, the dispensation and work of the Holy Spirit of God with respect unto the new creation, and the recovery of mankind or the church of God thereby. A matter this is of the highest importance unto them that sincerely believe, but most violently, and of late virulently, opposed by all the enemies of the grace of God and our Lord Jesus Christ. The weight and concernment of the doctrine hereof have in part been spoken unto before. I shall at present add no farther considerations to the same purpose, but leave all that fear the name of God to make a judgment of it by what is revealed concerning it in the Scriptures, and the uses whereunto it is in them directed. Many, we know, will not receive these things; but whilst we keep ourselves, in the handling of them, unto that word whereby one day both we and they must either stand or fall, we need not be moved at their ignorance or pride, nor at the fruits and effects of them, in reproaches, contempt, and scorn: for ἔχει Θεὸς ἔνδικον ὄμμα.

Now, the works of the Spirit, in reference unto the new creation, are of two sorts:—

First, Such as were preparatory unto it, under the Old Testament; for I reckon that the state of the old creation, as unto our living unto God, ended with the entrance of sin and giving the first promise. Whatever ensued thereon, in a way of grace, was preparatory for and unto the new. Secondly, Such as were actually wrought about it under the new. Those acts and workings of his which are common to both states of the church, — as is his effectual dispensation of sanctifying grace towards the elect of God, — I shall handle in common under the second head. Under the first, I shall only reckon up those that were peculiar unto that state. To make way hereunto I shall premise two general positions:—

1. There is nothing excellent amongst men, whether it be absolutely extraordinary, and every way above the production of natural principles, or whether it consist in an eminent and peculiar improvement of those principles and abilities, but it is ascribed unto the Holy Spirit of God, as the immediate operator and efficient cause of it. This we shall afterward confirm by instances. Of old he was all; now, some would have him nothing.

2. Whatever the Holy Spirit wrought in an eminent manner under the Old Testament, it had generally and for the most part, if not absolutely and always, a respect unto our Lord Jesus Christ and the gospel; and so was preparatory unto the completing of the great work of the new creation in and by him.

And these works of the Holy Spirit may be referred unto the two sorts mentioned, namely, — 1. Such as were extraordinary, and exceeding the whole compass of the abilities of nature, however improved and advanced; and, 2. Those which consist in the improving and exaltation of those abilities, to answer the occasions of life and use of the church.

Those of the first sort may be reduced unto three heads:— 1. Prophecy. 2. Inditing of the Scripture. 3. Miracles. Those of the other sort we shall find:— 1. In things political, as skill for government and rule amongst men. 2. In things moral, as fortitude and courage. 3. In things natural, as increase of bodily strength. 4. In gifts intellectual, — (1.) For things sacred, as to preach the word of God; (2.) In things artificial, as in Bezaleel and Aholiab. The work of grace on the hearts of men being more fully revealed under the New Testament than before, and of the same kind and nature in every state of the church since the fall, I shall treat of it once for all in its most proper place.

I. 1. The first eminent gift and work of the Holy Ghost under the Old Testament, and which had the most direct and immediate respect unto Jesus Christ, was that of prophecy: for the chief and principal end hereof in the church was to foresignify him, his sufferings, and the glory that should ensue, or to appoint such things to be observed in divine worship as might be types and representations of him; for the chiefest privilege of the church of old was but to hear tidings of the things which we enjoy, Isa. xxxiii. 17. As Moses on the top of Pisgah saw the land of Canaan, and in spirit, the beauties of holiness to be erected therein, which was his highest attainment; so the best of those saints was to contemplate the King of saints in the land that was yet very far from them, or Christ in the flesh. And this prospect, which by faith they obtained, was their chiefest joy and glory, John viii. 56; yet they all ended their days as Moses did, with respect unto the type of the gospel state, Deut. iii. 24, 25. So did they, Luke x. 23, 24; "God having provided some better thing for us, that they without us should not be made perfect," Heb. xi. 40. That this was the principal end of the gift of prophecy Peter declares, 1 Epist. i. 9–12: "Receiving the end of your faith, the salvation of your souls. Of which salvation the prophets have inquired and searched diligently, who prophesied of the grace that should come unto you: searching what, or what manner of time the Spirit of Christ which was in them did signify, when it testified beforehand the sufferings of Christ, and the glory that should follow. Unto whom it was revealed, that not unto themselves, but unto us they did minister the things, which are now reported unto you." Some of the ancients apprehended that some things were spoken obscurely by the prophets, and not to be understood without great search, especially such as concerned the rejection of the Jews, lest they should have been provoked to abolish the Scripture itself;[1] but the sum and substance of the prophetical work under the Old Testament, with the light, design, and ministry of the prophets themselves, are declared in those words. The work was, to give testimony unto the truth of God in the first promise, concerning the coming of the blessed Seed. This was God's method:— First, he gave himself immediately that promise which was the foundation of the church, Gen. iii. 15; then by revelation unto the prophets he confirmed that promise; after all which the Lord Christ was sent to make them all good unto the church, Rom. xv. 8. Herewithal they received fresh revelations concerning his person and his sufferings, with the glory that was to ensue thereon, and the grace which was to come thereby unto the church. Whilst they were thus employed and acted by the Holy Ghost, or the Spirit of Christ, they diligently endeavoured to come to an acquaintance with the things themselves, in their nature and efficacy, which were revealed unto them;[2] yet so as considering that not themselves, but some succeeding generations, should enjoy them in their actual exhibition. And whilst they were intent on these things, they searched also, as far as intimation was given thereof by the Spirit, after the time wherein all these things should be accomplished; both when it should be, and what manner of time it should be, or what would be the state and condition of the people of God in those days. This was the principal end of the gift of prophecy, and this the principal work and employment of the prophets: The first promise was given by God in the person of the Son, as I have proved elsewhere, Gen. iii. 15; but the whole explication, confirmation, and declaration of it, was carried on by the gift of prophecy.

The communication of this gift began betimes in the world, and continued, without any known interruption, in the possession of someone or more in the church at all times, during its preparatory or subservient estate. After the finishing of the canon of the Old Testament, it ceased in the Judaical church until it had a revival in John the Baptist; who was therefore greater than any prophet that went before, because he made the nearest approach unto and the clearest discovery of the Lord Jesus Christ, the end of all prophecies. Thus God "spake by the mouth of his holy prophets," τῶν ἀπ' αἰῶνος, "which have been since the world began," Luke i. 70. Adam himself had many things revealed unto him, without which he could not have worshipped God aright in that state and condition whereinto he was come; for although his natural light was sufficient to direct him unto all religious services required by the law of creation, yet was it not so unto all duties of that state whereinto he was brought by the giving of the promise after the entrance of sin. So was he guided unto the observance of such ordinances of worship as were needful for him and accepted with God, — as were sacrifices. The prophecy of Enoch is not only remembered, but called over and recorded, Jude 14, 15. And it is a matter neither curious nor difficult to demonstrate, that all the patriarchs of old, before the flood, were guided by a prophetical spirit in the imposition of names on those children who were to succeed them in the sacred line. Concerning Abraham, God expressly saith himself that he was a prophet, Gen. xx. 7, — that is, one who used to receive divine revelations.

Now, this gift of prophecy was always the immediate effect of the operation of the Holy Spirit. So it is both affirmed in general and in all the particular instances of it. In the first way, we have the illustrious testimony of the apostle Peter: 2 Epist. i. 20, 21, "Knowing this first, that no prophecy of the Scripture is of any private interpretation. For the prophecy came not in old time by the will of man, but holy men of God spake as they were moved by the Holy Ghost." This is a principle among believers, this they grant and allow in the first place, as that which they resolve their faith into, — namely, that the "sure word of prophecy," which they in all things take heed unto, verse 19, was not a fruit of any men's private conceptions, nor was subject to the wills of men, so as to attain it or exercise it by their own ability;[3] but it was given by "inspiration of God," 2 Tim. iii. 16: for the Holy Ghost, by acting, moving, guiding the minds of holy men, enabled them thereunto. This was the sole fountain and cause of all true divine prophecy that ever was given or granted to the use of the church. And, in particular, the coming of the Spirit of God upon the prophets, enabling them unto their work, is frequently mentioned. Micah declares in his own instance how it was with them all: Chap. iii. 8, "But truly I am full of power by the Spirit of the Lord, and of judgment, and of might, to declare unto Jacob his transgression, and to Israel his sin." It was from the Spirit of God alone that he had all his ability for the discharge of that prophetical office whereunto he was called. And when God would endow seventy elders with a gift of prophecy, he tells Moses that he would "take of the Spirit that was upon him," and give unto them for that purpose; that is, he would communicate of the same Spirit unto them as was in him. And where it is said at any time that God spake by the prophets, or that the word of God came to them, or God spake to them, it is always intended that this was the immediate work of the Holy Ghost. So says David of himself, "The Spirit of the Lord spake by me," or in me, "and his word was in my tongue," 2 Sam. xxiii. 2. Hence our apostle, repeating his words, ascribes them directly to the Holy Ghost: Heb. iii. 7, "Wherefore, as the Holy Ghost saith, To-day if ye will hear his voice;" and chap. iv. 7, "Saying in David." So the words which are ascribed unto the "Lord of hosts," Isa. vi. 9, 10, are asserted to be the words of the Holy Ghost, Acts xxviii. 25–27. He spake to them, or in them, by his holy inspirations; and he spake by them in his effectual infallible guidance of them, to utter, declare, and write what they received from him, without mistake or variation.

And this prophecy, as to its exercise, is considered two ways:— First, precisely for the prediction or foretelling things to come; as the Greek word, and the Latin traduced from thence, do signify. So prophecy is a divine prediction of future things, proceeding from divine revelation. But the Hebrew נָבָא, — whence are נָבִיא, "a prophet," and נְבוּאָה, "prophecy," — is not confined unto any such signification, although predictions from supernatural revelation are constantly expressed by it. But in general, secondly, the word signifies no more but to speak out, interpret, and declare the mind or words of another. So God tells Moses that he would "make him a god unto Pharaoh," — one that should deal with him in the name, stead, and power of God; and "Aaron his brother should be his prophet," Exod. vii. 1, — that is, one that should interpret his meaning and declare his words unto Pharaoh, Moses having complained of the defect of his own utterance. So prophets are the "interpreters," the declarers of the word, will, mind, or oracles of God unto others. Such a one is described,

Job xxxiii. 23. Hence, those who expounded the Scripture unto the church under the New Testament were called "prophets," and their work "prophecy," Rom. xii. 6, 1 Cor. xiv. 31, 32; and under the Old Testament those that celebrated the praises of God with singing in the temple, according to the institution of David, are said therein to "prophesy," 1 Chron. xxv. 2. And this name, נָבִיא, a "prophet," was of ancient use; for so God termed Abraham, Gen. xx. 7. Afterward, in common use, a prophet was called רֹאֶה and חֹזֶה, "a seer," because of their divine visions (and this was occasioned from those words of God concerning Moses, Num. xii. 6–8; and this being the ordinary way of his revealing himself, — namely, by dreams and visions, — prophets in those days, even from the death of Moses, were commonly called seers, which continued in use until the days of Samuel, 1 Sam. ix. 9); and אִישׁ־אֱלֹהִים, "a man of God," 1 Sam. ii. 27; which name Paul gives to the preachers of the gospel, 1 Tim. vi. 11, 2 Tim. iii. 17. And it is not altogether unworthy of observation what Kimchi notes, that the verb נָבָא is most frequently used in the passive conjugation niphal, because it denotes a receiving of that from God by way of revelation which is spoken unto others in a way of prophecy. And as it lies before us as an extraordinary gift of the Holy Ghost, it is neither to be confined to the strict notion of prediction and foretelling, nor to be extended to every true declaration of the mind of God, but only to that which is obtained by immediate revelation.

This peculiar gift, therefore, of the Holy Spirit we may a little distinctly inquire into; and two things concerning it may be considered:— First, Its general nature; Secondly, The particular ways whereby especial revelation was granted unto any. First, For its nature in general, it consisted in inspiration.[4] So the apostle speaks of the prophecies recorded in the Scripture, 2 Tim. iii. 16: θεοπνευστία, divine inspiration, was the original and cause of it. And the acting of the Holy Ghost in communicating his mind unto the prophets was called "inspiration" on a double account:— First, In answer unto his name and nature. The name whereby he is revealed unto us signifieth "breath;" and he is called the "breath of God," whereby his essential relation to the Father and Son, with his eternal natural emanation from them, is expressed. And, therefore, when our Saviour gave him unto his disciples, as a proper instructive emblem of what he gave, he breathed upon them, John xx. 22. So also in the great work of the infusion of the reasonable soul into the body of man, it is said, God "breathed into his nostrils the breath of life," Gen. ii. 7. From hence, I say, it is, — namely, from the nature and name of the Holy Spirit, — that his immediate actings on the minds of men, in the supernatural communication of divine revelations unto them, is called "inspiration" or inbreathing. And the unclean spirit, counterfeiting his actings, did inspire his worshippers with a preternatural afflatus, by ways suited unto his own filthy vileness. Secondly, This holy work of the Spirit of God, as it is expressed suitably to his name and nature, so the meekness, gentleness, facility wherewith he works is intended hereby. He did, as it were, gently and softly breathe into them the knowledge and comprehension of holy things. It is an especial and immediate work, wherein he acts suitably unto his nature as a spirit, the spirit or breath of God, and suitably unto his peculiar, personal properties of meekness, gentleness, and peace. So his acting is inspiration, whereby he came within the faculties of the souls of men, acting them with a power that was not their own. It is true, when he had thus inspired any with the mind of God, they had no rest, nor could have, unless they declared it in its proper way and season: Jer. xx. 9, "Then I said, I will not make mention of him, nor speak any more in his name: but his word was in mine heart as a burning fire shut up in my bones, and I was weary with forbearing, and I could not stay." But this disturbance was from a moral sense of their duty, and not from any violent agitations of his upon their natures. And whereas sometimes trouble and consternation of spirit did befall some of the prophets in and under the revelations they received from him, it was on a double account:— First, Of the dreadful representations of things that were made unto them in visions. Things of great dread and terror were represented unto their fancies and imaginations. Secondly, Of the greatness and dread of the things themselves revealed, which sometimes were terrible and destructive, Dan. vii. 15, 28, viii. 27; Hab. iii. 16; Isa. xxi. 2–4. But his inspirations were gentle and placid.

Secondly, The immediate effects of this inspiration were, that those inspired were moved or acted by the Holy Ghost: "Holy men of God spake," ὑπὸ Πνεύματος Ἁγίου φερόμενοι, 2 Pet. i. 21, — "moved" or acted "by the Holy Ghost." And two things are intended hereby:— First, The preparation and elevation of their intellectual faculties, their minds and understandings, wherein his revelations were to be received. He prepared them for to receive the impressions he made upon them, and confirmed their memories to retain them. He did not, indeed, so enlighten and raise their minds as to give them a distinct understanding and full comprehension of all the things themselves that were declared unto them; there was more in their inspirations than they could search into the bottom of.[5] Hence, although the prophets under the Old Testament were made use of to communicate the clearest revelations and predictions concerning Jesus Christ, yet in the knowledge and understanding of the meaning of them they were all inferior to John Baptist, as he was in this matter to the meanest believer, or "least in the kingdom of heaven." Therefore, for their own illumination and edification did they diligently inquire, by the ordinary means of prayer and meditation, into the meaning of the Spirit of God in those prophecies which themselves received by extraordinary revelation, 1 Pet. i. 10, 11. Nor did Daniel, who had those express representations and glorious visions concerning the monarchies of the world, and the providential alterations which should be wrought in them, understand what and how things would be in their accomplishment. That account he doth give of himself in the close of his visions, chap. xii. 8, 9. But he so raised and prepared their minds as that they might be capable to receive and retain those impressions of things which he communicated unto them. So a man tunes the strings of an instrument, that it may in a due manner receive the impressions of his finger, and give out the sound he intends. He did not speak in them or by them, and leave it unto the use of their natural faculties, their minds, or memories, to understand and remember the things spoken by him, and so declare them to others; but he himself acted their faculties, making use of them to express his words, not their own conceptions. And herein, besides other things, consists the difference between the inspiration of the Holy Spirit and those so called of the devil. The utmost that Satan can do, is to make strong impressions on the imaginations of men, or influence their faculties, by possessing, wresting, distorting the organs of the body and spirits of the blood. The Holy Spirit is in the faculties, and useth them as his organs. And this he did, secondly, with that light and evidence of himself, of his power, truth, and holiness, as left them liable to no suspicion whether their minds were under his conduct and influence or no. Men are subject to fall so far under the power of their own imaginations, through the prevalency of a corrupt distempered fancy, as to suppose them supernatural revelations; and Satan may, and did of old, and perhaps doth so still, impose on the minds of some, and communicate unto them such a conception of his insinuations, as that they shall for awhile think them to be from God himself. But in the inspirations of the Holy Spirit, and his actings of the minds of the holy men of old, he gave them infallible assurance that it was himself alone by whom they were acted, Jer. xxiii. 28. If any shall ask by what τεκμήρια, or infallible tokens, they might know assuredly the inspirations of the Holy Spirit, and be satisfied, with such a persuasion as was not liable to mistake, that they were not imposed upon, I must say plainly that I cannot tell, for these are things whereof we have no experience; nor is any thing of this nature, whatever some falsely and foolishly impute unto them who profess and avow an interest in the ordinary gracious workings of the Holy Ghost, pretended unto. What some frenetical persons, in their distempers or under their delusions, have boasted of, no sober or wise man esteems worthy of any sedate consideration. But this I say, it was the design of the Holy Ghost to give those whom he did thus extraordinarily inspire an assurance, sufficient to bear them out in the discharge of their duty, that they were acted by himself alone; for in the pursuit of their work, which they were by him called unto, they were to encounter various dangers, and some of them to lay down their lives for a testimony unto the truth of the message delivered by them. This they could not be engaged into without as full an evidence of his acting them as the nature of man in such cases is capable of. The case of Abraham fully confirms it. And it is impossible but that in those extraordinary workings there was, such an impression of himself, his holiness, and authority, left on their minds, as did secure them from all fear of delusion. Even upon the word, as delivered by them unto others, he put those characters of divine truth, holiness, and power, as rendered it ἀξιόπιστον, "worthy to be believed," and not to be rejected without the highest sin by them unto whom it came. Much more was there such an evidence in it unto them who enjoyed its original inspiration. Secondly, He acted and guided them as to the very organs of their bodies whereby they expressed the revelation which they had received by inspiration from him. They spake as they were acted by the Holy Ghost. He guided their tongues in the declaration of his revelations, as the mind of a man guideth his hand in writing to express its conceptions. Hence David, having received revelations from him, or being inspired by him, affirms, in his expression of them, that "his tongue was the pen of a ready writer," Ps. xlv. 1; that is, it was so guided by the Spirit of God to express the conceptions received from him. And on this account God is said to speak by their mouths: "As he spake by the mouth of his holy prophets," Luke i. 70; — all of whom had but one mouth on the account of their absolute consent and agreement in the same predictions; for this is the meaning of "one voice" or "one mouth" in a multitude. "The Holy Ghost spake by the mouth of David," Acts i. 16. For whatever they received by revelation, they were but the pipes through which the waters of it were conveyed, without the least mixture with any alloy from their frailties or infirmities. So, when David had received the pattern of the temple, and the manner of the whole worship of God therein by the Spirit, 1 Chron. xxviii. 12, he says, "All this the Lord made me understand in writing by his hand upon me, even all the works of this pattern,"[6] verse 19. The Spirit of God not only revealed it unto him, but so guided him in the writing of it down as that he might understand the mind of God out of what himself had written; or, he gave it him so plainly and evidently as if every particular had been expressed in writing by the finger of God.

(1.) It remaineth that, as unto this first extraordinary work and gift of the Holy Ghost, we consider those especial ways and means which he made use of in the communication of his mind unto the prophets, with some other accidental adjuncts of prophecy. Some, following Maimonides in his "More Nebuchim," have, from the several ways of the communication of divine revelations, distinguished the degrees of prophecy or of the gifts of it, preferring one above another. This I have elsewhere disproved, "Exposition of the Epistle to the Hebrews," chap. 1. Neither, indeed, is there, either hence or from any other ground, the least occasion to feign those eleven degrees of prophecy which he thought he had found out; much less may the spirit or gift of prophecy be attained by the ways he prescribes, and with Tatianus seems to give countenance unto.[7] The distinct outward manners and ways of revelation mentioned in the Scriptures may be reduced unto three heads:— 1. Voices; 2. Dreams; 3. Visions. And the accidental adjuncts of it are two:— 1. Symbolical actions; 2. Local mutations. The schoolmen, after Aquinas, 22. q. 174, a. 1, do commonly reduce the means of revelation unto three heads. For whereas there are three ways whereby we come to know any thing, — 1. By our external senses; 2. By impressions on the fantasy or imagination; 3. By pure acts of the understanding: so God by three ways revealed his will unto the prophets, — 1. By objects of their senses, as by audible voices; 2. By impressions on the imagination in dreams and visions; 3. By illustration or enlightening of their minds. But as this last way expresseth divine inspiration, I cannot acknowledge it as a distinct way of revelation by itself, for it was that which was absolutely necessary to give an infallible assurance of mind in the other ways also; and setting that aside, there is none of them but is obnoxious to delusion.

First, God sometimes made use of an articulate voice, speaking out those things which he did intend to declare in words significant of them. So he revealed himself or his mind unto Moses, when he "spake unto him face to face, as a man speaketh unto his friend," Exod. xxxiii. 11; Num. xii. 8. And as far as I can observe, the whole revelation made unto Moses was by outward, audible, articulate voices, whose sense was impressed on his mind by the Holy Spirit; for an external voice without an inward elevation and disposition of mind is not sufficient to give security and assurance of truth unto him that doth receive it. So God spake to Elijah, 1 Kings xix. 12–18, as also to Samuel and Jeremiah, and it may be to all the rest of the prophets at their first calling and entrance into their ministry; for words formed miraculously by God, and conveyed sensibly unto the outward ears of men, carry a great majesty and authority with them. This was not the usual way of God's revealing his mind, nor is it signified by that phrase of speech, "The word of the Lord came unto me;" whereby no more is intended but an immediate revelation, by what way or means soever it was granted. Mostly this was by that secret effectual impression on their minds which we have before described. And these voices were either immediately created by God himself, as when he spake unto Moses, — wherein the eminency of the revelation made unto him principally consisted, — or the ministry of angels was used in the formation and pronunciation of them. But, as we observed before, the divine certainty of their minds to whom they were spoken, with their abilities infallibly to declare them unto others, was from an immediate internal work of the Spirit of God upon them. Without this the prophets might have been imposed on by external audible voices, nor would they by themselves give their minds an infallible assurance.

Secondly, Dreams were made use of under the Old Testament to the same purpose, and unto them also I refer all those visions which they had in their sleep, though not called dreams;[8] and these, in this case, were the immediate operation of the Holy Ghost, as to the divine and infallible impressions they conveyed to the minds of men. Hence, in the promise of the plentiful pouring out of the Spirit, or communication of his gifts, mention is made of dreams: Acts ii. 17, "I will pour out of my Spirit upon all flesh: and your sons and your daughters shall prophesy, and your young men shall see visions, and your old men shall dream dreams." Not that God intended much to make use of this way of dreams and nocturnal visions under the New Testament; but the intention of the words is, to show that there should be a plentiful effusion of that Spirit which acted by these various ways and means then under the Old. Only, as to some particular directions God did sometimes continue his intimations by visions in the rest of the night. Such a vision had Paul, Acts xvi. 10. But of old this was more frequent. So God made a signal revelation unto Abraham, when the "deep sleep fell upon him, and horror of great darkness," Gen. xv. 12–16; and Daniel "heard the voice of the words" of him that spake unto him "when he was in a deep sleep," Dan. x. 9. But this sleep of theirs I look not on as natural, but as that which God sent and cast them into, that therein he might represent the image of things unto their imaginations. So of old he caused a "deep sleep to fall upon Adam," Gen. ii. 21. The Jews distinguish between dreams and those visions in sleep, as they may be distinctly considered; but I cast them together under one head, of revelation in sleep. And this way of revelation was so common, that one who pretended to prophesy would cry out, חָלַמְתִּי חָלָמְתִּי, "I have dreamed, I have dreamed," Jer. xxiii. 25. And by the devil's imitation of God's dealing with his church, this became a way of vaticination among the heathen also: Hom. i. 63, Καὶ γὰρ τ' ὄναρ ἐκ Διός ἐστιν, — "A dream is from Jupiter." And when the reprobate Jews were deserted as to all divine revelations, they pretended unto a singular skill in the interpretation of dreams; on the account of their deceit wherein they were sufficiently infamous.

> "Qualiacumque voles Judaei somia vendunt."
> [Juv., vi. 546.]

Thirdly, God revealed himself in and by visions or representations of things to the in ward or outward senses of the prophets. And this way was so frequent that it bare the name for a season of all prophetical revelations; for so we observed before, that a prophet of old time was called a "seer," and that because in their receiving of their prophecies they saw visions also. So Isaiah terms his whole glorious prophecy, חָזוֹן אֲשֶׁר חָזָה, "The vision which he saw," chap. i. 1; partly from the especial representations of things that were made unto him, chap. vi. 1–4; and partly, it may be, from the evidence of the things revealed unto him, which were cleared as fully to his mind as if he had had an ocular inspection of them.

So, from the matter of them, prophecies began in common to be called "The burden of the Lord;" for he burdened their consciences with his word, and their persons with its execution. But when false prophets began to make frequent use and to serve themselves of this expression, it was forbidden, Jer. xxiii. 33, 36; and yet we find that there is mention hereof about the same time, it may be, by Hab. i. 1; as also after the return from the captivity, Zech. ix. 1, Mal. i. 1. Either, therefore, this respected that only season wherein false prophets abounded, whom God would thus deprive of their pretence; or, indeed, the people, by contempt and scorn, did use that expression as that which was familiar unto the prophets in their denunciation of God's judgments against them, which God here rebukes them for and threatens to revenge. But none of the prophets had all their revelations by visions; nor doth this concern the communication of the gift of prophecy, but its exercise. And their visions are particularly recorded. Such were those of Isa. vi.; Jer. i. 11–16; Ezek. i., and the like. Now, these visions were of two sorts:[9] — 1. Outward representations of things unto the bodily eyes of the prophets; 2. Inward representations unto their minds. 1. There were sometimes appearances of persons or things made to their outward senses; and herein God made use of the ministry of angels. Thus three men appeared unto Abraham, Gen. xviii. 1, 2; one whereof was the Son of God himself; the other two, ministering angels; as hath been proved elsewhere. So was the burning bush which Moses saw, Exod. iii. 2; the appearances without similitude of any living thing on mount Sinai at the giving of the law, Exod. xix.; the man that Joshua saw at the siege of Jericho, chap. v. 13, 14. Such were the seething-pot and almond-rod seen by Jeremiah, chap. i. 11, 13, as also his baskets of figs, [chap. xiv. 1–3;] and many more of the like kind might be instanced in. In these cases God made representations of things unto their outward senses. 2. They were made sometimes only to their minds. So it is said expressly that when Peter saw his vision of a sheet knit at the four comers, and let down from heaven to earth, he was in a "trance:" Ἐπέπεσεν ἐπ' αὐτὸν ἔκστασις, Acts x. 10. An "ecstasy seized on him," whereby for a season he was deprived of the use of his bodily senses. And to this head I refer Daniel's and the apocalyptical visions. Especially I do so [refer] all those wherein a representation was made of God himself and his glorious throne; such as that of Micaiah, 1 Kings xxii. 19–22; and Isa. vi.; and Ezek. i. It is evident that in all these there was no use of the bodily senses of the prophets, but only their minds were affected with the ideas and representation of things; but this was so effectual as that they understood not but that they also made use of their visive faculty. Hence Peter, when he was actually delivered out of prison, thought a good while that he had only "seen a vision," Acts xii. 9; for he knew how powerfully the mind was wont to be affected by them. Now, these visions of both sorts were granted unto the prophets to confirm their minds in the apprehension of the things communicated unto them for the instruction of others; for hereby they were deeply affected with them, whereunto a clear idea and representation of things doth effectually tend. But yet two things were required to render these visions direct and complete parts of divine revelation:— 1. That the minds of the prophets were acted, guided, and raised in a due manner by the Holy Spirit for the receiving of them. This gave them their assurance that their visions were from God. 2. His enabling them faithfully to retain, and infallibly to declare, what was so represented unto them. For instance, Ezekiel receiveth a vision, by way of representation unto his mind of a glorious fabric of a temple, to instruct the church in the spiritual glory and beauty of gospel-worship which was to be introduced, chap. xli.–xlvi. It seems utterly impossible for the mind of man to conceive and retain at once all the harmonious structure, dimensions, and laws of the fabric represented. This was the peculiar work of the Holy Ghost, — namely, to implant and preserve the idea presented unto him on his mind, and to enable him accurately and infallibly to declare it. So David affirms that the Spirit of God made him to understand the pattern of the temple built by Solomon, "in writing by his hand upon him."

(2.) There were some accidental adjuncts of prophecy, which at some times accompanied it:—

First, In the revelation of the will of God to the prophets, they were sometimes enjoined symbolical actions. So Isaiah was commanded to "walk naked and bare-foot," chap. xx. 1–3; Jeremiah, to dispose of a "linen girdle," chap. xiii. 1–5; Ezekiel, to "lie in the siege," chap. iv. 1–3, and to remove the "stuff of his house," chap. xii. 3, 4; Hosea, to take "a wife of whoredoms, and children of whoredoms," chap. i. 2. I shall be brief in what is frequently spoken unto. Some of these things, as Isaiah's going naked, and Hosea's taking a wife of whoredoms, contain things in them against the light of nature and the express law of God, and of evil example unto others. None of these, therefore, can be granted to have been actually done; only these things were represented unto them in visions, to take the deeper impression upon them. And what they saw or did in vision they speak positively of their so seeing or doing: see Ezek. viii. For the other instances, I know nothing but that the things reported might be really performed, and not in vision only. And it is plain that Ezekiel was commanded to do the things he did in the sight of the people, for their more evident conviction, chap. xii. 4–6; and on the sight whereof they made inquiry what those things belonged unto them, chap. xxiv. 19.

Secondly, Their revelations were accompanied with local mutations, or rather being carried and transported from one place unto another. So was it with chap. viii. 3, xi. 24. And it is expressly said that it was "in the visions of God." Falling, by divine dispensation, into a trance or ecstasy, wherein their outward senses were suspended [in] their operation, their minds and understandings were, unto their own apprehension, carried in a holy rapture from one place unto another: which was effected only by a divine and efficacious representation of the things unto them which were done in the places from whence they were really absent.

And these are some of those accidents of prophetical revelations which are recorded in the Scripture; and it is possible that some other instances of the like nature may be observed. And all these belong to the πολυτροπία τῆς θείας ἐπιλύσεως, or manifold variety of divine revelations, mentioned Heb. i. 1.

But here a doubt of no small difficulty nor of less importance presents itself unto us, — namely, whether the Holy Ghost did ever grant the holy inspirations, and the gift of prophecy thereby, unto men wicked and unsanctified;[10] for the apostle Peter tells us that "holy men spake of old as they were moved by the Holy Ghost," 2 Pet. i. 21, which seems to intimate that all those who were inspired and moved by him, as to this gift of prophecy, were holy men of God.[11] And yet, on the other hand, we shall find that true prophecies have been given out by men seeming utterly void of all sanctifying grace. And, to increase the difficulty, it is certain that great predictions, and those with respect unto Christ himself, have been given and made by men guided and acted for the most part by the devil. So was it with Balaam, who was a sorcerer that gave himself to diabolical enchantments and divinations;

and, as such an one, was destroyed by God's appointment. Yea, at or about the same time wherein he uttered a most glorious prophecy concerning the Messiah, the Star of Jacob, being left unto his own spirit and inclination, he gave cursed advice and counsel for the drawing of the people of God into destructive and judgment-procuring sins, Num. xxxi. 16. And in the whole of his enterprise he thought to have satisfied his covetousness with a reward for cursing them by his enchantments. And yet this man not only professeth of himself that he "heard the words of God," and "saw the vision of the Almighty," Num. xxiv. 4, but did actually foretell and prophesy glorious things concerning Christ and his kingdom. Shall we, then, think that the Holy Spirit of God will immix his own holy inspirations with the wicked suggestions of the devil in a soothsayer? or shall we suppose that the devil was the author of those predictions, whereas God reproacheth false gods, and their prophets acted by them, that they could not declare the things that should happen, nor show the things that were to come afterward? Isa. xli. 22, 23. So, also, it is said of Saul that "the Spirit of the Lord departed from him, and an evil spirit terrified him," 1 Sam. xvi. 14; and yet, afterward, that the "Spirit of God came upon him, and he prophesied," chap. xix. 23. The old prophet at Bethel who lied unto the prophet that came from Judah, and that in the name of the Lord, seducing him unto sin and destruction, and probably defiled with the idolatry and false worship of Jeroboam, was yet esteemed a prophet, and did foretell what came to pass, 1 Kings xiii. 11–29.

Sundry things may be offered for the solution of this difficulty; for, — 1. As to that place of the apostle Peter, (1.) It may not be taken universally that all who prophesied at any time were personally holy, but only that for the most part so they were. (2.) He seems to speak particularly of them only who were penmen of the Scripture, and of those prophecies which remain therein for the instruction of the church; concerning whom I no way doubt but that they were all sanctified and holy. (3.) It may be that he understandeth not real inherent holiness, but only a separation and dedication unto God by especial office; which is a thing of another nature. 2. The gift of prophecy is granted not to be in itself and its own nature a sanctifying grace, nor is the inspiration so whereby it is wrought; for whereas it consists in an affecting of the mind with a transient irradiation of light in hidden things, it neither did nor could of itself produce faith, love, or holiness in the heart. Another work of the Holy Ghost was necessary hereunto. 3. There is, therefore, no inconsistency in this matter, that God should grant an immediate inspiration unto some that were not really sanctified. And yet I would not grant this to have been actually done without a just limitation; for whereas some were established to be prophets unto the church in the whole course of their lives, after their first call from God, as Samuel, Elijah, Elisha, Jeremiah, and the rest of the prophets mentioned in the Scripture, in like manner I no way doubt but they were all of them really sanctified by the Holy Spirit of God. But others there were who had only some occasional discoveries of hidden or future things made unto them, or fell into some ecstasies or raptures, with a supernatural agitation of their minds (as it is twice said of Saul), for a short season. And I see no reason why we may not grant, — yea, from Scripture testimonies we must grant, — that many such persons may be so acted by the Holy Spirit of God. So was it with wicked Caiaphas, who is said to "prophesy," John xi. 51; and a great prophecy indeed it was which his words expressed, greater than which there is none in the

Scripture. But the wretch himself knew nothing of the importance of what was uttered by him. A sudden impression of the Spirit of God caused him, against his intention, to utter a sacred truth, and that because he was high priest; whose words were of great reputation with the people.[12] And as Balaam was overruled to prophesy and speak good of Israel, when he really designed and desired to curse them; so this Caiaphas, designing the destruction of Jesus Christ, brought forth those words which expressed the salvation of the world by his death.

4. For the difficulty about Balaam himself, who was a sorcerer, and the devil's prophet, I acknowledge it is of importance. But sundry things may be offered for the removal of it. Some do contend that Balaam was a prophet of God only; that indeed he gave himself unto judicial astrology, and the conjecture of future events from natural causes, but as to his prophecies, they were all divine; and the light of them, affecting only the speculative part of his mind, had no influence upon his will, heart, and affections, which were still corrupt. This Tostatus pleadeth for. But as it is expressly said that he "sought for enchantments," Num. xxiv. 1, so the whole description of his course and end gives him up as a cursed sorcerer: and he is expressly called הַקּוֹסֵם, "the soothsayer," Josh. xiii. 22; which word though we have once rendered by "prudent," — that is, one who prudently conjectureth at future events according unto present appearing causes, Isa. iii. 2, — yet it is mostly used for a diabolical diviner or soothsayer. And for what he said of himself, that he "heard the words of God," and "saw the vision of the Almighty," it might be only his own boasting to procure veneration to his diabolical incantations. But in reputation we find he was in those days in the world; and supposed he was to utter divine oracles unto men. This God in his providence made use of to give out a testimony to the nations concerning the coming of the Messiah, the report whereof was then almost lost amongst men. In this condition it may be granted that the good Spirit of God, without the least reflection on the majesty and purity of his own holiness, did overrule the power of the devil, cast out his suggestions from the man's mind, and gave such an impression of sacred truths in the room of them as he could not but utter and declare: for that instant he did, as it were, take the instrument out of the hand of Satan, and, by his impression on it, caused it to give a sound according to his mind; which when he had done, he left it again unto his possession. And I know not but that he might do so sometimes with others among the Gentiles who were professedly given up to receive and give out the oracles of the devil. So he made the damsel possessed with a spirit of divination and soothsaying to acknowledge Paul and his companions to be "servants of the most high God," to "show to men the way of salvation," Acts xvi. 16, 17. And this must be acknowledged by them who suppose that the sibyls gave out predictions concerning Jesus Christ, seeing the whole strain of their prophetical oracles were expressly diabolical. And no conspiracy of men or devils shall cause him to forego his sovereignty over them, and the using of them to his own glory. 5. The case of Saul is plain. The Spirit of the Lord who departed from him was the Spirit of wisdom, moderation, and courage, to fit him for rule and government, — that is, the gifts of the Holy Ghost unto that purpose, which he withdrew from him; and the evil spirit that was upon him proceeded no farther but to the stirring up vexatious and disquieting affections of mind. And notwithstanding this molestation and punishment inflicted on him, the Spirit of God might at a season fall upon him, so as to cast him into a rapture or ecstasy, wherein his mind was acted and

exercised in an extraordinary manner, and himself transported into actions that were not at all according unto his own inclinations. So is this case well resolved by Augustine.[13] And [as] for the old prophet at Bethel, 1 Kings xiii. 11–32, although he appears to have been an evil man, yet he was one whom God made use of to reveal his mind sometimes to that people; nor is it probable that he was under satanical delusions, like the prophets of Baal, for he is absolutely called a prophet, and the word of the Lord did really come unto him, verses 20–22.

2. The writing of the Scripture was another effect of the Holy Ghost, which had its beginning under the Old Testament. I reckon this as a distinct gift from prophecy in general, or rather, a distinct species or kind of prophecy: for many prophets there were divinely inspired who yet never wrote any of their prophecies, nor any thing else for the use of the church; and many penmen of the Scripture were no prophets, in the strict sense of that name. And the apostle tells us that the γραφή, the scripture or writing itself, was by "inspiration of God," 2 Tim. iii. 16; as David affirms that he had the pattern of the temple from the Spirit of God in writing, because of his guidance of him in putting its description into writing, 1 Chron. xxviii. 19. Now, this ministry was first committed unto Moses, who, besides the five books of the Law, probably also wrote the story of Job. Many prophets there were before him, but he was the first who committed the will of God to writing after God himself, who wrote the law in tables of stone; which was the beginning and pattern of the Scriptures. The writers of the historical books of the Old Testament before the captivity are unknown. The Jews call them ראשונים נביאים, "the first" or "former prophets." Who they were in particular is not known; but certain it is that they were of the number of those holy men of God who of old wrote and spake as they were moved by the Holy Ghost. Hence are they called "prophets;" for although they wrote in an historical manner, as did Moses also, concerning things past and gone in their days, or it may be presently acted in their own times, yet they did not write them either from their own memory nor from tradition, nor from the rolls or records of time (although they might be furnished with and skilled in these things), but by the inspiration, guidance, and direction of the Holy Ghost. Hence are they called "prophets," in such a latitude as the word may be used in to signify any that are divinely inspired, or receive immediate revelations from God. And thus was it with all the penmen of the holy Scripture. As their minds were under that full assurance of divine inspiration which we before described, so their words which they wrote were under the especial care of the same Spirit; and were of his suggestion or inditing.

There were, therefore, three things concurring in this work:— First, The inspiration of the minds of these prophets with the knowledge and apprehension of the things communicated unto them. Secondly, The suggestion of words unto them to express what their minds conceived. Thirdly, The guidance of their hands in setting down the words suggested, or of their tongues in uttering them unto those by whom they were committed to writing, as Baruch wrote the prophecy of Jeremiah from his mouth, Jer. xxxvi. 4, 18. If either of these were wanting, the Scripture could not be absolutely and every way divine and infallible; for if the penmen of it were left unto themselves in any thing wherein that writing was concerned, who can secure us that nihil humani, no human imperfection, mixed itself therewithal? I know some think that the matter and substance of things only was communicated unto them, but as for the words whereby it was to be expressed, that was left unto themselves and their own abilities: and this they suppose is evident from that variety of style which, according to their various capacities, education, and abilities, is found amongst them. "This argues," as they say, "that the wording of their revelations was left unto themselves, and was the product of their natural abilities." This, in general, I have spoken unto elsewhere, and manifested what mistakes sundry have run into about the style of the holy penmen of the Scripture. Here I shall not take up what hath been argued and evinced in another place. I only say that the variety intended ariseth mostly from the variety of the subject-matters treated of; nor is it such as will give any countenance to the profaneness of this opinion, for the Holy Ghost in his work on the minds of men doth not put a force upon them, nor act them any otherwise than they are in their own natures, and with their present endowments and qualifications, meet to be acted and used. He leads and conducts them in such paths as wherein they are able to walk. The words, therefore, which he suggests unto them are such as they are accustomed unto, and he causeth them to make use of such expressions as were familiar unto themselves. So he that useth diverse seals maketh different impressions, though the guidance of them all be equal and the same; and he that toucheth skilfully several musical instruments, variously tuned, maketh several notes of music. We may also grant, and do, that they used their own abilities of mind and understanding in the choice of words and expressions: so the Preacher "sought to find out acceptable words," Eccles. xii. 10. But the Holy Spirit, who is more intimate unto the minds and skill of men than they are themselves, did so guide, act, and operate in them, as that the words they fixed upon were as directly and certainly from him as if they had been spoken to them by an audible voice. Hence "that which was written was upright, even words of truth," as in that place. This must be so, or they could not speak as they were moved by the Holy Ghost, nor could their writing be said to be of divine inspiration. Hence, ofttimes, in the original, great senses and significations depend on a single letter; as, for instance, in the change of the name of Abraham: and our Saviour affirms that every apex and iota of the law is under the care of God, as that which was given by inspiration from himself, Matt. v. 18. But I have on other occasions treated of these things, and shall not, therefore, here enlarge upon them.[14]

3. The third sort of the immediate extraordinary operations of the Holy Ghost, absolutely exceeding the actings and compliance of human faculties, are miracles of all sorts, which were frequent under the Old Testament. Such were many things wrought by Moses and Joshua, Elijah and Elisha, with some others; those by Moses exceeding, if the Jews fail not in their computation, all the rest that are recorded in the Scripture. Now, these were all the immediate effects of the divine power of the Holy Ghost. He is the sole author of all real miraculous operations; for by "miracles" we understand such effects as are really beyond and above the power of natural causes, however applied unto operation. Now, it is said expressly that our Lord Jesus Christ wrought miracles (for instance, the casting out of devils from persons possessed) by the Holy Ghost; and if their immediate production were by him in the human nature of Jesus Christ, personally united unto the Son of God, how much more must it be granted that it was he alone by whose power they were wrought in those who had no such relation unto the divine nature! And, therefore, where they are said

to be wrought by the "hand" or "finger of God," it is the person of the Holy Spirit which is precisely intended, as we have declared before. And the persons by whom they were wrought were never the real subjects of the power whereby they were wrought, as though it should be inherent and residing in them as a quality, Acts iii. 12, 16; only, they were infallibly directed by the Holy Ghost by word or action to pre-signify their operation. So was it with Joshua when he commanded the sun and moon to stand still, chap. x. 12. There was no power in Joshua, no, not [even] extraordinarily communicated to him, to have such a real influence upon the whole frame of nature as to effect so great an alteration therein: only, he had a divine warranty to speak that which God himself would effect; whence it is said that therein "the Lord hearkened unto the voice of a man," verse 14. It is a vanity of the greatest magnitude in some of the Jews, as Maimonides, ("More Nebuch.," page 2, cap. xxxv.,) Levi B. Gerson on the place, and others, who deny any fixation of the sun and moon, and judge that it is only the speed of Joshua in subduing his enemies before the close of that day which is intended. This they contend for, lest Joshua should be thought to have wrought a greater miracle than Moses! But as the prophet Habakkuk is express to the contrary, chap. iii. 11, and their own Sirachides, cap. xlv., xlvi., so it is no small prevarication in some Christians to give countenance unto such a putid fiction. See Grot. in loc. It is so in all other miraculous operations, even where the parts of the bodies of men were made instrumental of the miracle itself, as in the gift of tongues. They who had that gift did not so speak from any skill or ability residing in them, but they were merely organs of the Holy Ghost, which he moved at his pleasure. Now, the end of all these miraculous operations was, to give reputation to the persons, and to confirm the ministry of them by whom they were wrought; for as at first they were the occasion of wonder and astonishment, so upon their consideration they evidenced the respect and regard of God unto such persons and their work. So when God sent Moses to declare his will in an extraordinary manner unto the people of Israel, he commands him to work several miracles or signs before them, that they might believe that he was sent of God, Exod. iv. 8, 9. And such works were called signs, because they were tokens and pledges of the presence of the Spirit of God with them by whom they were wrought. Nor was this gift ever bestowed on any man alone, or for its own sake; but it was always subordinate unto the work of revealing or declaring the mind of God.

And these are the general heads of the extraordinary operations of the Holy Spirit of God in works exceeding all human or natural abilities, in their whole kind.

II. The next sort of the operations of the Holy Ghost under the Old Testament, whose explanation was designed, is of those whereby he improved, through immediate impressions of his own power, the natural faculties and abilities of the minds of men; and these, as was intimated, have respect to things political, moral, natural, and intellectual, with some of a mixed nature:—

1. He had in them respect unto things political. Such were his gifts whereby he enabled sundry persons unto rule and civil government amongst men. Government, or supreme rule, is of great concernment unto the glory of God in the world, and of the highest usefulness unto mankind. Without it the whole world would be filled with violence, and become a stage for all wickedness visibly and openly to act itself upon in disorder and confusion. And all men confess that unto a due management hereof unto its proper ends, sundry

peculiar gifts and abilities of mind are required in them and needful for them who are called thereunto. These are they themselves to endeavour after, and sedulously to improve the measures which they have attained of them, — and where this is by any neglected, the world and themselves will quickly feed on the fruits of that negligence; — but yet, because the utmost of what men may of this kind obtain by their ordinary endeavours, and an ordinary blessing thereon, is not sufficient for some especial ends which God aimed at in and by their rule and government, the Holy Ghost did oftentimes give an especial improvement unto their abilities of mind by his own immediate and extraordinary operation; and in some cases he manifested the effects of his power herein by some external, visible signs of his coming on them in whom he so wrought. So, in the first institution of the sanhedrim, or court of seventy elders, to bear together with Moses the burden of the people in their rule and government, the Lord is said to "put his Spirit upon them;" and [it is said] that "the Spirit rested on them:" Num. xi. 16, 17, "And the Lord said unto Moses, Gather unto me seventy men of the elders of Israel, whom thou knowest to be the elders of the people, and officers over them. And I will take of the Spirit which is upon thee, and will put it upon them; and they shall bear the burden of the people with thee." Verse 25, "And the Lord took of the Spirit that was upon Moses, and gave it unto the seventy elders, and the Spirit rested upon them." That which these elders were called unto was a share in the supreme role and government of the people, which was before entirely in the hand of Moses. This the occasion of their call declares, verses 11–15. And they were שֹׁטְרִים, "inferior officers" before, such as they had in Egypt, who influenced the people by their counsel and arbitration, Exod. iii. 16, v. 6, xxiv. 1, 9. Now they had a supreme power in judgment committed to them, and were thence called אֱלֹהִים, or "gods;" for these were they "unto whom the word of God came," who were thence called gods, John x. 34–36, Ps. lxxxii. 6, and not the prophets, who had neither power nor rule. And on them the Spirit of God that was in Moses rested; that is, wrought the same abilities for government in them as he had received, — that is, wisdom, righteousness, diligence, courage, and the like, that they might judge the people wisely, and look to the execution of the law impartially. Now, when the Spirit of God thus rested on them, it is said "They prophesied, and did not cease," Num. xi. 25, 26; that is, they sang or spake forth the praises of God in such a way and manner as made it evident unto all that they were extraordinarily acted by the Holy Ghost. So is that word used, 1 Sam. x. 10, and elsewhere. But this gift and work of prophecy was not the especial end for which they were endowed by the Spirit, for they were now called, as hath been declared, unto rule and government; but because their authority and rule was new among the people, God gave that visible sign and pledge of his calling them to their office, that they might have a due veneration of their persons, and acquiesce in their authority. And hence, from the ambiguity of that word יָסָפוּ וְלֹא, which we render "And did not cease," — "They prophesied, and did not cease," verse 25, — which may signify to "add" as well as to "cease," many of the Jews affirm that they so prophesied no more but that day only: "They prophesied then, and added not," — that is, to do so anymore. So when God would erect a kingdom amongst them, which was a new kind of government unto them, and designed Saul to be the person that should reign, it is said that he "gave him another heart," 1 Sam. x. 9, — that is, "the Spirit of God came upon him," as it is elsewhere expressed, to endow him with that wisdom and magnanimity that might make him meet for kingly rule. And because he was new called from a low condition unto royal dignity, the communication of the Spirit of God unto him was accompanied with a visible sign and token, that the people might acquiesce in his government, who were ready to despise his person; for he had also an extraordinary afflatus of the Spirit, expressing itself in a "visible rapture," verses 10, 11. And in like manner he dealt with others. For this cause, also, he instituted the ceremony of anointing at their inauguration; for it was a token of the communication of the gifts of the Holy Ghost unto them, though respect was had therein to Jesus Christ, who was to be anointed with all his fullness, of whom they were types unto that people. Now, these gifts for government are natural and moral abilities of the minds of men; such as are prudence, righteousness, courage, zeal, clemency, and the like. And when the Holy Ghost fell upon any persons to enable them for political rule and the administration of the civil power, he did not communicate gifts and abilities unto them quite of another kind, but only gave them an extraordinary improvement of their own ordinary abilities. And, indeed, so great is the burden wherewith a just and useful government is attended, so great and many are the temptations which power and a confluence of earthly things will invite and draw towards them, that without some especial assistance of the Holy Spirit of God, men cannot choose but either sink under the weight of it, or wretchedly miscarry in its exercise and management. This made Solomon, when God, in the beginning of his reign, gave him his option of all earthly desirable thing, to prefer wisdom and knowledge for rule before them all, 2 Chron. i. 7–12; and this he received from him who is the "Spirit of wisdom and understanding," Isa. xi. 2. And if the rulers of the earth would follow this example, and be earnest with God for such supplies of his Spirit as might enable them unto a holy, righteous discharge of their office, it would, in many places, be better with them and the world than it is or can be where is the state of things described Hos. vii. 3–5. Now, God of old did carry this dispensation out of the pale of the church, for the effecting of some especial ends of his own, and I no way question but that he continueth still so to do. Thus he anointed Cyrus, and calls him his "anointed" accordingly, Isa. xlv. 1; for Cyrus had a double work to do for God, in both parts whereof he stood in need of his especial assistance. He was to execute his judgments and vengeance on Babylon, as also to deliver his people, that they might reedify the temple. For both these he stood in need of, and did receive, especial aid from the Spirit of God, though he was in himself but a "ravenous bird" of prey, chap. xlvi. 11: for the gifts of this Holy One in this kind wrought no real holiness in them on whom they were bestowed; they were only given them for the good and benefit of others, with their own success in what they attempted unto that purpose. Yea, and many on whom they are bestowed never consider the author of them, but sacrifice to their own nets and drags, and look on themselves as the springs of their own wisdom and ability. But it is no wonder that all regard unto the gifts of the Holy Ghost in the government of the world is despised, when his whole work in and towards the church itself is openly derided.

2. We may add hereunto those especial endowments with some moral virtues, which he granted unto sundry persons for the accomplishment of some especial design. So he came upon Gideon and upon Jephthah, to anoint them unto the work of delivering the people from their adversaries in battle, Judges vi. 34, xi. 29. It is said before of them both that they were "men of valour,"

chap. vi. 12, xi. 1. This coming, therefore, of the Spirit of God upon them, and clothing of them, was his especial excitation of their courage, and his fortifying of their minds against those dangers they were to conflict withal. And this he did by such an efficacious impression of his power upon them as that both themselves received thereby a confirmation of their call, and others might discern the presence of God with them. Hence it is said that the "Spirit of the Lord clothed them," they being warmed in themselves and known to others by his gifts to and actings of them.

3. There are sundry instances of his adding unto the gifts of the mind, whereby he qualified persons for their duties, even bodily strength, when that also was needful for the work whereunto he called them. Such was his gift unto Samson. His bodily strength was supernatural, a mere effect of the power of the Spirit of God; and, therefore, when he put it forth in his calling, it is said that "the Spirit of the Lord came mightily upon him," Judges xiv. 6, xv. 14, or wrought powerfully in him. And he gave him this strength in the way of an ordinance, appointing the growing of his hair to be the sign and pledge of it; the care whereof being violated by him, he lost for a season the gift itself.

4. He also communicated gifts intellectual, to be exercised in and about things natural and artificial. So he endowed Bezaleel and Aholiab with wisdom and skill in all manner of curious workmanship, about all sorts of things, for the building and beautifying of the tabernacle, Exod. xxxi. 2, 3. Whether Bezaleel was a man that had before given himself unto the acquisition of those arts and sciences is altogether uncertain; but certain it is that his present endowments were extraordinary. The Spirit of God heightened, and improved, and strengthened the natural faculties of his mind to a perception and understanding of all the curious works mentioned in that place, and unto a skill how to contrive and dispose of them into the order designed by God himself. And, therefore, although the skill and wisdom mentioned differed not in the kind of it from that which others attained by industry, yet he received it by an immediate afflatus or inspiration of the Holy Ghost, as to that degree, at least, which he was made partaker of.

Lastly, The assistance given unto holy men for the publishing and preaching of the word of God to others, — as to Noah, who was "a preacher of righteousness," 2 Pet. ii. 5, for the conviction of the world and conversion of the elect, wherein the Spirit of God strove with men, Gen. vi. 3, and preached unto them that were disobedient, 1 Pet. iii. 19, 20, — might here also be considered, but that the explanation of his whole work in that particular will occur unto us in a more proper place.

And thus I have briefly passed through the dispensation of the Spirit of God under the Old Testament. Nor have I aimed therein to gather up his whole work and all his actings, for then everything that is praise-worthy in the church must have been inquired into; for all without him is death, and darkness, and sin. All life, light, and power are from him alone. And the instances of things expressly assigned unto him which we have insisted on are sufficient to manifest that the whole being and welfare of the church depended solely on his will and his operations. And this will yet be more evident when we have also considered those other effects and operations of his, which being common to both states of the church, under the Old Testament and the New, are purposely here omitted, because the nature of them is more fully cleared in the gospel, wherein also their exemplifications are more illustrious. From him, therefore, was the word of promise and the gift of prophecy, whereon the church was founded and whereby it was built; from him was the revelation and institution of all the ordinances of religious worship; from him was that communication of gifts and gracious abilities which any persons received for the edification, rule, protection, and deliverance of the church. All these things were wrought by "that one and the self-same Spirit, which divideth to every man severally as he will." And if this were the state of things under the Old Testament, a judgment may thence be made how it is under the New. The principal advantage of the present state above that which is past, next unto the coming of Christ in the flesh, consists in the pouring out of the Holy Ghost upon the disciples of Christ in a larger manner than formerly; and yet I know not how it is come to pass that some men think that neither he nor his work is of any great use unto us. And whereas we find everything that is good, even under the Old Testament, assigned unto him as the sole immediate author of it, it is hard to persuade, with many, that he continues now to do almost any good at all; and what he is allowed to have any hand in, it is sure to be so stated as that the principal praise of it may redound unto ourselves. So diverse, yea, so adverse, are the thoughts of God and men in these things, where our thoughts are not captivated unto the obedience of faith! But we must shut up this discourse. It is a common saying among the Jewish masters that the gift of the Holy Ghost ceased under the second temple, or after the finishing of it. Their meaning must be, that it did so as to the gifts of ministerial prophecy, of miracles, and of writing the mind of God by inspiration for the use of the church. Otherwise there is no truth in their observation; for there were afterward especial revelations of the Holy Ghost granted unto many, as unto Simeon and Anna, Luke ii. 25–38; and others constantly receive of his gifts and graces, to enable them unto obedience, and fit them for their employments; for without a continuance of these supplies the church itself must absolutely cease.

Footnotes:

1. Σημείωση δ' ὥς τινα μὲν εἴρηται δι' αἰνιγμάτων, τινὰ δὶ φανερώτερον. Τὰ μὲν οὖν δι' ἐπικρύψεως ἡγοῦμαι τῶν ἐκ περιτομῆς ἕνεκα κεκαλλυμμένως ἀποδεδόσθαι, διὰ τὰ θεσπιζόμενα κατ' αὐτῶν σκυθρωπά. Δι' ἅπερ εἰκὸς ἦν καὶ ἀφανίσαι αὐτοῦς τὴν γραφὴν, εἰ ἐκ τοῦ προφανοῦς τὴν ἐσχάτην αὐτῶν ἀποβολὴν ἐσήμαινεν — Euseb. Demonst. Evangel. lib. vi. Procem.

2. "Omnes prophetæ illa tantummodo sciebant quæ illis fuissent a Domino revelata. Unde et rex Hieremiam dubio interrogat, Si in ea hora qua cum illo loquebatur apud eum sermo Domini haberetur. Sed et Eliseus dicit, Quomodo hæc Dominus abscondit a me; et Elias præter se esse alios qui Deum colerent ignoravit." — Hieron. Comment. in Epist. ad Roman. cap. ii.

3. Οἳ δὲ τοῦ Θεοῦ ἄνθρωποι πνευματοφόροι πνεύματος ἁγίου, καὶ προφῆται γενόμενοι ὑπ' αὐτοῦ τοῦ Θεοῦ ἐμπνευσθέντες καὶ σοφισθέντες ἐγένοντο θεοδίδακτοι, καὶ ὅσιοι καὶ δίκαιοι. — Theophil. ad Autolycum. lib. ii."Prophetæ voces itemque virtutes ad fidem divinitatis edebant." — Tertul. Apol. cap. xviii.Οὐδ' ἀνδρὸς τοῦτο ποιεῖν, ἢ σοφοῦ τινος καὶ θείου; ἢ θεὸς ἂν ἔχοι φαίη τις ἂν, τοῦτο τὸ γέρας. Καὶ γὰρ οὐ τοῦ μάντεως, τό διότι, ἀλλὰ τὸ ὅτι μόνον εἰποῦ. — Plotin. Ennead. iii. lib. 3.

4. "Sed et hoc notandum ex eo quod dixerat; ut videam quid loquatur, in me; prophetiam visionem et eloquium Dei non extrinsecus ad prophetas fieri, sed intrinsecus et interiori homini respondere. Unde et Zacharias, et angelus inquit, qui loquebatur in me." — Hieron. Comment. in Hab. cap. ii.

5. And whereas the ancients contend, against the Ebionites, Marcionites, and Montanists, (as Epiphanius, Advers. Hæres. lib. ii. tom. 1; Hæres. xlviii.; Hieron. Procem. Comment. in Isa.,) that the prophets were not used ecstatically, but understood the things that were spoken to them, they

did not intend that they had, by virtue of their inspiration, a full comprehension of the whole sense of the revelations made unto them, but only that they were not in or by prophecy deprived of the use of their intellectual faculties, as it befell satanical enthusiasts. Ταῦτα γὰρ ἀληθῶς προφητῶν ἐν ἁγίῳ πνεύματι, ἐρρωμένην ἐχόντων τὴν διάνοιαν καὶ τὴν διδασκαλίαν καὶ τὴν διαλογίαν, as Epiphanius speaks. Wherefore, upon these words of Austin, "Per quosdam scientes, per quosdam nescientes, id quod ex adventu Christi usque nunc et deinceps agitur prænunciaretur esse venturum," de Civitat. Dei, lib. vii. cap. 32, one well adds, "Prophetæ nec omnes sua vaticinia intelligebant, nec qui intelligebant omnia intelligebant; non enim ex se loquebantur sed ex superiore Dei afflatu; cujus consilia non onmia eis erant manifesta; utebaturque Deus illis non velut consultis futurorum, sed instrumentis quibus homines alloqueretur."

6. "Nec aer voce pulsatus ad aures eorum perveniebat, sed Deus loquebatur in animo prophetarum." — Hieron. Proœm., in lib. i. Comment. in Isa.

7. Πνεῦμα δὲ τοῦ Θεοῦ πατὰ πᾶσιν μὲν οὐκ ἔστιν. Παρὰ δέ τισι τοῖς δικαίοις πολιτευομένοις καταγομένον, καὶ συμπλεκόμενον τῇ ψυχῇ, διὰ προαγορεύσεων ταῖς λοιπαῖς ψυχαῖς τὸ κεκρυμμένον ἀνήγγειλε. — Tatian. Assyr. Contra. Græcos.

8. "Sunt autem multa genera prophetandi, quorum unum est somniorum quale fuit in Daniele." — Hieron. in Hieremian, cap. 23.

9. "Propheta Deum, qui corporaliter invisibilis est, non corporaliter sed spiritualiter videt. Nam multa genera visionis in Scripturis sanctis inveniuntur. Unum secundum oculos corporis, sicut vidit Abraham tres viros sub ilice Mambre; alterum secundum quod imaginamur ea quæ per corpus sentimus. Nam et pars ipsa nostra cum Divinitus assumitur, multa revelantur non per oculos corperis, aut aures, aliumve sensum carnalem, sed tamen his similia, sicut vidit Petrus discum illum submitti a cœlo cum variis animalibus. Tertium autem genus visionis est secundum mentis intuitum quo intellectu conspiciuntur veritas et sapientia; sine quo genere illa duo quæ prius posui vel infructuosa sunt vel etiam in errorem mittunt." — August. contra Adamantum, cap. xxviii.

10. "Prophetæ erant Baal, et prophetæ confusionis, et alii offensionum, et quoscunque vitiosos prophetas Scriptura commemorat." — Hieron. Comment. in Epist. ad Titum. cap. i.

11. Ζητήσεις δὲ εἰ πάντες, εἴ τις προφητεύει, ἐκ πνεύματος ἁγίου προφητεύει; πῶς δὲ οὐ ζητήσεως ἄξιόν ἐστιν, εἴγε Δαβὶδ μετὰ τὴν ἐπὶ τοῦ Οὐρίου ἁμαρτίαν εὐλαβούμενος ἀφαιρεθῆναι ἀπ' αὐτοῦ τὸ ἅγιον πνεῦμά φησι. Τὸ πνεῦμα τὸ ἅγιον σου μὴ ἀντανέλῃς ἀπ' ἐμοῦ ... Οὕτω δὲ ζητήσεως ἄξιόν ἐστι τὸ περὶ τοῦ αγίου πνεύματος εἰ δύναται εἶναι καὶ ἐν ἁμαρτωλῷ ψυχῇ — Origen. Commentar. in Johan. tom. 30."Prophetiæ mysterio usi sunt etiam qui exorbitaverant a vera religione, quia et illis dedit Deus verbum suum ut mysteria futura pronunciarent hominibus." — Hieron. Comment. in Job. cap. xxxiii."Nam et prophetare et dæmonia excludere et virtutes magnas in terris facere sublimis utique et admirabilis res est, non tamen regnum cœleste consequitur quisquis in his omnibus invenitur, nisi recti et justi itineris observatione gradiatur." — Cyprian. de Unitat. Ecclesiæ.

12. Εἴ τις μὲν οὖν Προφήτης ἐστὶ πάντως προφητεύει· εἰ δέ τις προφητεύει οὐ πάντως ἐστὶ Προφήτης ... Ἐκ δὲ τῶν περὶ τὸν Καϊάφαν ἀναγεγραμμένων, προφητεύσαντα περὶ τοῦ σωτῆρος, ἔστιν ὅτι καὶ μοχθηρὰ ψυχὴ ἐπιδέχεται τοτὲ τὸ προφητεύειν. —Origen. Comment. in Johan. sect. 30.

13. "Saul invidiæ stimulo suscitatus et malo spiritu sæpe arreptus, cum David occidere vellet, et ipse David tunc cum Samuele et cæterorum prophetarum cuneo prophetaret, misit Saul nuncios et ipsum interficiendum de medio prophetarum rapere jubet. — Sed et ipse cum inter prophetas venerat prophetabat. — Quoniam Spiritus Sancti verba non dicentium merito pensantur, sed ipsius voluntate ubicunque voluerit proferuntur. At vero quidam in hoc loco æstimant quod Saul non Divino Spiritu sed malo illo quo sæpe arripiebatur per totum illum diem prophetaret ... Sed qualiter hoc sentiri potest cum ita scribitur; et factus est super eum Spiritus Domini et ambulans prophetabat? nisi forte sic in hoc loco accipitur Spiritus Domini quomodo et alio loco Spiritus Domini malus Saul arripiebat. Verumtamen ubicunque sine additamento Spiritus Dei vel Spiritus Domini vel Spiritus Christi in Scripturis sanctis invenitur, Spiritus Sanctus esse a nullo sano sensu dubitatur. Ubicunque vero cum additamento Spiritus Domini malus dicitur esse, intelligitur diabolus esse, qui Domini propter ministerium, malus propter vitium dictus videtur." — August. de Mirabil. Scripturæ, lib. ii. cap. 10.

14. See his treatises on "The Divine Original of the Scriptures," "Vindication of Greek and Hebrew Texts," and "Exercitationes adversus Fanaticos," vol. xvi. of his works. — Ed.

Chapter II - General dispensation of the Holy Spirit with respect unto the new creation

The work of the Spirit of God in the new creation proposed to consideration — The importance of the doctrine hereof — The plentiful effusion of the Spirit the great promise respecting the times of the New Testament — Ministry of the gospel founded on the promise of the Spirit — How this promise is made unto all believers — Injunction to all to pray for the Spirit of God — The solemn promise of Christ to send his Spirit when he left the world — The ends for which he promised him — The work of the new creation the principal means of the revelation of God and his glory — How this revelation is made in particular herein.

We are now arrived at that part of our work which was principally intended in the whole, and that because our faith and obedience are principally therein concerned; — this is, the dispensation and work of the Holy Ghost with respect to the gospel, or the new creation of all things in and by Jesus Christ. And this, if any thing in the Scripture, is worthy of our most diligent inquiry and meditation; nor is there any more important principle and head of that religion which we do profess. The doctrine of the being and unity of the divine nature is common to us with the rest of mankind, and hath been so from the foundation of the world, however some, "like brute beasts," have herein also "corrupted themselves." The doctrine of the Trinity, or the subsistence of three persons in the one divine nature or being, was known to all who enjoyed divine revelation, even under the Old Testament, though to us it be manifested with more light and convincing evidence. The incarnation of the Son of God was promised and expected from the first entrance of sin, and received its actual accomplishment in the fullness of time, during the continuance of the Mosaical pedagogy. But this dispensation of the Holy Ghost whereof we now proceed to treat is so peculiar unto the New Testament, that the evangelist speaking of it says, "The Holy Ghost was not yet given, because that Jesus was not yet glorified," John vii. 39; and they who were instructed in the doctrine of John the Baptist only, knew not "whether there were any Holy Ghost," Acts xix. 2. Both which sayings concerned his dispensation under the New Testament; for his eternal being and existence they were not ignorant of, nor did he then first begin to be, as we have fully manifested in our foregoing discourses. To stir us up, therefore, unto diligence in this inquiry, unto what was in general laid down before I shall add some considerations evidencing the greatness and necessity of this duty, and then proceed to the matter itself that we have proposed to handle and explain:—

1. The plentiful effusion of the Spirit is that which was principally prophesied of and foretold as the great privilege and pre-eminence of the gospel church-state; this was that good wine which was kept until the last. This all the prophets bear witness unto: see Isa. xxxv. 7, xliv. 3; Joel ii. 28; Ezek. xi. 19, xxxvi. 27, with other places innumerable. The great promise of the Old

Testament was that concerning the coming of Christ in the flesh. But he was so to come as to put an end unto that whole church-state wherein his coming was expected. To prove this was the principal design of the apostle in his Epistle to the Hebrews. But this promise of the Spirit, whose accomplishment was reserved for the times of the gospel, was to be the foundation of another church-state, and the means of its continuance. If, therefore, we have any interest in the gospel itself, or desire to have; if we have either part or lot in this matter, or desire to be made partakers of the benefits which attend thereon, — which are no less than our acceptation with God here and our salvation hereafter, — it is our duty to search the Scriptures, and inquire diligently into these things. And let no man deceive us with vain words, as though the things spoken concerning the Spirit of God and his work towards them that do believe were fanatical and unintelligible by rational men; for because of this contempt of him, the wrath of God will come on the children of disobedience. And if the "world in wisdom," and their reason, "know him not," nor can "receive him," yet they who believe do know him; for "he dwelleth with them, and shall be in them," John xiv. 17. And the present practice of the world, in despising and slighting the Spirit of God and his work, gives light and evidence into those words of our Saviour, that "the world cannot receive him;" and it cannot do so, because it "neither seeth him nor knoweth him," or hath no experience of his work in them, or of his power and grace. Accordingly [so] doth it, [so] is it come to pass. Wherefore, not to avow the Spirit of God in his work, is to be ashamed of the gospel and of the promise of Christ, as if it were a thing not to be owned in the world.

2. The ministry of the gospel, whereby we are begotten again, that we should be a kind of first-fruits of his creatures unto God, is from his promised presence with it and work in it, called the ministry of the Spirit, even of the Spirit that giveth life, 2 Cor. iii. 8; and it is so in opposition to the "ministration of the law," wherein yet there were a multitude of ordinances of worship and glorious ceremonies. And he who knows no more of the ministry of the gospel but what consists in an attendance unto the letter of institutions and the manner of their performance knows nothing of it. Nor yet is there any extraordinary afflatus or inspiration now intended or attended unto, as we are slanderously reported, and as some affirm that we pretend; but there is that presence of the Spirit of God with the ministry of the gospel, in his authority, assistance, communication of gifts and abilities, guidance, and direction, as without which it will be useless and unprofitable in and unto all that take the work thereof upon them. This will be more fully declared afterward; for, —

3. The promise and gift of the Spirit under the gospel is not made nor granted unto any peculiar sort of persons only, but unto all believers, as their conditions and occasions do require. They are not, therefore, the especial interest of a few, but the common concern of all Christians. The Papists grant that this promise is continued; but they would confine it to their pope or their councils, things nowhere mentioned in the Scripture, nor the object of any one gospel promise whatever. It is all believers in their places and stations, churches in their order, and ministers in their office, unto whom the promise of him is made, and towards whom it is accomplished, as shall be shown. Others, also, grant the continuance of this gift, but understand no more by it but an ordinary blessing upon men's rational endeavours, common and exposed unto all alike. This is no less than to overthrow his whole work, to take his

sovereignty out of his hand, and to deprive the church of all especial interest in the promise of Christ concerning him. In this inquiry, therefore, we look after what at present belongs unto ourselves, if so be we are disciples of Christ, and do expect the fulfilling of his promises; for whatever men may pretend, unto this day, "if they have not the Spirit of Christ, they are none of his," Rom. viii. 9: for our Lord Jesus Christ hath promised him as a comforter, to abide with his disciples forever, John xiv. 16, and by him it is that he is present with them and among them to the end of the world, Matt. xxviii. 20, xviii. 20; — that we speak not as yet of his sanctifying work, whereby we are enabled to believe, and are made partakers of that holiness without which no man shall see God. Wherefore, without him all religion is but a body without a soul, a carcass without an animating spirit. It is true, in the continuation of his work he ceaseth from putting forth those extraordinary effects of his power which were needful for the laying the foundation of the church in the world; but the whole work of his grace, according to the promise of the covenant, is no less truly and really carried on at this day, in and towards all the elect of God, than it was on the day of Pentecost and onwards; and so is his communication of gifts necessary for the edification of the church, Eph. iv. 11–13. The owning, therefore, and avowing the work of the Holy Ghost in the hearts and on the minds of men, according to the tenor of the covenant of grace, is the principal part of that profession which at this day all believers are called unto.

4. We are taught in an especial manner to pray that God would give his Holy Spirit unto us, that through his aid and assistance we may live unto God in that holy obedience which he requires at our hands, Luke xi. 9–13. Our Saviour, enjoining an importunity in our supplications, verses 9, 10, and giving us encouragement that we shall succeed in our requests, verses 11, 12, makes the subject-matter of them to be the Holy Spirit: "Your heavenly Father shall give the Holy Spirit to them that ask him," verse 13; which in the other evangelist is "good things," Matt. vii. 11, because he is the author of them all in us and to us, nor doth God bestow any good thing on us but by his Spirit. Hence, the promise of bestowing the Spirit is accompanied with a prescription of duty unto us, that we should ask him or pray for him; which is included in every promise where his sending, giving, or bestowing is mentioned. He, therefore, is the great subject-matter of all our prayers. And that signal promise of our blessed Saviour, to send him as a comforter, to abide with us forever, is a directory for the prayers of the church in all generations. Nor is there any church in the world fallen under such a total degeneracy but that, in their public offices, there are testimonies of their ancient faith and practice, in praying for the coming of the Spirit unto them, according to this promise of Christ. And therefore our apostle, in all his most solemn prayers for the churches in his days, makes this the chief petition of them, that God would give unto them, and increase in them, the gifts and graces of the Holy Spirit, with the Spirit himself, for sundry especial effects and operations whereof they stood in need, Eph. i. 17, iii. 16; Col. ii. 2. And this is a full conviction of what importance the consideration of the Spirit of God and his work is unto us. We must deal in this matter with that confidence which the truth instructs us unto, and therefore say, that he who prayeth not constantly and diligently for the Spirit of God, that he may be made partaker of him for the ends for which he is promised, is a stranger from Christ and his gospel. This we are to attend unto, as that whereon our eternal happiness doth depend. God knows our state and condition, and we

may better learn our wants from his prescription of what we ought to pray for than from our sense and experience; for we are in the dark unto our own spiritual concerns, through the power of our corruptions and temptations, and "know not what we should pray for as we ought," Rom. viii. 26. But our heavenly Father knows perfectly what we stand in need of; and, therefore, whatever be our present apprehensions concerning ourselves, which are to be examined by the word, our prayers are to be regulated by what God hath enjoined us to ask and what he hath promised to bestow.

5. What was before mentioned may here be called over again and farther improved, yea, it is necessary that so it should be. This is, the solemn promise of Jesus Christ when he was [about] to leave this world by death, [John xiv. 15–17.] And whereas he therein made and confirmed his testament, Heb. ix. 15–17, he bequeathed his Spirit as his great legacy unto his disciples; and this he gave unto them as the great pledge of their future inheritance, 2 Cor. i. 22, which they were to live upon in this world. All other good things he hath, indeed, bequeathed unto believers, as he speaks of peace with God in particular: "Peace I leave with you, my peace I give unto you," John xiv. 27. But he gives particular graces and mercies for particular ends and purposes. The Holy Spirit he bequeaths to supply his own absence, John xvi. 13; that is, for all the ends of spiritual and eternal life. Let us, therefore, consider this gift of the Spirit either formally, under this notion that he was the principal legacy left unto the church by our dying Saviour, or materially, as to the ends and purposes for which he is so bequeathed, and it will be evident what valuation we ought to have of him and his work. How would some rejoice if they could possess any relic of any thing that belonged unto our Saviour in the days of his flesh, though of no use or benefit unto them! Yea, how great a part of men called Christians do boast in some pretended parcels of the tree whereon he suffered! Love abused by superstition lies at the bottom of this vanity; for they would embrace any thing left them by their dying Saviour. But he left them no such things, nor did ever bless and sanctify them unto any holy or sacred ends; and therefore hath the abuse of them been punished with blindness and idolatry. But this [gift of the Spirit] is openly testified unto in the gospel. Then when his heart was overflowing with love unto his disciples and care for them, when he took a holy prospect of what would be their condition, their work, duty, and temptations in the world, and thereon made provision of all that they could stand in need of, he promiseth to leave and give unto them his Holy Spirit to abide with them forever, directing us to look unto him for all our comforts and supplies. According, therefore, unto our valuation and esteem of him, to our satisfaction and acquiescency in him, is our regard to the love, care, and wisdom of our blessed Saviour to be measured. And, indeed, it is only in his word and Spirit wherein we can either honour or despise him in this world; in his own person he is exalted at the right hand of God, far above all principalities and powers, so that nothing of ours can immediately reach him or affect him. But it is in our regard to these that he makes a trial of our faith, love, and obedience. And it is a matter of lamentation to consider the contempt and scorn that, on various pretences, is cast upon this Holy Spirit, and the work whereunto he is sent by God the Father and by Jesus Christ; for there is included therein a contempt of them also. Nor will a pretence of honouring God in their own way secure such persons as shall contract the guilt of this abomination; for it is an idol, — and not the God and Father of our Lord Jesus Christ, — who doth not work

effectually in the elect by the Holy Ghost, according to the Scriptures. And if we consider this promise of the Spirit to be given unto us, as to the ends of it, then, —

6. He is promised and given as the sole cause and author of all the good that in this world we are or can be made partakers of;[15] for, (1.) there is no good communicated unto us from God, but it is bestowed on us or wrought in us by the Holy Ghost. No gift, no grace, no mercy, no privilege, no consolation, do we receive, possess, or use, but it is wrought in us, collated on us, or manifested unto us, by him alone. Nor, (2.) is there any good in us towards God, any faith, love, duty, obedience, but what is effectually wrought in us by him, by him alone; for "in us, that is, in our flesh" (and by nature we are but flesh), "there dwelleth no good thing." All these things are from him and by him, as shall, God assisting, be made to appear by instances of all sorts in our ensuing discourse. And these considerations I thought meet to premise unto our entrance into that work which now lieth before us.

(1.) The great work whereby God designed to glorify himself ultimately in this world was that of the new creation, or of the recovery and restoration of all things by Jesus Christ, Heb. i. 1–3; Eph. i. 10. And as this is in general confessed by all Christians, so I have elsewhere insisted on the demonstration of it. (2.) That which God ordereth and designeth as the principal means for the manifestation of his glory must contain the most perfect and absolute revelation and declaration of himself, his nature, his being, his existence, and excellencies; for from their discovery and manifestation, with the duties which as known they require from rational creatures, doth the glory of God arise, and no otherwise. (3.) This, therefore, was to be done in this great work; and it was done accordingly. Hence is the Lord Christ, in his work of mediation, said to be "The image of the invisible God," Col. i. 15; "The brightness of his glory, and the express image of his person," Heb. i. 3; in whose face the knowledge of the glory of God shineth forth unto us, 2 Cor. iv. 6; — because in and by him, in his work of the new creation, all the glorious properties of the nature of God are manifested and displayed incomparably above what they were in the creation of all things in the beginning. I say, therefore, in the contrivance, projection, production, carrying on, disposal, and accomplishment of this great work, God hath made the most eminent and glorious discovery of himself unto angels and men, Eph. iii. 8–10, 1 Pet. i. 10–12; that we may know, love, trust, honour, and obey him in all things as God, and according to his will. (4.) In particular, in this new creation he hath revealed himself in an especial manner as three in one. There was no one more glorious mystery brought to light in and by Jesus Christ than that of the holy Trinity, or the subsistence of the three persons in the unity of the same divine nature. And this was done not so much in express propositions or verbal testimonies unto that purpose, — which yet is done also, as by the declaration of the mutual, divine, internal acts of the persons towards one another, and the distinct, immediate, divine, external actings of each person in the work which they did and do perform, — for God revealeth not himself unto us merely doctrinally and dogmatically, but by the declaration of what he doth for us, in us, and towards us, in the accomplishment of "the counsel of his own will;" see Eph. i. 4–12. And this revelation is made unto us, not that our minds might be possessed with the notions of it, but that we may know aright how to place our trust in him, how to obey him and live unto him, how to obtain and exercise communion with him, until we come to the enjoyment of him.

We may make application of these things unto, and exemplify them yet farther in, the work under consideration. Three things in general are in it proposed unto our faith:— 1. The supreme purpose, design, contrivance, and disposal of it. 2. The purchasing and procuring cause and means of the effects of that design, with its accomplishment in itself and with respect unto God. 3. The application of the supreme design and actual accomplishment of it, to make it effectual unto us.

The first of these is absolutely in the Scripture assigned unto the Father, and that uniformly and everywhere. His will, his counsel, his love, his grace, his authority, his purpose, his design, are constantly proposed as the foundation of the whole work, as those which were to be pursued, effected, accomplished: see Isa. xlii. 1–4; Ps. xl. 6–8; John iii. 16; Isa. liii. 10–12; Eph. i. 4–12, and other places innumerable. And on this account, because the Son undertook to effect whatever the Father had so designed and purposed, there were many acts of the will of the Father towards the Son, — [as] in sending, giving, appointing of him; in preparing him a body; in comforting and supporting him; in rewarding and giving a people unto him, — which belong unto the Father, on the account of the authority, love, and wisdom, that were in them, their actual operation belonging particularly unto another person. And in these things is the person of the Father in the divine being proposed unto us to be known and adored. Secondly, The Son condescendeth, consenteth, and engageth to do and accomplish in his own person the whole work which, in the authority, counsel, and wisdom of the Father, was appointed for him, Phil. ii. 5–8. And in these divine operations is the person of the Son revealed unto us to be "honoured even as we honour the Father." Thirdly, The Holy Ghost doth immediately work and effect whatever was to be done in reference unto the person of the Son or the sons of men, for the perfecting and accomplishment of the Father's counsel and the Son's work, in an especial application of both unto their especial effects and ends. Hereby is he made known unto us, and hereby our faith concerning him and in him is directed.

And thus, in this great work of the new creation by Jesus Christ, doth God cause all his glory to pass before us, that we may both know him and worship him in a due manner. And what is the peculiar work of the Holy Ghost herein we shall now declare.

Footnotes:

15. "Gratias ago tibi clementissime Deus, quis quod quæsivi mane prior ipse donasti." — Cypr. de Baptism. Christi.

Chapter III - Work of the Holy Spirit with respect unto the head of the new creation the human nature of Christ

The especial works of the Holy Spirit in the new creation — His work on the human nature of Christ — How this work could be, considering the union of the human nature unto and in the person of the Son of God — Assumption of the human nature into union, the only act of the person of the Son towards it — Personal union the only necessary consequent of this assumption — All other actings of the person of the Son in and on the human nature voluntary — The Holy Spirit the immediate efficient cause of all divine operations — -He is the Spirit of the Son or of the Father — How all the works of the Trinity are undivided — The body of Christ formed in the womb by the Holy Ghost, but of the substance of the blessed Virgin; why this was necessary — Christ not hence the Son of the Holy Ghost according to the human nature — Difference between the assumption of the human nature by the Son and the creation of it by the Holy Ghost — The conception of Christ, how ascribed to the Holy Ghost, and how to the blessed Virgin — Reasons of the espousal of the blessed Virgin to Joseph before the conception of Christ — The actual purity and holiness of the soul and body of Christ from his miraculous conception.

The dispensation and work of the Holy Ghost in this new creation respect, first, The Head of the church, the Lord Jesus Christ, in his human nature, as it was to be, and was, united unto the person of the Son of God. Secondly, It concerns the members of that mystical body in all that belongs unto them as such. And under these two heads we shall consider them.

First, therefore, we are to inquire what are the operations of the Holy Ghost in reference unto Jesus Christ, the Head of the church. And these were of two sorts:— 1. Such as whereof the person of Christ in his human nature was the immediate object. 2. Such as he performs towards others on his behalf; that is, with direct respect unto his person and office.

I. But yet, before we enter upon the first sort of his works which we shall begin withal, an objection of seeming weight and difficulty must be removed out of our way; which I shall the rather do because our answer unto it will make the whole matter treated of the more plain and familiar unto us. It may, therefore, be, and it is objected, "That whereas the human nature of Christ is assigned as the immediate object of these operations of the Holy Ghost, and that nature was immediately, inseparably, and undividedly united unto the person of the Son of God, there doth not seem to be any need, nor indeed room, for any such operations of the Spirit; for could not the Son of God himself, in his own person, perform all things requisite both for the forming, supporting, sanctifying, and preserving of his own nature, without the especial assistance of the Holy Ghost? nor is it easy to be understood how an immediate work of the Holy Ghost should be interposed, in the same person, between the one nature and the other." And this seeming difficulty is vehemently pressed by the Socinians, who think to entangle our whole doctrine of the blessed Trinity and incarnation of the Son of God thereby. But express testimonies of Scripture, with the clear and evident analogy of faith, will carry us easily and safely through this seeming difficulty. To which end we may observe, that, —

1. The only singular immediate act of the person of the Son on the human nature was the assumption of it into subsistence with himself. Herein the Father and the Spirit had no interest nor concurrence, εἰ μὴ κατ' εὐδοκίαν καὶ βούλησιν, "but by approbation and consent," as Damascen speaks: for the Father did not assume the human nature, he was not incarnate; neither did the Holy Spirit do so; but this was the peculiar act and work of the Son. See John i. 14; Rom. i. 3; Gal. iv. 4; Phil. ii. 6, 7; Heb. ii. 14, 16; which places, with many others to the same purpose, I have elsewhere expounded, and vindicated from the exceptions of the Socinians.

2. That the only necessary consequent of this assumption of the human nature, or the incarnation of the Son of God, is the personal union of Christ, or the inseparable subsistence of the assumed nature in the person of the Son. This was necessary and indissoluble, so that it was not impeached nor shaken in the least by the temporary dissolution of that nature by the separation of the soul and body: for the union of the soul and body in Christ did not constitute him a person, that the dissolution of them should destroy his personality; but he was a person by the uniting of both unto the Son of God.

3. That all other actings of God in the person of the Son towards the human nature were voluntary, and did not necessarily ensue on the union mentioned; for there was no transfusion of the properties of one nature into the other, nor real physical communication of divine essential excellencies unto the humanity. Those who seem to contend for any such thing resolve all at last into a true assignation by way of predication, as necessary on the union mentioned, but contend not for a real transfusion of the properties of one nature into the other. But these communications were voluntary. Hence were those temporary dispensations, when, under his great trial, the human nature complained of its desertion and dereliction by the divine, Matt. xxvii. 46; for this forsaking was not as to personal union, or necessary subsistence and supportment, but as to voluntary communications of light and consolation. Hence himself declares that the human nature was not the residential subject of omnisciency; for so he speaks, Mark xiii. 32, "But of that day and that hour knoweth no man, no, not the angels which are in heaven, neither the Son, but the Father." For the exposition given by some of the ancients, that the Lord Christ speaks not this absolutely, but only "that he knew it not to declare it unto them," is unworthy of him; for no more did the Father so know it, seeing he hath not declared it. But this was the opinion only of some of them; the more advised were otherwise minded. He[16] speaks of himself with respect unto his human nature only, and thereunto all communications were voluntary. So after his ascension, God gave him that revelation that he made to the apostle, Rev. i. 1. The human nature, therefore, however inconceivably advanced, is not the subject of infinite, essentially divine properties; and the actings of the Son of God towards it, consequential unto its assumption, and that indissoluble subsistence in its union which ensued thereon, are voluntary.

1. The Holy Ghost, as we have proved before, is the immediate, peculiar, efficient cause of all external divine operations: for God worketh by his Spirit, or in him immediately applies the power and efficacy of the divine excellencies unto their operation; whence the same work is equally the work of each person.

2. The Holy Spirit is the Spirit of the Son, no less than the Spirit of the Father. He proceedeth from the Son, as from the Father. He is the "Spirit of the Son," Gal. iv. 6. And hence is he the immediate operator of all divine acts of the Son himself, even on his own human nature. Whatever the Son of God wrought in, by, or upon the human nature, he did it by the Holy Ghost, who is his Spirit, as he is the Spirit of the Father.

3. To clear the whole matter, it must be yet farther observed that the immediate actings of the Holy Ghost are not spoken of him absolutely, nor ascribed unto him exclusively, as unto the other persons and their concurrence in them. It is a saying generally admitted, that Opera Trinitatis ad extra sunt indivisa. There is no such division in the external operations of God that any one of them should be the act of one person, without the concurrence of the others; and the reason of it is, because the nature of God, which is the principle of all divine operations, is one and the same, undivided in them all. Whereas, therefore, they are the effects of divine power, and that power is essentially the same in each person, the works themselves belong equally unto them: as, if it were possible that three men might see by the same eye, the act of seeing would be but one, and it would be equally the act of all three. But the things we insist on are ascribed eminently unto the Holy Ghost, on the account of the order of his subsistence in the holy Trinity, as he is the Spirit of the Father and the Son; whence, in every divine act, the authority of the Father, the love and wisdom of the Son, with the immediate efficacy and power of the Holy Ghost, are to be considered. Yea, and there is such a distinction in their operations, that one divine act may produce a peculiar respect and relation unto one person, and not unto another; as the assumption of the human nature did to the Son, for he only was incarnate.

And such are the especial actings of the Holy Ghost towards the head of the church, our Lord Jesus Christ, in this work of the new creation, as we shall demonstrate in sundry instances:—

First, The framing, forming, and miraculous conception of the body of Christ in the womb of the blessed Virgin was the peculiar and especial work of the Holy Ghost.[17] This work, I acknowledge, in respect of designation, and the authoritative disposal of things, is ascribed unto the Father; for so the Lord Christ speaketh unto him: "A body hast thou prepared me," Heb. x. 5. But this preparation does not signify the actual forming and making ready of that body, but the eternal designation of it: it was prepared in the counsel and love of the Father. As to voluntary assumption, it is ascribed to the Son himself: chap. ii. 14, "Forasmuch as the children are partakers of flesh and blood, he also himself likewise took part of the same;" he took upon him a body and soul, entire human nature, as the children, or all believers, have the same, synecdochically expressed by "flesh and blood." Verse 16, "He took on him the seed of Abraham." But the immediate divine efficiency in this matter was the peculiar work of the Holy Ghost: Matt. i. 18, "When as his mother Mary was espoused to Joseph, before they came together, she was found with child of the Holy Ghost." Verse 20, "That which is conceived in her is of the Holy Ghost." Luke i. 35, "The angel answered and said unto her, The Holy Ghost shall come upon thee, and the power of the Highest shall overshadow thee: therefore also that holy thing which shall be born of thee shall be called the Son of God." 1. The person working is the Holy Ghost. He is the wonderful operator in this glorious work. And therein the power of the Most High was exerted; for "The power of the Highest" is neither explicatory of the former expression, "The Holy Ghost," as though he were only the power of the Most High, nor is it the adjoining of a distinct agent or cause unto him, as though the Holy Ghost and the power of the Most High were different agents in this matter. Only the manner of his effecting this wonderful matter, concerning which the blessed Virgin had made that inquiry, verse 34, "How shall this be, seeing I know not a man?" is expressed. "The Holy Ghost," saith the angel, "acting the power of the Most High," or in the infinite power of God, "shall accomplish it." 2. For his access unto his work, it is expressed by his "coming upon her." The importance of this expression, and what is signified thereby, hath been declared before. And it is often used to declare his actings with reference unto the production of miraculous works: Acts i. 8, "Ye shall receive power, after that the Holy Ghost is come upon you;" — "He will so come upon you as to put forth the power of the Most High in you and by you, in gifts and operations miraculous;" for he is said to come, with respect unto his beginning of any marvellous operation, where before he did not work to the like purpose. 3. The act of the Holy Ghost in this matter was a creating act; not, indeed, like the first creating act, which produced the matter and substance of all things out of nothing, causing that to be which was not before, neither in matter, nor form, nor passive disposition; but like those subsequent acts of creation, whereby, out of matter before made and prepared, things were made that which before they were not, and which of themselves they had no active disposition unto nor concurrence in. So man was created or formed of the dust of the earth, and woman of a rib taken from man. There was a previous matter unto their creation, but such as gave no assistance nor had any active disposition to the production of that particular kind of creature whereinto they were formed by the creating power of God. Such was this act of the Holy Ghost in forming the body of our Lord Jesus Christ; for although it was effected by an act of infinite creating power, yet it was formed or made of the substance of the blessed Virgin. That it should be so was absolutely necessary, — (1.) For the accomplishment of the promises made unto Abraham and David, that the Messiah should be of their seed, and proceed from their loins. (2.) So was it also on the account of the first original promise, that the "seed of the woman should bruise the serpent's head:" for the Word was to be "made flesh," John i. 14; to be "made of a woman," Gal. iv. 4; or "made of the seed of David according to the flesh," Rom. i. 3; and to take upon him "the seed of Abraham," Heb. ii. 16. (3.) To confirm the truth hereof is his genealogy according to the flesh given us by two of the evangelists; which were neither to the purpose nor true if he were not made of the substance or flesh of the blessed Virgin. (4.) Besides, all our cognation and alliance unto him, whence he was meet to be our Saviour, suffering in the same nature wherein we have sinned, do depend hereon, Heb. ii. 14; for if he had not been made like us in all things, sin only excepted, if he had not been partaker of our nature, there had been no foundation for the imputing that unto us which he did, suffered, and wrought, Rom. viii. 3, 4. And hence these things are accounted unto us, and cannot be so unto angels, whose nature he did not take upon him, Heb. ii. 16. This, therefore, was the work of the Holy Ghost in reference unto the human nature of Christ in the womb of his mother: By his omnipotent power he formed it of the substance of the body of the holy Virgin, — that is, as unto his body. And hence sundry things do ensue:—

1. That the Lord Christ could not on this account, no, not with respect unto his human nature only, be said to be the Son of the Holy Ghost, although he supplied the place and virtue of a natural father in generation; for the relation of filiation dependeth only on and ariseth from a perfect generation, and not on every effect of an efficient cause. When one fire is kindled by another, we do not say that it is the son of that other, unless it be very improperly; much less when a man builds a house do we say that it is his son. There was, therefore, no other relation between the person of the Holy Ghost and the human nature of Christ but that of a creator and a creature. And the Lord Christ is, and is called, "The Son of God' with respect only unto the Father and his eternal, ineffable generation, communicating being and subsistence unto him, as the fountain and original of the Trinity. Filiation, therefore, is a personal adjunct, and belongs unto Christ as he was a divine person, and not with respect unto his human nature. But that nature being assumed, whole Christ was the Son of God.

2. That this act of the Holy Ghost, in forming of the body of Christ, differs from the act of the Son in assuming the human nature into personal union with himself: for this act of the Son was not a creating act, producing a being out of nothing, or making any thing by the same power to be what in its own nature it was not; but it was an ineffable act of love and wisdom, taking the nature so formed by the Holy Ghost, so prepared for him, to be his own in the instant of its formation, and thereby preventing the singular and individual subsistence of that nature in and by itself. So, then, as the creating act of the Holy Ghost, in forming the body of our Lord Jesus Christ in the womb, doth not denominate him to be his father, no, not according to the human nature, but he is the Son of God upon the account of his eternal generation only; so it doth not denote an assumption of that nature into union with himself, nor was he incarnate. He made the human nature of Christ, body and soul, with, in, and unto a subsistence in the second person of the Trinity, not [in] his own.

3. It hence also follows that the conception of Christ in the womb, being the effect of a creating act, was not accomplished successively and in process of time, but was perfected in an instant;[18] for although the creating acts of infinite power, where the works effected have distinct parts, may have a process or duration of time allotted unto them, as the world was created in six days, yet every part of it that was the object of an especial creating act was instantaneously produced. So was the forming of the body of Christ, with the infusion of a rational soul to quicken it, though it increased afterwards in the womb unto the birth. And as it is probable that this conception was immediate upon the angelical salutation, so it was necessary that nothing of the human nature of Christ should exist of itself antecedently unto its union with the Son of God: for in the very instant of its formation, and therein, was the "Word made flesh," John i. 14; and the Son of God was "made of a woman," Gal. iv. 4; so that the whole essence of his nature was created in the same instant. Thus far the Scriptures go before, and herein it is necessary to assert the forming of the body and soul of Christ by the Holy Spirit. The curious inquiries of some of the schoolmen and others are to be left unto themselves, or rather, to be condemned in them; for what was farther in this miraculous operation of the Holy Ghost, it seems purposely to be hid from us in that expression, Δύναμισ

Ὑψίστου ἐπισκιάσει σοι, — "The power of the Most High shall overshadow thee." Under the secret, glorious covert hereof we may learn to adore that holy work here, which we hope to rejoice in and bless God for unto eternity. And I suppose, also, that there is in the word an allusion unto the expression of the original acting of the Holy Spirit towards the newlyproduced mass of the old creation, whereof we spake before. Then it is said of him that he was מְרַחֶפֶת, as it were "hovering" and "moving" over it for the formation and production of all things living; for both the words include in them an allusion unto a covering like that of a fowl over its eggs, communicating, by its cognate warmth and heat, a principle of life unto their seminal virtue.

It remaineth only that we consider how the same work of the conception of Christ is assigned unto the Holy Ghost and to the blessed Virgin; for of her it is said expressly in prophecy, הָרָה הָעַלְמָה, Isa. vii. 14, "A virgin shall conceive," — the same word that is used to express the conception of any other woman, Gen. iv. 1. Hence she is termed by the ancients Θεοτόκος and Dei genetrix; which last, at least, I wish had been forborne. Compare it with the Scripture, and there will appear an unwarrantable καινοφωνία in it. So Luke i. 31. The words of the angel to her are, Συλλήψη ἐν γαστρὶ, καὶ τέξῃ υἱόν, — "Thou shalt conceive in thy womb, and bring forth a son;" where her conception of him is distinguished from her bringing of him forth. And yet in the ancient creed commonly called the Apostles', and generally received by all Christians as a summary of religion, it is said he was "conceived by the Holy Ghost," and only "born of the Virgin Mary." Ans. The same work is assigned to both as causes of a different kind, — unto the Holy Spirit as the active, efficient cause, who by his almighty power produced the effect. And the disputes managed by some of the ancients about "de Spiritu Sancto" and "ex Spiritu Sancto" were altogether needless; for it is his creating efficiency that is intended. And his conceiving is ascribed unto the holy Virgin as the passive, material cause; for his body was formed of her substance, as was before declared. And this conception of Christ was after her solemn espousals unto Joseph, and that for sundry reasons; for, — 1. Under the covering of her marriage to him she was to receive a protection of her spotless innocency. And besides, 2. God provided one that should take care of her and her child in his infancy. And, 3. Hereby, also, was our blessed Saviour freed from the imputation of an illegitimate birth, until by his own miraculous operations he should give testimony unto his miraculous conception; concerning which before his mother could not have been believed. 4. That he might have one on whose account his genealogy might be recorded, to manifest the accomplishment of the promise unto Abraham and David; for the line of a genealogy was not legally continued by the mother only. Hence Matthew gives us his genealogy by Joseph, to whom his mother was legally espoused. And although Luke gives us the true, natural line of his descent, by the progenitors of the blessed Virgin, yet he nameth her not; only mentioning her espousals, he begins with Heli, who was her father, chap. iii. 23. And this is the first thing ascribed peculiarly to the Holy Spirit with respect unto the head of the church, Christ Jesus.

From this miraculous creation of the body of Christ, by the immediate power of the Holy Ghost, did it become a meet habitation for his holy soul, every way ready and complying with all actings of grace and virtue. We have not only the depravation of our natures in general, but the obliquity of our particular constitutions, to conflict withal. Hence it is that one is disposed to passion, wrath, and anger; another, to vanity and lightness; a third, to sensuality and fleshly pleasures; and so others to sloth and idleness. And although this disposition, so far as it is the result of our especial constitutions and complexion, is not sin in itself, yet it dwells at the next door unto it, and, as it is excited by the moral pravity of our natures, a continual occasion of it. But the body of Christ being formed pure and exact by the Holy Ghost, there was no disposition or tendency in his constitution to the least deviation from perfect holiness in any kind. The exquisite harmony of his natural temperature made love, meekness, gentleness, patience, benignity, and goodness, natural and cognate unto him, as having an incapacity of such motions as should be subservient unto or compliant with any thing different from them. Hence, secondly, also, although he took on him those infirmities which belong unto our human nature as such, and are inseparable from it until it be glorified, yet he took none of our particular infirmities which cleave unto our persons, occasioned either by the vice of our constitutions or irregularity in the use of our bodies. Those natural passions of our minds which are capable of being the means of affliction and trouble, as grief, sorrow, and the like, he took upon him; as also those infirmities of nature which are troublesome to the body, as hunger, thirst, weariness, and pain, — yea, the purity of his holy constitution made him more highly sensible of these things than any of the children of men; — but as to our bodily diseases and distempers, which personally adhere unto us, upon the disorder and vice of our constitutions, he was absolutely free from [them].

Footnotes:

16. Δῆλόν ἐστιν ὅτι καὶ τὴν τοῦ παντὸς τέλους ὥραν ὡς μὲν λόγος γινώσκει, ὡς δὲ ἄνθρωπος ἀγνοεῖ. Ἀνθρώπου γὰρ ἴδιον τὸ ἀγνοεῖν, καὶ μάλιστα ταῦτα. Ἀλλὰ καὶ τοῦτο τῆς φιλανθρωπίας ἴδιον τοῦ σωτῆρος. Ἐπειδὴ γὰρ γέγονεν ἄνθρωπος, οὐκ ἐπῃσχύνετο διὰ τὴν σάρκα τὴν ἀγνοοῦσαν εἰπεῖν, οὐκ οἶδα. Ἵνα δείξῃ ὅτι εἰδὼς ὡς θεὸς ἀγνοεῖ σαρκικῶς. — Athanas. Orat. iv. ad Arian.Ἀγνοεῖ τοίνυν κατὰ τὸ σχῆμα τῆς ἀνθρωπότητος, ὁ γινώσκων τὰ πάντα κατὰ τὴν δύναμιν τῆς θεότητος. — Chrysost. tom. vii. serm. 117.Πλὴν ἰστέον, ὅτι οἱ πολλοὶ τῶν πατέρων, σχεδὸν δὲ πάντες, φαίνονται λέγοντες αὐτὸν ἀγνοειν. Εἰ γὰρ κατὰ πάντα λέγεται ἡμῖν ὁμοούσιος, ἀγνοοῦμεν δὲ καὶ ἡμεῖς, δῆλον ὅτι καὶ αὐτὸς ἠγνόει. — Leontius Byzantinus, de Sectis.

17. "Maximum in totâ creaturâ testimonium de divinitate Spiritus Sancti corpus Domini est; quod ex Spiritu Sancto esse creditur secundum evangelistam, Matt. i., sicut angelus ad Josephum dicit, Quod in ea natum est de Spiritu Sancto est." — Athanas. de Fid. Un. et Trin."Creatrix virtus altissimi, superveniente Spiritu Sancto in virginem Mariam, Christi corpus fabricavit; quo ille usus templo sine viri natus est semine" — Didym. de Spir. Sanc. lib. ii.

18. Εἴ τις λέγει πρῶτον πεπλάσθαι τὸ σῶμα τοῦ κυρίου ἡμῶν Ἰησοῦ Χριστοῦ ἐν τῇ μήτρᾳ τῆς ἁγίας παρθένου, καὶ μετὰ ταῦτα ἑνωθῆναι αὐτῷ τὸν Θεὸν λόγον, καὶ τὴν ψυχὴν ὡς προϋπάρξασαν, ἀνάθεμα ἔστω. — Concil. Constantinop. ad Origenistas.

Chapter IV - Work of the Holy Spirit in and on the human nature of Christ

The actual sanctification of the human nature of Christ by the Holy Ghost — On what ground spotless and free from sin — Positively endowed with all grace — Original holiness and sanctification in Christ, how carried on by the Spirit — Exercise of grace in Christ by the rational faculties of his soul — Their improvement — Wisdom and knowledge, how increased objectively in the human nature of Christ — The anointing of Christ by the Holy Spirit with power and gifts — Collated eminently on him at his baptism — John iii. 34 explained and vindicated — Miraculous works wrought in Christ by the Holy Ghost — Christ guided, conducted, and supported by the Spirit in his whole work — Mark i. 12 opened — How the Lord Christ offered himself unto God through the eternal Spirit — His sanctification thereunto — Graces acting eminently therein — Love, zeal, submission, faith, and truth, all exercised therein — The work of the Spirit of God towards Christ whilst he was in the state of the dead; in his resurrection and glorification — The office of the Spirit to bear witness unto Christ, and its discharge — The true way and means of coming unto the knowledge of Christ, with the necessity thereof — Danger of mistakes herein — What it is to love Christ as we ought.

Secondly, The human nature of Christ being thus formed in the womb by a creating act of the Holy Spirit, was in the instant of its conception sanctified, and filled with grace according to the measure of its receptivity. Being not begotten by natural generation, it derived no taint of original sin or corruption from Adam, that being the only way and means of its propagation; and being not in the loins of Adam morally before the fall, the promise of his incarnation being not given until afterward, the sin of Adam could on no account be imputed unto him. All sin was charged on him as our mediator and surety of the covenant; but on his own account he was obnoxious to no charge of sin, original or actual. His nature, therefore, as miraculously created in the manner described, was absolutely innocent, spotless, and free from sin, as was Adam in the day wherein he was created. But this was not all; it was by the Holy Spirit positively endowed with all grace. And hereof it was afterward only capable of farther degrees as to actual exercise, but not of any new kind of grace. And this work of sanctification, or the original infusion of all grace into the human nature of Christ, was the immediate work of the Holy Spirit; which was necessary unto him: for let the natural faculties of the soul, the mind, will, and affections, be created pure, innocent, undefiled, — as they cannot be otherwise immediately created of God, — yet there is not enough to enable any rational creature to live to God; much less was it all that was in Jesus Christ. There is, moreover, required hereunto supernatural endowments of grace, superadded unto the natural faculties of our souls. If we live unto God, there must be a principle of spiritual life in us, as well [as] of life natural. This was the image of God in Adam, and was wrought in Christ by the Holy Spirit: Isa. xi. 1–3,

"There shall come forth a rod out of the stem of Jesse, and a Branch shall grow out of his roots: and the Spirit of the Lord shall rest upon him, the Spirit of wisdom and understanding, the Spirit of counsel and might, the Spirit of knowledge and of the fear of the Lord; and shall make him of quick understanding in the fear of the Lord." It is granted that the following work of the Spirit in and upon the Lord Christ, in the execution of his office as the king and head of the church, is included in these words; but his first sanctifying work in the womb is principally intended: for these expressions, "A rod out of the stem of Jesse," and "A Branch out of his roots," with respect whereunto the Spirit is said to be communicated unto him, do plainly regard his incarnation; and the soul of Christ, from the first moment of its infusion, was a subject capable of a fullness of grace, as unto its habitual residence and in-being, though the actual exercise of it was suspended for a while, until the organs of the body were fitted for it. This, therefore, it received by this first unction of the Spirit. Hence, from his conception, he was "holy," as well as "harmless" and "undefiled," Heb. vii. 26; a "holy thing," Luke i. 35; radically filled with a perfection of grace and wisdom, inasmuch as the Father "gave him not the Spirit by measure," John iii. 34. See to this purpose our commentary on Heb. i. 1; see also John i. 14–17.

Thirdly, The Spirit carried on that work whose foundation he had thus laid. And two things are to be here diligently observed:—

1. That the Lord Christ, as man, did and was to exercise all grace by the rational faculties and powers of his soul, his understanding, will, and affections; for he acted grace as a man, "made of a woman, made under the law." His divine nature was not unto him in the place of a soul, nor did immediately operate the things which he performed, as some of old vainly imagined; but being a perfect man, his rational soul was in him the immediate principle of all his moral operations, even as ours are in us. Now, in the improvement and exercise of these faculties and powers of his soul, he had and made a progress after the manner of other men; for he was made like unto us "in all things," yet without sin. In their increase, enlargement, and exercise, there was required a progression in grace also; and this he had continually by the Holy Ghost: Luke ii. 40, "The child grew, and waxed strong in spirit." The first clause refers to his body, which grew and increased after the manner of other men; as verse 52, he "increased in stature." The other respects the confirmation of the faculties of his mind, — he "waxed strong in spirit." So, verse 52, he is said to "increase in wisdom and stature."[19]

He was πληρούμενος σοφίας, continually "filling and filled" with new degrees "of wisdom," as to its exercise, according as the rational faculties of his mind were capable thereof; an increase in these things accompanied his years, verse 52. And what is here recorded by the evangelist contains a description of the accomplishment of the prophecy before mentioned, Isa. xi. 1–3. And this growth in grace and wisdom was the peculiar work of the Holy Spirit; for as the faculties of his mind were enlarged by degrees and strengthened, so the Holy Spirit filled them up with grace for actual obedience.

2. The human nature of Christ was capable of having new objects proposed to its mind and understanding, whereof before it had a simple nescience. And this is an inseparable adjunct of human nature as such, as it is to be weary or hungry, and no vice or blamable defect. Some have made a great outcry about the ascribing of ignorance by some protestant divines unto the human soul of

Christ: Bellarm. de Anim. Christi. Take" ignorance" for that which is a moral defect in any kind, or an unacquaintedness with that which anyone ought to know, or is necessary unto him as to the perfection of his condition or his duty, and it is false that ever any of them ascribed it unto him. Take it merely for a nescience of some things, and there is no more in it but a denial of infinite omniscience, — nothing inconsistent with the highest holiness and purity of human nature. So the Lord Christ says of himself that he knew not the day and hour of the end of all things, [Mark xiii. 32]; and our apostle of him, that he "learned obedience by the things that he suffered," Heb. v. 8. In the representation, then, of things anew to the human nature of Christ, the wisdom and knowledge of it was objectively increased, and in new trials and temptations he experimentally learned the new exercise of grace. And this was the constant work of the Holy Spirit in the human nature of Christ. He dwelt in him in fullness; for he received him not by measure. And continually, upon all occasions, he gave out of his unsearchable treasures grace for exercise in all duties and instances of it. From hence was he habitually holy, and from hence did he exercise holiness entirely and universally in all things.

Fourthly, The Holy Spirit, in a peculiar manner, anointed him with all those extraordinary powers and gifts which were necessary for the exercise and discharging of his office on the earth:[20] Isa. lxi. 1, "The Spirit of the Lord God is upon me; because the Lord hath anointed me to preach good tidings unto the meek; he hath sent me to bind up the brokenhearted, to proclaim liberty to the captives, and the opening of the prison to them that are bound."

It is the prophetical office of Christ, and his discharge thereof in his ministry on the earth, which is intended. And he applies these words unto himself with respect unto his preaching of the gospel, Luke iv. 18, 19; for this was that office which he principally attended unto here in the world, as that whereby he instructed men in the nature and use of his other offices. For his kingly power, in his human nature on the earth, he exercised it but sparingly. Thereunto, indeed, belonged his sending forth of apostles and evangelists to preach with authority. And towards the end of his ministry he instituted ordinances of gospel worship, and appointed the order of his church in the foundation and building of it up; which were acts of kingly power. Nor did he perform any act of his sacerdotal office but only at his death, when he "gave himself for us an offering and a sacrifice to God for a sweet-smelling savour," Eph. v. 2; wherein God "smelled a savour of rest," and was appeased towards us. But the whole course of his life and ministry was the discharge of his prophetical office unto the Jews, Rom. xv. 8; which he was to do according to the great promise, Deut. xviii. 18, 19: and on the acceptance or refusal of him herein depended the life and death of the church of Israel, verse 19; Acts iii. 23; Heb. ii. 3; John viii. 24. Hereunto was he fitted by this unction of the Spirit. And here, also, is a distinction between the "Spirit that was upon him," and his being "anointed to preach," which contains the communication of the gifts of that Spirit unto him; as it is said, Isa. xi. 2, 3, "The Spirit rested upon him as a Spirit of wisdom," to make him "of quick understanding in the fear of the Lord." Now, this was in a singular manner and in a measure inexpressible, whence he is said to be "anointed with the oil of gladness above his fellows," or those who were partakers of the same Spirit with him, Ps. xlv. 7; Heb. i. 8, 9; although I acknowledge that there was in that expression a peculiar respect unto his glorious exaltation, which afterward ensued, as hath been declared on that place. And this collation of extraordinary gifts for the discharge of his prophetical office was at his baptism, Matt. iii. 17.

They were not bestowed on the Head of the church, nor are any gifts of the same nature in general bestowed on any of his members, but for use, exercise, and improvement. And that they were then collated appears; for, —

1. Then did he receive the visible pledge which confirmed him in, and testified unto others his calling of God to, the exercise of his office; for then "the Spirit of God descended like a dove, and lighted upon him: and lo a voice came from heaven, saying, This is my beloved Son, in whom I am well pleased," Matt. iii. 16, 17. Hereby was he "sealed of God the Father," John vi. 27, in that visible pledge of his vocation, setting the great seal of heaven to his commission. And this also was to be a testimony unto others, that they might own him in his office, now he had undertaken to discharge it, chap. i. 33.

2. He now entered on his public ministry, and wholly gave himself up unto his work; for before, he did only occasionally manifest the presence of God with him, somewhat to prepare the minds of men to attend unto his ministry, as when he filled them with astonishment at his discourses with the doctors in the temple, Luke ii. 46, 47. And although it is probable that he might be acted by the Spirit in and unto many such extraordinary actions during his course of a private life, yet the fullness of gifts for his work he received not until the time of his baptism, and, therefore, before that he gave not himself up wholly unto his public ministry.

3. Immediately hereon it is said that he was "full of the Holy Ghost," Luke iv. 1. Before, he was said to "wax strong in spirit," πληρούμενος σοφίας, chap. ii. 40, "continually filling;" but now he is πλήρης Πνεύματος Ἁγίου, "full of the Holy Ghost." He was actually possessed of and furnished with all that fullness of spiritual gifts which were any way needful for him or useful unto him, or which human nature is capable of receiving. With respect hereunto doth the evangelist [baptist?] use that expression, Οὐ γὰρ ἐκ μέτρου δίδωσιν ὁ Θεὸς τὸ Πνεῦμα, John iii. 34, — "For God giveth not the Spirit by measure." That it is the Lord Jesus Christ who is here intended, unto whom the Spirit is thus given, is evident from the context, although it be not express[ed] in the text. He is spoken of, and is the subject of the whole discourse: Verse 31, "He that cometh from above is above all: he that cometh from heaven is above all." None doubts but that this is a description of the person of Christ. And in the beginning of this verse, "He whom God hath sent speaketh the words of God;" which is the usual periphrasis of the Lord Christ, used at least twenty times in this Gospel. Of him this account is given, that he "testifieth what he hath seen and heard," verse 32; and that he "speaketh the words of God," verse 34. Different events are also marked upon his testimony, for many refused it, verse 32, but some received it, who therein "set to their seal that God is true," verse 33; for he that "believeth not the record that he gave of his Son hath made him a liar," 1 John v. 10. As a reason of all this, it is added that "God gave not the Spirit by measure unto him;" so that he was fully enabled to "speak the words of God," and those by whom his testimony was rejected were justly liable to "wrath," verse 36. Vain, therefore, is the attempt of Crellius, de Spir. Sanc., followed by Schlichtingius in his comment on this place, who would exclude the Lord Christ from being intended in these words; for they would have them signify no more but only in general that God is not bound up to measures in the dispensation of the Spirit, but gives to one according unto one measure, and to another according to

another. But as this gloss overthrows the coherence of the words, disturbing the context, so it contradicts the text itself: for God's not giving the Spirit ἐκ μέτρου, "by measure," is his giving of him ἀμέτρως, "immeasurably," without known bounds or limits, and so the Spirit was given unto the Lord Christ only; for "unto every one of us is given grace according to the measure of the gift of Christ," Eph. iv. 7, — that is, in what measure he pleaseth to communicate and distribute it. But the effects of this giving of the Spirit unto the Lord Christ not by measure belonged unto that fullness from whence we "receive grace for grace," John i. 16; for hereby the Father accomplished his will, when "it pleased him that in him should all fullness dwell," that "in all things he might have the pre-eminence," Col. i. 18, 19. Nor can any difficulty of weight be cast on this interpretation from the use of the word in the present tense, which is by Crellius insisted on, — δίδωσι, "he giveth:" "For Christ," they say, "had before received the Spirit, for this is spoken of him after his baptism. If, therefore, he had been intended, it should rather have been, 'he hath given,' or 'he hath not given unto him by measure.'" But, — (1.) This was immediately on his baptism, and therefore the collation of the fullness of the Spirit might be spoken of as a thing present, being but newly past; which is an ordinary kind of speech on all occasions. Besides, (2.) The collation of the Spirit is a continued act, in that he was given him to abide with him, to rest upon him, wherein there was a continuance of the love of God towards and his care over him in his work. Hence the Lord Christ saith of himself, or the prophet in his person, that the Spirit sent him: "Now the Lord God, and his Spirit, hath sent me," Isa. xlviii. 16. The same work in sending of Christ is ascribed unto the "Lord God," that is, the Father, and to the "Spirit," but in a different manner. He was sent by the Father authoritatively; and the furniture he received by the Spirit, of gifts for his work and office, is called his sending of him; as the same work is assigned unto different persons in the Trinity on different accounts. Fifthly, It was in an especial manner by the power of the Holy Spirit he wrought those great and miraculous works whereby his ministry was attested unto and confirmed. Hence it is said that God wrought miracles by him: Acts ii. 22, "Jesus of Nazareth, a man approved of God by miracles and wonders and signs, which God did by him;" for they are all immediate effects of divine power. So when he cast out devils with a word of command, he affirms that he did it by the "finger of God," Luke xi. 20, — that is, by the infinite divine power of God. But the power of God acted in an especial manner by the Holy Spirit, as is expressly declared in the other evangelist, Matt. xii. 28; and, therefore, on the ascription of his mighty works unto Beelzebub, the prince of devils, he lets the Jews know that therein they blasphemed the Holy Spirit, whose works indeed they were, verses 31, 32. Hence these mighty works are called δυνάμεις, "powers," because of the power of the Spirit of God put forth for their working and effecting: see Mark vi. 5, ix. 39; Luke iv. 36, v. 17, vi. 19, viii. 46, ix. 1. And in the exercise of this power consisted the testimony given unto him by the Spirit that he was the Son of God; for this was necessary unto the conviction of the Jews, to whom he was sent, John x. 37, 38.

Sixthly, By him was he guided, directed, comforted, supported, in the whole course of his ministry, temptations, obedience, and sufferings. Some few instances on this head may suffice. Presently after his baptism, when he was full of the Holy Ghost, he was "led by the Spirit into the wilderness," Luke iv. 1. 1. The Holy Spirit guided him to begin his contest and conquest with the devil. Hereby he made an entrance into his ministry; and it teacheth us all what we must look for if we solemnly engage ourselves to follow him in the work of preaching the gospel. The word used in Mark to this purpose hath occasioned some doubt what spirit is intended in these words, Τὸ πνεῦμα αὐτὸν ἐκβάλλει εἰς τὴν ἔρημον, chap. i. 12, "The spirit driveth him into the wilderness." It is evident that the same spirit and the same act are intended in all the evangelists, here, and Matt. iv. 1, Luke iv. 1. But how the Holy Spirit should be said ἐκβάλλειν, to "drive him," is not so easy to be apprehended. But the word in Luke is ἤγετο, which denotes a guiding and rational conduct; and this cannot be ascribed unto any other spirit, with respect unto our Lord Jesus, but only the Spirit of God. Matthew expresseth the same effect by ἀνήχθη, chap. iv. 1, — he was "carried," or "carried up," or "taken away," from the midst of the people. And this was ὑπὸ τοῦ Πνεύματος, "of that Spirit," — namely, which descended on him and rested on him immediately before, chap. iii. 16. And the continuation of the discourse in Luke will not admit that any other spirit be intended: "And Jesus being full of the Holy Spirit returned from Jordan, and was led by the Spirit into the wilderness," — namely, by that Spirit which he was full of. By ἐκβάλλει, therefore, in Mark, no more is intended but the sending of him forth by a high and strong impression of the Holy Spirit on his mind. Hence the same word is used with respect unto the sending of others, by the powerful impression of the Spirit of God on their hearts, unto the work of preaching the gospel: Matt. ix. 38, "Pray ye therefore the Lord of the harvest," ὅπως ἐκβάλλῃ ἐργάλλῃ ἐργάτας εἰς τὸν θερισμὸν αὐτοῦ, "that he would thrust forth labourers into his harvest," — namely, by furnishing them with the gifts of his Spirit, and by the power of his grace constraining them to their duty. So also Luke x. 2. So did he enter upon his preparation unto his work under his conduct; and it were well if others would endeavour after a conformity unto him within the rules of their calling. 2. By his assistance was he carried triumphantly through the course of his temptations unto a perfect conquest of his adversary as to the present conflict, wherein he sought to divert him from his work; which afterward he endeavoured by all ways and means to oppose and hinder. 3. The temptation being finished, he returned again out of the wilderness, to preach the gospel "in the power of the Spirit," chap. iv. 14. He returned ἐν τῇ δυνάμει τοῦ Πνεύματος, "in the power of the Spirit" into Galilee, — that is, powerfully enabled by the Holy Spirit unto the discharge of his work; and hence, in his first sermon at Nazareth, he took these words of the prophet for his text, "The Spirit of the Lord is upon me, because he hath anointed me to preach the gospel to the poor," verse 18. The issue was, that they "all bare him witness, and wondered at the gracious words which proceeded out of his mouth," verse 22. And as he thus began his ministry in the power of the Spirit, so, having received him not by measure, he continually on all occasions put forth his wisdom, power, grace, and knowledge, to the astonishment of all, and the stopping of the mouths of his adversaries, shutting them up in their rage and unbelief. 4. By him was he directed, strengthened, and comforted, in his whole course, — in all his temptations, troubles, and sufferings, from first to last; for we know that there was a confluence of all these upon him in his whole way and work, a great part of that whereunto he humbled himself for our sakes consisting in these things. In and under them he stood in need of mighty supportment and strong consolation. This God promised unto him, and this he expected, Isa. xlii. 4, 6, xlix. 5–8, l. 7, 8. Now, all the voluntary communications of the divine nature unto the human were, as we have showed, by the Holy Spirit.

Seventhly, He offered himself up unto God through the eternal Spirit, Heb. ix. 14. I know many learned men do judge that by the "eternal Spirit" in that place, not the third person is intended, but the divine nature of the Son himself; and there is no doubt but that also may properly be called the eternal Spirit. There is also a reason in the words themselves strongly inclining unto that sense and acceptation of them: for the apostle doth show whence it was that the sacrifice of the Lord Christ had an efficacy beyond and above the sacrifices of the law, and whence it would certainly produce that great effect of "purging our consciences from dead works;" and this was, from the dignity of his person, on the account of his divine nature. It arose, I say, from the dignity of his person, his deity giving sustentation unto his human nature in the sacrifice of himself; for by reason of the indissoluble union of both his natures, his person became the principle of all his mediatory acts, and from thence had they their dignity and efficacy. Nor will I oppose this exposition of the words. But, on the other side, many learned persons, both of the ancient and modern divines, do judge that it is the person of the Holy Spirit that is intended.

And because this is a matter of great importance, — namely, how the Lord Christ offered up himself unto God as a sacrifice by the eternal Spirit, — I shall farther explain it, though but briefly. Those who look only on the outward part of the death of Christ can see nothing but suffering in it. The Jews took him, and they with the soldiers both scourged and slew him, hanging him on the tree. But the principal consideration of it is his own offering himself a sacrifice unto God, as the great high priest of the church, to make atonement and reconciliation for sinners, which was hid from the world by those outward acts of violence which were upon him; and this he did by the eternal Spirit, wherein we may take notice of the ensuing instances:—

1. He sanctified, consecrated, or dedicated himself unto God for to be an offering or sacrifice: John xvii. 19, "For their sakes," — that is, the elect, — "I sanctify myself." The Lord Christ was before this perfectly sanctified as to all inherent holiness, so that he could not speak of sanctifying himself afresh in that sense. Neither was it the consecration of himself unto his office of a priest; for this was the act of him who called him: "He glorified not himself to be made an high priest; but he that said unto him, Thou art my Son," Heb. v. 5. He made him a priest by his death, "after the power of an endless life," chap. vii. 16, 20, 21. Wherefore, he consecrated himself to be a sacrifice, as the beast to be sacrificed of old was first devoted unto that purpose. Therefore it is said that he thus sanctified or consecrated himself that we might be sanctified. Now, "we are sanctified through the offering of the body of Jesus Christ once for all," Heb. x. 10. This was his first sacerdotal act. He dedicated himself to be an offering to God; and this he did through the effectual operation of the eternal Spirit in him.

2. He went voluntarily and of his own accord to the garden; which answered the adduction or bringing of the beast to be sacrificed unto the door of the tabernacle, according to the law: for there he did not only give up himself into the hands of those who were to shed his blood, but also actually entered upon the offering up of himself unto God in his agony, when he "offered up prayers and supplications with strong crying and tears," Heb. v. 7; which declares not the matter, but the manner of his offering.

3. In all that ensued, all that followed hereon, unto his giving up the ghost, he offered himself to God in and by those actings of the grace of the Holy Spirit in him, which accompanied him to the last. And these are diligently to be considered, because on them depend the efficacy of the death of Christ as to atonement and merit, as they were enhanced and rendered excellent by the worth and dignity of his person; for it is not the death of Christ, merely as it was penal and undergone by the way of suffering, that is the means of our deliverance, but the obedience of Christ therein, which consisted in his offering of himself through the eternal Spirit unto God, that gave efficacy and success unto it. We may, therefore, inquire what were those principal graces of the Spirit which he acted in this offering of himself unto God; and they were, —

(1.) Love to mankind, and compassion towards sinners. This the holy soul of the Lord Jesus was then in the highest and most inconceivable exercise of. This, therefore, is frequently expressed where mention is made of this offering of Christ: Gal. ii. 20, "Who loved me, and gave himself for me." Rev. i. 5, "Who loved us and washed us from our sins in his own blood." And compassion is the first grace required in a high priest or sacrificer, Heb. v. 2. God being now upon a design of love (for it was in the pursuit of eternal love that Christ was sent into the world, John iii. 16; Tit. iii. 4–6), this love, that was now in its most inconceivable advancement in the heart of Christ, was most grateful and acceptable unto him. And this intenseness of love did also support the mind of Christ under all his sufferings; as Jacob, through the greatness of his love unto Rachel, made light of the seven years' service that he endured for her, Gen. xxix. 20. And so did the Lord Christ "endure the cross and despise the shame for the joy" of saving his elect "which was set before him," Heb. xii. 2. And this was one grace of the eternal Spirit whereby he offered himself unto God.

(2.) That which principally acted him in the whole was his unspeakable zeal for, and ardency of affection unto, the glory of God. These were the coals which with a vehement flame, as it were, consumed the sacrifice. And there were two things that he aimed at with respect unto the glory of God:— [1.] The manifestation of his righteousness, holiness, and severity against sin. His design was, to repair the glory of God, wherein it had seemed to suffer by sin. Ps. xl. 6–8, Heb. x. 5–7, He came to do that, with full desire of soul, (expressed in these words, "Lo, I come,") which legal sacrifices could not do, — namely, to make satisfaction to the justice of God for sin, to be "a propitiation, to declare his righteousness," Rom. iii. 25. And this he doth, as to the manner of it, with inexpressible ardency of zeal and affections: Ps. xl. 8, "I delight to do thy will, O my God: yea, thy law is in the midst of my bowels." He doubles the expression of the intenseness of his mind hereon. And, therefore, when he was to prepare himself in his last passover for his suffering, he expresseth the highest engagement of heart and affections unto it: Luke xxii. 15, "With desire I have desired to eat this passover with you before I suffer;" as with respect unto the same work he had before expressed it, "I have a baptism to be baptized with, and how am I straitened," or pained, "till it be accomplished!" chap. xii. 50. His zeal to advance the glory of God, in the manifestation of his righteousness and holiness, by the offering up of himself as a sin-offering to make atonement, gave him no rest and ease until he was engaged in it, whence it wrought unto the utmost. [2.] The exercise of his grace and love. This he knew was the way to open the treasures of grace and love, that they might be poured out on sinners, to the everlasting glory of God; for this was the design of God in the whole, Rom. iii. 24–26. This zeal and affection unto the glory of God's righteousness, faithfulness, and grace, which was wrought in the heart of Christ by the eternal Spirit, was that wherein principally he offered up himself unto God.

(3.) His holy submission and obedience unto the wilt of God, which were now in the height of their exercise, and grace advanced unto the utmost in them, was another especial part of this his offering up of himself. That this was wrought in him by the holy or eternal Spirit was before declared. And it is frequently expressed as that which had an especial influence into the efficacy and merit of his sacrifice: Phil. ii. 8, "He humbled himself, and became obedient unto death, even the death of the cross." And when he "offered up prayers and supplications, though he were a Son, yet learned he obedience by the things which he suffered," Heb. v. 7, 8; that is, he experienced obedience in suffering. It is true that the Lord Christ, in the whole course of his life, yielded obedience unto God, as he was "made of a woman, made under the law," Gal. iv. 4; but now he came to the great trial of it, with respect unto the especial command of the Father "to lay down his life," and to "make his soul an offering for sin," Isa. liii. 10. This was the highest act of obedience unto God that ever was, or ever shall be to all eternity; and therefore doth God so express his satisfaction therein and acceptance of it, Isa. liii. 11, 12; Phil. ii. 9, 10. This was wrought in him, this he was wrought unto, by the Holy Spirit; and therefore by him he offered himself unto God.

(4.) There belongs also hereunto that faith and trust in God which, with fervent prayers, cries, and supplications, he now acted on God and his promises, both with respect unto himself and to the covenant which he was sealing with his blood. This our apostle represents as an especial work of his, testified unto in the Old Testament: Heb. ii. 13, "I will put my trust in him." And, [1.] This respected himself, namely, that he should be supported, assisted, and carried through the work he had undertaken unto a blessed issue. Herein, I confess, he was horribly assaulted, until he cried out, "My God, my God, why hast thou forsaken me?" Ps. xxii. 1; but yet, after and through all his dreadful trial, his faith and trust in God were victorious. This he expressed in the depth and extremity of his trials, verses 9–11; and made such an open profession of it that his enemies, when they supposed him lost and defeated, reproached him with it, verse 8; Matt. xxvii. 43. To this purpose he declares himself at large, Isa. l. 7–9. So his faith and trust in God, as to his own supportment and deliverance, with the accomplishment of all the promises that were made unto him upon his engagement into the work of mediation, were victorious. [2.] This respected the covenant, and all the benefits that the church of the elect was to be made partaker of thereby. The blood that he now shed was the "blood of the covenant," and it was shed for his church, namely, that the blessings of the covenant, might be communicated unto them, Gal. iii. 13, 14. With respect hereunto did he also exercise faith in God, as appears fully in his prayer which he made when he entered on his oblation, John xvii.

Now, concerning these instances we may observe three things to our present purpose:— (1.) These and the like gracious actings of the soul of Christ were the ways and means whereby, in his death and blood-shedding, — which was violent and by force inflicted on him as to the outward instruments, and was penal as to the sentence of the law, — he voluntarily and freely offered up himself a sacrifice unto God for to make atonement; and these were the things which, from the dignity of his person, became efficacious and victorious.

Without these his death and blood-shedding had been no oblation.

(2.) These were the things which rendered his offering of himself a "sacrifice to God of a sweet-smelling savour," Eph. v. 2. God was so absolutely delighted and pleased with these high and glorious acts of grace and obedience in Jesus Christ that he smelled, as it were, a "savour of rest" towards mankind, or those for whom he offered himself, so that he would be angry with them no more, curse them no more, as it is said of the type of it in the sacrifice of Noah, Gen. viii. 20, 21. God was more pleased with the obedience of Christ than he was displeased with the sin and disobedience of Adam, Rom. v. 17–21. It was not, then, [by] the outward suffering of a violent and bloody death, which was inflicted on him by the most horrible wickedness that ever human nature brake forth into, that God was atoned, Acts ii. 23; nor yet was it merely his enduring the penalty of the law that was the means of our deliverance; but the voluntary giving up of himself to be a sacrifice in these holy acts of obedience was that upon which, in an especial manner, God was reconciled unto us. (3.) All these things being wrought in the human nature by the Holy Ghost, who, in the time of his offering, acted all his graces unto the utmost, he is said thereon to "offer himself unto God through the eternal Spirit," by whom, as our high priest, he was consecrated, spirited, and acted thereunto.

Eighthly, There was a peculiar work of the Holy Spirit towards the Lord Christ whilst he was in the state of the dead; for here our preceding rule must be remembered, — namely, that notwithstanding the union of the human nature of Christ with the divine person of the Son, yet the communications of God unto it, beyond subsistence, were voluntary. Thus in his death the union of his natures in his person was not in the least impeached; but yet for his soul or spirit, he commends that in an especial manner into the hands of God his Father, — Ps. xxxi. 5, Luke xxiii. 46, "Father, into thy hands I commend my spirit," — for the Father had engaged himself in an eternal covenant to take care of him, to preserve and protect him even in death, and to show him again the "way and path of life," Ps. xvi. 11. Notwithstanding, then, the union of his person, his soul in its separate state was in an especial manner under the care, protection, and power of the Father, preserved in his love until the hour came wherein he showed him again the path of life. His holy body in the grave continued under the especial care of the Spirit of God; and hereby was accomplished that great promise, that "his soul should not be left in hell, nor the Holy One see corruption," Ps. xvi. 10; Acts ii. 31. It is the body of Christ which is here called "The Holy One," as it was made a "holy thing" by the conception of it in the womb by the power of the Holy Ghost. And it is here spoken of in contradistinction unto his soul, and opposed by Peter unto the body of David, which when it died saw corruption, Acts ii. 29. This pure and holy substance was preserved in its integrity by the overshadowing power of the Holy Spirit, without any of those accidents of change which attend the dead bodies of others. I deny not but there was use made of the ministry of angels about the dead body of Christ whilst it was in the grave, even those which were seen sitting afterward in the place where he lay, John xx. 12; by these was it preserved from all outward force and violation; — but this also was under the peculiar care of the Spirit of God, who how he worketh by angels hath been before declared.

Ninthly, There was a peculiar work of the Holy Spirit in his resurrection, this being the completing act in laying the foundation of the church, whereby Christ entered into his rest, — the great testimony given unto the finishing of the work of redemption, with the satisfaction of God therein, and his acceptation of the person of the Redeemer. It is, on various accounts, assigned distinctly to each person in the Trinity; and this not only as all the external works of God are undivided, each person being equally concerned in their operation, but also upon the account of their especial respect unto and interest in the work of redemption, in the manner before declared. Unto the Father it is ascribed, on the account of his authority, and the declaration therein of Christ's perfect accomplishment of the work committed unto him: Acts ii. 24, "Him hath God raised up, having loosed the pains of death: because it was not possible that he should be holden of it." It is the Father who is spoken of, and he is said, as in other places, to raise Christ from the dead; but this he doth with respect unto "his loosing the pains of death," — λύσας τὰς ὠδῖνας τοῦ θανάτου. These are the חֶבְלֵי־מָוֶת, which, with a little alteration of one vowel,[21] signify the "sorrows of death," or the "cords of death;" for חֶבְלֵי־מָוֶת, are the "sorrows of death," and חֶבְלֵי־מָוֶת, are the "cords of death." See Ps. xviii. 4, cxvi. 3. And the "sorrows of death" here intended were the "cords" of it, — that is, the power it had to bind the Lord Christ for a season under it; for the "pains of death," that is, the ὠδῖνες, "tormenting pains," ended in his death itself. But the consequents of them are here reckoned unto them, or the continuance under the power of death, according unto the sentence of the law. These God loosed, when, the law being fully satisfied, the sentence of it was taken off, and the Lord Christ was acquitted from its whole charge. This was the act of God the Father, as the supreme rector and judge of all. Hence he is said to "raise him from the dead," as the judge by his order delivereth an acquitted prisoner or one who hath answered the law. The same work he also takes unto himself: John x. 17, 18, "I lay down my life, that I might take it again. No man taketh it from me, but I lay it down of myself. I have power to lay it down, and I have power to take it again." For although men by violence took away his life, when "with wicked hands they crucified and slew him," Acts ii. 23, iii. 15, yet because they had neither authority nor ability so to do without his own consent, he saith no man did, or could, take away his life, — that is, against his will, by power over him, as the lives of other men are taken away; for this neither angels nor men could do. So, also, although the Father is said to raise him from the dead by taking off the sentence of the law, which he had answered, yet he himself also took his life again by an act of the love, care, and power of his divine nature, his living again being an act of his person, although the human nature only died. But the peculiar efficiency in the reuniting of his most holy soul and body was an effect of the power of the Holy Spirit: 1 Pet. iii. 18, "He was put to death in the flesh, but quickened by the Spirit;" ζωοποιηθεὶς δὲ τῷ Πνεύματι, — "he was restored to life by the Spirit." And this was that Spirit whereby he preached unto them that were disobedient in the days of Noah, verses 19, 20; or that Spirit of Christ which was in the prophets from the foundation of the world, chap. i. 11; by which he preached in Noah unto that disobedient generation, 2 Pet. ii. 5, whereby the Spirit of God strove for a season with those inhabitants of the old world, Gen. vi. 3; — that is, the Holy Spirit of God. To the same purpose we are instructed by our apostle: Rom. viii. 11, "If the Spirit of him that raised up Jesus from the dead dwell in you, he that raised up Christ from the dead shall also quicken your mortal bodies by his Spirit that dwelleth in you;" — "God shall quicken our mortal bodies also by the same Spirit whereby he raised Christ from the dead;" for so the relation of the one work to the other requires the words to be understood. And he asserts again the same expressly, Eph. i. 17–20. He prays that God would give his Holy Spirit unto them as a Spirit of wisdom and revelation, verse 17. The effects thereof in them and upon them are described, verse 18. And this he desires that they may so be made partakers of as that, by the work of the Spirit of God in themselves, renewing and quickening them, they might have an experience of that exceeding greatness of his power which he put forth in the Lord Christ when he raised him from the dead. And the evidence or testimony given unto his being the Son of God, by his resurrection from the dead, is said to be "according to the Spirit of holiness," or the Holy Spirit, Rom. i. 4. He was positively declared to be the Son of God by his resurrection from the dead, ἐν δυνάμει κατὰ Πνεῦμα ἁγιωσύνης, — that is, by the "powerful working of the Holy Spirit." This, also, is the intendment of that expression, 1 Tim. iii. 16, "Justified in the Spirit." God was "manifest in the flesh," by his incarnation and passion therein; and "justified in the Spirit," by a declaration of his acquitment from the sentence of death and all the evils which he underwent, with the reproaches wherewith he was contemptuously used, by his quickening and resurrection from the dead, through the mighty and effectual working of the Spirit of God.

Tenthly, It was the Holy Spirit that glorified the human nature [of Christ], and made it every way meet for its eternal residence at the right hand of God, and a pattern of the glorification of the bodies of them that believe on him. He who first made his nature holy, now made it glorious. And as we are made conformable unto him in our souls here, his image being renewed in us by the Spirit, so he is in his body, now glorified by the effectual operation of the same Spirit, the exemplar and pattern of that glory which in our mortal bodies we shall receive by the same Spirit; for "when he shall appear, we shall be like him," 1 John iii. 2, seeing he will "change our vile bodies, that they may be fashioned like unto his glorious body, according to the working whereby he is able even to subdue all things unto himself," Phil. iii. 21.

And these are some of the principal instances of the operation of the Holy Spirit on the human nature of the Head of the church. The whole of them all, I confess, is a work that we can look but little into; only what is plainly revealed we desire to receive and embrace, considering that if we are his, we are predestinated to be made conformable in all things unto him, and that by the powerful and effectual operation of that Spirit which thus wrought all things in him, to the glory of God. And as it is a matter of unspeakable consolation unto us to consider what hath been done in and upon our nature by the application of the love and grace of God through his Spirit unto it; so it is of great advantage, in that it directs our faith and supplications in our endeavours after conformity with him, which is our next end, under the enjoyment of God in glory. What, therefore, in these matters we apprehend, we embrace; and for the depth of them, they are the objects of our admiration and praise.

II. There is yet another work of the Holy Spirit, not immediately in and upon the person of the Lord Christ, but towards him, and on his behalf, with respect unto his work and office; and it compriseth the head and fountain of the whole office of the Holy Spirit towards the church. This was his witness-bearing unto the Lord Christ, — namely, that he was the Son of God, the true

Messiah, and that the work which he performed in the world was committed unto him by God the Father to accomplish. And this same work he continueth to attend unto unto this day, and will do so to the consummation of all things. It is known how the Lord Christ was reproached whilst he was in this world, and how ignominiously he was sent out of it by death. Hereon a great contest ensued amongst mankind, wherein heaven and hell were deeply engaged. The greatest part of the world, the princes, rulers, and wise men of it, affirmed that he was an impostor, a seducer, a malefactor, justly punished for his evil deeds. He, on the other side, chose twelve apostles to bear testimony unto the holiness of his life, the truth and purity of his doctrine, the accomplishment of the prophecies of the Old Testament in his birth, life, work, and death; and, in especial, unto his resurrection from the dead, whereby he was justified and acquitted from all the reproaches of hell and the world, and their calumnies refelled. But what could the testimony of twelve poor men, though never so honest, prevail against the confronting suffrage of the world? Wherefore, this work of bearing witness unto the Lord Christ was committed unto Him who is above and over all, who knoweth how, and is able, to make his testimony prevalent: John xv. 26, "When the Comforter is come, whom I will send unto you from the Father, even the Spirit of truth, which proceedeth from the Father, he shall testify of me." Accordingly, the apostles plead his concurring testimony: Acts v. 32, "We are his witnesses of these things; and so also is the Holy Ghost, whom God hath given to them that obey him." And how he thus gave his testimony our apostle declares, Heb. ii. 4, "God also bearing witness with them" (that is, the apostles), "both with signs and wonders, and with divers miracles, and gifts of the Holy Spirit, according to his own will." The first principal end why God gave the Holy Spirit to work all those miraculous effects in them that believed in Jesus, was, to bear witness unto his person that he was indeed the Son of God, owned and exalted by him; for no man not utterly forsaken of all reason and understanding, not utterly blinded, would once imagine that the Holy Spirit of God would work such marvellous operations in and by them who believed on him, if he designed not to justify his person, work, and doctrine thereby. And this in a short time, together with that effectual power which he put forth in and by the preaching of the word, carried not only his vindication against all the machinations of Satan and his instruments throughout the world, but also subdued the generality of mankind unto faith in him and obedience unto him, 2 Cor. x. 4, 5. And upon this testimony it is that there is real faith in him yet maintained in the world. This is that which he promised unto his disciples whilst he was yet with them in the world, when their hearts were solicitous how they should bear up against their adversaries upon his absence. "I will," saith he, "send the Comforter unto you. And when he is come, he will reprove the world of sin, and of righteousness, and of judgment: of sin, because they believe not on me; of righteousness, because I go to my Father, and ye see me no more; of judgment, because the prince of this world is judged," John xvi. 7–11. The reason why the world believed not on Christ was, because they believed not that he was sent of God, chap. ix. 29. By his testimony the Spirit was to reprove the world of their infidelity, and to convince them of it by evidencing the truth of his mission; for hereon the whole issue of the controversy between him and the world did depend. Whether he were righteous or a deceiver was to be determined by his being sent or not sent of God; and, consequently, God's acceptance or disapprobation of him. That he was so sent, so approved, the Holy Spirit convinced the world by his testimony, manifesting that he "went to the Father," and was exalted by him; for it was upon his ascension and exaltation that he received and poured out the promise of the Spirit to this purpose, Acts ii. 33. Moreover, whilst he was in the world there was an unrighteous judgment, by the instigation of Satan, passed upon him. On this testimony of the Spirit, that judgment was to be reversed, and a contrary sentence passed on the author of it, the prince of this world; for by the gospel so testified unto was he discovered, convicted, judged, condemned, and cast out of that power and rule in the world which, by the darkness of the minds of men within and idolatry without, he had obtained and exercised. And that the Holy Spirit continueth to do the same work, though not absolutely by the same means, unto this very day, shall be afterward declared.

And by these considerations may we be led into that knowledge of and acquaintance with our Lord Jesus Christ, which is so necessary, so useful, and so much recommended unto us in the Scripture. And the utter neglect of learning the knowledge of Christ, and of the truth as it is in him, is not more pernicious unto the souls of men than is the learning of it by undue means, whereby false and mischievous ideas or representations of him are infused into the minds of men. The Papists would learn and teach him by images, the work of men's hands, and teachers of lies: for besides that they are forbidden by God himself to be used unto any such purposes, and therefore cursed with barrenness and uselessness, as to any end of faith or holiness, they are in themselves suited only to ingenerate low and carnal thoughts in depraved superstitious minds; for as the worshippers of such images know not what is the proper cause nor the proper object of that reverence and those affections they find in themselves, when they approach unto them and adore before them, so the apprehensions which they can have hereby tend but to the "knowing after the flesh," which the apostle looked on as no part of his duty, 2 Cor. v. 16. But the glory of the human nature, as united unto the person of the Son of God, and engaged in the discharge of his office of mediator, consists alone in these eminent, peculiar, ineffable communications of the Spirit of God unto him, and his powerful operations in him; this is represented unto us in the glass of the gospel, which we beholding by faith, are changed into the same image by the same Spirit, 2 Cor. iii. 18.

Our Lord Christ himself did foretell us that there would be great inquiries after him, and that great deceits would be immixed therewithal. "If," saith he, "they shall say unto you, Behold, he is in the desert, go not forth: behold, he is in the secret chambers, believe it not," Matt. xxiv. 26. It is not a wilderness, low, persecuted, inglorious, and invisible condition, as to outward profession, that our Saviour here intendeth: for himself foretold that his church should be driven into the wilderness, and nourished there, and that for a long season, Rev. xii. 6; and where his church is, there is Christ, for his promise is, to be with them and among them unto the end of the world, Matt. xxviii. 20. Nor by "secret chambers" doth he intend those private places of meeting for security which all his disciples, for some hundreds of years, were compelled unto and did make use of, after his apostles, who met sometimes in an upper room, sometimes in the night, for fear of the Jews; and such, it is notorious, were all the meetings of the primitive Christians. But our Saviour here foretells the false ways that some would pretend he is taught by and found in; for, first, some would say he was ἐν τῇ ἐρήμῳ, "in the desert" or wilderness, and if men would go forth thither, there they would see him and find him. And there is nothing intended hereby but the ancient superstitious monks, who, under a pretence of religion, retired themselves into deserts and solitary places; for there they pretended great intercourse with Christ, great visions and appearances of him, being variously deluded and imposed on by Satan and their own imaginations. It is ridiculous on the one hand, and deplorable on the other, to consider the woeful follies, delusions, and superstitions this sort of men fell into; yet was in those days nothing more common than to say that Christ was in the desert, conversing with the monks and anchorites. "Go not forth unto them," saith our Lord Christ; "for in so doing ye will be deceived." And again saith he, "If they say unto you, He is ἐν τοῖς ταμείοις, in the secret chambers, believe it not." There is, or I am much deceived, a deep and mysterious instruction in these words.

Ταμεῖα signifies those secret places in a house where bread and wine and cates[22] of all sorts are laid up and stored. This is the proper signification and use of the word. What pretence, then, could there be for any to say that Christ was in such a place? Why, there ensued so great a pretence hereof, and so horrible a superstition thereon, that it was of divine wisdom to foresee it, and of divine goodness to forewarn us of it; for it is nothing but the popish figment of transubstantiation that is intended. Christ must be in the secret places where their wafer and wine were deposited, — that is, ἐν τοῖς ταμείοις. Concerning this, saith our Saviour, "Believe them not." All crafts, and frauds, and bloody violences, will be used to compel you to believe a Christ in the pix and repository; but, if you would not be seduced, "believe them not." Such are the false ways whereby some have pretended to teach Christ and to learn him, which have led them from him into hurtful snares and perdition. The consideration that we have insisted on will guide us, if attended to, unto a spiritual and saving knowledge of him. And we are to learn thus to know him, —

First, That we may love him with a pure unmixed love. It is true, it is the person of Christ as God and man that is the proper and ultimate object of our love towards him; but a clear distinct consideration of his natures and their excellencies is effectual to stir up and draw forth our love towards him. So the spouse in the Canticles, rendering a reason of her intense affections towards him, says that "he is white and ruddy, the chiefest of ten thousand;" that is, perfect in the beauty of the graces of the Holy Spirit, which rendered him exceeding amiable. So also Ps. xlv. 2. Would you, therefore, propose Christ unto your affections, so as that your love unto him may be sincere and without corruption, as it is required to be, Eph. vi. 24, that you may not lavish away the actings of your souls upon a false object, and think you love Christ, when you love only the imaginations of your own breasts? — consider his human nature, as it was rendered beautiful and lovely by the work of the Spirit of God upon it, before described. Do you love him because he was and is so full of grace, so full of holiness, because in him there was an all-fullness of the graces of the Spirit of God? Consider aright what hath been delivered concerning him, and if you can and do, on the account thereof, delight in him and love him, your love is genuine and spiritual; but if your love be merely out of an apprehension of his being now glorious in heaven, and there able to do you good or evil, it differs not much from that of the Papists, whose love is much regulated in its actings by the good or bad painting of the images whereby they represent him. You are often pressed to direct your love unto the person of Christ, and it is that which is your principal duty in this world; but this you cannot do without a distinct notion and knowledge of him. There are, therefore, three things in general that you are to consider to this purpose:— 1. The blessed union of his two natures in the same person. Herein he is singular, God having taken that especial state on him, which in no other thing or way had any consideration. This, therefore, is to have a speciality in our divine love to the person of Christ. 2. The uncreated glories of the divine nature, whence our love hath the same object with that which we owe unto God absolutely. 3. That perfection and fullness of grace which dwelt in his human nature, as communicated unto him by the Holy Spirit, whereof we have treated. If we love the person of Christ, it must be on these considerations; which whilst some have neglected, they have doted on their own imaginations, and whilst they have thought themselves even sick of love for Christ, they have only languished in their own fancies.

Secondly, We are to know Christ so as to labour after conformity unto him. And this conformity consists only in a participation of those graces whose fullness dwells in him. We can, therefore, no other way regularly press after it, but by an acquaintance with and due consideration of the work of the Spirit of God upon his human nature; which is therefore worthy of our most diligent inquiry into.

And so have we given a brief delineation of the dispensation and work of the Holy Spirit in and towards the person of our Lord Jesus Christ, the head of the church. His preparation of a mystical body for him, in his powerful gracious work on the elect of God, doth nextly ensue.

Footnotes:

19. "Quomodo proficiebat sapientiâ Dei? doceat te ordo verborum. Profectus est ætatis, profectus est sapientiæ, sed humanæ. Ideo ætatem ante præmisit, ut secundum homines crederes dictum; ætas enim non divinitatis sed corporis est. Ergo si proficiebat ætate hominis proficiebat sapientiâ hominis. Sapientia autem sensu proficit, quia a sensu sapientia." — Ambros. de Incarnat. Dom. Mysterio, chap. vii."Nam et Dominus homo accepit communicationem Spiritus Sancti; sicut in evangeliis legitur, 'Jesus ergo repletus Spiritu Sancto, regressus est a Iordane.' Hæc autem absque ullâ calumniâ de dominico homine, qui totus Christus, unus est Jesus Filius Dei, sensu debemus pietatis accipere, non quod alter et alter sit, sed quod de uno atque eodem quasi de altero, secundum naturam Dei, et hominis disputatur." — Didym. de Spir. Sanc. lib. ii.

20. Εἰ ποίνυν ἡ σὰρξ ἡ δεσποτικὴ, τὸ κυριακὸν πλάσμα, ὁ ξένος ἄνθρωπος, ὁ οὐράνιος, τὸ νέον βλάστημα, τὸ ἀπὸ τῆς ξένης ὠδῖνος ἀνθήσαν οὗτος λαμβάνει τὸ πνεῦμα ἅγιον, etc. — Chrysost. Homil. de Spir. Sanc.

21. Our author must allude to a difference in the vowel-points; חֵבֶל as in Isa. lxvi. 7, signifying pains, and חֶבֶל, with the seghol instead of the tsere, being translated cord or rope. The word occurs also in composition with בְּ under the meaning of "cords," or "fetters," as in Job xxxvi. 8, בְּחַבְלֵי־עֹנִי. — Ed.

22. Cates, viands. — Ed.

Chapter V - The general work of the Holy Spirit in the new creation with respect unto the members of that body whereof Christ is the head

Christ the head of the new creation — Things premised in general unto the remaining work of the Spirit — Things presupposed unto the work of the Spirit towards the church — The love and grace of Father and Son — The whole work of the building of the church committed to the Holy Spirit — Acts ii. 33 opened — The foundation of the church in the promise of the Spirit, and its building by him alone — -Christ present with his church only by his Spirit — Matt. xxviii. 19, 20; Acts i. 9, 10, iii. 21; Matt. xviii. 19, 20; 2 Cor. vi. 16; 1 Cor. iii. 16, compared — The Holy Spirit works the work of Christ — John xvi. 13–15 opened — The Holy Spirit the peculiar author of all grace — The Holy Spirit worketh all this according to his own will — 1. His will and pleasure is in all his works — 2. He works variously as to the kinds and degrees of his operations — How he may be resisted, how not — How the same work is ascribed unto the Spirit distinctly, and to others with him — The general heads of his operations towards the church.

We have considered the work of the Spirit of God in his laying the foundation of the church of the New Testament, by his dispensations towards the head of it, our Lord Jesus Christ. He is the foundation-stone of this building, with seven eyes engraven on him, or filled with an absolute perfection of all the gifts and graces of the Spirit, Zech. iii. 9, which when he is exalted also as "the headstone of the corner," there are shoutings in heaven and earth, crying, "Grace, grace unto him!" chap. iv. 7. As upon the laying of the foundation and placing of the corner-stone of the earth in the old creation, "the morning stars sang together, and all the sons of God shouted for joy," Job xxxviii. 6, 7; so upon the laying of this foundation, and placing of this corner-stone in the new creation, all things sing together and cry, "Grace, grace unto it!" The same hand which laid this foundation doth also finish the building. The same Spirit which was given unto him, "not by measure," John iii. 34, giveth grace unto every one of us, "according to the measure of the gift of Christ," Eph. iv. 7. And this falleth now under our consideration, — namely, the perfecting the work of the new creation by the effectual operation and distributions of the Spirit of God. And this belongs unto the establishment of our faith, that he who prepared, sanctified, and glorified the human nature, the natural body of Jesus Christ, the head of the church, hath undertaken to prepare, sanctify, and glorify his mystical body, or all the elect given unto him of the Father. Concerning which, before we come to consider particular instances, some things in general must be premised, which are these that follow:—

First, Unto the work of the Holy Spirit towards the church some things are supposed, from whence it proceeds, which it is built upon and resolved into. It is not an original but a perfecting work. Some things it supposeth, and bringeth all things to perfection; and these are, —

1. The love, grace, counsel, and eternal purpose of the Father; 2. The whole work of the mediation of Jesus Christ, (which things I have handled elsewhere;) — for it is the peculiar work of the Holy Spirit to make those things of the Father and Son effectual unto the souls of the elect, to the praise of the glory of the grace of God. God doth all things for himself, and his supreme end is the manifestation of his own glory. And in the old or first creation, he seems principally, or firstly, to intend the demonstration and exaltation of the glorious essential properties of his nature, his goodness, power, wisdom, and the like, as Ps. xix. 1–4, Rom. i. 19–21, Acts xiv. 15–17, xvii. 24–28; leaving only on the works of his hands some obscure impressions of the distinction of persons, subsisting in the unity of that Being whose properties he had displayed and glorified. But in the work of the new creation, God firstly and principally intends the especial revelation of each person of the whole Trinity distinctly, in their peculiar distinct operations; all which tend ultimately to the manifestation of the glory of his nature also. And herein consists the principal advantage of the New Testament above the Old; for although the work of the new creation was begun and carried on secretly and virtually under the Old Testament, yet they had not a full discovery of the economy of the holy Trinity therein, which was not evidently manifest until the whole work was illustriously brought to light by the gospel. Hence, although there appear a vigorous acting of faith and ardency of affection in the approaches of the saints unto God under the Old Testament, yet as unto a clear access to the Father through the Son by the Spirit, as Eph. ii. 18, wherein the life and comfort of our communion with God do consist, we hear nothing of it. Herein, therefore, God plainly declares that the foundation of the whole was laid in the counsel, will, and grace of the Father, chap. i. 3–6; then that the making way for the accomplishing of that counsel of his, so that it might be brought forth to the praise of his glory, is by the mediation of the Son, God having designed in this work to bring things so about, that "all men should honour the Son, even as they honour the Father," John v. 23. There yet remains the actual application of all to the souls of men, that they may be partakers of the grace designed in the counsel of the Father, and prepared in the mediation of the Son; and herein is the Holy Spirit to be manifested and glorified, that he also, together with the Father and the Son, may be known, adored, worshipped, according unto his own will. This is the work that he hath undertaken. And hereon, upon the solemn initiation of any person into the covenant of God, in answer unto this design and work, he is baptized into "the name of the Father, and of the Son, and of the Holy Ghost," Matt. xxviii. 19. And these things have been discoursed of before, though necessarily here called over again.

Secondly, From the nature and order of this work of God it is, that after the Son was actually exhibited in the flesh, according to the promise, and had fulfilled what he had taken upon him to do in his own person, the great promise of carrying on and finishing the whole work of the grace of God in our salvation concerns the sending of the Holy Spirit to do and perform what he also had undertaken.[23] Thus, when our Lord Jesus Christ was ascended into heaven, and began conspicuously and gloriously to carry on the building of his church upon himself, the rock and foundation of it, it is said, that, "being by the right hand of God exalted, he received of the Father the promise of the Holy Spirit," Acts ii. 33; which must be a little opened:— 1. Before he departed from his disciples, as hath been mentioned on several occasions, he comforted and cheered their drooping spirits with the promise of sending him unto them, which he often repeated and inculcated on their minds, John xiv. 15–17. And, 2. When he was actually leaving them, after his resurrection, he gives them order to sit still, and not to engage in the public work of building the church, whereunto he had designed them, until that promise were actually accomplished towards them: Acts i. 4, "Being assembled together with them, he commanded them that they should not depart from Jerusalem, but wait for the promise of the Father;" and verse 8, "Ye shall receive power, after that the Holy Ghost is come upon you; and ye shall be witnesses unto me both in Jerusalem, and in all Judea, and in Samaria, and unto the utmost part of the earth." He would have them look neither for assistance in their work, nor success unto it, but from the promised Spirit alone; and lets them know, also, that by his aid they should be enabled to carry their testimony of him to the uttermost parts of the earth. And herein lay, and herein doth lie, the foundation of the ministry of the church, as also its continuance and efficacy. The kingdom of Christ is spiritual, and, in the animating principles of it, invisible. If we fix our minds only on outward order, we lose the rise and power of the whole. It is not an outward visible ordination by men, — though that be necessary, by rule and precept, — but Christ's communication of that Spirit, the everlasting promise whereof he received of the Father, that gives being, life, usefulness, and success, to the ministry. Wherefore, also, 3. Upon his ascension, in the accomplishment of the great promises given unto the church under the Old Testament, Isa. xliv. 3, Joel ii. 28, 29, as also of his own, newly given unto his disciples, he poured forth his Spirit on them. This the apostle Peter declares in this place: "Being exalted by the right hand of God, and having received of the Father the promise of the Holy Spirit, he shed forth what they then saw and heard," in the miraculous operations and effects of it. And he is said then to receive the promise of the Father, because he then received the thing promised. The promise was not then first given unto him, nor did he then receive it for himself; for as the promise was given long before, so in his own person he had received the fullness of the Spirit from his incarnation, as hath been declared: but now he had power given him actually to fulfil and accomplish the promise in the collation of the thing promised, and is thence said to receive the promise. So Heb. xi. 13, 39, it is said of all believers under the Old Testament, that they "died in faith, not having received the promise;" that is, the thing promised was not actually exhibited in their days, though they had the promise of it, as it is expressly said of Abraham, chap. vii. 6. The promise, therefore, itself was given unto the Lord Christ, and actually received by him in the covenant of the mediator, when he undertook the great work of the restoration of all things, to the glory of God; for herein had he the engagement of the Father that the Holy Spirit should be poured out on the sons of men, to make effectual unto their souls the whole work of his mediation: wherefore, he is said now to "receive this promise," because on his account, and by him as exalted, it was now solemnly accomplished in and towards the church. In the same manner the same thing is described, Ps. lxviii. 18, "Thou hast ascended on high, thou hast led captivity captive; thou hast received gifts for men;" which is rendered, Eph.

iv. 8, "Thou hast given gifts unto men:" for he received the promise at this time only to give out the Spirit and his gifts unto men. And if any are so fond as to expect strength and assistance in the work of the ministry without him, or such success in their labours as shall find acceptance with God, they do but deceive their own souls and others.

Here lay the foundation of the Christian church: The Lord Christ had called his apostles to the great work of building his church, and the propagation of his gospel in the world. Of themselves, they were plainly and openly defective in all qualifications and abilities that might contribute any thing thereunto. But whatever is wanting in themselves, whether light, wisdom, authority, knowledge, utterance, or courage, he promiseth to supply them withal. And this he would not do, nor did, any otherwise but by sending the Holy Spirit unto them; on whose presence and assistance alone depended the whole success of their ministry in the world. It was "through the Holy Ghost that he gave commandments unto them," Acts i. 2. Those commandments concern the whole work in preaching the gospel and founding of the church; and these he gives unto them through the actings of divine wisdom in the human nature by the Holy Ghost. And on their part, without his assistance he forbids them to attempt any thing, verses 4, 8. In this promise, then, the Lord Christ founded the church itself, and by it he built it up. And this is the hinge whereon the whole weight of it doth turn and depend unto this day. Take it away, suppose it to cease as unto a continual accomplishment, and there will be an absolute end of the church of Christ in this world; — no dispensation of the Spirit, no church. He that would utterly separate the Spirit from the word had as good burn his Bible. The bare letter of the New Testament will no more ingenerate faith and obedience in the souls of men, no more constitute a church-state among them who enjoy it, than the letter of the Old Testament doth so at this day among the Jews, 2 Cor. iii. 6, 8. But blessed be God, who hath knit these things together towards his elect, in the bond of an everlasting covenant! Isa. lix. 21. Let men, therefore, cast themselves into what order they please, institute what forms of government and religious worship they think good; let them do it either by an attendance according unto the best of their understandings unto the letter of the Scripture, or else in an exercise of their own wills, wisdom, and invention, — if the work of the Spirit of God be disowned or disclaimed by them, if there be not in them and upon them such a work of his as he is promised [for] by our Lord Jesus Christ, there is no church-state amongst them, nor as such is it to be owned or esteemed. And on the ministry and the church do all ordinary communications of grace from God depend.

Thirdly, It is the Holy Spirit who supplies the bodily absence of Christ, and by him doth he accomplish all his promises to the church. Hence, some of the ancients call him "Vicarium Christi," "The vicar of Christ," or him who represents his person, and dischargeth his promised work: Operam navat Christo vicariam. When our Lord Jesus was leaving the world, he gave his disciples command to "preach the gospel," Mark xvi. 15, and to "disciple all nations" into the faith and profession thereof, Matt. xxviii. 19. For their encouragement herein, he promiseth his own presence with them in their whole work, wherever any of them should be called unto it, and that whilst he would have the gospel preached on the earth. So saith he, "I am with you alway, even unto the end of the world," or the consummation of all things, verse 20. Immediately after he had thus spoken unto them, "while they beheld, he was taken up, and a cloud received him out of their sight," and they "looked steadfastly toward heaven as he went up," Acts i. 9, 10. Where now is the accomplishment of his promise that he would be with them unto the end of all things, which was the sole encouragement he gave them unto their great undertaking? It may be that after this his triumphant ascension into heaven, to take possession of his kingdom and glory, he came again unto them, and made his abode with them. "No," saith Peter; "the heaven must receive him until the times of restitution of all things," Acts iii. 21. How, then, is this promise of his made good, which had such a peculiar respect unto the ministry and ministers of the gospel, that without it none can ever honestly or conscientiously engage in the dispensation of it, or expect the least success upon their so doing? Besides, he had promised unto the church itself, that "wherever two or three were gathered together in his name, that he would be in the midst of them," Matt. xviii. 19, 20. Hereon do all their comforts and all their acceptance with God depend. I say, all these promises are perfectly fulfilled by his sending of the Holy Spirit. In and by him he is present with his disciples in their ministry and their assemblies. And whenever Christ leaves the world, the church must do so too; for it is his presence alone which puts men into that condition, or invests them with that privilege: for so he saith, "I will dwell in them, and walk in them; and I will be their God, and they shall be my people," 2 Cor. vi. 16; Lev. xxvi. 12. Their being the "people of God," so as therewithal to be "the temple of the living God," — that is, to be brought into a sacred church-state for his worship, — depends on his "dwelling in them and walking in them." And this he doth by his Spirit alone; for, "Know ye not that ye are the temple of God, and that the Spirit of God dwelleth in you?" 1 Cor. iii. 16. He, therefore, so far represents the person, and supplies the bodily absence of Christ, that on his presence the being of the church, the success of the ministry, and the edification of the whole, do absolutely depend. And this, if any thing in the whole gospel, deserves our serious consideration; for, — 1. The Lord Jesus hath told us that his presence with us by his Spirit is better and more expedient for us than the continuance of his bodily presence. Now, who is there that hath any affection for Christ but thinks that the carnal presence of the human nature of Christ would be of unspeakable advantage unto him? And so, no doubt, it would, had any such thing been designed or appointed in the wisdom and love of God. But so it is not; and, on the other side, we are commanded to look for more advantage and benefit by his spiritual presence with us, or his presence with us by the Holy Ghost. It is, therefore, certainly incumbent on us to inquire diligently what valuation we have hereof, and what benefit we have hereby; for if we find not that we really receive grace, assistance, and consolation, from this presence of Christ with us, we have no benefit at all by him nor from him, for he is now no otherwise for these ends with any but by his Spirit. And this they will one day find whose profession is made up of such a sottish contradiction as to avow an honour for Jesus Christ, and yet blaspheme his Spirit in all his holy operations. 2. The Lord Christ having expressly promised to be present with us to the end of all things, there are great inquiries how that promise is accomplished. Some say he is present with us by his ministers and ordinances; but how, then, is he present with those ministers themselves, unto whom the promise of his presence is made in an especial manner? The Papists would have him carnally and bodily present in the sacrament; but he himself hath told us that "the flesh," in such a sense, "profiteth nothing," John vi. 63, and that it is the "Spirit alone that quickeneth." The Lutherans fancy an omnipresence, or ubiquity of his human nature, by virtue of its personal union; but this is destructive of that nature itself, which being made to be everywhere, as such a nature, is truly nowhere; and the most learned among them are ashamed of this imagination. The words of Schmidt on Eph. iv. 10, Ἵνα πληρώσῃ τὰ πάντα, are worthy of consideration:— "Per τὰ πάντα, aliqui intelligunt totum mundum, seu totum universum hoc, exponuntque ut omnipræsentia sua omnibus in mundo locis adesset, loca omnia implendo: et hi verbum πληρώσῃ de physicâ et crassâ impletione accipiunt; quam tamen talis πλήρωσις seu impletio locorum in mundo omnium quæ vel expansionem corpoream in quantitate continuâ, vel multiplicationem, imo infinitam multitudinem unius ejusdemque corperis in discreta præsupponit, et ex humana speculatione orta est, falsoque nostris ecclesiis affingitur" (wherein yet he confesseth that it is taught); "ne cogitanda quidem sit pio homini; sed potius omnipræsentia Christi hominis — uti promissa est, modo nobis ineffabili credi, et multo certius aliunde sciri possit ex ipsius promissione," Matt. xxviii. 20. This way, as we say with the Scripture, is by his Spirit, the perfect manner of whose presence and operation is ineffable.

Fourthly, As he represents the person and supplies the room and place of Jesus Chest, so he worketh and effecteth whatever the Lord Christ hath taken upon himself to work and effect towards his disciples. Wherefore, as the work of the Son was not his own work, but rather the "work of the Father who sent him," and in whose name he performed it, so the work of the Holy Spirit is not his own work, but rather the work of the Son, by whom he is sent, and in whose name he doth accomplish it: John xvi. 13–15, "Howbeit when the Spirit of truth is come, he will guide you into all truth: for he shall not speak of himself; but whatsoever he shall hear, that shall he speak: and he will show you things to come. He shall glorify me: for he shall receive of mine, and shall show it unto you. All things that the Father hath are mine: therefore said I, that he shall take of mine, and shall show it unto you." He comes to reveal and communicate truth and grace to the disciples of Christ; and in his so doing he "speaks not of himself," that is, of himself only. He comes not with any absolute new dispensation of truth or grace, distinct or different from that which is in and by the Lord Christ, and which they had heard from him. The Holy Spirit being promised unto the disciples, and all their work and duty being suspended on the accomplishment of that promise, whereas he is God, they might suppose that he would come with some absolute new dispensation of truth, so that what they had learned and received from Christ should pass away and be of no use unto them. To prevent any such apprehension, he lets them know that the work he had to do was only to carry on and build on the foundation which was laid in his person or doctrine, or the truth which he had revealed from the bosom of the Father. And, — 1. This I take to be the meaning of that expression, "He shall not speak of himself;" — "He shall reveal no other truth, communicate no other grace, but what is in, from, and by myself." This was the Holy Spirit to do; and this he did. And hereby may we try every spirit whether it be of God. That spirit which revealeth any thing, or pretendeth to reveal any thing, any doctrine, any grace, any truth, that is contrary unto, that is not consonant to, yea, that is not the doctrine, grace, or truth of Christ, as now revealed in the word, that brings any thing new, his own, or of himself, that spirit is not of God. So it is added, — 2. "Whatsoever he shall hear, that shall he speak." This which he hears is the whole counsel of the Father and the Son concerning the salvation of the church. And how is he said to "hear" it? which word, in its proper signification, hath no place in the mutual internal actings of the divine persons of the holy Trinity. Being the Spirit of the Father and the Son, proceeding from both, he is equally participant of their counsels. So the outward act of hearing is mentioned as the sign of his infinite knowledge of the eternal counsels of the Father and Son; he is no stranger unto them. And this is a general rule, — That those words which, with respect unto us, express the means of any thing, as applied unto God, intend no more but the signs of it. Hearing is the means whereby we come to know the mind of another who is distinct from us; and when God is said to hearken or hear, it is a sign of his knowledge, not the means of it. So is the Holy Spirit said to "hear" those things, because he knows them; as he is also on the same account said to "search the deep things of God." Add hereunto that the counsel of these things is originally peculiar to the Father, and unto him it is everywhere peculiarly ascribed; therefore is the participation of the Spirit therein as a distinct person called his hearing. Hereunto, 3. His great work is subjoined: "He," saith Christ, "shall glorify me." This is the design that he is sent upon, this is the work that he comes to do; even as it was the design and work of Jesus Christ to glorify the Father, by whom he was sent. And this are they always to bear in mind who stand in need of or pray for his assistance in their work or office in the church of God: He is given unto them, that through him they may give and bring glory to Jesus Christ. And, 4. How the Holy Spirit doth glorify the Lord Christ is also declared: "He shall receive of mine, and shall show it unto you." The communication of spiritual things from Christ by the Spirit is here called "his receiving" of them; as the communication of the Spirit from the Father by the Lord Christ to his disciples is called "his receiving of the promise." The Spirit cannot receive any thing subjectively which he had not, as an addition unto him; it is therefore the economy of these things that is here intended. He is not said to receive them, as though before he had them not; for what can he who is God so receive? Only, when he begins to give them unto us, because they are peculiarly the things of Christ, he is said to receive them; for we can give nothing of another's but what we receive of him. Good things are given unto us from Christ by the Spirit; for so it is added, "And shall show them unto you;" — "He shall make them known unto you; so declare them, and manifestly evidence them to you and in you, that ye shall understand and have experience of them in yourselves; show them by revelation, instructing you in them, by communication imparting them to you." And what are those things that he shall so declare? They are τὰ ἐμά, "my things," saith our Saviour. The things of Christ may be referred unto two heads, — his truth and his grace, John i. 17. The first he shows by revelation, the latter by effectual communication. His truth he showed unto them by revelation, as we have declared him to be the immediate author of all divine revelations. This he did unto the apostles by his inspirations, enabling them infallibly to receive, understand, and declare the whole counsel of God in Christ; for so, according unto the promise, he led them into all truth. And his grace he showed unto them in his pouring out both of his sanctifying graces and extraordinary gifts upon them in an abundant measure. And so he still continues to show the truth and grace of Christ unto all believers, though not in the same manner as unto the former, nor unto the same degree as unto the latter: for he shows unto us the "truth of Christ," or the truth that "came by Jesus Christ," by the word as written and preached, instructing us in it, and enlightening our minds spiritually and savingly to understand the mind of God therein; and of his grace he imparts unto us in our sanctification, consolation, and communication of spiritual gifts, according unto the measure of the gift of Christ unto every one of us, as the present use of the church doth require; — which things must be afterward declared. 5. And the reason of the assertion is added in the last place: "All things that the Father hath are mine; therefore said I, that he shall take of mine, and shall show it unto you." Two things may be observed in these words:—

(1.) The extent of the things of Christ, which are to be showed unto believers by the Spirit; and they are, "All the things that the Father hath." "They are mine," saith our Saviour. And these "all things" may be taken either absolutely and personally, or with a restriction unto office. [1.] All things that the Father hath absolutely were the Son's also; for, receiving his personality from the Father, by the communication of the whole entire divine nature, all the things of the Father must needs be his. Thus, "as the Father hath life in himself, so hath he given unto the Son to have life in himself," John v. 26. And the like may be said of all other essential properties of the Godhead. [2.] But these seem not to be the "all things" here intended. They are not the "all things" of the divine nature, which he had by eternal generation, but the "all things" of spiritual grace and power, which he had by voluntary donation, Matt. xi. 27; John iii. 35, "The Father loveth the Son, and hath given all things into his hand." That is, all the effects of the love, grace, and will of the Father, whatever he had purposed in himself from eternity, and whatever his infinite power and goodness would produce in the pursuit thereof, were all given and committed unto Jesus Christ. So all things that the Father hath were his.

(2.) That these things may be rightly understood and apprehended, we must consider a twofold operation of God as three in one. The first hereof is absolute in all divine works whatever; the other respects the economy of the operations of God in our salvation. In those of the first sort, both the working and the work do in common and undividedly belong unto and proceed from each person. And the reason hereof is, because they are all effects of the essential properties of the same divine nature, which is in them all, or rather, which is the one nature of them all. But yet as they have one nature, so there is an order of subsistence in that nature, and the distinct persons work in the order of their subsistence: John v. 19, 20, "Verily, verily, I say unto you, The Son can do nothing of himself, but what he seeth the Father do: for what things soever he doeth, these also doeth the Son likewise." The Father doth not first work in order of time, and then the Son, seeing of it, work another work like unto it; but the Son doth the same work that the Father doth. This is absolutely necessary, because of their union in nature. But yet in the order of their subsistence, the person of the Father is the original of all divine works, in the principle and beginning of them, and that in order of nature antecedently unto the operation of the Son. Hence he is said to "see" what the Father doth; which, according unto our former rule in the exposition of such expressions, when ascribed unto the divine nature, is the sign and evidence, and not the means, of his knowledge. He sees what the Father doth, as he is his eternal Wisdom. The like must be said of the Holy Spirit, with respect both unto the Father and Son. And this order of operation in the Holy Trinity is not voluntary, but natural and necessary from the one essence and distinct subsistences thereof. Secondly, There are those operations which, with respect unto our salvation, the Father, Son, and Holy Spirit do graciously condescend unto, which are those treated of in this place. Now, though the designing of this work was absolutely voluntary, yet, upon a supposition thereof, the order of its accomplishment was made necessary from the order of the subsistence of the distinct persons in the Deity; and that is here declared. Thus, [1.] The things to be declared unto us and bestowed on us are originally the Father's things. He is the peculiar fountain of them all. His love, his grace, his wisdom, his goodness, his counsel, his will, are their supreme cause and spring. Hence are they said to be the "things that the Father hath." [2.] They are made the things of the Son, — that is, they are given and granted in and unto his disposal, — on the account of his mediation; for thereby they were to be prepared for us and given out unto us, to the glory of God. Answerable hereunto, as the Lord Christ is mediator, all the things of grace are originally the Father's, and then given unto him. [3.] They are actually communicated unto us by the Holy Spirit: "Therefore said I, he shall take of mine and shall show it unto you." He doth not communicate them unto us immediately from the Father. We do not so receive any grace from God, — that is, the Father; nor do we so make any return of praise or obedience unto God. We have nothing to do with the person of the Father immediately. It is the Son alone by whom we have an access unto him, and by the Son alone that he gives out of his grace and bounty unto us. He that hath not the Son hath not the Father. With him, as the great treasurer of heavenly things, are all grace and mercy intrusted. The Holy Spirit, therefore, shows them unto us, works them in us, bestows them on us, as they are the fruits of the mediation of Christ, and not merely as effects of the divine love and bounty of the Father; and this is required from the order of subsistence before mentioned. Thus the Holy Spirit supplies the bodily absence of Jesus Christ, and effects what he hath to do and accomplish towards his [people] in the world; so that whatever is done by him, it is the same as if it were wrought immediately by the Lord Christ himself in his own person, whereby all his holy promises are fully accomplished towards them that believe. And this instructs us in the way and manner of that communion which we have with God by the gospel; for herein the life, power, and freedom of our evangelical state do consist, and an acquaintance herewith gives us our translation "out of darkness into the marvellous light of God." The person of the Father, in his wisdom, will, and love, is the original of all grace and glory. But nothing hereof is communicated immediately unto us from him. It is from the Son, whom he loves, and hath given all things into his hand. He hath made way for the communication of these things unto us, unto the glory of God; and he doth it immediately by the Spirit, as hath been declared. Hereby are all our returns unto God to be regulated. The Father, who is the original of all grace and glory, is ultimately intended by us in our faith, thankfulness, and obedience; yet not so but that the Son and Spirit are considered as one God with him. But we cannot address ourselves with any of them immediately unto him. "There is no going to the Father," saith Christ, "but by me," John xiv. 6. "By him we believe in God," 1 Pet. i. 21. But yet neither can we do so unless we are enabled thereunto by the Spirit, the author in us of faith, prayer, praise, obedience, and whatever our souls tend unto God by. As the descending of God towards us in love and grace issues or ends in the work of the Spirit in us and on us, so all our ascending towards him begins therein; and as the first instance of the proceeding of grace and love towards us from the Father is in and by the

Son, so the first step that we take towards God, even the Father, is in and by the Son. And these things ought to be explicitly attended unto by us, if we intend our faith, and love, and duties of obedience should be evangelical. Take an instance of the prayers of wicked men under their convictions, or their fears, troubles, and dangers, and the prayers of believers. The former is merely vox naturæ clamantis ad Dominum naturæ, — an outcry that distressed nature makes to the God of it, — and as such alone it considers him. But the other is vox Spiritus adoptionis clamantis per Christum, Abba, Pater; it is the voice of the Spirit of adoption addressing itself in the hearts of believers unto God as a Father. And a due attendance unto this order of things gives life and spirit unto all that we have to do with God. Woe to professors of the gospel who shall be seduced to believe that all they have to do with God consists in their attendance unto moral virtue! It is fit for them so to do who, being weary of Christianity, have a mind to turn Pagans. But "our fellowship is," in the way described, "with the Father, and with his Son Jesus Christ." It is, therefore, of the highest importance unto us to inquire into and secure unto ourselves the promised workings of the Holy Spirit; for by them alone are the love of the Father and the fruits of the mediation of the Son communicated unto us, without which we have no interest in them, and by them alone are we enabled to make any acceptable returns of obedience unto God. It is sottish ignorance and infidelity to suppose that, under the gospel, there is no communication between God and us but what is, on his part, in laws, commands, and promises; and on ours, by obedience performed in our strength, and upon our convictions unto them. To exclude hence the real internal operations of the Holy Ghost, is to destroy the gospel. And, as we shall see farther afterward, this is the true ground and reason why there is a sin against the Holy Spirit that is irremissible: for he coming unto us to make application of the love of the Father and grace of the Son unto our souls, in the contempt of him there is a contempt of the whole actings of God towards us in a way of grace; for which there can be no remedy.

Fifthly, Whereas the Holy Spirit is the Spirit of grace, and the immediate efficient cause of all grace and gracious effects in men, wherever there is mention made of them or any fruits of them, it is to be looked on as a part of his work, though he be not expressly named, or it be not particularly attributed unto him. I know not well, or do not well understand, what some men begin to talk about moral virtue. Something they seem to aim at (if they would once leave the old Pelagian ambiguous expressions, and learn to speak clearly and intelligibly) that is in their own power, and so, consequently, [in the power] of all other men; at least, it is so with an ordinary blessing upon their own endeavours: which things we must afterward inquire into. But for grace, I think all men will grant that, as to our participation of it, it is of the Holy Spirit, and of him alone. Now, grace is taken two ways in the Scripture:— 1. For the gracious free love and favour of God towards us; and, 2. For gracious, free, effectual operations in us and upon us. In both senses the Holy Spirit is the author of it as unto us: in the first, as to its manifestation and application; in the latter, as to the operation itself. For although he be not the principal cause nor procurer of grace in the first sense, which is the free act of the Father, yet the knowledge, sense, comfort, and all the fruits of it, are by him alone communicated unto us, as we shall see afterward; and the latter is his proper and peculiar work. This, therefore, must be taken for granted, that wherever any gracious actings of God in or towards men are mentioned, it is the Holy Spirit who is peculiarly and principally intended.

Sixthly, It must be duly considered, with reference unto the whole work of the Holy Spirit, that in whatever he doth, he acts, works, and distributes according to his own will. This our apostle expressly affirmeth. And sundry things of great moment do depend hereon in our walking before God; as, —

1. That the will and pleasure of the Holy Spirit is in all the goodness, grace, love, and power, that he either communicates unto us or worketh in us. He is not as a mere instrument or servant, disposing of the things wherein he hath no concern, or over which he hath no power; but in all things he worketh towards us according to his own will. We are, therefore, in what we receive from him and by him, no less to acknowledge his love, kindness, and sovereign grace, than we do those of the Father and the Son.

2. That he doth not work, as a natural agent, ad ultimum virium, to the utmost of his power, as though in all he did he came and did what he could. He moderates all his operations by his will and wisdom. And, therefore, whereas some are said to "resist the Holy Ghost," Acts vii. 51, and so to frustrate his work towards them, it is not because they can do so absolutely, but only they can do so as to some way, kind, or degree of his operations. Men may resist some sort or kind of means that he useth, as to some certain end and purpose, but they cannot resist him as to his purpose and the end he aims at; for he is God, and "who hath resisted his will?" Rom. ix. 19. Wherefore, in any work of his, two things are to be considered:— (1.) What the means he maketh use of tend unto in their own nature; and, (2.) What he intends by it. The first may be resisted and frustrated, but the latter cannot be so. Sometimes in and by that word which in its own nature tends to the conversion of sinners, he intendeth by it only their hardening, Isa. vi. 9, 10; John xii. 40, 41; Acts xxviii. 26, 27; Rom. xi. 8; and he can, when he pleaseth, exert that power and efficacy in working as shall take away all resistance. Sometimes he will only take order for the preaching and dispensation of the word unto men; for this also is his work, Acts xiii. 2. Herein men may resist his work, and reject his counsel concerning themselves; but when he will put forth his power, in and by the word, to the creating of a new heart in men and the opening of the eyes of them that are blind, he doth therein so take away the principle of resistance, that he is not, that he cannot be, resisted.

3. Hence, also, it follows that his works may be of various kinds, and that those which are of the same kind may yet be carried on unequally as to degrees. It is so in the operations of all voluntary agents, who work by choice and judgment. They are not confined to one sort of works, nor to the production of the same kind of effects; and where they design so to do, they moderate them as to degrees, according to their power and pleasure. Thus we shall find some of the works of the Holy Spirit to be such as may be perfect in their kind, and men may be made partakers of the whole end and intention of them, and yet no saving grace be wrought in them; such are his works of illumination, conviction, and sundry others. Men, I say, may have a work of the Holy Spirit on their hearts and minds, and yet not be sanctified and converted unto God; for the nature and kind of his works are regulated by his own will and purpose. If he intend no more but their conviction and illumination, no more shall be effected; for he works not by a necessity of nature, so that all his operations should be of the same kind, and have their especial form from his nature, and

not from his will. So, also, where he doth work the same effect in the souls of men, I mean the same in the kind of it, as in their regeneration he doth, yet he doth it by sundry means, and carrieth it on to a great inequality, as to the strengthening of its principle, and increase of its fruits unto holiness; and hence is that great difference as to light, holiness, and fruitfulness, which we find among believers, although all alike partakers of the same grace for the kind thereof. The Holy Spirit worketh in all these things according to his own will, whereof there neither is nor can be any other rule but his own infinite wisdom. And this is that which the apostle minds the Corinthians of, to take away all emulation and envy about spiritual gifts, that everyone should orderly make use of what he had received to the profit and edification of others. "They are," saith he, "given and distributed by the same Spirit, according to his own will, to one after one manner, unto another after another; so that it is an unreasonable thing for any to contend about them."

But it may be said, "That if not only the working of grace in us, but also the effects and fruits of it, in all its variety of degrees, is to be ascribed unto the Holy Spirit and his operations in us according to his own will, then do we signify nothing ourselves; nor is there any need that we should either use our endeavours and diligence, or at all take any care about the furtherance or growth of holiness in us, or attend unto any duties of obedience. To what end and purpose, then, serve all the commands, threatenings, promises, and exhortations of the Scripture, which are openly designed to excite and draw forth our own endeavours?" And this is indeed the principal difficulty wherewith some men seek to entangle and perplex the grace of God. But I answer, —

1. Let men imagine what absurd consequences they please thereon, yet that the Spirit of God is the author and worker of all grace in us, and of all the degrees of it, of all that is spiritually good in us, is a truth which we must not forego, unless we intend to part with our Bibles also: for in them we are taught "that in us, that is, in our flesh, dwelleth no good thing," Rom. vii. 18; that "we are not sufficient of ourselves to think any thing as of ourselves, but our sufficiency is of God," 2 Cor. iii. 5, "who is able to make all grace abound toward us, that we may always have all sufficiency in all things, abounding to every good work," chap. ix. 8; that "without Christ we can do nothing," John xv. 5, "for it is God which worketh in us both to will and to do of his good pleasure," Phil. ii. 13.

To grant, therefore, that there is any spiritual good in us, or any degree of it, that is not wrought in us by the Spirit of God, both overthrows the grace of the gospel and denies God to be the only, first, supreme, and chiefest good, as also the immediate cause of what is so; which is to deny his very being. It is therefore certain, whatever any pretend, that nothing can hence ensue but what is true and good, and useful to the souls of men; for from truth, especially such great and important truths, nothing else will follow.

2. It is brutish ignorance in any to argue in the things of God, from the effectual operations of the Spirit, unto a sloth and negligence of our own duty. He that doth not know that God hath promised to "work in us" in a way of grace what he requires from us in a way of duty, hath either never read the Bible or doth not believe it, either never prayed or never took notice of what he prayed for. He is a heathen, he hath nothing of the Christian in him, who doth not pray that God would work in him what he requires of him. This we know,

that what God commands and prescribes unto us, what he encourageth us unto, we ought with all diligence and earnestness, as we value our souls and their eternal welfare, to attend unto and comply withal. And we do know that whatever God hath promised he will do himself in us, towards us, and upon us, it is our duty to believe that he will so do. And to fancy an inconsistency between these things is to charge God foolishly.

3. If there be an opposition between these things, it is either because the nature of man is not meet to be commanded, or because it needs not to be assisted. But that both these are false and vain suppositions shall be afterward declared. The Holy Spirit so worketh in us as that he worketh by us, and what he doth in us is done by us. Our duty it is to apply ourselves unto his commands, according to the conviction of our minds; and his work it is to enable us to perform them.

4. He that will indulge, or can do so, unto sloth and negligence in himself, on the account of the promised working of the Spirit of grace, may look upon it as an evidence that he hath no interest or concern therein; for he ordinarily giveth not out his aids and assistances anywhere but where he prepares the soul with diligence in duty. And whereas he acts us no otherwise but in and by the faculties of our own minds, it is ridiculous, and implies a contradiction, for a man to say he will do nothing, because the Spirit of God doth all; for where he doth nothing, the Spirit of God doth nothing, unless it be merely in the infusion of the first habit or principle of grace, whereof we shall treat afterward.

5. For degrees of grace and holiness which are inquired after, they are peculiar unto believers. Now, these are furnished with an ability and power to attend unto and perform those duties whereon the increase of grace and holiness doth depend; for although there is no grace nor degree of grace or holiness in believers but what is wrought in them by the Spirit of God, yet, ordinarily and regularly, the increase and growth of grace, and their thriving in holiness and righteousness, depend upon the use and improvement of grace received, in a diligent attendance unto all those duties of obedience which are required of us, 2 Pet. i. 5–7. And methinks it is the most unreasonable and sottish thing in the world, for a man to be slothful and negligent in attending unto those duties which God requireth of him, which all his spiritual growth depends upon, which the eternal welfare of his soul is concerned in, on pretence of the efficacious aids of the Spirit, without which he can do nothing, and which he neither hath nor can have whilst he doth nothing.

Here lies the ground and foundation of our exercising faith in particular towards him, and of our acting of it in supplications and thanksgivings. His participation of the divine nature is the formal reason of our yielding unto him divine and religious worship in general; but his acting towards us according to the sovereignty of his own will is the especial reason of our particular addresses unto him in the exercise of grace, for we are baptized into his name also.

Seventhly, We may observe that, in the actings and works of the Holy Spirit, some things are distinctly and separately ascribed unto him, although some things be of the same kind wrought by the person in and by whom he acts; or, he is said at the same time to do the same thing distinctly by himself, and in and by others. So John xv. 26, 27: "I will," saith our Saviour, "send the Spirit of truth, and he shall testify of me, and ye also shall bear witness." The witness of the Spirit unto Christ is proposed as distinct and separate from the witness given by the apostles: "He shall testify of me, and ye also shall bear witness." And yet they also were enabled to give their witness by him alone. So it is expressly declared, Acts i. 8, "Ye shall receive power, after that the Holy Ghost is come upon you; and ye shall be witnesses unto me." Their witnessing unto Christ was the effect of the power of the Holy Spirit upon them, and the effect of his work in them; and he himself gave no other testimony but in and by them. What, then, is the distinct testimony that is ascribed unto him? It must be somewhat that, in or by whomsoever it was wrought, did of its own nature discover its relation unto him as his work. So it was in this matter; for it was no other but those signs and wonders, or miraculous effects, which he wrought in the confirmation of the testimony given by the apostles, all which clearly evidenced their own original. So our apostle, Heb. ii. 3, 4. The word was "confirmed, συνεπιμαρτυροῦντος τοῦ Θεοῦ σημείοις τε καὶ τέρασι," — "God cowitnessing by signs and wonders." He enabled the apostles to bear witness unto Christ by their preaching, sufferings, holiness, and constant testimony which they gave unto his resurrection. But in this he appeared not, he evidenced not himself unto the world, though he did so in and by them in whom he wrought. But, moreover, he wrought such visible, miraculous works by them as evidenced themselves to be effects of his power, and were his distinct witness to Christ. So our apostle tells us, Rom. viii. 16, "The Spirit itself beareth witness with our spirit, that we are the children of God." The witness which our own spirits do give unto our adoption is the work and effect of the Holy Spirit in us. If it were not, it would be false, and not confirmed by the testimony of the Spirit himself, who is the Spirit of truth; and none "knoweth the things of God but the Spirit of God," 1 Cor. ii. 11. If he declare not our sonship in us and to us, we cannot know it. How, then, doth he bear witness with our spirits? what is his distinct testimony in this matter? It must be some such act of his as evidenceth itself to be from him immediately unto them that are concerned in it, — that is, those unto whom it is given. What this is in particular, and wherein it doth consist, we shall afterward inquire. So Rev. xxii. 17, "The Spirit and the bride say, Come." The bride is the church, and she prayeth for the coming of Christ. This she doth by his aid and assistance who is the Spirit of grace and supplications. And yet distinctly and separately the Spirit saith, "Come;" that is, he puts forth such earnest and fervent desires as have upon them an impression of his immediate efficiency. So verse 20 carrieth the sense of the place, — namely, that it is Christ himself unto whom she says "Come;" or they pray for the hastening of his coming. Or they say "Come" unto others, in their invitation of them unto Christ, as the end of verse 17 seems to apply it: then is it the prayers and preaching of the church for the conversion of souls that is intended; and with both the Spirit works eminently to make them effectual. Or it may be, in this place, "the Spirit" is taken for the Spirit in the guides and leaders of the church. They, praying by his especial guidance and assistance, say, "Come;" or preachers say unto others, "Come;" and "the bride," or the body of the church, acted by the same Spirit, joins with them in this great request and supplication. And thereunto all believers are invited in the following words: "And let him that heareth say, Come."

All these things were necessary to be premised in general, as giving some insight into the nature of the operations of the Holy Spirit in us and towards us; and hereby we have made our way plain to the consideration of his especial works, in the calling, building, and carrying on the church unto perfection. Now, all his works of this kind may be reduced unto three heads:— 1. Of sanctifying grace; 2. Of especial gifts; 3. Of peculiar evangelical privileges. Only, we must observe that these things are not so distinguished as to be negatively contradistinct to each other; for the same thing, under several considerations, may be all these, — a grace, a gift, and a privilege. All that I intend is to reduce the operations of the Holy Spirit unto these heads, casting each of them under that which it is most eminent in, and as which it is most directly proposed unto us; and I shall begin with his work of grace.

Footnotes:

23. Καὶ μάλιστά γε τὸ ἀπολαύειν τοῦς ἀναπλασθέντας τοῦ ἁγιασμοῦ καὶ διαμένειν ἐν τῇ ἀναπλάσει, τῆς τοῦ παναγίου πνεύματος ἐστι δημουργίας τε καὶ συνοχῆς. — Jobius apud. Photium. lib. cxxii.

Book III

Chapter I - Work of the Holy Spirit in the new creation by regeneration

The new creation completed — Regeneration the especial work of the Holy Spirit — Wrought under the Old Testament, but clearly revealed in the New; and is of the same kind in all that are regenerate, the causes and way of it being the same in all — It consisteth not in baptism alone, nor in a moral reformation of life; but a new creature is formed in it, whose nature is declared, and farther explained — Denial of the original depravation of nature the cause of many noxious opinions — Regeneration consisteth not in enthusiastic raptures; their nature and danger — The whole doctrine necessary, despised, corrupted, vindicated.

We have formerly declared the work of the Holy Spirit in preparing and forming the natural body of Christ. This was the beginning of the new creation, the foundation of the gospel state and church. But this was not the whole of the work he had to do. As he had provided and prepared the natural body of Christ, so he was to prepare his mystical body also. And hereby the work of the new creation was to be completed and perfected. And as it was with respect unto him and his work in the old creation, so was it also in the new. All things in their first production had darkness and death upon them; for "the earth was without form and void, and darkness was upon the face of the deep," Gen. i. 2. Neither was there any thing that had either life in it, or principle of life, or any disposition thereunto. In this condition he moved on the prepared matter, preserving and cherishing of it, and communicating unto all things a principle of life, whereby they were animated, as we have declared. It was no otherwise in the new creation. There was a spiritual darkness and death came by sin on all mankind; neither was there in any man living the least principle of spiritual life, or any disposition thereunto. In this state of things, the Holy Spirit undertaketh to create a new world, new heavens and a new earth, wherein righteousness should dwell. And this, in the first place, was by his effectual communication of a new principle of spiritual life unto the souls of God's elect, who were the matter designed of God for this work to be wrought upon. This he doth in their regeneration, as we shall now manifest.

First, Regeneration in Scripture is everywhere assigned to be the proper and peculiar work of the Holy Spirit: John iii. 3–6, "Jesus answered and said unto Nicodemus, Verily, verily, I say unto thee, Except a man be born again, he cannot see the kingdom of God. Nicodemus saith unto him, How can a man be born when he is old? can he enter the second time into his mother's womb, and be born? Jesus answered, Verily, verily, I say unto thee, Except a man be born of water and of the Spirit, he cannot enter into the kingdom of God. That which is born of the flesh is flesh; and that which is born of the Spirit is spirit." It was an ancient knowing teacher of the church of the Jews, a "master in Israel," whom our blessed Saviour here discourseth withal and instructs; for on the consideration of his miracles he concluded that "God was with him," and came to inquire of him about the kingdom of God.

Our Saviour knowing how all our faith and obedience to God, and all our acceptance with him, depend on our regeneration, or being born again, acquaints him with the necessity of it; wherewith he is at first surprised. Wherefore he proceeds to instruct him in the nature of the work whose necessity he had declared; and this he describes both by the cause and the effect of it. For the cause of it, he tells him it is wrought by "water and the Spirit;" — by the Spirit, as the principal efficient cause; and by water, as the pledge, sign, and token[1] of it, in the initial seal of the covenant, the doctrine whereof was then preached amongst them by John the Baptist: or, the same thing is intended in a redoubled expression, the Spirit being signified by the water also, under which notion he is often promised.

Hereof, then, or of this work, the Holy Spirit is the principal efficient cause; whence he in whom it is wrought is said to be "born of the Spirit:" Verse 8, "So is every one that is born of the Spirit." And this is the same with what is delivered, chap. i. 13, "Who are born, not of blood, nor of the will of the flesh, nor of the will of man, but of God." The natural and carnal means of blood, flesh, and the will of man, are rejected wholly in this matter, and the whole efficiency of the new birth is ascribed unto God alone. His work answers whatever contribution there is unto natural generation from the will and nature of man; for these things are here compared, and from its analogy unto natural generation is this work of the Spirit called "regeneration." So in this place is the allusion and opposition between these things expressed by our Saviour: "That which is born of the flesh is flesh; and that which is born of the Spirit is spirit," chap. iii. 6. And herein also we have a farther description of this work of the Holy Spirit by its effect, or the product of it; it is "spirit," — a new spiritual being, creature, nature, life, as shall be declared. And because there is in it a communication of a new spiritual life, it is called a "vivification" or "quickening," with respect unto the state wherein all men are before this work is wrought in them and on them, Eph. ii. 1, 5; which is the work of the Spirit alone, for "it is the Spirit that quickeneth, the flesh profiteth nothing," John vi. 63. See Rom. viii. 9, 10; Tit. iii. 4–6, where the same truth is declared and asserted: "But after that the kindness and love of God our Saviour toward man appeared, not by works of righteousness which we have done, but according to his mercy he saved us, by the washing of regeneration, and renewing of the Holy Spirit; which he shed on us richly through Jesus Christ our Saviour."

What we have frequently mentioned occurreth here expressly, — namely, the whole blessed Trinity, and each person therein, acting distinctly in the work of our salvation. The spring or fountain of the whole lieth in the kindness and love of God, even the Father. Thereunto it is everywhere ascribed in the Scripture. See John iii. 16; Eph. i. 3–6. Whatever is done in the accomplishment of this work, it is so in the pursuit of his will, purpose, and counsel, and is an effect of his love and grace. The procuring cause of the application of the love and kindness of God unto us is Jesus Christ our Saviour, in the whole work of his mediation, verse 6. And the immediate efficient cause in the communication of the love and kindness of the Father, through the mediation of the Son, unto us, is the Holy Spirit. And this he doth in the renovation of our natures, by the washing of regeneration, wherein we are purged from our sins, and sanctified unto God.

More testimonies unto this purpose need not be insisted on. This truth, of the Holy Spirit being the author of our regeneration, which the ancients esteemed a cogent argument to prove his deity, even from the greatness and dignity of the work,[2] is, in words at least, so far as I know, granted by all who pretend to sobriety in Christianity. That by some others it hath been derided and exploded is the occasion of this vindication of it. It must not be expected that I should here handle the whole doctrine of regeneration practically, as it may be educed by inferences from the Scripture, according to the analogy of faith and the experiences of them that believe; it hath been done already by others. My present aim is only to confirm the fundamental principles of truth concerning those operations of the Holy Spirit, which at this day are opposed with violence and virulence. And what I shall offer on the present subject may be reduced unto the ensuing heads:—

First, Although the work of regeneration by the Holy Spirit was wrought under the Old Testament, even from the foundation of the world, and the doctrine of it was recorded in the Scriptures, yet the revelation of it was but obscure in comparison of that light and evidence which it is brought forth into by the gospel. This is evident from the discourse which our blessed Saviour had with Nicodemus on this subject; for when he acquainted him clearly with the doctrine of it, he was surprised, and fell into that inquiry, which argued some amazement, "How can these things be?" But yet the reply of our Saviour manifests that he might have attained a better acquaintance with it out of the Scripture than he had done: "Art thou," saith he, "a master in Israel, and knowest not these things?" — "Dost thou take upon thee to teach others what is their state and condition, and what is their duty towards God, and art ignorant thyself of so great and fundamental a doctrine, which thou mightst have learned from the Scripture?" For if he might not so have done, there would have been no just cause of the reproof given him by our Saviour; for it was neither crime nor negligence in him to be ignorant of what God had not revealed. This doctrine, therefore, — namely, that everyone who will enter into the kingdom of God must be born again of the Holy Spirit, — was contained in the writings of the Old Testament. It was so in the promises, that God would circumcise the hearts of his people, — that he would take away their heart of stone, and give them a heart of flesh, with his law written in it, and other ways, as shall be afterward proved.

But yet we see that it was so obscurely declared that the principal masters and teachers of the people knew little or nothing of it. Some, indeed, would have this regeneration, if they knew what they would have, or as to what may be gathered of their minds out of their "great swelling words of vanity," to be nothing but reformation of life, according to the rules of the Scripture. But Nicodemus knew the necessity of reformation of life well enough, if he had ever read either Moses or the Prophets; and to suppose that our Lord Jesus Christ proposed unto him the thing which he knew perfectly well, only under a new name or notion, which he had never heard of before, so to take an advantage of charging him of being ignorant of what indeed he full well knew and understood, is a blasphemous imagination. How they can free themselves from the guilt hereof who look on "regeneration" as no more but a metaphorical expression of amendment of life, I know not. And if it be so, if there be no more in it but, as they love to speak, becoming a new moral man, — a thing which all the world, Jews and Gentiles, understood, — our Lord Jesus was so far from bringing it forth into more light and giving it more perspicuity, by what he teacheth concerning regeneration, the nature, manner, causes, and effects of it, that he cast it thereby into more darkness and obscurity than ever it was delivered in, either by Jewish masters or Gentile philosophy; for although the gospel do really teach all duties of morality with more exactness and clearness, and press unto the observance of them on motives incomparably more cogent, than any thing that otherwise ever befell the mind of man to think or apprehend, yet if it must be supposed to intend nothing else in its doctrine of the new birth or regeneration but those moral duties and their observance, it is dark and unintelligible. I say, if there be not a secret, mysterious work of the Spirit of God in and upon the souls of men intended in the writings of the New Testament, but only a reformation of life, and the improvement of men's natural abilities in the exercise of moral virtue, through the application of outward means unto their minds and understandings, conducting and persuading thereunto, they must be granted to be obscure beyond those of any other writers whatsoever, as some have not feared already to publish unto the world concerning the epistles of Paul. But so long as we can obtain an acknowledgment from men that they are true, and in any sense the word of God, we doubt not but to evince that the things intended in them are clearly and properly expressed, so as they ought to be, and so as they are capable to be expressed; the difficulties which seem to be in them arising from the mysterious nature of the things themselves contained in them, and the weakness of our minds in apprehending such things, and not from any obscurity or intricacy in the declaration of them. And herein, indeed, consists the main contest whereinto things with the most are reduced. Some judge that all things are so expressed in the Scripture, with a condescension unto our capacity, as that there is still to be conceived an inexpressible grandeur in many of them, beyond our comprehension; others judge, on the other hand, that under a grandeur of words and hyperbolical expressions, things of a meaner and a lower sense are intended and to be understood. Some judge the things of the gospel to be deep and mysterious, the words and expressions of it to be plain and proper; others think the words and expressions of it to be mystical and figurative, but the things intended to be ordinary and obvious to the natural reason of every man. But to return.

Both regeneration and the doctrine of it were under the Old Testament. All the elect of God, in their several generations, were regenerate by the Spirit of God. But in that ampliation and enlargement of truth and grace under the gospel which came by Jesus Christ, who brought life and immortality to light, as more persons than of old were to be made partakers of the mercy of it, so the nature of the work itself is far more clearly, evidently, and distinctly revealed and declared. And because this is the principal and internal remedy of that disease which the Lord Christ came to cure and take away, one of the first things that he preached was the doctrine of it. All things of this nature before, even "from the beginning of the world, lay hid in God," Eph. iii. 9. Some intimations were given of them, in "parables" and "dark sayings," מִנִּי־קֶדֶם חִידוֹת, Ps. lxxviii. 2, in types, shadows, and ceremonies, so as the nature of the grace in them was not clearly to be discerned. But now, when the great Physician of our souls came, who was to heal the wound of our natures, whence we "were dead in trespasses and sins," he lays naked the disease itself, declares the greatness of it, the ruin we were under from it; that we might know and be thankful for its reparation. Hence, no doctrine is more fully and plainly declared in the gospel than this of our regeneration by the effectual and ineffable operation of the Holy Spirit; and it is a consequent and fruit of the depravation of our nature, that, against the full light and evidence of truth, now clearly manifested, this great and holy work is opposed and despised.

Few, indeed, have yet the confidence in plain and intelligible words to deny it absolutely; but many tread in the steps of him who first in the church of God undertook to undermine it.[3] This was Pelagius, whose principal artifice, which he used in the introduction of his heresy, was in the clouding of his intentions with general and ambiguous expressions, as some would by making use of his very words and phrases. Hence, for a long time, when he was justly charged with his sacrilegious errors, he made no defence of them, but reviled his adversaries as corrupting his mind, and not understanding his expressions. And by this means, as he got himself acquitted in the judgment of some, less experienced in the sleights and cunning craftiness of them who lie in wait to deceive, and[4] juridically freed in an assembly of bishops; so in all probability he had suddenly infected the whole church with the poison of those opinions, which the proud and corrupted nature of man is so apt to receive and embrace, if God had not stirred up some few holy and learned persons, Austin especially, to discover his frauds, to repel his calumnies, and to confute his sophisms; which they did with indefatigable industry and good success. But yet these tares, being once sown by the envious one, found such a suitable and fruitful soil in the darkened minds and proud hearts of men, that from that day to this they could never be fully extirpated; but the same bitter root hath still sprung up, unto the defiling of many, though various new colours have been put upon its leaves and fruit. And although those who at present amongst us have undertaken the same cause with Pelagius do not equal him either in learning or diligence, or an appearance of piety and devotion, yet do they exactly imitate him in declaring their minds in cloudy, ambiguous expressions, capable of various constructions until they are fully examined, and thereon reproaching (as he did) those that oppose them as not aright representing their sentiments, when they judge it their advantage so to do; as the scurrilous, clamorous writings of S. P.[5] do sufficiently manifest.

Secondly, Regeneration by the Holy Spirit is the same work, for the kind of it, and wrought by the same power of the Spirit in all that are regenerate, or ever were, or shall be so, from the beginning of the world unto the end thereof. Great variety there is in the application of the outward means which the Holy Spirit is pleased to use and make effectual towards the accomplishment of this great work; nor can the ways and manner hereof be reduced unto any certain order, for the Spirit worketh how and when he pleaseth, following the sole rule of his own will and wisdom. Mostly, God makes use of the preaching of the word; thence called "the ingrafted word, which is able to save our souls," James i. 21; and the "incorruptible seed," by which we are "born again," 1 Pet. i. 23. Sometimes it is wrought without it; as in all those who are regenerate before they come to the use of reason, or in their infancy. Sometimes men are called, and so regenerate, in an extraordinary manner; as was Paul. But mostly they are so in and by the use of ordinary means, instituted, blessed, and sanctified of

God to that end and purpose. And great variety there is, also, in the perception and understanding of the work itself in them in whom it is wrought, for in itself it is secret and hidden, and is no other ways discoverable but in its causes and effects; for as "the wind bloweth where it listeth, and thou hearest the sound thereof, but canst not tell whence it cometh, and whither it goeth, so is every one that is born of the Spirit," John iii. 8.

In the minds and consciences of some, this is made known by infallible signs and tokens. Paul knew that Christ was formed and revealed in himself, Gal. i. 15, 16. So he declared that whoever is in Christ Jesus "is a new creature," 2 Cor. v. 17, — that is, is born again, — whether they know themselves so to be or no. And many are in the dark as to their own condition in this matter all their days; for they "fear the Lord, and obey the voice of his servant" (Christ Jesus), and yet "walk in darkness, and have no light," Isa. l. 10. They are "children of light," Luke xvi. 8, John xii. 36, Eph. v. 8, 1 Thess. v. 5; and yet "walk in darkness, and have no light:" which expressions have been well used and improved by some, and by others of late derided and blasphemed.

And there is great variety in the carrying on of this work towards perfection, — in the growth of the new creature, or the increase of grace implanted in our natures by it: for some, through the supplies of the Spirit, make a great and speedy progress towards perfection, others thrive slowly and bring forth little fruit; the causes and occasions whereof are not here to be enumerated. But notwithstanding all differences in previous dispositions, in the application of outward means, in the manner of it, ordinary or extraordinary, in the consequents of much or less fruit, the work itself in its own nature is of the same kind, one and the same. The elect of God were not regenerate one way, by one kind of operation of the Holy Spirit, under the Old Testament, and those under the New Testament [by] another. They who were miraculously converted, as Paul, or who upon their conversion had miraculous gifts bestowed on them, as had multitudes of the primitive Christians, were no otherwise regenerate, nor by any other internal efficiency of the Holy Spirit, than everyone is at this day who is really made partaker of this grace and privilege. Neither were those miraculous operations of the Holy Spirit which were visible unto others any part of the work of regeneration, nor did they belong necessarily unto it; for many were the subjects of them, and received miraculous gifts by them, who were never regenerate, and many were regenerate who were never partakers of them. And it is a fruit of the highest ignorance and unacquaintedness imaginable with these things, to affirm that in the work of regeneration the Holy Spirit wrought of old miraculously, in and by outwardly visible operations, but now only in a human and rational way, leading our understanding by the rules of reason, unless the mere external mode and sign of his operation be intended: for all ever were, and ever shall be, regenerate by the same kind of operation, and the same effect of the Holy Spirit on the faculties of their souls; which will be farther manifest if we consider, —

1. That the condition of all men, as unregenerate, is absolutely the same. One is not by nature more unregenerate than another. All men since the fall, and the corruption of our nature by sin, are in the same state and condition towards God. They are all alike alienated from him, and all alike under his curse, Ps. li. 5; John iii. 5, 36; Rom. iii. 19, v. 15–18; Eph. ii. 3; Tit. iii. 3, 4. There are degrees of wickedness in them that are unregenerate, but there is no

difference as to state and condition between them, — all are unregenerate alike; as amongst those who are regenerate there are different degrees of holiness and righteousness, one, it may be, far exceeding another, yet there is between them no difference of state and condition, — they are all equally regenerate. Yea, some may be in a greater forwardness and preparation for the work itself, and thereby in a greater nearness to the state of it than others; but the state itself is incapable of such degrees. Now, it must be the same work, for the kind and nature of it, which relieves and translates men out of the same state and condition. That which gives the formal reason of the change of their state, of their translation from death to life, is and must be the same in all. If you can fix on any man, from the foundation of the world, who was not equally born in sin, and by nature dead in trespasses and sins, with all other men, the man Christ Jesus only excepted, I would grant that he might have another kind of regeneration than others have, but that I know he would stand in need of none at all.

2. The state whereinto men are brought by regeneration is the same. Nor is it, in its essence or nature, capable of degrees, so that one should be more regenerate than another. Everyone that is born of God is equally so, though one may be more beautiful than another, as having the image of his heavenly Father more evidently impressed on him, though not more truly. Men may be more or less holy, more or less sanctified, but they cannot be more or less regenerate. All children that are born into the world are equally born, though some quickly outstrip others in the perfections and accomplishments of nature; and all born of God are equally so, though some speedily outgo others in the accomplishments and perfections of grace. There was, then, never but one kind of regeneration in this world, the essential form of it being specifically the same in all.

3. That the efficient cause of this work, the grace and power whereby it is wrought, with the internal manner of the communication of that grace, are the same, shall be afterward declared. To this standard, then, all must come. Men may bear themselves high, and despise this whole work of the Spirit of God, or set up an imagination of their own in the room thereof; but whether they will or no, they must be tried by it, and no less depends on their interest in it than their admission into the kingdom of God. And let them pretend what they please, the true reason why any despise the new birth is, because they hate a new life. He that cannot endure to live to God will as little endure to hear of being born of God. But we shall by the Scripture inquire what we are taught concerning it, and declare both what it is not, of things which falsely pretend thereunto, and then what it is indeed.

First, Regeneration doth not consist in a participation of the ordinance of baptism and a profession of the doctrine of repentance. This is all that some will allow unto it, to the utter rejection and overthrow of the grace of our Lord Jesus Christ: for the dispute in this matter is not, whether the ordinances of the gospel, as baptism, do really communicate internal grace unto them that are, as to the outward manner of their administration, duly made partakers of them, whether ex opere operato, as the Papists speak, or as a federal means of the conveyance and communication of that grace which they betoken and are the pledges of; but, whether the outward susception of the ordinance, joined with a profession of repentance in them that are adult, be not the whole of what is called regeneration. The vanity of this presumptuous folly, destructive of all the grace of the gospel, invented to countenance men in their sins, and to hide from them the necessity of being born again, and therein of turning unto God, will be laid open in our declaration of the nature of the work itself. For the present, the ensuing reasons will serve to remove it out of our way:—

1. Regeneration doth not consist in these things, which are only outward signs and tokens of it, or at most instituted means of effecting it; for the nature of things is different and distinct from the means and evidences or pledges of them: but such only is baptism, with the profession of the doctrine of it, as is acknowledged by all who have treated of the nature of that sacrament. 2. The apostle really states this case, 1 Pet. iii. 21, "In answer whereunto even baptism doth also now save us (not the putting away of the filth of the flesh, but the answer of a good conscience toward God), by the resurrection of Jesus Christ." The outward administration of this ordinance, considered materially, reacheth no farther but to the washing away of "the filth of the flesh;" but more is signified thereby. There is denoted in it the restipulation of a "good conscience toward God, by the resurrection of Jesus Christ" from the dead, or a "conscience purged from dead works to serve the living God," Heb. ix. 14, and quickened by virtue of his resurrection unto holy obedience. See Rom. vi. 3–7. 3. The apostle Paul doth plainly distinguish between the outward ordinances, with what belongs unto a due participation of them, and the work of regeneration itself: Gal. vi. 15, "In Christ Jesus neither circumcision availeth any thing, nor uncircumcision, but a new creature;" — for as by "circumcision" the whole system of Mosaical ordinances is intended, so the state of "uncircumcision," as then it was in the professing Gentiles, supposed a participation of all the ordinances of the gospel; but from them all he distinguisheth the new creation, as that which they may be without, and which being so, they are not available in Christ Jesus. 4. If this were so, then all that are duly baptized, and do thereon make profession of the doctrine of it, — that is, of repentance for the forgiveness of sins, — must of necessity be regenerate. But this we know to be otherwise. For instance, Simon the magician was rightly and duly baptized, for he was so by Philip the evangelist; which he could not be without a profession of faith and repentance. Accordingly, it is said that he "believed," Acts viii. 13, — that is, made a profession of his faith in the gospel. Yet he was not regenerate; for at the same time he had "neither part nor lot in that matter," his "heart not being right in the sight of God," but was "in the gall of bitterness, and in the bond of iniquity," verses 21, 23; which is not the description of a person newly regenerate and born again. Hence the cabalistical Jews, who grope in darkness after the old notions of truth that were among their forefathers, do say, that at the same instant wherein a man is made "a proselyte of righteousness," there comes a new soul into him from heaven, his old pagan soul vanishing or being taken away. The introduction of a new spiritual principle to be that unto the soul which the soul is unto the body naturally is that which they understand; or they choose thus to express the reiterated promise of taking away the "heart of stone," and giving a "heart of flesh" in the place of it. Secondly, Regeneration doth not consist in a moral reformation of life and conversation.

Let us suppose such a reformation, to be extensive unto all known instances. Suppose a man be changed from sensuality unto temperance, from rapine to righteousness, from pride and the dominion of irregular passions unto humility and moderation, with all instances of the like nature which we can imagine, or are prescribed in the rules of the strictest moralists; suppose this change be laboured, exact, and accurate, and so of great use in the world; suppose, also, that a man hath been brought and persuaded unto it through the preaching of the gospel, so "escaping the pollutions that are in the world through lust, even by the knowledge of our Lord and Saviour Jesus Christ," or the directions of his doctrine delivered in the gospel; — yet I say, all this, and all this added unto baptism, accompanied with a profession of faith and repentance, is not regeneration, nor do they comprise it in them. And I have extended this assertion beyond what some among us, so far as I can see, do so much as pretend unto in their confused notions and sophistical expressions about morality, when they make it the same with grace. But whatever there may be of actual righteousness in these things, they do not express an inherent, habitual righteousness; which whosoever denies overthrows the gospel, and all the whole work of the Spirit of God, and of the grace of our Lord Jesus Christ.

But we must stay a while. This assertion of ours is by some not only denied but derided. Neither is that all; but whoever maintains it is exposed as an enemy to morality, righteousness, and reformation of life. All virtue, they say, is hereby excluded, to introduce I know not what imaginary godliness. But whether we oppose or exclude moral virtue or no, by the doctrine of regeneration, or any other, God and Christ will in due time judge and declare. Yea, were the confession of the truth consistent with their interests, the decision of this doubt might be referred unto their own consciences. But being not free to commit any thing to that tribunal, unless we had better security of its freedom from corrupt principles and prejudices than we have, we shall at present leave all the world to judge of our doctrine, with respect unto virtue and morality, by the fruits of it, compared with theirs by whom it is denied. In the meantime, we affirm that we design nothing in virtue and morality but to improve them, by fixing them on a proper foundation, or ingrafting them into that stock whereon alone they will thrive and grow, to the glory of God and the good of the souls of men. Neither shall we be moved in this design by the clamorous or calumnious outcries of ignorant or profligate persons. And for the assertion laid down, I desire that those who despise and reproach it would attempt an answer unto the ensuing arguments whereby it is confirmed, with those others which shall be insisted on in our description of the nature of the work of regeneration itself, and that upon such grounds and principles as are not destructive of Christian religion nor introductive of atheism, before they are too confident of their success.

If there be in and required unto regeneration, the [6]infusion of a new, real, spiritual principle into the soul and its faculties, of spiritual life, light, holiness, and righteousness, disposed unto and suited for the destruction or expulsion of a contrary, inbred, habitual principle of sin and enmity against God, enabling unto all acts of holy obedience, and so in order of nature antecedent unto them, then it doth not consist in a mere reformation of life and moral virtue, be they never so exact or accurate. Three things are to be observed for the clearing of this assertion, before we come to the proof and confirmation of it; as, — 1. That this reformation of life, which we say is not regeneration, or that regeneration doth not consist therein, is a necessary duty, indispensably required of all men; for we shall take it here for the whole course of actual obedience unto God, and that according to the gospel. Those, indeed, by whom it is urged and pressed in the room of regeneration, or as that wherein regeneration doth consist, do give such an account and description of it as that it is, or at least may be, foreign unto true gospel-obedience, and so not contain in it one acceptable duty unto God, as shall afterward be declared; but here I shall take it, in our present inquiry, for that whole course of duties which, in obedience towards God, are prescribed unto us. 2. That the principle before described, wherein regeneration as passively considered, or as wrought in us, consists, doth always certainly and infallibly produce the reformation of life in tended. In some it doth it more completely, in others more imperfectly, in all sincerely; for the same grace in nature and kind is communicated unto several persons in various degrees, and is by them used and improved with more or less care and diligence. In those, therefore, that are adult, these things are inseparable. Therefore, 3. The difference in this matter cometh unto this head: We say and believe that regeneration consists in spirituali renovatione naturæ, — "in a spiritual renovation of our nature;" our modem Socinians, that it doth so in morali reformatione vitæ, — "in a moral reformation of life." Now, as we grant that this spiritual renovation of nature will infallibly produce a moral reformation of life; so if they will grant that this moral reformation of life doth proceed from a spiritual renovation of our nature, this difference will be at an end. And this is that which the ancients intend by first receiving the Holy Ghost, and then all graces with him.[7] However, if they only design to speak ambiguously, improperly, and unscripturally, confounding effects and their causes, habits and actions, faculties or powers and occasional acts, infused principles and acquired habits, spiritual and moral, grace and nature, that they may take an opportunity to rail at others for want of better advantage, I shall not contend with them; for allow a new spiritual principle, an infused habit of grace, or gracious abilities, to be required in and unto regeneration, or to be the product or the work of the Spirit therein, that which is "born of the Spirit being spirit," and this part of the nature of this work is sufficiently cleared. Now, this the Scripture abundantly testifieth unto. 2 Cor. v. 17, "If any man be in Christ he is a new creature." This new creature is that which is intended, that which was before described, which being born of the Spirit is spirit. This is produced in the souls of men by a creating act of the power of God,[8] or it is not a creature. And it is superinduced into the essential faculties of our souls, or it is not a new creature; for whatever is in the soul of power, disposition, ability, or inclination unto God, or for any moral actions, by nature, it belongs unto the old creation, it is no new creature. And it must be somewhat that hath a being and subsistence of its own in the soul, or it can be neither new nor a creature. And by our apostle it is opposed to all outward privileges, Gal. v. 6, vi. 15. That the production of it also is by a creating act of almighty power the Scripture testifieth, Ps. li. 10; Eph. ii. 10; and this can denote nothing but a new spiritual principle or nature wrought in us by the Spirit of God. "No," say some; "a new creature is no more but a changed man." It is true; but then this change is internal also. "Yes, in the purposes, designs, and inclinations of the mind." But is it by a real infusion of a new principle of spiritual life and holiness? "No; it denotes no more but a new course of conversation, only the expression is metaphorical. A new creature is a moral man that hath changed his course and way; for if he were always a moral man, that he was never in any vicious way or course, as it was with him, Matt. xix. 16–22, then he was always a new creature." This is good gospel, at once overthrowing original sin and the grace of our Lord Jesus Christ! This doctrine, I am sure, was not learned from the fathers, whereof some used to boast; nay, it is much more fulsome than any thing ever taught by Pelagius himself, who, indeed, ascribed more unto grace than these men do, although he denied this creation of a new principle of grace in us antecedent unto acts of obedience.[9] And this turning all Scripture expressions of spiritual things into metaphors is but a way to turn the whole into a fable, or at least to render the gospel the most obscure and improper way of teaching the truth of things that ever was made use of in the world.

This new creature, therefore, doth not consist in a new course of actions, but in renewed faculties, with new dispositions, power, or ability to them and for them. Hence it is called the "divine nature:" 2 Pet. i. 4, "He hath given unto us exceeding great and precious promises, that by these ye might be partakers of the divine nature." This θεία φύσις, this "divine nature," is not the nature of God, whereof in our own persons we are not subjectively partakers; and yet a nature it is which is a principle of operation, and that divine or spiritual, — namely, an habitual holy principle, wrought in us by God, and bearing his image. By the "promises," therefore, we are made partakers of a divine, supernatural principle of spiritual actions and operations; which is what we contend for. So the whole of what we intend is declared, Eph. iv. 22–24, "Put off concerning the former conversation the old man, which is corrupt according to the deceitful lusts; and be renewed in the spirit of your mind; and put on the new man, which after God is created in righteousness and true holiness." It is the work of regeneration, with respect both to its foundation and progress, that is here described. 1. The foundation of the whole is laid in our being "renewed in the spirit of our mind;" which the same apostle elsewhere calls being "transformed in the renovation of our minds," Rom. xii. 2. That this consists in the participation of a new, saving, supernatural light, to enable the mind unto spiritual actings, and to guide it therein, shall be afterward declared. Herein consists our "renovation in knowledge, after the image of him who created us," Col. iii. 10. And, 2. The principle itself infused into us, created in us, is called the "new man," Eph. iv. 24, — that is, the new creature before mentioned; and it is called the "new man," because it consists in the universal change of the whole soul, as it is the principle of all spiritual and moral action. And, (1.) It is opposed unto the "old man," "Put off the old man, and put on the new man," verses 22, 24. Now, this "old man" is the corruption of our nature, as that nature is the principle of all religious, spiritual, and moral actions, as is evident, Rom. vi. 6. It is not a corrupt conversation, but the principle and root of it; for it is distinguished both from the conversation of men, and those corrupt lusts which are exercised therein, as to that exercise. And, (2.) It is called the "new man," because it is the effect and product of God's creating power, and that in a way of "a new creation," see Eph. i. 19; Col. ii. 12, 13; 2 Thess. i. 11; and it is here said to be "created after God," Eph. iv. 24. Now, the object of a creating act is an instantaneous production. Whatever preparations there may be for it and dispositions unto it, the bringing forth of a new form and being by creation is in an instant. This, therefore, cannot consist in a mere reformation of life. So are we said herein to be the "workmanship of God, created in Christ Jesus unto good works," chap. ii. 10. There is a work of God in us preceding all our good works towards him; for before we can work any of them, in order of nature, we must be the workmanship of God, created unto them, or enabled spiritually for the performance of them.

Again: This new man, whereby we are born again, is said to be created in righteousness and true holiness. That there is a respect unto man created in innocency, wherein he was made in the image of God, I suppose will not be denied. It is also expressed Col. iii. 10, "Ye have put on the new man, which is renewed in knowledge after the image of him that created him." Look, then, what was, or wherein consisted, the image of God in the first man, thereunto answers this new man which is created of God. Now, this did not consist in reformation of life, no, nor in a course of virtuous actions; for he was created in the image of God before he had done anyone good thing at all, or was capable of so doing. But this image of God consisted principally, as we have evinced elsewhere, in the uprightness, rectitude, and ability of his whole soul, his mind, will, and affections, in, unto, and for the obedience that God required of him. This he was endowed withal antecedently unto all voluntary actions whereby he was to live to God. Such, therefore, must be our regeneration, or the creation of this new man in us. It is the begetting, infusing, creating, of a new saving principle of spiritual life, light, and power in the soul, antecedent unto true evangelical reformation of life, in [the] order of nature, [and] enabling men thereunto, according unto the mind of God.

Hereunto accords that of our Saviour, Luke vi. 43, "A good tree bringeth not forth corrupt fruit, neither doth a corrupt tree bring forth good fruit;" compared with Matt. vii. 18. The fruit followeth the nature of the tree; and there is no way to change the nature of the fruit, but by changing the nature of the tree which brings it forth. Now, all amendment of life in reformation is but fruit, chap. iii. 10; but the changing of our nature is antecedent hereunto. This is the constant course and tenor of the Scripture, to distinguish between the grace of regeneration, which it declares to be an immediate supernatural work of God in us and upon us, and all that obedience, holiness, righteousness, virtue, or whatever is good in us, which is the consequent, product, and effect of it. Yea, God hath declared this expressly in his covenant, Ezek. xxxvi. 25–27; Jer. xxxi. 33, xxxii. 39, 40. The method of God's proceeding with us in his covenant is, that he first washeth and cleanseth our natures, takes away the heart of stone, gives a heart of flesh, writes his law in our hearts, puts his Spirit in us; wherein, as shall be evidenced, the grace of regeneration doth consist. The effect and consequent hereof is, that we shall walk in his statutes, keep his judgments and do them, — that is, reform our lives, and yield all holy obedience unto God. Wherefore these things are distinguished as causes and effects. See to the same purpose, Rom. vi. 3–6; Col. iii. 1–5; Eph. ii. 10, iv. 23–25. This I insist upon still, on supposition that by "reformation of life" all actual obedience is intended; for as to that kind of life which is properly called a moral course of life, in opposition to open debaucheries and unrighteousness, which doth not proceed from an internal principle of saving grace, it is so far from being regeneration or grace, as that it is a thing of no acceptation with God absolutely, whatever use or reputation it may be of in the world.

And yet farther: This work is described to consist in the sanctification of the whole spirit, soul, and body, 1 Thess. v. 23. And if this be that which some men intend by "reformation of life" and "moral virtue," they must needs win much esteem for their clearness and perspicuity in teaching spiritual things; for who would not admire them for such a definition of morality, — namely, that it is the principal sanctification of the whole spirit, soul, and body, of a believer, by the Holy Ghost? But not to dwell longer on this subject, there is no description of the work of regeneration in the Scripture, in its nature, causes, or effects, no name given unto it, no promise made of it, nothing spoken of the ways, means, or power, by which it is wrought, but is inconsistent with this bold Pelagian figment, which is destructive of the grace of Jesus Christ.

The ground of this imagination, that regeneration consists in a moral reformation of life, ariseth from a denial of original sin, or an inherent, habitual corruption of nature; for the masters unto the men of this persuasion tell us that whatever is of vice or defilement in us, it is contracted by a custom of sinning only. And their conceptions hereof do regulate their opinions about regeneration; for if man be not originally corrupted and polluted, if his nature be not depraved, if it be not possessed by, and under the power of, evil dispositions and inclinations, it is certain that he stands in no need of an inward spiritual renovation of it. It is enough for such an one that, by change of life, he renounce a custom of sinning, and reform his conversation according to the gospel; which in himself he hath power to do. But as it hath been in part already manifested, and will fully, God assisting, be evinced afterward, that in our regeneration the native ignorance, darkness, and blindness of our minds are dispelled, saving and spiritual light being introduced by the power of God's grace into them; that the pravity and stubbornness of our wills are removed and taken away, a new principle of spiritual life and righteousness being bestowed on them; and that the disorder and rebellion of our affections are cured by the infusion of the love of God into our souls: so the corrupt imagination of the contrary opinion, directly opposite to the doctrine of the Scriptures, the faith of the ancient church, and the experience of all sincere believers, hath amongst us of late nothing but ignorance and ready confidence produced to give countenance unto it.

Thirdly, The work of the Holy Spirit in regeneration doth not consist, in enthusiastical raptures, ecstasies, voices, or any thing of the like kind. It may be some such things have been, by some deluded persons, apprehended or pretended unto; but the countenancing of any such imaginations is falsely and injuriously charged on them who maintain the powerful and effectual work of the Holy Spirit in our regeneration. And this some are prone to do; wherein whether they discover more of their ignorance or of their malice I know not, but nothing is more common with them. All whom in this matter they dissent from, so far as they know what they say or whereof they affirm, do teach men to look after enthusiastic inspirations or unaccountable raptures, and to esteem them for conversion unto God, although, in the meantime, they live in a neglect of holiness and righteousness of conversation. I answer, If there be those who do so, we doubt not but that, without their repentance, the wrath of God will come upon them, as upon other children of disobedience. And yet, in the meantime, we cannot but call aloud that others would discover their diligence in attendance unto these things, who, as far as I can discern, do cry up the names of virtue and righteousness in opposition to the grace of Jesus Christ, and that holiness which is a fruit thereof. But for the reproach now under consideration, it is, as applied, no other but a calumny and false accusation; and that it is so, the writings and preachings of those who have most diligently laboured in the declaration of the work of the Holy Spirit in our regeneration will bear testimony at the great day of the Lord. We may, therefore, as unto this negative principle, observe three things:— 1. That the Holy Spirit in this work doth ordinarily put forth his power in and by the use of means. He worketh also on men suitably unto their natures, even as the faculties of their souls, their minds, wills, and affections, are meet to be affected and wrought upon. He doth not come upon them with involuntary raptures, using their faculties and powers as the evil spirit wrests the bodies of them whom he possesseth. His whole work, therefore, is rationally to be accounted for by and unto them who believe the Scripture, and have received the Spirit of truth, whom the world cannot receive. The formal efficiency of the Spirit, indeed, in the putting forth the exceeding greatness of his power in our quickening, — which the ancient church constantly calleth his "inspiration of grace," both in private writing and canons of councils, — is no otherwise to be comprehended by us than any other creating act of divine power; for as we hear the wind, but know not whence it cometh, and whither it goeth, "so is every one that is born of the Spirit." Yet these two things are certain herein:— (1.) That he worketh nothing, nor any other way, nor by any other means, than what are determined and declared in the word. By that, therefore, may and must everything really belonging, or pretended to belong, unto this work of regeneration, be tried and examined. (2.) That he acts nothing contrary unto, puts no force upon, any of the faculties of our souls, but works in them and by them suitably to their natures; and being more intimate unto them, as Austin speaks, than they are unto themselves, by an almighty facility he produceth the effect which he intendeth.

This great work, therefore, neither in part nor whole consists in raptures, ecstasies, visions, enthusiastic inspirations, but in the effect of the power of the Spirit of God on the souls of men, by and according to his word, both of the law and the gospel. And those who charge these things on them who have asserted, declared, and preached it according to the Scriptures, do it, probably, to countenance themselves in their hatred of them and of the work itself. Wherefore, —

2. Where, by reason of distempers of mind, disorder of fancy, or long continuance of distressing fears and sorrows, in and under such preparatory works of the Spirit, which sometimes cut men to their hearts in the sense of their sin, and sinful, lost condition, any do fall into apprehensions or imaginations of any thing extraordinary in the ways before mentioned, if it be not quickly and strictly brought unto the rule, and discarded thereby, it may be of great danger unto their souls, and is never of any solid use or advantage. Such apprehensions, for the most part, are either conceptions of distempered minds and discomposed fancies, or delusions of Satan transforming himself into an angel of light, which the doctrine of regeneration ought not to be accountable for. Yet I must say, —

3. That so it is come to pass, that many of those who have been really made partakers of this gracious work of the Holy Spirit have been looked on in the world, which knows them not, as mad, enthusiastic, and fanatical. So the captains of the host esteemed the prophet that came to anoint Jehu, 2 Kings ix. 11. And the kindred of our Saviour, when he began to preach the gospel, said he was "beside himself," or ecstatical, Mark iii. 21, and "they went out to lay hold on him." So Festus judged of Paul, Acts xxvi. 24, 25. And the author of the Book of Wisdom gives us an account what acknowledgments some will make when it shall be too late, as to their own advantage: Chapter v. 3–5, "They shall say, crying out, because of the trouble of their minds, This is he whom we accounted a scorn, and a common reproach. We fools esteemed his life madness, and his latter end to have been shameful, but how is he reckoned

among the sons of God, and his lot is among the holy ones!" From what hath been spoken it appears, —

Fourthly, That the work of the Spirit of God in regenerating the souls of men is diligently to be inquired into by the preachers of the gospel, and all to whom the word is dispensed. For the former sort, there is a peculiar reason for their attendance unto this duty; for they are used and employed in the work itself by the Spirit of God, and are by him made instrumental for the effecting of this new birth and life. So the apostle Paul styles himself the father of them who were converted to God or regenerated through the word of his ministry: 1 Cor. iv. 15, "Though ye have ten thousand instructors in Christ, yet have ye not many fathers: for in Christ Jesus I have begotten you through the gospel." He was used in the ministry of the word for their regeneration, and therefore was their spiritual father, and he only, though the work was afterward carried on by others. And if men are fathers in the gospel to no more than are converted unto God by their personal ministry, it will be no advantage unto any one day to have assumed that title, when it hath had no foundation in that work as to its effectual success. So, speaking of Onesimus, who was converted by him in prison, he calls him "his son, whom he had begotten in his bonds," Philem. 10. And this he declared to have been prescribed unto him as the principal end of his ministry, in the commission he had for preaching the gospel, Acts xxvi. 17, 18. Christ said unto him, "I send thee unto the Gentiles, to open their eyes, to turn them from darkness to light, and from the power of Satan unto God;" which is a description of the work under consideration. And this is the principal end of our ministry also. Now, certainly it is the duty of ministers to understand the work about which they are employed, as far as they are able, that they may not work in the dark and fight uncertainly, as men beating the air. What the Scripture hath revealed concerning it, as to its nature and the manner of its operation, as to its causes, effects, fruits, evidences, they ought diligently to inquire into. To be spiritually skilled therein is one of the principal furnishments of any for the work of the ministry, without which they will never be able to divide the word aright, nor show themselves workmen that need not be ashamed. Yet it is scarcely imaginable with what rage and perversity of spirit, with what scornful expressions, this whole work is traduced and exposed to contempt. Those who have laboured herein are said "to prescribe long and tedious trains of conversion, to set down nice and subtile processes of regeneration, to fill people's heads with innumerable swarms of superstitious fears and scruples about the due degrees of godly sorrow, and the certain symptoms of a thorough humiliation,"[10] pp. 306, 307. Could any mistake be charged on particular persons in these things, or the prescribing of rules about conversion to God and regeneration that are not warranted by the word of truth, it were not amiss to reflect upon them and refute them; but the intention of these expressions is evident, and the reproach in them is cast upon the work of God itself: and I must profess that I believe the degeneracy from the truth and power of Christian religion, the ignorance of the principal doctrines of the gospel, and that scorn which is cast, in these and the like expressions, on the grace of our Lord Jesus Christ, by such as not only profess themselves to be ministers, but of a higher degree than ordinary, will be sadly ominous unto the whole state of the reformed church amongst us, if not timely repressed and corrected. But what at present I affirm in this matter is, — 1. That it is a duty indispensably incumbent on all ministers of the gospel to acquaint themselves thoroughly with the nature of this work, that they may be able to comply with the will of God and grace of the Spirit in the effecting and accomplishment of it upon the souls of them unto whom they dispense the word. Neither, without some competent knowledge hereof, can they discharge any one part of their duty and office in a right manner. If all that hear them are born dead in trespasses and sins, if they are appointed of God to be the instruments of their regeneration, it is a madness, which must one day be accounted for, to neglect a sedulous inquiry into the nature of this work, and the means whereby it is wrought. And the ignorance hereof or negligence herein, with the want of an experience of the power of this work in their own souls, is one great cause of that lifeless and unprofitable ministry which is among us.

2. It is likewise the duty of all to whom the word is preached to inquire also into it. It is unto such to whom the apostle speaks, 2 Cor. xiii. 5, "Examine yourselves, whether ye be in the faith; prove your own selves. Know ye not your own selves, how that Jesus Christ is in you, except ye be reprobates?" It is the concernment of all individual Christians, or professors of Christian religion, to try and examine themselves what work of the Spirit of God there hath been upon their hearts; and none will deter them from it but those who have a design to hoodwink them to perdition. And, — (1.) The doctrine of it is revealed and taught us; for "secret things belong unto the Lord our God, but those things which are revealed belong unto us and to our children for ever, that we may do all the words of the law," Deut. xxix. 29. And we speak not of curious inquiries into or after hidden things, or the secret, veiled actions of the Holy Spirit; but only of an upright endeavour to search into and comprehend the doctrine concerning this work, to this very end, that we might understand it. (2.) It is of such importance unto all our duties and all our comforts to have a due apprehension of the nature of this work, and of our own concernment therein, that an inquiry into the one and the other cannot be neglected without the greatest folly and madness. Whereunto we may add, (3.) The danger that there is of men being deceived in this matter, which is the hinge whereon their eternal state and condition doth absolutely turn and depend. And certain it is that very many in the world do deceive themselves herein: for they evidently live under one of these pernicious mistakes, — namely, either, [1.] That men may go to heaven, or "enter into the kingdom of God," and not be "born again," contrary to that of our Saviour, John iii. 5; or, [2.] That men may be "born again," and yet live in sin, contrary to 1 John iii. 9.

Footnotes:

1. "Si in gratiâ, non ex naturâ aquæ, sed ex præsentiâ est Spiritus Sancti: numquid in aquâ vivimus, sicut in Spiritu? numquid in aquâ signamur sicut in Spiritu?" — Ambros. de Spir. Sanc. lib. i. cap. 6.

2. "Similiter ex Spiritu secundum gratiam nos renasci, Dominus ipse testatur dicens, Quod natum est ex carne, caro est, quia de carne natum est; et quod natum est de Spiritu, Spiritus est, quia Spiritus Deus est. Claret igitur spiritualis quoque generationis authorem esse Spiritum Sanctum, quia secundum Deum creamur et Filii Dei sumus. Ergo cum ille nos in regnum suum per adoptionem sacræ regenerationis assumpserit, nos ei quod suum est denegamus? ille nos supernæ generationis hæredes fecit, nos hæreditatem vindicamus, refutamus authorem; sed non potest manere beneficium cum author excluditur, nec author sine munere, nec sine authore munus. Si vindicas gratiam, crede potentiam; si refutas potentiam, gratiam ne requiras. Sancti igitur Spiritus opus est regeneratio ista præstantior, et novi hujus hominis qui creatur ad imaginem Dei author est Spiritus, quem utique meliorem hoe exteriori esse nostro homine nemo

dubitaverit." — Ambros. de Spir. Sanc lib. ii. cap. 9.

3. "Denique quomodo respondeat advertite, et videte latebras ambiguitatis falsitati præparare refugia, ita ut etiam nos cum primum ea legimus, recta vel correcta propemodum gauderemus." — August. de Peccat. Orig., cap. 18."Mihi pene persuaserat hanc illam gratiam de qua quæstio est confiteri; quominus in multis ejus opusculi locis sibi ipsi contradicere videretur. Sed cum in manus meas et alia venissent quæ posterius latiusque scripsit, vidi quemadmodum etiam illic gratiam nominare sed ambigua generalitate quid sentiret abscondens, gratiæ tamen vocabulo frangens invidiam, offensionemque declinans." — Id. de Grat. Christ., lib. i. cap. 37.Vid. August. lib. i. cont. Julianum, cap. 5, lib. iii., cap. 1, Lib. de Gest.; Pelag., cap. 30, Epist. 95, ad Innocent.; Epist. Innocent. ad August."Negant etiam quam ad sacram Christi virginem Nemehiadem in oriente conscripsimus, et noverint nos ita hominis laudare naturam ut Dei semper addamus auxilium (verba Pelagii quibus respondet Augustinus), istam sane lege, mihique pene persuaserat, hanc illam gratiam de qua quæstio est confiteri." — Id. ubi supra.

4. "Fefellit judicium Palæstinum, propterea ibi videtur purgatus; Romanam vero ecclesiam, ubi eum esse notissimum scitis fallere usque quaque non potuit, quamvis et hoc fuerit utrumque conatus. Tanto judices fefellit occultius, quanto exponit ista versutius." — August. Lib. de Peccat. Orig. cap. 16.

5. Samuel Parker; see page 121 of this vol. — Ed.

6. "Per inhærentem justitiam intelligimus supernaturale donum gratiæ sanctificantis, oppositum originali peccato, et in singulis animæ facultatibus reparans et renovans illam Dei imaginem, quæ per peccatum originale fœdata ac disspata fuit. Origlnale peccatum mentem tenebris implevit, hæc infusa gratia lumine cœlesti collustrat. Istud cor humanum obstinatione et odio Dei ac divinæ legis maculavit, hæc infusa justitia cor emollit et amore boni accendit et inflammat. Postremo illud affectus omnes atque ipsum appetitum rebellione infecit; hæc renovata sanctitas in ordinem cogit perturbatas affectiones, et ipsam rebellem concupiscentiam dominio spoliat, et quasi sub jugum mittit." — Davenant. de Justit. Habit. cap. iii."Fides tanquam radix imbre suscepto hæret in animæ solo; ut cum per legem Dei excoli cœperit surgant in ea rami qui fructus operum ferant. Non ergo ex operibus radix justitiæ, sed ex radice justitiæ fructus operum crescit." — Origen. lib. iv. in Epist. ad Roman.

7. "Is qui Spiritus Sancti particeps efficitur, per communionem ejus fit spiritualis pariter et sanctus." — Didym. lib. i. de Spir. Sanc., p. 218, inter opera Hieronymi."Qui Spiritu Sancto plenus est statim universis donationibus Dei repletur, sapientia, scientia, fide, cæterisque virtutibus." — Id. ibid."Nunquam enim accipit quisquam spirituales benedictiones Dei, nisi præcesserit Spiritus Sanctus; qui enim habet Spiritum Sanctum consequenter habebit benedictiones." — Idem, p. 220.

8. "Sicut in nativitate carnali omnem nascentis hominis voluntatem præcedit operis divini formatio, sic in spirituali nativitate qua veterem hominem deponere incipimus."— Fulgent. de Incarnat. et Grat. Christ. cap. 29."Forma præcessit in carne Christi, quam in nostra fide spiritualiter agnoscamus; nam Christus Filius Dei, secundum carnem de Spiritu Sancto conceptus et natus est: carnem autem illam nec concipere virgo posset nec parere, nisi ejus carnis Spiritus Sanctus operetur exordium. Sic etiam in hominis corde nec concipi fides potuit nec augeri, nisi eam Spiritus Sanctus effundat et nutriat. Ex eodem namque Spiritu renati sumus, ex quo Christus natus est." — Idem, cap. xx.

9. "Adjuvat nos Deus" (the words of Pelagius), "per doctrinam et revelationem suam, dum cordis nostri oculos aperit, dum nobis, ne præsentibus occupemur, futura demonstrat, dum diaboli pandit insidias, dum nos multiformi et ineffabili dono gratiæ cælestis illuminat." — August. Lib. de Grat. cont. Pelag. et Cælest. cap. vii.

10. Our author quotes from Parker's "Defence and Continuation of the Eccleaiastical Polity," etc. See page 121 of this volume. — Ed.

Chapter II - Works of the Holy Spirit preparatory unto regeneration

Sundry things preparatory to the work of conversion — Material and formal dispositions, with their difference — Things in the power of our natural abilities required of us in a way of duty — Internal, spiritual effects wrought in the souls of men by the word — Illumination — Conviction of sin — Consequents thereof — These things variously taught — Power of the word and energy of the Spirit distinct — Subject of this work; mind, affections, and conscience — Nature of this whole work, and difference from saving conversion farther declared.

First, in reference unto the work of regeneration itself, positively considered, we may observe, that ordinarily there are certain previous and preparatory works, or workings in and upon the souls of men, that are antecedent and dispositive unto it. But yet regeneration doth not consist in them, nor can it be educed out of them. This is, for the substance of it, the position of the divines of the church of England at the synod of Dort, two whereof died bishops, and others of them were dignified in the hierarchy. I mention it, that those by whom these things are despised may a little consider whose ashes they trample on and scorn. Lawful, doubtless, it is for any man, on just grounds, to dissent from their judgments and determinations;[11] but to do it with an imputation of folly, with derision, contempt, scorn, and scoffing, at what they believed and taught, becometh only a generation of new divines amongst us. But to return; I speak in this position only of them that are adult, and not converted until they have made use of the means of grace in and by their own reasons and understandings; and the dispositions I intend are only materially so, not such as contain grace of the same nature as is regeneration itself. A material disposition is that which disposeth and some way maketh a subject fit for the reception of that which shall be communicated, added, or infused into it as its form. So wood by dryness and a due composure is made fit and ready to admit of firing, or continual fire. A formal disposition is where one degree of the same kind disposeth the subject unto farther degrees of it; as the morning light, which is of the same kind, disposeth the air to the reception of the full light of the sun. The former we allow here, not the latter. Thus, in natural generation there are sundry dispositions of the matter before the form is introduced. So the body of Adam was formed before the rational soul was breathed into it; and Ezekiel's bones came together with a noise and shaking before the breath of life entered into them.

I shall in this place give only a summary account of this preparatory work, because in the close of these discourses I shall handle it practically and more at large. Wherefore what I have here to offer concerning it shall be reduced unto the ensuing observations:—

First, There are some things required of us in a way of duty in order unto our regeneration, which are so in the power of our own natural abilities as that nothing but corrupt prejudices and stubbornness in sinning do keep or hinder men from the performance of them. And these we may reduce unto two heads:— 1. An outward attendance unto the dispensation of the word of God, with those other external means of grace which accompany it or are appointed therein. "Faith cometh by hearing, and hearing by the word of God," Rom. x. 17; that is, it is hearing the word of God which is the ordinary means of ingenerating faith in the souls of men. This is required of all to whom the gospel doth come; and this they are able of themselves to do, as well as any other natural or civil action. And where men do it not, where they despise the word at a distance, yea, where they do it not with diligence and choice, it is merely from supine negligence of spiritual things, carnal security, and contempt of God; which they must answer for. 2. A diligent intension of mind, in attendance on the means of grace, to understand and receive the things revealed and declared as the mind and will of God. For this end hath God given men their reasons and understandings, that they may use and exercise them about their duty towards him, according to the revelation of his mind and will. To this purpose he calls upon them to remember that they are men, and to turn unto him. And there is nothing herein but what is in the liberty and power of the rational faculties of our souls, assisted with those common aids which God affords unto all men in general. And great advantages both may be and are daily attained hereby. Persons, I say, who diligently apply their rational abilities in and about spiritual things, as externally revealed in the word and the preaching of it, do usually attain great advantages by it, and excel their equals in other things; as Paul did when he was brought up at the feet of Gamaliel. Would men be but as intent and diligent in their endeavours after knowledge in spiritual things, as revealed in a way suited unto our capacities and understandings, as they are to get skill in crafts, sciences, and other mysteries of life, it would be much otherwise with many than it is. A neglect herein also is the fruit of sensuality, spiritual sloth, love of sin, and contempt of God; all which are the voluntary frames and actings of the minds of men.

These things are required of us in order unto our regeneration, and it is in the power of our own wills to comply with them. And we may observe concerning them that, — 1. The omission of them, the neglect of men in them, is the principal occasion, and cause of the eternal ruin of the souls of the generality of them to whom or amongst whom the gospel is preached: "This is the condemnation, that light is come into the world, and men loved darkness rather than light, because their deeds were evil," John iii. 19. The generality of men know full well that they do in this matter no more what they are able than what they should. All pleadable pretences of inability and weakness are far from them. They cannot but know here, and they shall be forced to confess hereafter, that it was merely from their own cursed sloth, with love of the world and sin, that they were diverted from a diligent attendance on the means of conversion and the sedulous exercise of their minds about them. Complaints hereof against themselves will make up a great part of their last dreadful cry. 2. In the most diligent use of outward means, men are not able of themselves to attain unto regeneration, or complete conversion to God, without an especial, effectual, internal work of the Holy Spirit of grace on their whole souls. This containing the substance of what is principally proposed unto confirmation in the ensuing discourses, need not here be insisted on. 3. Ordinarily, God, in the effectual dispensation of his grace, meeteth with them who attend with diligence on the outward administration of the means of it. He doth so, I say, ordinarily, in comparison of them who are despisers and neglecters of them. Sometimes, indeed, he goeth, as it were, out of the way to meet with and bring home unto himself a persecuting Saul, taking of him in, and taking him off from, a course of open sin and rebellion; but ordinarily he dispenseth his peculiar especial grace among them who attend unto the common means of it: for he will both glorify his word thereby, and give out pledges of his approbation of our obedience unto his commands and institutions.

Secondly, There are certain internal spiritual effects wrought in and upon the souls of men, whereof the word preached is the immediate instrumental cause, which ordinarily do precede the work of regeneration, or real conversion unto God. And they are reducible unto three heads:— 1. Illumination; 2. Conviction; 3. Reformation. The first of these respects the mind only; the second, the mind, conscience, and affections; and the third, the life and conversation:—

1. The first is illumination, of whose nature and causes we must afterward treat distinctly. At present, I shall only consider it as it is ordinarily previous unto regeneration, and materially disposing the mind thereunto. Now, all the light which by any means we attain unto, or knowledge that we have in or about spiritual things, things of supernatural revelation, come under this denomination of illumination. And hereof there are three degrees:— (1.) That which ariseth merely from an industrious application of the rational faculties of our souls to know, perceive, and understand the doctrines of truth as revealed unto us; for hereby much knowledge of divine truth may be obtained, which others, through their negligence, sloth, and pride, are unacquainted with. And this knowledge I refer unto illumination, — that is, a light superadded to the innate conceptions of men's minds, and beyond what of themselves they can extend unto, — because it is concerning such things as the heart of man could never of itself conceive, but the very knowledge of them is communicated by their revelation, 1 Cor. ii. 9, 11. And the reason why so very few do exercise themselves to the attaining of this knowledge, according to their abilities, is because of the enmity which is in the carnal minds of all men by nature unto the things themselves that are revealed. And within the compass of this degree I comprise all knowledge of spiritual things that is merely natural. (2.) There is an illumination which is an especial effect of the Holy Ghost by the word on the minds of men. With respect hereunto, some who fall totally from God and perish eternally are said to have been "once enlightened," Heb. vi. 4. This light variously affects the mind, and makes a great addition unto what is purely natural, or attainable by the mere exercise of our natural abilities.

For, [1.] It adds perspicuity unto it, making the things discerned in it more clear and perspicuous to the mind. Hence men endowed with it are said to "know the way of righteousness," 2 Pet. ii. 21, — clearly and distinctly to apprehend the doctrine of the gospel as the way of righteousness. They know it not only or merely as true, but as a way of righteousness, — namely, the way of God's righteousness, which is therein "revealed from faith to faith," Rom. i. 17, and the way of righteousness for sinners in the sight of God, chap. x. 3, 4. [2.] It adds a greater assent unto the truth of the things revealed than mere natural reason can rise up unto. Hence those thus illuminated are frequently said to "believe," their faith being only the naked assent of their minds unto the truth revealed to them. So it is said of Simon the magician, Acts viii. 13, and of sundry of the Jews, John ii. 23, xii. 42. [3.] It adds unto them some kind of evanid joy. These "receive the word with joy," and yet have "no root in themselves," Luke viii. 13. They "rejoice in the light" of it, at least "for a season," John v. 35. Persons that are thus enlightened will be variously affected with the word, so as they are not whose natural faculties are not spiritually excited. [4.] It adds ofttimes gifts also, whereof this spiritual light is, as it were, the common matter, which in exercise is formed and fashioned in great variety. I say, this kind of spiritual light, the effect of this illumination, is the subject-matter, and contains in it the substance, of all spiritual gifts. One sort of gift it is when put forth and exercised in one way, or one kind of duty, and another as in another. And where it is improved into gifts, which principally it is by exercise, there it wonderfully affects the mind, and raiseth its apprehensions in and of spiritual things. Now, concerning this degree of illumination, I say, first, That it is not regeneration, nor doth it consist therein, nor doth necessarily or infallibly ensue upon it. A third degree is required thereunto, which we shall afterward explain. Many, therefore, may be thus enlightened, and yet never be converted. Secondly, That in order of nature it is previous unto a full and real conversion to God, and is materially preparatory and dispositive thereunto; for saving grace enters into the soul by light. As it is therefore a gift of God, so it is the duty of all men to labour after a participation of it, however by many it be abused.

2. Conviction of sin is another effect of the preaching of the word antecedaneous unto real conversion to God. This in general the apostle describes, 1 Cor. xiv. 24, 25, "If all prophesy, and there come in one that believeth not, he is convinced of all: and thus are the secrets of his heart made manifest; and so falling down on his face he will worship God."

And sundry things are included herein, or do accompany it; as, — (1.) A disquieting sense of the guilt of sin with respect unto the law of God, with his threatenings and future judgment. Things that before were slighted and made a mock of do now become the soul's burden and constant disquietment. "Fools make a mock of sin;" they traverse their ways, and snuff up the wind like the wild ass; but in their month, when conviction hath burdened them, you may find them. And hereby are the minds of men variously affected with fears and anguish, in various degrees,[12] according as impressions are made upon them by the word. And these degrees are not prescribed as necessary duties unto persons under their convictions, but only described as they usually fall out, to the relief and direction of such as are concerned in them; — as a man going to give directions unto another how to guide his course in a voyage at sea, he tells him that in such a place he will meet with rocks and shelves, storms and cross winds, so that if he steer not very heedfully he will be in danger to miscarry and to be cast away; he doth not prescribe it unto him as his duty to go among such rocks and into such storms, but only directs him how to guide himself in them where he doth meet with them, as assuredly he will, if he miss not his proper course. (2.) Sorrow or grief for sin committed, because past and irrecoverable; which is the formal reason of this condemning sorrow. This the Scripture calls "sorrow of the world," 2 Cor. vii. 10; divines, usually, legal sorrow, as that which, in conjunction with the sense of the guilt of sin mentioned, brings men into bondage under fear, Rom. viii. 15. (3.) Humiliation for sin, which is the exercise or working of sorrow and fear in outward acts of confession, fasting, praying, and the like. This is the true nature of legal humiliation, 1 Kings xxi. 29. (4.) Unless by these things the soul be swallowed up in despair, it cannot be but that it will be filled with thoughts, desires, inquiries, and contrivances about a deliverance out of that state and condition wherein it is; as Acts ii. 37, xvi. 30. 3. Oftentimes a great reformation of life and change in affections doth ensue hereon; as Matt. xiii. 20; 2 Pet. ii. 20; Matt. xii. 44.

All these things may be wrought in the minds of men by the dispensation of the word, and yet the work of regeneration be never perfected in them. Yea, although they are good in themselves, and fruits of the kindness of God towards us, they may not only be lost as unto any spiritual advantage, but also be abused unto our great disadvantage. And this comes not to pass but by our own sin, whereby we contract a new guilt upon our souls. And it commonly so falls out one of these three ways; for, — 1. Some are no way careful or wise to improve this light and conviction unto the end whereunto they tend and are designed.

Their message is, to turn the minds of men, and to take them off from their self-confidence, and to direct them unto Christ. Where this is not attended unto, where they are not used and improved unto the pursuit of this end, they insensibly wither, decay, and come to nothing. 2. In some they are overborne by the power and violence of their lusts, the love of sin, and efficacy of temptation. They are sinned away everyday, and leave the soul in ten times a worse condition than they found it. 3. Some rest in these things, as though they comprised the whole work of God towards them, and guided them in all the duties required of them. This is the state of many where they extend their power, in the last instance, unto any considerable reformation of life, and attendance unto duties of religious worship. But this, as was said, falls out through the abuse which the carnal minds of men, retaining their enmity against God, do put these things unto. In their own nature they are good, useful, and material preparations unto regeneration, disposing the mind unto the reception of the grace of God.

And the doctrine concerning these things hath been variously handled, distinguished, and applied, by many learned divines and faithful ministers of the gospel. Unto that light which they received into them from the infallible word of truth, they joined those experiences which they had observed in their own hearts and the consciences of others with whom they had to do, which were suitable thereunto; and in the dispensation of this truth, according to the "measure of the gift of the grace of Christ," which they severally received, they had a useful and fruitful ministry in the world, to the converting of many unto God. But we have lived to see all these things decried and rejected. And the way which some have taken therein is as strange and uncouth as the thing itself; for they go not about once to disprove by Scripture or reason what hath been taught or delivered by any sober persons to this purpose, nor do they endeavour themselves to declare from or by the Scriptures what is the work of regeneration, what are the causes and effects of it, in opposition thereunto. These and such like ways, made use of by all that have treated of spiritual things from the foundation of Christianity, are despised and rejected; but horrible and contemptuous reproaches are cast upon the things themselves, in words heaped together on purpose to expose them unto scorn among persons ignorant of the gospel and themselves. Those that teach them are "ecstatical and illiterate;" and those that receive them are "superstitious, giddy, and fanatical."

All conviction, sense of and sorrow for sin; all fear of the curse and wrath due unto sin; all troubles and distresses of mind by reason of these things, — are "foolish imaginations, the effects of bodily diseases and distempers, enthusiastic notions, arising from the disorders of men's brains," and I know not what untoward "humours in their complexions and constitutions." The same or the like account is also given concerning all spiritual desertions, or joys and refreshments; and the whole doctrine concerning these things is branded with novelty, and hopes expressed of its sudden vanishing out of the world. This contempt and scorn of the gospel have we lived to see, whereof, it may be, other ages and places have not had experience; for as all these things are plentifully taught by some of the ancients in their expositions of the scriptures wherein they are expressed, especially by Austin, who had occasion particularly to inquire into them, so the doctrine concerning them is in a great measure retained in the church of Rome itself. Only some amongst ourselves are weary of them; who, being no way able to oppose the principles and foundations whereon they are built, nor to disprove them by Scripture or reason, betake themselves to these revilings and reproaches; and, as if it were not enough for them to proclaim their own ignorance and personal unacquaintance with those things which inseparably accompany that conviction of sin, righteousness, and judgment which our Lord Jesus Christ hath promised to send the Holy Spirit to work in all that should believe, they make the reproaching of it in others a principal effect of that religion which they profess. "Nevertheless the foundation of God standeth sure, The Lord knoweth them that are his." But we must return to our purpose.

Thirdly, All the things mentioned as wrought instrumentally by the word are effects of the power of the Spirit of God. The word itself, under a bare proposal to the minds of men, will not so affect them. We need go no farther for the confirmation hereof than merely to consider the preaching (with the effects which it had towards many) of the prophets of old, Isa. xlix. 4, Jer. xv. 20, Ezek. xxxiii. 31, 32; of Jesus Christ himself, John viii. 59; and of the apostles, Acts xiii. 41, 45, 46. Hence to this day, the Jews, who enjoy the letter of the Old Testament, without the administration of the Spirit, are as full of blindness, hardness, and obstinacy, as any in the world who are utterly deprived of it. Many amongst ourselves sit all their days under the preaching of the word, and yet have none of the effects mentioned wrought upon them, when others, their associates in hearing, are really affected, convinced, and converted. It is, therefore, the ministration of the Spirit, in and by the word, which produceth all or any of these effects on the minds of men; he is the fountain of all illumination. Hence, they that are "enlightened" are said to be made "partakers of the Holy Spirit," Heb. vi. 4. And he is promised by our Saviour "to convince the world of sin," John xvi. 8; which, although in that place it respects only one kind of sin, yet it is sufficient to establish a general rule, that all conviction of sin is from and by him. And no wonder if men live securely in their sins, to whom the light which he gives and the convictions which he worketh are a scorn and reproach.

There is, indeed, an objection of some moment against the ascription of this work unto the energy of the Holy Spirit; for "whereas it is granted that all these things may be wrought in the minds and souls of men, and yet they may come short of the saving grace of God, how can he be thought to be the author of such a work? Shall we say that he designs only a weak and imperfect work upon the hearts of men? or that he deserts and gives over the work of grace which he hath undertaken towards them, as not able to accomplish it?"

Ans. 1. In many persons, it may be in the most, who are thus affected, real conversion unto God doth ensue, the Holy Spirit by these preparatory actings making way for the introduction of the new spiritual life into the soul: so they belong unto a work that is perfect in its kind. 2. Wherever they fail and come short of what in their own nature they have a tendency unto, it is not from any weakness and imperfection in themselves, but from the sins of them in whom they are wrought. For instance, even common illumination and conviction of sin have, in their own nature, a tendency unto sincere conversion. They have so in the same kind as the law hath to bring us unto Christ. Where this end is not attained, it is always from the interposition of an act of wilfulness and stubbornness in those enlightened and convicted. They do not sincerely improve what they have received, and faint not merely for want of strength to proceed, but, by a free act of their own wills, they refuse the grace which is farther tendered unto them in the gospel. This will, and its actual resistance unto the work of the Spirit, God is pleased in some to take away. It is, therefore, of sovereign grace when and where it is removed. But the sin of men and their guilt is in it where it is continued; for no more is required hereunto but that it be voluntary. It is will, and not power, that gives rectitude or obliquity unto moral actions. 3. As we observed before, the Holy Spirit in his whole work is a voluntary agent. He worketh what, when, and how he pleaseth. No more is required unto his operations, that they may be such as become him, but these two things:— First, That in themselves they be good and holy. Secondly, That they be effectual as unto the ends whereunto by him they are designed. That he should always design them to the utmost length of what they have a moral tendency towards, though no real efficiency for, is not required. And these things are found in these operations of the Holy Spirit. They are in their own nature good and holy. Illumination is so; so is conviction and sorrow for sin, with a subsequent change of affections and amendment of life.

Again: What he worketh in any of these effectually and infallibly accomplisheth the end aimed at; which is no more but that men be enlightened, convinced, humbled, and reformed, wherein he faileth not. In these things he is pleased to take on him the management of the law, so to bring the soul into bondage thereby, that it may be stirred up to seek after deliverance; and he is thence actively called the "Spirit of bondage unto fear," Rom. viii. 15. And this work is that which constitutes the third ground in our Saviour's parable of the sower. It receives the seed and springs up hopefully, until, by cares of the world, temptations, and occasions of life, it is choked and lost, Matt. xiii. 22. Now, because it oftentimes maketh a great appearance and resemblance of regeneration itself, or of real conversion to God, so that neither the world nor the church is able to distinguish between them, it is of great concernment unto all professors of the gospel to inquire diligently whether they have in their own souls been made partakers of any other work of the Spirit of God or no; for although this be a good work, and doth lie in a good subserviency unto regeneration, yet if men attain no more, if they proceed no farther, they will perish, and that eternally. And multitudes do herein actually deceive themselves, speaking peace unto their souls on the effects of this work; whereby it is not only insufficient to save them, as it is to all persons at all times, but also becomes a means of their present security and future destruction. I shall, therefore, give some few instances of what this work, in the conjunction of all the parts of it, and in its utmost improvement, cannot effect; whereby men may make a judgment how things stand in their own souls in respect unto it:—

1. It may be observed, that we have placed all the effects of this work in the mind, conscience, affections, and conversation. Hence it follows, notwithstanding all that is or may be spoken of it, that the will is neither really changed nor internally renewed by it. Now, the will is the ruling, governing faculty of the soul, as the mind is the guiding and leading. Whilst this abides unchanged, unrenewed, the power and reign of sin continue in the soul, though not undisturbed yet unruined. It is true, there are many checks and controls, from the light of the mind and reflections of conscience, cast in this state upon the actings of the will, so that it cannot put itself forth in and towards sin with that freedom, security, and licentiousness as it was wont to do. Its fierceness and rage, rushing into sin as the horse into the battle, running on God and the thick bosses of his buckler, may be broken and abated by those hedges of thorns which it finds set in its way, and those buffetings it meets withal from light and convictions; its delight and greediness in sinning may be calmed and quieted by those frequent representations of the terror of the Lord on the one hand, and the pleasure of eternal rest on the other, which are made unto it: but yet still, setting aside all considerations foreign unto its own principle, the bent and inclination of the will itself is to sin and evil always and continually. The will of sinning may be restrained upon a thousand considerations, which light and convictions will administer, but it is not taken away. And this discovers itself when the very first motions of the soul towards sinful objects have a sensible complacency, until they are controlled by light and fear. This argues an unrenewed will, if it be constant and universal.

2. The effects of this work on the mind, which is the first subject affected with it, proceeds not so far as to give it delight, complacency, and satisfaction in the lively spiritual nature and excellencies of the things revealed unto it. The true nature of saving illumination consists in this, that it gives the mind such a direct intuitive insight and prospect into spiritual things as that, in their own spiritual nature, they suit, please, and satisfy it, so that it is transformed into them, cast into the mould of them, and rests in them, Rom. vi. 17, xii. 2; 1 Cor. ii. 13–15; 2 Cor. iii. 18, iv. 6. This the work we have insisted on reacheth not unto; for, notwithstanding any discovery that is made therein of spiritual things unto the mind, it finds not an immediate, direct, spiritual excellency in them, but only with respect unto some benefit or advantage which is to be attained by means thereof. It will not give such a. spiritual insight into the mystery of God's grace by Jesus Christ, called "his glory shining in the face of Jesus Christ," 2 Cor. iv. 6, as that the soul, in its first direct view of it, should, for what it is in itself, admire it, delight in it, approve it, and find spiritual solace with refreshment in it. But such a light, such a knowledge it communicates, as that a man may like it well in its effects, as a way of mercy and salvation.

3. This work extends itself to the conscience also; but yet it doth not purge the conscience from dead works, that we should serve the living God. This is the effect of a real application of the blood of Christ by faith unto our souls, Heb. ix. 14. Two things it effects upon the conscience:— (1.) It renders it more ready, quick, and sharp in the reproving and condemning of all sin than it was before. To condemn sin, according unto its light and guidance, is natural unto

and inseparable from the conscience of man; but its readiness and ability to exercise this condemning power may, by custom and course of sinning in the world, be variously weakened and impeded. But when conscience is brought under the power of this work, having its directing light augmented, whereby it sees more of the evil of sin than formerly, and having its self-reflections sharpened and multiplied, it is more ready and quick in putting forth its judging and condemning power than it was. (2.) Conscience is assisted and directed hereby to condemn many things in sin which before it approved of; for its judging power is still commensurate unto its light, and many things are thereby now discovered to be sinful which were not so by the mere natural guidance under which before it was. But yet, notwithstanding all this, it doth not purge the conscience from dead works; that is, conscience is not hereby wrought unto such an abhorrency of sin for itself as continually to direct the soul unto an application to the blood of Christ for the cleansing of itself and the purging of it out. It contents itself to keep all things in a tumult, disorder, and confusion, by its constant condemning both sin and sinners.

4. This work operates greatly on the affections. We have given instances in the fear, sorrow, joy, and delight about spiritual things that are stirred up and acted thereby. But yet it comes short in two things of a thorough work upon the affections themselves: for, (1.) it doth not fix them; and, (2.) it doth not fill them. (1.) It is required that our affections be fixed on heavenly and spiritual things, and true grace will effect it: Col. iii. 1, 2, "If ye be risen with Christ, seek those things which are above, where Christ sitteth on the right hand of God. Set your affection on things above." The joys, the fears, the hopes, the sorrows, with reference unto spiritual and eternal things, which the work before mentioned doth produce, are evanid, uncertain, unstable, not only as to the degrees, but as to the very being of them. Sometimes they are as a river ready to overflow its banks, — men cannot but be pouring them out on all occasions; and sometimes as waters that fail, — no drop comes from them. Sometimes they are hot, and sometimes cold; sometimes up, and sometimes down; sometimes all heaven, and sometimes all world; without equality, without stability. But true grace fixeth the affections on spiritual things. As to the degrees of their exercise, there may be and is in them great variety, according as they may be excited, aided, assisted, by grace and the means of it, or obstructed and impeded by the interposition of temptations and diversions. But the constant bent and inclination of renewed affections is unto spiritual things, as the Scripture everywhere testifieth and experience doth confirm. (2.) The forementioned work doth not fill the affections, however it may serve to take them up and pacify them. It comes like many strangers to an inn to lodge, which take up a great deal of room, and make an appearance as if none were in the house but themselves; and yet they turn not out the family which dwelleth there, but there they make their abode still. Light and conviction, with all their train and attendants, come into the mind and affections as if they would fill them, and possess them for themselves alone; but yet, when they have done all, they leave the quiet places of the house for the world, and sin, and self. They do not thrust them out of the affections, and fill up their places with spiritual things. But saving grace fills up the affections with spiritual things, fills the soul with spiritual love, joy, and delight, and exerciseth all other affections about their proper objects. It denies not a room to any other things, relations, possessions, enjoyments, merely as they are natural, and are content to be

subordinate unto God and spiritual things; but if they would be carnal, disorderly, or predominant, it casts them out.

5. This work is oftentimes carried on very far in reformation of life and conversation, so that it will express the whole form of godliness therein. But herein, also, it is subject unto a threefold defect and imperfection; for, — (1.) It will consist with and allow of raging and reigning sins of ignorance. The conducting light in this work not leading unto the abhorrency of all sin as sin, nor into a pursuit of holiness out of a design to be universally conformable unto Christ, but being gathered up from this and that particular command, it ofttimes leaves behind it great sins unregarded. So it left persecution in Paul before his conversion; and so it leaves hatred and a desire of persecution in many at this day. And other sins of the like nature may escape its utmost search, to the ruin of the soul. (2.) Its reformation of the conversation is seldom universal as to all known sins, unless it be for a season, whilst the soul is under a flagrant pursuit of self-righteousness. Paul in that condition had preserved himself so as that, according to the law, he was blameless; and the young man thought he had kept all the commandments from his youth. But setting aside this consideration, notwithstanding the utmost that this work can attain unto, after the efficacy of its first impressions begin to abate, lust will reserve some peculiar way of venting and discovering itself; which is much spoken unto. (3.) The conversations of persons who live and abide under the power of this work only is assuredly fading and decaying. Coldness, sloth, negligence, love of the world, carnal wisdom, and security, do everyday get ground upon them. Hence, although by a long course of abstinence from open sensual sins, and stating of a contrary interest, they are not given up unto them, yet, by the decays of the power of their convictions, and the ground that sin gets upon them, they become walking and talking skeletons in religion, — dry, sapless, useless, worldlings. But where the soul is inlaid with real saving grace, it is in a state of thriving continually. Such an one will go on from strength to strength, from grace to grace, from glory to glory, and will be fat and flourishing in old age. By these things may we learn to distinguish in ourselves between the preparatory work mentioned, and that of real saving conversion unto God. And these are some of the heads of those operations of the Holy Spirit on the minds of men, which oftentimes are preparatory unto a real conversion unto God; and sometimes, [by] their contempt and rejection, a great aggravation of the sin and misery of them in whom they were wrought.

And these things, as they are clearly laid down in the Scripture and exemplified in sundry instances, so, for the substance of them, they have been acknowledged (till of late) by all Christians; only some of the Papists have carried them so far as to make them formally dispositive unto justification, and to have a congruous merit thereof. But this the ancients denied, who would not allow that either any such preparation or any moral virtues did capacitate men for real conversion, observing that others were often called before those who were so qualified.[13] And in them there are goads and nails, which have been fastened by wise and experienced masters of the assemblies, to the great advantage of the souls of men; for, observing the usual ways and means whereby these effects are wrought in the minds of the hearers of the word, with their consequences, in sorrow, troubles, fear, and humiliations, and the courses which they take to improve them, or to extricate themselves from the perplexity of them, they have managed the rules of Scripture with their own and others' experience suitable thereunto, to the great benefit of the church of God. That these things are now despised and laughed to scorn is no part of the happiness of the age wherein we live, as the event will manifest.

And in the meantime, if any suppose that we will forego these truths and doctrines, which are so plainly revealed in the Scripture, the knowledge whereof is so useful unto the souls of men, and whose publication in preaching hath been of so great advantage to the church of God, merely because they understand them not, and therefore reproach them, they will be greatly mistaken. Let them lay aside that unchristian way of treating about these things which they have engaged in, and plainly prove that men need not be convinced of sin, that they ought not to be humbled for it, nor affected with sorrow with respect unto it; that they ought not to seek for a remedy or deliverance from it; that all men are not born in a state of sin; that our nature is not depraved by the fall; that we are able to do all that is required of us, without the internal aids and assistances of the Spirit of God, — and they shall be diligently attended unto.

Footnotes:

11. "Sunt quædam opera externa, ab hominibus ordinariè requisita, priusquam ad statum regenerationis, aut conversionis perducantur, quæ ab iisdem quandoque libere fieri, quandoque liberè omitti solent; ut adire ecclesiam, audire verbi præconium, et id genus alia."Sunt quædam effecta interna ad conversionem sive regenerationem prævia, quæ virtute verbi, spiritusque in nondum regeneratorum cordibus excitantur; qualia sunt notitia voluntatis divinæ, sensus peccati, timor pœnæ; cogitatio de liberatione, spes aliqua veniæ." — Synod. Dordrec. Sententia Theolog. Britan. ad Artic. quartum, thes. 1, 2, p. 139.

12. "Heu miserum, nimisque miserum quem torquet conscientia sua, quam fugere non potest; nimis miserum quem expectat damnatio sua quam vitare non potest, nisi Deus eripiat. Nimis est infelix cui mors æterna est sensibilis; nimis ærumnosus quem terrent continui de sua infelicitate horrores." — August. de Contritione Cordis.

13. "Nonne advertimus multos fideles nostros ambulantes viam Dei, ex nulla parte ingenio comparari, non dicam quorundam hæreticorum, sed etiam minorum? Item nonne videmus quosdam homines utriusque sexus in conjugali castitate viventes sine querela, et tamen vel hæreticos vel Paganos, vel etiam in vera fide et vera ecclesia sic tepidos, ut eos miremur meretricum et histrionum subito conversorum, non solum sapientiâ et temperantiâ sed etiam fide, spe et charitate superari." — August. lib. ii. Quæs. ad Simplician. q. 2.

Chapter III - Corruption or depravation of the mind by sin

Contempt and corruption of the doctrine of regeneration — All men in the world regenerate or unregenerate — General description of corrupted nature — Depravation of the mind — Darkness upon it — The nature of spiritual darkness — Reduced unto two heads — Of darkness objective; how removed — Of darkness subjective; its nature and power proved — Eph. iv. 17, 18, opened and applied — The mind "alienated from the life of God" — The" life of God," what it is — The power of the mind with respect unto spiritual things examined — 1 Cor. ii. 14 opened — Ψυχικὸς ἄνθρωπος, or the "natural man," who — Spiritual things, what they are — How the natural man cannot know or receive spiritual things — Difference between understanding doctrines and receiving of things — A twofold power and ability of mind with respect unto spiritual things explained — Reasons why a natural man cannot discern spiritual things — How and wherefore spiritual things are foolishness to natural men — Why natural men cannot receive the things of God — A double impotency in the mind of man by nature — 1 Cor. ii. 14 farther vindicated — Power of darkness in persons unregenerate — The mind filled with wills or lusts, and enmity thereby — The power and efficacy of spiritual darkness at large declared.

We have, I hope, made our way plain for the due consideration of the great work of the Spirit in the regeneration of the souls of God's elect. This is that whereby he forms the members of the mystical body of Christ, and prepares living stones for the building of a temple wherein the living God will dwell. Now, that we may not only declare the truth in this matter, but also vindicate it from those corruptions wherewith some have endeavoured to debauch it, I shall premise a description lately given of it, with confidence enough, and it may be not without too much authority; and it is in these words: "What is it to be born again, and to have a new spiritual life in Christ, but to become sincere proselytes to the gospel, to renounce all vicious customs and practices, and to give an upright and uniform obedience to all the laws of Christ. And, therefore, if they are all but precepts of moral virtue, to be born again, and to have a new spiritual life, is only to become a new moral man. But their account" (speaking of Nonconformist ministers) "of this article is so wild and fantastic, that had I nothing else to make good my charge against them, that alone would be more than enough to expose the prodigious folly of their spiritual divinity," pp. 343, 344.[14] I confess these are the words of one who seems not much to consider what he says, so as that it may serve his present turn in reviling and reproaching other men; for he considers not that, by this description of it, he utterly excludes the baptismal regeneration of infants, which is so plainly professed by the church wherein he is dignified. But this is publicly declared, avowed, and vended, as allowed doctrine amongst us, and therefore deserves to be noticed, though the person that gives it out be at irreconcilable feuds with himself and his church. Of morality and grace an account shall be given elsewhere. At present, the work of regeneration is that which is under our consideration. And concerning this, those so severely treated teach no other doctrine but what, for the substance of it, is received in all the reformed churches in Europe, and which so many learned divines of the church of England confirmed with their suffrage at the synod of Dort. Whether this deserve all the scorn which this haughty person pours upon it by his swelling words of vanity will, to indifferent persons, be made appear in the ensuing discourse; as also what is to be thought of the description of it given by that author, which, whether it savour more of ignorance and folly, or of pride and fulsome errors, is hard to determine. I know some words in it are used with the old Pelagian trick of ambiguity, so as to be capable of having another sense and interpretation put upon them than their present use and design will admit of; but that artifice will be immediately rendered useless.

There is a twofold state of men with respect unto God, which is comprehensive of all individuals in the world; for all men are either unregenerate or regenerate. There being an affirmation and a negation concerning the state of regeneration in the Scripture, one of them may be used concerning every capable subject; every man living is so, or he is not so. And herein, as I suppose, there is a general consent of Christians. Again, it is evident in the Scripture, and we have proved it in our way, that all men are born in an unregenerate condition. This is so positively declared by our Saviour that there is no rising up against it, John iii. 3–8. Now, regeneration being the delivery of men (or the means of it) from that state and condition wherein they are born or are by nature, we cannot discover wherein it doth consist without a declaration of that state which it gives us deliverance from. And this, in the first place, we shall insist upon at large, giving an account of the state of lapsed nature under a loss of the original grace of God. And these things I shall handle practically, for the edification of all sorts of believers, and not in the way and method of the schools; which yet shall be done elsewhere.

In the declaration of the state of corrupted nature after the fall, and before the reparation of it by the grace of Jesus Christ, — that is, the effectual operation of the Holy Spirit, — the Scripture principally insists on three things:[15] — 1. The corruption and depravation of the mind; which it calls by the name of darkness and blindness, with the consequents of vanity, ignorance, and folly. 2. The depravation of the will and affections; which it expresseth several ways, as by weakness or impotency, and stubbornness or obstinacy. 3. By the general name of death, extended to the condition of the whole soul. And these have various effects and consequences, as in our explanation of them will appear.

All men by nature, not enlightened, not renewed in their minds by the saving, effectual operation of the Holy Spirit, are in a state of darkness and blindness with respect unto God and spiritual things, with the way of pleasing him and living unto him. Be men otherwise and in other things never so wise, knowing, learned, and skilful, in spiritual things they are dark, blind, ignorant, unless they are renewed in the spirit of their minds by the Holy Ghost. This is a matter which the world cannot endure to hear of, and it is ready to fall into a tumult upon its mention. They think it but an artifice which some weak men have got up, to reflect on and condemn them who are wiser than themselves On the like occasion did the Pharisees ask of our Saviour that question with pride and scorn, "Are we blind also?" John ix. 40. But as he lets them know that their presumption of light and knowledge would serve only to aggravate their sin and condemnation, verse 41; so he plainly tells them, that notwithstanding all their boasting, "they had neither heard the voice of God at any time, nor seen his shape," chap. v. 37.

Some at present talk much about the power of the intellectual faculties of our souls, as though they were neither debased, corrupted, impaired, nor depraved. All that disadvantage which is befallen our nature by the entrance of sin is but in "the disorder of the affections and the inferior sensitive parts of the soul, which are apt to tumultuate and rebel against that pure untainted light which is in the mind!" And this they speak of it without respect unto its renovation by the Holy Spirit; for if they include that also, they are in their discourses most notorious confused triflers. Indeed, some of them write as if they had never deigned once to consult with the Scriptures, and others are plainly gone over into the tents of the Pelagians. But, setting aside their modern artifices of confident boasting, contemptuous reproaches, and scurrilous railings, it is no difficult undertaking so to demonstrate the depravation of the minds of men by nature, and their impotency thence to discern spiritual things in a spiritual manner,[16] without a saving, effectual work of the Holy Spirit in their renovation, as that the proudest and most petulant of them shall not be able to return any thing of a solid answer thereunto. And herein we plead for nothing but the known doctrine of the ancient catholic church, declared in the writings of the most learned fathers and determinations of councils against the Pelagians, whose errors and heresies are again revived among us by a crew of Socinianized Arminians.

We may to this purpose first consider the testimonies given in the Scripture unto the assertion as laid down in general: Matt. iv. 16; "The people which sat in darkness saw great light; and to them which sat in the region and shadow of death light is sprung up." Of what kind this darkness was in particular shall be afterward declared. For the present it answers what is proposed, — that before the illumination given them by the preaching of the gospel, the people mentioned "sat in darkness," or lived under the power of it. And such as was the light whereby they were relieved, of the same kind was the darkness under which they were detained. And in the same sense, when Christ preached the gospel, "the light shined in darkness, and the darkness comprehended it not," John i. 5, — gave not place to the light of the truth declared by him, that it might be received in the souls of men. The commission which he gave to Paul the apostle, when he sent him to preach the gospel, was, "To open the eyes of men, and to turn them from darkness to light," Acts xxvi. 18; — not to a light within them; for internal light is the eye or seeing of the soul, but the darkness was such as consisted in their blindness, in not having their eyes open: "To open their eyes, and turn them from darkness." Eph. v. 8, "Ye were sometimes darkness, but now are ye light in the Lord." What is the change and alteration made in the minds of men intended in this expression will afterward appear; but that a great change is proposed none can doubt. Col. i. 13, "Who hath delivered us from the power of darkness;" as also 1 Pet. ii. 9, "Who hath called us out of darkness into his marvellous light." And the darkness which is in these testimonies ascribed unto persons in an unregenerate condition is by Paul compared to that which was at the beginning, before the creation of light: Gen. i. 2, "Darkness was upon the face of the deep." There was no creature that had a visive faculty; there was darkness subjectively in all; and there was no light to see by, but all was objectively wrapped up in darkness. In this state of things, God by an almighty act of his power created light: Verse 3, "God said, Let there be light: and there was light." And no otherwise is it in this new creation: "God, who commanded the light to shine out of darkness, shines in the hearts of men, to give them the light of the knowledge of his glory in the face of Jesus Christ," 2 Cor. iv. 6. Spiritual darkness is in and upon all men, until God, by an almighty and effectual work of the Spirit, shine into them, or create light in them. And this darkness is that light within which some boast to be in themselves and others!

To clear our way in this matter, we must consider, — first, the nature of this spiritual darkness, what it is, and wherein it doth consist; and then, secondly, show its efficacy and power in and on the minds of men, and how they are corrupted by it.

First, The term "darkness" in this case is metaphorical, and borrowed from that which is natural. What natural darkness is, and wherein it consists, all men know; if they know it not in its cause and reason, yet they know it by its effects. They know it is that which hinders men from all regular operations which are to be guided by the outward senses. And it is twofold:— 1. When men have not light to see by, or when the usual light, the only external medium for the discovery of distant objects, is taken from them. So was it with the Egyptians during the three days' darkness that was on their land. They could not see for want of light; they had their visive faculty continued unto them, yet having "no light," they "saw not one another, neither arose any from his place," Exod. x. 23: for God, probably, to augment the terror of his judgment, restrained the virtue of artificial light, as well as he did that which was natural. 2. There is darkness unto men when they are blind, either born so or made so: Ps. lxix. 23, "Let their eyes be darkened, that they see not." So the angels smote the Sodomites with blindness, Gen. xix. 11; and Paul the sorcerer, Acts xiii. 11. However the sun shineth, it is all one perpetual night unto them that are blind.

Answerable hereunto, spiritual darkness may be referred unto two heads; for there is an objective darkness, a darkness that is on men, and a subjective darkness, a darkness that is in them. The first consists in the want of those means whereby alone they may be enlightened in the knowledge of God and spiritual things. This is intended, Matt. iv. 16. This means is the word of God, and the preaching of it. Hence it is called a "light," Ps. cxix. 105, and is said to "enlighten," Ps. xix. 8, or to be "a light shining in a dark place," 2 Pet. i. 19; and it is so termed, because it is the outward means of communicating the light of the knowledge of God unto the minds of men. What the sun is unto the world as unto things natural, that is the word and the preaching of it unto men as to things spiritual; and hence our apostle applies what is said of the sun in the firmament, as to the enlightening of the world, Ps. xix. 1–4, unto the gospel and the preaching of it, Rom. x. 15, 18.

And this darkness is upon many in the world, even all unto whom the gospel is not declared, or by whom it is not received, where it is or hath been so. Some, I know, have entertained a vain imagination about a saving revelation of the knowledge of God by the works of creation and providence, objected[17] to the rational faculties of the minds of men. It is not my purpose here to divert unto the confutation of that fancy. Were it so, it were easy to demonstrate that there is no saving revelation of the knowledge of God unto sinners, but as he is in Christ reconciling the world unto himself; and that so he is not made known but by the word of reconciliation committed unto the dispensers of the gospel. Whatever knowledge, therefore, of God may be attained by the means mentioned, as he is the God of nature ruling over men, and requiring obedience from them according to the covenant and law of their creation, yet the knowledge of him as a God in Christ pardoning sin and saving sinners is attainable by the gospel only. But this I have proved and confirmed elsewhere.[18]

It is the work of the Holy Spirit to remove and take away this darkness; which until it is done no man can see the kingdom of God, or enter into it. And this he doth by sending the word of the gospel into any nation, country, place, or city, as he pleaseth. The gospel does not get ground in any place, nor is restrained from any place or people, by accident, or by the endeavours of men; but it is sent and disposed of according to the sovereign will and pleasure of the Spirit of God. He gifteth, calls, and sends men unto the work of preaching it, Acts xiii. 2, 4, and disposeth them unto the places where they shall declare it, either by express revelation, as of old, chap. xvi. 6–10, or guides them by the secret operations of his providence. Thus the dispensation of the "light of the gospel," as to times, places, and persons, depends on his sovereign pleasure, Ps. cxlvii. 19, 20. Wherefore, although we are to take care and pray much about the continuance of the dispensation of the gospel in any place, and its propagation in others, yet need we not to be over-solicitous about it. This work and care the Holy Ghost hath taken on himself, and will carry it on according to the counsel of God and his purposes concerning the kingdom of Jesus Christ in this world. And thus far the dispensation of the gospel is only a causa sine quâ non of the regeneration of men, and the granting of it depends solely on the will of the Spirit of God.

It is subjective darkness which is of more direct and immediate consideration in this matter, the nature whereof, with what it doth respect, and the influence of it on the minds of men, must be declared, before we can rightly apprehend the work of the Holy Spirit in its removal by regeneration.

This is that whereby the Scripture expresseth the natural depravation and corruption of the minds of men, with respect unto spiritual things and the duty that we owe to God, according to the tenor of the covenant. And two things must be premised to our consideration of it; as, —

1. That I shall not treat of the depravation or corruption of the mind of man by the fall, with respect unto things natural, civil, political, or moral, but merely with regard to things spiritual, heavenly, and evangelical. It were easy to evince, not only by testimonies of the Scripture, but by the experience of all mankind, built on reason and the observation of instances innumerable, that the whole rational soul of man since the fall, and by the entrance of sin, is weakened, impaired, vitiated, in all its faculties and all their operations about their proper and natural objects. Neither is there any relief against these evils, with all those unavoidable perturbations wherewith it is possessed and actually disordered in all its workings, but by some secret and hidden operation of the Spirit of God, such as he continually exerts in the rule and government of the world. But it is concerning the impotency, defect, depravation, and perversity of the mind with respect unto spiritual things alone, that we shall treat at present. I say, then, —

2. That, by reason of that vice, corruption, or depravation of the minds of all unregenerate men, which the Scripture calls darkness and blindness, they are not able of themselves, by their own reasons and understandings, however exercised and improved, to discern, receive, understand, or believe savingly, spiritual things, or the mystery of the gospel, when and as they are outwardly revealed unto them, without an effectual, powerful work of the Holy Spirit, creating, or by his almighty power inducing, a new saving light into them.[19] Let it be supposed that the mind of a man be no way hurt or impaired by any natural defect, such as doth not attend the whole race of mankind, but is personal only and accidental; suppose it free from contracted habits of vice or voluntary prejudices, — yet upon the proposal of the doctrine and mysteries of the gospel, let it be done by the most skilful masters of the assemblies, with the greatest evidence and demonstration of the truth, it is not able of itself, spiritually and savingly, to receive, understand, and assent unto them, without the especial aid and assistance and operation of the Holy Spirit.[20]

To evince this truth, we may consider, in one instance, the description given us in the Scripture of the mind itself, and its operations with respect unto spiritual things. This we have, Eph. iv. 17, 18, "This I say therefore, and testify in the Lord, that ye henceforth walk not as other Gentiles walk, in the vanity of their mind, having the understanding darkened, being alienated from the life of God through the ignorance that is in them, because of the blindness of their heart." It is of the Gentiles that the apostle speaks, but the apostle speaks of them on the account of that which is common unto all men by nature; for he treats of their condition with respect unto the faculties of their minds and souls, wherein there is, as unto the life of God, or spiritual things, no difference naturally among men. And their operations and effects are, for the substance of them, the same.

Some, indeed, give such an account of this text as if the apostle had said, "Do not ye live after the manner of the heathens, in the vileness of those practices, and in their idol-worship. That long course of sin having blinded their understandings, so that they see not that which by the light of nature they are enabled to see, and, by that gross ignorance and obduration of heart, run into all impiety, [they] are far removed from that life which God and nature require of them." It is supposed in this exposition, — (1.) That the apostle hath respect, in the first place, to the practice of the Gentiles, not to their state and condition. (2.) That this practice concerns only their idolatry and idol-worship. (3.) That what is here ascribed unto them came upon them by a long course of sinning. (4.) That the darkness mentioned consists in a not discerning of what might be seen by the light of nature. (5.) That their alienation from the life of God consisted in running into that impiety which was distant or removed from the life that God and nature require. But all these sentiments are so far from being contained in the text as that they are expressly contrary unto it; for, — (1.) Although the apostle doth carry on his description of this state of the Gentiles unto the vile practices that ensued thereon, verse 19, yet it is their state by nature, with respect unto the "life of God," which is first intended by him. This is apparent from what he prescribes unto Christians in opposition thereunto, — namely, "The new man, which after God is created in righteousness and true holiness," verse 24. (2.) The "vanity" mentioned is subjective in their minds, and so hath no respect to idol-worship, but as it was an effect thereof. The "vanity of their minds" is the principle whereof this walking, be what it will, was the effect and consequent. (3.) Here is no mention nor intimation of any long course of sinning, much less that it should be the cause of the other things ascribed to the Gentiles; whereof, indeed, it was the effect. The description given is that of the state of all men by nature, as is plain from chap. ii. 1–3. (4.) The "darkness" here mentioned is opposed unto being "light in the Lord," chap. v. 8; which is not mere natural light, nor can any by that light alone discern spiritual things, or the things that belong to the life of God. (5.) The life of God here is not that life which God and nature require, but that life which God reveals in, requires, and communicates by, the gospel, through Jesus Christ, as all learned expositors acknowledge. Wherefore the apostle treateth here of the state of men by nature with respect unto spiritual and supernatural things. And three heads he reduceth all things in man unto:— 1. He mentions τὸν νοῦν, the "mind;" 2. Τὴν διάνοιαν, the "understanding;" and, 3. Τὴν καρδίαν, the "heart." And all these are one entire principle of all our moral and spiritual operations, and are all affected with the darkness and ignorance whereof we treat.

1. There is ὁ νοῦς, the "mind." This is the τὸ ἡγεμονικόν, the leading and ruling faculty of the soul. It is that in us which looketh out after proper objects for the will and affections to receive and embrace. Hereby we have our first apprehensions of all things, whence deductions are made to our practice. And hereunto is ascribed ματαιότης, "vanity:" "They walk in the vanity of their mind." Things in the Scripture are said to be vain which are useless and fruitless. Μάταιος, "vain," is from μάτην, "to no purpose," Matt. xv. 9. Hence the apostle calls the idols of the Gentiles, and the rites used in their worship, μάταια, "vain things," Acts xiv. 15. So he expresseth the Hebrew, הַבְלֵי־שָׁוְא, Jonah ii. 8, "lying vanities," or אָוֶן; which is as much as ἀνωφελές, a thing altogether useless and unprofitable, according to the description given of them, 1 Sam. xii. 21, יַצִּילוּ וְלֹא לֹא־יוֹעִילוּ אֲשֶׁר הַתֹּהוּ הֵמָּה כִּי־תֹהוּ, — "Vain things, which cannot profit nor deliver; for they are vain." There is no profit in nor use of that which is vain. As the mind is said to be vain, or under the power of vanity, two things are intended:— (1.) Its natural inclination unto things that are vain, — that is, such as are not a proper nor useful object unto the soul and its affections.

It seeks about to lead the soul to rest and satisfaction, but always unto vain things, and that in great variety. Sin, the world, pleasures, the satisfaction of the flesh, with pride of life, are the things which it naturally pursues. And in actings of this nature a vain mind abounds; it multiplies vain imaginations, like the sand on the seashore. These are called "The figments of the hearts of men," Gen. vi. 5, which are found to be only "evil continually." These it feigns and frames, abundantly bringing them forth, as the earth doth grass, or as a cloud pours out drops of water. And herein, (2.) It is unstable; for that which is vain is various, inconstant, unfixed, light, as a natural mind is, so that it is like hell itself for confusion and disorder, or the whorish woman described by Solomon, Prov. vii. 11, 12. And this hath befallen it by the loss of that fixed regularity which it was created in. There was the same cogitative or imaginative faculty in us in the state of innocency as there remains under the power of sin; but then all the actings of it were orderly and regular, — the mind was able to direct them all unto the end for which we were made. God was, and would have been, the principal object of them, and all other things in order unto him. But now, being turned off from him, the mind in them engageth in all manner of confusion; and they all end in vanity or disappointment. They offer, as it were, their service unto the soul, to bring it in satisfaction. And although they are rejected one after another, as not answering what they pretend unto, yet they constantly arise under the same notion, and keep the whole soul under everlasting disappointments. And from hence it is that the mind cannot assent unto the common principles of religion in a due manner, which yet it cannot deny. This will be farther cleared afterward. Hereon in conversion unto God, we are said to have our minds renewed, Rom. xii. 2, and to be "renewed in the spirit of our mind," Eph. iv. 23. By the "mind" the faculty itself is intended, the rational principle in us of apprehension, of thinking, discoursing, and assenting. This is renewed by grace, or brought into another habitude and frame, by the implantation of a ruling, guiding, spiritual light in it. The "spirit" of the mind, is the inclination and disposition in the actings of it; these also must be regulated by grace.

2. There is the δάνοια, the "understanding." This is the τὸ διακριτικόν, the directive, discerning, judging faculty of the soul, that leads it unto practice. It guides the soul in the choice of the notions which it receives by the mind. And this is more corrupt than the mind itself; for the nearer things come to practice, the more prevalent in them is the power of sin. This, therefore, is said to be "darkened;" and being so, it is wholly in vain to pretend a sufficiency in it to discern spiritual things without a supernatural illumination. Light, in the dispensation of the gospel, shines, or casts out some rays of itself, into this darkened understanding of men, but that receives it not, John i. 5.

3. There is καρδία, the "heart." This in Scripture is τὸ πρακτικόν in the soul, the practical principle of operation, and so includes the will also. It is the actual compliance of the will and affections with the mind and understanding, with respect unto the objects proposed by them. Light is received by the mind, applied by the understanding, used by the heart. Upon this, saith the apostle, there is πώρωσις, "blindness." It is not a mere ignorance or incomprehensiveness of the notions of truth that is intended, but a stubborn resistance of light and conviction. An obstinate and obdurate hardness is upon the heart, whence it rejects all the impressions that come upon it from notions of truth. And on these considerations men themselves before conversion are said to be "darkness," Eph. v. 8. There may be degrees in a moral privation, but when it is expressed in the abstract, it is a sign that it is at its height, that it is total and absolute. And this is spoken with respect unto spiritual and saving light only, or a saving apprehension of spiritual truths. There is not in such persons so much as any disposition remaining to receive saving knowledge, any more than there is a disposition in darkness itself to receive light. The mind, indeed, remains a capable subject to receive it, but hath no active power nor disposition in itself towards it; and, therefore, when God is pleased to give us a new ability to understand and perceive spiritual things in a due manner, he is said to give us a new faculty, because of the utter disability of our minds naturally to receive them, 1 John v. 20. Let vain men boast whilst they please of the perfection and ability of their rational faculties with respect unto religion and the things of God, this is the state of them by nature, upon His judgment that must stand forever.

And, by the way, it may not be amiss to divert here a little unto the consideration of that exposition which the whole world and all things in it give unto this text and testimony concerning the minds of natural men being under the power of vanity, for this is the spring and inexhaustible fountain of all that vanity which the world is filled with. There is, indeed, a vanity which is penal, — namely, that vexation and disappointment which men finally meet withal in the pursuit of perishing things, whereof the wise man treats at large in his Ecclesiastes; but I intend that sinful vanity which the mind itself produces, and that in all sorts of persons, ages, sexes, and conditions in the world. This some of the heathens saw, complained of, reproved, and derided, but yet could never reach to the cause of it, nor free themselves from being under the power of the same vanity, though in a way peculiar and distinct from the common sort, as might easily be demonstrated. But the thing is apparent; almost all that our eyes see or our ears hear of in the world is altogether vain. All that which makes such a noise, such a business, such an appearance and show among men, may be reduced unto two heads:— (1.) The vanity that they bring into the things that are, and that are either good in themselves and of some use, or at least indifferent. So men do variously corrupt their buildings and habitations, their trading, their conversation, their power, their wealth, their relations. They join innumerable vanities with them, which render them loathsome and contemptible, and the meanest condition to be the most suitable to rational satisfaction. (2.) Men find out, and as it were create, things to be mere supporters, countenancers, and nourishers of vanity. Such, in religion, are carnal, pompous ceremonies, like those of the church of Rome, which have no end but to bring in some kind of provision for the satisfaction of vain minds; stage-players, mimics, with innumerable other things of the same nature, which are nothing but theatres for vanity to act itself upon. It were endless but to mention the common effects of vanity in the world. And men are mightily divided about these things. Those engaged in them think it strange that others run not out into the "same compass of excess and riot with themselves, speaking evil of them," 1 Pet. iv. 4. They wonder at the perverse, stubborn, and froward humour which befalls some men, that they delight not in, that they approve not of, those things and ways wherein they find so great a suitableness unto their own minds. Others, again, are ready to admire whence it is that the world is mad on such vain and foolish things as it is almost wholly given up unto. The consideration we have insisted on gives us a satisfactory account of the grounds and reasons hereof. The mind of man by nature is wholly vain, under the power of vanity, and is an endless, fruitful womb of all monstrous births. The world is now growing towards six thousand years old, and yet is no nearer the bottom of the springs of its vanity, or the drawing out of its supplies, than it was the first day that sin entered into it. New sins, new vices, new vanities, break forth continually; and all is from hence, that the mind of man by nature is altogether vain. Nor is there any way or means for putting a stop hereunto in persons, families, cities, nations, but so far as the minds of men are cured and renewed by the Holy Ghost. The world may alter its shape and the outward appearances of things, it may change its scenes, and act its part in new habits and dresses, but it will still be altogether vain so long as natural uncured vanity is predominant in the minds of men; and this will sufficiently secure them from attaining any saving acquaintance with spiritual things.

Again: It is one of the principal duties incumbent on us, to be acquainted with, and diligently to watch over, the remainders of this vanity in our own minds. The sinful distempers of our natures are not presently cured at once, but the healing and removing of them is carried on by degrees unto the consummation of the course of our obedience in this world. And there are three effects of this natural vanity of the mind in its depraved condition to be found among believers themselves:— (1.) An instability in holy duties, as meditation, prayer, and hearing of the word. How ready is the mind to wander in them, and to give entertainment unto vain and fond imaginations, at least unto thoughts and apprehensions of things unsuited to the duties wherein we are engaged! How difficult is it to keep it up unto an even, fixed, stable frame of acting spiritually in spiritual things! How is it ready at every breath to unbend and let down its intension! All we experience or complain of in this kind is from the uncured relics of this vanity. (2.) This is that which inclines and leads men towards a conformity with and unto a vain world, in its customs, habits, and ordinary converse; which are all vain and foolish. And so prevalent is it herein, and such arguments hath it possessed itself withal to give it countenance, that in many instances of vanity it is hard to give a distinction between them and the whole world that lies under the power of it. Professors, it may be, will not comply with the world in the things before mentioned, that have no other use nor end but merely to support, act, and nourish vanity; but from other things, which, being indifferent in themselves, are yet filled with vanity in their use, how ready are many for a compliance with the course of the world, which lieth in evil and passeth away! (3.) It acts itself in fond and foolish imaginations, whereby it secretly makes provision for the flesh and the lusts thereof; for they all generally lead unto self-exaltation and satisfaction. And these, if not carefully checked, will proceed to such an excess as greatly to taint the whole soul. And in these things lie the principal cause and occasion of all other sins and miscarriages. We have, therefore, no more important duty incumbent on us than mightily to oppose this radical distemper. It is so, also, to attend diligently unto the remedy of it; and this consists, (1.) In a holy fixedness of mind, and an habitual inclination unto things spiritual; which is communicated unto us by the Holy Ghost, as shall be afterward declared, Eph. iv. 23, 24. (2.) In the due and constant improvement of that gracious principle, — [1.] By constant watchfulness against the mind's acting itself in vain, foolish, unprofitable imaginations, so far at least [as] that vain thoughts may not lodge in us; [2.] By exercising it continually unto holy spiritual meditations, "minding always the things that are above," Col. iii. 2; [3.] By a constant, conscientious humbling of our souls, for all the vain actings of our minds that we do observe; — all which might be usefully enlarged on, but that we must return.

[Secondly], The minds of men unregenerate being thus depraved and corrupted, being thus affected with darkness, and thereby being brought under the power of vanity, we may yet farther consider what other effects and consequents are on the same account ascribed unto it. And the mind of man in this state may be considered, either, — 1. As to its dispositions and inclinations; [or], 2. As to its power and actings, with respect unto spiritual, supernatural things:—

1. As to its dispositions, it is (from the darkness described) perverse and depraved, whereby men are" alienated from the life of God," Eph. iv. 18; for this alienation of men from the divine life is from the depravation of their minds. Hence are they said to be "alienated and enemies in their mind by wicked works," or by their mind in wicked works, being fixed on them and under the power of them, Col. i. 21. And that we may the better understand what is intended hereby, we may consider both what is this "life of God," and how the unregenerate mind is alienated from it:—

(1.) All life is from God. The life which we have in common with all other living creatures is from him, Acts xvii. 28; Ps. civ. 30. And, (2.) That peculiar vital life which we have by the union of the rational soul with the body is from God also, and that in an especial manner, Gen. ii. 7; Job x. 12. But neither of these is anywhere called the "life of God." But it is an especial life unto God which is intended; and sundry things belong thereunto, or sundry things are applied unto the description of it:— (1.) It is the life which God requireth of us, that we may please him here and come to the enjoyment of him hereafter; the life of faith and spiritual obedience by Jesus Christ, Rom. i. 17; Gal. ii. 20, "I live by the faith of the Son of God;" Rom. vi., vii. (2.) It is that life which God worketh in us, not naturally by his power, but spiritually by his grace; and that both as to the principle and all the vital acts of it, Eph. ii. 1, 5; Phil. ii. 13. (3.) It is that life whereby God liveth in us, that is, in and by his Spirit through Jesus Christ: Gal. ii. 20, "Christ liveth in me." And where the Son is, there is the Father; whence, also, this life is said to be "hid with him in God," Col. iii. 3. (4.) It is the life whereby we live to God, Rom. vi., vii., whereof God is the supreme and absolute end, as he is the principal efficient cause of it. And two things are contained herein:— [1.] That we do all things to his glory. This is the proper end of all the acts and actings of this life, Rom. xiv. 7, 8. [2.] That we design in and by it to come unto the eternal enjoyment of him as our blessedness and reward, Gen. xv. 1. (5.) It is the life whereof the gospel is the law and rule, John vi. 68; Acts v. 20. (6.) A life all whose fruits are holiness and spiritual, evangelical obedience, Rom. vi. 22; Phil. i. 11. Lastly, It is a life that dieth not, that is not obnoxious unto death, "eternal life," John xvii. 3. These things contain the chief concerns of that peculiar spiritual, heavenly life, which is called the "life of God."

The carnal mind is alienated from this life. It hath no liking of it, no inclination to it, but carrieth away the whole soul with an aversation from it. And this alienation or aversation appears in two things:— (1.) In its unreadiness and unaptness to receive instruction in and about the concernments of it. Hence are men dull and "slow of heart to believe," Luke xxiv. 25; νωθροὶ ταῖς ἀκοαῖς, Heb. v. 11, 12, "heavy in hearing;" and slow in the apprehension of what they hear. So are all men towards what they do not like, but have an aversation from. This God complains of in his people of old: "My people are foolish, they have not known me; they are sottish children, and they have none understanding: they are wise to do evil, but to do good they have no knowledge," Jer. iv. 22. (2.) In the choice and preferring of any other life before it. The first choice a natural mind makes is of a life in sin and pleasure; which is but a death, a death to God, 1 Tim. v. 6, James v. 5, — a life without the law, and before it comes, Rom. vii. 9. This is the life which is suited to the carnal mind, which it desires, delights in, and which willingly it would never depart from. Again, if, by afflictions or convictions, it be in part or wholly forced to forsake and give up this life, it will choose, magnify, and extol a moral life, a life in, by, and under the law; though at the last it will stand it in no more stead than the life of sin and pleasure which it hath been forced to forego, Rom. ix. 32, x. 3. The thoughts of this spiritual life, this "life of God," it cannot away with. The notions of it are uncouth, the description of it is unintelligible, and the practice of it either odious folly or needless superstition. This is the disposition and inclination of the mind towards spiritual things, as it is corrupt and depraved.

2. The power also of the mind with respect unto its actings towards spiritual things may be considered; and this, in short, is none at all, in the sense which shall be explained immediately, chap. v. 6. For this is that which we shall prove concerning the mind of a natural man, or of a man in the state of nature: However it may be excited and improved under those advantages of education and parts which it may have received, yet [it] is not able, hath not a power of its own, spiritually and savingly, or in a due manner, to receive, embrace, and assent unto spiritual things, when proposed unto it in the dispensation and preaching of the gospel, unless it be renewed, enlightened, and acted by the Holy Ghost.

This the apostle plainly asserts, 1 Cor. ii. 14, "The natural man receiveth not the things of the Spirit of God: for they are foolishness unto him: neither can he know them, because they are spiritually discerned."

(1.) The subject spoken of is ψυχικὸς ἄνθρωπος, "animalis homo," the "natural man," he who is a natural man. This epithet is in the Scripture opposed unto πνευματικός, "spiritual," 1 Cor. xv. 44, Jude 19, where ψυχικοί are described by πνεῦμα μὴ ἔχοντες, such as have not the Spirit of God. The foundation of this distinction, and the distribution of men into these two sorts thereby, is laid in that of our apostle, 1 Cor. xv. 45, Ἐγένετο ὁ πρῶτος ἄνθρωπος Ἀδὰμ εἰς ψυχὴν ζῶσαν· ὁ ἔσχατος Ἀδὰμ εἰς πνεῦμα ζωοποιοῦν· — "The first Adam was made a living soul." Hence every man who hath no more but what is traduced from him is called ψυχικός, — he is a "living soul," as was the first Adam. And, "The last Adam was made a quickening spirit." Hence he that is of him, partaker of his nature, that derives from him, is πνευμστικός, a "spiritual man." The person, therefore, here spoken of, or ψυχικός, is one that hath all that is or can be derived from the first Adam, one endowed with a "rational soul," and who hath the use and exercise of all its rational faculties.

Some who look upon themselves almost so near to advancements as to countenance them in magisterial dictates and scornful reflections upon others, tell us that by this "natural man," "a man given up to his pleasures, and guided by brutish affections," and no other, is intended, — "one that gives himself up to the government of his inferior faculties;" but no rational man, no one that will attend unto the dictates of reason, is at all concerned in this assertion. But how is this proved? If we are not content with bare affirmations, we must at length be satisfied with railing and lying, and all sorts of reproaches. But the apostle in this chapter distributes all men living into πνευματικοί and ψυχικοί, "spiritual" and "natural." He who is not a spiritual man, be he who and what he will, be he as rational as some either presume themselves to be or would beg of the world to believe that they are, is a natural man. The supposition of a middle state of men is absolutely destructive of the whole discourse of the apostle as to its proper design. Besides, this of ψυχικὸς is the best and softest term that is given in the Scripture to unregenerate men, with respect unto the things of God; and there is no reason why it should be thought only to express the worst sort of them thereby. The Scripture terms not men peculiarly captivated unto brutish affections, ἀνθρώπους ψυχικούς, "natural men," but rather ἄλογσ ζῶα φυσικά, 2 Pet. ii. 12, "natural brute beasts." And Austin gives us a better account of this expression, Tractat. 98, in Johan:— "Animalis homo, i.e., qui secundum hominem sapit, animalis dictus ab anima, carnalis a carne, quia ex anima et carne constat omnis homo, non percipit ea quæ sunt Spiritus Dei, i.e., quid gratiæ credentibus conferat crux Christi." And another: "Carnales dicimur, quando totos nos voluptatibus damus; spirituales, quando Spiritum Sanctum prævium sequimur; id est, cum ipso sapimus instruente, ipso ducimur auctore. Animales reor esse philosophos qui proprios cogitatus putant esse sapientiam, de quibus recte dicitur, animalis autem homo non recipit ea quæ sunt Spiritus, stultitia quippe est ei," Hieronym. Comment. in Epist. ad Galatians cap. v. And another: Ψυχικός ἐστιν ὁ τὸ πᾶν τοῖς λογισμοῖς τῆς ψυχῆς[21] διδοὺς, καὶ μὴ νομίζων ἄνωθέν τινος δεῖσθαι βοηθείας, ὅπερ ἐστὶν ἀνοίας, καὶ γὰρ ἔδωκεν αὐτὴν ὁ Θεὸς ἵνα μανθάνῃ, καὶ δέχηται τὸ παρ' αὐτοῦ, οὐχ ἵνα ἑαυτῇ αὐτὴν ἀρκεῖν νομίζῃ. Καὶ γὰρ οἱ ὀφθαλμοὶ καλοὶ καὶ χρήσιμοι, ἀλλ' ἐὰν βούλωνται χωρὶς φωτὸς ὁρᾷν, οὐδὲν αὐτοὺς τὸ κάλλος ὀνίνησιν, οὐδὲ ἡ οἰκεία ἰσχὺς, ἀλλὰ καὶ παραβλάπει. Ὅυτω τοίνυν ἡ ψυγὴ ἐὰν βουληθῇ χωρὶς πνεύματος βλέπειν, καὶ ἐμποδὼν ἑαυτῇ γίνεται, Chrysost. in 1 Cor. ii. 15; — "The natural man is he who ascribes all things to the power of the reasonings of the mind, and doth not think that he stands in need of aid from above: which is madness; for God hath given the soul that it should learn and receive what he bestows, what is from him, and not suppose that it is sufficient of itself or to itself. Eyes are beautiful and profitable; but if they would see without light, this beauty and power will not profit but hurt them. And the mind, if it would see" (spiritual things) "without the Spirit of God, it doth but ensnare itself." And it is a sottish supposition, that there is a sort of unregenerate, rational men who are not under the power of corrupt affections in and about spiritual things, seeing the "carnal mind is enmity against God." This, therefore, is the subject of the apostle's proposition, — namely, "a natural man," everyone that is so, that is no more but so, that is, everyone who is not "a spiritual man," is one who hath not received the Spirit of God, verses 11, 12, one that hath [only] the spirit of a man, enabling him to search and know the things of a man, or to attain wisdom in things natural, civil, or political.

(2.) There is in the words a supposition of the proposal of some things unto the mind of this "natural man;" for the apostle speaks with respect unto the dispensation and preaching of the gospel, whereby that proposal is made, verses 4–7. And these things are τὰ τοῦ Πνεύματος τοῦ Θεοῦ, "the things of the Spirit of God;" which are variously expressed in this chapter. Verse 2, they are called "Jesus Christ, and him crucified;" verse 7, the "wisdom of God in a mystery, the hidden wisdom, which God hath ordained;" verse 12, "the things that are freely given to us of God;" verse 16, "the mind of Christ;" and sundry other ways to the same purpose. There are in the gospel, and belong to the preaching of it, precepts innumerable concerning moral duties to be observed towards God, ourselves, and other men; and all these have a coincidence with and a suitableness unto the inbred light of nature, because the principles of them all are indelibly ingrafted therein. These things being in some sense the "things of a man," may be known by the "spirit of a man that is in him," verse 11: howbeit they cannot be observed and practised according to the mind of God without the aid and assistance of the Holy Ghost. But these are not the things peculiarly here intended, but the mysteries, which depend on mere sovereign supernatural revelation, and that wholly; things that "eye hath not seen, nor ear heard, neither have entered into the heart of man" to conceive, verse 9; things of God's sovereign counsel, whereof there were no impressions in the mind of man in his first creation: see Eph. iii. 8–11.

(3.) That which is affirmed of the natural man with respect unto these spiritual things is doubly expressed:— [1.] By οὐ δέχεται, — "He receiveth them not;" [2.] By οὐ δύναται γνῶναι, — "He cannot know them." In this double assertion, — 1st. A power of receiving spiritual things is denied: "He cannot know them; he cannot receive them;" as Rom. viii. 7, "The carnal mind is not subject to the law of God, neither indeed can be." And the reason hereof is subjoined: "Because they are spiritually discerned;" a thing which such a person hath no power to effect. 2dly. A will of rejecting them is implied: "He receiveth them not;" and the reason hereof is, "For they are foolishness unto him." They are represented unto him under such a notion as that he will have nothing to do with them. 3dly. Actually (and that both because he cannot and because he will not), he receives them not. The natural man neither can, nor will, nor doth, receive the things of the Spirit of God; — is altogether incapable of giving them admission in the sense to be explained.

To clear and free this assertion from objections, it must be observed, —

(1.) That it is not the mere literal sere of doctrines or propositions of truth that is intended.[22] For instance, "That Jesus Christ was crucified," mentioned by the apostle, 1 Cor. ii. 2, is a proposition whose sense and importance any natural man may understand, and assent unto its truth, and so be said to receive it. And all the doctrines of the gospel may be taught and declared in propositions and discourses, the sense and meaning whereof a natural man may understand. And in the due investigation of this sense, and judging thereon concerning truth and falsehood, lies that use of reason in religious things which some would ignorantly confound with an ability of discerning spiritual things in themselves and their own proper nature. This, therefore, is granted; but it is denied that a natural man can receive the things themselves. There is a wide difference between the mind's receiving doctrines notionally, and its receiving the things taught in them really. The first a natural man can do. It is done by all who, by the use of outward means, do know the doctrine of the Scripture, in distinction from ignorance, falsehood, and error. Hence, men unregenerate are said to "know the way of righteousness," 2 Pet. ii. 21, — that is, notionally and doctrinally; for really, saith our apostle, they cannot. Hereon "they profess that they know God," — that is, the things which they are taught concerning him and his will, — whilst "in works they deny him, being abominable and disobedient," Tit. i. 16; Rom. ii. 23, 24. In the latter way they only receive spiritual things in whose minds they are so implanted as to produce their real and proper effects, Rom. xii. 2; Eph. iv. 22–24. And there are two things required unto the receiving of spiritual things really and as they are in themselves:—

[1.] That we discern, assent unto them, and receive them, under an apprehension of their conformity and agreeableness to the wisdom, holiness, and righteousness of God, 1 Cor. i. 23, 24. The reason why men receive not Christ crucified, as preached in the gospel, is because they see not a consonancy in it unto the divine perfections of the nature of God. Neither can any receive it until they see in it an expression of divine power and wisdom. This, therefore, is required unto our receiving the things of the Spirit of God in a due manner, — namely, that we spiritually see and discern their answerableness unto the wisdom, goodness, and holiness of God; wherein lies the principal rest and satisfaction of them that really believe. This a natural man cannot do.

[2.] That we discern their suitableness unto the great ends for which they are proposed as the means of accomplishing. Unless we see this clearly and distinctly, we cannot but judge them weakness and foolishness. These ends being the glory of God in Christ, with our deliverance from a state of sin and misery, with a translation into a state of grace and glory, unless we are acquainted with these things, and the aptness, and fitness, and power of the things of the Spirit of God to effect them, we cannot receive them as we ought; and this a natural man cannot do. And from these considerations, unto which sundry others of the like nature might be added, it appears how and whence it is that a natural man is not capable of receiving the things of the Spirit of God.

(2.) It must be observed that there is, or may be, a twofold capacity or ability of receiving, knowing, or understanding spiritual things in the mind of a man:—

[1.] There is a natural power, consisting in the suitableness and proportionableness of the faculties of the soul to receive spiritual things in the way that they are proposed unto us. This is supposed in all the exhortations, promises, precepts, and threatenings of the gospel; for in vain would they be proposed unto us had we not rational minds and understandings to apprehend their sense, use, and importance, and [were we not] also meet subjects for the faith, grace, and obedience which are required of us. None pretend that men are, in their conversion to God, like stocks and stones, or brute beasts, that have no understanding; for although the work of our conversion is called a "turning of stones into children of Abraham," because of the greatness of the change, and because of ourselves we contribute nothing thereunto, yet if we were every way as such as to the capacity of our natures, it would not become the wisdom of God to apply the means mentioned for effecting of that work. God is said, indeed, herein to "give us an understanding," 1 John v. 20; but the natural faculty of the understanding is not thereby intended, but only the renovation of it by grace, and the actual exercise of that grace in apprehending spiritual things. There are two adjuncts of the commands of God:— 1st. That they are equal; 2dly. That they are easy, or not grievous. The former they have from the nature of the things commanded, and the fitness of our minds to receive such commands, Ezek. xviii. 25; the latter they have from the dispensation of the Spirit and grace of Christ, which renders them not only possible unto us, but easy for us.

Some pretend that whatever is required of us or prescribed unto us in a way of duty, we have a power in and of ourselves to perform.[23] If by this power they intend no more but that our minds, and the other rational faculties of our souls, are fit and meet, as to their natural capacity, for and unto such acts as wherein those duties do consist, it is freely granted; for God requires nothing of us but what must be acted in our minds and wills, and which they are naturally meet and suited for. But if they intend such an active power and ability as, being excited by the motives proposed unto us, can of itself answer the commands of God in a due manner, they deny the corruption of our nature by the entrance of sin, and render the grace of Christ useless, as shall be demonstrated.

[2.] There is, or may be, a power in the mind to discern spiritual things, whereby it is so able to do it as that it can immediately exercise that power in the spiritual discerning of them upon their due proposal unto it, that is, spiritually; as a man that hath the visive faculty sound and entire, upon the due proposal of visible objects unto him can discern and see them. This power must be spiritual and supernatural; for whereas to receive spiritual things spiritually is so to receive them as really to believe them with faith divine and supernatural, to love them with divine love, to conform the whole soul and affections unto them, Rom. vi. 17, 2 Cor. iii. 18, no natural man hath power so to do: this is that which is denied in this place by the apostle. Wherefore, between the natural capacity of the mind and the act of spiritual discerning there must be an interposition of an effectual work of the Holy Ghost enabling it thereunto, 1 John v. 20; 2 Cor. iv. 6.

Of the assertion thus laid down and explained the apostle gives a double reason: the first taken from the nature of the things to be known, with respect unto the mind and understanding of a natural man; the other from the way or manner whereby alone spiritual things may be acceptably discerned:—

(1.) The first reason, taken from the nature of the things themselves, with respect unto the mind, is, that "they are foolishness." In themselves they are the "wisdom of God," 1 Cor. ii. 7; — effects of the wisdom of God, and those which have the impress of the wisdom of God upon them. And when the dispensation of them was said to be "foolishness," the apostle contends not about it, but tells them, however, it is the "foolishness of God," chap. i. 25; which he doth to cast contempt on all the wisdom of men, whereby the gospel is despised. And they are the "hidden wisdom" of God; such an effect of divine wisdom as no creature could make any discovery of, Eph. iii. 9, 10; Job xxviii. 20–22. And they are the "wisdom of God in a mystery," or full of deep, mysterious wisdom. But to the natural man they are "foolishness," not only although they are the wisdom of God, but peculiarly because they are so, and as they are so; for "the carnal mind is enmity against God." Now, that is esteemed foolishness which is looked on either as weak and impertinent, or as that which contains or expresseth means and ends disproportionate, or as that which is undesirable in comparison of what may be set up in competition with it, or is on any other consideration not eligible or to be complied with on the terms whereon it is proposed. And for one or other or all of these reasons are spiritual things, — namely, those here intended, wherein the wisdom of God in the mystery of the gospel doth consist, — foolishness unto a natural man; which we shall demonstrate by some instances:—

[1.] That they were so unto the learned philosophers of old, both our apostle doth testify and the known experience of the first ages of the church makes evident, 1 Cor. i. 22, 23, 26–28. Had spiritual things been suited unto the minds or reasons of natural men, it could not be but that those who had most improved their minds, and were raised unto the highest exercise of their reasons, must much more readily have received and embraced the mysteries of the gospel than those who were poor, illiterate, and came many degrees behind them in the exercise and improvement thereof. So we see it is as to the reception of any thing in nature or morality which, being of any worth, is proposed unto the minds of men; it is embraced soonest by them that are wisest and know most. But here things fell out quite otherwise. They were the wise, the knowing, the rational, the learned men of the world, that made the greatest and longest opposition unto spiritual things, and that expressly and avowedly because they were "foolishness unto them," and that on all the accounts before mentioned; and their opposition unto them they managed with pride, scorn, and contempt, as they thought "foolish things" ought to be handled.

The profound ignorance and confidence whence it is that some of late are not ashamed to preach and print that it was the learned, rational, wise part of mankind, as they were esteemed or professed of themselves, the philosophers, and such as under their conduct pretended unto a life according to the dictates of reason, who first embraced the gospel, as being more disposed unto its reception than others, cannot be sufficiently admired or despised. Had they once considered what is spoken unto this purpose in the New Testament, or known any thing of the entrance, growth, or progress of Christian religion in the world, they would themselves be ashamed of this folly. But every day in this matter, "prodeunt oratores novi, stulti adolescentuli," who talk confidently, whilst they know neither what they say nor whereof they do affirm.

[2.] The principal mysteries of the gospel, or the spiritual things intended, are by many looked on and rejected as foolish, because false and untrue; though, indeed, they have no reason to think them false, but because they suppose them foolish. And they fix upon charging them with falsity to countenance themselves in judging them to be folly. Whatever concerns the incarnation of the Son of God, the satisfaction that he made for sin and sinners, the imputation of his righteousness unto them that believe, the effectual working of his grace in the conversion of the souls of men, — which, with what belongs unto them, comprise the greatest part of the spiritual things of the gospel, — are not received by many because they are false, as they judge; and that which induceth them so to determine is, because they look on them as foolish, and unsuited unto the rational principles of their minds.

[3.] Many plainly scoff at them, and despise them as the most contemptible notions that mankind can exercise their reasons about. Such were of old prophesied concerning, 2 Pet. iii. 3, 4; and things at this day are come to that pass. The world swarms with scoffers at spiritual things, as those which are unfit for rational, noble, generous spirits to come under a sense or power of, because they are so foolish. But these things were we foretold of, that when they came to pass we should not be troubled or shaken in our minds; yea, the atheism of some is made a means to confirm the faith of others!

[4.] It is not much otherwise with some, who yet dare not engage into an open opposition to the gospel with them before mentioned; for they profess the faith of it, and avow a subjection to the rules and laws of it. But the things declared in the gospel may be reduced unto two heads, as was before observed:— 1st. Such as consist in the confirmation, direction, and improvement of the moral principles and precepts of the law of nature. 2dly. Such as flow immediately from the sovereign will and wisdom of God, being no way communicated unto us but by supernatural revelation only. Such are all the effects of the wisdom and grace of God, as he was in Christ reconciling the world unto himself; the offices of Christ, his administration of them, and dispensation of the Spirit; with the especial, evangelical, supernatural graces and duties which are required in us with respect thereunto. The first sort of these things many will greatly praise and highly extol; and they will declare how consonant they are to reason, and what expressions suitable unto them may be found in the ancient philosophers. But it is evident, that herein also they fall under a double inconvenience: for, — 1st. Mostly, they visibly transgress what they boast of as their rule, and that above others; for where shall we meet with any, at least with many, of this sort of men, who in any measure comply with that modesty, humility, meekness, patience, self-denial, abstinence, temperance, contempt of the world, love of mankind, charity, and purity, which the gospel requires under this head of duties? Pride, ambition, insatiable desires after earthly advantages and promotions, scoffing, scorn and contempt of others, vanity of converse, envy, wrath, revenge, railing, are none of the moral duties required in the gospel. And, — 2dly. No pretence of an esteem for any one part of the gospel will shelter men from the punishment due to the rejection of the whole by whom any essential part of it is refused. And this is the condition of many. The things which most properly belong to the mysteries of the gospel, or the unsearchable riches of the grace of God in Christ Jesus, are foolishness unto them; and the preaching of them is called "canting and folly." And some of these, although they go not so far as the friar at Rome, who said that "St Paul fell into great excesses in these things," yet they have dared to accuse his writings of darkness and obscurity; for no other reason, so far as I can understand, but because he insists on the declaration of these spiritual mysteries: and it is not easy to express what contempt and reproach is cast by some preachers on them. But it is not amiss that some have proclaimed their own shame herein, and have left it on record, to the abhorrency of posterity.

[5.] The event of the dispensation of the gospel manifesteth that the spiritual things of it are foolishness to the most; for as such are they rejected by them, Isa. liii. 1–3. Suppose a man of good reputation for wisdom and sobriety should go unto others, and inform them, and that with earnestness, evidence of love to them, and care for them, with all kinds of motives to beget a belief of what he proposeth, that by such ways as he prescribeth they may exceedingly increase their substance in this world, until they exceed the wealth of kings, — a thing that the minds of men in their contrivances and designs are intent upon; — if in this case they follow not his advice, it can be for no other reason but because they judge the things proposed by him to be no way suited or expedient unto the ends promised, — that is, to be foolish things. And this is the state of things with respect unto the mysteries of the gospel. Men are informed, in and by the ways of God's appointment, how great and glorious they are, and what blessed consequents there will be of a spiritual reception of them. The beauty and excellency of Christ, the inestimable privilege of divine adoption, the great and precious promises made unto them that do believe, the glory of the world to come the necessity and excellency of holiness and gospel obedience unto the attaining of everlasting blessedness, are preached unto men, and pressed on them with arguments and motives filled with divine authority and wisdom; yet after all this, we see how few eventually do apply themselves with any industry to receive them, or at least actually do receive them: for "many are called, but few are chosen." And the reason is, because, indeed, unto their darkened minds these things are foolishness, whatsoever they pretend unto the contrary.

(2.) As the instance foregoing compriseth the reasons why a natural man will never receive the things of the Spirit of God, so the apostle adds a reason why he cannot; and that is taken from the manner whereby alone they may be usefully and savingly received, which he cannot attain unto, "Because they are spiritually discerned." In this whole chapter he insists on an opposition between a natural and a spiritual man, natural things and spiritual things, natural light and knowledge and spiritual. The natural man, he informs us, will, by a natural light, discern natural things: "The things of a man knoweth the spirit of a man." And the spiritual man, by a spiritual light received from Jesus Christ, discerneth spiritual things; for "none knoweth the things of God, but the Spirit of God, and he to whom he will reveal them." This ability the apostle denies unto a natural man; and this he proves, — [1.] Because it is the work of the Spirit of God to endow the minds of men with that ability, which there were no need of in case men had it of themselves by nature; and, [2.] (as he shows plentifully elsewhere), The light itself whereby alone spiritual things can be spiritually discerned is wrought, effected, created in us, by an almighty act of the power of God, 2 Cor. iv. 6.

From these things premised, it is evident that there is a twofold impotency in the minds of men with respect unto spiritual things:— (1.) That which immediately affects the mind, a natural impotency, whence it cannot receive them for want of light in itself. (2.) That which affects the mind by the will and affections, a moral impotency, whereby it cannot receive the things of the Spirit of God, because unalterably it will not; and that because, from the unsuitableness of the objects unto its will and affections, and to the mind by them, they are foolishness unto it.

(1.) There is in unregenerate men a natural impotency, through the immediate depravation of the faculties of the mind or understanding, whereby a natural man is absolutely unable, without an especial renovation by the Holy Ghost, to discern spiritual things in a saving manner.[24] Neither is this impotency, although absolutely and naturally insuperable, and although it have in it also the nature of a punishment, any excuse or alleviation of the sin of men when they receive not spiritual things as proposed unto them; for although it be our misery, it is our sin; — it is the misery of our persons, and the sin of our natures. As by it there is an unconformity in our minds to the mind of God, it is our sin; as it is a consequent of the corruption of our nature by the fall, it is an effect of sin; and as it exposeth us unto all the ensuing evil of sin and unbelief, it is both the punishment and cause of sin. And no man can plead his sin or fault as an excuse of another sin in any kind. This impotency is natural, because it consists in the deprivation of the light and power that were originally in the faculties of our minds or understandings, and because it can never be taken away or cured but by an immediate communication of a new spiritual power and ability unto the mind itself by the Holy Ghost in its renovation, so curing the depravation of the faculty itself. And this is consistent with what was before declared [concerning] the natural power of the mind to receive spiritual things: for that power respects the natural capacity of the faculties of our minds; this impotency, the depravation of them with respect unto spiritual things.

(2.) There is in the minds of unregenerate persons a moral impotency, which is reflected on them greatly from the will and affections, whence the mind never will receive spiritual things, — that is, it will always and unchangeably reject and refuse them, — and that because of various lusts, corruptions, and prejudices invincibly fixed in them, causing them to look on them as foolishness. Hence it will come to pass that no man shall be judged and perish at the last day merely on the account of his natural impotency. Everyone to whom the gospel hath been preached, and by whom it is refused, shall be convinced of positive actings in their minds, rejecting the gospel from the love of self, sin, and the world. Thus our Saviour tells the Jews that "no man can come unto him, except the Father draw him," John vi. 44. Such is their natural impotency that they cannot. Nor is it to be cured but by an immediate divine instruction or illumination; as it is written, "They shall be all taught of God," verse 45. But this is not all; he tells them elsewhere, "Ye will not come to me, that ye might have life," chap. v. 40. The present thing in question was not the power or impotency of their minds, but the obstinacy of their wills and affections, which men shall principally be judged upon at the last day; for "this is the condemnation, that light is come into the world, and men loved darkness rather than light, because their deeds were evil," chap. iii. 19. Hence it follows, —

That the will and affections being more corrupted than the understanding, — as is evident from their opposition unto and defeating of its manifold convictions, — no man doth actually apply his mind to the receiving of the things of the Spirit of God to the utmost of that ability which he hath; for all unregenerate men are invincibly impeded therein by the corrupt stubbornness and perverseness of their wills and affections. There is not in any of them a due improvement of the capacity of their natural faculties, in the use of means, for the discharge of their duty towards God herein. And what hath been pleaded may suffice for the vindication of this divine testimony concerning the disability of the mind of man in the state of nature to understand and receive the things of the Spirit of God in a spiritual and saving manner, however they are proposed unto it; which those who are otherwise minded may despise whilst they please, but are no way able to answer or evade.

And hence we may judge of that paraphrase and exposition of this place which one hath given of late: "But such things as these, they that are led only by the light of human reason, the learned philosophers, etc., do absolutely despise, and so hearken not after the doctrine of the gospel; for it seems folly to them. Nor can they, by any study of their own, come to the knowledge of them; for they are only to be had by understanding the prophecies of the Scripture, and other such means, which depend on divine revelation, the voice from heaven, descent of the Holy Ghost, miracles," etc. (1.) The natural man is here allowed to be the rational man, the learned philosopher, one walking by the light of human reason; which complies not with their exception to this testimony who would have only such an one as is sensual and given up unto brutish affections to be intended. But yet neither is there any ground (though some countenance be given to it by Hierom) to fix this interpretation unto that expression. If the apostle may be allowed to declare his own mind, he tells us that he intends everyone, of what sort and condition soever, "who hath not received the Spirit of Christ." (2.) Οὐ δέχεται is paraphrased by, "Doth absolutely despise;" which neither the word here, nor elsewhere, nor its disposal in the present connection, will allow of or give countenance unto. The apostle in the whole discourse gives an account why so few received the gospel, especially of those who seemed most likely so to do, being wise and learned men, and the gospel being no less than the wisdom of God; and the reason hereof he gives from their disability to receive the things of God, and their hatred of them, or opposition to them, neither of which can be cured but by the Spirit of Christ. (3.) The apostle treats not of what men could find out by any study of their own, but of what they did and would do, and could do no otherwise, when the gospel was proposed, declared, and preached unto them. They did not, they could not, receive, give assent unto, or believe, the spiritual mysteries therein revealed. (4.) This preaching of the gospel unto them was accompanied with and managed by those evidences mentioned, — namely, the testimonies of the prophecies of Scripture, miracles, and the like, — in the same way and manner, and unto the same degree, as it was towards them by whom it was received and believed. In the outward means of revelation and its proposition there was no difference. (5.) The proper meaning of οὐ δέχεται, "receiveth not," is given us in the ensuing reason and explanation of it: Οὐ δύναται γνῶναι, "He cannot know them," — that is, unless he be spiritually enabled thereunto by the Holy Ghost. And this is farther confirmed in the reason subjoined, "Because they are spiritually discerned." And to wrest this unto the outward means of revelation, which is directly designed to express the internal manner of the mind's reception of things revealed, is to wrest the Scripture at pleasure. How much better doth the description given by Chrysostom of a natural and spiritual man give light unto and determine the sense of this place: Ψυχικὸς ἄνθρωπος, ὁ διὰ σάρκα ζῶν, καὶ μήπω φωτισθεὶς τὸν νοῦν διὰ Πνεύματος, ἀλλὰ μόνην τὴν ἔμφυτον καὶ ἀνθρωπίνην σύνεσιν ἔχων, ἣν τῶν ἁπάντων ψυχαῖς ἐμβάλλει ὁ Δημιουργός· — "A natural man is he who lives in or by the flesh, and hath not his mind as yet enlightened by the Spirit, but only hath that inbred human understanding which the Creator hath endued the minds of all men with." And, Ὁ πνευματικὸς, ὁ διὰ Πνεῦμα ζῶν, φωτισθεὶς τὸν νοῦν διὰ πνεύματος, οὐ μόνην τὴν ἔμφυτον καὶ ἀνθρωπίνην σύνεσιν ἔχων, ἀλλὰ μᾶλλον τὴν χαρισθεῖσαν πνευματικὴν, ἣν τῶν πιστῶν ψυχαῖς ἐμβάλλει τὸ Ἅγιον Πνεῦμα· — "The spiritual man is he who liveth by the Spirit, having his mind enlightened by him; having not only an inbred human understanding, but rather a spiritual understanding, bestowed on him graciously, which the Holy Ghost endues the minds of believers withal" But we proceed.

3. Having cleared the impotency to discern spiritual things spiritually that is in the minds of natural men, by reason of their spiritual blindness, or that darkness which is in them, it remains that we consider what is the power and efficacy of this darkness to keep them in a constant and unconquerable aversion from God and the gospel. To this purpose, some testimonies of Scripture must be also considered; for notwithstanding all other notions and disputes in this matter, for the most part compliant with the inclinations and affections of corrupted nature, by them must our judgments be determined, and into them is our faith to be resolved. I say, then, that this spiritual darkness hath a power over the minds of men to alienate them from God; that is, this which the Scripture so calleth is not a mere privation, with an impotency in the faculty ensuing thereon, but a depraved habit, which powerfully, and, as unto them in whom it is, unavoidably, influenceth their wills and affections into an opposition unto spiritual things, the effects whereof the world is visibly filled withal at this day. And this I shall manifest, first in general, and then in particular instances. And by the whole it will be made to appear that not only the act of believing and turning unto God is the sole work and effect of grace, — which the Pelagians did not openly deny, and the semiPelagians did openly grant, — but also that all power and ability for it, properly so called, is from grace also.

(1.) Col. i. 13, We are said to be delivered ἐκ τῆς ἐξουσίας τοῦ σκότους, from "the power of darkness." The word signifies such a power as consists in authority or rule, that bears sway, and commands them who are obnoxious unto it. Hence the sins of men, especially those of a greater guilt than ordinary, are called "works of darkness," Eph. v. 11; not only such as are usually perpetrated in the dark, but such as the darkness also of men's minds doth incline them unto and naturally produce. That, also, which is here called "the power of darkness" is called "the power of Satan," Acts xxvi. 18; for I acknowledge that it is not only or merely the internal darkness or blindness of the minds of men in the state of nature that is here intended, but the whole state of darkness, with what is contributed thereunto by Satan and the world. This the prophet speaks of, Isa. lx. 2, "Behold, the darkness shall cover the earth, and gross darkness the people: but the Lord shall arise upon thee." Such a darkness it is, as nothing can dispel but the light of the Lord arising on and in the souls of men. But all is resolved into internal darkness: for Satan hath no power in men, nor authority over them, but what he hath by means of this darkness; for by this alone doth that "prince of the power of the air" work effectually in "the children of disobedience," Eph. ii. 2. Hereby doth he seduce, pervert, and corrupt them; nor hath he any way to fortify and confirm their minds against the gospel but by increasing this blindness or darkness in them, 2 Cor. iv. 4. An evidence of the power and efficacy of this darkness we may find in the devil himself.

The apostle Peter tells us that the angels who sinned are "reserved unto judgment" under "chains of darkness," 2 Pet. ii. 4. It is plain that there is an allusion in the words unto the dealing of men with stubborn and heinous malefactors. They do not presently execute them upon their offences, nor when they are first apprehended; they must be kept unto a solemn day of trial and judgment. But yet, to secure them that they make no escape, they are bound with chains which they cannot deliver themselves from. Thus God deals with fallen angels; for although yet they "go to and fro in the earth, and walk up and down in it," as also in the air, in a seeming liberty and at their pleasure, yet are they under such chains as shall securely hold them unto the great day of their judgment and execution. That they may not escape their appointed doom, they are held in "chains of darkness." They are always so absolutely and universally under the power of God as that they are not capable of the vanity of a thought for the subducting themselves from under it. But whence is it that, in all their wisdom, experience, and the long-continued prospect which they have had of their future eternal misery, none of them ever have attempted, nor ever will, a mitigation of their punishment or deliverance from it, by repentance and compliance with the will of God? This is alone from their own darkness, in the chains whereof they are so bound that although they believe their own everlasting ruin, and tremble at the vengeance of God therein, yet they cannot but continue in their course of mischief, disobedience, and rebellion. And although natural men are not under the same obdurateness with them, as having a way of escape and deliverance provided for them and proposed unto them, which they have not; yet this darkness is no less effectual to bind them in a state of sin, without the powerful illumination of the Holy Ghost, than it is in the devils themselves. And this may be farther manifested by the consideration of the instances wherein it puts forth its efficacy in them:—

(1.) It fills the mind with enmity against God, and all the things of God: Col. i. 21, "Ye were enemies in your mind." Rom. viii. 7, "The carnal mind is enmity against God: for it is not subject to the law of God, neither indeed can be." And the carnal mind there intended is that which is in every man who hath not received, who is not made partaker of, the Spirit of God, in a peculiar saving manner, as is at large declared in the whole discourse of the apostle, verses 5, 6, 9–11; so that the pretence is vain, and directly contradictory to the apostle, that it is only one sort of fleshly, sensual, unregenerate men, whom he intends. This confidence, not only in perverting, but openly opposing, the

Scripture, is but of a late date, and that which few of the ancient enemies of the grace of God did rise up unto. Now God in himself is infinitely good and desirable. "How great is his goodness and how great is his beauty!" Zech. ix. 17. There is nothing in him but what is suited to draw out, to answer, and fill the affections of the soul. Unto them that know him, he is the only delight, rest, and satisfaction. Whence, then, doth it come to pass that the minds of men should be filled and possessed with enmity against him? Enmity against and hatred of him who is absolute and infinite goodness seem incompatible unto our human affections; but they arise from this darkness, which is the corruption and depravation of our nature, by the ways that shall be declared.

It is pretended and pleaded by some in these days, that upon an apprehension of the goodness of the nature of God, as manifested in the works and light of nature, men may, without any other advantages, love him above all, and be accepted with him. But as this would render Christ and the gospel, as objectively proposed, if not useless, yet not indispensably necessary, so I desire to know how this enmity against God, which the minds of all natural men are filled withal, if we may believe the apostle, comes to be removed and taken away, so as that they should love him above all, seeing these things are absolute extremes and utterly irreconcilable? This must be either by the power of the mind itself upon the proposal of God's goodness unto it, or by the effectual operation in it and upon it of the Spirit of God. Any other way is not pretended unto; and the latter is that which we contend for. And as to the former, the apostle supposeth the goodness of God, and the proposal of this goodness of God unto the minds of men, not only as revealed in the works of nature, but also in the law and gospel, and yet affirms that "the carnal mind," which is in every man, "is enmity against him;" and in enmity there is neither disposition nor inclination to love. In such persons there can be no more true love of God than is consistent with enmity to him and against him.

All discourses, therefore, about the acceptance they shall find with God who love him above all for his goodness, without any farther communications of Christ or the Holy Spirit unto them, are vain and empty, seeing there never was, nor ever will be, any one dram of such love unto God in the world; for, whatever men may fancy concerning the love of God, where this enmity arising from darkness is unremoved by the Spirit of grace and love, it is but a self-pleasing with those false notions of God which this darkness suggests unto them. With these they either please themselves or are terrified, as they represent things to their corrupt reason and fancies. Men in this state, destitute of divine revelation, did of old seek after God, Acts xvii. 27, as men groping in the dark; and although they did in some measure find him and know him, so far as that from the things that were made they came to be acquainted with "his eternal power and Godhead," Rom. i. 20, yet he was still absolutely unto them "the unknown God," Acts xvii. 23, whom they "ignorantly worshipped," — that is, they directed some worship to him in the dedication of their altars, but knew him not: Ὃν ἀγνοοῦντες εὐσεβεῖτε. And that they entertained all of them false notions of God is from hence evident, that none of them either, by virtue of their knowledge of him, did free themselves from gross idolatry, which is the greatest enmity unto him, or did not countenance themselves in many impieties or sins from those notions they had received of God and his goodness, Rom. i. 20, 21. The issue of their disquisitions after the nature of God was, that "they glorified him not, but became vain in their imaginations, and their foolish hearts were darkened." Upon the common principles of the first Being and the chiefest good, their fancy or imaginations raised such notions of God as pleased and delighted them, and drew out their affections; which was not, indeed, unto God and his goodness, but unto the effect and product of their own imaginations. And hence it was that those that had the most raised apprehensions concerning the nature, being, and goodness of God, with the highest expressions of a constant admiration of him and love unto him, when by any means the true God indeed was declared unto them as he hath revealed himself and as he will be known, these great admirers and lovers of divine goodness were constantly the greatest opposers of him and enemies unto him. And an uncontrollable evidence this is that the love of divine goodness, which some do fancy in persons destitute of supernatural revelation and other aids of grace, was, in the best of them, placed on the products of their own imaginations, and not on God himself.

But omitting them, we may consider the effects of this darkness working by enmity in the minds of them who have the word preached unto them. Even in these, until effectually prevailed on by victorious grace, either closely or openly, it exerts itself. And however they may be doctrinally instructed in true notions concerning God and his attributes, yet in the application of them unto themselves, or in the consideration of their own concernment in them, they "always err in their hearts." All the practical notions they have of God tend to alienate their hearts from him, and that either by contempt or by an undue dread and terror; for some apprehend him slow and regardless of what they do, at least one that is not so severely displeased with them as that it should be necessary for them to seek a change of their state and condition. They think that God is such an one as themselves, Ps. l. 21; at least, that he doth approve them, and will accept them, although they should continue in their sins. Now, this is a fruit of the highest enmity against God, though palliated with the pretence of the most raised notions and apprehensions of his goodness; for as it is a heinous crime to imagine an outward shape of the divine nature, and that God is like to men or beasts, — the height of the sin of the most gross idolaters, Rom. i. 23, Ps. cvi. 20, — so it is a sin of a higher provocation to conceive him so far like unto bestial men as to approve and accept of them in their sins. Yet this false notion of God, even when his nature and will are objectively revealed in the word, this darkness doth and will maintain in the minds of men, whereby they are made obstinate in their sin to the uttermost. And where this fails, it will on the other hand represent God all fire and fury, inexorable and untractable. See Mic. vi. 6, 7; Isa. xxxiii. 14; Gen. iv. 13.

Moreover, this darkness fills the mind with enmity against all the ways of God; for as "the carnal mind is enmity against God," so "it is not subject unto his law, neither indeed can be." So the apostle informs us that men are "alienated from the life of God," or dislike the whole way and work of living unto him, by reason of the ignorance and blindness that is in them, Eph. iv. 18; and it esteems the whole rule and measure of it to be "foolishness," 1 Cor. i. 18, 21. But I must not too long insist on particulars, although in these days, wherein some are so apt to boast in proud swelling words of vanity concerning the power and sufficiency of the mind, even with respect unto religion and spiritual things, it cannot be unseasonable to declare what is the judgment of the Holy Ghost, plainly expressed in the Scriptures, in this matter; and one testimony thereof will be of more weight with the disciples of Jesus Christ than a thousand declamations to the contrary.

(2.) This darkness fills the mind with wills or perverse lusts that are directly contrary to the will of God, Eph. ii. 3. There are θελήματα διανοιῶν, the wills or "lusts of the mind," — that is, the habitual inclinations of the mind unto sensual objects; it "minds earthly things," Phil. iii. 19. And hence the mind itself is said to be "fleshly," Col. ii. 18. As unto spiritual things, it is "born of the flesh," and "is flesh." It likes, savours, approves of nothing but what is carnal, sensual, and vain. Nothing is suited unto it but what is either curious, or needless, or superstitious, or sensual and earthly. And therefore are men said to "walk in the vanity of their minds." In the whole course of their lives they are influenced by a predominant principle of vanity. And in this state the thoughts and imaginations of the mind are always set on work to provide sensual objects for this vain and fleshly frame; hence are they said to be "evil continually," Gen. vi. 5. This is the course of a darkened mind. Its vain frame or inclination, the fleshly will of it, stirs up vain thoughts and imaginations; it "minds the things of the flesh," Rom. viii. 5. These thoughts fix on and represent unto the mind objects suited unto the satisfaction of its vanity and lust. With these the mind committeth folly and lewdness, and the fleshly habit thereof is thereby heightened and confirmed, and this multiplies imaginations of its own kind, whereby men "inflame themselves," Isa. lvii. 5, waxing worse and worse. And the particular bent of these imaginations doth answer the predominancy of any especial lust in the heart or mind.

It will be objected, "That although these things are so in many, especially in persons that are become profligate in sin, yet, proceeding from their wills and corrupt, sensual affections, they argue not an impotency in the mind to discern and receive spiritual things, but, notwithstanding these enormities of some, the faculty of the mind is still endued with a power of discerning, judging, and believing spiritual things in a due manner."

Ans. 1. We do not now discourse concerning the weakness and disability of the mind in and about these things, which is as it were a natural impotency, like blindness in the eyes, which hath been both explained and confirmed before; but it is a moral disability, and that as unto all the powers of nature invincible, as unto the right receiving of spiritual things, which ensues on that corrupt depravation of the mind in the state of nature, that the Scripture calls "darkness" or "blindness," which we intend.

2. Our present testimonies have sufficiently confirmed that all the instances mentioned do proceed from the depravation of the mind. And whereas this is common unto and equal in all unregenerate men, if it produce not in all effects to the same degree of enormity, it is from some beams of light and secret convictions from the Holy Spirit, as we shall afterward declare.

3. Our only aim is, to prove the indispensable necessity of a saving work of illumination on the mind, to enable it to receive spiritual things spiritually; which appears sufficiently from the efficacy of this darkness, whence a man hath no ability to disentangle or save himself; for, also, —

(3.) It fills the mind with prejudices against spiritual things, as proposed unto it in the gospel; and from these prejudices it hath neither light nor power to extricate itself. No small part of its depravation consists in its readiness to embrace them, and pertinacious adherence unto them. Some few of these prejudices may be instanced:—

[1.] The mind, from the darkness that is in it, apprehends that spiritual things, the things of the gospel, as they are proposed, have an utter inconsistency with true contentment and satisfaction. These are the things which all men, by various ways, do seek after. This is the scent and chase which they so eagerly pursue, in different tracks and paths innumerable. Something they would attain or arrive unto which should satisfy their minds and fill their desires; and this commonly, before they have had any great consideration of the proposals of the gospel, they suppose themselves in the way at least unto, by those little tastes of satisfaction unto their lusts which they have obtained in the ways of the world. And these hopeful beginnings they will not forego: Isa. lvii. 10, "Thou art wearied in the greatness of thy way; yet saidst thou not, There is no hope: thou hast found the life of thine hand; therefore thou wast not grieved." They are ready ofttimes to faint in the pursuit of their lusts, because of the disappointments which they find in them or the evils that attend them; for, which way soever they turn themselves in their course, they cannot but see or shrewdly suspect that the end of them is, or will be, vanity and vexation of spirit. But yet they give not over the pursuit wherein they are engaged; they say not, "There is no hope." And the reason hereof is, because they "find the life of their hand." Something or other comes in daily, either from the work that they do, or the company they keep, or the expectation they have, which preserves their hope alive, and makes them unwilling to forego their present condition. They find it to be none of the best, but do not think there can be a better; and, therefore, their only design is to improve or to thrive in it. If they might obtain more mirth, more wealth, more strength and health, more assurance of their lives, more power, more honour, more suitable objects unto their sensual desires, then they suppose it would be better than it is; but as for any thing which differeth from these in the whole kind, they can entertain no respect for it. In this state and condition, spiritual things, the spiritual, mysterious things of the gospel, are proposed unto them. At first view they judge that these things will not assist them in the pursuit or improvement of their carnal satisfactions. And so far they are in the right; they judge not amiss. The things of the gospel will give neither countenance nor help to the lusts of men. Nay, it is no hard matter for them to come to a discovery that the gospel, being admitted in the power of it, will crucify and mortify those corrupt affections which hitherto they have been given up to the pursuit of; for this it plainly declares, Col. iii. 1–5; Tit. ii. 11, 12.

There are but two things wherein men seeking after contentment and satisfaction are concerned:— first, the objects of their lusts or desires, and then those lusts and desires themselves. The former may be considered in their own nature, as they are indifferent, or as they are capable of being abused to corrupt and sinful ends. In the first way, as the gospel condemns them not, so it adds nothing to them unto those by whom it is received. It gives not men more riches, wealth, or honour, than they had before in the world. It promises no such thing unto them that do receive it, but rather the contrary. The latter consideration of them it condemns and takes away. And for the desires of men themselves, the avowed work of the gospel is, to mortify them. And hereby the naturally corrupt relation which is between these desires and their objects is broken and dissolved. The gospel leaves men, unless upon extraordinary occasions, their names, their reputations, their wealth, their honours, if lawfully obtained and possessed; but the league that is between the mind and these things in all natural men must be broken. They must no more be looked on as the chiefest good, or in the place thereof, nor as the matter of satisfaction, but must give place to spiritual, unseen, eternal things. This secretly alienates the carnal mind, and a prejudice is raised against it, as that which would deprive the soul of all its present satisfactions, and offer nothing in the room of them that is suitable to any of its desires or affections; for, by reason of the darkness that it is under the power of, it can neither discern the excellency of the spiritual and heavenly things which are proposed unto it, nor have any affections whereunto they are proper and suited, so that the soul should go forth after them. Hereby this prejudice becomes invincible in their souls. They neither do, nor can, nor will admit of those things which are utterly inconsistent with all things wherein they hope or look for satisfaction. And men do but please themselves with dreams and fancies, who talk of such a reasonableness and excellency in gospel truths as that the mind of a natural man will discern such a suitableness in them unto itself, as thereon to receive and embrace them; nor do any, for the most part, give a greater evidence of the prevalency of the darkness and enmity that are in carnal minds against the spiritual things of the gospel, as to their life and power, than those who most pride and please themselves in such discourses.

[2.] The mind by this darkness is filled with prejudices against the mystery of the gospel in a peculiar manner. The hidden spiritual wisdom of God in it, as natural men cannot receive, so they do despise it, and all the parts of its declaration they look upon as empty and unintelligible notions. And this is that prejudice whereby this darkness prevails in the minds of men, otherwise knowing and learned. It hath done so in all ages, and in none more effectually than in that which is present. But there is a sacred, mysterious, spiritual wisdom in the gospel and the doctrine of it. This is fanatical, chimerical, and foolish to the wisest in the world, whilst they are under the power of this darkness. To demonstrate the truth hereof is the design of the apostle Paul, 1 Cor. i., ii.: for he directly affirms that the doctrine of the gospel is the wisdom of God in a mystery; that this wisdom cannot be discerned nor understood by the wise and learned men of the world, who have not received the Spirit of Christ, and, therefore, that the things of it are weakness and foolishness unto them. And that which is foolish is to be despised, yea, folly is the only object of contempt. And hence we see that some, with the greatest pride, scorn, and contempt imaginable, do despise the purity, simplicity, and whole mystery of the gospel, who yet profess they believe it. But to clear the whole nature of this prejudice, some few things may be distinctly observed:—

There are two sorts of things declared in the gospel:— 1st. Such as are absolutely its own, that are proper and peculiar unto it, — such as have no footsteps in the law or in the light of nature, but are of pure revelation, peculiar to the gospel. Of this nature are all things concerning the love and will of God in Christ Jesus. The mystery of his incarnation, of his offices and whole mediation, of the dispensation of the Spirit, and our participation thereof, and our union with Christ thereby, our adoption, justification, and effectual sanctification, thence proceeding, in brief, everything that belongs unto the purchase and application of saving grace, is of this sort. These things are purely and properly evangelical, peculiar to the gospel alone. Hence the apostle Paul, unto whom the dispensation of it was committed, puts that eminency upon them, that, in comparison, he resolved to insist on nothing else in his preaching,

1 Cor. ii. 2; and to that purpose doth he describe his ministry, Eph. iii. 7–11. 2dly. There are such things declared and enjoined in the gospel as have their foundation in the law and light of nature. Such are all the moral duties which are taught therein. And two things may be observed concerning them:— (1st.) That they are in some measure known unto men aliunde from other principles. The inbred concreated light of nature doth, though obscurely, teach and confirm them. So the apostle, speaking of mankind in general, saith, Τὸ γνωστὸν τοῦ Θεοῦ φανερόν ἐστιν ἐν αὐτοῖς, Rom. i. 19; — "That which may be known of God is manifested in themselves." The essential properties of God, rendering our moral duty to him necessary, are known by the light of nature; and by the same light are men able to make a judgment of their actions whether they be good or evil, Rom. ii. 14, 15. And this is all the light which some boast of, as they will one day find to their disappointment. (2dly.) There is on all men an obligation unto obedience answerable to their light concerning these things. The same law and light which discovereth these things doth also enjoin their observance. Thus is it with all men antecedently unto the preaching of the gospel unto them.

In this estate the gospel superadds two things unto the minds of men:— (1st.) It directs us unto a right performance of these things, from a right principle, by a right rule, and to a right end and purpose; so that they, and we in them, may obtain acceptance with God. Hereby it gives them a new nature, and turns moral duties into evangelical obedience. (2dly.) By a communication of that Spirit which is annexed unto its dispensation, it supplies us with strength for their performance in the manner it prescribes.

Hence it follows that this is the method of the gospel:— first, it proposeth and declareth things which are properly and peculiarly its own. So the apostle sets down the constant entrance of his preaching, 1 Cor. xv. 3. It reveals its own mysteries, to lay them as the foundation of faith and obedience. It inlays them in the mind, and thereby conforms the whole soul unto them. See Rom. vi. 17; Gal. iv. 19; Tit. ii. 11, 12; 1 Cor. iii. 11; 2 Cor. iii. 18. This foundation being laid, — without which it hath, as it were, nothing to do with the souls of men, nor will proceed unto any other thing with them by whom this its first work is refused, — it then grafts all duties of moral obedience on this stock of faith in Christ Jesus. This is the method of the gospel, which the apostle Paul observeth in all his epistles: first, he declares the mysteries of faith that are peculiar to the gospel, and then descends unto those moral duties which are regulated thereby.

But the prejudice we mentioned inverts the order of these things. Those who are under the power of it, when, on various accounts, they give admittance unto the gospel in general, yet fix their minds, firstly and principally, on the things which have their foundation in the law and light of nature. These they know and have some acquaintance with in themselves, and therefore cry them up, although not in their proper place, nor to their proper end. These they make the foundation, according to the place which they held in the law of nature and covenant of works, whereas the gospel allows them to be only necessary superstructions on the foundation. But resolving to give unto moral duties the pre-eminence in their minds, they consider afterward the peculiar doctrines of the gospel, with one or other of these effects; for, first, Some in a manner wholly despise them, reproaching those by whom they are singularly professed. What is contained in them is of no importance, in their judgment, compared with the more necessary duties of morality, which they pretend to embrace;

and, to acquit themselves of the trouble of a search into them, they reject them as unintelligible or unnecessary. Or, secondly, They will, by forced interpretations, enervating the spirit and perverting the mystery of them, square and fit them to their own low and carnal apprehensions. They would reduce the gospel and all the mysteries of it to their own light, as some; to reason, as others; to philosophy, as the rest; — and let them who comply not with their weak and carnal notions of things expect all the contemptuous reproaches which the proud pretenders unto science and wisdom of old cast upon the apostles and first preachers of the gospel. Hereby advancing morality above the mystery and grace of the gospel, they at once reject the gospel and destroy morality also; for, taking it off from its proper foundation, it falls into the dirt, — whereof the conversation of the men of this persuasion is no small evidence.

From this prejudice it is that the spiritual things of the gospel are by many despised and condemned. So God spake of Ephraim, Hos. viii. 12, "I have written to him the great things of my law, but they were counted as a strange thing." The things intended were תּוֹרָתִי [תֲּבֵי Keri] רֻבֵּי, — the "great, manifold, various things of the law." That which the law was then unto that people, such is the gospel now unto us. The "torah" was the entire means of God's communicating his mind and will unto them, as his whole counsel is revealed unto us by the gospel. These things he wrote unto them, or made them in themselves and their revelation plain and perspicuous. But when all was done, they were esteemed by them כְּמוֹ־זָר, as is also the gospel, "a thing foreign" and alien unto the minds of men, which they intend not to concern themselves in. They will heed the things that are cognate unto the principles of their nature, things morally good or evil; but for the hidden wisdom of God in the mystery of the gospel, it is esteemed by them as "a strange thing." And innumerable other prejudices of the same nature doth this darkness fill the minds of men withal, whereby they are powerfully, and, as unto any light or strength of their own, invincibly, kept off from receiving of spiritual things in a spiritual manner.

4. Again; the power and efficacy of this darkness in and upon the souls of unregenerate men will be farther evidenced by the consideration of its especial subject, or the nature and use of that faculty which is affected with it. This is the mind or understanding. Light and knowledge are intellectual virtues or perfections of the mind, and that in every kind whatever, whether in things natural, moral, or spiritual. The darkness whereof we treat is the privation of spiritual light, or the want of it; and therefore are they opposed unto one another: "Ye were sometimes darkness, but now are ye light in the Lord," Eph. v. 8. It is, therefore, the mind or understanding which is affected with this darkness, which is vitiated and depraved by it.

Now, the mind may be considered two ways:— (1.) As it is theoretical or contemplative, discerning and judging of things proposed unto it. So it is its office to find out, consider, discern, and apprehend the truth of things. In the case before us, it is the duty of the mind to apprehend, understand, and receive, the truths of the gospel as they are proposed unto it, in the manner of and unto the end of their proposal. This, as we have manifested, by reason of its depravation, it neither doth nor is able to do, John i. 5; 1 Cor. ii. 14. (2.) It may be considered as it is practical, as to the power it hath to direct the whole soul, and determine the will unto actual operation, according to its light. I shall not inquire at present whether the will, as to the specification of its acts, do necessarily follow the determination of the mind or practical understanding. I aim at no more but that it is the directive faculty of the soul as unto all moral and spiritual operations. Hence it follows:—

(1.) That nothing in the soul, nor the will and affections, can will, desire, or cleave unto any good, but what is presented unto them by the mind, and as it is presented. That good, whatever it be, which the mind cannot discover, the will cannot choose nor the affections cleave unto. All their actings about and concerning them are not such as answer their duty. This our Saviour directs us to the consideration of, Matt. vi. 22, 23, "The light of the body is the eye: if therefore thine eye be single, thy whole body shall be full of light. But if thine eye be evil, thy whole body shall be full of darkness. If therefore the light that is in thee be darkness, how great is that darkness!" As the eye is naturally the light of the body, or the means thereof, so is the mind unto the soul. And if darkness be in the eye, not only the eye but the whole body is in darkness, because in the eye alone is the light of the whole; so if the mind be under darkness, the whole soul is so also, because it hath no light but by the mind. And hence both is illumination sometimes taken for the whole work of conversion unto God, and the spiritual actings of the mind, by the renovation of the Holy Ghost, are constantly proposed as those which precede any gracious actings in the will, heart, and life; as we shall show afterward.

(2.) As the soul can no way, by any other of its faculties, receive, embrace, or adhere unto that good in a saving manner which the mind doth not savingly apprehend; so where the mind is practically deceived, or any way captivated under the power of prejudices, the will and the affections can no way free themselves from entertaining that evil which the mind hath perversely assented unto. Thus, where the mind is reprobate or void of a sound judgment, so as to call good evil, and evil good, the heart, affections, and conversation will be conformable thereunto, Rom. i. 28–32. And in the Scripture the deceit of the mind is commonly laid down as the principle of all sin whatever, 1 Tim. ii. 14; Heb. iii. 12, 13; 2 Cor. xi. 3.

And this is a brief delineation of the state of the mind of man whilst unregenerate, with respect unto spiritual things. And from what hath been spoken, we do conclude that the mind in the state of nature is so depraved, vitiated, and corrupted, that it is not able, upon the proposal of spiritual things unto it in the dispensation and preaching of the gospel, to understand, receive, and embrace them in a spiritual and saving manner, so as to have the sanctifying power of them thereby brought into and fixed in the soul, without an internal, especial, immediate, supernatural, effectual, enlightening act of the Holy Ghost; which what it is, and wherein it doth consist, shall be declared.

Footnotes:

14. See Samuel Parker's "Defence and Continuation of the Ecclesiastical Polity." — Ed.

15. "Dico veterem Nativitatem atque adeo omnes vires naturæ, quæ naturali propagatione transfunduntur in sobolem in scriptura damnari; maledictam cordis nostri imaginationem, rationem, os, manus, pedes peccato et tenebris involuta in nobis omnia." — Johan. Ferus in Evang. Joh. cap. i. v. 23. "Fide perdita, spe relicta, intelligentia obcæcata, voluntate captiva, homo quo in se reparetur non invenit." — De Vocat. Gent. lib. vii. cap. 3.

16. "Si quis per naturæ vigorem evangelizanti predicationi nos consentire posse confirmet absque illuminatione Spiritus Sancti; hæretico fallitur spiritu." — Conc. Arausic. ii. can. 7.

17. In the sense of "placed before," "presented." — Ed.

18. See treatise, "Communion with God," and his "Vindication" of it in reply to Dr Sherlock, vol ii. — Ed.

19. "Quomodo nempe lux incassum circumfundit oculos cæcos vel clausos, ita animalis homo non percipit ea quæ sunt Spiritus Dei." — 1 Cor. ii. 14; Bernard. Ser. i. sup. Cantic.

20. "Si quis per naturæ vigorem bonum aliquod quod ad salutem pertinet vitæ æternæ, cogitare ut expedit, aut eligere, sive salutari, id est, Evangelicæ prædicationi consentire posse confirmat, absque illuminatione et inspiratione Spiritus Sancti, qui dat omnibus suavitatem consentiendo et credendo veritati, hæretico fallitur spiritu." — Conc. Arausic. ii. can. 7."Ideo dictum est quia nullus hominum illuminatur nisi illo lumine veritatis quod Deus est; ne quisquam putaret ab eo se illuminari, a quo aliquid audit ut discat, non dico si quenquam magnum hominem, sed nec si angelum ei contingat habere doctorem. Adhibetur enim sermo veritatis extrinsecus vocis ministerio corporali; verumtamen neque qui plantat est aliquid, neque qui rigat, sed qui incrementum dat Deus. Audit quippe homo dicentem vel hominem vel angelum, sed ut sentiat et cognoscat verum esse quod dicitur, illo lumine mens ejus intus aspergitur, quod æternum manet, quod etiam in tenebris lucet." — August. de Peccat. Meritis et Remissione, lib. i. cap. 25.

21. Τοῖς ψυχροῖς, ex editione Parisiensi, 1733. — Ed.

22. "Firmissime tene et nullatenus dubites, posse quidem hominem, quem nec ignorantia literarum, neque aliqua prohibet imbecillitas vel adversitas, verba sanctæ legis et evangelii sive legere sive ex ore cujusquam prædicatoris audire; sed divinis mandatis obedire neminem posse, nisi quem Deus gratiâ suâ prævenerit, ut quod audit corpore, etiam corde percipiat et æcepta divinitus bonâ voluntate atque virtute, mandata Dei facere et velit et possit." — August. de Fide ad Petrum, cap. 34.

23. "Magnum aliquid Pelagiani se scire putant quando dicunt, non juberet Deus quod sciat non posse ab homine fieri; quis hoc nesciat? sed ideo jubet aliqua quæ non possumus ut noverimus quid ab illo petere debeamus. Ipsa enim est quæ orando impetrat, quod lex imperat." — August. de Grat. et Lib. Arbit. cap. 19."Mandando impossibilia non prævaricatores homines fecit, sed humiles; ut omne os obstruatur; et subditus fiat omnis mundus Deo; quia ex operibus legis non justificatibur omnis caro coram illo. Accipientes quippe mandatum, sentientes defectum, clamabimus in cœlum, et miserebitur nostri Deus." — Bernard. Serm. 50, in Cantic.

24. "In nullo gloriandum, quia nihil nostrum est." — Cypr. lib. 3. ad Quirin."Fide perdita, spe relicta, intelligentia obcæcata, voluntate captiva, homo qua in se reparetur non invenit." — Prosp. de Vocat. Gent. lib. i. cap. 7."Quicunque tribuit sibi bonum quod facit, etiamsi nihil videtur mali manibus operari, jam cordis innocentiam perdidit, in quo se largitori bonorum prætulit." — Hieron. in Prov. cap. xvi.

Chapter IV - Life and death, natural and spiritual, compared

Of death in sin — All unregenerate men spiritually dead — Spiritual death twofold: legal; metaphorical — Life natural, what it is, and wherein it consists — Death natural, with its necessary consequents — The supernatural life of Adam in innocency, in its principle, acts, and power — Differences between it and our spiritual life in Christ — Death spiritual a privation of the life we had in Adam; a negation of the life of Christ — Privation of a principle of all life to God — Spiritual impotency therein — Differences between death natural and spiritual — The use of precepts, promises, and threatenings — No man perisheth merely for want of power — No vital acts in an state of death — The way of the communication of spiritual life — Of what nature are the best works of persons unregenerate — No disposition unto spiritual life under the power of spiritual death.

Another description that the Scripture gives of unregenerate men, as to their state and condition, is, that they are spiritually dead; and hence, in like manner, it follows that there is a necessity of an internal, powerful, effectual work of the Holy Ghost on the souls of men, to deliver them out of this state and condition by regeneration. And this principally respects their wills and affections, as the darkness and blindness before described doth their minds and understandings. There is a spiritual life whereby men live unto God; this they being strangers unto and alienated from, are spiritually dead. And this the Scripture declares concerning all unregenerate persons, partly in direct words, and partly in other assertions of the same importance. Of the first sort the testimonies are many and express: Eph. ii. 1, "Ye were dead in trespasses and sins;" Verse 5, "When we were dead in sins;" Col. ii. 13, "And ye being dead in your sins, and the uncircumcision of your flesh;" 2 Cor. v. 14, "If one died for all, then were all dead;" Rom. v. 15, "Through the offence of one many are dead;" Verse 12, "Death passed upon all men, for that all have sinned." And the same is asserted in the second way, where the recovery and restoration of men by the grace of Christ is called their "quickening," or the bestowing of a new life upon them: for this supposeth that they were dead, or destitute of that life which in this revivification is communicated unto them; for that alone can be said to be quickened which was dead before. See Eph. ii. 5; John v. 21, vi. 63.

This death that unregenerate persons are under is twofold:—

1. Legal, with reference unto the sentence of the law. The sanction of the law was, that upon sin man should die: "In the day that thou eatest thereof thou shalt die the death," Gen. ii. 17. Upon this sentence Adam and all his posterity became dead in law, morally dead, or obnoxious unto death penally, and adjudged unto it. This death is intended in some of the places before mentioned; as Rom. v. 12, and it may be also, 2 Cor. v. 14: for as Christ died, so were all dead. He died penally under the sentence of the law, and all were obnoxious unto death, or dead on that account. But this is not the death which I

intend, neither are we delivered from it by regeneration, but by justification, Rom. viii. 1.

2. There is in them a spiritual death, called so metaphorically, from the analogy and proportion that it bears unto death natural. Of great importance it is to know the true nature hereof, and how by reason thereof unregenerate men are utterly disabled from doing any thing that is spiritually good, until they are quickened by the almighty power and irresistible efficacy of the Holy Ghost. Wherefore, to declare this aright, we must consider the nature of life and death natural, in allusion whereunto the spiritual estate of unregenerate men is thus described.

Life in general, or the life of a living creature, is "Actus vivificantis in vivificatum[25] per unionem utriusque;" — "The act of a quickening principle on a subject to be quickened, by virtue of their union." And three things are to be considered in it:—

1. The principle of life itself; and this in man is the rational, living soul, called נִשְׁמַת חַיִּים : Gen. ii. 7, "God breathed into his nostrils the breath of life, and man became a living soul." Having formed the body of man of the dust of the earth, he designed him a principle of life superior unto that of brute creatures, which is but the exurgency and spirit of their temperature and composition, though peculiarly educed by the formative virtue and power of the Holy Ghost, as hath been before declared. He creates for him, therefore, a separate, distinct, animating soul, and infuseth it into the matter prepared for its reception. And as he did thus in the beginning of the creation of the species or kind of the human race, in its first individuals, so he continueth to do the same in the ordinary course of the works of his providence for the continuation of it; for having ordained the preparation of the body by generation, he immediately infuseth into it the "living soul," the "breath of life."

2. There is the "actus primus," or the quickening act of this principle on the principle quickened, in and by virtue of union. Hereby the whole man becomes חַיָּה נֶפֶשׁ, — a "living soul;" ψυχικὸς ἄνθρωπος, — a person quickened by a vital principle, and enabled for all naturally vital actions.

3. There are the acts of this life itself; and they are of two sorts:— (1.) Such as flow from life as life. (2.) Such as proceed from it as such a life, from the principle of a rational soul. Those of the first sort are natural and necessary, as are all the actings and energies of the senses, and of the locomotive faculty, as also what belongs unto the receiving and improving of nutriment. These are acts of life, whence the psalmist proves idols to be dead things from the want of them; so far are they from having a divine life, as that they have no life at all, Ps. cxv. 4–7. These are acts of life as life, inseparable from it; and their end is, to preserve the union of the whole between the quickening and quickened principles. (3.) There are such acts of life as proceed from the especial nature of this quickening principle. Such are all the elicit[26] and imperate[27] acts of our understandings and wills; all actions that are voluntary, rational, and peculiarly human. These proceed from that special kind of life which is given by the especial quickening principle of a rational soul.

Hence it is evident wherein death natural doth consist; and three things may be considered in it:— 1. The separation of the soul from the body. Hereby the act of infusing the living soul ceaseth unto all its ends; for as a principle of life unto the whole, it operates only by virtue of its union with the subject to be quickened by it. 2. A cessation of all vital actings in the quickened subject; for that union from whence they should proceed is dissolved. 3. As a consequent of these, there is in the body an impotency for and an ineptitude unto all vital operations. Not only do all operations of life actually cease, but the body is no more able to effect them. There remains in it, indeed, "potentia obedientialis," a "passive power" to receive life again, if communicated unto it by an external efficient cause, — so the body of Lazarus being dead had a receptive power of a living soul, — but an active power to dispose itself unto life or vital actions it hath not.

From these things we may, by a just analogy, collect wherein life and death spiritual do consist. And to that end some things must be previously observed; as, — 1. That Adam in the state of innocency, besides his natural life, whereby he was a living soul, had likewise a supernatural life with respect unto its end, whereby he lived unto God. This is called the "life of God," Eph. iv. 18, which men now in the state of nature are alienated from; — the life which God requires, and which hath God for its object and end. And this life was in him supernatural: for although it was concreated in and with the rational soul, as a perfection due unto it, in the state wherein and with respect unto the end for which it was made, yet it did not naturally flow from the principles of the rational soul; nor were the principles, faculties, or abilities of it, inseparable from those of the soul itself, being only accidental perfections of them, inlaid in them by especial grace. This life was necessary unto him with respect unto the state wherein and the end for which he was made. He was made to live unto the living God, and that in a peculiar manner; — to live unto his glory in this world, by the discharge of the rational and moral obedience required of him; and to live afterward in his glory and the eternal enjoyment of him, as his chiefest good and highest reward. That whereby he was enabled hereunto was that life of God, which we are alienated from in the state of nature. 2. In this life, as in life in general, three things are to be considered:— (1.) Its principle; (2.) Its operation; (3.) Its virtue; or habit, act, and power.

(1.) There was a quickening principle belonging unto it; for every life is an act of a quickening principle. This in Adam was the image of God, or an habitual conformity unto God, his mind and will, wherein the holiness and righteousness of God himself was represented, Gen. i. 26, 27. In this image he was created, or it was concreated with him, as a perfection due to his nature in the condition wherein he was made. This gave him an habitual disposition unto all duties of that obedience that was required of him; it was the rectitude of all the faculties of his soul with respect unto his supernatural end, Eccles. vii. 29.

(2.) There belonged unto it continual actions from, or by virtue of, and suitable unto, this principle. All the acts of Adam's life should have been subordinate unto his great moral end. In all that he did he should have lived unto God, according unto the law of that covenant wherein he walked before him. And an acting in all things suitably unto the light in his mind, unto the righteousness and holiness in his will and affections, that uprightness, or integrity, or order, that was in his soul, was his living unto God.

(3.) He had herewithal power or ability to continue the principle of life in suitable acts of it, with respect unto the whole obedience required of him; that is, he had a sufficiency of ability for the performance of any duty, or of all, that the covenant required.

And in these three [things] did the supernatural life of Adam in innocency consist; and it is that which the life whereunto we are restored by Christ doth answer. It answers unto it, I say, and supplies its absence with respect unto the end of living unto God according unto the new covenant that we are taken into; for neither would the life of Adam be sufficient for us to live unto God according to the terms of the new covenant, nor is the life of grace we now enjoy suited to the covenant wherein Adam stood before God. Wherefore, some differences there are between them, the principal whereof may be reduced into two heads:—

1. The principle of this life was wholly and entirely in man himself. It was the effect of another cause, of that which was without him, — namely, the good-will and power of God; but it was left to grow on no other root but what was in man himself. It was wholly implanted in his nature, and therein did its springs lie. Actual excitations, by influence of power from God, it should have had; for no principle of operation can subsist in an independence of God, nor apply itself unto operation without his concurrence. But in the life whereunto we are renewed by Jesus Christ, the fountain and principle of it is not in ourselves, but in him, as one common head unto all that are made partakers of him. He is "our life;" and our life (as to the spring and fountain of it) is hid with him in God, Col. iii. 3, 4; for he quickeneth us by his Spirit, Rom. viii. 11. And our spiritual life, as in us, consists in the vital actings of this Spirit of his in us; for "without him we can do nothing," John xv. 5. By virtue hereof we "walk in newness of life," Rom. vi. 4. We live, therefore, hereby; yet not so much we, as "Christ liveth in us," Gal. ii. 20.

2. There is a difference between these lives with respect unto the object of their vital acts, for the life which we now lead by the faith of the Son of God hath sundry objects of its actings which the other had not; for whereas all the actings of our faith and love, — that is, all our obedience, — doth respect the revelation that God makes of himself and his will unto us, there are now new revelations of God in Christ, and consequently new duties of obedience required of us; as will afterward appear. And other such differences there are between them. The life which we had in Adam and that which we are renewed unto in Christ Jesus are so far of the same nature and kind, as our apostle manifests in sundry places, Eph. iv. 23, 24, Col. iii. 10, as that they serve to the same end and purpose.

There being, therefore, this twofold spiritual life, or ability of living unto God, that which we had in Adam and that which we have in Christ, we must inquire with reference unto which of these it is that unregenerate men are said to be spiritually dead, or dead in trespasses and sins. Now this, in the first place, hath respect unto the life we had in Adam; for the deprivation of that life was in the sanction of the law, "Thou shalt die the death." This spiritual death is comprised therein, and that in the privation of that spiritual life, or life unto God, which unregenerate men never had, neither de facto nor de jure, in any state or condition. Wherefore, with respect hereunto they are dead only negatively, — they have it not; but with respect unto the life we had in Adam, they are dead privatively, — they have lost that power of living unto God which they had.

From what hath been discoursed, we may discover the nature of this spiritual death, under the power whereof all unregenerate persons do abide: for there are three things in it:

1. A privation of a principle of spiritual life enabling us to live unto God; 2. A negation of all spiritual, vital acts, — that is, of all acts and duties of holy obedience, acceptable unto God, and tending to the enjoyment of him; 3. A total defect and want of power for any such acts whatever. All these are in that death which is a privation of life, such as this is.

First, There is in it a privation of a principle of spiritual life, namely, of that which we had before the entrance of sin, or a power of living unto God according to the covenant of works; and a negation of that which we have by Christ, or a power of living unto God according to the tenor of the covenant of grace. Those, therefore, who are thus dead have no principle or first power of living unto God, or for the performance of any duty to be accepted with him, in order to the enjoyment of him, according to either covenant. It is with them, as to all the acts and ends of life spiritual, as it is with the body, as to the acts and ends of life natural, when the soul is departed from it. Why else are they said to be dead?

It is objected "That there is a wide difference between death natural and spiritual. In death natural, the soul itself is utterly removed and taken from the body; but in death spiritual it continues. A man is still, notwithstanding this spiritual death, endowed with an understanding, will, and affections; and by these are men enabled to perform their duty unto God, and yield the obedience required of them."

Ans. 1. In life spiritual the soul is unto the principle of it as the body is unto the soul in life natural; for in life natural the soul is the quickening principle, and the body is the principle quickened. When the soul departs, it leaves the body with all its own natural properties, but utterly deprived of them which it had by virtue of its union with the soul. So in life spiritual, the soul is not, in and by its essential properties, the quickening principle of it, but it is the principle that is quickened. And when the quickening principle of spiritual life departs, it leaves the soul with all its natural properties entire as to their essence, though morally corrupted; but of all the power and abilities which it had by virtue of its union with a quickening principle of spiritual life, it is deprived. And to deny such a quickening principle of spiritual life, superadded unto us by the grace of Christ, distinct and separate from the natural faculties of the soul, is, upon the matter, to renounce the whole gospel It is all one as to deny that Adam was created in the image of God which he lost, and that we are renewed unto the image of God by Jesus Christ. Hence, 2. Whatever the soul acts in spiritual things by its understanding, will, and affections, as deprived of or not quickened by this principle of spiritual life, it doth it naturally, not spiritually, as shall be instantly made to appear.

There is, therefore, in the first place, a disability or impotency unto all spiritual things to be performed in a spiritual manner, in all persons not born again by the Spirit; because they are spiritually dead. Whatever they can do, or however men may call what they do, unless they are endowed with a quickening principle of grace, they can perform no act spiritually vital, no act of life whereby we live to God, or that is absolutely accepted with him. Hence it is said, "The carnal mind is enmity against God: for it is not subject to the law of God, neither indeed can be," Rom. viii. 7. "So then they that are in the flesh cannot please God," verse 8. Men may cavil whilst they please about this carnal mind, and contend that it is only the sensitive part of the soul, or the affections, as corrupted by prejudices and [by] depraved habits of vice, two things are plain in the text; first, That this carnal mind is in all mankind, whoever they be, who are not partakers of the Spirit of God and his quickening power; secondly, That where it is, there is a disability of doing any thing that should please God: which is the sum of what we contend for, and which men may with as little a disparagement of their modesty deny as reject the authority of the apostle. So our Saviour, as to one instance, tells us that "no man can come to him except the Father draw him," John vi. 44. And so is it figuratively expressed where, all men being by nature compared unto evil trees, it is affirmed of them that they cannot bring forth good fruit unless their nature be changed, Matt. vii. 18, xii. 33. And this disability as to good is also compared by the prophet unto such effects as lie under a natural impossibility of accomplishment, Jer. xiii. 23. We contend not about expressions. This is that which the Scripture abundantly instructeth us in: There is no power in men by nature whereby they are of themselves, — upon the mere proposal of their duty in spiritual obedience, and exhortations from the word of God unto the performance of it, accompanied with all the motives which are meet and suited to prevail with them thereunto, — [able] to perceive, know, will, or do any thing in such a way or manner as that it should be accepted with God, with respect unto our spiritual life unto him, according to his will, and future enjoyment of him, without the efficacious infusion into them, or creation in them, of a new gracious principle or habit enabling them thereunto; and that this is accordingly wrought in all that believe by the Holy Ghost, we shall afterward declare.

But it will be objected, and hath against this doctrine been ever so since the days of Pelagius, "That a supposition hereof renders all exhortations, commands, promises, and threatenings, — which comprise the whole way of the external communication of the will of God unto us, — vain and useless; for to what purpose is it to exhort blind men to see or dead men to live, or to promise rewards unto them upon their so doing? Should men thus deal with stones, would it not be vain and ludicrous, and that because of their impotency to comply with any such proposals of our mind unto them; and the same is here supposed in men as to any ability in spiritual things."

Ans. 1. There is nothing, in the highest wisdom, required in the application of any means to the producing of an effect, but that in their own nature they are suited thereunto, and that the subject to be wrought upon by them is capable of being affected according as their nature requires.[28] And thus exhortations, with promises and threatenings, are in their kind, as moral instruments, suited and proper to produce the effects of faith and obedience in the minds of men. And the faculties of their souls, their understandings, wills, and affections, axe meet to be wrought upon by them unto that end; for by men's rational abilities they are able to discern their nature and judge of their tendency. And because these faculties are the principle and subject of all actual obedience, it is granted that there is in man a natural, remote, passive power to yield obedience unto God, which yet can never actually put forth itself without the effectual working of the grace of God, not only enabling but working in them to will and to do.

2. Exhortations, promises, and threatenings respect not primarily our present ability, but our duty. Their end is, to declare unto us, not what we can do, but what we ought to do; and this is done fully in them. On the other hand, make a general rule, that what God commands or exhorts us unto, with promises made unto our obedience, and threatenings annexed unto a

supposition of disobedience, we have power in and of ourselves to do, or we are of ourselves able to do, and you quite evacuate the grace of God, or at least make it only useful for the more easy discharge of our duty, not necessary unto the very being of duty itself; which is the Pelagianism anathematized by so many councils of old. But in the church it hath hitherto been believed that the command directs our duty, but the promise gives strength for the performance of it.

3. God is pleased to make these exhortations and promises to be "vehicula gratiæ," — the means of communicating spiritual life and strength unto men; and he hath appointed them unto this end, because, considering the moral and intellectual faculties of the minds of men, they are suited thereunto. Hence, these effects are ascribed unto the word, which really are wrought by the grace communicated thereby, James i. 18; 1 Pet. i. 23. And this, in their dispensation under the covenant of grace, is their proper end. God may, therefore, wisely make use of them, and command them to be used towards men, notwithstanding all their own disability savingly to comply with them, seeing he can, will, and doth himself make them effectual unto the end aimed at.

But it will be farther objected, "That if men are thus utterly devoid of a principle of spiritual life, of all power to live unto God, — that is, to repent, believe, and yield obedience, — is it righteous that they should perish eternally merely for their disability, or their not doing that which they are not able to do? This would be to require brick and to give no straw, yea, to require much where nothing is given. But the Scripture everywhere chargeth the destruction of men upon their wilful sin, not their weakness or disability."

Ans. 1. Men's disability to live to God is their sin. Whatever, therefore, ensues thereon may be justly charged on them. It is that which came on us by the sin of our nature in our first parents, all whose consequents are our sin and our misery, Rom. v. 12. Had it befallen us without a guilt truly our own, according to the law of our creation and covenant of our obedience, the case would have been otherwise; but on this supposition (sufficiently confirmed elsewhere), those who perish do but feed on the fruit of their own ways.

2. In the transactions between God and the souls of men, with respect unto their obedience and salvation, there is none of them but hath a power in sundry things, as to some degrees and measures of them, to comply with his mind and will, which they voluntarily neglect; and this of itself is sufficient to bear the charge of their eternal ruin. But, —

3. No man is so unable to live unto God, to do any thing for him, but that withal he is able to do any thing against him. There is in all men by nature a depraved, vicious habit of mind, wherein they are alienated from the life of God; and there is no command given unto men for evangelical faith or obedience, but they can and do put forth a free positive act of their wills in the rejection of it, either directly or interpretatively, in preferring somewhat else before it. As "they cannot come to Christ except the Father draw them," so "they will not come that they may have life;" wherefore their destruction is just and of themselves.

This is the description which the Scripture giveth us concerning the power, ability, or disability, of men in the state of nature, as unto the performance of spiritual things. By some it is traduced as fanatical and senseless; which the Lord Christ must answer for, not we, for we do nothing but plainly represent what he hath expressed in his word; and if it be "foolishness" unto any, the day will determine where the blame must lie.

Secondly, There is in this death an actual cessation of all vital acts. From this defect of power, or the want of a principle of spiritual life, it is that men in the state of nature can perform no vital act of spiritual obedience, — nothing that is spiritually good, or saving, or acceptable with God, according to the tenor of the new covenant; which we shall, in the second place, a little explain.

The whole çourse of our obedience to God in Christ is the "life of God," Eph. iv. 18, — that life which is from him in a peculiar manner, whereof he is the especial author, and whereby we live unto him, — which is our end. And the gospel, which is the rule of our obedience, is called "The words of this life," Acts v. 20, — that which guides and directs us how to live to God. Hence all the duties of this life are vital acts, spiritually vital acts, acts of that life whereby we live to God.

Where, therefore, this life is not, all the works of men are dead works. Where persons are dead in sin, their works are "dead works." They are so all of them, either in their own nature, or with respect unto them by whom they are performed, Heb. ix. 14. They are dead works because they proceed not from a principle of life, are unprofitable as dead things, Eph. v. 11, and end in death eternal, James i. 15.

We may, then, consider how this spiritual life, which enableth us unto these vital acts, is derived and communicated unto us:—

1. The original spring and fountain of this life is with God: Ps. xxxvi. 9, "With thee is the fountain of life." The sole spring of our spiritual life is in an especial way and manner in God. And hence our life is said to be "hid with Christ in God," Col. iii. 3; that is, as to its internal producing and preserving cause. But it is thus also with respect unto all life whatever. God is the "living God." All other things are in themselves but dead things; their life, whatever it be, is in him efficiently and eminently, and in them it is purely derivative. Wherefore, —

2. Our spiritual life, as unto the especial nature of it, is specificated and discerned from a life of any other kind, in that the fulness of it is communicated unto the Lord Christ as mediator, Col. i. 19; and from his fullness we do receive it, John i. 16. There is a principle of spiritual life communicated unto us from his fullness thereof, whence he quickeneth whom he pleaseth. Hence he is said to be "our life," Col. iii. 4. And in our life, it is not so much we who live, as "Christ that liveth in us," Gal. ii. 20; because we act nothing but as we are acted by virtue and power from him, 1 Cor. xv. 10.

3. The fountain of this life being in God, and the fullness of it being laid up in Christ for us, he communicates the power and principle of it unto us by the Holy Ghost, Rom. viii. 11. That he is the immediate efficient cause hereof, we shall afterward fully evince and declare. But yet he doth it so as to derive it unto us from Jesus Christ, Eph. iv. 15, 16; for he is "the life," and "without him," or power communicated from him, "we can do nothing," John xv. 5.

4. This spiritual life is communicated unto us by the Holy Ghost, according unto and in order for the ends of the new covenant: for this is the promise of it, That God will first write his law in our hearts, and then we shall walk in his statutes; that is, the principle of life must precede all vital acts. From this principle of life, thus derived and conveyed unto us, are all those vital acts whereby we live to God. Where this is not, — as it is not in any that are "dead

in sins," for from the want hereof are they denominated "dead," — no act of obedience unto God can so be performed as that it should be an act of the "life of God;" and this is the way whereby the Scripture doth express it. The same thing is intended when we say in other words, that without an infused habit of internal inherent grace, received from Christ by an efficacious work of the Spirit, no man can believe or obey God, or perform any duty in a saving manner, so as it should be accepted with him. And if we abide not in this principle, we let in the whole poisonous flood of Pelagianism into the church. To say that we have a sufficiency in ourselves so much as to think a good thought, or to do any thing as we ought, any power, any ability that is our own, or in us by nature, however externally excited and guided by motives, directions, reasons, encouragements, of what sort soever, to believe or obey the gospel savingly in any one instance, is to overthrow the gospel and the faith of the catholic church in all ages.

But it may be objected, "That whereas many unregenerate persons may and do perform many duties of religious obedience, if there be nothing of spiritual life in them then are they all sins, and so differ not from the worst things they do in this world, which are but sins; and if so, unto what end should they take pains about them? Were it not as good for them to indulge unto their lusts and pleasures, seeing all comes to one end? It is all sin, and nothing else. Why do the dispensers of the gospel press any duties on such as they know to be in that estate? What advantage shall they have by a compliance with them? Were it not better to leave them to themselves, and wait for their conversion, than to spend time and labour about them to no purpose?"

Ans. 1. It must be granted that all the duties of such persons are in some sense sins. It was the saying of Austin,[29] that the virtues of unbelievers are splendida peccata. This some are now displeased with; but it is easier to censure him than to confute him. Two things attend in every duty that is properly so:— (1.) That it is accepted with God; and, (2.) That it is sanctified in them that do it. But neither of these is in the duties of unregenerate men; for they have not faith, and "without faith it is impossible to please God," Heb. xi. 6. And the apostle also assures us that unto the defiled and unbelieving, — that is, all unsanctified persons, not purified by the Spirit of grace, — all things are unclean, because their consciences and minds are defiled, Tit. i. 15. So their praying is said to be an "abomination," and their plowing "sin." It doth not, therefore, appear what is otherwise in them or to them. But as there are good duties which have sin adhering to them, Isa. lxiv. 6, so there are sins which have good in them; for bonum oritur ex integris, malum ex quocunque defectu. Such are the duties of men unregenerate. Formally, and unto them, they are sin; materially, and in themselves, they are good. This gives them a difference from, and a preference above, such sins as are every way sinful. As they are duties, they are good; as they are the duties of such persons, they are evil, because necessarily defective in what should preserve them from being so. And on this ground they ought to attend unto them, and may be pressed thereunto.

2. That which is good materially and in itself, though vitiated from the relation which it hath to the person by whom it is performed, is approved, and hath its acceptation in its proper place; for duties may be performed two ways:— (1.) In hypocrisy and pretence. So they are utterly abhorred of God, in matter and manner. That is such a poisonous ingredient as vitiates the whole, Isa. i. 11–15; Hos. i. 4. (2.) In integrity, according unto present light and

conviction; which, for the substance of them, are approved. And no man is to be exhorted to do any thing in hypocrisy: see Matt. x. 26. And on this account also, that the duties themselves are acceptable, men may be pressed to them. But, —

3. It must be granted that the same duty, for the substance of it in general, and performed according to the same rule as to the outward manner of it, may be accepted in or from one and rejected in or from another. So was it with the sacrifices of Cain and Abel. And not only so, but the same rejected duty may have degrees of evil for which it is rejected, and be more sinful in and unto one than unto another. But we must observe, that the difference doth not relate merely unto the different states of the persons by whom such are performed, — as, because one is in the state of grace, whose duties are accepted, and another in the state of nature, whose duties are rejected, as their persons are: for although the acceptation of our persons be a necessary condition for the acceptation of our duties, as God first had respect unto Abel, and then unto his offering, yet there is always a real specifical difference between the duties themselves whereof one is accepted and the other rejected, although, it may be, unto us it be every way imperceptible; as in the offerings of Cain and Abel, that of Abel was offered in faith, the defect whereof in the other caused it to be refused. Suppose duties, therefore, to be every way the same, as to the principles, rule, and ends, or whatever is necessary to render them good in their kind, and they would be all equally accepted with God, by whomsoever they are performed, for he is "no respecter of persons." But this cannot be but where those that perform them are partakers of the same grace. It is, therefore, the wills of men only that vitiate their duties, which are required of them as good; and if so, they may justly be required of them. The defect is not immediately in their state, but in their wills and their perversity.

4. The will of God is the rule of all men's obedience. This they are all bound to attend unto; and if what they do, through their own defect, prove eventually sin unto them, yet the commandment is just and holy, and the observance of it justly prescribed unto them. The law is the moral cause of the performance of the duties it requires, but not of the sinful manner of their performance; and God hath not lost his right of commanding men, because they by their sin have lost their power to fulfil his command. And if the equity of the command doth arise from the proportioning of strength that men have to answer it, he that contracts the highest moral disability that depraved habits of mind can introduce or a course of sinning produce in him, is freed from owing obedience unto any of God's commands, seeing all confess that such a habit of sin may be contracted as will deprive them in whom it is of all power of obedience! Wherefore, —

5. Preachers of the gospel and others have sufficient warrant to press upon all men the duties of faith, repentance, and obedience, although they know that in themselves they have not a sufficiency of ability for their due performance; for, — (1.) It is the will and command of God that so they should do, and that is the rule of all our duties. They are not to consider what man can do or will do, but what God requires. To make a judgment of men's ability, and to accommodate the commands of God unto them accordingly, is not committed unto any of the sons of men. (2.) They have a double end in pressing on men the observance of duties, with a supposition of the state of impotency described:— [1.] To prevent them from such courses of sin as would harden

them, and so render their conversion more difficult, if not desperate. [2.] To exercise a means appointed of God for their conversion, or the communication of saving grace unto them. Such are God's commands, and such are the duties required in them. In and by them God doth use to communicate of his grace unto the souls of men; not with respect unto them as their duties, but as they are ways appointed and sanctified by him unto such ends. And hence it follows that even such duties as are vitiated in their performance, yet are of advantage unto them by whom they are performed; for, — 1st. By attendance unto them they are preserved from many sins. 2d. In an especial manner from the great sin of despising God, which ends commonly in that which is unpardonable. 3d. They are hereby made useful unto others, and many ends of God's glory in the world. 4th. They are kept in God's way, wherein they may gradually be brought over unto a real conversion unto him.

Thirdly, In this state of spiritual death there is not, in them who are under the power of it, any disposition active and inclining unto life spiritual. There is not so in a dead carcase unto life natural. It is a subject meet for an external power to introduce a living principle into. So the dead body of Lazarus was quickened and animated again by the introduction of his soul; but in itself it had not the least active disposition nor inclination thereunto. And no otherwise is it with a soul dead in trespasses and sins. There is in it potentia obedientialis, a power rendering it meet to receive the communications of grace and spiritual life; but a disposition thereunto of its own it hath not. There is in it a remote power, in the nature of its faculties, meet to be wrought upon by the Spirit and grace of God; but an immediate power, disposing and enabling it unto spiritual acts, it hath not. And the reason is, because natural corruption cleaves unto it as an invincible, unmovable habit, constantly inducing unto evil, wherewith the least disposition unto spiritual good is not consistent. There is in the soul, in the Scripture language (which some call "canting"), "the body of the sins of the flesh," Col. ii. 11; which unless it be taken away by spiritual circumcision, through the virtue of the death of Christ, it will lie dead into eternity. There is, therefore, in us that which may be quickened and saved; and this is all we have to boast of by nature. Though man by sin be made like the beasts that perish, being brutish and foolish in his mind and affections, yet he is not so absolutely; he retains that living soul, those intellectual faculties, which were the subject of original righteousness, and are meet to receive again the renovation of the image of God by Jesus Christ.

But this also seems obnoxious to an objection from the instances that are given in the Scripture, and whereof we have experience, concerning sundry good duties performed by men unregenerate, and that in a tendency unto living unto God, which argues a disposition to spiritual good. So Balaam desired to "die the death of the righteous;" and Herod "heard John the Baptist gladly, doing many things willingly;" and great endeavours after conversion unto God we find in many who never attain thereunto. So that to say there is no disposition unto spiritual life in any unregenerate person is to make them all equal, which is contrary to experience.

Ans. 1. There is no doubt but that unregenerate men may perform many external duties which are good in themselves, and lie in the order of the outward disposal of the means of conversion; nor is it questioned but they may have real designs, desires, and endeavours after that which is presented unto them as their chiefest good; — but so far as these desires or actings are merely natural, there is no disposition in them unto spiritual life, or that which is spiritually good. So far as they are supernatural, they are not of themselves; for, —

2. Although there are no preparatory inclinations in men, yet there are preparatory works upon them. Those who have not the word, yet may have convictions of good and evil, from the authority of God in their consciences, Rom. ii. 14, 15. And the law, in the dispensation of it, may work men unto many duties of obedience, much more may the gospel so do; but whatever effects are hereby produced, they are wrought by the power of God, exerted in the dispensation of the word. They are not educed out of the natural faculties of the minds of men, but are effects of the power of God in them and upon them, for we know that "in the flesh there dwelleth no good thing;" and all unregenerate men are no more, for "that which is born of the flesh is flesh."

3. The actings thus effected and produced in men unregenerate are neither fruits of, nor dispositions unto spiritual life. Men that are spiritually dead may have designs and desires to free themselves from dying eternally, but such a desire to be saved is no saving disposition unto life.

Footnotes:

25. Vivificandum? according to the translation. — Ed.

26. Elicit, brought into actual existence. — Ed.

27. Imperate, done by the direction of the mind. — Ed.

28. "Magnum aliquid Pelagiani se scire putant quando dicunt, non juberet Deus quod scit non posse ab homine fieri, quis hoc nesciat? sed ideo jubet aliqua quæ non possumus ut noverimus quid ab illo petere debeamus. Ipsa enim est fides quæ orando impetrat, quod lex imperat." — August. de Grat. et Lib. Arbit. cap. xvi."O homo cognosce in præceptione quid debeas habere; in corruptione cognosce tuo te vitio non habere; in oratione cognosce unde accipias quod vis habere." — Idem, de Corrupt. et Grat. cap. iii."Mandando impossibilia, non prevaricatores homines fecit, sed humiles; ut omne os obstruatur; et subditus fiat omnis mundus Deo. Accipientes nempe mandatum, sentientes defectum, clamabimus in cœlum." — Bernard. Serm. 50 in Cant."Quamvis dicamus Dei donum esse obedientiam, tamen homines exhortamur ad eam: sed illis qui veritatis exhortationem obedienter audiunt, ipsum donum Dei datum est, hoc est, obedienter audire; illis autem qui non sic audiunt, non est datum." August. de Dono Perseverant. cap. xiv.

29. "Manifestissimè patet in impiorum animis nullam habitare virtutem; sed omnia opera eorum immunda esse atque polluta, habentium sapientiam non spiritualem sed animalem, non cœlestem sed terrenam." — Prosper. ad Collat. cap. xiii. "Omne etenim probitatis opus nisi semine veræ Exoritur fidei, peccatum est, inque reatum Vertitur, et sterilis cumulat sibi gloria pœnam." Prosper. de Ingratis. cap. xvi. 407–409."Multa laudabilia atque miranda possunt in homine reperiri, quæ sine charitatis medullis habent quidem pietatis similitudinem, sed non habent veritatem." — Idem, ad Rufin. de Lib. Arbit.

Chapter V - The nature, causes, and means of regeneration

Description of the state of nature necessary unto a right understanding of the work of the Spirit in regeneration — No possibility of salvation unto persons living and dying in a state of sin — Deliverance from it by regeneration only — The Holy Ghost the peculiar author of this work — Differences about the manner and nature of it — Way of the ancients in explaining the doctrine of grace — The present method proposed — Conversion not wrought by moral suasion only — The nature and efficacy of moral suasion, wherein they consist — Illumination preparatory unto conversion — The nature of grace morally effective only, opened; not sufficient for conversion — The first argument, disproving the working of grace in conversion to be by moral suasion only — The second — The third — The fourth — Wherein the work of the Spirit in regeneration positively doth consist — The use and end of outward means — Real internal efficiency of the Spirit in this work — Grace victorious and irresistible — The nature of it explained; proved — The manner of God's working by grace on our wills farther explained — Testimonies concerning the actual collation of faith by the power of God — Victorious efficacy of internal grace proved by sundry testimonies of Scripture — From the nature of the work wrought by it, in vivification and regeneration — Regeneration considered with respect unto the distinct faculties of the soul; the mind, the will, the affections.

Unto the description we are to give of the work of regeneration, the precedent account of the subject of it, or the state and condition of them that are to be regenerated, was necessarily to be premised; for upon the knowledge thereof doth a due apprehension of the nature of that work depend. And the occasion of all the mistakes and errors that have been about it, either of old or of late, hath been a misunderstanding of the true state of men in their lapsed condition, or of nature as depraved. Yea, and those by whom this whole work is derided do now countenance themselves therein by their ignorance of that state, which they will not learn either from the Scripture or experience; for, "natura sic apparet vitiata ut hoc majoris vitii sit non videre," as Austin speaks. It is an evidence of the corruption of nature, that it disenables the minds of men to discern their own corruption. We have previously discharged this work so far as it is necessary unto our present purpose. Many other things might be added in the explication of it, were that our direct design. Particularly, having confined myself to treat only concerning the depravation of the mind and will, I have not insisted on that of the affections, which yet is effectual to retain unregenerate men under the power of sin; though it be far enough from truth that the whole corruption of nature consists therein, as some weakly and atheologically have imagined. Much less have I treated concerning that increase and heightening of the depravation of nature which is contracted by a custom of sinning, as unto all the perverse ends of it. Yet this also the Scripture much insists upon, as that which naturally and necessarily ensues in all in whom it is not prevented by the effectual transforming grace of the Spirit of God; and it is that which seals up the impossibility of their turning themselves to God, Jer. xiii. 23; Rom. iii. 10–19. But that the whole difficulty of conversion should arise from men's contracting a habit or custom of sinning is false, and openly contradictory to the Scripture. These things are personal evils, and befall individuals, through their own default, in various degrees. And we see that amongst men, under the same use of means, some are converted unto God who have been deeply immersed in an habitual course of open sins, whilst others, kept from them by the influence of their education upon their inclinations and affections, remain unconverted. So was it of old between the publicans and harlots on the one hand, and the Pharisees on the other. But my design was only to mention that which is common unto all, or wherein all men universally are equally concerned, who are partakers of the same human nature in its lapsed condition. And what we have herein declared from the Scriptures will guide us in our inquiry after the work of the Holy Spirit of grace in our deliverance from it.

It is evident, and needs no farther confirmation, that persons living and dying in this estate cannot be saved. This hitherto hath been allowed by all that are called Christians; nor are we to be moved that some who call themselves so do begin to laugh at the disease, and despise the remedy of our nature. Among those who lay any serious and real claim unto Christianity, there is nothing more certain nor more acknowledged than that there is no deliverance from a state of misery for those who are not delivered from a state of sin. And he who denies the necessary perishing of all that live and die in the state of corrupted nature, denies all the use of the incarnation and mediation of the Son of God: for if we may be saved without the renovation of our natures, there was no need nor use of the new creation of all things by Jesus Christ, which principally consists therein; and if men may be saved under all the evils that came upon us by the fall, then did Christ die in vain. Besides, it is frequently expressed that men in that state are "enemies to God," "alienated from him," "children of wrath," "under the curse;" and if such may be saved, so may devils also. In brief, it is not consistent with the nature of God, his holiness, righteousness, or truth, with the law or gospel, nor possible in the nature of the thing itself, that such persons should enter into or be made possessors of glory and rest with God. A deliverance, therefore, out of and from this condition is indispensably necessary to make us meet for the inheritance of the saints in light.

This deliverance must be and is by regeneration. The determination of our Saviour is positive, both in this and the necessity of it, before asserted: John iii. 3, "Except a man be born again," or from above, "he cannot see the kingdom of God." Whatever sense the "kingdom of God" is taken in, either for that of grace here or of glory hereafter, it is all the same as unto our present purpose. There is no interest in it to be obtained, no participation of the benefits of it, unless a man be born again, unless he be regenerate. And this determination of our Saviour, as it is absolute and decretory, so it is applicable unto and equally compriseth every individual of mankind. And the work intended by their regeneration, or in being born again, which is the spiritual conversion and quickening of the souls of men, is everywhere ascribed unto them that shall be saved. And although men may have, through their ignorance and prejudices, false apprehensions about regeneration and the nature of it, or wherein it doth consist, yet, so far as I know, all Christians are agreed that it is the way and means of our deliverance from the state of sin or corrupted nature, or rather our deliverance itself; for this both express testimonies of Scripture and the nature of the thing itself put beyond contradiction, Tit. iii. 3–5. And those by whom it is exposed unto scorn, who esteem it a ridiculous thing for any one to inquire whether he be regenerate or no, will one day understand the necessity of it, although, it may be, not before it is too late to obtain any advantage thereby.

The Holy Ghost is the immediate author and cause of this work of regeneration. And herein again, as I suppose, we have in general the consent of all. Nothing is more in words acknowledged than that all the elect of God are sanctified by the Holy Ghost. And this regeneration is the head, fountain, or beginning of our sanctification, virtually comprising the whole in itself, as will afterward appear. However, that it is a part thereof is not to be denied. Besides, as I suppose, it is equally confessed to be an effect or work of grace, the actual dispensation whereof is solely in the hand of the Holy Spirit. This, I say, is in words acknowledged by all, although I know not how some can reconcile this profession unto other notions and sentiments which they declare concerning it; for setting aside what men do herein themselves, and others do towards them in the ministry of the word, I cannot see what remains, as they express their loose imaginations, to be ascribed unto the Spirit of God. But at present we shall make use of this general concession, that regeneration is the work of the Holy Ghost, or an effect of his grace. Not that we have any need so to do, but that we may avoid contesting about those things wherein men may shroud their false opinions under general, ambiguous expressions; which was the constant practice of Pelagius and those who followed him of old. But the Scripture is express in testimonies to our purpose. What our Saviour calls being "born again," John iii. 3, he calls being "born of the Spirit," verses 5, 6, because he is the sole, principal, efficient cause of this new birth; for "it is the Spirit that quickeneth," John vi. 63; Rom. viii. 11. And God saveth us "according to his mercy, by the washing of regeneration, and renewing of the Holy Ghost," Tit. iii. 5. Whereas, therefore, we are said to be "born of God," or to be "begotten again of his own will," John i. 13, James i. 18, 1 John iii. 9, it is with respect unto the especial and peculiar operation of the Holy Spirit.

These things are thus far confessed, even by the Pelagians themselves, both those of old and those at present, at least in general; nor hath any as yet been so hardy as to deny regeneration to be the work of the Holy Spirit in us, unless we must except those deluded souls who deny both him and his work. Our sole inquiry, therefore, must be after the manner and nature of this work; for the nature of it depends on the manner of the working of the Spirit of God herein. This, I acknowledge, was variously contended about of old; and the truth concerning it hath scarce escaped an open opposition in any age of the church. And at present this is the great ball of contention between the Jesuits and the Jansenists; the latter keeping close to the doctrine of the principal ancient writers of the church; the former, under new notions, expressions, and distinctions, endeavouring the re-enforcement of Pelagianism, whereunto some of the elder schoolmen led the way, of whom our Bradwardine so long ago complained. But never was it with so much impudence and ignorance traduced and reviled as it is by some among ourselves; for a sort of men we have who, by stories of wandering Jews, rhetorical declamations, pert cavillings, and proud revilings of those who dissent from them, think to scorn and banish truth out of the world, though they never yet durst attempt to deal openly and plainly with any one argument that is pleaded in its defence and confirmation.

The ancient writers of the church, who looked into these things with most diligence, and laboured in them with most success, as Austin, Hilary, Prosper, and Fulgentius, do represent the whole work of the Spirit of God towards the souls of men under certain heads or distinctions of grace; and herein were they followed by many of the more sober schoolmen, and others of late without number. Frequent mention we find in them of grace, as "preparing, preventing, working, co-working, and confirming." Under these heads do they handle the whole work of our regeneration or conversion unto God. And although there may be some alteration in method and ways of expression, — which may be varied as they are found to be of advantage unto them that are to be instructed, — yet, for the substance of the doctrine, they taught the same which hath been preached amongst us since the Reformation, which some have ignorantly traduced as novel. And the whole of it is nobly and elegantly exemplified by Austin in his Confessions; wherein he gives us the experience of the truth he had taught in his own soul. And I might follow their footsteps herein, and perhaps should for some reasons have chosen so to have done, but that there have been so many differences raised about the explication and application of these terms and distinctions, and the declaration of the nature of the acts and effects of the spirit of grace intended in them, as that to carry the truth through the intricate perplexities which under these notions have been cast upon it, would be a longer work than I shall here engage into, and too much divert me from my principal intention. I shall, therefore, in general, refer the whole work of the Spirit of God with respect unto the regeneration of sinners unto two heads:— First, That which is preparatory for it; and, secondly, That which is effective of it. That which is preparatory for it is the conviction of sin; this is the work of the Holy Spirit, John xvi. 8. And this also may be distinctly referred unto three heads:— 1. A discovery of the true nature of sin by the ministry of the law, Rom. vii. 7. 2. An application of that discovery made in the mind or understanding unto the conscience of the sinner. 3. The excitation of affections suitable unto that discovery and application, Acts ii. 37. But these things, so far as they belong unto our present design, have been before insisted on. Our principal inquiry at present is after the work itself, or the nature and manner of the working of the Spirit of God in and on the souls of men in their regeneration; and this must be both negatively and positively declared:— First, The work of the Spirit of God in the regeneration of sinners, or the quickening of them who are dead in trespasses and sins, or in their first saving conversion to God, doth not consist in a moral suasion only. By suasion we intend such a persuasion as may or may not be effectual; so absolutely we call that only persuasion whereby a man is actually persuaded. Concerning this we must consider, —

1. What it is that is intended by that expression, and wherein its efficacy doth consist; and, 2. Prove that the whole work of the Spirit of God in the conversion of sinners doth not consist therein. And I shall handle this matter under this notion, as that which is known unto those who are conversant in these things from the writings of the ancient and modern divines; for it is to no purpose to endeavour the reducing of the extravagant, confused discourses of some present writers unto a certain and determinate stating of the things in difference among us. That which they seem to aim at and conclude may be

reduced unto these heads:— (1.) That God administers grace unto all in the declaration of the doctrine of the law and gospel. (2.) That the reception of this doctrine, the belief and practice of it, is enforced by promises and threatenings. (3.) That the things revealed, taught, and commanded, are not only good in themselves, but so suited unto the reason and interest of mankind as that the mind cannot but be disposed and inclined to receive and obey them, unless overpowered by prejudices and a course of sin. (4.) That the consideration of the promises and threatenings of the gospel is sufficient to remove these prejudices and reform that course. (5.) That upon a compliance with the doctrine of the gospel and obedience thereunto, men are made partakers of the Spirit, with other privileges of the New Testament, and have a right unto all the promises of the present and future life. Now, this being a perfect system of Pelagianism, condemned in the ancient church as absolutely exclusive of the grace of our Lord Jesus Christ, will be fully removed out of our way in our present discourse, though the loose, confused expressions of some be not considered in particular; for if the work of our regeneration do not consist in a moral suasion, — which, as we shall see, contains all that these men will allow to grace, — their whole fabric falls to the ground of its own accord:—

1. As to the nature of this moral suasion, two things may be considered:— (1.) The means, instrument, and matter of it, and this is the word of God; the word of God, or the Scripture, in the doctrinal instructions, precepts, promises, and threatenings of it. This is that, and this is that alone, whereby we are commanded, pressed, persuaded, to turn ourselves and live to God. And herein we comprise the whole, both the law and the gospel, with all the divine truths contained in them, as severally respecting the especial ends where-unto they are designed; for although they are distinctly and peculiarly suited to produce distinct effects on the minds of men, yet they all jointly tend unto the general end of guiding men how to live unto God, and to obtain the enjoyment of him. As for those documents and instructions which men have concerning the will of God, and the obedience which he requires of them from the light of nature, with the works of creation and providence, I shall not here take them into consideration: for either they are solitary, or without any superaddition of instructive light by revelation, and then I utterly deny them to be a sufficient outward means of the conversion of any one soul; or they may be considered as improved by the written word as dispensed unto men, and so they are comprised under it, and need not to be considered apart. We will, therefore, suppose that those unto whom the word is declared have antecedaneously thereunto all the help which the light of nature will afford.

(2.) The principal way of the application of this means to produce its effect on the souls of men is the ministry of the church. God hath appointed the ministry for the application of the word unto the minds and consciences of men for their instruction and conversion. And concerning this we may observe two things:— [1.] That the word of God, thus dispensed by the ministry of the church, is the only ordinary outward means which the Holy Ghost maketh use of in the regeneration of the adult unto whom it is preached. [2.] That it is every way sufficient in its own kind, — that is, as an outward means; for the revelation which is made of God and his mind thereby is sufficient to teach men all that is needful for them to believe and do that they may be converted unto God, and yield him the obedience that he requires. Hence two things do ensue:— 1st. That the use of those means unto men in the state of sin, if they are not complied withal, is sufficient, on the grounds before laid down, to leave them by whom they are rejected inexcusable: so Isa. v. 3–5; Prov. xxix. 1; 2 Chron. xxxvi. 14–16.

2d. That the effect of regeneration or conversion unto God is assigned unto the preaching of the word, because of its efficacy there-unto in its own kind and way, as the outward means thereof, 1 Cor. iv. 15; James i. 18; 1 Pet. i. 23.

2. We may consider what is the nature and wherein the efficacy of this moral work doth consist. To which purpose we may observe, — (1.) That in the use of this means for the conversion of men, there is, preparatory unto that wherein this moral persuasion doth consist, an instruction of the mind in the knowledge of the will of God and its duty towards him. The first regard unto men in the dispensation of the word unto them is their darkness and ignorance, whereby they are alienated from the life of God. This, therefore, is the first end of divine revelation, — namely, to make known the counsel and will of God unto us: see Matt. iv. 15, 16; Luke iv. 18, 19; Acts xxvi. 16–18, xx. 20, 21, 26, 27. By the preaching of the law and the gospel, men are instructed in the whole counsel of God and what he requires of them; and in their apprehension hereof doth the illumination of their minds consist, whereof we must treat distinctly afterward. Without a supposition of this illumination there is no use of the persuasive power of the word; for it consists in affecting the mind with its concernment in the things that it knows, or wherein it is instructed. Wherefore we suppose in this case that a man is taught by the word both the necessity of regeneration, and what is required of himself thereunto.

(2.) On this supposition, that a man is instructed in the knowledge of the will of God, as revealed in the law and the gospel, there is accompanying the word of God, in the dispensation of it, a powerful persuasive efficacy unto a compliance with it and observance of it. For instance, suppose a man to be convinced by the word of God of the nature of sin; of his own sinful condition, of his danger from thence with respect unto the sin of nature, on which account he is a child of wrath; and of his actual sin, which farther renders him obnoxious unto the curse of the law and the indignation of God; of his duty hereon to turn unto God, and the way whereby he may so do, — there are in the precepts, exhortations, expostulations, promises, and threatenings of the word, especially as dispensed in the ministry of the church, powerful motives to affect, and arguments to prevail with, the mind and will of such a man to endeavour his own regeneration or conversion unto God, rational and cogent above all that can be objected unto the contrary. On some it is acknowledged that these things have no effect; they are not moved by them, they care not for them, they do despise them, and live and die in rebellion against the light of them, "having their eyes blinded by the god of this world." But this is no argument that they are not powerful in themselves, although, indeed, it is that they are not so towards us of themselves, but only as the Holy Spirit is pleased to act them towards us. But in these motives, reasons, and arguments, whereby men are, in and from the word and the ministry of it, urged and pressed unto conversion to God, doth this moral persuasion whereof we speak consist. And the efficacy of it unto the end proposed ariseth from the things ensuing, which are all resolved into God himself:— [1.] From an evidence of the truth of the things from whence these motives and arguments were taken. The foundation of all the efficacy of the dispensation of the gospel lies in an evidence that the things proposed in it are not " cunningly-devised fables," 2 Pet. i. 16. Where this is not admitted, where it is not firmly assented unto, there can be no persuasive efficacy in it; but where there is, namely, a prevalent persuasion of the truth of the things proposed, there the mind is under a disposition unto the things whereunto it is persuaded. And hereon the whole efficacy of the word in and upon the souls of men is resolved into the truth and veracity of God; for the things contained in the Scripture are not proposed unto us merely as true, but as divine truths, as immediate revelations from God, which require not only a rational but a sacred religious respect unto them. They are things that the "mouth of the Lord hath spoken."

[2.] There is a proposal unto the wills and affections of men in the things so assented unto, on the one hand as good, amiable, and excellent, wherein the chiefest good, happiness, and utmost end of our natures are comprised, to be pursued and attained; and on the other of things evil and terrible, the utmost evil that our nature is obnoxious unto, to be avoided: for this is urged on them, that to comply with the will of God in the proposals of the gospel, to conform thereunto, to do what he requires, to turn from sin unto him, is good unto men, best for them, — assuredly attended with present satisfaction and future glory. And therein is also proposed the most noble object for our affections, even God himself, as a friend, as reconciled unto us in Christ; and that in a way suited unto his holiness, righteousness, wisdom, and goodness, which we have nothing to oppose unto nor to lay in the balance against. The way, also, of the reconciliation of sinners unto God by Jesus Christ is set out as that which hath such an impress of divine wisdom and goodness upon it, as that it can be refused by none but out of a direct enmity against God himself. Unto the enforcing of these things on the minds of men, the Scripture abounds with reasons, motives, and arguments; the rendering whereof effectual is the principal end of the ministry. On the other hand, it is declared and evidenced that sin is the great debasement of our natures, — the ruin of our souls, the only evil in the world, in its guilt and punishment; and that a continuance in a state of it, with a rejection of the invitation of the gospel unto conversion to God, is a thing foolish, unworthy of a rational creature, and that which will be everlastingly pernicious. Whereas, therefore, in the judgment of every rational creature, spiritual things are to be preferred before natural, eternal things before temporal, and these things are thus disposed of in infinite goodness, love, and wisdom, they must needs be apt to affect the wills and take the affections of men. And herein the efficacy of the word on the minds and consciences of men is resolved into the authority of God. These precepts, these promises, these threatenings are his, who hath right to give them and power to execute them. And with his authority, his glorious greatness and his infinite power come under consideration; so also doth his goodness and love in an especial manner, with many other things, even all the known properties of his holy nature; — all which concur in giving weight, power, and efficacy unto these motives and arguments.

(3.) Great power and efficacy is added hereunto from the management of these motives in the preaching of the word. Herein with some the rhetorical faculty of them by whom it is dispensed is of great consideration; for hereby are they able to prevail very much on the minds of men. Being acquainted with the inclinations and dispositions of all sorts of persons, the nature of their affections and prejudices, with the topics or kinds and heads of arguments meet to affect them and prevail with them, as also the ways of insinuating persuasive motives into their minds, they express the whole in words elegant, proper, expressive, and suited to allure, draw, and engage them unto the ways and duties proposed unto them.[30] Herein do some place the principal use and efficacy of the ministry in the dispensation of the word; with me it is of no consideration, for our apostle rejects it utterly from any place in his ministry: 1 Cor. ii. 4. "My speech and my preaching was not with enticing words of man's wisdom, but in demonstration of the Spirit and of power." Some of late have put in faint and weak exceptions unto the latter clause, as though not an evidence of the powerful presence of the Spirit of God in the dispensation of the gospel were intended therein, but the power of working miracles, contrary to the whole scope of the place and consent of the best expositors; but that, by the first clause, the persuasive art of human oratory is excluded from use and efficacy in the preaching of the gospel, none as yet hath had the impudence to deny. But let this also be esteemed to be as useful and efficacious in this work, as to the end of preaching in the conversion of the souls of men, as any can imagine, it shall be granted; only I shall take leave to resolve the efficacy of preaching into two other causes:— [1.] The institution of God. He hath appointed the preaching of the word to be the means, the only outward ordinary means, for the conversion of the souls of men, 1 Cor. i. 17–20; Mark xvi. 15, 16; Rom. i. 16. And the power or efficacy of any thing that is used unto an end in spiritual matters depends solely on its divine appointment unto that end.

[2.] The especial gifts that the Spirit of God doth furnish the preachers of the gospel withal, to enable them unto an effectual discharge of their work, Eph. iv. 11–13, whereof we shall treat afterward. All the power, therefore, that these things are accompanied withal is resolved into the sovereignty of God; for he hath chosen this way of preaching for this end, and he bestows these gifts on whom he pleaseth. From these things it is that the persuasive motives which the word abounds withal unto conversion, or turning to God from sin, have that peculiar efficacy on the minds of men which is proper unto them.

(4.) We do not therefore, in this case, suppose that the motives of the word are left unto a mere natural operation, with respect unto the ability of them by whom it is dispensed, but, moreover, that it is blessed of God, and accompanied with the power of the Holy Spirit, for the producing of its effect and end upon the souls of men. Only, the operation of the Holy Ghost on the minds and wills of men in and by these means is supposed to extend no farther but unto motives, arguments, reasons, and considerations, proposed unto the mind, so to influence the will and the affections. Hence his operation is herein moral, and so metaphorical, not real, proper, and physical.

Now, concerning this whole work I affirm these two things:—

1. That the Holy Spirit doth make use of it in the regeneration or conversion of all that are adult, and that either immediately in and by the preaching of it, or by some other application of light and truth unto the mind derived from the word; for by the reasons, motives, and persuasive arguments which the word affords are our minds affected, and our souls wrought upon in our conversion unto God, whence it becomes our reasonable obedience.

And there are none ordinarily converted, but they are able to give some account by what considerations they were prevailed on thereunto. But, —

2. We say that the whole work, or the whole of the work of the Holy Ghost in our conversion, doth not consist herein; but there is a real physical work, whereby he infuseth a gracious principle of spiritual life into all that are

effectually converted and really regenerated, and without which there is no deliverance from the state of sin and death which we have described; which, among others, may be proved by the ensuing arguments.

The principal arguments in this case will ensue in our proofs from the Scriptures that there is a real physical work of the Spirit on the souls of men in their regeneration. That all he doth consisteth not in this moral suasion, the ensuing reasons do sufficiently evince:— First, If the Holy Spirit work no otherwise on men, in their regeneration or conversion, but by proposing unto them and urging upon them reasons, arguments, and motives to that purpose,[31] then after his whole work, and notwithstanding it, the will of man remains absolutely indifferent whether it will admit of them or no, or whether it will convert itself unto God upon them or no; for the whole of this work consists in proposing objects unto the will, with respect whereunto it is left undetermined whether it will choose and close with them or no. And, indeed, this is that which some plead for: for they say that "in all men, at least all unto whom the gospel is preached, there is that grace present or with them that they are able to comply with the word if they please, and so believe, repent, or do any act of obedience unto God according to his will; and if they will, they can refuse to make use of this assistance, aid, power, or grace, and so continue in their sins." What this grace is, or whence men have this power and ability, by some is not declared. Neither is it much to be doubted but that many do imagine that it is purely natural; only they will allow it to be called grace, because it is from God who made us. Others acknowledge it to be the work or effect of grace internal, wherein part of the difference lay between the Pelagians and semi-Pelagians of old. But they all agree that it is absolutely in the power of the will of man to make use of it or not, — that is, of the whole effect on them, or product in them, of this grace communicated in the way described; for notwithstanding any thing wrought in us or upon us thereby, the will is still left various, flexible, and undetermined. It is true, that notwithstanding the grace thus administered, the will hath power to refuse it and to abide in sin; but that there is no more grace wrought in us but what may he so refused, or that the will can make use of that grace for conversion which it can refuse, is false.

For, — 1. This ascribes the whole glory of our regeneration and conversion unto ourselves, and not to the grace of God; for that act of our wills, on this supposition, whereby we convert unto God, is merely an act of our own, and not of the grace of God. This is evident; for if the act itself were of grace, then would it not be in the power of the will to hinder it. 2. This would leave it absolutely uncertain, notwithstanding the purpose of God and the purchase of Christ, whether ever any one in the world should be converted unto God or no; for when the whole work of grace is over, it is absolutely in the power of the will of man whether it shall be effectual or no, and so absolutely uncertain: which is contrary to the covenant, promise, and oath of God unto and with Jesus Christ. 3. It is contrary to express testimonies of Scripture innumerable, wherein actual conversion unto God is ascribed unto his grace, as the immediate effect thereof. This will farther appear afterward. "God worketh in us both to will and to do," Phil. ii. 13. The act, therefore, itself of willing in our conversion is of God's operation; and although we will ourselves, yet it is he who causeth us to will, by working in us to will and to do. And if the act of our will, in believing and obedience, in our conversion to God, be not the effect of his grace in us, he doth not "work in us both to will and to do of his good pleasure."

Secondly, This moral persuasion, however advanced or improved, and supposed to be effectual, yet confers no new real supernatural strength unto the soul; for whereas it worketh, yea, the Spirit or grace of God therein and thereby, by reasons, motives, arguments, and objective considerations, and no otherwise, it is able only to excite and draw out the strength which we have, delivering the mind and affections from prejudices and other moral impediments. Real aid, and internal spiritual strength, neither are nor can be conferred thereby.[32]

And he who will acknowledge that there is any such internal spiritual strength communicated unto us must also acknowledge that there is another work of the Spirit of God in us and upon us than can be effected by these persuasions. But thus it is in this case, as some suppose: "The mind of man is affected with much ignorance, and usually under the power of many prejudices, which, by the corrupt course of things in the world, possess it from its first actings in the state of infancy. The will and the affections likewise are vitiated with depraved habits, which by the same means are contracted. But when the gospel is proposed and preached unto them, the thinks contained in it, the duties it requires, the promises it gives, are so rational, or so suited unto the principles of our reason, and the subject-matter of them is so good, desirable, and beautiful, unto an intellectual appetite, that, being well conveyed unto the mind, they are able to discard all the prejudices and disadvantages of a corrupt course under which it hath suffered, and prevail with the soul to desist from sin, — that is, a course of sinning, — and to become a new man in all virtuous conversation." And that this is in the liberty and power of the will is "irrefragably proved" by that sophism of Biel[33] out of Scotus and Occam, which contains the substance of what they plead in this cause. Yea, "thus to do is so suitable unto the rational principles of a well-disposed mind, that to do otherwise is the greatest folly and madness in the world." "Especially will this work of conversion be unquestionably wrought if the application of these means of it be so disposed, in the providence of God, as that they may be seasonable with respect unto the frame and condition of the mind whereunto they are applied. And as sundry things are necessary to render the means of grace thus seasonable and congruous unto the present frame, temper, and disposition of the mind, so in such a congruity much of its efficacy doth consist. "And this," as it is said, "is the work of the Holy Ghost, and an effect of the grace of God; for if the Spirit of God did not by the word prevent, excite, stir up, and provoke the minds of men, did he not help and assist them, when endeavouring to turn to God, in the removal of prejudices and all sorts of moral impediments, men would continue and abide, as it were, dead in trespasses and sins, at least their endeavours after deliverance would be weak and fruitless."

This is all the grace, all the work of the Spirit of God, in our regeneration and conversion, which some will acknowledge, so far as I can learn from their writings and discourses.[34]

But that there is more required thereunto I have before declared; as also, it hath been manifested what is the true and proper use and efficacy of these means in this work. But to place the whole of it herein is that which Pelagius contended for of old; yea, he granted a greater use and efficacy of grace than I can find to be allowed in the present confused discourses of some on this subject.[35] Wherefore it is somewhat preposterous to endeavour an imposition of such rotten errors upon the minds of men, and that by crude assertions, without any pretence of proof, as is the way of many. And that the sole foundation of all their harangues, — namely, the suitableness of gospel principles and promises unto our wisdom and reason, antecedently unto any saving work of the Spirit on our minds, — is directly contradictory to the doctrine of our apostle, shall afterward be declared. But, it may be, it will be said that it is not so much what is Pelagian and what is not, as what is truth and what is not, that is to be inquired after; and it is granted that this is, and ought to he, our first and principal inquiry; but it is not unuseful to know in whose steps they tread who at this day oppose the doctrine of the effectual grace of Christ, and what judgment the ancient church made of their principles and opinions.

It is pretended yet farther, that "grace in the dispensation of the word doth work really and efficiently, especially by illumination, internal excitations of the mind and affections; and if thereon the will do put forth its act, and thereby determine itself in the choice of that which is good, in believing and repenting, then the grace thus administered concurs with it, helps and aids it in the perfecting of its act; so that the whole work is of grace." So pleaded the semi-Pelagians, and so do others continue to do. But all this while the way whereby grace, or the Spirit of God, worketh this illumination, excites the affections, and aids the will, is by moral persuasion only, no real strength being communicated or infused but what the will is at perfect liberty to make use of or to refuse at pleasure. Now this, in effect, is no less than to overthrow the whole grace of Jesus Christ, and to render it useless; for it ascribes unto man the honour of his conversion, his will being the principal cause of it. It makes a man to beget himself anew, or to be born again of himself — to make himself differ from others by that which he hath not in an especial manner received. It takes away the analogy that there is between the forming of the natural body of Christ in the womb, and the forming of his mystical body in regeneration. It makes the act of living unto God by faith and obedience to be a mere natural act, no fruit of the mediation or purchase of Christ; and allows the Spirit of God no more power or efficacy in or towards our regeneration than is in a minister who preacheth the word, or in an orator who eloquently and pathetically persuades to virtue and dehorts from vice. And all these consequences, it may be, will be granted by some amongst us, and allowed to be true; to that pass are things come in the world, through the confident pride and ignorance of men. But not only it may be, but plainly and directly, the whole gospel and grace of Christ are renounced where they are admitted.

Thirdly, This is not all that we pray for,[36] either for ourselves or others, when we beg effectual grace for them or ourselves. There was no argument that the ancients more pressed the Pelagians withal than that the grace which they acknowledged did not answer the prayers of the church, or what we are taught in the Scripture to pray for. We are to pray only for what God hath promised, and for the communication of it unto us in that way whereby he will work it and effect it. Now, he is at a great indifferency in this matter who only prays that God would persuade him or others to believe and to obey, to be converted or to convert himself. The church of God hath always prayed that God would work these things in us; and those who have a real concernment in them do pray continually that God would effectually work them in their hearts. They pray that he would convert them; that he would create a clean heart and renew a right spirit in them; that he would give them faith for Christ's sake, and increase it in them; and that in all these things he would work in them by the exceeding greatness of his power both to will and to do according to his good pleasure. And there is not a Pelagian in the world who ever once prayed for grace, or gracious assistance against sin and temptation, with a sense of his want of it, but that his prayers contradicted his profession. To think that by all these petitions, with others innumerable dictated unto us in the Scripture, and which a spiritual sense of our wants will engage into, we desire nothing but only that God would persuade, excite, and stir us up to put forth a power and ability of our own in the performance of what we desire, is contrary unto all Christian experience. Yea, for a man to lie praying with importunity, earnestness, and fervency, for that which is in his own power, and can never be effected but by his own power, is fond and ridiculous; and they do but mock God who pray unto him to do that for them which they can do for themselves, and which God cannot do for them but only when and as they do it themselves. Suppose a man to have a power in himself to believe and repent; suppose these to be such acts of his will as God doth not, indeed cannot, by his grace work in him, but only persuade him thereunto, and show him sufficient reason why he should so do, — to what purpose should this man, or with what congruity could he, pray that God would give him faith and repentance? This some of late, as it seems, wisely observing, do begin to scoff at and reproach the prayers of Christians; for whereas, in all their supplications for grace, they lay the foundation of them in an humble acknowledgment of their own vileness and impotency unto any thing that is spiritually good, yea, and a natural aversation from it, and a sense of the power and working of the remainder of indwelling sin in them, hereby exciting themselves unto that earnestness and importunity in their requests for grace which their condition makes necessary[37] (which hath been the constant practice of Christians since there was one in the world), this is by them derided and exposed to contempt. In the room, therefore, of such despised prayers, I shall supply them with an ancient form that is better suited unto their principles.[38] The preface unto it is, "Ille ad Deum digne elevat manus, ille orationem bonâ conscientiâ effundit qui potest dicere." The prayer followeth:—"Tu nosti Domine quam sanctæ et puræ et mundæ sint ab omni malitia, et iniquitate, et rapina quas ad te extendo manus: quemadmodum justa et munda labia et ab omni mendacio libera quibus offero tibi deprecationes, ut mihi miserearis." This prayer Pelagius taught a widow to make, as it was objected unto him in the Diospolitan Synod, that is at Lydda in Palestine, cap. vi.; only he taught her not to say that she had no deceit in her heart, as one among us doth wisely and humbly vaunt that he knoweth of none in his, so every way perfect is the man! Only to balance this of Pelagius, I shall give these men another prayer, but in the margin,[39] not declaring whose it is, lest they should censure him to the gallows. Whereas, therefore, it seems to be the doctrine of some that we have no grace from Christ but only that of the gospel teaching us our duty, and proposing a reward, I know not what they have to pray for, unless it be riches, wealth, and preferments, with those things that depend thereon.

Fourthly, This kind of the operation of grace, where it is solitary, — that is, where it is asserted exclusively to an internal physical work of the Holy Spirit, — is not suited to effect and produce the work of regeneration or conversion unto God in persons who are really in that state of nature which we have before described. The most effectual persuasions cannot prevail with such men to convert themselves, any more than arguments can prevail with a blind, man to see, or with a dead man to rise from the grave, or with a lame man to walk steadily. Wherefore, the whole description before given from the Scripture of the state of lapsed nature must be disproved and removed out of the way before this grace can be thought to be sufficient for the regeneration and conversion of men in that estate. But some proceed on other principles. "Men," they say, "have by nature certain notions and principles concerning God and the obedience due unto him, which are demonstrable by the light of reason; and certain abilities of mind to make use of them unto their proper end." But they grant, at least some of them do,[40] that "however these principles may be improved and acted by those abilities, yet they are not sufficient, or will not eventually be effectual, to bring men unto the life of God, or to enable them so to believe in him, love him, and obey him, as that they may come at length unto the enjoyment of him; at least, they will not do this safely and easily, but through much danger and confusion: wherefore God, out of his goodness and love to mankind, hath made a farther revelation of himself by Jesus Christ in the gospel, with the especial way whereby his anger against sin is averted, and peace made for sinners; which men had before only a confused apprehension and hope about. Now, the things received, proposed, and prescribed in the gospel, are so good, so rational, so every way suited unto the principles of our being, the nature of our intellectual constitutions, or the reason of men, and those fortified with such rational and powerful motives, in the promises and threatenings of it, representing unto us on the one hand the chiefest good which our nature is capable of, and on the other the highest evil to be avoided that we are obnoxious unto, that they can be refused or rejected by none but out of a brutish love of sin, or the efficacy of depraved habits, contracted by a vicious course of living. And herein consists the grace of God towards men, especially as the Holy Ghost is pleased to make use of these things in the dispensation of the gospel by the ministry of the church; for when the reason of men is by these means excited so far as to cast off prejudices, and enabled thereby to make a right judgment of what is proposed unto it, it prevails with them to convert to God, to change their lives, and yield obedience according to the rule of the gospel, that they may be saved." And no doubt this were a notable system of Christian doctrine especially as it is by some rhetorically blended or theatrically represented in feigned stories and apologues, were it not defective in one or two things: for, first, it is exclusive of a supposition of the fall of man, at least as unto the depravation of our nature which ensued thereon, and, secondly, of all real effective grace dispensed by Jesus Christ;[41] which render it a fantastic dream, alien from the design and doctrine of the gospel. But it is a fond thing to discourse with men about either regeneration or conversion unto God by whom these things are denied.

Such a work of the Holy Spirit we must, therefore, inquire after as whereby the mind is effectually renewed, the heart changed, the affections sanctified, all actually and effectually, or no deliverance will be wrought, obtained, or ensue, out of the estate described; for notwithstanding the utmost improvement of our minds and reasons that can be imagined, and the most eminent proposal of the truths of the gospel, accompanied with the most powerful enforcements of duty and obedience that the nature of the things themselves will afford, yet the mind of man in the state of nature, without a supernatural elevation by grace, is not able so to apprehend them as that its apprehension should he spiritual, saving, or proper unto the things apprehended. And notwithstanding the perception which the mind may attain unto in the truth of gospel proposals, and the conviction it may have of the necessity of obedience, yet is not the will able to apply itself unto any spiritual act thereof, without an ability wrought immediately in it by the power of the Spirit of God; or rather, unless the Spirit of God by his grace do effect the act of willing in it. Wherefore, not to multiply arguments, we conclude that the most effectual use of outward means alone is not all the grace that is necessary unto, nor all that is actually put forth in, the regeneration of the souls of men.

Having thus evidenced wherein the work of the Holy Spirit in the regeneration of the souls of men doth not consist, — namely, in a supposed congruous persuasion of their minds, where it is alone, —

Secondly, I shall proceed to show wherein it doth consist, and what is the true nature of it. And to this purpose I say, —

1. Whatever efficacy that moral operation which accompanies, or is the effect of, the preaching of the word, as blessed and used by the Holy Spirit, is of, or may be supposed to be of, or is possible that it should be of, in and towards them that are unregenerate, we do willingly ascribe unto it. We grant that in the work of regeneration, the Holy Spirit, towards those that are adult, doth make use of the word, both the law and the gospel, and the ministry of the church in the dispensation of it, as the ordinary means thereof; yea, this is ordinarily the whole external means that is made use of in this work, and an efficacy proper unto it is accompanied withal. Whereas, therefore, some contend that there is no more needful to the conversion of sinners but the preaching of the word unto them who are congruously disposed to receive it, and that the whole of the grace of God consists in the effectual application of it unto the minds and affections of men, whereby they are enabled to comply with it, and turn unto God by faith and repentance, they do not ascribe a greater power unto the word than we do, by whom this administration of it is denied to be the total cause of conversion; for we assign the same power to the word as they do, and more also, only we affirm that there is an effect to be wrought in this work which all this power, if alone, is insufficient for. But in its own kind it is sufficient and effectual, so far as that the effect of regeneration or conversion unto God is ascribed thereunto. This we have declared before.

2. There is not only a moral but a physical immediate operation of the Spirit, by his power and grace, or his powerful grace, upon the minds or souls of men in their regeneration.[42] This is that which we must cleave to, or all the glory of God's grace is lost, and the grace administered by Christ neglected. So is it asserted, Eph. i. 18–20, "That ye may know what is the exceeding greatness of his power to us-ward who believe, according to the working of his mighty power, which he wrought in Christ when he raised him from the dead." The power here mentioned hath an "exceeding greatness" ascribed unto it, with respect unto the effect produced by it. The power of God in itself is, as unto all acts, equally infinite, — he is omnipotent; but some effects are greater than others, and carry in them more than ordinary impressions of it. Such is that here intended, whereby God makes men to be believers, and preserves them when they are so. And unto this power of God there is an actual operation or efficiency ascribed, — the "working of his mighty power." And the nature of this operation or efficiency is declared to be of the same kind with that which

was exerted in the raising of Christ from the dead; and this was by a real physical efficiency of divine power. This, therefore, is here testified, that the work of God towards believers, either to make them so or preserve them such, — for all is one as unto our present purpose, — consists in the acting of his divine power by a real internal efficiency. So God is said to "fulfil in us all the good pleasure of his goodness, and the work of faith with power," 2 Thess. i. 11; 2 Pet. i. 3. And hence the work of grace in conversion is constantly expressed by words denoting a real internal efficiency; such as creating, quickening, forming, giving a new heart, whereof afterward. Wherever this word is spoken with respect unto an active efficiency, it is ascribed unto God; he creates us anew, he quickens us, he begets us of his own will. But where it is spoken with respect unto us, there it is passively expressed; we are created in Christ Jesus, we are new creatures, we are born again, and the like; which one observation is sufficient to evert the whole hypothesis of Arminian grace. Unless a work wrought by power, and that real and immediate, be intended herein, such a work may neither be supposed possible, nor can be expressed. Wherefore, it is plain in the Scripture that the Spirit of God works internally, immediately, efficiently, in and upon the minds of men in their regeneration. The new birth is the effect of an act of his power and grace; or, no man is born again but it is by the inward efficiency of the Spirit.

3. This internal efficiency of the Holy Spirit on the minds of men, as to the event, is infallible,[43] victorious, irresistible, or always efficacious. But in this assertion we suppose that the measure of the efficacy of grace and the end to be attained are fixed by the will of God. As to that end whereunto of God it is designed, it is always prevalent or effectual, and cannot be resisted, or it will effectually work what God designs it to work: for wherein he "will work, none shall let him;" and "who hath resisted his will?" There are many motions of grace, even in the hearts of believers, which are thus far resisted, as that they attain not that effect which in their own nature they have a tendency unto. Were it otherwise, all believers would be perfect. But it is manifest in experience that we do not always answer the inclinations of grace, at least as unto the degree which it moves towards. But yet even such motions also, if they are of and from saving grace, are effectual so far, and for all those ends which they are designed unto in the purpose of God; for his will shall not be frustrated in any instance. And where any work of grace is not effectual, God never intended it should be so, nor did put forth that power of grace which was necessary to make it so. Wherefore, in or towards whomsoever the Holy Spirit puts forth his power, or acts his grace for their regeneration, he removes all obstacles, overcomes all oppositions, and infallibly produceth the effect intended.[44] This proposition being of great importance to the glory of God's grace, and most signally opposed by the patrons of corrupted nature and man's free-will in the state thereof, must be both explained and confirmed. We say, therefore, —

(1.) The power which the Holy Ghost puts forth in our regeneration is such, in its acting or exercise, as our minds, wills, and affections, are suited to be wrought upon, and to be affected by it, according to their natures and natural operations: "Turn thou me, and I shall be turned; draw me, and I shall run after thee." He doth not act in them any otherwise than they themselves are meet to be moved and move, to be acted and act, according to their own nature, power, and ability. He draws us with "the cords of a man." And the work itself is expressed by persuading, — "God shall persuade Japheth;" and alluring, — "I will allure her into the wilderness, and speak comfortably unto her:" for as it is certainly effectual, so it carries no more repugnancy unto our faculties than a prevalent persuasion doth. So that, —

(2.) He doth not, in our regeneration, possess the mind with any enthusiastical impressions, nor act absolutely upon us as he did in extraordinary prophetical inspirations of old, where the minds and organs of the bodies of men were merely passive instruments, moved by him above their own natural capacity and activity, not only as to the principle of working, but as to the manner of operation; but he works on the minds of men in and by their own natural actings, through an immediate influence and impression of his power: "Create in me a clean heart, O God." He "worketh both to will and to do."

(3.) He therefore offers no violence or compulsion unto the will.[45] This that faculty is not naturally capable to give admission unto. If it be compelled, it is destroyed. And the mention that is made in the Scripture of compelling ("Compel them to come in") respects the certainty of the event, not the manner of the operation on them. But whereas the will, in the depraved condition of fallen nature, is not only habitually filled and possessed with an aversion from that which is good spiritually ("Alienated from the life of God"), but also continually acts an opposition unto it, as being under the power of the "carnal mind," which is "enmity against God; and whereas this grace of the Spirit in conversion doth prevail against all this opposition, and is effectual and victorious over it, — it will be inquired how this can any otherwise be done but by a kind of violence and compulsion, seeing we have evinced already that moral persuasion and objective allurement is not sufficient thereunto? Ans. It is acknowledged that in the work of conversion unto God, though not in the very act of it, there is a reaction between grace and the will, their acts being contrary; and that grace is therein victorious, and yet no violence or compulsion is offered unto the will; for, —

[1.] The opposition is not ad idem. The enmity and opposition that is acted by the will against grace is against it as objectively proposed unto it. So do men "resist the Holy Ghost," — that is, in the external dispensation of grace by the word. And if that be alone, they may always resist it; the enmity that is in them will prevail against it: "Ye do always resist the Holy Ghost." The will, therefore, is not forced by any power put forth in grace, in that way wherein it is capable of making opposition unto it, but the prevalency of grace is of it as it is internal, working really and physically; which is not the object of the will's opposition, for it is not proposed unto it as that which it may accept or refuse, but worketh effectually in it.

[2.] The will, in the first act of conversion (as even sundry of the schoolmen acknowledge), acts not but as it is acted, moves not but as it is moved; and therefore is passive therein, in the sense immediately to be explained. And if this be not so, it cannot be avoided but that the act of our turning unto God is a mere natural act, and not spiritual or gracious; for it is an act of the will, not enabled thereunto antecedently by grace. Wherefore it must be granted, and it shall he proved, that, in order of nature, the acting of grace in the will in our conversion is antecedent unto its own acting; though in the same instant of time wherein the will is moved it moves, and when it is acted it acts itself, and preserves its own liberty in its exercise. There is, therefore, herein an inward almighty secret act of the power of the Holy Ghost, producing or effecting in us the will of conversion unto God, so acting our wills as that they also act themselves, and that freely. So Austin, cont. Duas Epistol. Pelag. lib. i. cap. 19: "Trahitur [homo] miris modis ut velit, ab illo qui novit intus in ipsis cordibus hominum operari; non ut homines, quod fieri non potest, nolentes credant, sed ut volentes ex nolentibus fiant." The Holy Spirit, who in his power and operation is more intimate, as it were, unto the principles of our souls than they are to themselves, doth, with the preservation and in the exercise of the liberty of our wills, effectually work our regeneration and conversion unto God.

This is the substance of what we plead for in this cause, and which declares the nature of this work of regeneration, as it is an inward spiritual work. I shall, therefore, confirm the truth proposed with evident testimonies of Scripture, and reasons contained in them or educed from them.

First, The work of conversion itself, and in especial the act of believing,[46] or faith itself, is expressly said to be of God, to be wrought in us by him, to be given unto us from him. The Scripture says not that God gives us ability or power to believe only, — namely, such a power as we may make use of if we will, or do otherwise; but faith, repentance, and conversion themselves are said to be the work and effect of God. Indeed, there is nothing mentioned in the Scriptures concerning the communicating of power, remote or next unto the mind of man, to enable him to believe antecedently unto actual believing. A "remote power," if it may be so called, in the capacities of the faculties of the soul, the reason of the mind, and liberty of the will, we have given an account concerning; but for that which some call a "next power,"[47] or an ability to believe in order of nature antecedent unto believing itself, wrought in us by the grace of God, the Scripture is silent. The apostle Paul saith of himself, Πάντα ἰσχύω ἐν τῷ ἐνδυναμοῦτί με Χριστῷ, Phil. iv. 13, — "I can do all things," or prevail in all things, "through Christ who enableth me;" where a power or ability seems to be spoken of antecedent unto acting: but this is not a power for the, first act of faith, but a power in them that believe. Such a power I acknowledge, which is acted in the co-operation of the Spirit and grace of Christ with the grace which believers have received, unto the performance of all acts of holy obedience; whereof I must treat elsewhere. Believers have a stock of habitual grace; which may be called indwelling grace in the same sense wherein original corruption is called indwelling sin. And this grace, as it is necessary unto every act of spiritual obedience, so of itself, without the renewed co-working of the Spirit of Christ, it is not able or sufficient to produce any spiritual act. This working of Christ upon and with the grace we have received is called enabling of us; but with persons unregenerate, and as to the first act of faith, it is not so.

But it will be objected, "That every thing which is actually accomplished was in potentia before; there must, therefore, be in us a power to believe before we do so actually." Ans. The act of God working faith in us is a creating act: "We are his workmanship, created in Christ Jesus," Eph. ii. 10; and he that is in Christ Jesus "is a new creature," 2 Cor. v. 17. Now, the effects of creating acts are not in potentia anywhere but in the active power of God; so was the world itself before its actual existence. This is termed potentia logica, which is no more but a negation of any contradiction to existence; not potentia physica, which includes a disposition unto actual existence. Notwithstanding, therefore, all these preparatory works of the Spirit of God which we allow in this matter, there is not by them wrought in the minds and wills of men such a next power, as they call it, as should enable them to believe without farther actual grace working faith itself. Wherefore, with respect to believing, the first act of God is to work in us "to will:" Phil. ii. 13, "He worketh in us to will." Now, to will to believe is to believe. This God works in us by that grace which Austin and the schoolmen call gratia operans, because it worketh in us without us, the will being merely moved and passive therein. That there is a power or faculty of believing given unto all men unto whom the gospel is preached, or who are called by the outward dispensation of it, some do pretend; and that "because those unto whom the word is so preached, if they do not actually believe, shall perish eternally, as is positively declared in the gospel, Mark xvi. 16; but this they could not justly do if they had not received a power or faculty of believing."

Ans. 1. Those who believe not upon the proposal of Christ in the gospel are left without remedy in the guilt of those other sins, for which they must perish eternally. "If ye believe not," saith Christ, "that I am he, ye shall die in your sins," John viii. 24.

2. The impotency that is in men, as to the act of believing, is contracted by their own fault, both as it ariseth from the original depravation of nature, and as it is increased by corrupt prejudices and contracted habits of sin: wherefore, they justly perished of whom yet it is said that "they could not believe," John xii. 39.

3. There is none by whom the gospel is refused, but they put forth an act of the will in its rejection, which all men are free unto and able for: "I would have gathered you, but ye would not," Matt. xxiii. 37. "Ye will not come to me, that ye may have life," [John v. 40.]

But the Scripture positively affirms of some to whom the gospel was preached that "they could not believe," John xii. 39; and of all natural men, that " they cannot receive the things of God," 1 Cor. ii. 14. Neither is it "given" unto all to "know the mysteries of the kingdom of heaven," but to some only, Matt. xi. 25, xiii. 11; and those to whom it is not so given have not the power intended. Besides, faith is not of all, or "all have not faith," 2 Thess. iii. 2, but it is peculiar to the "elect of God," Tit. i. 1; Acts xiii. 48; and these elect are but some of those that are called, Matt. xx. 16.

Yet farther to clear this, it may be observed, that this first act of willing may be considered two ways:— 1. As it is wrought in the will subjectively, and so it is formally only in that faculty; and in this sense the will is merely passive, and only the subjeet moved or acted. And in this respect the act of God's grace in the will is an act of the will. But, 2. It may be considered as it is efficiently also in the will, as, being acted, it acts itself. So it is from the will as its principle, and is a vital act thereof, which gives it the nature of obedience. Thus the will in its own nature is mobilis, fit and meet to be wrought upon by the grace of the Spirit to faith and obedience; with respect unto the creating act of grace working faith in us, it is mota, moved and acted thereby; and in respect of its own elicit act, as it so acted and moved, it is movens, the next efficient cause thereof.

These things being premised for the clearing of the nature of the operation of the Spirit in the first communication of grace unto us, and the will's compliance therewithal, we return unto our arguments or testimonies given unto the actual collation of faith[48] upon us by the Spirit and grace of God, which must needs be effectual and irresistible; for the contrary implies a contradiction, — namely, that God should "work what is not wrought:" — Phil.

i. 29, "To you it is given in the behalf of Christ, not only to believe on him, but also to suffer for his sake," To "believe on Christ" expresseth saving faith itself. This is "given" unto us. And how is it given us? Even by the power of God "working in us both to will and to do of his good pleasure," chap. ii. 13. Our faith is our coming to Christ. "And no man," saith he, "can come unto me, except it be given unto him of my Father," John vi. 65. All power in ourselves for this end is utterly taken away: "No man can come unto me."[49] However we may suppose men to be prepared or disposed, whatever arguments may be proposed unto them, and in what season soever, to render things congruous and agreeable unto their inclinations, yet no man of himself can believe, can come to Christ, unless faith itself be "given unto him," — that is, be wrought in him by the grace of the Father, Phil. i. 29. So it is again asserted, and that both negatively and positively, Eph. ii. 8, "By grace are ye saved through faith; and that not of yourselves: it is the gift of God." Our own ability, be it what it will, however assisted and excited, and God's gift, are contradistinguished. If it be "of ourselves," it is not "the gift of God;" if it be "the gift of God," it is not "of ourselves." And the manner how God bestows this gift upon us is declared, verse 10, "We are his workmanship, created in Christ Jesus unto good works." Good works, or gospel obedience, are the things designed. These must proceed from faith, or they are not acceptable with God, Heb. xi. 6. And the way whereby this is wrought in us, or a principle of obedience, is by a creating act of God: "We are his workmanship, created in Christ Jesus." In like manner God is said to "give us repentance," 2 Tim. ii. 25; Acts xi. 18. This is the whole of what we plead: God in our conversion, by the exceeding greatness of his power, as he wrought in Christ when he raised him from the dead, actually worketh faith and repentance in us, gives them unto us, bestows them on us; so that they are mere effects of his grace in us. And his working in us infallibly produceth the effect intended, because it is actual faith that he works, and not only a power to believe, which we may either put forth and make use of or suffer to be fruitless, according to the pleasure of our own wills.

Secondly, As God giveth and worketh in us faith and repentance, so the way whereby he doth it, or the manner how he is said to effect them in us, makes it evident that he doth it by a power infallibly efficacious, and which the will of man doth never resist; for this way is such as that he thereby takes away all repugnancy, all resistance, all opposition, every thing that lieth in the way of the effect intended: Deut. xxx. 6, "The Lord thy God will circumcise thine heart, and the heart of thy seed, to love the Lord thy God with all thine heart, and with all thy soul, that thou mayest live." A denial of the work here intended is expressed chap. xxix. 4, "The Lord hath not given you an heart to perceive, and eyes to see, and ears to hear, unto this day." What it is to have the heart circumcised the apostle declares, Col. ii. 11. It is the "putting off the body of the sins of the flesh by the circumcision of Christ," — that is, by our conversion to God. It is the giving "an heart to perceive, and eyes to see, and ears to hear," — that is, spiritual light and obedience, — by the removal of all obstacles and hinderances. This is the immediate work of the Spirit of God himself. No man ever circumcised his own heart. No man can say he began to do it by the power of his own will, and then God only helped him by his grace. As the act of outward circumcision on the body of a child was the act of another, and not of the child, who was only passive therein, but the effect was in the body of the child only, so is it in this spiritual circumcision, — it is the act of God, whereof our hearts are the subject. And whereas it is the blindness, obstinacy, and stubbornness in sin that is in us by nature, with the prejudices which possess our minds and affections, which hinder us from conversion unto God, by this circumcision they are taken away; for by it the "body of the sins of the flesh is put off." And how should the heart resist the work of grace, when that whereby it should resist is effectually taken away?

Ezek. xxxvi. 26, 27, "A new heart also will I give you, and a new spirit will I put within you: and I will take away the stony heart out of your flesh, and I will give you a heart of flesh. And I will put my Spirit within you, and cause you to walk in my statutes, and ye shall keep my judgments, and do them." To which may be added, Jer. xxiv. 7, "I will give them a heart to know me, that I am the Lord: and they shall be my people, and I will be their God: so they shall return unto me with their whole heart." As also, Isa. xliv. 3–5, "I will pour water upon him that is thirsty, and floods upon the dry ground: I will pour my Spirit upon thy seed, and my blessing upon thine offspring: and they shall spring up as among the grass, as willows by the water-courses. One shall say, I am the Lord's," etc. So Jer. xxxi. 33, "I will put my law in their inward parts, and write it in their hearts." I shall first inquire two things about these concurrent testimonies:—

1. Is it lawful for us, is it our duty, to pray that God would do and effect what he hath promised to do, and that both for ourselves and others? — [We may pray] for ourselves, that the work of our conversion may be renewed, carried on, and consummated in the way and by the means whereby it was begun, that so "he which hath begun the good work in us may perfect it until the day of Jesus Christ," Phil. i. 6; for those who are converted and regenerated, and are persuaded on good and infallible grounds that so they are, may yet pray for those things which God promiseth to work in their first conversion. And this is because the same work is to be preserved and carried on in them by the same means, the same power, the same grace, wherewith it was begun. And the reason is, though this work, as it is merely the work of conversion, is immediately perfected and completed as to the being of it; yet as it is the beginning of a work of sanctification, it is continually to be renewed and gone over again, because of the remainder of sin in us and the imperfection of our grace. [And we may pray] for others, that it may be both begun and finished in them. And do we not in such prayers desire that God would really, powerfully, effectually, by the internal efficiency of his Spirit, take away all hinderances, oppositions, and repugnancy in our minds and wills, and actually collate upon us, give unto us, and work in us, a new principle of obedience, that we may assuredly love, fear, and trust in God always? or do we only desire that God would so help us as to leave us absolutely undetermined whether we will make use of his help or no? Did ever any pious soul couch such an intention in his supplications? He knows not how to pray who prays not that God would, by his own immediate power, work those things in him which he thus prayeth for. And unto this prayer, also, grace effectual is antecedently required.[50] Wherefore, I inquire, —

2. Whether God doth really effect and work in any the things which he here promiseth that he will work and effect? If he do not, where is his truth and faithfulness? It is said that "he doth so, and will so do, provided that men do not refuse his tender of grace nor resist his operations, but comply with them." But this yields no relief, —

For, (1.) What is it not to refuse the grace of conversion, but to comply with it? Is it not to believe, to obey, — to convert ourselves? So, then, God promiseth to convert us, on condition that we convert ourselves; to work faith in us, on condition that we do believe; and a new heart, on condition that we make our hearts new ourselves! To this are all the adversaries of the grace of God brought by those conditions which they feign of its efficacy to preserve the sovereignty of free-will in our conversion, — that is, unto plain and open contradictions, which have been charged sufficiently upon them by others, and from which they could never extricate themselves. (2.) Where God promiseth[51] thus to work, as these testimonies do witness, and doth not effectually do so, it must be either because he cannot or because he will not. If it be said that he doth it not because he will not, then this is that which is ascribed unto God, — that he promiseth indeed to take away our stony heart, and to give us a new heart with his law written in it, but he will not do so; which is to overthrow his faithfulness, and to make him a liar. If they say it is because he cannot, seeing that men oppose and resist the grace whereby he would work this effect, then where is the wisdom of promising to work that in us which he knew he could not effect without our compliance, and which he knew that we would not comply withal? But it will be said that God promiseth to work and effect these things, but in such a way as he hath appointed, — that is, by giving such supplies of grace as may enable us thereunto, — which if we refuse to make use of, the fault is merely our own. Ans. It is the things themselves that are promised, and not such a communication of means to effect them as may produce them or may not, as the consideration of the place will manifest; whereof observe, —

[1.] The subject spoken of in these promises is the heart. And the heart in the Scripture is taken for the whole rational soul, not absolutely, but as all the faculties of the soul are one common principle of all our moral operations. Hence it hath such properties assigned unto it as are peculiar to the mind or understanding, as to see, perceive, to be wise, and to understand; and, on the contrary, to be blind and foolish; and sometimes such as belong properly to the will and affections, as to obey, to love, to fear, to trust in God. Wherefore, the principle of all our spiritual and moral operations is intended hereby.

[2.] There is a description of this heart, as it is in us antecedent unto the effectual working of the grace of God in us: it is said to be stony, — "The heart of stone." It is not absolutely that it is said so to be, but with respect unto some certain end. This end is declared to be our walking in the ways of God, or our fearing of him. Wherefore, our hearts by nature, as unto living to God or his fear, are a stone, or stony; and who hath not experience hereof from the remainders of it still abiding in them? And two things are included in this expression:— 1st. An ineptitude unto any actings towards that end. Whatever else the heart can do of itself, in things natural or civil, in outward things, as to the end of living unto God it can of itself, without his grace, do no more than a stone can do of itself unto any end whereunto it may be applied. 2dly. An obstinate, stubborn opposition unto all things conducing unto that end. Its hardness or obstinacy, in opposition to the pliableness of a heart of flesh, is principally intended in this expression. And in this stubbornness of the heart consists all that repugnancy to the grace of God which is in us by nature, and hence all that resistance doth arise, which some say is always sufficient to render any operation of the Spirit of God by his grace fruitless.

[3.] This heart, — that is, this impotency and enmity which is in our natures unto conversion and spiritual obedience, — God says he will take away; that is, he will do so in them who are to be converted according to the purpose of his will, and whom he will turn unto himself.[52] He doth not say that he will endeavour to take it away, nor that he will use such or such means for the taking of it away, but absolutely that he will take it away. He doth not say that he will persuade men to remove it or do it away, that he will aid and help them in their so doing, and that so far as that it shall wholly be their own fault if it be not done, — which no doubt it is where it is not removed; but positively that he himself will take it away. Wherefore, the act of taking it away is the act of God by his grace, and not the act of our wills but as they are acted thereby; and that such an act as whose effect is necessary. It is impossible that God should take away the stony heart, and yet the stony heart not be taken away. What, therefore, God promiseth herein, in the removal of our natural corruption, is as unto the event infallible, and as to the manner of operation irresistible.

[4.] As what God taketh from us in the cure of our original disease, so what he bestoweth on us or works in us is here also expressed; and this is, a new heart and a new spirit: "I will give you a new heart." And withal it is declared what benefit we do receive thereby: for those who have this new heart bestowed on them or wrought in them, they do actually, by virtue thereof, "fear the Lord and walk in his ways;" for so it is affirmed in the testimonies produced: and no more is required thereunto, as nothing less will effect it. There must, therefore, be in this new heart thus given us a principle of all holy obedience unto God: the creating of which principle in us is our conversion to him; for God doth convert us, and we are converted. And how is this new heart communicated unto us? "I will," saith God, "give them a new heart." "That is, it may be, he will do what is to be done on his part that they may have it; but we may refuse his assistance, and go without it." No; saith he, "I will put a new spirit within them;" which expression is capable of no such limitation or condition. And to make it more plain yet, he affirms that he "will write his law in our hearts." It is confessed that this is spoken with respect unto his writing of the law of old in the tables of stone. As, then, he wrote the letter of the law in the tables of stone, so that thereon and thereby they were actually engraven therein; so by writing the law, that is, the matter and substance of it, in our hearts, it is as really fixed therein as the letter of it was of old in the tables of stone. And this can be no otherwise but in a principle of obedience and love unto it, which is actually wrought of God in us. And the aids or assistances which some men grant that are left unto the power of our own wills to use or not to use, have no analogy with the writing of the law in tables of stone. And the end of the work of God described is not a power to obey, which may be exerted or not; but it is actual obedience in conversion, and all the fruits of it. And if God do not in these promises declare a real efficiency of internal grace, taking away all repugnancy of nature unto conversion, curing its depravation actually and effectually, and communicating infallibly a principle of scriptural obedience, I know not in what words such a work may be expressed. And whatever is excepted as to the suspending of the efficacy of this work upon conditions in ourselves, it falls immediately into gross and sensible contradictions. An especial instance of this work we have, Acts xvi. 14.

A third argument is taken from the state and condition of men by nature, before described; for it is such as that no man can be delivered from it, but by that powerful, internal, effectual grace which we plead for, such as wherein the mind and will of man can act nothing in or towards conversion to God but as they are acted by grace. The reason why some despise, some oppose, some deride the work of the Spirit of God in our regeneration or conversion, or fancy it to be only an outward ceremony, or a moral change of life and conversation, is, their ignorançe of the corrupted and depraved estate of the souls of men, in their minds, wills, and affections, by nature; for if it be such as we have described, — that is, such as in the Scripture it is represented to be, — they cannot be so brutish as once to imagine that it may be cured, or that men may be delivered from it, without any other aid but that of those rational considerations which some would have to be the only means of our conversion to God. We shall, therefore, inquire what that grace is, and what it must be, whereby we are delivered from it:—

1. It is called a vivification or quickening. We are by nature "dead in trespasses and sins," as hath been proved, and the nature of that death at large explained. In our deliverance from thence, we are said to be "quickened," Eph. ii. 5. Though dead, we "hear the voice of the Son of God, and live," John v. 25; being made "alive unto God through Jesus Christ," Rom. vi. 11. Now, no such work can be wrought in us but by an effectual communication of a principle of spiritual life; and nothing else will deliver us. Some think to evade the power of this argument by saying that "all these expressions are metaphorical, and arguings from them are but fulsome metaphors:" and it is well if the whole gospel be not a metaphor unto them. But if there be not an impotency in us by nature unto all acts of spiritual life, like that which is in a dead man unto the acts of life natural; if there be not an alike power of God required unto our deliverance from that condition, and the working in us a principle of spiritual obedience, as is required unto the raising of him that is dead, — they may as well say that the Scripture speaks not truly as that it speaks metaphorically. And that it is almighty power, the "exceeding greatness of God's, power," that is put forth and exercised herein; we have proved from Eph. i. 19, 20; Col. ii. 12, 13; 2 Thess. i. 11; 2 Pet. i. 3. And what do these men intend by this quickening, this raising us from the dead by the power of God? A persuasion of our minds by rational motives taken from the word, and the things contained in it! But was there ever heard such a monstrous expression, if there be nothing else in it? What could the holy writers intend by calling such a work as this by a "quickening of them who were dead in trespasses and sins through the mighty power of God," unless it were, by a noise of insignificant words, to draw us off from a right understanding of what is intended? And it is well if some are not of that mind.

2. The work itself wrought is our regeneration. I have proved before that this consists in a new, spiritual, supernatural, vital principle or habit of grace, infused into the soul, the mind, will, and affections, by the power of the Holy Spirit, disposing and enabling them in whom it is unto spiritual, supernatural, vital acts of faith and obedience. Some men seem to be inclined to deny all habits of grace. And on such a supposition, a man is no longer a believer than he is in the actual exercise of faith; for there is nothing in him from whence he should be so denominated. But this would plainly overthrow the covenant of God, and all the grace of it. Others expressly deny all gracious, supernatural,

infused habits, though they may grant such as are or may be acquired by the frequent acts of those graces or virtues whereof they are the habits. But the Scripture giveth us another description of this work of regeneration, for it consists in the renovation of the image of God in us: Eph. iv. 23, 24, "Be renewed in the spirit of your mind, and put on the new man, which after God is created in righteousness and true holiness." That Adam in innocency had a supernatural ability of living unto God habitually residing in him is generally acknowledged; and although it were easy for us to prove that whereas he was made for a super-natural end, — namely, to live to God, and to come to the enjoyment of him, — it was utterly impossible that he should answer it or comply with it by the mere strength of his natural faculties, had they not been endued with a supernatural ability, which, with respect unto that end, was created with them and in them, yet we will not contend about terms. Let it be granted that he was created in the image of God, and that he had an ability to fulfil all God's commands, and that in himself, and no more shall be desired. This was lost by the fall. When this is by any denied, it shall be proved. In our regeneration, there is a renovation of this image of God in us: "Renewed in the spirit of your mind." And it is renewed in us by a creating act of almighty power: "Which after God," or according to his likeness, "is created in righteousness and true holiness." There is, therefore, in it an implantation of a new principle of spiritual life, of a life unto God in repentance, faith, and obedience, or universal holiness, according to gospel truth, or the truth which came by Jesus Christ, John i. 17. And the effect of this work is called "spirit:" John iii. 6, "That which is born of the Spirit is spirit." It is the Spirit of God of whom we are born; that is, our new life is wrought in us by his efficiency. And that which in us is so born of him is spirit; not the natural faculties of our souls, — they are once created, once born, and no more, — but a new principle of spiritual obedience, whereby we live unto God. And this is the product of the internal immediate efficiency of grace.

This will the better appear if we consider the faculties of the soul distinctly, and what is the especial work of the Holy Spirit upon them in our regeneration or conversion to God:— (1.) The leading, conducting faculty of the soul is the mind or understanding. Now, this is corrupted and vitiated by the fall; and how it continues depraved in the state of nature hath been declared before. The sum is, that it is not able to discern spiritual things in a spiritual manner; for it is possessed with spiritual blindness or darkness, and is filled with enmity against God and his law, esteeming the things of the gospel to be foolishness; because it is alienated from the life of God through the ignorance that is in it. We must, therefore, inquire what is the work of the Holy Spirit on our minds in turning of us to God, whereby this depravation is removed and this vicious state cured, whereby we come to see and discern spiritual things in a spiritual manner, that we may savingly know God and his mind as revealed in and by Jesus Christ. And this is several ways declared in the Scripture:—

[1.] He is said to give us an understanding: 1 John v. 20, "The Son of God is come, and hath given us an understanding, that we may know him that is true;" which he doth by his Spirit. Man by sin is become like the "beasts that perish, which have no understanding," Ps. xlix. 12, 20. Men have not lost their natural intellective faculty or reason absolutely. It is continued unto them, with the free though impaired use of it, in things natural and civil.

And it hath an advance in sin; men are "wise to do evil:"[53] but it is lost as to the especial use of it in the saving knowledge of God and his will, "To do good they have no knowledge," Jer. iv. 22; for naturally, "there is none that understandeth, there is none that seeketh after God," Rom. iii. 11. It is corrupted not so much in the root and principle of its actings, as with respect unto their proper object, term, and end. Wherefore, although this giving of an understanding be not the creating in us anew of that natural faculty, yet it is that gracious work in it without which that faculty in us, as depraved, will no more enable us to know God savingly than if we had none at all. The grace, therefore, here asserted in the giving of an understanding is the causing of our natural understandings to understand savingly. This David prays for: Ps. cxix. 34, "Give me understanding, and I shall keep thy law." The whole work is expressed by the apostle, Eph. i. 17, 18, "That the God of our Lord Jesus Christ, the Father of glory, may give unto you the Spirit of wisdom and revelation in the knowledge of him: the eyes of your understanding being opened; that ye may know what is the hope of his calling," etc. That "the Spirit of wisdom and revelation" is the Spirit of God working those effects in us, we have before evinced. And it is plain that the "revelation" here intended is subjective, in enabling us to apprehend what is revealed, and not objective, in new revelations, which the apostle prayed not that they might receive. And this is farther evidenced by the ensuing description of it: "The eyes of your understanding being opened." There is an eye in the understanding of man, — that is, the natural power and ability that is in it to discern spiritual things. But this eye is sometimes said to be "blind," sometimes to be "darkness," sometimes to be "shut" or closed; and nothing but the impotency of our minds to know God savingly, or discern things spiritually when proposed unto us, can be intended thereby. It is the work of the Spirit of grace to open this eye,[54] Luke iv. 18; Acts xxvi. 18; and this is by the powerful, effectual removal of that depravation of our minds, with all its effects, which we before described. And how are we made partakers thereof? It is of the gift of God, freely and effectually working it: for, first, he "giveth us the Spirit of wisdom and revelation" to that end; and, secondly, works the thing itself in us. He "giveth us a heart to know him," Jer. xxiv. 7, without which we cannot so do, or he would not himself undertake to work it in us for that end. There is, therefore, an effectual, powerful, creating act of the Holy Spirit put forth in the minds of men in their conversion unto God, enabling them spiritually to discern Spiritual things; wherein the seed and substance of divine faith is contained.

[2.] This is called the renovation of our minds: "Renewed in the spirit of your mind," Eph. iv. 23; which is the same with being "renewed in knowledge," Col. iii. 10. And this renovation of our minds hath in it a transforming power to change the whole soul into an obediential frame towards God, Rom. xii. 2. And the work of renewing our minds is peculiarly ascribed unto the Holy Spirit: Tit. iii. 5, "The renewing of the Holy Ghost." Some men seem to fancy, yea, do declare, that there is no such depravation in or of the mind of man, but that he is able, by the use of his reason, to apprehend, receive, and discern those truths of the gospel which are objectively proposed unto it. But of the use of reason in these matters, and its ability to discern and judge of the sense of propositions and force of inferences in things of religion, we shall treat afterward. At present, I only inquire whether men unregenerate be of themselves able spiritually to discern spiritual things when they are proposed unto them in the dispensation of the gospel, so as their knowledge may be saving in and unto themselves, and acceptable unto God in Christ, and that without any especial, internal, effectual work of the Holy Spirit of grace in them and upon them? If they say they are, as they plainly plead them to be, and will not content themselves with an ascription unto them of that notional, doctrinal knowledge which none deny them to be capable of, I desire to know to what purpose are they said to be "renewed by the Holy Ghost?" to what purpose are all those gracious actings of God in them before recounted? He that shall consider what, on the one band, the Scripture teacheth us concerning the blindness, darkness, impotency of our minds, with respect unto spiritual things, when proposed unto us, as in the state of nature; and, on the other, what it affirms concerning the work of the Holy Ghost in their renovation and change, in giving them new power, new ability, a new, active understanding, — will not be much moved with the groundless, confident, unproved dictates of some concerning the power of reason in itself to apprehend and discern religious things, so far as we are required in a way of duty. This is all one as if they should say, that if the sun shine clear and bright, every blind man is able to see.

God herein is said to communicate a light unto our minds, and that so as that we shall see by it, or perceive by it, the things proposed unto us in the gospel usefully and savingly: 2 Cor. iv. 6, "God, who commanded the light to shine out of darkness, hath shined in our hearts, to give the light of the knowledge of the glory of God in the face of Jesus Christ." Did God no otherwise work on the minds of men but by an external, objective proposal of truth unto them, to what purpose doth the apostle mention the almighty act of creating power which he put forth and exercised in the first production of natural light out of darkness? What allusion is there between that work and the doctrinal proposal of truth to the minds of men? It is, therefore, a confidence not to be contended with, if any will deny that the act of God in the spiritual illumination of our minds be of the same nature, as to efficacy and efficiency, with that whereby he created light at the beginning of all things. And because the effect produced in us is called "light," the act itself is described by "shining:" " God bath shined in our hearts," — that is, our minds. So he conveys light unto them by an act of omnipotent efficiency. And as that which is so wrought in our minds is called "light," so the apostle, leaving his metaphor, plainly declares what he intends thereby, — namely, the actual "knowledge of the glory of God in the face of Jesus Christ;" that is, as God is revealed in Christ by the gospel, as he declares, verse 4. Having, therefore, first, compared the mind of man by nature, with respect unto a power of discerning spiritual things, to the state of all things under darkness before the creation of light; and, secondly, the powerful working of God in illumination unto the act of his omnipotency in the production or creation of light natural, — he ascribes our ability to know, and our actual knowledge of God in Christ, unto his real efficiency and operation. And these things in part direct us towards an apprehension of that work of the Holy Spirit upon the minds of men in their conversion unto God whereby their depravation is cured, and without which it will not so be. By this means, and no otherwise, do we who were "darkness" become "light in the Lord," or come to know God in Christ savingly, looking into and discerning spiritual things with a proper intuitive sight, whereby all the other faculties of our souls are guided and influenced unto the obedience of faith.

(2.) It is principally with respect unto the will and its depravation by nature that we are said to be dead in sin. And herein is seated that peculiar obstinacy, whence it is that no unregenerate person doth or can answer his own convictions, or walk up unto his light in obedience. For the will may be considered two ways:— first, As a rational, vital faculty of our souls; secondly, As a free principle,[55] freedom being of its essence or nature. This, therefore, in our conversion to God, is renewed by the Holy Ghost, and that by an effectual implantation in it of a principle of spiritual life and holiness in the room of that original righteousness which it lost by the fall. That he doth so is proved by all the testimonies before insisted on:— First, This is its renovation as it is a rational, vital faculty; and of this vivification see before. Secondly, As it is a free principle, it is determined unto its acts in this case by the powerful operation of the Holy Ghost, without the least impeachment of its liberty or freedom; as hath been declared. And that this is so might be fully evinced, as by others so by the ensuing arguments; for if the Holy Ghost do not work immediately and effectually upon the will, producing and creating in it a principle of faith and obedience, infallibly determining it in its free acts, then is all the glory of our conversion to be ascribed unto ourselves, and we make ourselves therein, by the obediential actings of our own free will, to differ from others who do not so comply with the grace of God; which is denied by the apostle, 1 Cor. iv. 7. Neither can any purpose of God concerning the conversion of any one soul he certain and determinate, seeing after he hath done all that is to be done, or can be done towards it, the will, remaining undetermined, may not be converted, contrary to those testimonies of our Saviour, Matt. xi. 25, 26; John vi. 37; Rom. viii. 29. Neither can there be an original infallibility in the promises of God made to Jesus Christ concerning the multitudes that should believe in him, seeing it is possible no one may so do, if it depend on the undetermined liberty of their wills whether they will or no. And then, also, must salvation of necessity be "of him that willeth, and of him that runneth," and not "of God, that showeth mercy on whom he will have mercy," contrary to the apostle, Rom. ix. 15, 16. And the whole efficacy of the grace of God is made thereby to depend on the wills of men; which is not consistent with our being the "workmanship of God, created in Christ Jesus unto good works," Eph. ii. 10. Nor, on this supposition, do men know what they pray for, when they pray for their own or other men's conversion to God; as hath been before declared. There is, therefore, necessary such a work of the Holy Spirit upon our wills as may cure and take away the depravation of them before described, freeing us from the state of spiritual death, causing us to live unto God, and determining them in and unto the acts of faith and obedience. And this he doth whilst and as he makes us new creatures, quickens us who are dead in trespasses and sins, gives us a new heart and puts a new spirit within us, writes his law in our hearts, that we may do the mind of God and walk in his ways, worketh in us to will and to do, making them who were unwilling and obstinate to become willing and obedient, and that freely and of choice.

(3.) In like manner a prevailing love is implanted upon the affections by the Spirit of grace, causing the soul with delight and complacency to cleave to God and his ways. This removes and takes away the enmity before described, with the effects of it: Deut. xxx. 6, "The Lord thy God will circumcise thine heart, and the heart of thy seed, to love the Lord thy God with all thine heart, and with all thy soul, that thou mayest live." This circumcision of the heart consists in the "putting off the body of the sins of the flesh," as the apostle speaks, Col. ii. 11. He "crucifies the flesh, with the affections and lusts" thereof. Some men are inclined to think that all the depravation of our nature consists in that of the sensitive part of the soul, or our affections; the vanity and folly of which opinion bath been before discovered. Yet it is not denied but that the affections are signally depraved, so that by them principally the mind and will do act those lusts that are peculiarly seated in them, or by them do act according to their perverse and corrupt inclinations, Gal. v. 24; James i. 14, 15. Wherefore, in the circumcision of our hearts, wherein the flesh, with the lusts, affections, and deeds thereof, is crucified by the Spirit, he takes from them their enmity, carnal prejudices, and depraved inclinations, really though not absolutely and perfectly; and instead of them he fills us with holy spiritual love, joy, fear, and delight, not changing the being of our affections, but sanctifying and guiding them by the principle of saving light and knowledge before described, and uniting them unto their proper object in a due manner.

From what hath been spoken in this third argument, it is evident that the Holy Spirit, designing the regeneration or conversion of the souls of men, worketh therein effectually, powerfully, and irresistibly; which was proposed unto confirmation.

From the whole it appears that our regeneration is a work of the Spirit of God, and that not any act of our own, which is only so, is intended thereby.[56] I say it is not so our own as by outward helps and assistance to be educed out of the principles of our natures. And herein is the Scripture express; for, mentioning this work directly with respect unto its cause, and the manner of its operation in the effecting of it, it assigns it positively unto God or his Spirit 1 Pet. i. 3, "God, according to his abundant mercy, hath begotten us again." James i. 18, "Of his own will begat he us with the word of truth." John iii. 5, 6, 8, "Born of the Spirit." 1 John iii. 9, "Born of God." And, on the other hand, it excludes the will of man from any active interest herein; I mean, as to the first beginning of it: 1 Pet. i. 23, "Born again, not of corruptible seed, but of incorruptible, by the word of God, which liveth and abideth for ever." John i. 13, "Which were born, not of blood, nor of the will of the flesh, nor of the will of man, but of God." See Matt. xvi. 17; Tit. iii. 5; Eph. ii. 9, 10. It is, therefore, incumbent on them who plead for the active interest of the will of man in regeneration to produce some testimonies of Scripture where it is assigned unto it, as the effect unto its proper cause. Where is it said that a man is born again or begotten anew by himself? And if it be granted, — as it must be so, unless violence be offered not only to the Scripture but to reason and common sense, — that whatever be our duty and power herein, yet these expressions must denote an act of God, and not ours, the substance of what we contend for is granted, as we shall be ready at any time to demonstrate. It is true, God doth command us to circumcise our hearts and to make them new: but he doth therein declare our duty, not our power; for himself promiseth to work in us what he requireth of us. And that power which we have and do exercise in the progress of this work, in sanctification and holiness, proceeds from the infused principle which we receive in our regeneration; for all which ends we ought to pray for Him, according to the example of holy men of old.[57]

Footnotes:

30. Τί τὸ ὄφελος, ἐὰν εὐσύνθετος μὲν ὁ λόγος, κακοσύνθετος δὲ ὁ τρόπος; εἰ μὲν γὰρ σοφιστοῦ διδασκαλεῖον ἦ ἡ ἐκκλησία εὐγλωττίας ἦν ὁ καιρός. Ἐπειδὴ δὲ τρόπων ἀγὼν καὶ καρποφορία τὸ προκείμενον, καὶ προσδοκία οὐρανῶν τὸ προσδοκώμενον, μὴ γλυπτα ζητείσθω ἀλλ' ὁ τρόπος. —Athanas. de Semente.

31. "Non est igitur gratia Dei in natura liberi arbitrii, et in lege atque doctrina sicut Pelagius desipit, sed ad singulos actus datur illius voluntate de quo scriptum est; pluviam voluntariam segregabis Deus hæreditati tuæ. Quia et liberum arbitrium ad diligendum Deum primi peccati granditate perdidimus; et lex Dei atque doctrina quamvis sancta et justa et bona, tamen occidit, si non vivificet Spiritus, per quem fit non ut audiendo sed ut obediendo, neque ut lectione sed ut dilectione teneatur. Quapropter ut in Deum credamus et pie vivamus, non volentis neque currentis sed miserentis est Dei; non quia velle non debemus et currere, sed quia ipse in nobis et velle operatur et currere. Non ergo gratiam dicamus esse doctrinam, sed agnoscamus gratiam quæ facit prodesse doctrinam; quæ gratia si desit, videmus etiam obesse doctrinam." — August. Epist. ccxvii, ad Vitalem.

32. "Sed quid illud est quo corporum sensus pulsantur, in agro cordis cui impenditur ista cultura, nec radicem potest figere nec germen emittere, nisi ille summus et verus Agricola potentia sui operis adhibuerit, et ad vitalem profectum ea quæ sunt plantata perduxerit?" — Epist. ad Demetriadem.

33. "Omni dictamini rectæ rationis potest voluntas se conformare; sed diligere Deum super omnia est dictamen rectæ rationis; ratio enim dictat inter omnia diligenda esse aliquid summe diligendum. Item homo errans potest diligere creaturam super omnia, ergo etiam Deum; mirum enim valde esset, quod voluntas se conformare possit dictamini erroneo et non recto." — Biel, ii. Sent. distinc. 27, q. art. 4.

34. "Hoc piarum mentium est, ut nihil sibi tribuant, sed totum gratiæ Dei; unde quantumcunque aliquis det gratiæ Dei, etiamsi subtrahat potestati naturæ aut liberi arbitrii a pietate non recedit; cum vero aliquid gratiæ Dei subtrahitur et naturæ tribuitur quod gratiæ est, ibi potest periculum intervenire." — Cassander. Lib. Consult. art. lxviii.

35. "Pelagiana hæresis quo dogmate catholicam fidem destruere adorta sit, et quibus impietatum venenis viscera ecclesiæ atque ipsa vitalia corporis Christi voluerit occupare, notiora sunt quam ut opere narrationis indigeant. Ex his tamen una est blasphemia, nequissimum et subtilissimum germen aliarum, quâ dicunt gratiam Dei secundum merita hominum dari. Cum enim primum tantam naturæ humanæ vellent astruere sanitatem, ut per solum liberum arbitrium posset assequi Dei regnum; eo quod tam plene ipso conditionis suæ præsidio juvaretur; ut habens naturaliter rationalem intellectum facile bonum eligeret malumque vitaret, et ubi in utrâque parte libera essent opera voluntatis, non facultatem his qui mali sunt ad bonum deesse, sed studium. Cum ergo, ut dixi, totam justitiam hominis ex naturali vellent rectitudine ac possibilitate subsistere, atque hanc definitionem doctrina sana respueret, damnatum a catholicis sensum et multis postea hæreticæ fraudis varietatibus coloratum, hoc apud se ingenio servaverunt, ut ad incipiendum, et ad proficiendum, et ad perseverandum in bono necessariam homini Dei gratiam profiterentur. Sed in hac professione quo dolo vasa iræ molirentur irrepere, ipsa Dei gratia vasis misericordiæ revelavit. Intellectum est enim, saluberrimeque perspectum hoc tantum eos de gratia confiteri, quod quædam libero Arbitrio sit magistra, seque per cohortationes, per legem, per doctrinam, per creaturarum contemplationem, per miracula, perque terrores extrinsecus judicio ejus ostentet; quo unusquisque secundum voluntatis suæ motum, si quæsierit inveniat; si petierit, recipiat, si pulsaverit, introeat." — Prosp. ad Rufin. de Lib. Arbit.

36. "Inaniter et perfunctorie potius quam veraciter pro eis, ut doctrinæ cui adversantur credendo consentiant, Deo fundimus preces, si ad ejus non pertinet gratiam convertere ad fidem suam, ipsi fidei contrarias hominum voluntates." — August. Epist. ccxvii.

37. "Prima divini muneris gratia est, ut erudiat nos ad nostræ humilitatis confessionem, et agnoscere faciat, quod, si quid boni agimus, per illum possumus, sine quo nihil possumus." — Prosp. Sentent. cv. ex August.

38. "Quicunque tribuit sibi bonum quod facit etiamsi videtur nihil mali manibus operari, jam cordis innocentiam perdidit in quo se largitori bonorum prætulit." — Hieron. in cap. xvi. Proverb.

39. "O bone Domine Jesu, etsi ego admisi unde me damnare potes, tu non amisisti unde salvare soles. — Verum est conscientia mea meretur damnationem, et pœnitentia mea non sufficit ad satisfactionem. Sed certum est quod

misericordia tua superat omnem offensionem. Parce ergo mihi, Domine, qui es salus vera et non vis mortem peccatoris: miserere, Domine, peccatrici animæ meæ, solve vincula ejus, sana vulnera ejus. Ecce misericors Deus coram te exhibeo animam meam virtutum muneribus desolatam, catenis vitiorum ligatam, pondere peccatorum gravatam, delictorum sordibus fœdatam, discissam vulneribus dæmonum, putidam et fœtidam ulceribus criminum: his et aliis gravioribus malis quæ tu melius vides quam ego obstrictam, oppressam, circumdatam, obvolutam, bonorum omuium relevamine destitutam," etc.

40. "Gratia qua Christi populus sumus hoc cohibetur Limite vobiscum, et formam hanc ascribitis illi, Ut cunctos vocet illa quidem invitetque; neque ullum Præteriens, studeat communem adferre salutem Omnibus, et totum peccato absolvere mundum. Sed proprio quemque Arbitrio parere vocanti, Judicioque suo, mota se extendere mente Ad lucem oblatam, quæ se non substrahat ulli; Sed cupidos recti juvet, illustretque volentes. Hinc adjutoris Domini bonitate magistra Crescere virtutum studia, ut quid quisque petendum Mandatis didicit, jugi sectetur amore." Prosp. de Ingrat. cap. x. 251–262.

41. "Ploremus coram Domino qui fecit nos et homines et salvos. Nam si ille nos fecit homines, nos autem ipsi nos fecimus salvos, aliquid illo melius fecimus; melior est enim salvus homo quam quilibet homo. Si ergo te Deus fecit hominem, et tu te fecisti bonum hominem, quod tu fecisti melius est." — August. de Verb. Apost. Serm. x."Natura humana, etiamsi in illa integritate in qua est condita, permanet, nullo modo seipsam, creatore sua non adjuvante, servaret. Unde cum sine Dei gratia salutem non posset custodire quam accepit, quomodo sine Dei gratia potest recuperare quam perdidit?" — Prosp. Sentent. 308.

42. "At vero onmipotens hominem cum gratia salvat, Ipsa suum consummat opus, cui tempus agendi Semper adest quæ gesta velit: non moribus illi Fit mora, non causis anceps suspenditur ullis. Nec quod sola potest curâ officioque ministri Exequitur, famulisve vicem committit agendi. Qui quamvis multa admoveat mandata vocantis, Pulsant non intrant animas; Deus ergo sepultos Suscitat et solvit peccati compede vinctos. Ille obscuratis dat cordibus intellectum: Ille ex injustis justos facit, indit amorem Quo redametur amans, et amor quem conserit, ipse est. Hunc itaque affectum quo sumunt mortua vitam, Quo tenebræ fiunt lumen, quo immunda nitescunt; Quo stulti sapere incipiunt ægrique valescunt Nemo alii dat, nemo sibi." Prosp. de Ingrat. cap. xv. 384–398."Legant ergo et intelligant, intueantur atque fateantur, non lege atque doctrina insonante forinsecus, sed internâ atque occultâ, mirabili atque ineffabili potestate operari Deum in cordibus hominum non solum veras revelationes, sed bonas etiam voluntates." — August. Lib. de Grat. Christ. adv. Pelagium et Cælest., cap. xxiv.

43. "Quid est, Omnis qui audivit a Patre, et didicit, venit ad me; nisi nullus est qui audiat a Patre, et discat et non veniat ad me? Si enim omnis qui audivit a Patre et didicit, venit, profecto omnis qui non venit non audivit a Patre nec didicit; nam si audisset et didicisset veniret; — hæc itaque gratia quæ occulte humanis cordibus divina largitate tribuitur, a nullo duro corde respuitur; ideo quippe tribuitur ut cordis duritia primitus auferatur." — August. de Prædest. Sanct. lib. i. cap. 8.

44. "O qualis est artifex ille Spiritus! nulla ad discendum mora agitur in omne quod voluerit. Mox enim ut eligeret mentem docet; solumque tetigisse docuisse est. Nam humanum subito ut illustrat immutat affectum; abnegat hoc repente quod erat, exhibet repente quod non erat." — Gregor. Hom. xxx. in Evangel.

45. "Christus non dicit, duxerit, ut illic aliquo modo intelligamus præcedere voluntatem; sed dicit, traxerit, quis autem trahitur si jam volebat; et tamen nemo venit nisi velit, trahitur ergo miris modis ut velit, ab illo qui novit intus in ipsis hominum cordibus operari; non ut homines, quod fieri non potest, nolentes credant, sed ut volentes ex nolentibus fiant." — August. cont. Duas Epist. Pelag. cap. xix."Certum est nos velle cum volumus, sed ille facit ut velimus bonum, de quo dictum est, Deus est qui operatur in nobis velle." — Idem de Grat. et Lib. Arbit. cap. xvi.

46. "Restat ut ipsam fidem unde omnis justitia sumit initium, non humano, quo isti extolluntur, tribuamus arbitrio, nec ullis precedentibus meritis, quoniam inde incipiunt bona quæcunque sunt merita, sed gratuitum Dei donum esse fateamur, si gratiam veram, id est, sine meritis cogitemus." — August. Epist. cv."Nolens ergo his tam claris testimoniis repugnare, et tamen volens a seipso sibi esse quod credidit quasi componat cum Deo ut partem fidei sibi vendicet, atque illi partem relinquat; et quod est elatius, primam tollit ipse, sequentem dat illi; et in eo quod dicit esse amborum, priorem se, facit posteriorem Deum." — August. de Prædest. Sanct. cap. ii.

47. "Quando Deus docet per Spiritus gratiam, ita docet ut quod quisque didicerit non tantum cognoscendo videat, sed etiam volendo appetat agendoque perficiat. Et ipso divino docendi modo etiam ipsa voluntas, et ipsa operatio non sola volendi et operandi naturalis possibilitas adjuvatur. Si enim solum posse nostrum hac gratia juvaretur, ita diceret Dominus, Omnis qui audivit a Patre, et didicit, potest venire ad me." — August. de Grat. Christ. contra Pelagium, cap. xiv.

48. "Si quis sine gratia Dei credentibus, volentibus, desiderantibus, conantibus misericordiam dicit conferri divinitus; non autem ut credamus, velimus, per infusionem et inspirationem Spiritus Sancti in nobis fieri confitetur, anathema sit." — Conc. Arausic. 2. can. 6."Datur potestas ut filii Dei fiant qui credunt in eum, cum hoc ipsum datur ut credant in eum. Quæ potestas nisi detur a Deo nulla esse potest ex libero arbitrio, quia nec liberum bono erit quod liberator non liberaverit." — August, lib. i. cont. Duas Epist. Pelag. cap. 3.

49. "Restat ut ipsam fidem unde omnis justitia sumit initium, non humano, quo isti extolluntur, tribuamus arbitrio, nec ullis precedentibus meritis, quoniam inde incipiunt bona quæcunque sunt merita, sed gratuitum Dei donum esse fateamur, si gratiam veram, id est, sine meritis cogitamus." — August. Epist. cv.

50. "Semper quidem adjutorium gratiæ nobis est a Deo poscendum, sed nec ipsum quod possumus viribus nostris assignem. Neque enim haberi potest ipse saltem orationis affectus nisi divinitus fuerit attributus. Ut ergo desideremus adjutorium gratiæ, hoc ipsum quoque est gratiæ, ipsa namque incipit effundi ut incipiat posci." — Fulgent. Epist. vi. ad Theod.

51. "Hoc est enim, promittit Deus quod ipse facit; non enim ipse promittit et alius facit; quod jam non est promittere sed prædicere. Ideo non ex operibus sed ex vocante, ne ipsorum sit, non Dei." — August. de Spir. et Lit. cap. xxiv.

52. "Hæc gratia quæ occultè humanis cordibus divina largitate tribuitur, a nullo duro corde respuitur; ideo quippe tribuitur, ut cordis durities primitus auferatur" — August. de Prædest. Sanct. cap. viii.

53. "Prorsus si Dei adjutorium defuerit, nihil boni agere poteris; agis quidem illo non adjuvente libera voluntate, sed male; ad hoc idonea est voluntas tua quæ vocatur libera, et male agendo fit damnabilis ancilla." — August. Serm. xiii. de Verb. Apost.

54. "Erat lumen verum quæ illuminat omnem hominem venientem in hunc mundum; ideo dictum est, quia nullus hominum illuminatur, nisi illo lumine veritatis quod Deus est, ne quisquam putaret ab eo se illuminari a quo aliquid audit ut discat; non dico si quenquam magnum hominem, sed nec si angelum ei contingat habere doctotem. Adhibetur enim sermo veritatis extrinsecus vocis ministerio corporalis; verumtamen neque qui plantat est aliquid, neque qui rigat, sed qui incrementum dat Deus. Audit quippe homo dicentem vel hominem vel angelum, sed ut sentiat et cognoscat verum esse quod dicitur, illo lumine intus mens ejus aspergitur quod æternum manet, quod etiam in tenebris lucet." — August. de Peccat. Merit. et Remiss. lib. i. cap. 25.

55. "Libertas sine gratia nihil est nisi contumacia, non libertas." — August. Epist. lxxxix.

56. "Quis istis corda mutavit, nisi qui finxit singillatim corda eorum? Quis hujus rigoris duritiem ad obediendi mollivit affectum, nisi qui potens est de lapidibus Abrahæ filios excitare?" — Prosp. ad Rufin. de Lib. Arbit."Ploremus coram Domino qui fecit nos et homines et salvos. Nam si ille nos fecit homines, nos autem ipsi nos fecimus salvos, aliquid illo melius fecimus. Melior enim est salvus homo quam quilibet homo. Si ergo te Deus fecit hominem et tu te fecisti bonum hominem, quod tu fecisti melius est. Noli te extollere super Deum, ... confitere illi qui fecit te, quia nemo recreat nisi qui creat, nemo reficit nisi qui fecit." — August. de Verb. Apost. Serm. x."Nemo quisquam hominum sive ad cogitandum, sive ad operandum quodcunque bonum potest esse idoneus; nisi qui fuerit munere gratuito divinæ opitulationis adjutus; ab ipso namque est initium bonæ voluntatis, ab ipso facultas boni operis, ab ipso perseveantia bonæ conversationis." — Fulgent. lib. i. ad Monim.

57. "Jam divini amor Numinis, Patris omnipotentis prolisque beatissimæ sancta communicatio; omnipotens Paraclete Spiritus; mœrentium consolator clementissime, jam cordis mei penetralibus potenti illabere virtute, et tenebrosa quæque laris neglecti latibula, corusci luminis fulgore pius habitator lætifica, tuique roris abundantia, longo ariditatis marcentia squalore, visitando fecunda."

Chapter VI - The manner of conversion explained in the instance of Augustine[58]

The outward means and manner of conversion to God, or regeneration, with the degrees of spiritual operations on the minds of men and their effects, exemplified in the conversion of Augustine, as the account is given thereof by himself.

As among all the doctrines of the gospel, there is none opposed with more violence and subtlety than that concerning our regeneration by the immediate, powerful, effectual operation of the Holy Spirit of grace; so there is not scarce any thing more despised or scorned by many in the world than that any should profess that there hath been such a work of God upon themselves, or on any occasion declare aught of the way and manner whereby it was wrought. The very mentioning hereof is grown a derision among some that call themselves Christians; and to plead an interest or concern in this grace is to forfeit all a man's reputation with many who would be thought wise, and boast themselves to be rational. Neither is this a practice taken up of late, in these declining times of the world, but seems to have been started and followed from days of old, — possibly from the beginning; yea, the enmity of Cain against Abel was but a branch of this proud and perverse inclination. The instance of Ishmael in the Scripture is representative of all such as, under an outward profession of the true religion, did or do scoff at those who, being, as Isaac, children of the promise, do profess and evidence an interest in the internal power of it, which they are unacquainted withal. And the same practice may be traced in succeeding ages. Hence, holy Austin, entering upon the confession of his greater sins, designing thereby to magnify the glory and efficacy of the grace of God in his conversion, provides against this scorn of men, which he knew he should meet withal. "Irrideant," saith he, "me arrogantes et nondum salubriter prostrati et elisi a te, Deus meus, ego tamen confitear tibi dedecora mea, in laude tua," Confess. lib. iv. cap. 1; — "Let arrogant men deride or scorn me, who were never savingly cast down nor broken in pieces by thee, my God, yet I will [rather, let me] confess my own shame, unto thy praise." Let none be offended with these expressions, of being "savingly or wholesomely cast down and broken of God;" for, in the judgment of this great person, they are not fanatical. We may not, therefore, think it strange if the same truth, the same practice, and profession of it, do still meet with the same entertainment. Let them deride and scorn it who were never humbled savingly, nor broken with a sense of sin, nor relieved by grace; the holy work of God's Spirit is to be owned, and the truth to be avowed as it is in Jesus.

Of the original depravation of our nature we have treated so far as is needful unto our present purpose; yet some things must be added concerning the effects of that depravation, which will conduce unto the right understanding of the way and manner whereby the Spirit of God proceedeth for the healing and removal of it, which we have now under especial consideration. And we may observe, —

First, That the corrupt principle of sin, the native habitual inclination that is in us unto evil, worketh early in our natures, and for the most part preventeth all the actings of grace in us. Though some may be sanctified in or from the womb, yet in order of nature this native corruption hath first place in them; for a clean thing cannot be brought out of an unclean, but "that which is born of the flesh is flesh:" Ps. lviii. 3, "The wicked are estranged from the womb: they go astray as soon as they be born, speaking lies." It is to no purpose to say that he speaks of wicked men, — that is, such who are habitually and profligately so; for, whatever any man may afterward run into by a course of sin, all men are morally alike from the womb, and it is an aggravation of the wickedness of men that it begins so early, and holds on an uninterrupted course. Children are not able to speak from the womb, as soon as they are born; yet here are they said to speak lies. It is, therefore, the perverse acting of depraved nature in infancy that is intended; for everything that is irregular, that answers not the law of our creation and rule of our obedience, is a lie. And among the many instances collected by Austin of such irregular actings of nature in its infant state, one is peculiarly remarkable: Confess. lib. i. cap. 6, "Paulatim sentiebam ubi essem, et voluntates meas volebam ostendere eis per quos implerentur, et non poteram … Itaque jactabam membra, et voces, signa similia voluntatibus meis, pauca quæ poteram, qualia poteram; et cum mihi non obtemperabatur, vel non intellecto, vel ne obesset, indignabar non subditis majoribus, et liberis non servientibus, et me de illis flendo vindicabam." This again he repeats, cap. 7: "An pro tempore illa bona erant, flendo petere etiam quod noxie daretur; indignari acriter non subjectis hominibus, liberis et majoribus, hisque a quibus genitus est; multisque præterea prudentioribus, non ad nutum voluntatis obtemperantibus, feriendo nocere niti, quantum potest, quia non obeditur imperiis quibus perniciose obediretur? Ita imbecillitas membrorum infantilium innocens est, non animus infantium." Those irregular and perverse agitations of mind, and of the will or appetite, not yet under the conduct of reason, which appear in infants, with the indignation and little self-revenges wherewith they are accompanied in their disappointments when all about them do not subject themselves unto their inclinations, it may be to their hurt, are from the obliquity of our nature, and effects of that depraved habit of sin wherewith it is wholly possessed. And by the frequency of these lesser actings are the mind and will prepared for those more violent and impetuous motions which, by the improving of their natural capacities, and the incitation of new objects presented unto their corruptions, they are exposed unto and filled withal. God did not originally thus create our nature, — a condition worse than and inferior unto that of other creatures, in whose young ones there are none of these disorders, but a regular compliance with their natural instinct prevails in them. And as the dying of multitudes of infants, notwithstanding the utmost care for their preservation, whereas the young ones of other creatures all generally live, if they have whereby their nature may be sustained, argues the imputation of sin unto them, — for death entered by sin, and passed upon all, inasmuch as all have sinned, — so those irregular actings, peculiar unto them, prove sin inherent in them, or the corruption of their nature from their conceptions.

Secondly, With the increase of our natural faculties, and the strengthening of the members of our bodies, which by nature are become ready "instruments of unrighteousness unto sin," Rom. vi. 13, this perverse principle acts itself with more evidence, frequency, and success in the production of actual sin, or inordinate actings of the mind, will, and affections. So the wise man tells us that "childhood and youth are vanity," Eccles. xi. 10. The mind of man, in the state of childhood and youth, puts itself forth in all kinds of vain actings, in foolish imaginations, perverse and froward appetites, falseness in words, with sensible effects of corrupt inclinations in every kind. Austin's first book of Confessions is an excellent comment on that text, wherein the "vanity of childhood and youth" are graphically described, with pathetical self-reflecting complaints concerning the guilt of sin which is contracted in them. Some, perhaps, may think light of those ways of folly and vanity wherein childhood doth, or left alone would, consume itself; — that there is no moral evil in those childish innocencies. That good man was of another mind. "Istane est," saith he, "innocentia puerilis? non est, Domine, non est, oro to, Deus meus. Nam hæc ipsa sunt quæ a pædagogis et magistris, a nucibus et pilulis et passeribus, ad præfectos et reges, aurum, prædia, mancipia, hæc ipsa omnino quæ succedentibus majoribus ætatibus transeunt [sicuti ferulis majora supplicia succedunt]," lib. i. cap. 19. This is not innocency; it is not so. The same principle and habit of mind, carried over unto riper age and greater occasions, bring forth those greater sins which the lives of men are filled withal in this world. And who is there, who hath a serious reverence of God, with any due apprehension of his holiness, and a clear conviction of the nature of sin, who is not able to call over such actings in childhood, which most think meet to connive at, wherein they may remember that perversity whereof they are now ashamed? By this means is the heart prepared for a farther obduration in sin, by the confirmation of native obstinacy.

Thirdly, Unto those more general irregularities actual sins do succeed, — such, I mean, as are against the remaining light of nature, or committed in rebellion unto the dictates and guidance of our minds and consciences, the influence of those intelligences of moral good and evil which are inseparable from the faculties of our souls; for although in some they may be stifled and overborne, yet can they never be utterly obliterated or extinguished, but will accompany the nature of man unto eternity, even in that condition wherein they shall be of no other use but to add to and increase its misery. Amongst those we may call over one or two instances. Lying is such a sin, which the depravation of nature in youth is prone to exert itself by, and that on sundry reasons, not now to be inquired into: "They go astray from the womb, speaking lies." The first inducement of our nature unto sin was by a lie, and we fell in Adam by giving credit thereunto; and there is in every sin a particular lie. But speaking falsely, contrary unto what they know to be true, is that which children are prone unto, though some more than others, according as other vicious habits prevail in them, whose actings they foolishly think to thatch over and cover thereby. This that holy person whom we instance in acknowledgeth, and bewaileth in himself: "Non videbam voraginem turpitudinis in quam projectus eram ab oculis tuis. Nam in illis jam quid me fœdius fuit, [ubi etiam talibus displicebam], fallendo innumerabilibus mendaciis, et pædagogum et magistros et parentes amore ludendi, studio spectandi nugatoria [et imitandi ludicra inquietudine?]" lib. i. cap. 19; — "I saw not (O God) into what a gulf of filth I was cast out from before thee; for what was more filthy than I, whilst out of love of plays, and desire of looking after vanities, I deceived teachers and parents with innumerable lies?" And this the good man was afterward exceedingly humbled for, and from it learned much of the vileness of his own nature. And we find by experience that a sense of this sin ofttimes accompanies the first real convictions that befall the souls of men; for when they seriously reflect upon themselves, or do view themselves in the glass of the law, they are not only sensible of the nature of this sin, but also how much they indulged themselves therein, partly whilst they remember how on the least occasions they were surprised into it, which yet they neglected to watch against, and partly understanding how sometimes they made it their business, by premeditated falsehoods, so to cover other sins as to escape rebuke and correction. The mention of these things will probably be entertained with contempt and scorn in this age, wherein the most prodigious wickednesses of men are made but a sport; but God, his holiness, and his truth, are still the same, whatever alterations there may be in the world. And the holy psalmist seems to have some reflection on this vice of youth, when he prays that God would take from him the "way of lying." Of the same nature are those lesser thefts, in despoiling their parents and governors of such things as they are not allowed to take and make use of for themselves: "They rob their father or mother, and say, It is no transgression," Prov. xxviii. 24. So saith the same person, "Furta etiam faciebam de cellario parentum et de mensa, vel gula imperitante, vel ut haberem quod darem pueris, ludum suum mihi, quo pariter delectabantur tamen, vendentibus," lib. i. cap. 19. He sometimes stole from his parents, either to gratify his own sensual appetite, or to give unto his companions. In such instances doth original pravity exert itself in youth or childhood, and thereby both increase its own power and fortify the mind and the affections against the light and efficacy of conviction.

Fourthly, As men grow up in the state of nature, sin gets ground in them and upon them, subjectively and objectively. Concupiscence gets strength with age, and grows in violence as persons arrive to ability for its exercise; the instruments of it, in the faculties of the soul, organs of the senses, and members of the body, growing everyday more serviceable unto it, and more apt to receive impressions from it or to comply with its motions. Hence some charge the sins of youth on the heat of blood and the restlessness of the animal spirits, which prompt men unto irregularities and extravagancies; — but these are only vehicula concupiscentiæ, things which it makes use of to exert its poison by; for sin turns everything in this state unto its own advantage, and abuseth even "the commandment" itself, to "work in us all manner of concupiscence," Rom. vii. 8. Again, the objects of lust, by the occasions of life, are now multiplied. Temptations increase with years and the businesses of the world, but especially by that corruption of conversation which is among the most. Hence sundry persons are in this part of their youth, one way or other, overtaken with some gross actual sin or sins. That all are not so is a mere effect of preventing grace, and not at all from themselves. This the apostle respects in his charge, 2 Tim. ii. 22, "Flee youthful lusts;" such lusts as work effectually and prevail mightily in those that are young, if not subdued by the grace of God. And David, in a sense and from experience hereof, prays that God would not remember "the sins of his youth," Ps. xxv. 7. And a reflection from them is sometimes the torment of age, Job xx. 11: so he in whom we have chosen to exemplify the instances of such a course. He humbly confesseth unto God his falling into and being overtaken with great sins, such as fornication and uncleanness, in his younger days; in the mire whereof he was long detained. To this purpose he discourseth at large, lib. ii. cap. 1–3. And of the reason of this his humble and public acknowledgment he gives this holy account: "Neque enim tibi, Deus meus, sed apud te narro hæc generi meo, generi humano, quantulacunque ex particula incidere potest in istas meas literas. Et ut quid hoc? Ut videlicet ego et quisquis hæc legit, cogitemus de quam profundo clamandum sit ad te," cap. 3; — "I declare these things, O my God, not unto thee, but before thee" (or in thy presence), "unto my own race, unto human kind, whatever portion thereof may fall on these writings of mine. And unto what end? Namely, that I and everyone who shall read these things may consider out of what great depths we are to cry unto thee." So he, who lived not to see the days wherein humble confession of sin was made a matter of contempt and scorn.

Now, there is commonly a twofold event of men's falling under the power of temptations, and thereby into great actual sins: —

1. God sometimes takes occasion from them to awaken their consciences unto a deep sense not only of that sin in particular whose guilt they have contracted, but of their other sins also. The great Physician of their souls turns this poison into a medicine, and makes that wound which they have given themselves to be the lancing of a festered sore; for whereas their oscitancy, prejudices, and custom of sinning, have taken away the sense of lesser sins, and secure them from reflections from them, the stroke on their consciences from those greater provocations pierceth so deep as that they are forced to entertain thoughts of looking out after a release or remedy. So did they of old at the sermon of Peter, when he charged them with the guilt of a consent to the crucifying of Jesus Christ: "They were pricked in their heart, and said, Men and brethren, what shall we do?" Acts ii. 36, 37.

2. With others it proves a violent entrance into a farther pursuit of sin. The bounds of restraints, with the influence of natural light, being broken up and rejected, men's lusts being let loose, do break through all remaining obstacles, and run out into the greatest compass of excess and riot; observing no present evil to ensue on what they have done, according to their first fears, they are emboldened to greater wickedness, Eccles. viii. 11. And by this means is their conversion unto God rendered more difficult, and men thus wander away more and more from him unto the greatest distance that is recoverable by grace; for, —

Fifthly, A course in, and a custom of, sinning with many ensues hereon. Such the apostle treats concerning, Eph. iv. 18, 19, "Being past feeling, have given themselves over unto lasciviousness, to work all uncleanness with greediness." Custom of sinning takes away the sense of it; the course of the world takes away the shame of it; and love to it makes men greedy in the pursuit of it. See Confess. lib. 2. cap. 6. And this last effect of sin, as incited, provoked, and assisted by temptations, hath great variety in the effects and degrees of it. Hence are the various courses of unhumbled sinners in the world, wherein the outrage and excess of some seems to justify others in their more sedate irregularities and less conspicuous provocations. Yea, some who are not in any better state and condition as to their interest in the covenant of God than others, will yet not only startle at but really abhor those outrages of sin and wickedness which they fall into. Now, this difference ariseth not from hence, that the nature of all men is not equally corrupt and depraved, but that God is pleased to make his restraining grace effectual towards some, to keep them within those bounds of sinning which they shall not pass over, and to permit others so to fall under a conjunction of their lusts and temptations as that they proceed unto all manner of evil. Moreover, there are peculiar inclinations unto some sins, if not inlaid in, yet much enhanced and made obnoxious unto incitations by, the temperature of the body; and some are more exposed unto temptations in the world from their outward circumstances and occasions of life. Hereby are some even precipitated to all manner of evil. But still "the old man, which is corrupt according to the deceitful lusts," is the same naturally in all. All difference as to good from evil, — I mean not as to the nature of the things themselves, but as to men's interest in them, so as to adhere to the one and avoid the other, — is from the will of God. Thus he secretly prepares for some a better temperature of nature, docile and pliable unto such notices of things as may entertain their minds, and satisfy them above sensual delights. And some he disposeth, in their education, callings, societies, aims, and designs in the world, into ways inconsistent with open lewdness, which will much balance their inclinations, besides his secret internal actings on their hearts and minds, whereof afterward. This is excellently expressed by Austin, Confess. lib. ii. cap. 7: "Diligam te, Domine, et gratias agam, et confitear nomini tuo, quoniam tanta dimisisti mihi mala et nefaria opera mea. Gratiæ tuæ deputo et misericordia tuæ quod peccata mea tanquam glaciem solvisti, gratiæ tuæ deputo et quæcunque non feci mala; quid enim non facere potui qui etiam gratuitum facinus amavi? Et omnia mihi dimissa esse fateor, et quæ mea sponte feci mala, et quæ te duce non feci. Quis est hominum, qui suam cogitans infirmitatem, audet viribus suis tribuere castitatem atque innocentiam suam, ut minus amet te, quasi minus ei necessaria fuerit misericordia tua, quâ condonas peccata conversis ad te? Qui enim vocatus ad te secutus est vocem tuam et vitavit, et quæ me de meipso recordantem et fatentem legit, non me derideat ab eo medico ægrum sanari, a quo sibi prestitum est ut non ægrotaret, vel potius ut minus ægrotaret; et ideo te tantundem imo vero amplius diligat, quia per quem me videt tantis peccatorum meorum languoribus exui, per eum se videt tantis peccatorum languoribus non implicari;" — "I will love thee, O Lord, and thank thee, and confess unto thy name, because thou hast forgiven me my evil and nefarious deeds. I impute it to thy grace and mercy that thou hast made my sins to melt away as ice, and I impute it to thy grace as to all the evils which I have not done; for what could not I have done who loved wickedness for itself? All I acknowledge are forgiven me, both the evils that I have done of my own accord, and what through thy guidance I have not done. Who is there who, considering his own weakness, dare ascribe his chastity or innocency unto his own strength, that he may less love thee, as though thy mercy were less necessary unto him, whereby thou forgivest the sins of them that are converted to thee. For let not him who, being called of thee, and having heard thy voice, hath avoided the evils which I have confessed, deride me that, being sick, was healed of that physician from whom he received the mercy not to be sick, or not to be so sick; [and therefore let him love thee so much the more, as he sees himself prevented from having fallen into the great maladies of sin, through that God by whom he sees me delivered from the great maladies of the sin into which I had actually fallen.]"

This brief account of the actings of corrupted nature, until it comes unto the utmost of a recoverable alienation from God, may somewhat illustrate and set off the work of his grace towards us. And thus far, whatever habit be contracted in a course of sin, yet the state of men is absolutely recoverable by the grace of Jesus Christ administered in the gospel, 1 Cor. vi. 9–11. No state of sin is absolutely unhealable until God hath variously dealt with men by his Spirit. His word must be rejected, and he must be sinned against in a peculiar manner, before remission be impossible. All sins and blasphemies antecedent thereunto may be forgiven unto men, and that before their conversion unto God, Matt. xii. 31, 32; Luke xii.

10. Wherefore, the manner and degrees of the operations of this Spirit of God on the minds of men, towards and in their conversion, is that which we shall now inquire into, reducing what we have to offer concerning it unto certain heads or instances:—

First, Under the ashes of our collapsed nature there are yet remaining certain sparks of celestial fire, consisting in inbred notices of good and evil, of rewards and punishments, of the presence and all-seeing eye of God, of help and assistance to be had from him, with a dread of his excellencies where any thing is apprehended unworthy of him or provoking unto him; and where there are any means of instruction from supernatural revelation, by the word preached, or the care of parents in private, there they are insensibly improved and increased. Hereby men do obtain an objective, distinct knowledge of what they had subjectively and radically, though very imperfectly, before. These notices, therefore, God oftentimes excites and quickens even in them that are young, so that they shall work in them some real regard of and applications unto him. And those great workings about the things of God, and towards him, which are sometimes found in children, are not mere effects of nature; for that would not so act itself were it not, by one occasion or other, for that end administered by the providence of God, effectually excited. And many can call over such divine visitations in their youth, which now they understand to be so. To this purpose speaks the person mentioned: "Puer cœpi rogare te auxilium et refugium meum, et in tuam invocationem rumpebam nodos linguæ meæ, et rogabam te parvus non parvo affectu, ne in schola vapularem." He prayed earnestly to God as a refuge, when he was afraid to be beat at school. And this he resolves into instruction, or what he had observed in others: "Invenimus homines rogantes te, et didicimus ab eis, sentientes te ut poteramus esse magnum aliquem; qui posses etiam non adparens sensibus nostris, exaudire nos et subvenire nobis," lib. i. cap. 9. And hereunto he adds some general instruction which he had from the word, cap. 11. And from the same principles, when he was a little after surprised with a fit of sickness, he cried out with all earnestness that he might be baptized, that so he might, as he thought, go to heaven; for his father was not yet a Christian, whence he was not baptized in his infancy: "Vidisti, Domine, cum adhuc puer essem, et quodam die pressus stomachi dolore repente æstuarem pene moriturus; vidisti, Deus meus, quoniam custos meus jam eras, quo motu animi et qua fide baptismum Christi tui, Dei et Domini mei flagitavi," cap. 11. Such affections and occasional actings of soul towards God are wrought in many by the Spirit. With the most they wear off and perish, as they did with him, who after this cast himself into many flagitious sins. But in some God doth, in and by the use of these means, inlay their hearts with those seeds of faith and grace which he gradually cherisheth and increaseth.

Secondly, God works upon men by his Spirit in outward means, to cause them to take some real and steady consideration of him, their own distance from him, and obnoxiousness unto his righteousness on the account of sin. It is almost incredible to apprehend, but that it is testified unto by daily experience, how men will live even where the word is read and preached; how they will get a form of speaking of God, yea, and of performing some duties of religion, and yet never come to have any steady thoughts of God, or of their relation to him, or of their concernment in his will. Whatever they speak of God, "he is not in all their thoughts," Ps. x. 4. Whatever they do in religion, they do it not unto him, Amos v. 25. They have "neither heard his voice at any time, nor seen his shape," John v. 37; knowing nothing for themselves, which is their duty, Job v. 27. And yet it is hard to convince them that such is their condition. But when God is pleased to carry on his work of light and grace in them, they can call to mind and understand how it was with them in their former darkness. Then will they acknowledge that in truth they never had serious, steady thoughts of God, but only such as were occasional and transient. Wherefore God begins here with them. And thereby to subduct them from under the absolute power of the vanity of their minds, by one means or other he fixeth in them steady thoughts concerning himself, and their relation unto him. And there are several ways which he proceedeth in for the effecting hereof; as, —

1. By some sudden amazing judgments, whereby he "revealeth his wrath from heaven against the ungodliness of men," Rom. i. 18. So Waldo was affected when his companion was stricken dead as he walked with him in the fields; which proved the occasion of his conversion unto God. So the psalmist describes the affections and thoughts of men when they are surprised with a storm at sea, Ps. cvii. 25–28; an instance whereof we have in the mariners of Jonah's ship, chap. i. 4–7. And that Pharaoh who despised one day, saying, "Who is the Lord, that I should regard him?" being the next day terrified with thunder and lightning, cries out, "Entreat the Lord for me that it may be so no more," Exod. ix. 28. And such like impressions from divine power most men, at one time or other, have experience of.

2. By personal afflictions, Job xxxiii. 19, 20; Ps. lxxviii. 34, 35; Hos. v. 15. Affliction naturally bespeaks anger, and anger respects sin. It bespeaks itself to be God's messenger to call sin to remembrance, 1 Kings xvii. 18; Gen. xlii. 21, 22. The time of affliction is a time of consideration, Eccles. vii. 14; and if men be not obdurate and hardened almost unto practical atheism by a course of sinning, they cannot but bethink themselves who sends affliction, and for what end it is sent. Hence great thoughts of the holiness of God and of his hatred of sin, with some sense of men's own guilt and especial crimes, will arise; and these effects many times prove preparatory and materially dispositive unto conversion. And not what these things are in themselves able to operate is to be considered, but what they are designed unto and made effectual for by the Holy Ghost.

3. By remarkable deliverances and mercies: so it was with Naaman the Syrian, 2 Kings v. 15–17. Sudden changes from great dangers and distresses by unexpected reliefs deeply affect the minds of men, convincing them of the power, presence, and goodness of God; and this produceth a sense and acknowledgment of their own unworthiness of what they have received. Hence,

also, some temporary effects of submission to the divine will and gratitude do proceed.

4. An observation of the conversation of others hath affected many to seek into the causes and ends of it; and this inclines them unto imitation, 1 Pet. iii. 1, 2.

5. The word, in the reading or preaching of it, is the principal means hereof. This the Holy Spirit employeth and maketh use of in his entrance into this work, 1 Cor. xiv. 24, 25; for those convictions befall not men from the word universally or promiscuously, but as the Holy Spirit willeth and designeth. It is by the law that men have the knowledge of sin, Rom. vii. 7; yet we see by experience that the doctrine of the law is despised by the most that hear it. Wherefore, it hath not in itself a force or virtue always to work conviction of sin in them unto whom it is outwardly proposed; only towards some the Spirit of God is pleased to put forth an especial energy in the dispensation thereof.

By these and the like means doth God ofttimes put the wildness of corrupted nature unto a stand, and stir up the faculties of the soul, by an effectual though not saving impression upon them, seriously to consider of itself, and its relation unto him and his will. And hereby are men ofttimes incited and engaged unto many duties of religion, as prayer for the pardon of sin, with resolutions of amendment. And although these things in some are subordinated unto a farther and more effectual work of the Spirit of God upon them, yet with many they prove evanid and fading, their goodness in them being "as a morning cloud, and as the early dew which passeth away," Hos. vi. 4. And the reasons whence it is that men cast off these warnings of God, and pursue not their own intentions under them, nor answer what they lead unto, are obvious; for, —

(1.) The darkness of their minds being yet uncured, they are not able to discern the true nature of these divine intimations and instructions, but after awhile regard them not, or reject them as the occasions of needless scruples and fears. (2.) Presumption of their present condition, that it is as good as it need be, or as is convenient in their present circumstances and occasions, makes them neglect the improvement of their warnings. (3.) Profane societies and relations, such as, it may be, scoff at and deride all tremblings at divine warnings, with ignorant ministers, that undertake to teach what they have not learned, are great means of hardening men in their sins, and of forfeiting the benefit of these divine intimations. (4.) They will, as to all efficacy, and the motions they bring on the affections of men, decay and expire of themselves, if they are not diligently improved: wherefore in many they perish through mere sloth and negligence. (5.) Satan applies all his engines to the defeatment of these beginnings of any good in the souls of men. (6.) That which effectually and utterly overthrows this work, which causeth them to cast off these heavenly warnings, is mere love of lusts and pleasures, or the unconquered adherence of a corrupted heart unto sensual and sinful objects, that offer present satisfaction unto its carnal desires. By this means is this work of the Spirit of God in the hearts and minds of many utterly defeated, to the increase of their guilt, an addition to their natural hardness, and the ruin of their souls. But in some of them he is graciously pleased to renew his work, and by more effectual means to carry it on to perfection, as shall be afterward declared.

Now, there is scarce any of these instances of the care and watchfulness of God over the souls of men whom he designs either to convince or convert, for the ends of his own glory, but the holy person whom we have proposed as an example gives an account of them in and towards himself, declaring in like manner how, by the ways and means mentioned, they were frustrated, and came to nothing. Such were the warnings which he acknowledged that God gave him by the persuasions and exhortations of his mother, lib. 2. cap. 3; such were those which he had in sicknesses of his own, and in the death of his dear friend and companion, lib. 4. cap. 5–7. And in all the several warnings he had from God, he chargeth the want and guilt of their non-improvement on his natural blindness, his mind being not illuminated, and the corruption of his nature not yet cured, with the efficacy of evil society, and the course of the world in the places where he lived. But it would be tedious to transcribe the particular accounts that he gives of these things, though all of them singularly worthy of consideration: for I must say, that, in my judgment, there is none among the ancient or modem divines unto this day, who, either in the declarations of their own experiences, or their directions unto others, have equalled, much less him, in an accurate search and observation of all the secret actings of the Spirit of God on the minds and souls of men, both towards and in their recovery or conversion; and in order hereunto, scarce anyone not divinely inspired hath so traced the way of the serpent, or the effectual working of original sin in and on the hearts of men, with the efficacy communicated thereunto by various temptations and occasions of life in this world. The ways, also, whereby the deceitfulness of sin, in compliance with objective temptations, doth seek to elude and frustrate the work of God's grace, when it begins to attempt the strongholds of sin in the heart, were exceedingly discovered unto him. Neither hath any man more lively and expressly laid open the power of effectual and victorious grace, with the manner of its operation and prevalency. And all these things, by the guidance of the good Spirit of God and attendance unto the word, did he exemplify from his own experience in the whole work of God towards him; only it must be acknowledged that he declareth these things in such a way and manner, as also with such expressions, as many in our days would cry out on as fulsome and fanatical.

Thirdly, In the way of calling men unto the saving knowledge of God, the Holy Spirit convinceth them of sin, or he brings them under the power of a work of conviction.

It is not my design, nor here in my way, to handle the nature of the work of conviction, the means, causes, and effects of it. Besides, it hath been done at large by others. It is sufficient unto my purpose, — 1. To show the nature of it in general; 2. The causes of it; 3. The ways whereby men lose their convictions, and so become more and more hardened in sin; 4. How the Holy Spirit doth carry on the work in some unto complete conversion unto God:—

1. For the nature of it in general, it consists in a fixing the vain mind of a sinner upon a due consideration of sin, its nature, tendency, and end, with his own concernment therein, and a fixing of a due sense of sin upon the secure mind of the sinner, with suitable affections unto its apprehensions. The warnings, before insisted on, whereby God excites men to some steady notices of him and themselves, are like calls given unto a man in a profound sleep, whereat being startled he lifts up himself for a little space, but oppressed with the power of his deep slumber, quickly lays him down again, as Austin

expresseth it; but this work of conviction abides with men, and they are no way able speedily to disentangle themselves from it.

Now, the mind of man, which is the subject of this work of conviction, hath two things distinctly to be considered in it:— first, The understanding, which is the active, noetical, or contemplative power and faculty of it; second, The affections, wherein its passive and sensitive power doth consist. With respect hereunto there are two parts of the work of conviction:— (1.) The fixing of the mind, the rational, contemplative power of it, upon a due consideration of sin; (2.) The fixing of a due sense of sin on the practical, passive, sensible part of the mind, — that is, the conscience and affections, as was aid before:—

(1.) It is a great work, to fix the vain mind of an unregenerate sinner on a due consideration of sin, its nature and tendency. The darkness of their own mind and inexpressible vanity, — wherein I place the principal effect of our apostasy from God, — do disenable, hinder, and divert them from such apprehensions. Hence God so often complains of the foolishness of the people, that they would not consider, that they would not be wise to consider their latter end. We find by experience this folly and vanity in many unto an astonishment. No reasons, arguments, entreaties, by all that is naturally dear to them, no necessities, can prevail with them to fix their minds on a due consideration of sin. Moreover, Satan now employs all his engines to beat off the efficacy and power of this work; and when his temptations and delusions are mixed with men's natural darkness and vanity, the mind seems to be impregnably fortified against the power of conviction: for although it be [only] real conversion unto God that overthrows the kingdom of Satan in us, yet this work of conviction raiseth such a combustion in it that he cannot but fear it will be its end; and this strong man armed would, if possible, keep his goods and house in peace. Hence all sorts of persons have daily experience, in their children, servants, relations, how difficult, yea, how impossible, it is to fix their minds on a due consideration of sin, until it be wrought in them by the exceeding greatness of the power of the Spirit of God. Wherefore, herein consists the first part of this work of conviction, — it fixeth the mind on a due consideration of sin. So it is expressed, Ps. li. 3, "My sin is ever before me." God "reproves men," and "sets their sins in order before their eyes," Ps. l. 21. Hence they are necessitated, as it were, always to behold them, and that which way soever they turn themselves. Fain they would cast them behind their backs, or cast out the thoughts of them, but the arrows of God stick in them, and they cannot take off their minds from their consideration. And whereas there are three things in sin, — 1st. The original of it, and its native inherence in us, as Ps. li. 5, 2dly. The state of it, or the obnoxiousness of men to the wrath of God on the account thereof, Eph. ii. 1–3, 3dly. The particular sins of men's lives; — in the first part of the work of conviction, the minds of men are variously exercised with respect unto them, according as the Spirit of God is pleased to engage and fix them.

(2.) As the mind is hereby fixed on the consideration of sin, so a sense of sin must also be fixed on the mind, — that is, the conscience and affections. A bare contemplation of the concernments of sin is of little use in this matter. The Scripture principally evidenceth this work of conviction, or placeth it in this effect of a sense of sin, in trouble, sorrow, disquietment of mind, fear of ruin, and the like: see Acts ii. 37, xxiv. 25. But this I must not enlarge upon. This, therefore, is the second thing which we observe in God's gracious actings towards the recovery of the souls of men from their apostasy and from under the power of sin.

2. The principal efficient cause of this work is the Holy Ghost; the preaching of the word, especially of the law, being the instrument which he maketh use of therein. The knowledge of sin is by the law, both the nature, guilt, and curse belonging to it, Rom. vii. 7. There is, therefore, no conviction of sin but what consists in an emanation of light and knowledge from the doctrine of the law, with an evidence of its power and a sense of its curse. Other means, as afflictions, dangers, sicknesses, fears, disappointments, may be made use of to excite, stir up, and put an edge upon the minds and affections of men; yet it is, by one means or other, from the law of God that such a discovery is made of sin unto them, and such a sense of it wrought upon them, as belong unto this work of conviction. But it is the Spirit of God alone that is the principal efficient cause of it, for he works these effects on the minds of men. God takes it upon himself, as his own work, to "reprove men, and set their sins in order before their eyes," Ps. l. 21. And that this same work is done immediately by the Spirit is expressly declared, John xvi. 8. He alone it is who makes all means effectual unto this end and purpose. Without his especial and immediate actings on us to this end, we may hear the law preached all the days of our lives and not be once affected with it. And it may, by the way, be worth our observation to consider how God, designing the calling or conversion of the souls of men, doth, in his holy, wise providence, overrule all their outward concernments, so as that they shall be disposed into such circumstances as conduce to the end aimed at. Either by their own inclinations and choice, or by the intervention of accidents crossing their inclinations and frustrating their designs, he will lead them into such societies, acquaintances, relations, places, means, as he hath ordained to be useful unto them for the great ends of their conviction and conversion. So, in particular, Austin aboundeth in his contemplation on the holy, wise providence of God, in carrying of him from Carthage to Rome, and from thence to Milan, where he heard Ambrose preach every Lord's day; which proved at length the means of his thorough conversion to God. And in that whole course, by his discourse upon it, he discovers excellently, as, on the one hand, the variety of his own projects and designs, his aims and ends, which ofttimes were perverse and froward; so, on the other, the constant guidance of divine Providence, working powerfully through all occurrences towards the blessed end designed for him. And I no way doubt but that God exercised him unto those distinct experiences of sin and grace in his own heart and ways, because he had designed him to be the great champion of the doctrine of his grace against all its enemies, and that not only in his own age, wherein it met with a fierce opposition, but also in all succeeding ages, by his excellent labours, preserved for the use of the church: see Confess. lib. 5. cap. 7–9, etc. "Tu spes mea [et portio mea] in terra viventium, ad mutandum terrarum locum pro salute animæ mea, et Carthagini stimulos quibus inde avellerer admovebas, et Romæ illecebras quibus attraherer, proponebas mihi per homines, qui diligunt vitam mortuam, hinc insana facientes, inde vana pollicentes, et ad corrigendos gressus meos, utebaris occulte et illorum et mea perversitate," cap. 8; — "Thou who art my hope [and my portion] in the land of the living, that I might remove from one country to another, for the salvation of my soul, didst both apply goads unto me at Carthage, whereby I might be driven from thence, and proposedst allurements unto me at Rome, whereby I

might be drawn thither; and this thou didst by men: who love the dead life in sin, here doing things outrageous, there promising things desirable to vain minds, whilst thou, to correct and reform my ways, didst secretly make use of their frowardness and mine."

3. It must be granted that many on whom this work hath been wrought, producing great resolutions of amendment and much reformation of life, do lose all the power and efficacy of it, with all the impressions it had made on their affections. And some of these wax worse and more profligate in sinning than ever they were before; for having broken down the dam of their restraints, they pour out their lusts like a flood, and are more senseless than ever of those checks and fears with which before they were bridled and awed, 2 Pet. ii. 20–22. So the person lately mentioned declares, that after many convictions which he had digested and neglected, he was grown so obdurate and senseless, that falling into a fever, wherein he thought he should die and go immediately unto hell, he had not that endeavour afar deliverance and mercy which he had many years before on lesser dangers. And this perverse effect is variously brought about:—

(1.) It is with most an immediate product of the power of their own lust. Especially is it so with them who together with their convictions receive no gifts of the Holy Ghost; for, as we observed, their lusts being only checked and controlled, not subdued, they get new strength by their restraint, and rebel with success against conviction. Such as these fall away from what they have attained suddenly, Matt. xiii. 5, 21. One day they seem to lie in hell by the terror of their convictions, and the next to be hasting towards it by their sins and pollutions: see Luke xi. 24–26; Hos. vi. 4.

(2.) This apostasy is promoted and hastened by others; as, — [1.] Such as undertake to be spiritual guides and instructors of men in their way towards rest, who being unskilful in the word of righteousuess, do heal their wounds slightly, or turn them out of the way. Seducers also, it may be, interpose their crafty deceits, whereby they lie in wait to deceive, and so turn men off from those good ways of God whereinto they would otherwise enter. So it fell out with Austin, who, beginning somewhat to inquire after God, fell into the society and heresy of the Manichees, which frustrated all the convictions which by any means he had received. [2.] Such as directly, and that perhaps with importunity and violence, will endeavour to draw men back into the ways of the world and the pursuit of their lusts, Prov. i. 11–14. So the same person declares with what earnestness and restless importunities some of his companions endeavoured to draw him unto the spectacles and plays at Rome. And it is not easily imagined with what subtlety some persons will entice others into sinful courses, nor what violence they will use in their temptations, under a pretence of love and friendship. [3.] The awe that is put on the minds of men in their convictions, arising from a dread of the terror of the law, and the judgments of God threatened therein, is apt of itself to wear off when the soul is a little accustomed unto it, and yet sees no evil actually to ensue, Eccles. viii. 11; 2 Pet. iii. 4.

4. In some the Holy Spirit of God is pleased to carry on this work of conviction towards a farther blessed issue, and then two things ensue thereon in the minds of them who are so convinced:—

(1.) There will follow great and strange conflicts between their corruptions and their convictions. And this doth especially manifest itself in them who have been accustomed unto a course of sinning, or have any particular sin wherein they delight, and by which they have given satisfaction unto their lusts; for the law, coming with power and terror on the conscience, requires a relinquishment of all sins, at the eternal peril of the soul. Sin hereby is incited and provoked,[59] and the soul begins to see its disability to conflict with that which before it thought absolutely in its own power: for men that indulge themselves in their sins doubt not but that they can leave them at their pleasure; but when they begin to make head against them on the command of the law, they find themselves to be in the power of that which they imagined to be in theirs. So doth sin take occasion by the commandment to work in men all manner of concupiscence; and those who thought themselves before to be alive do find that it is sin which lives, and that themselves are dead, Rom. vii. 7–9. Sin rising up in rebellion against the law, discovers its own power, and the utter impotency of them in whom it is to contest with it or destroy it. But yet men's convictions in this condition will discover themselves, and operate two ways, or in a twofold degree:—

[1.] They will produce some endeavours and promises of amendment and reformation of life. These men are unavoidably cast upon or wrought unto, to pacify the voice of the law in their consciences, which bids them do so or perish. But such endeavours or promises, for the most part, hold only unto the next occasion of sinning or temptation. An access of the least outward advantage or provocation unto the internal power of sin slights all such resolutions, and the soul gives up itself unto the power of its old ruler. Such effects of the word are described, Hos. vi. 4. So Austin expresseth his own experience after his great convictions and before his full conversion, lib. 8. cap. 5: "Suspirabam ligatus non ferro alieno, sed mea ferrea voluntate. Velle meum tenebat inimicus, et inde mihi catenam fecerat et constrinxerat me. Quippe ex voluntate perversa facta est libido, et dum servitur libidini, facta est consuetudo; et dum consuetudini non resistitur, facta est necessitas. Quibus quasi ansulis sibimet innexis, unde catenam appellavi, tenebat me obstrictum dura servitus." And he shows how faint and languid his endeavours were for reformation and amendment: "Sarcinâ sæculi, velut somno adsolet, dulciter premebar, et cogitationes quibus meditabar in te, similes erant conatibus expergisci volentium, qui tamen superati soporis altitudine remerguntur." And he confesseth that although, through the urgency of his convictions, he could not but pray that he might be freed from the power of sin, yet, through the prevalency of that power in him, he had a secret reserve and desire not to part with that sin which he prayed against, cap 7: "Petieram a te castitatem et dixeram, Da mihi castitatem et continentiam, sed noli modo. Timebam enim ne me cito exaudires, et cito sanares a morbo concupiscentiæ, quam malebam expleri quam extingui."

[2.] These endeavours do arise unto great perplexities and distresses; for after awhile, the soul of a sinner is torn and divided between the power of corruption and the terror of conviction.[60] And this falls out upon a double account:— 1st. Upon some occasional sharpening of former convictions, when the sense of them has been ready to wear off. 2dly. From the secret insinuation of a principle of spiritual life and strength into the will, whose nature and power the soul is as yet unacquainted withal. Of both these we have signal instances in the person before mentioned; for after all the means which God had used towards him for his conversion, whilst yet he was detained under the power of sin, and ready on every temptation to revert to his former courses, he occasionally heard one Pontitianus giving an account of the conversion of two eminent courtiers, who immediately renounced the world, and betook themselves wholly to the service of God. This discourse God was pleased to make use of farther to awake him, and even to amaze him. Lib. viii. cap. 7: "Narrabat hoc Pontitianus; tu autem, Domine, inter verba ejus retorquebas me ad meipsum, auferens me a dorso meo ubi me posueram, dum nollem me attendere, et constituebas me ante faciem meam, ut viderem quam turpis essem, quam distortus et sordidus, maculosus et ulcerosus: et videbam et horrebam, et quo a me fugerem non erat. Et si conabar a me avertere aspectum narrabat ille quod narrabat, et tu me rursus opponebas mihi, et impingebas me in oculos meos, ut invenirem iniquitatem meam et odissem." And a little after, "Ita rodebar intus et confundebar pudore horribili vehementer, cum Pontitianus talia loqueretur." The substance of what he says is, that in and by that discourse of Pontitianus, God held him to the consideration of himself, caused him to see and behold his own filth and vileness, until he was horribly perplexed and confounded in himself. So it often falls out in this work of the Spirit of God. When his first warnings are not complied withal, when the light he communicates is not improved, upon the return of them they shall be mixed with some sense of severity.

This effect, I say, proceeds from hence, that under this work God is pleased secretly to communicate a principle of grace or spiritual life unto the will. This, therefore, being designed to rule and bear sway in the soul, begins its conflict effectually to eject sin out of its throne and dominion; for whereas, when we come under the power of grace, sin can no longer have dominion over us, Rom. vi. 14; so the Spirit begins now to "lust against the flesh," as Gal. v. 17, aiming at and intending a complete victory or conquest. There was, upon bare conviction, a contest before in the soul, but it was merely between the mind and conscience on the one hand, and the will on the other. The will was still absolutely bent on sin, only some head was made against its inclinations by the light of the mind before sin, and rebukes of conscience after it; but the conflict begins now to be in the will itself. A new principle of grace being infused thereinto, opposeth those habitual inclinations unto evil which were before predominant in it. This fills the mind with amazement, and in some brings them to the very door of despair, because they see not how nor when they shall be delivered. So was it with the person instanced in. Lib. viii. cap. 5: "Voluntas nova quæ mihi esse cœperat, ut te gratis colerem fruique te vellem, Deus, sola certa jucunditas, nondum erat idonea ad superandam priorem vetustate roboratam. Ita duæ voluntates meæ, una vetus, alia nova, illa carnalis, illa spiritualis, confligebant inter se, atque discordando dissipabant animam meam. Sic intelligebam in me ipso experimento id quod legeram, quomodo 'caro concupisceret adversus Spiritum, et Spiritus adversus carnem.' Ego quidem in utroque, sed magis ego in eo quod in me approbabam quam in eo quod in me improbabam. Ibi enim magis jam non ego, quia ex magna parte id patiebar invitus, quod faciebam volens;" — "The new will which began to be in me, whereby I would love thee, O my God, the only certain sweetness, was not yet able to overcome my former will, confirmed by long continuance. So my two wills, the one old, the other new, the one carnal, the other spiritual, conflicted between themselves, and rent my soul by their disagreement. Then did I understand by experience in myself what I had read, how 'the flesh lusteth against the Spirit, and the Spirit against the flesh.' I was myself on both sides, but more in that which I approved in myself than in what I condemned in myself. I was not more in that which I condemned, because for the most part I suffered it unwillingly, rather than did it willingly." This conflict between grace and sin in the will he most excellently expresseth, cap. 9–11, delivering those things which more or less are evident in the experience of those who have passed through this work. His fluctuations, his promises, his hopes and fears, the ground he got and lost, the pangs of conscience and travail of soul which he underwent in the new birth, are all of them graphically represented by him.

In this tumult and distress of the soul, God oftentimes quiets it by some suitable word of truth, administered unto it either in the preaching of the gospel, or by some other means disposed in his providence unto the same end. In the midst of this storm and disorder, he comes and says, "Peace, be still;" for, together with his word, he communicates some influence of his grace that shall break the rebellious strength, and subdue the power of sin, and give the mind satisfaction in a full resolution for its everlasting relinquishment. So was it with him mentioned. When in the condition described, he was hurried up and down almost like a distracted person, whilst he suffered the terrors of the Lord, sometimes praying, sometimes weeping, sometimes alone, sometimes in the company of his friends, sometimes walking, and sometimes lying on the ground, he was, by an unusual occurrence, warned to take up a book and read. The book next him was that of Paul's Epistle, which taking up and opening, the place he first fixed his eyes upon was Rom. xiii. 13, 14, "Let us walk honestly, as in the day; not in rioting and drunkenness, not in chambering and wantonness, not in strife and envying. But put ye on the Lord Jesus Christ, and make not provision for the flesh, to fulfil the lusts thereof." Immediately on the reading of these words, there was an end put unto his perplexing conflict. He found his whole soul, by the power of almighty grace, subdued wholly to the will of God, and fixed unto a prevalent resolution of adhering to him with a relinquishment of sin, with an assured composure upon the account of the success he should have therein through Jesus Christ. Immediately he declared what he had done, what had befallen him, first to his friend, then to his mother; which proved the occasion of conversion to the one and inexpressible joy to the other. The end of the story deserves to be reported in his own words: "Arripui librum, aperui, et legi … Nec ultra volui legere, nec opus erat; statim quippe cum fine hujusce sententiæ, quasi luce securitatis infusâ cordi meo, omnes dubitationis tenebræ diffugerunt. Tum interjecto aut digito aut nescio quo alio signo, codicem clausi, et tranquillo jam vultu indicavi Alypio. At ille quid in se ageretur, quod ego nesciebam, sic indicavit: petit videre quid legissem. Ostendi, et attendit etiam ultra quam ego legeram, et ignorabam quid sequeretur. Sequebatur vero, 'Infirmum autem in fide recipite,' quod ille ad se retulit, mihique aperuit. Sed tali admonitione firmatus est, placitoque ac proposito bono, et congruentissimo suis moribus, quibus a me in melius jam olim valde longeque distabat, sine ulla turbulenta cunctatione conjunctus est. Inde ad matrem ingredimur. Indicamus, gaudet. Narramus quemadmodum gestum sit; exultat et triumphat, et benedicit tibi, qui potens es ultra quam petimus aut intelligimus facere," lib. viii. cap. 12; — "Having read these verses, I would read no more, nor was there any need that so I should do; for upon the end of that sentence, as if a light of peace or security had been infused into my heart, all darkness of doubts fled away. Marking the book with my finger put into it, or by some other sign, I shut it, and with a quiet countenance declared what was done to Alypius; and hereupon he also declared what was at work in himself, whereof I was ignorant. He desired to see what I had read; which when I had showed him, he looked farther than I had read, nor did I know what followed. But it was this, 'Him that is weak in the faith receive;' which he applied unto himself, and declared it unto me. Confirmed by this admonition, with a firm purpose, and suitable to his manners, wherein he formerly much excelled me, he was joined to me without any turbulent delay. We go in hereon unto my mother, and declare what was done; she rejoiceth. We make known the manner of it how it was done; she exulteth and triumpheth, and blesseth thee, O God, who art able to do for us more than we know how to ask or understand." And these things doth the holy man express to bear witness, as he says, "adversus typhum humani generis," — to "repress the swelling pride of mankind." And in the example of Alypius we have an instance how variously God is pleased to effect this work in men, carrying some through strong convictions, deep humiliations, great distresses, and perplexing terrors of mind, before they come to peace and rest; leading others gently and quietly, without any visible disturbances, unto the saving knowledge of himself by Jesus Christ.

(2.) A second thing which befalls men under this work of conviction, is a dread and fear as to their eternal condition. There doth befall them an apprehension of that wrath which is due to their sins, and threatened in the curse of the law to be inflicted on them. This fills them with afflictive perturbations of mind, with dread and terror, consternation and humbling of their souls thereon. And what befalls the minds of men on this account is handled by some distinctly, under the names or titles of "dolor legalis," "timor servilis," "attritio mentis," "compunctio cordis," "humiliatio animæ," — "legal sorrow," "servile fear," "attrition of mind," "compunction," and "humiliation," and the like. And as these things have been handled most of them by modern divines, and cast into a certain series and dependence on one another, with a discovery of their nature and degrees, and how far they are required in order unto sincere conversion and sound believing; so they are all of them treated on, in their way, by the schoolmen, as also they were before them by many of the fathers. The charge, therefore, of novelty, which is laid by some against the doctrine of these things, ariseth from a fulsome mixture of ignorance and confidence. Whether, therefore, all things that are delivered concerning these things be right or no, sure enough I am that the whole doctrine about them, for the substance of it, is no newer than the gospel, and that it hath been taught in all ages of the church. What is needful to be received concerning it I shall reduce to the ensuing heads:—

[1.] Conviction of sin being ordinarily by the law, either immediately or by light and truth thence derived, there doth ordinarily accompany it a deep sense and apprehension of the eternal danger which the soul is liable unto on the account of the guilt of the sin whereof it is convinced; for the law comes with its whole power upon the mind and conscience. Men may be partial in the law; the law will not be partial. It doth not only convince by its light, but also at the same time condemns by its authority; for what the law speaks, "it speaks unto them that are under the law." It takes men under its power, then, shutting them under sin, it speaks unto them in great severity. This is called the coming of the commandment, and slaying of a sinner, Rom. vii. 9.

[2.] This apprehension will ordinarily ingenerate disquieting and perplexing affections in the minds of men; nor can it be otherwise where it is fixed and prevalent; as, — 1st. Sorrow and shame for and of what they have done. Shame was the first thing wherein conviction of sin discovered itself, Gen. iii. 7. And sorrow always accompanieth it. Acts ii. 37, hearing these things, κατενύγησαν τῇ καρδίᾳ, — "they were pierced with perplexing grief in their heart." Their eyes are opened to see the guilt and sense of sin, which pierceth them through with dividing sorrow. 2dly. Fear of eternal wrath. This keeps the soul in bondage, Heb. ii. 15, and is accompanied with torment. The person so convinced believes the threatening of the law to be true, and trembles at it; an eminent instance whereof we have in our first parents also, Gen. iii. 8, 10. 3dly. Perplexing unsatisfactory inquiries after means and ways for deliverance out of this present distress and from future misery. "What shall we do? what shall we do to be saved?" is the restless inquiry of such persons, Mic. vi. 6, 7; Acts ii. 37, xvi. 30.

[3.] These things will assuredly put the soul on many duties, as prayer for deliverance, abstinence from sin, endeavours after a general change of life; in all which, and the like, this conviction puts forth and variously exerciseth its power.

[4.] We do not ascribe the effects intended unto the mere working of the passions of the minds of men upon the rational consideration of their state and condition; which yet cannot but be grievous and afflictive. These things may be so proposed unto men and pressed on them as that they shall not be able to avoid their consideration, and the conclusions which naturally follow on them; and yet they may not be in the least affected with them, as we see by experience. Wherefore we say, moreover, that the law or the doctrine of it, when the consciences of men are effectually brought under its power, is accompanied with a secret virtue from God, called a "spirit of bondage;" which causeth a sense of the curse of it to take a deep impression on the soul, to fill it with fear and dread, yea, sometimes with horror and despair. This the apostle calls the "spirit of bondage unto fear," Rom. viii. 15, and declares at large how all that are under the law, — that is, the convincing and condemning power of it, — are in bondage; nor doth the law in the administration of it lead or gender unto any thing else but bondage, Gal. iv. 22–24.

[5.] The substance of these things is ordinarily found in those who are converted unto God when grown up unto the use of reason, and capable of impressions from external administrations. Especially are they evident in the minds and consciences of such as have been engaged in any open sinful course or practice. But yet no certain rule or measure of them can be prescribed as necessary in or unto any antecedaneously unto conversion. To evince the truth hereof two things may be observed:— 1st. That perturbations, sorrows, dejections, dread, fears, are no duty unto any; only they are such things as sometimes ensue or are immitted into the mind upon that which is a duty indispensable, namely, conviction of sin. They belong not to the precept of the law, but to its curse. They are no part of what is required of us, but of what is inflicted on us. There is a gospel sorrow and humiliation after believing that is a duty, that is both commanded and hath promises annexed unto it; but this legal sorrow is an effect of the curse of the law, and not of its command. 2dly. God is pleased to exercise a prerogative and sovereignty in this whole matter, and deals with the souls of men in unspeakable variety. Some he leads by the gates of death and hell unto rest in his love, like the people of old through the waste and howling wilderness into Canaan; and the paths of others he makes plain and easy unto them. Some walk or wander long in darkness; in the souls of others Christ is formed in the first gracious visitation.

[6.] There is, as was said, no certain measure or degree of these accidents or consequents of conviction to be prescribed unto any as antecedaneously necessary to sincere conversion and sound believing; but these two things in general are so:— 1st. Such a conviction of sin, — that is, of a state of sin, of a course of sin, of actual sins, against the light of natural conscience, — as that the soul is satisfied that it is thereby obnoxious unto the curse of the law and the wrath of God. Thus, at least, doth God conclude and shut up everyone under sin on whom he will have mercy; for "every mouth must be stopped, and all the world become guilty before God," Rom. iii. 19; Gal. iii. 22. Without this no man ever did, nor ever will, sincerely believe in Jesus Christ; for he calleth none unto him but those who in some measure are weary or thirsty, or one way or other seek after deliverance. "The whole," he tells us, — that is, those who so conceit themselves, — "have no need of a physician;" they will neither inquire after him nor care to go unto him when they are invited so to do. See Isa. xxxii. 2. 2dly. A due apprehension and resolved judgment that there is no way within the compass of a man's own contrivance to find out, or his ability to make use of and to walk in, nor any other way of God's appointment or approbation, which will deliver the soul in and from the state and condition wherein it is and that which it fears, but only that which is proposed in the gospel by Jesus Christ.

[7.] Where these things are, the duty of a person so convinced is, — 1st, To inquire after and to receive the revelation of Jesus Christ, and the righteousness of God in him, John i. 12. And in order hereunto, he ought, — (1st.) To own the sentence of the law under which he suffereth, justifying God in his righteousness and the law in its holiness, whatever be the issue of this dispensation towards himself, Rom. iii. 19, 20, vii. 12, 13; for God in this work intends to break the stubbornness of men's hearts, and to hide pride from them, chap. iii. 4. (2dly.) Not hastily to believe everything that will propose itself unto him as a remedy or means of relief, Mic. vi. 6, 7. The things which will present themselves in such a case as means of relief are of two sorts:— [1st.] Such as the fears and superstitions of men have suggested or will suggest. That which hath raised all the false religion which is in the world is nothing but a contrivance for the satisfaction of men's consciences under convictions. To pass by Gentilism, this is the very life and soul of Popery. What is the meaning of the sacrifice of the mass, of purgatory, of pardons, penances, indulgences, abstinences, and the like things innumerable, but only to satisfy conscience by them, perplexed with a sense of sin? Hence many among them, after great and outrageous wickednesses, do betake themselves to their highest monastical severity. The life and soul of superstition consists in endeavours to quiet and charm the consciences of men convinced of sin. [2dly.] That which is pressed with most vehemency and plausibility, being suggested by the law itself, in a way of escape from the danger of its sentence, as the sense of what it speaks, represented in a natural conscience, is legal righteousness, to be sought after in amendment of life. This proposeth itself unto the soul, as with great importunity, so with great advantages, to further its acceptance; for, — First, The matter of it is unquestionably necessary, and without it in its proper place, and with respect unto its proper end, there is no sincere conversion unto God. Secondly, It is looked on as the sense of the law, or as that which will give satisfaction thereunto. But there is a deceit in all these things as to the end proposed, and if any amendment of life be leaned on to that purpose, it will prove a broken reed, and pierce the hand of him that rests upon it; for although the law require at all times an abstinence from sin, and so for the future, which in a sinner is amendment of life, yet it proposeth it not as that which will deliver any soul from the guilt of sin already contracted, which is the state under consideration. And if it win upon the mind to accept of its terms unto that end or purpose, it can do no more, nor will do less, than shut up the person under its curse. 2dly. It is the duty of persons in such a condition to beware of entangling temptations; as, — (1st.) That they have not attained such a degree of sorrow for sin and humiliation as is necessary unto them that are called to believe in Jesus Christ. There was, indeed, more reason of giving caution against temptations of this kind in former days, when preachers of the gospel dealt more severely, — I wish I may not also say more sincerely, — with the consciences of convinced sinners, than it is the manner of most now to do. But it is yet possible that herein may lie a mistake, seeing no such degrees of these things as some may be troubled about are prescribed for any such end either in the law or gospel. (2dly.) That those who persuade them to believe know not how great sinners they are. But yet they know that Christ called the greatest; and it is an undervaluation of the grace of Christ to suppose that the greatest sins should disappoint the effects of it in any that sincerely come unto him.

Fourthly, The last thing, whereby this work of conversion to God is completed, as to the outward means of it, which is the ingenerating and acting of faith in God by Jesus Christ, remains alone to be considered, wherein all possible brevity and plainness shall be consulted; and I shall comprise what I have to offer on this head in the ensuing observations:—

1. This is the proper and peculiar work of the gospel, and ever was so from the first giving of the promise. "The law was given by Moses, but grace and truth came by Jesus Christ," John i. 17; Rom. i. 16; 1 Pet. i. 23; James i. 18; Eph. iii. 8–10.

2. To this purpose it is necessary that the gospel, — that is, the doctrine of it concerning redemption, righteousness, and salvation, by Jesus Christ, — be declared and made known to convinced sinners. And this also is an effect of sovereign wisdom and grace, Rom. x. 13–15.

3. The declaration of the gospel is accompanied with a revelation of the will of God with respect unto the faith and obedience of them unto whom it is declared. "This is the work of God," the work which he requires at our hands, "that we believe on him whom he hath sent," John vi. 29. And this command of God unto sinners, to believe in the Lord Jesus Christ for life and salvation, the gospel teacheth us to press from the manifold aggravations which attend the sin of not complying therewith: for it is, as therein declared, — (1.) A rejection of the testimony of God, which he gives unto his wisdom, love, and grace, with the excellency and certainty of the way of salvation of sinners by Jesus Christ; which is to make God a liar,1 John v. 10; John iii. 33. (2.) A contempt of love and grace, with the way and means of their communication to lost sinners by

the blood of the Son of God; which is the highest provocation that can be offered unto the divine Majesty.

4. In the declaration of the gospel, the Lord Christ is in an especial manner proposed as crucified and lifted up for the especial object of our faith, John iii. 14, 15; Gal. iii. 1. And this proposition of Christ hath included in it an invitation unto all convinced sinners to come unto him for life and salvation, Isa. lv. 1–3, lxv. 1.

5. The Lord Christ being proposed unto sinners in the gospel, and their acceptance or receiving of him being urged on them, it is withal declared for what end he is so proposed; and this is, in general, to "save them from their sins," Matt. i. 21, or "the wrath to come," whereof they are afraid, 1 Thess. i. 10: for in the evangelical proposition of him there is included, — (1.) That there is a way yet remaining for sinners whereby they may escape the curse of the law and the wrath of God, which they have deserved, Ps. cxxx. 4; Job xxxiii. 24; Acts iv. 12. (2.) That the foundation of these ways lies in an atonement made by Jesus Christ unto the justice of God, and satisfaction to his law for sin, Rom. iii. 25; 2 Cor. v. 21; Gal. iii. 13. (3.) That God is well pleased with this atonement, and his will is that we should accept of it and acquiesce in it, 2 Cor. v. 18–20; Isa. liii. 11, 12; Rom. v. 10, 11.

6. It is proposed, and promised that through and upon their believing, — that is, on Christ as proposed in the gospel, for the only way of redemption and salvation, — convinced sinners shall be pardoned, justified, and acquitted before God, discharged of the law against them, through the imputation unto them of what the Lord Christ hath done for them and suffered in their stead, Rom. viii. 1, 3, 4, x. 3, 4; 1 Cor. i. 30, 31; 2 Cor. v. 21; Eph. ii. 8–10.

7. To prevail with and win over the souls of men unto a consent to receive Christ on the terms wherein he is proposed, — that is, to believe in him and trust unto him, to what he is, hath done and suffered, and continueth to do, for pardon of sin, life, and salvation, — the gospel is filled with arguments, invitations, encouragements, exhortations, promises, all of them designed to explain and declare the love, grace, faithfulness, and good-will of God herein. In the due management and improvement of these parts of the gospel consists the principal wisdom and skill of the ministers of the New Testament.

8. Among these various ways or means of the declaration of himself and his will, God frequently causeth some especial word, promise, or passage to fix itself on the mind of a sinner; as we saw it in the instance before insisted on. Hereby the soul is first excited to exert and act the faith wherewith it is endued by the effectual working of the Spirit of God before described; and by this means are men directed unto rest, peace, and consolation, in that variety of degrees wherein God is pleased to communicate them.

9. This acting of faith on Christ, through the promise of the gospel, for pardon, righteousness, and salvation, is inseparably accompanied with, and that faith is the root and infallible cause of, a universal engagement of heart unto all holy obedience to God in Christ, with a relinquishment of all known sin, necessarily producing a thorough change and reformation of life and fruitfulness in obedience: for as, upon a discovery of the love of God in Christ, the promises whereby it is exhibited unto us being mixed with faith, the soul of a poor sinner will be filled with godly sorrow and shame for its former sins, and will be deeply humbled for them; so all the faculties of it being now renewed and inwardly changed, it can no more refrain from the love of holiness and

from an engagement into a watchful course of universal obedience unto God, by such free actings as are proper unto it, than one that is newborn can refrain from all acts of life natural, in motion, desire of food, and the like. Vain and foolish, therefore, are the reproaches of some, who, in a high course of a worldly life and profane, do charge others with preaching a justification by faith alone in Christ Jesus, unto a neglect of holiness, righteousness, and obedience to God, which such scoffers and fierce despisers of all that are good do so earnestly plead for. Those whom they openly reflect upon do unanimously teach that the faith which doth not purify the heart and reform the life, which is not fruitful in good works, which is not an effectual cause and means of repentance and newness of life, is not genuine nor pleadable unto justification, but empty, dead, and that which, if trusted unto, will eternally deceive the souls of men. They do all of them press the indispensable necessity of universal holiness, godliness, righteousness, or obedience to all the commands of God, on surer principles, with more cogent arguments, in a more clear compliance with the will, grace, and love of God in Christ, than any they pretend unto who ignorantly and falsely traduce them as those who regard them not. And as they urge an obediential holiness which is not defective in any duty, either towards God or man, which they either plead for or pretend unto, so it contains that in it which is more sublime, spiritual, and heavenly than what they are either acquainted with or do regard; which in its proper place shall be made more fully to appear.

10. Those who were thus converted unto God in the primitive times of the church were, upon their confession or profession hereof, admitted into church-society and to a participation of all the mysteries thereof. And this being the common way whereby any were added unto the fellowship of the faithful, it was an effectual means of intense love without dissimulation among them all, on the account of their joint interest in the grace of our Lord Jesus Christ. And I shall shut up this discourse with one instance hereof, given us by Austin, in the conversion and admission into church-society of Victorinus, a Platonical philosopher, as he received the story from Simplicianus, by whom he was baptized: "Ut ventum est ad horam profitendæ fidei quæ verbis certis conceptis retentisque memoriter, de loco eminentiore, in conspectu populi fidelis, Romæ reddi solet ab eis qui accessuri sunt ad gratiam tuam, oblatum esse dicebat Victorino a presbyteris, ut secretius redderet, sicut nonnullis qui verecundia trepidaturi videbantur, offerri mos erat; illum autem maluisse salutem suam in conspectu sanctæ multitudinis profiteri. Non enim erat salus, quam docebat in rhetorica, et tamen eam publice professus erat. Quanto minus ergo vereri debuit mansuetum gregem tuum pronuncians verbum tuum, qui non verebatur in verbis suis turbas insanorum! Itaque ubi ascendit ut redderet, omnes sibimet invicem quisque ut eum noverant, instrepuerunt nomen ejus strepitu gratulationis, (quis autem ibi eum non noverat?) et sonuit presso sonitu per ora cunctorum collætantium, Victorinus, Victorinus. Cito sonuerunt exultatione quia videbant eum, et cito siluerunt intentione ut audirent eum. Pronunciavit ille fidem veracem præclara fiducia, et volebant eum omnes rapere intro in cor suum; et rapiebant amando et gaudendo. Hæ rapientium manus erant," lib. 8. cap. 2. Not a few things concerning the order, discipline, and fervent love of the primitive Christians in their church-societies are intimated and represented in these words, which I shall not here reflect upon.

And this is the second great work of the Spirit of God in the new creation. This is a summary description of his forming and creating the members of that mystical body, whose head is Christ Jesus. The latter part of our discourse, concerning the external manner of regeneration or conversion unto God, with the gradual preparation for it and accomplishment of it in the souls of men, is that subject which many practical divines of this nation have in their preaching and writings much insisted on and improved, to the great profit and edification of the church of God. But this whole doctrine, with all the declarations and applications of it, is now, by some among ourselves, derided and exposed to scorn, although it be known to have been the constant doctrine of the most learned prelates of the church of England. And as the doctrine is exploded, so all experience of the work itself in the souls of men is decried as fanatical and enthusiastical.

To obviate the pride and wantonness of this filthy spirit, I have, in the summary representation of the work itself now given, confirmed the several instances of it with the experience of the great and holy man so often named; for whereas some of those by whom this doctrine and work are despised are puffed up with a conceit of their excellency in the theatrical, sceptical faculty of these days, unto a contempt of all by whom they are contradicted in the most importune of their dictates, yet if they should swell themselves until they break, like the frog in the fable, they would never prevail with their fondest admirers to admit them into a competition with the immortal wit, grace, and learning of that eminent champion of the truth and light of the age wherein he lived.

Footnotes:

58. After a youth spent in vicious excess, Augustine was converted to the faith of the gospel, and admitted into the church by Ambrose at Milan, a. d. 387. Ten years afterwards he wrote his "Confessions," in thirteen books; of which ten are occupied with a detail of his sinful conduct in early life, the circumstances of his conversion, and his personal history up to the period of his mother's death, while the remaining three are devoted to an exposition of the Mosaic account of creation. The work is altogether of an unique and extraordinary character, — a direct address to the Deity, sustained with considerable skill and occasionally in strains of animated devotion, abounding in the most humble confession of the sins of the author's youth, and marked everywhere with the vigour of genius. As a faithful and minute record of the internal workings of his heart, these "Confessions" of Augustine are of great service in illustrating the nature of the spiritual change implied in conversion. It is on this account Owen draws from them so largely in this chapter. Milner, for similar purposes, has embodied the substance of them in his "History of the Church."The quotations made by Owen have been compared with Bruder's edition of the "Confessions" (1837). In some instances these quotations are translated by Owen, but wherever a formal translation is not supplied, the reader may understand that the substance of what is quoted is given immediately afterwards in our author's own words. — Ed.

59. "Libera me, Domine, ab his hostibus meis, a quibus me liberare non valeo. Perversum et pessimum est cor meum, ad deploranda propria peccata mea est lapideum et aridum, ad resistendum insultantibus molle et luteum, ad inutilia et noxia pertractanda velox et infatigabile, ad cogitanda salubria fastidiosum et immobile. Anima mea distorta et depravata est ad percipiendum bonum; sed ad voluptatum vitia nimis facilis et prompta, ad salutem reminiscendam nimis etiam difficilis et pigra." — Lib. de Contritione Cordis, inter opera August. cap. iv.

60. "Vere abyssus peccata mea sunt, quia incomprehensibilia profunditate, et inestimabilia sunt numero et immensitate. O abyssus abyssum invocans! O peccata mea, tormenta quibus me servatis abyssus sunt, quia infinita et incomprehensibilia sunt. Est et tertia abyssus, et est nimis terribilis; judicia Dei abyssus multa, quia super omnem sensum occulta. Hæ omnes abyssi terribiles sunt mihi undique, quia timor super timorem et dolor super dolorem.

Abyssus judiciorum Dei super me, abyssus inferni subtus me, abyssus peccatorum meorum est intra me. Illam quæ super me est timeo ne in me irruat; et me cum abysso mea, in illam quæ subtus me latet, obruat." — Lib. de Contritione Cordis, inter opera August. cap. ix.

Book IV

Chapter I - The nature of sanctification and gospel holiness explained

Regeneration the way whereby the Spirit forms living members for the mystical body of Christ — Carried on by sanctification — 1 Thess. v. 23 opened — God the only author of our sanctification and holiness, and that as the God of peace — Sanctification described — A diligent inquiry into the nature whereof, with that of holiness, proved necessary — Sanctification twofold: 1. By external dedication; 2. By internal purification — Holiness peculiar to the gospel and its truth — Not discernible to the eye of carnal reason — Hardly understood by believers themselves — It passeth over into eternity — Hath in it a present glory — Is all that God requireth of us, and in what sense — Promised unto us — How we are to improve the command for holiness.

In the regeneration or conversion of God's elect, the nature and manner whereof we have before described, consists the second part of the work of the Holy Spirit, in order unto the completing and perfecting of the new creation. As in the former he prepared a natural body for the Son of God, wherein he was to obey and suffer according to his will, so by this latter he prepares him a mystical body, or members spiritually living, by uniting them unto him who is their head and their life, Col. iii. 4. "For as the body is one, and hath many members, and all the members of that one body, being many, are one body, so also is Christ," 1 Cor. xii. 12. Nor doth he leave this work in that beginning of it whereof we have treated, but unto him also it belongs to continue it, to preserve it, and to carry it on to perfection; and this he doth in our sanctification, whose nature and effects we are in the next place to inquire into.

Our apostle, in his First Epistle to the Thessalonians, chap. v., having closely compiled a great number of weighty, particular, evangelical duties, and annexed sundry motives and enforcements unto them, closeth all his holy prescriptions with a fervent prayer for them: Verse 23, "And the very God of peace sanctify you wholly; and let your whole spirit and soul and body be preserved blameless unto the coming of our Lord Jesus Christ;" — or, as I had rather read the words, "And God himself, even the God of peace, sanctify you throughout, that your whole spirit and soul and body may be preserved blameless." The reason hereof is, because all the graces and duties which he had enjoined them did belong unto their sanctification, which, though their own duty, was not absolutely in their own power, but was a work of God in them and upon them. Therefore, that they might be able thereunto, and might actually comply with his commands, he prays that God would thus sanctify them throughout. That this shall be accomplished in them and for them, he gives them assurance from the faithfulness (and consequently power and unchangeableness, which are included therein) of him who had undertaken to effect it: Verse 24, "Faithful is he that calleth you, who also will do it." Now, whereas this assurance did not arise nor was taken from any thing that was peculiar unto them, but merely from the consideration of the faithfulness of God himself, it is equal with respect unto all that are effectually called. They shall all infallibly be sanctified throughout, and preserved blameless to the coming of Jesus Christ. This, therefore, being the great privilege of believers, and their eternal safety absolutely depending thereon, it requires our utmost diligence to search into the nature and necessity of it; which may be done from this and the like places of Scripture.

And in this place, — 1. The author of our sanctification, who only is so, is asserted to be "God." He is the eternal spring and only fountain of all holiness; there is nothing of it in any creature but what is directly and immediately from him; there was not in our first creation. He made us in his own image. And to suppose that we can now sanctify or make ourselves holy is proudly to renounce and cast off our principal dependence upon him. We may as wisely and rationally contend that we have not our being and our lives from God, as that we have not our holiness from him, when we have any. Hereunto are the proud opinions of educing a holiness out of the principles of nature to be reduced. I know all men will pretend that holiness is from God; it was never denied by Pelagius himself: but many, with him, would have it to be from God in a way of nature, and not in a way of especial grace. It is this latter way which we plead for; — and what is from ourselves, or educed by any means out of our natural abilities, is not of God in that way; for God, as the author of grace, and the best of corrupted nature are opposed, as we shall see farther afterward. 2. And, therefore, is he that is the author of our sanctification so emphatically here expressed: Αὐτὸς δὲ ὁ Θεὸς, "Even God himself." If he doth it not, none other can do it; it is no otherwise to be wrought nor effected. There is no other way whereby it may be brought about, nor doth it fall under the power or efficacy of any means absolutely whatever, but it must be wrought by God himself. He doth it of himself, from his own grace; by himself, or his own power; for himself, or his own glory. 3. And that, under this especial consideration, as he is the "God of peace."

This title is ascribed unto God only by our apostle, and by him frequently, Rom. xv. 33, xvi. 20; 2 Cor. xiii. 11; Phil. iv. 9; Heb. xiii. 20. Were it unto our present purpose to discourse concerning the general nature of peace, I might show how it is comprehensive of all order, rest, and blessedness, and all that is in them. On this account the enclosure of it in this title unto God, as its only possessor and author, belongs to the glory of his sovereign diadem. Everything that is contrary unto it is evil, and of the evil one; yea, all that is evil is so, because of its contrariety unto peace. Well, therefore, may God be styled "The God of peace." But these things I may not here stay to explain, although the words are so comprehensive and expressive of the whole work of sanctification, and that holiness which is the effect thereof, as that I shall choose to found my whole discourse concerning this subject upon them. That which offers itself unto our present design from this expression is the peculiar respect unto the work of our sanctification which lies in this especial property of God. Wherefore is he said to sanctify us as the God of peace! 1. Because it is a fruit and effect of that peace with himself which he hath made and prepared for us by Jesus Christ; for he was in Christ reconciling the world unto himself, destroying the enmity which entered by sin, and laying the foundation of eternal peace. From hence it is that he will sanctify us, or make us holy; without a respect whereunto he would no more do so than he will sanctify again the angels that have sinned, for whom there is no peace made nor atonement. 2. God, by the sanctification of our natures and persons, preserves that peace with himself in its exercise which he made and procured by the mediation of Christ, without which it could not be kept or continued; for in the duties and fruits thereof consist all those actings towards God which a state of reconciliation, peace, and friendship, do require. It is holiness that keeps up a sense of peace with God, and prevents those spiritual breaches which the remainders of our enmity would occasion. Hence God, as the author of our peace, is the author of our holiness. God, even God himself, the God of peace, doth sanctify us. How this is done immediately by the Holy Ghost, the Spirit of love and peace, and wherein the nature of this work doth consist, are the things which must afterward be more fully declared. And he is here said to sanctify us ὁλοτελεῖς, that is, "universally and completely," carrying on the work until it comes to perfection; for two things are intended in that expression:— First, That our whole nature is the subject of this work, and not any one faculty or part of it. Second, That as the work itself is sincere and universal, communicating all parts of real holiness unto our whole nature, so it is carried on to completeness and perfection. Both these, in the ensuing words, the apostle expresseth as the end and design of his prayer for them, and the effect of the work of grace which he prayed for: for, first, The subject of this sanctification he makes to be our whole natures, which he distributes unto our entire spirits, souls, and bodies; and, second, The end of the whole is, the preservation of us blameless in the peace of God unto the coming of Christ; — which will both of them be, immediately, more fully spoken unto. Wherefore, — Sanctification, as here described, is the immediate work of God by his Spirit upon our whole nature, proceeding from the peace made for us by Jesus Christ, whereby, being changed into his likeness, we are kept entirely in peace with God, and are preserved unblamable, or in a state of gracious acceptation with him, according to the terms of the covenant, unto the end. The nature of this work, and its effect, which is our holiness, with the necessity of them both, we must on many accounts, with our utmost diligence, inquire and search into. This both the importance of the truth itself, and the opposition that is made unto it, render necessary. Besides, whereas we are in the declaration of the especial operations of the Holy Ghost, although he be not so denominated originally from this peculiar work, as though he should be called "holy" merely because he is the author of holiness in all that are made partakers of it, which we have before disproved, yet there is a general consent, in words at least, among all who are called Christians, that this is his immediate and proper work, or that he is the only sanctifier of all them that do believe; — and this I shall take as yet for granted, although some among us, who not only pretend high to the preaching of holiness (whatever be their practice), but reproach others as weakening the necessity of it, do talk at such a rate as if in the holiness which they pleaded for he had nothing to do in a peculiar manner; for it is no news to meet with quaint and gilded discourses about holiness, intermixed with scoffing reflections on the work of the Holy Ghost therein. This work, therefore, of his, we are in an especial manner to attend unto, unless we would be found among the number of such as those who own themselves, and teach their children, that "the Holy

Ghost sanctifies all the elect of God," and yet not only despise the work of holiness in themselves, but deride those who plead an interest therein as an effect of the sanctification of the Spirit; for such fruits of secret atheism doth the world abound withal. But our principal duty in this world is, to know aright what it is to be holy, and so to be indeed.

One thing we must premise to clear our ensuing discourse from ambiguity; and this is, that there is mention in the Scripture of a twofold sanctification, and consequently of a twofold holiness. The first is common unto persons and things, consisting in the peculiar dedication, consecration, or separation of them unto the service of God by his own appointment, whereby they become holy. Thus the priests and Levites of old, the ark, the altar, the tabernacle, and the temple, were sanctified and made holy; and indeed in all holiness whatever, there is a peculiar dedication and separation unto God. But in the sense mentioned, this was solitary and alone. No more belonged unto it but this sacred separation, nor was there any other effect of this sanctification. But, secondly, there is another kind of sanctification and holiness, wherein this separation to God is not the first thing done or intended, but a consequent and effect thereof. This is real and internal, by the communicating of a principle of holiness unto our natures, attended with its exercise in acts and duties of holy obedience unto God. This is that which, in the first place, we inquire after; and how far believers are therein and thereby peculiarly separated and dedicated unto God shall be afterward declared. And unto what we have to deliver concerning it we shall make way by the ensuing observations:—

1. This whole matter of sanctification and holiness is peculiarly joined with and limited unto the doctrine, truth, and grace of the gospel; for holiness is nothing but the implanting, writing, and realizing of the gospel in our souls. Hence it is termed Ὁσιότης τῆς ἀληθείας, Eph. iv. 24, — "The holiness of truth;" which the truth of the gospel ingenerates, and which consists in a conformity thereunto. And the gospel itself is Ἀλήθεια κατ' εὐσέβειαν, Tit. i. 1, — "The truth which is according unto godliness," which declares that godliness and holiness which God requireth. The prayer, also, of our Saviour for our sanctification is conformed thereunto: John xvii. 17, "Sanctify them in" (or by) "thy truth: thy word is truth." And he sanctified himself for us to be a sacrifice, that "we might be sanctified in the truth." This alone is that truth which makes us free, John viii. 32, — that is, from sin and the law, unto righteousness in holiness. It belongs neither to nature nor the law, so as to proceed from them or to be effected by them. Nature is wholly corrupted and contrary unto it. The "law," indeed, for certain ends, "was given by Moses," but all "grace and truth came by Jesus Christ." There neither is, nor ever was, in the world, nor ever shall be, the least dram of holiness, but what, flowing from Jesus Christ, is communicated by the Spirit, according to the truth and promise of the gospel. There may be something like it as to its outward acts and effects (at least some of them), something that may wear its livery in the world, that is but the fruit of men's own endeavours in compliance with their convictions; but holiness it is not, nor of the same kind or nature with it. And this men are very apt to deceive themselves withal. It is the design of corrupted reason to debase all the glorious mysteries of the gospel, and all the concernments of them. There is nothing in the whole mystery of godliness, from the highest crown of it, which is the person of Christ, "God manifested in the flesh," unto the lowest and nearest effect of this grace, but it labours to deprave, dishonour, and debase. The Lord

Christ, it would have in his whole person to be but a mere man, in his obedience and suffering to be but an example, in his doctrine to be confined unto the capacity and comprehension of carnal reason, and the holiness which he communicates by the sanctification of his Spirit to be but that moral virtue which is common among men as the fruit of their own endeavours.

Herein some will acknowledge that men are guided and directed to a great advantage by the doctrine of the gospel, and thereunto excited by motions of the Holy Ghost himself, put forth in the dispensation of that truth; but any thing else in it more excellent, more mysterious, they will not allow. But these low and carnal imaginations are exceedingly unworthy of the grace of Christ, the glory of the gospel, the mystery of the recovery of our nature, and healing of the wound it received by the entrance of sin, with the whole design of God in our restoration unto a state of communion with himself. Moral virtue is, indeed, the best thing amongst men that is of them. It far exceeds in worth, use, and satisfaction, all that the honours, powers, profits, and pleasures of the world can extend unto. And it is admirable to consider what instructions are given concerning it, what expressions are made of its excellency, what encomiums of its use and beauty, by learned contemplative men among the heathen; the wisest of whom did acknowledge that there was yet something in it which they could only admire, and not comprehend. And very eminent instances of the practice of it were given in the lives and conversations of some of them; and as the examples of their righteousness, moderation, temperance, equanimity, in all conditions, rise up at present unto the shame and reproach of many that are called Christians, so they will be called over at the last day as an aggravation of their condemnation. But to suppose that this moral virtue, whatever it be really in its own nature, or however advanced in the imaginations of men, is that holiness of truth which believers receive by the Spirit of Christ, is to debase it, to overthrow it, and to drive the souls of men from seeking an interest in it. And hence it is that some, pretending highly a friendship and respect unto it, do yet hate, despise, and reproach what is really so, pleasing themselves with the empty name or withered carcass of virtue, every way inferior, as interpreted in their practice, to the righteousness of heathens. And this, in the first place, should stir up our diligence in our inquiries after its true and real nature, that we deceive not ourselves with a false appearance of it, and that unto our ruin.

2. It is our duty to inquire into the nature of evangelical holiness, as it is a fruit or effect in us of the Spirit of sanctification, because it is abstruse and mysterious, and (be it spoken with the good leave of some, or whether they will or no) undiscernible unto the eye of carnal reason. We may say of it in some sense as Job of wisdom: “Whence cometh wisdom? and where is the place of understanding? seeing it is hid from the eyes of all living, and kept close from the fowls of heaven. Destruction and death say, We have heard the fame thereof with our ears. God understandeth the way thereof, and he knoweth the place thereof. And unto man he said, Behold, the fear of the Lord, that is wisdom; and to depart from evil is understanding,” chap. xxviii. 20–23, 28. This is that wisdom whose ways, residence, and paths, are so hidden from the natural reason and understandings of men. No man, I say, by his mere sight and conduct, can know and understand aright the true nature of evangelical holiness; and it is, therefore, no wonder if the doctrine of it be despised by many as an enthusiastical fancy. It is of the things of the Spirit of God, yea, it is the principal effect of all his operations in us and towards us; and these “things

of God knoweth no man, but the Spirit of God," 1 Cor. ii. 11. It is by him alone that we are enabled to "know the things that are freely given to us of God," verse 12, as this is, if ever we receive any thing of him in this world, or shall do so to eternity. "Eye hath not seen, nor ear heard, neither have entered into the heart of man, the things which God hath prepared for them that love him;" the comprehension of these things is not the work of any of our natural faculties, but "God reveals them unto us by his Spirit," verses 9, 10. Hence it often falls out, as it did in the Jews and Pharisees of old, that those who are most zealous and industrious for and after a legal righteousness, walking in a strict attendance unto duties proportionable unto light and convictions, pretending to be it, and bearing some resemblance of it, are the most fierce and implacable enemies of true evangelical holiness. They know it not, and therefore hate it; they have embraced something else in its place and stead, and therefore despise and persecute it; as it befalls them who embrace error for truth in any kind.

3. Believers themselves are ofttimes much unacquainted with it, either as to their apprehension of its true nature, causes, and effects, or, at least, as to their own interest and concernment therein. As we know not of ourselves the things that are wrought in us of the Spirit of God, so we seldom attend as we ought unto his instructing of us in them. It may seem strange, indeed, that whereas all believers are sanctified and made holy, they should not understand or apprehend what is wrought in them and for them, and what abideth with them; but, alas! how little do we know of ourselves, of what we are, and whence are our powers and faculties, even in things natural! Do we know how the members of the body are fashioned in the womb? We are apt to be seeking after and giving reasons for all things, and to describe the progress of the production of our natures from first to last, so as if not to satisfy ourselves, yet to please and amuse others; for "vain man would be wise, though he be born like the wild ass's colt." The best issues of our consideration hereof is that of the psalmist: "Thou, O Lord, hast possessed my reins: thou hast covered me in my mother's womb. I will praise thee; for I am fearfully and wonderfully made: marvellous are thy works; and that my soul knoweth right well. My substance was not hid from thee, when I was made in secret, and curiously wrought in the lowest parts of the earth. Thine eyes did see my substance, yet being unperfect; and in thy book all my members were written, which in continuance were fashioned, when as yet there was none of them," Ps. cxxxix. 13–16. By diligent consideration of these things we may obtain a firm foundation to stand on, in a holy admiration of the infinite wisdom and goodness of that sovereign Architect who hath raised this fabric unto his own glory; and what we farther attempt is vanity and curiosity. How little do we know of these souls of ours! and all that we do so is by their powers and operations, which are consequential unto their being. Now, these things are our own naturally, — they dwell and abide with us; they are we, and we are they, and nothing else; yet is it no easy thing for us to have a reflex and intimate acquaintance with them. And is it strange if we should be much in the dark unto this new nature, this new creature, which comes from above, from God in heaven, wherewith our natural reason hath no acquaintance? It is new, it is wonderful, it is a work supernatural, and is known only by supernatural revelation.

Besides, there are other things which pretend to be this gospel holiness and are not, whereby unspeakable multitudes are deluded and deceived. With some, any reformation of life and abstinence from flagitious sins, with the performance of the common duties of religion, is all which they suppose is required unto this head of their duty. Others contend with violence to substitute moral virtues, — by which they know not themselves what they intend, — in the room thereof. And there is a work of the law which, in the fruits of it, internal and external, in the works of righteousness and duties, is hardly, and not but by spiritual light and measures, to be distinguished from it. This also adds to the difficulty of understanding it aright, and should to our diligent inquiry into it.

4. We must also consider that holiness is not confined to this life, but passeth over into eternity and glory. Death hath no power over it to destroy it or divest us of it; for, — (1.) Its acts, indeed, are transient, but its fruits abide forever in their reward. They who "die in the Lord rest from their labours, and their works do follow them," Rev. xiv. 13. "God is not unrighteous to forget their labour of love," Heb. vi. 10. There is not any effect or fruit of holiness, not the least, not the giving of a cup of cold water to a disciple of Christ in the name of a disciple, but it shall be had in everlasting remembrance, and abide forever in its eternal reward. Nothing shall be lost, but all the fragments of it shall be gathered up and kept safe forever. Everything else, how specious soever it be in this world, shall be burnt up and consumed, as hay and stubble; when the least, the meanest, the most secret fruit of holiness, shall be gathered as gold and silver, durable substance, into God's treasury, and become a part of the riches of the inheritance of the saints in glory. Let no soul fear the loss of any labour, in any of the duties of holiness, in the most secret contest against sin, for inward purity, for outward fruitfulness; in the mortification of sin, resistance of temptations, improvement of grace; in patience, moderation, self-denial, contentment; — all that you do know, and what you do not know, shall be revived, called over, and abide eternally in your reward. Our Father, who now "seeth in secret," will one day reward openly; and the more we abound in these things, the more will God be glorified in the recompense of reward. But this is not all, nor that which I intend. (2.) It abides forever, and passeth over into glory in its principle or nature. The love wherewith we now adhere to God, and by which we act the obedience of faith towards the saints, faileth not; it ends not when glory comes on, but is a part of it, 1 Cor. xiii. 8. It is true, some gifts shall be done away, as useless in a state of perfection and glory, as the apostle there discourseth; and some graces shall cease, as to some especial acts and peculiar exercise, as faith and hope, so far as they respect things unseen and future; — but all those graces whereby holiness is constituted, and wherein it doth consist, for the substance of them, as they contain the image of God, as by them we are united and do adhere unto God in Christ, shall in their present nature, improved into perfection, abide forever. In our knowledge of them, therefore, have we our principal insight into our eternal condition in glory; and this is, as a firm foundation of consolation, so a part of our chiefest joy in this world. Is it not a matter of unspeakable joy and refreshment, that these poor bodies we carry about us, after they have been made a prey unto death, dust, worms, and corruption, shall be raised and restored to life and immortality, freed from pain, sickness, weakness, weariness, and vested with those qualities, in conformity to Christ's glorious body, which yet we understand not? It is so, also, that these souls, which now animate and rule in us, shall be delivered from all their darkness, ignorance, vanity, instability, and alienation from things spiritual and heavenly. But this is not all. Those poor low graces, which now

live and are acting in us, shall be continued, preserved, purified, and perfected; but in their nature be the same as now they are, as our souls and bodies shall be. That love whereby we now adhere to God as our chiefest good; that faith whereby we are united to Christ, our everlasting head; that delight in any of the ways or ordinances of God wherein he is enjoyed, according as he hath promised his presence in them; that love and goodwill which we have for all those in whom is the Spirit, and on whom is the image of Christ; with the entire principle of spiritual life and holiness, which is now begun in any of us, — shall be all purified, enhanced, perfected, and pass into glory. That very holiness which we here attain, those inclinations and dispositions, those frames of mind, those powers and abilities in obedience and adherence unto God, which here contend with the weight of their own weakness and imperfection, and with the opposition that is continually made against them by the body of death that is utterly to be abolished, shall be gloriously perfected into immutable habits, unchangeably acting our souls in the enjoyment of God. And this also manifesteth of how much concernment it is unto us to be acquainted with the doctrine of it, and of how much more to be really interested in it. Yea, —

5. There is spiritual and heavenly glory in it in this world. From hence is the church, the "King's daughter," said to be "all glorious within," Ps. xlv. 13. Her inward adorning with the graces of the Spirit, making her beautiful in holiness, is called "glory;" and is so. So also the progress and increase of believers herein is called by our apostle their being "changed from glory to glory," 2 Cor. iii. 18, — from one degree of glorious grace unto another. As this, next unto the comeliness of the righteousness of Christ, put upon us by the free grace of God, is our only beauty in his sight, so it is such as hath a real spiritual glory in it. It is the first-fruits of heaven. And as the apostle argueth concerning the Jews, that if the "first-fruits" were holy, then is the whole lump holy, so may we on the other side, if the whole "weight," as he calls it, and fullness of our future enjoyment be glory, then are the first-fruits in their measure so also. There is in this holiness, as we shall see farther afterward, a ray of eternal light, a principle of eternal life, and the entire nature of that love whereby we shall eternally adhere unto God. The divine nature, the new immortal creature, the life of God, the life of Christ, are all comprised in it. It represents unto God the glory of his own image renewed in us; and unto the Lord Christ the fruits of his Spirit and effect of his mediation, wherein he sees of the travail of his soul, and is satisfied. There is, therefore, nothing more to be abhorred than those carnal, low, and unworthy thoughts which some men vent of this glorious work of the Holy Spirit, who would have it wholly to consist in a legal righteousness or moral virtue.

6. This is that which God indispensably requireth of us. The full prosecution of this consideration we must put off unto our arguments for the necessity of it, which will ensue in their proper place. At present I shall show that not only God requireth holiness indispensably in all believers, but also that this is all which he requireth of them or expecteth from them; for it compriseth the whole duty of man. And this surely rendereth it needful for us both to know what it is, and diligently to apply ourselves unto the obtaining an assured participation of it; for what servant who hath any sense of his relation and duty, if he be satisfied that his master requireth but one thing of him, will not endeavour an acquaintance with it and the performance of it? Some, indeed, say

that their holiness (such as it is) is the chief or only design of the gospel. If they intend that it is the first, principal design of God in and by the gospel, and that not only as to the preceptive part of it, but also as unto its doctrinal and promissory parts, whence it is principally and emphatically denominated, it is a fond imagination. God's great and first design, in and by the gospel, is eternally to glorify himself, his wisdom, goodness, love, grace, righteousness, and holiness, by Jesus Christ, Eph. i. 5, 6. And in order to this his great and supreme end, he hath designed the gospel; and designs by the gospel (which gives the gospel its design), — (1.) To reveal that love and grace of his unto lost sinners, with the way of its communication through the mediation of his Son incarnate, as the only means whereby he will be glorified and whereby they may be saved, Acts xxvi. 18. (2.) To prevail with men, in and by the dispensation of its truth, and encouragement of its promises, to renounce their sins and all other expectations of relief or satisfaction, and to betake themselves by faith unto that way of life and salvation which is therein declared unto them, 2 Cor. v. 18–21; Col. i. 25–28. (3.) To be the means and instrument of conveying over unto them, and giving them a title unto and a right in, that grace and mercy, that life and righteousness, which is revealed and tendered unto them thereby, Mark xvi. 16. (4.) To be the way and means of communicating the Spirit of Christ with grace and strength unto the elect, enabling them to believe and receive the atonement, Gal. iii. 2. (5.) Hereby to give them union with Christ as their spiritual and mystical head; as also to fix their hearts and souls in their choicest actings, in their faith, trust, confidence, and love, immediately on the Son of God, as incarnate, and their mediator, John xiv. 1. Wherefore, the first and principal end of the gospel towards us is, to invite and encourage lost sinners unto the faith and approbation of the way of grace, life, and salvation, by Jesus Christ; without a compliance wherewith, in the first place, the gospel hath no more to do with sinners, but leaves them to justice, the law, and themselves. But now, upon a supposition of these things, and of our giving glory to God by faith in them, the whole that God requireth of us in the gospel in a way of duty is, that we should be holy, and abide in the use of those means whereby holiness may be attained and improved in us; for if he require any other thing of us, it must be on one of these four accounts:— (1.) To make atonement for our sins; or, (2.) To be our righteousness before him; or, (3.) To merit life and salvation by; or, (4.) To supererogate in the behalf of others. No other end can be thought of, besides what are the true ends of holiness, whereon God should require any thing of us; and all the false religion that is in the world leans on a supposition that God doth require somewhat of us with respect unto these ends.

But, — (1.) He requires nothing of us (which we had all the reason in the world to expect that he would) to make atonement or satisfaction for our sins, that might compensate the injuries we have done him by our apostasy and rebellion; for whereas we had multiplied sins against him, lived in an enmity and opposition to him, and had contracted insupportable and immeasurable debts upon our own souls, terms of peace being now proposed, who could think but that the first thing required of us would be, that we should make some kind of satisfaction to divine justice for all our enormous and heinous provocations? yea, who is there that indeed doth naturally think otherwise? So he apprehended who was contriving a way in his own mind how he might come to an agreement with God: Mic. vi. 6, 7, "Wherewith shall I come before the Lord, and bow myself before the high God? shall I come before him with burnt-offerings, with calves of a year old? Will the Lord be pleased with thousands of rams, or with ten thousands of rivers of oil? shall I give my firstborn for my transgression, the fruit of my body for the sin of my soul?" This, or something of this nature, seems to be but a very reasonable inquiry for a guilty self-condemned sinner, when first he entertains thoughts of an agreement with the holy sin-avenging God. And this was the foundation of all that cruel and expensive superstition that the world was in bondage unto for so many ages. Mankind generally thought that the principal thing which was required of them in religion was to atone and pacify the wrath of the divine Power, and to make a compensation for what had been done against him. Hence were their sacrifices of hecatombs of beasts, of mankind, of their children, and of themselves, as I have elsewhere declared. And the same principle is still deep rooted in the minds of convinced sinners: and many an abbey, monastery, college, and alms-house hath it founded; for in the fruits of this superstition, the priests, which set it on work, always shared deeply. But quite otherwise; in the gospel there is declared and tendered unto sinners an absolute free pardon of all their sins, without any satisfaction or compensation made or to be made on their part, that is, by themselves, — namely, on the account of the atonement made for them by Jesus Christ. And all attempts or endeavours after works or duties of obedience in any respect satisfactory to God for sin or meritorious of pardon do subvert and overthrow the whole gospel. See 2 Cor. v. 18–21. Wherefore, in answer to the inquiry before mentioned, the reply in the prophet is, that God looks for none of these things, and that all such contrivances were wholly vain: "He hath showed thee, O man, what is good; and what doth the Lord require of thee, but to do justly, and to love mercy, and to walk humbly with thy God?" Mic. vi. 8; which last expression compriseth the whole of our covenant obedience, Gen. xvii. 1, as the two former are eminent instances of it in particular.

(2.) He requireth nothing of us in a way of righteousness for our justification for the future. That this also he would have done we might have justly expected; for a righteousness we must have, or we cannot be accepted with him. And here, also, many are at a loss, and resolve that it is a thing fond and inconvenient to think of peace with God without some righteousness of their own, on the account whereof they may be justified before him; and rather than they will forego that apprehension, they will let go all other thoughts of peace and acceptance. "Being ignorant of the righteousness of God, they go about to establish their own righteousness, and do not submit themselves unto the righteousness of God;" nor will they acquiesce in it "that Christ is the end of the law for righteousness to every one that believeth," as Rom. x. 4. But so it is, that God requireth not this of us in the gospel; for we are "justified freely by his grace, through the redemption that is in Christ Jesus," chap. iii. 24. And we do "therefore conclude that a man is justified by faith without the deeds of the law," verse 28. So chap. viii. 3, 4. Neither is there any mention in the whole gospel of God's requiring a righteousness in us upon the account whereof we should be justified before him, or in his sight; for the justification by works mentioned in James consists in the evidencing and declaration of our faith by them.

(3.) God requireth not any thing of us whereby we should purchase or merit for ourselves life and salvation: for "by grace are we saved through faith; not of works, lest any man should boast," Eph. ii. 8, 9. God doth save us neither by nor for the" works of righteousness which we have done," but "according to his mercy," Tit. iii. 5: so that although, on the one side, the "wages of sin is death," there being a proportion in justice between sin and punishment, yet there is none between our obedience and our salvation; and therefore "eternal life is the gift of God through Jesus Christ our Lord," Rom. vi. 23. God, therefore, requires nothing at our hands under this notion or consideration, nor is it possible that in our condition any such thing should be required of us; for whatever we can do is due beforehand on other accounts, and so can have no prospect to merit what is to come. Who can merit by doing his duty? Our Saviour doth so plainly prove the contrary as none can farther doubt of it than of his truth and authority, Luke xvii. 10. Nor can we do any thing that is acceptable to him but what is wrought in us by his grace; and this overthrows the whole nature of merit, which requires that that be every way our own whereby we would deserve somewhat else at the hands of another, and not his more than ours. Neither is there any proportion between our duties and the reward of the eternal enjoyment of God; for besides that they are all weak, imperfect, and tainted with sin, so that no one of them is able to make good its own station for any end or purpose, in the strictness of divine justice, they altogether come infinitely short of the desert of an eternal reward by any rule of divine justice. And if any say "That this merit of our works depends not on, nor is measured by, strict justice, but wholly by the gracious condescension of God, who hath appointed and promised so to reward them," I answer, in the first place, That this perfectly overthrows the whole nature of merit; for the nature of merit consists entirely and absolutely in this, that "to him that worketh, is the reward not reckoned of grace, but of debt," Rom. iv. 4. And these two are contrary and inconsistent; for what is "by grace is no more of works, otherwise grace is no more grace;" and what is "of works is no more of grace, otherwise work is no more work," chap. xi. 6. And those who go about to found a merit of ours in the grace of God do endeavour to unite and reconcile those things which God hath everlastingly separated and opposed. And I say, secondly, That although God doth freely, graciously, and bountifully reward our duties of obedience, and upon the account of his covenant and promise he is said to be, and he is, righteous in his so doing, yet he everywhere declares that what he so doth is an act of mere grace in himself, that hath not respect unto any thing but only the interposition and mediation of Jesus Christ. In this sense God in the gospel requireth of us nothing at all.

(4.) Much less doth he require of any that they should do such things as, being no way necessary unto that obedience which themselves personally owe unto him, may yet by their supererogation therein redound to the advantage and benefit of others. This monstrous fiction, which hath outdone all the Pharisaism of the Jews, we are engaged for to the church of Rome, as a pretence given to the piety, or rather covering of the impiety, of their votaries. But seeing, on the one hand, that they are themselves who pretend to these works but flesh, and so cannot on their own account be "justified in the sight of God," so it is extreme pride and cursed self-confidence for them to undertake to help others by the merit of those works whose worth they stand not in need of, concerning which it will be one day said unto them, "Who hath required these things at your hands?"

But now, whereas God requireth none of these things of us, nothing with respect unto any of these ends, such is the perverseness of our minds by nature, that many think that God requireth nothing else of us, or nothing of us but with respect unto one or other of these ends; nor can they in their hearts conceive why they should perform any one duty towards God unless it be with some kind of regard unto these things. If they may do any thing whereby they may make some recompense for their sins that are past, at least in their own minds and consciences, if any thing whereby they may procure an acceptance with God, and the approbation of their state and condition, they have something which, as they suppose, may quicken and animate their endeavours. Without these considerations, holy obedience is unto them a thing lifeless and useless. Others will labour and take pains, both in ways of outward mortification and profuse munificence in any way of superstitious charity, whilst they are persuaded, or can persuade themselves, that they shall merit eternal life and salvation thereby, without much being beholden to the grace of God in Christ Jesus. Yea, all that hath the face or pretence of religion in the Papacy consists in a supposition that all which God requireth of us, he doth it with respect unto these ends of atonement, justification, merit, and supererogation. Hereunto do they apply all that remains of the ordinances of God amongst them, and all their own inventions are managed with the same design. But by these things is the gospel and the faith of our Lord Jesus Christ made of none effect. Herein, then, I say, lies the express opposition that is between the "wisdom of God" in the mystery of the gospel and the φρόνημα τῆς σαρκός, — the "wisdom of the flesh," or our carnal reason. God, in his dealing with us by the gospel, takes upon his own grace and wisdom the providing of an atonement for our sins, a righteousness whereby we may be justified before him, and the collation of eternal life upon us; all in and by him who of God is "made unto us wisdom and righteousness, and sanctification and redemption." But withal he indispensably requires of us holiness and universal obedience, for the ends that shall be declared afterward. This way, thinks the wisdom of the flesh, or carnal reason, is mere "foolishness;" as our apostle testifies, 1 Cor. i. 18, 23. But such a foolishness it is as is "wiser than men," verse 25, — that is, a way so excellent and full of divine wisdom that men are not able to comprehend it. Wherefore, in opposition hereunto, carnal reason concludes that either what God requires of us is to be done with respect unto the ends mentioned, some or other or all of them, or that it is no great matter whether it be done or no. Neither can it discern of what use our holiness or obedience unto God should be if it serve not unto some of these purposes; for the necessity of conformity to God, of the renovation of his image in us, before we are brought unto the enjoyment of him in glory, the authority of his commands, the reverence of his wisdom, appointing the way of holiness and obedience as the means of expressing our thankfulness, glorifying him in the world, and of coming to eternal life, it hath no regard unto. But the first true saving light that shines by the gospel from Jesus Christ into our souls begins to undeceive us in this matter. And there is no greater evidence of our receiving an evangelical baptism, or of being baptized into the spirit of the gospel, than the clear compliance of our minds with the wisdom of God herein. When we find such constraining motives unto holiness upon us as will not allow the least subducting of our souls from a universal attendance unto it, purely on the ends of the gospel, without respect unto those now discarded, it is an evidence that the wisdom of God hath prevailed against that of the flesh in our minds.

Wherefore holiness, with the fruits of it, with respect unto their proper ends, which shall afterward be declared, is all that God requireth of us. And this he declares in the tenor of the covenant with Abraham, Gen. xvii. 1, "I am the Almighty God; walk before me, and be thou perfect;" — "This is that, and this is all, that I require of thee, namely, thy holy obedience; for all other things wherein thou art concerned, I take them all upon my own almighty power or all-sufficiency:" as he says elsewhere, that the "whole of man is to fear God and keep his commandments." And the consideration hereof, taken singly and by itself, is sufficient, with all that have any regard unto God or their own eternal welfare, to convince them of what importance these things are unto them.

7. But neither yet are we left in this matter merely under the authority of God's command, with an expectation of our compliance with it from our own ability and power: God, moreover, hath promised to sanctify us, or to work this holiness in us, the consideration whereof will give us yet a nearer prospect into its nature. He that requires it of us knows that we have it not of ourselves. When we were in our best condition by nature, in the state of original holiness, vested with the image of God, we preserved it not; and is it likely that now, in the state of lapsed and depraved nature, it is in our own power to restore ourselves, to re-introduce the image of God into our souls, and that in a far more eminent manner than it was at first created by God? What needed all that contrivance of infinite wisdom and grace for the reparation of our nature by Jesus Christ, if holiness, wherein it doth consist, be in our own power, and educed out of the natural faculties of our souls? There can no more fond imagination befall the minds of men than that defiled nature is able to cleanse itself, or depraved nature to rectify itself, or that we, who have lost that image of God which he created in us and with us, should create it again in ourselves by our own endeavours. Wherefore, when God commandeth and requireth us to be holy, he commands us to be that which by nature and of ourselves we are not; and not only so, but that which we have not of ourselves a power to attain unto. Whatever, therefore, is absolutely in our own power is not of that holiness which God requireth of us; for what we can do ourselves, there is neither necessity nor reason why God should promise to work in us by his grace. And to say that what God so promiseth to work, he will not work or effect indeed, but only persuade and prevail with us to do it, is, through the pride of unbelief, to defy the truth and grace of God, and with the spoils of them to adorn our own righteousness and power. Now, God hath multiplied his promises to this purpose, so that we shall need to call over only some of them in way of instance: Jer. xxxi. 33, "I will put my law in their inward parts, and write it in their hearts; and will be their God, and they shall be my people." Chap. xxxii. 39, 40, "I will give them one heart, and one way, that they may fear me for ever; and I will put my fear in their hearts, that they shall not depart from me." Ezek. xxxvi. 26, 27, "A new heart will I give you, and a new spirit will I put within you: and I will take away the stony heart out of your flesh, and I will give you an heart of flesh. And I will put my Spirit within you, and cause you to walk in my statutes, and ye shall keep my judgments, and do them." Verse 25, "I will sprinkle clean water upon you, and ye shall be clean; from all your filthiness will I cleanse you." Verse 29, "I will also save you from all your

uncleannesses." The whole of our sanctification and holiness is comprised in these promises. To be cleansed from the defilements of sin, whatever they be, to have a heart inclined, disposed, enabled, to fear the Lord always, and to walk in all his ways and statutes accordingly, with an internal habitual conformity of the whole soul unto the law of God, is to be sanctified or to be holy. And all this God promiseth directly to work in us and to accomplish himself. In the faith of these promises, and for the fulfilling of them, the apostle prayeth for the Thessalonians, as we observed at our entrance, that "the God of peace himself would sanctify them throughout," whereby "their whole spirits, souls, and bodies, might be preserved blameless to the coming of Jesus Christ." And hence is evident what we before observed, that what is absolutely in our own power is not of the nature of, nor doth necessarily belong unto, holiness, whatever it be. The best of the intellectual or moral habits of our minds, which are but the natural improvement and exercise of our faculties, neither are nor can be our holiness; nor do the best of our moral duties, as merely and only so, belong thereunto. By these moral habits and duties we understand the powers, faculties, or abilities of our souls, exercised with respect and in obedience unto the commands of God, as excited, persuaded, and guided by outward motives, rules, arguments, and considerations. Plainly, all the power we have of ourselves to obey the law of God, and all that we do in the pursuit and exercise of that power, upon any reasons, motives, or considerations whatever, — which may all be resolved into fear of punishment and hope of reward, with some present satisfaction of mind, on the account of ease in conscience within or outward reputation, whether in abstinence from sin or the performance of duties, — are intended hereby, and are not that holiness which we inquire after. And the reason is plain, even because those things are not wrought in us by the power of the especial grace of God, in the pursuit of the especial promise of the covenant, as all true holiness is. If any shall say that they are so wrought in us, they do expressly change the nature of them: for thereby those powers would be no more natural, but supernatural; and those duties would be no more merely moral, but evangelical and spiritual; — which is to grant all we contend for. Wherefore, that which men call "moral virtue" is so far from being the whole of internal grace or holiness, that if it be no more than so, it belongs not at all unto it, as not being effected in us by the especial grace of God, according to the tenor and promise of the covenant.

And we may here divert a little, to consider what ought to be the frame of our minds in the pursuit of holiness with respect unto these things, — namely, what regard we ought to have unto the command on the one hand, and to the promise on the other, — to our own duty, and to the grace of God. Some would separate these things, as inconsistent. A command they suppose leaves no room for a promise, at least not such a promise as wherein God should take on himself to work in us what the command requires of us; and a promise they think takes off all the influencing authority of the command. "If holiness be our duty, there is no room for grace in this matter; and if it be an effect of grace, there is no place for duty." But all these arguings are a fruit of the wisdom of the flesh before mentioned, and we have before disproved them. The "wisdom that is from above" teacheth us other things. It is true, our works and grace are opposed in the matter of justification, as utterly inconsistent; if it be of works it is not of grace, and if it be of grace it is not of works, as our apostle argues, Rom. xi. 6. [But] our duty and God's grace are nowhere opposed in the matter of sanctification, yea, the one doth absolutely suppose the other. Neither can we perform our duty herein without the grace of God; nor doth God give us this grace unto any other end but that we may rightly perform our duty. He that shall deny either that God commands us to be holy in a way of duty, or promiseth to work holiness in us in a way of grace, may with as much modesty reject the whole Bible. Both these, therefore, we are to have a due regard unto, if we intend to be holy. And, (1.) Our regard unto the command consisteth in three things, — [1.] That we get our consciences always affected with the authority of it, as it is the command of God. This must afterward be enlarged on. Where this is not, there is no holiness. Our holiness is our obedience; and the formal nature of obedience ariseth from its respect unto the authority of the command. [2.] That we see and understand the reasonableness, the equity, the advantage of the command. Our service is a reasonable service; the ways of God are equal, and in the keeping of his commands there is great reward. If we judge not thus, if we rest not herein, and are thence filled with indignation against everything within us or without us that opposeth it or riseth up against it, whatever we do in compliance with it in a way of duty, we are not holy. [3.] That hereon we love and delight in it, because it is holy, just, and good; because the things it requires are upright, equal, easy, and pleasant to the new nature, without any regard to the false ends before discovered. And, (2.) We have a due regard unto the promise to the same end, [1.] When, we walk in a constant sense of our own inability to comply with the command in any one instance from any power in ourselves; for we have no sufficiency of ourselves, our sufficiency is of God. As for him who is otherwise minded, his heart is lifted up. [2.] When we adore that grace which hath provided help and relief for us. Seeing without the grace promised we could never have attained unto the least part or degree of holiness, and seeing we could never deserve the least dram of that grace, how ought we to adore and continually praise that infinite bounty which hath freely provided us of this supply! [3.] When we act faith in prayer and expectation on the promise for supplies of grace enabling us unto holy obedience. And, [4.] When we have especial regard thereunto with respect unto especial temptations and particular duties. When on all such occasions we satisfy not ourselves with a respect unto the promise in general, but exercise faith in particular on it for aid and assistance, then do we regard it in a due manner.

8. To come yet nearer unto our principal design, I say it is the Holy Ghost who is the immediate peculiar sanctifier of all believers, and the author of all holiness in them. I suppose I need not insist upon the confirmation of this assertion in general. I have proved before that he is the immediate dispenser of all divine grace, or the immediate operator of all divine gracious effects in us, whereof this is the chief. Besides, it is such an avowed and owned principle among all that are called Christians, — namely, that the Holy Ghost is the sanctifier of all God's elect, — that as it is not questioned, so it need not in general be farther proved. Those who are less experienced in these things may consult Ps. li. 10–12; Ezek. xi. 19, xxxvi. 25–27; Rom. viii. 9–14; 1 Cor. vi. 11; 1 Pet. i. 2; Isa. iv. 4, xliv. 3, 4; Tit. iii. 4, 5. But it is the nature and manner of his work herein, with the effect produced thereby, that we are to inquire into; for as this belongs unto our general design of declaring the nature, power, and efficacy of all the gracious divine operations of the Holy Spirit, so it will give

us an acquaintance in particular with that work and the fruits of it, wherein we are so highly concerned.

Chapter II - Sanctification a progressive work

Sanctification described, with the nature of the work of the Holy Spirit therein; which is progressive — The way and means whereby holiness is increased in believers, especially by faith and love, whose exercise is required in all duties of obedience; as also those graces whose exercise is occasional — The growth of holiness expressed in an allusion unto that of plants, with an insensible progress — Renders grace therein to be greatly admired; and is discerned in the answerableness of the work of the Spirit in sanctification and supplication — Objections against the progressive nature of holiness removed.

Having passed through the consideration of the general concernments of the work of sanctification, I shall, in the next place, give a description of it, and then explain it more particularly in its principal parts. And this I shall do, but under this express caution, that I do not hope nor design at once to represent the life, glory, and beauty of it, or to comprise all things that eminently belong unto it; only I shall set up some way-marks that may guide us in our progress or future inquiry into the nature and glory of it. And so I say that, — Sanctification is an immediate work of the Spirit of God on the souls of believers, purifying and cleansing of their natures from the pollution and uncleanness of sin, renewing in them the image of God, and thereby enabling them, from a spiritual and habitual principle of grace, to yield obedience unto God, according unto the tenor and terms of the new covenant, by virtue of the life and death of Jesus Christ. Or more briefly:— It is the universal renovation of our natures by the Holy Spirit into the image of God, through Jesus Christ.

Hence it follows that our holiness, which is the fruit and effect of this work, the work as terminated in us, as it compriseth the renewed principle or image of God wrought in us, so it consists in a holy obedience unto God by Jesus Christ, according to the terms of the covenant of grace, from the principle of a renewed nature. Our apostle expresseth the whole more briefly yet, — namely, He that is in Christ Jesus is a new creature, 2 Cor. v. 17; for herein he expresseth both the renovation of our natures, the endowment of them with a new spiritual principle of life and operation, with actings towards God suitable thereunto. I shall take up the first general description of it, and in the consideration of its parts give some account of the nature of the work and its effects, and then shall distinctly prove and confirm the true nature of it, wherein it is opposed or called into question.

1. It is, as was before proved, and is by all confessed, the work in us of the Spirit of God. It is the renovation of the Holy Ghost whereby we are saved. And a real, internal, powerful, physical work it is, as we have proved before abundantly, and shall afterward more fully confirm. He doth not make us holy only by persuading us so to be. He doth not only require us to be holy, propose unto us motives unto holiness, give us convictions of its necessity, and thereby excite us unto the pursuit and attainment of it, though this he doth also by the word and ministration thereof. It is too high an impudency for anyone to

pretend an owning of the gospel, and yet to deny a work of the Holy Ghost in our sanctification; and, therefore, both the old and new Pelagians did and do avow a work of his herein. But what is it that really they ascribe unto him? Merely the exciting our own abilities, aiding and assisting us in and unto the exercise of our own native power; which, when all is done, leaves the work to be our own and not his, and to us must the glory and praise of it be ascribed. But we have already sufficiently proved that the things thus promised of God and so effected are really wrought by the exceeding greatness of the power of the Spirit of God; and this will yet afterward be made more particularly to appear.

2. This work of sanctification differs from that of regeneration, as on other accounts, so especially on that of the manner of their being wrought. The work of regeneration is instantaneous, consisting in one single creating act. Hence it is not capable of degrees in any subject. No one is more or less regenerate than another; everyone in the world is absolutely so, or not so, and that equally, although there are degrees in their state on other reasons. But this work of sanctification is progressive, and admits of degrees. One may be more sanctified and more holy than another, who is yet truly sanctified and truly holy. It is begun at once, and carried on gradually. But this observation being of great importance, and such as, if rightly weighed, will contribute much light unto the nature of the whole work of sanctification and holiness, I shall divert in this chapter unto such an explanation and confirmation of it as may give an understanding and furtherance herein.

An increase and growth in sanctification or holiness is frequently in the Scripture enjoined us, and frequently promised unto us. So speaks the apostle Peter in a way of command, 2 Pet. iii. 17, 18, "Fall not," be not cast down, "from your own steadfastness; but grow," or increase, "in grace." It is not enough that we decay not in our spiritual condition, that we be not diverted and carried off from a steady course in obedience by the power of temptations; but an endeavour after an improvement, an increase, a thriving in grace, that is, in holiness, is required of us. And a compliance with this command is that which our apostle so commendeth in the Thessalonians, 2 Epist. i. 3, — namely, the exceeding growth of their faith, and abounding of their love; that is, the thriving and increase of those graces in them, — that which is called "increasing with the increase of God," Col. ii. 19, or the increase in holiness which God requires, accepts, approves, by supplies of spiritual strength from Jesus Christ our head, as it is there expressed.

The work of holiness, in its beginning, is but like seed cast into the earth, — namely, the seed of God, whereby we are born again. And it is known how seed that is cast into the earth doth grow and increase. Being variously cherished and nourished, it is in its nature to take root and to spring up, bringing forth fruit. So is it with the principle of grace and holiness. It is small at first, but being received in good and honest hearts, made so by the Spirit of God, and there nourished and cherished, it takes root and brings forth fruit. And both these, even the first planting and the increase of it, are equally from God by his Spirit.

"He that begins this good work doth also perform it until the day of Jesus Christ," Phil. i. 6. And this he doth two ways:—

First, By increasing and strengthening those graces of holiness which we have received and been engaged in the exercise of. There are some graces whose exercise doth not depend on any outward occasions; but they are, and that in their actual exercise, absolutely necessary unto the least degree of the life of God: such are faith and love. No man doth, no man can, live to God, but in the exercise of these graces. Whatever duties towards God men may perform, if they are not enlivened by faith and love, they belong not unto that spiritual life whereby we live to God. And these graces are capable of degrees, and so of increase; for so we read expressly of little faith and great faith, weak and strong faith, both true and the same in the substance, but differing in degrees. So also is there fervent love, and that which comparatively is but cold. These graces, therefore, in carrying on the work of sanctification, are gradually increased. So the disciples prayed our Saviour that he would increase their faith, Luke xvii. 5; — that is, add unto its light, confirm it in its assent, multiply its acts, and make it strong against its assaults, that it might work more effectually in difficult duties of obedience; which they had an especial regard unto, as is evident from the context, for they pray for this increase of faith upon the occasion of our Saviour's enjoining frequent forgiveness of offending brethren, — a duty not at all easy nor pleasing to flesh and blood. And the apostle prays for the Ephesians, that they may be "rooted and grounded in love," chap. iii. 17; that is, that by the increase and strengthening of their love, they may be more established in all the duties of it. See 1 Thess. iii. 12, 13.

These graces being the springs and spirit of our holiness, in the increase of them in us the work of sanctification is carried on and universal holiness increased. And this is done by the Holy Spirit several ways:—

First, By exciting them unto frequent actings. Frequency of acts doth naturally increase and strengthen the habits whence they proceed; and in these spiritual habits of faith and love it is so, moreover, by God's appointment. They grow and thrive in and by their exercise, Hos. vi. 3. The want thereof is the principal means of their decay. And there are two ways whereby the Holy Spirit excites the graces of faith and love unto frequent acts:—

(1.) He doth it morally, by proposing their objects suitably and seasonably unto them. This he doth by his ordinances of worship, especially the preaching of the word. God in Christ, the promises of the covenant, and other proper objects of our faith and love, being proposed unto us, these graces are drawn out unto their exercise. And this is one principal advantage which we have by attendance on the dispensation of the word in a due manner, — namely, that by presenting those spiritual truths which are the object of our faith unto our minds, and those spiritual good things which are the object of our love unto our affections, both these graces are drawn forth into frequent actual exercise. And we are greatly mistaken if we suppose we have no benefit by the word beyond what we retain in our memories, though we should labour for that also. Our chief advantage lies in the excitation which is thereby given unto our faith and love to their proper exercise; and hereby are these graces kept alive, which without this would decay and wither. Herein doth the Holy Spirit "take the things of Christ, and show them unto us," John xvi. 14, 15. He represents them unto us in the preaching of the word as the proper objects of our faith and love, and so brings to remembrance the things spoken by Christ, chap. xiv. 26; that is, in the dispensation of the word, he minds us of the gracious words and truths of Christ, proposing them to our faith and love. And herein lies the secret profiting and thriving of believers under the preaching of the gospel; which, it may be, they are not sensible of themselves. By this means are many thousands of acts of faith and love drawn forth, whereby these graces are exercised and strengthened; and consequently holiness is increased: and the word, by the actings of faith being mixed with it, as Heb. iv. 2, increaseth it by its incorporation.

(2.) The Spirit doth it really and internally. He dwelleth in believers, preserving in them the root and principle of all their grace by his own immediate power. Hence all graces in their exercise are called "The fruits of the Spirit," Gal. v. 22, 23. He brings them forth from the stock that he hath planted in the heart. And we cannot act any one grace without his effectual operation therein: "God worketh in us both to will and to do of his good pleasure," Phil. ii. 13; — that is, there is no part of our wills singly and separately from him in obedience but it is the operation of the Spirit of God in us, so far as it is spiritual and holy. He is the immediate author of every good or gracious acting in us; for "in us, that is, in our flesh" (and of ourselves we are but flesh), "there dwelleth no good." Wherefore, the Spirit of God dwelling in believers doth effectually excite and stir up their graces unto frequent exercise and actings, whereby they are increased and strengthened. And there is nothing in the whole course of our walking before God that we ought to be more careful about than that we grieve not, that we provoke not, this good and holy Spirit, whereon he should withhold his gracious aids and assistances from us. This, therefore, is the first way whereby the work of sanctification is gradually carried on, by the Holy Ghost exciting our graces unto frequent actings, whereby they are increased and strengthened.

Secondly, He doth it by supplying believers with experiences of the truth, and reality, and excellency, of the things that are believed. Experience is the food of all grace, which it grows and thrives upon. Every taste that faith obtains of divine love and grace, or how gracious the Lord is, adds to its measure and stature. Two things, therefore, must briefly be declared:— (1.) That the experience of the reality, excellency, power, and efficacy of the things that are believed, is an effectual means of increasing faith and love; (2.) That it is the Holy Ghost which gives us this experience. (1.) For the first, God himself expostulates with the church how its faith came to be so weak, when it had so great experience of him, or of his power and faithfulness: Isa. xl. 27, 28, "Hast thou not known? hast thou not heard? How, then, sayest thou that God hath forsaken thee?" And our apostle affirms that the consolations which he had experimentally received from God enabled him unto the discharge of his duty towards others in trouble, 2 Cor. i. 4; for herein we prove, or do really approve of, as being satisfied in, "the good, and acceptable, and perfect will of God," Rom. xii. 2. And this is that which the apostle prayeth for in the behalf of the Col. ii. 2. I may say that he who knoweth not how faith is encouraged and strengthened by especial experiences of the reality, power, and spiritual efficacy on the soul of the things believed, never was made partaker of any of them. How often doth David encourage his own faith and [that of] others from his former experiences! which were pleaded also by our Lord Jesus Christ to the same purpose, in his great distress, Ps. xxii. 9, 10. (2.) That it is the Holy Ghost who giveth us all our spiritual experiences needs no other consideration to evince but only this, that in them consists all our consolation. His work and office it is to administer consolation unto believers, as being the only Comforter of the church. Now, he administereth comfort no other way but by giving unto the minds and souls of believers a spiritual, sensible experience of the reality and power of the things we do believe. He doth not comfort us by words, but by things. Other means of spiritual consolation I know none; and I am sure this never fails. Give unto a soul an experience, a taste, of the love and grace of God in Christ Jesus, and be its condition what it will, it cannot refuse to be comforted. And hereby doth he "shed abroad the love of God in our hearts," Rom. v. 5, whereby all graces are cherished and increased.

Thirdly, He doth it by working immediately an actual increase of these graces in us. I have showed that these are capable of improvement, and of an addition of degrees unto them. Now, they are originally the immediate work and product of the Spirit of God in us, as hath been abundantly evinced. And as he first works and creates them, so he increaseth them. Hereby they that are "feeble become as David," Zech. xii. 8; that is, those whose graces were weak, whose faith was infirm, and whose love was languid, shall, by the supplies of the Spirit, and the increase given by him unto them, become strong and vigorous. To this purpose are promises multiplied in the Scripture; which in our constant supplications we principally respect. This is that which the schoolmen, after Austin, call "Gratiam corroborantem;" that is, the working of the Holy Spirit in the increasing and strengthening of grace received. See Eph. iii. 16, 17; Col. i. 10, 11; Isa. xl. 29. And this is the principal cause and means of the gradual increase of holiness in us, or the carrying on of the work of sanctification, Ps. cxxxviii. 8.

Secondly, There are graces whose exercise is more occasional, and not always actually necessary as unto the life of God; that is, it is not necessary that they be always in actual exercise, as faith and love are to be. With respect unto these, holiness is increased by the addition of one to another, until we are brought on several occasions to the practice and exercise of them all; for the addition of the new exercise of any grace belongs unto the gradual carrying on of the work of sanctification. And hereunto all things that befall us in this world, all our circumstances, are laid in a subserviency by the wisdom of God. All our relations, all our afflictions, all our temptations, all our mercies, all our enjoyments, all occurrences, are suited to a continual adding of the exercise of one grace to another, wherein holiness is increased. And if we make not use of them to that purpose, we miss of all the benefit and advantage we might have of them, and disappoint, what lies in us, the design of divine love and wisdom in them. This is given us in charge, 2 Pet. i. 5–7: "Besides this, giving all diligence, add to your faith virtue; and to virtue knowledge; and to knowledge temperance; and to temperance patience; and to patience godliness; and to godliness brotherly-kindness; and to brotherlykindness charity." The end why this injunction is given us is, that we may "escape the corruption that is in the world through lust," verse 4; that is, have all our corruptions thoroughly subdued, and our souls thoroughly sanctified. To this end are the promises given us, and a divine, spiritual nature is bestowed upon us. But will that suffice, or is there no more required of us unto that end? "Yes," saith the apostle; "this great work will not be effected unless you use your utmost diligence, and endeavour to add the exercise of all the graces of the Spirit one to another, as occasion shall require." There is a method in this concatenation of graces from first to last, and an especial reason for each particular, or why the apostle requires that such a grace should be added unto such an one in the order laid down; which at present I shall not inquire into. But, in general, he intends that every grace is to be exercised according to its proper season and especial occasion. Hereby, also, is the work of sanctification gradually carried on, and holiness increased. And this addition of one grace unto another, with the progress of holiness thereby, is also from the Holy Ghost. And three ways there are whereby he accomplisheth his work herein:— 1. By ordering things so towards us, and bringing of us into such conditions as wherein the exercise of these graces shall be required and necessary. All the afflictions and trials which he bringeth the church into have no other end or design. So the apostle James expresseth it, chap. i. 2–4: "My brethren, count it all joy when ye fall into divers temptations; knowing this, that the trying of your faith worketh patience. But let patience have its perfect work, that ye may be perfect and entire, wanting nothing." These temptations are trials upon afflictions, troubles, persecutions, and the like; but take them in any other sense, it is the same unto our purpose. These are all guided unto us by Christ and his Spirit; for it is he who rebukes and chastens us. But what is his end therein? It is that faith may be exercised and patience employed, and one grace added unto another, that they may carry us on towards perfection. So he bringeth us into that condition as wherein we shall assuredly miscarry if we add not the exercise of one grace unto another.

2. In this state of things he effectually minds us of our duty, and what graces ought to be put upon their exercise. We may dispute whether it be better to act faith, or to despond; to add patience under the continuance of our trials, or to trust unto ourselves, and irregularly to seek after deliverance or divert unto other satisfactions. Then doth he cause us to "hear a word behind us, saying, This is the way, walk ye in it, when we turn to the right hand, and when we turn to the left," Isa. xxx. 21. When we are at a loss, and know not what to do, and are ready, it may be, to consult with flesh and blood, and to divert to irregular courses, he speaks effectually to us, saying, "No; that is not your way, but this is it," namely, to act faith, patience, submission to God, adding one grace to another, binding our hearts thereby to our duty. 3. He actually excites and sets all needful graces at work in the way and manner before spoken unto.

This, then, is to be fixed, that all this increase of holiness is immediately the work of the Holy Ghost, who therein gradually carries on his design of sanctifying us throughout, in our whole spirits, souls, and bodies. There is in our regeneration and habitual grace received a nature bestowed on us capable of growth and increase, and that is all; if it be left unto itself, it will not thrive, it will decay and die. The actual supplies of the Spirit are the waterings that are the immediate cause of its increase. It wholly depends on continual influences from God. He cherisheth and improves the work he hath begun with new and fresh supplies of grace every moment: Isa. xxvii. 3, "I the Lord will water it every moment." And it is the Spirit which is this water, as the Scripture everywhere declares. God the Father takes on him the care of this matter; "he watcheth over his vineyard to keep it." The Lord Christ is the head, fountain, and treasure of all actual supplies; and the Spirit is the efficient cause, communicating them unto us from him. From hence it is that any grace in us is kept alive one moment, that it is ever acted in one single duty, that ever it receives the least measure of increase or strengthening. With respect unto all these it is that our apostle saith, "Nevertheless, I live, yet not I, but Christ liveth in me," Gal. ii. 20. Spiritual life and living by it, in all the acts of it, are immediately from Christ.

I concern not myself much how moral virtue, that is no more, is preserved and sustained in the minds and lives of men, though I am not ignorant of the precepts, directions, and instructions, which are given unto that end by some of old and some of late. But for grace and holiness, we have infallible assurance that the being, life, continuance, and all the actings of it, in any of the sons of men, depend merely and only upon their relation unto that spring and fountain of all grace which is in Christ, and the continual supplies of it by the Holy Spirit, whose work it is to communicate them, Col. iii. 3; John xv. 5; Col. ii. 19.

There is no man who hath any grace that is true and saving, that hath any seed, any beginning of sanctification or holiness, but the Holy Spirit, by his watchful care over it, and supplies of it, is able to preserve it, to extricate it from difficulties, to free it from opposition, and to increase it unto its full measure and perfection. Wherefore, "let the hands that hang down be lifted up, and the feeble knees be strengthened." We have to do with him who "will not quench the smoking flax nor break the bruised reed." And, on the other side, there is none who hath received grace in such a measure, nor hath so confirmed it by constant, uninterrupted exercise, as that he can preserve it one moment, or act it in any one instance or duty, without the continual supplies of new actual grace and help from him who worketh in us to will and to do; for saith our Lord Christ unto his apostles, and in them to all believers, the best and strongest of them, "Without me ye can do nothing," John xv. 5. And they who of themselves can do nothing, — that is, in a way of living unto God, — cannot of themselves preserve grace, act it, and increase it; which are the greatest things we do or are wrought in us in this world. Wherefore God hath, in infinite wisdom, so ordered the dispensation of his love and grace unto believers, that all of them living upon the continual supplies of his Spirit, none may have cause, on the one hand, to faint or despond, nor occasion, on the other, unto self-confidence or elation of mind; that so "no flesh may glory in itself, but he that glorieth may glory in the Lord." And, therefore, as he greatly encourageth the weak, the fearful, the faint, the disconsolate and dejected, and that by the engagement of all the holy properties of his nature in and unto their assistance, Isa. xxxv. 3–6, xl. 27–31; so he warns them who suppose themselves strong, steadfast, and immovable, "not to be highminded, but to fear," Rom. xi. 20, because the whole issue of things depends on his sovereign supplies of grace. And seeing he hath promised in the covenant to continue faithfully these supplies unto us, there is ground of faith given unto all, and occasion of presumption administered unto none.

But it will be said, "That if not only the beginning of grace, sanctification, and holiness be from God, but the carrying of it on and the increase of it also be from him, and not only so in general, but if all the actings of grace, and every act of it, be an immediate effect of the Holy Spirit, then what need is there that we should take any pains in this thing ourselves, or use our own endeavours to grow in grace or holiness, as we are commanded? If God work all himself in us, and if without his effectual operation in us we can do nothing, there is no place left for our diligence, duty, or obedience."

Ans. 1. This objection we must expect to meet withal at every turn. Men will not believe there is a consistency between God's effectual grace and our diligent obedience; that is, they will not believe what is plainly, clearly, distinctly revealed in the Scripture, and which is suited unto the experience of all that truly believe, because they cannot, it may be, comprehend it within the compass of carnal reason. 2. Let the apostle answer this objection for this once: 2 Pet. i. 3, "His divine power hath given unto us all things that pertain to life and godliness, through the knowledge of him that hath called us to glory and virtue: whereby are given unto us exceeding great and precious promises: that by these ye might be partakers of the divine nature, having escaped the corruption that is in the world through lust." If all things that pertain unto life and godliness, — among which, doubtless, is the preservation and increase of grace, — be given unto us by the power of God, if from him we receive that divine nature by virtue whereof our corruptions are subdued, then, I pray, what need is there of any endeavours of our own? The whole work of sanctification is wrought in us, it seems, and that by the power of God; we, therefore, may let it alone, and leave it unto him whose it is, whilst we are negligent, secure, and at ease. "Nay," saith the apostle; "this is not the use which the grace of God is to be put unto. The consideration of it is, or ought to be, the principal motive and encouragement unto all diligence for the increase of holiness in us." For so he adds immediately, verse 5, Καὶ αὐτὸ τοῦτο δέ, — "But also for this cause," or, because of the gracious operations of the divine power in us, "giving all diligence, add to your faith virtue," as before. These objectors and this apostle were very diversely minded in these matters; what they make an insuperable discouragement unto diligence in obedience, that he makes the greatest motive and encouragement thereunto. 3. I say, from this consideration it will unavoidably follow that we ought continually to wait and depend on God for supplies of his Spirit and grace, without which we can do nothing. That God is more the author, by his grace, of the good we do than we ourselves ("Not I, but the grace of God which was with me"); that we ought to be careful that by our negligences and sins we provoke not the Holy Spirit to withhold his aids and assistances, and so to leave us to ourselves, in which condition we can do nothing that is spiritually good; — these things, I say, will unavoidably follow on the doctrine before declared; and if anyone be offended at them, it is not in our power to render them relief.

I shall close the discourse on this subject with some considerations of that similitude by which the Scripture so frequently represents the gradual improvement of grace and holiness; and this is the growth of trees and plants: Hos. xiv. 5, 6, "I will be as the dew unto Israel: he shall grow as the lily, and cast forth his roots as Lebanon. His branches shall spread, and his beauty shall be as the olive-tree, and his smell as Lebanon." Isa. xliv. 3, 4, "I will pour water on him that is thirsty, and floods upon the dry ground: I will pour my Spirit upon thy seed, and my blessing upon thine offspring: and they shall spring up as among the grass, as willows by the water-courses." And so in other places very many. And we may know that this similitude is singularly instructive, or it would not have been so frequently made use of to this purpose. Some few instances tending to administer light in this matter I shall briefly reflect upon:—

1. These trees and plants have the principle of their growth in themselves. They do not grow immediately from external adventitious aid and furtherance; they grow from their own seminal virtue and radical moisture. It is no otherwise in the progress of sanctification and holiness. It hath a root, a seed, a principle of growth and increase, in the soul of him that is sanctified. All grace is immortal seed, and contains in it a living, growing principle. That which hath

not in itself a life and power of growth is not grace; and therefore what duties soever any men do perform, whereunto they are either guided by natural light, or which they are urged unto by convictions from the word, if they proceed not from a principle of spiritual life in the heart, they are no fruits of holiness nor do belong thereunto. The water of grace which is from Christ is a "well of water springing up into everlasting life," in them on whom it is bestowed, John iv. 14. It is, therefore, the nature of holiness to thrive and grow, as it is of trees or plants, that have their seminal virtue in themselves after their kind.

2. A tree or plant must be watered from above, or it will not thrive and grow by virtue of its own seminal power. If a drought cometh, it will wither or decay. Wherefore, where God mentioneth this growth, he ascribes it unto his watering. "I will be as the dew," and "I will pour water," is the especial cause of it. It is so in this carrying on of holiness. There is a nature received capable of increase and growth; but if it be left unto itself, it will not thrive, it will decay and die. Wherefore God is unto it as the dew, and pours water on it by the actual supplies of the Spirit, as we have showed before.

3. The growth of trees and plants is secret and imperceptible, nor is discerned but in the effects and consequences of it. The most watchful eye can discern little of its motion. "Crescit occulto velut arbor ævo." It is no otherwise in the progress of holiness. It is not immediately discernible, either by themselves in whom it is, or by others that make observation of it. It lies only under the eye of him by whom it is wrought; only by the fruits and effects of it is it made manifest. And some, indeed, especially in some seasons, do plainly and evidently thrive and grow, springing up like the willows by the water-courses. Though their growth in itself is indiscernible, yet it is plain they have grown. Such we ought all to be. The growth of some, I say, is manifest on every trial, on every occasion; their profiting is visible to all. And as some say that the growth of plants is not by a constant insensible progress, but they increase by sudden gusts and motions, which may sometimes be discerned in the openings of buds and flowers, so the growth of believers consists principally in some intense vigorous actings of grace on great occasions, as of faith, love, humility, self-denial, bounty; and he who hath not some experience of such actings of grace in especial instances can have little evidence of his growth. Again, there are trees and plants that have the principle of life and growth in them but yet are so withering and unthrifty that you can only discern them to be alive. And so it is with too many believers. They are all "trees planted in the garden of God;" some thrive, some decay for a season, but the growth of the best is secret.

From what hath been proved it is evident that the work of sanctification is a progressive work, that holiness is gradually carried on in us by it towards perfection. It is neither wrought nor completed at once in us, as is regeneration, nor doth it cease under any attainments or in any condition of life, but is thriving and carried on. A river continually fed by a living fountain may as soon end its streams before it come to the ocean, as a stop be put to the course and progress of grace before it issue in glory; for "the path of the just is as the shining light, that shineth more and more unto the perfect day," Prov. iv. 18. So is their path wherein they are led and conducted by the Holy Spirit, even as the morning light; which after it once appears, though it may be sometimes clouded, yet faileth not until it arrive unto its perfection. And as the wisdom, patience, faithfulness, and power, which the Holy Spirit of God exerciseth herein are unutterable, so are they constantly admired by all that are interested in them: so are they by the psalmist, Ps. lxvi. 8, 9, xxxi. 19. Who is there who hath made any diligent observation of his own heart and ways, and what have been the workings of the grace of God in him and towards him, to bring him unto the stature and measure whereunto he is arrived, that doth not admire the watchful care and powerful workings of the Spirit of God therein? The principle of our holiness as in us is weak and infirm, because it is in us; in some to so low a degree as is ofttimes unto themselves imperceptible. This he preserves and cherisheth, that it shall not be overpowered by corruptions and temptations. Among all the glorious works of God, next unto that of redemption by Jesus Christ, my soul doth most admire this of the Spirit in preserving the seed and principle of holiness in us, as a spark of living fire in the midst of the ocean, against all corruptions and temptations wherewith it is impugned. Many breaches are made in and upon our course of obedience by the incursions of actual sins; these he cures and makes up, healing our backslidings and repairing our decays. And he acts the grace we have received by constant fresh supplies. He wants much of the comfort and joy of a spiritual life who doth not diligently observe the ways and means whereby it is preserved and promoted; and it is no small part of our sin and folly when we are negligent herein.

All believers are, no doubt, in some measure convinced hereof, not only from the testimonies given unto it in the Scripture, but also from their own experience; and there is nothing in themselves which they may more distinctly learn it from than the nature and course of their prayers, with the workings of their hearts, minds, and affections in them. Let profane persons deride it whilst they please, it is the Spirit of God, as a Spirit of grace, that enables believers to pray and make intercession according to the mind of God; and herein, as he is the Spirit of supplications, he copieth out and expresseth what he worketh in them as the Spirit of sanctification. In teaching us to pray, he teacheth us what and how he worketh in us; and if we wisely consider his working in our hearts by prayer, we may understand much of his working upon our hearts by grace. It is said that "he who searcheth the hearts," that is, God himself, "knoweth the mind of the Spirit," in the intercessions he maketh in us, Rom. viii. 27. There are secret powerful operations of the Spirit in prayer that are discernible only to the great Searcher of hearts. But we also ought to inquire and observe, so far as we may, what he leads us unto and guides us about; which is plainly his work in us. I do not think that the Spirit worketh supplications in us by an immediate, supernatural, divine afflatus, so as he inspired the prophets of old, who ofttimes understood not the things uttered by themselves, but inquired afterward diligently into them; but I do say (let the proud carnal world despise it whilst they please, and at their peril) that the Spirit of God doth graciously, in the prayers of believers, carry out and act their souls and minds in desires and requests, which, for the matter of them, are far above their natural contrivances and invention. And he who hath not experience hereof is a greater stranger unto these things than will at length be unto his advantage. By a diligent observance hereof we may know of what kind and nature the work of the Holy Ghost in us is, and how it is carried on. For how in general doth the Holy Spirit teach us and enable us to pray? It is by these three things:— 1. By giving us a spiritual insight into the promises of God and the grace of the covenant, whereby we know what to ask upon a spiritual view of the mercy and grace that God hath prepared for us. 2. By acquainting us with and giving us an experience of our wants, with a deep sense of them, such as we cannot bear without relief. 3. By creating and stirring up desires in the new creature for its own preservation, increase, and improvement. And in answer unto these things consisteth his whole work of sanctification in us; for it is his effectual communication unto us of the grace and mercy prepared in the promises of the covenant through Jesus Christ. Hereby doth he supply our spiritual wants, and set the new creature in life and vigour. So are our prayers an extract and copy of the work of the Holy Spirit in us, given us by himself. And, therefore, by whomsoever he is despised as a Spirit of supplication, he is so as a Spirit of sanctification also. Now, consider what it is that in your prayers you most labour about? Is it not that the body, the power, the whole interest, of sin in you may be weakened, subdued, and at length destroyed? Is it not that all the graces of the Spirit may be renewed daily, increased and strengthened, so as that you may be more ready and prepared for all duties of obedience? And what is all this for, but that holiness may be gradually progressive in your souls, that it may be carried on by new supplies and additions of grace, until it come to perfection?

It will be said, perhaps, by some, that they find neither in themselves nor others, by the best of their observation, that the work of sanctification is constantly progressive, or that holiness doth so grow and thrive wherever it is in sincerity: for as for themselves, they have found grace more vigorous, active, and flourishing, in former days than of late; the streams of it were fresher and stronger at the spring of conversion than since they find them to be in their course. Hence are those complaints among many of their leanness, their weakness, their deadness, their barrenness. Nor were many of the saints in the Scripture without such complaints. And many may cry, "Oh that it were with us as in our former days, in the days of our youth!" Complaints of this nature do everywhere abound, and some are ready to conclude, upon this consideration, that either sincere holiness is not so growing and progressive as is pretended, or that, indeed, they have no interest therein. Yea, the like may be said upon a diligent observation of others, churches and single professors. What evidence do they give that the work of holiness is thriving in them? doth it not appear rather to be retrograde and under a constant decay?

I shall so far consider and remove this objection as that the truth which we have asserted suffer not from it, and so be left as an empty notion; nor yet those be altogether discouraged who come not up unto a full compliance with it. And this I shall do in the ensuing rules and observations.

1. It is one thing what grace or holiness is suited unto in its own nature, and what is the ordinary or regular way of the procedure of the Spirit in the work of sanctification, according to the tenor of the covenant of grace; another, what may occasionally fall out by indisposition and irregularity, or any other obstructing interposition in them in whom the work is wrought. Under the first consideration, the work is thriving and progressive; in the latter, the rule is liable to sundry exceptions. A child that hath a principle of life, a good natural constitution, and suitable food, will grow and thrive; but that which hath obstructions from within, or distempers and diseases, or falls and bruises, may be weak and thriftless. When we are regenerated, we are as newborn babes, and ordinarily, if we have the sincere milk of the word, we shall grow thereby. But if we ourselves give way to temptations, corruptions, negligences, conformity to the world, is it any wonder if we are lifeless and thriftless? It suffices to

confirm the truth of what we have asserted, that everyone in whom is a principle of spiritual life, who is born of God, in whom the work of sanctification is begun, if it be not gradually carried on in him, if he thrive not in grace and holiness, if he go not from strength to strength, it is ordinarily from his own sinful negligence and indulgence unto carnal lusts, or love of this present world. Considering the time we have had and the means we have enjoyed, what grown, what flourishing plants, in faith, love, purity, self-denial, and universal conformity to Christ, might many of us have been, who now are weak, withering, fruitless, and sapless, scarce to be distinguished from the thorns and briers of the world! It is time for us rather to be casting off every weight and the sin that doth so easily beset us, to be by all means stirring up ourselves unto a vigorous recovery of our first faith and love, with an abundant growth in them, than to be complaining that the work of holiness doth not go on, and that before our wounds become incurable.

2. It is one thing to have holiness really thriving in any soul, another for that soul to know it and to be satisfied in it; and these things may be separated: whereof there are many reasons. But before I name them, I must premise one necessary observation, and that is, — Whereas this rule is proposed for the relief of such as are at a loss about their condition, and know not whether holiness be thriving in them or no, those have no concernment herein who may at any time, if they please, give themselves an account how matters go with them, and on what grounds: for if men do indulge unto any predominant lust, if they live in the neglect of any known duty or in the practice of any way of deceit, if they suffer the world to devour the choicest increase of their souls, and formality to eat out the spirit, vigour, and life of holy duties, or any of these in a remarkable manner, I have nothing to offer unto them to manifest that holiness may thrive in them although they discern it not; for undoubtedly it doth not do so, nor are they to entertain any hopes but that whilst they abide in such a condition it will decay more and more. Such are to be awaked with violence, like men falling into a deadly lethargy, to be snatched as brands out of the fire, to be warned to recover their first faith and love, to repent and do their first works, lest their end should be darkness and sorrow forevermore. But as unto those who walk with God humbly and in sincerity, there may be sundry reasons given whence it is that holiness may be thriving in them, and yet not be discerned by them so to be. And, therefore, though holiness be wrought within ourselves, and only there, yet there may be seasons wherein sincere, humble believers may be obliged to believe the increase and growth of it in them when they perceive it not, so as to be sensible of it; for, — (1.) It being the subject of so many gospel promises, it is a proper object of faith, or a thing that is to be believed. The promises are God's explanations of the grace of the covenant, both as to its nature and the manner of its operation; and they do not abound in any concernment of it more than this, that those who are partakers of it shall thrive and grow thereby. With what limitations they are bounded, and what is required on our part that we may have them fulfilled towards us, shall be afterward declared. But their accomplishment depends on God's faithfulness, and not on our sense of it. Where, therefore, we do not openly lay an obstruction against it, as in the case now mentioned, we may, we ought to believe that they are fulfilled towards us, although we are not continually sensible thereof. And, (2.) It is our duty to grow and thrive in holiness; and what God requires of us, we are to believe that he will help us in, and doth so,

whatever be our present sense and apprehension. And he who on these grounds can believe the growth of holiness in himself, though he have no sensible experience thereof, is, in my judgment, in as good, and perhaps a more safe, condition than he who, through the vigorous working of spiritual affections, is most sensible thereof: for it is certain that such an one doth not by any wilful neglect, or indulgence unto any sin, obstruct the growth of holiness, for he that doth so cannot believe that it doth thrive in him or is carried on, whatever his presumptions may be; and the life of faith, whereof this is a part, is every way a safe life. Besides, such a person is not in that danger of a vain elation of mind and carelessness thereon, as others may be; for wherein we live by faith, and not at all by sense, we shall be humble and fear always. Such an one not finding in himself the evidence of what he most desires, will be continually careful that he drive it not farther from him. But the reasons of this difficulty are:—

[1.] The work itself, as hath been before declared at large, is secret and mysterious; and, therefore (as in some), I hope in many, there is the reality and essence of holiness, who yet can find nothing of it in themselves, nor perhaps anyone else, but only Jesus Christ, who is of quick understanding in the fear of the Lord, so it may in the same secret manner thrive as to its degrees in them who yet perceive it not. There is not any thing in our whole course that we ought to be more awake unto than a diligent observation of the progress and decays of grace; for as the knowledge of them is of the same importance unto us with that of our duties and comforts, so they are very hardly and difficultly to be discerned, nor will be so truly for our good and advantage, without our utmost diligence and spiritual wisdom in their observation. Hence, as we before observed, it is compared in the Scripture frequently unto the growth of plants and trees, Hos. xiv. 5, 6; Isa. xliv. 3, 4. Now, we know that in those of them which are the most thrifty and flourishing, though we may perceive they are grown, yet we cannot discern their growing. And the apostle tells us, that as the "outward man perisheth, so the inward man is renewed day by day," 2 Cor. iv. 16. The perishing of the outward man is by those natural decays whereby it continually tends unto death and dissolution; and we know, many of us, how hardly these insensible decays are discerned, unless some great and violent disease befall us. We rather know that we are enfeebled and weakened by age and infirmities than perceive when or how. So is the inward man renewed in grace. It is by such secret ways and means as that its growth and decay are hardly to be apprehended. And yet he who is negligent in this inquiry walks at all peradventures with God, — knows not whereabout he is in his way, whether he be nearer or farther off from his journey's end than he was before. Write that man a fruitless and a thriftless Christian who calls not himself to an account about his increases and decays in grace. David knew this work to be of so great importance as that he would not trust to himself and ordinary assistances for the discharge of it, but earnestly calls on God to undertake it for him and to acquaint him with it, Ps. cxxxix. 23, 24.

[2.] There may some perplexing temptations befall the mind of a believer, or some corruption take advantage to break loose for a season, it may be for a long season, which may much gall the soul with its suggestions, and so trouble, disturb, and unquiet it, as that it shall not be able to make a right judgment of its grace and progress in holiness. A ship may be so tossed in a storm at sea as that the most skilful mariners may not be able to discern whether they make any way in their intended course and voyage, whilst they are carried on with success and speed. In such cases, grace in its exercise is principally engaged in an opposition unto its enemy, which it hath to conflict withal, and so its thriving other ways is not discernible. If it should be inquired how we may discern when grace is exercised and thrives in opposition unto corruptions and temptations, I say, that as great winds and storms do sometimes contribute to the fruit-bearing of trees and plants, so do corruptions and temptations unto the fruitfulness of grace and holiness. The wind comes with violence on the tree, ruffles its boughs, it may be breaks some of them, beats off its buds, loosens and shakes its roots, and threatens to cast the whole to the ground; but by this means the earth is opened and loosed about it, and the tree gets its roots deeper into the earth, whereby it receives more and fresh nourishment, which renders it fruitful, though it bring not forth fruit visibly, it may be, till a good while after. In the assaults of temptations and corruptions the soul is woefully ruffled and disordered, — its leaves of profession are much blasted, and its beginnings of fruit-bearing much broken and retarded; but, in the meantime, it secretly and invisibly casts out its roots of humility, self-abasement, [and] mourning, in a hidden and continual labouring of faith and love after that grace, whereby holiness doth really increase, and way is made for future visible fruitfulness: for, —

[3.] God, who in infinite wisdom manageth the new creature or whole life of grace by his Spirit, doth so turn the streams of it, and so renew and change the especial kinds of its operations, as that we cannot easily trace his paths therein, and may, therefore, be often at a loss about it, as not knowing well what he is doing with us. For instance, it may be the work of grace and holiness hath greatly put forth and evidenced itself in the affections, which are renewed by it. Hence persons have great experience of readiness unto, and delight and cheerfulness in, holy duties, especially those of immediate intercourse with God; for the affections are quick and vigorous, for the most part, in the youth of profession, and the operations of them being sensible unto them in whom they are, and their fruits visible, they make persons seem always fresh and green in the ways of holiness. But it may be, after awhile, it seems good to the sovereign Disposer of this affair to turn, as it were, the streams of grace and holiness into another channel. He sees that the exercise of humility, godly sorrow, fear, diligent conflicting with temptations, that, it may be, strike at the very root of faith and love, are more needful for them. He will, therefore, so order his dispensations towards them, by afflictions, temptations, occasions of life in the world, as that they shall have new work to do, and all the grace they have be turned into a new exercise. Hereon, it may be, they find not that sensible vigour in their spiritual affections, nor that delight in spiritual duties, which they have done formerly. This makes them sometimes ready to conclude that grace is decayed in them, that the springs of holiness are drying up, and they know neither where nor what they are. But yet, it may be, the real work of sanctification is still thriving and effectually carried on in them.

3. It is acknowledged that there may be, that there are in many, great decays in grace and holiness; that the work of sanctification goeth back in them, and that, it may be, universally and for a long season. Many actings of grace are lost in such persons, and the things that remain are ready to die. This the Scripture abundantly testifieth unto and giveth us instances of. How often doth God charge his people with backsliding, barrenness, decays in faith and love! And the experience of the days wherein we live sufficiently confirm the

truth of it. Are there not open and visible decays in many as to the whole spirit, all the duties and fruits, of holiness? Cannot the best among us contribute somewhat to the evidence hereof from our own experience? What shall we say, then? is there no sincere holiness where such decays are found? God forbid. But we must inquire the reasons whence this comes to pass, seeing this is contrary to the gradual progress of holiness in them that are sanctified, which we have asserted. And I answer two things unto it:—

(1.) That these decays are occasional and preternatural as to the true nature and constitution of the new creature, and a disturbance of the ordinary work of grace. They are diseases in our spiritual state, which it is not to be measured by. Are you dead and cold in duties, backward in good works, careless of your heart and thoughts, addicted to the world? — these things belong not to the state of sanctification, but are enemies unto it, sicknesses and diseases in the spiritual constitution of the persons in whom they are.

(2.) Although our sanctification and growth in holiness be a work of the Holy Spirit, as the efficient cause thereof, yet is it our own work also in a way of duty. He hath prescribed unto us what shall be our part, what he expects from us and requireth of us, that the work may be regularly carried on unto perfection, as was before declared. And there are two sorts of things which if we attend not unto in a due manner, the orderly progress of it will be obstructed and retarded; for, —

[1.] The power and growth of any lust or corruption, and a compliance from it with temptations, which is inseparable from the prevalency of any sin in us, lies directly against this progress. If we allow or approve of any such thing in us; if we indulge unto any actings of sin, especially when known and grown frequent, in any one kind; if we neglect the use of the best means for the constant mortification of sin, which every enlightened soul understands to be necessary thereunto, — there is, and will be increased, a universal decay in holiness, and not only in that particular corruption which is so spared and indulged. A disease in any one of the vitals, or principal parts of the body, weakens not only the part wherein it is, but the whole body itself, and vitiates the whole constitution by a sympathy of parts; and any particular lust indulged unto vitiates the whole spiritual health, and weakens the soul in all duties of obedience.

[2.] There are some things required of us to this end, that holiness may thrive and be carried on in us. Such are, the constant use of all ordinances and means appointed unto that end, a due observance of commanded duties in their season, with a readiness for the exercise of every especial grace in its proper circumstances. Now, if we neglect these things, if we walk at all peradventures with God, attending neither to means nor duties, nor the exercise of grace, as we should, we are not to wonder if we find ourselves decaying, yea, ready to die. Doth any man wonder to see a person formerly of a sound constitution grown weak and sickly, if he openly neglect all means of health, and contract all sorts of diseases by his intemperance? Is it strange that a nation should be sick and faint at heart, that grey hairs should be sprinkled upon it, that it should be poor and decaying, whilst consuming lusts, with a strange neglect of all invigorating means, do prevail in it? No more is it that a professing people should decay in holy obedience whilst they abide in the neglect expressed.

Having vindicated this assertion, I shall yet add a little farther improvement of it; and, if the work of holiness be such a progressive, thriving work in its own nature; if the design of the Holy Ghost, in the use of means, be to carry it on in us, and increase it more and more unto a perfect measure; then is our diligence still to be continued to the same end and purpose: for hereon depend our growth and thriving. It is required of us that we give all diligence unto the increase of grace, 2 Pet. i. 5–7, and that we abound therein, 2 Cor. viii. 7, "abounding in all diligence;" and not only so, but that we "show the same diligence unto the end," Heb. vi. 11. Whatever diligence you have used in the attaining or improving of holiness, abide in it unto the end, or we cast ourselves under decays and endanger our souls. If we slack or give over as to our duty, the work of sanctification will not be carried on in a way of grace. And this is required of us, this is expected from us, that our whole lives be spent in a course of diligent compliance with the progressive work of grace in us. There are three grounds on which men do or may neglect this duty, whereon the life of their obedience and all their comforts do depend:—

(1.) A presumption or groundless persuasion that they are already perfect. This some pretend unto in a proud and foolish conceit, destructive of the whole nature and duty of evangelical holiness or obedience; for this, on our part, consists in our willing compliance with the work of grace, gradually carried on unto the measure appointed unto us. If this be already attained, there is an end of all evangelical obedience, and men return again to the law unto their ruin. See Phil. iii. 12–14. It is an excellent description of the nature of our obedience which the apostle gives us in that place. All absolute perfection in this life is rejected as unattainable. The end proposed is blessedness and glory, with the eternal enjoyment of God; and the way whereby we press towards it, which compriseth the whole of our obedience, is by continual, uninterrupted following after, pressing, reaching out, — a constant progress, in and by our utmost diligence.

(2.) A foolish supposition that, being interested in a state of grace, we need not now be so solicitous about exact holiness and obedience in all things as we were formerly, whilst our minds hung in suspense about our condition. But so much as anyone hath this apprehension or persuasion prevailing in him or influencing of him, so much hath he cause deeply to question whether he have yet any thing of grace or holiness or no; for this persuasion is not of Him who hath called us. There is not a more effectual engine in the hand of Satan either to keep us off from holiness or to stifle it when it is attained, nor can any thoughts arise in the hearts of men more opposite to the nature of grace; for which cause the apostle rejects it with detestation, Rom. vi. 1, 2.

(3.) Weariness and despondencies, arising from oppositions. Some find so much difficulty in and opposition to the work of holiness and its progress from the power of corruptions, temptations, and the occasions of life in this world, that they are ready to faint and give over this diligence in duties and contending against sin. But the Scripture doth so abound with encouragements unto this sort of persons as that we need not to insist thereon.

Chapter III - Believers the only object of sanctification, and subject of gospel holiness

Believers the only subject of the work of sanctification — How men come to believe, if believers alone receive the Spirit of sanctification — The principal ends for which the Spirit is promised, with their order in their accomplishment — Rules to be observed in praying for the Spirit of God, and his operations therein — That believers only are sanctified or holy proved and confirmed — Mistakes about holiness, both notional and practical, discovered — The proper subject of holiness in believers.

That which we are next to inquire into is, the personal subject of this work of sanctification, or who, and of what sort, those persons are that are made holy. Now, these are all and only believers. All who unfeignedly believe in God through Jesus Christ are sanctified, and no others. Unto them is evangelical holiness confined. It is for them and them only that our Saviour prays for this mercy, grace, or privilege: John xvii. 17, "Sanctify them by thy truth." And concerning them he affirms, "For their sakes I sanctify myself, that they also may be sanctified through the truth," verse 19. And whereas, in the verses foregoing, he had immediate respect unto his apostles and present disciples, that we may know that neither his prayer nor his grace is confined or limited unto them, he adds, "Neither pray I for these alone," — that is, in this manner, and for these ends, — "but for them also which shall believe on me through their word," verse 20. It was, therefore, the prayer of our Lord Jesus Christ that all believers should be sanctified; and so also was it his promise: chap. vii. 38, 39, "He that believeth on me, as the Scripture hath said, out of his belly shall flow rivers of living water. But this spake he of the Spirit, which they that believe on him should receive." And it is with respect principally unto this work of sanctification that he is compared unto flowing and living water, as hath been declared before. It is for believers, the "church that is in God the Father and in the Lord Jesus Christ," — that is, by faith, — 1 Thess. i. 1, that our apostle prays that "the God of peace would sanctify them throughout," chap. v. 23.

But before we proceed to a farther confirmation of this assertion, an objection of some importance is to be removed out of our way: for on this supposition, that the Spirit of sanctification is given only unto believers, it may be inquired how men come so to be; for if we have not the Spirit until after we do believe, then is faith itself of ourselves. And this is that which some plead for, — namely, "That the gift of the Holy Ghost, unto all ends and purposes for which he is promised, is consequential unto faith, with the profession and obedience thereof, being, as it were, its reward." See Crell. de Spir. Sanc., cap. 5. To this purpose it is pleaded, "That the apostle Peter encourageth men unto faith and repentance with the promise that thereon they should 'receive the gift of the Holy Ghost,' Acts ii. 38; and so is that also of our Saviour, John xiv. 17, that 'the world,' — that is, unbelievers, — 'cannot receive the Spirit of truth:'

so that our faith and obedience are required as a necessary qualification unto the receiving of the Holy Ghost; and if they are so absolutely, then are they of ourselves, and not wrought in us by the grace of God;" — which is express Pelagianism.

Ans. I could dwell long on this inquiry concerning the especial subject of the Holy Spirit, seeing the right understanding of many places of Scripture doth depend thereon; but because I have much work yet before me, I will reduce what I have to offer on this head into as narrow a compass as possibly I may. In answer, therefore, to this objection, I say, —

1. That the Holy Spirit is said to be promised and received with respect unto the ends which he is promised for, and the effects which he worketh when he is received; for although he be himself but one, "the one and the self-same Spirit," and he himself is promised, given forth, and received, as we have declared, yet he hath many and diverse operations. And as his operations are divers, or [of] several sorts and kinds, so our receiving of him, as to the manner of it, is divers also, and suited unto the ends of his communications unto us. Thus, in some sense he is promised unto and received by believers; in another he is promised and received to make men so, or to make them believe. In the first way there may be some activity of faith in a way of duty, whereas in the latter we are passive, and receive him only in a way of grace.

2. The chief and principal ends for which the Holy Spirit is promised and received may be reduced to these four heads:— (1.) Regeneration; (2.) Sanctification; (3.) Consolation; (4.) Edification. There are, indeed, very many distinct operations and distributions of the Spirit, as I have in part already discovered, and shall yet farther go over them in particular instances; but they may be reduced unto these general heads, or at least they will suffice to exemplify the different manner and ends of the receiving of the Spirit. And this is the plain order and method of these things, as the Scripture both plainly and plentifully testifies:— (1.) He is promised and received as to the work of regeneration unto the elect; (2.) As to the work of sanctification unto the regenerate; (3.) As to the work of consolation unto the sanctified; and, (4.) As unto gifts for edification unto professors, according to his sovereign will and pleasure.

(1.) He is promised unto the elect, and received by them as to his work of regeneration. That this is his work in us wholly and entirely I have proved before at large. Hereunto the qualifications of faith and obedience are no way required as previously necessary in us. In order of nature, our receiving of the Spirit is antecedent to the very seed and principle of faith in us, as the cause is to the effect, seeing it is wrought in us by him alone; and the promises concerning the communication of the Spirit unto this end have been before explained and vindicated. Hereby doth the Holy Ghost prepare a habitation for himself, and make way for all the following work which he hath to do in us and towards us, unto the glory of God, and the perfecting of our salvation, or the making of us "meet for the inheritance of the saints in light," Col. i. 12.

(2.) He is promised and received as a Spirit of sanctification unto and by them that are regenerate, — that is, unto believers, — and only unto them. This will be fully confirmed immediately. And this puts an issue to the principal difficulty of the foregoing objection. It is no way inconsistent that faith should be required previously unto the receiving of the Spirit as a Spirit of sanctification, though it be not so as he is the author of regeneration. The same

Spirit first worketh faith in us, and then preserveth it when it is wrought. Only, to clear the manner of it, we may observe, — First, That sanctification may be considered two ways:— First, As to the original and essential work of it, which consists in the preservation of the principle of spiritual life and holiness communicated unto us in our regeneration. Secondly, As to those renewed actual operations whereby it is carried on, and is gradually progressive, as hath been declared. Secondly, Faith also, or believing, may be considered in this matter two ways:— First, As to its original communication, infusion, or creation in the soul; for it is the gift or work of God. In this respect, — that is, as to the seed, principle, and habit of it, — it is wrought in us, as all other grace is, in regeneration. Secondly, As to its actings in us, or as unto actual believing, or the exercise of faith and the fruits of it, in a constant profession and holy obedience. Sanctification in the first sense respects faith also in the first; that is, the preservation of the seed, principle, grace, habit of faith in us, belongs unto the sanctifying work of the Holy Spirit; and so believers only are sanctified. And in the latter sense it respects faith in the latter also; that is, the progress of the work of sanctification in us is accompanied with the actings and exercise of faith. But both ways faith is a necessary qualification in and unto them that are sanctified. Believers, therefore, are the adequate subject of the work of sanctification; which is all that at present is under our consideration. (3.) The Spirit is also promised as a comforter, or a Spirit of consolation. In this sense, or for this end and work, he is not promised unto them that are regenerate merely as such; for many may be regenerate who are not capable of consolation, nor do need it, as infants, who may be, and are, many of them, sanctified from the womb. Nor is he so promised unto them that are believers absolutely, who have the grace or habit of faith wrought in them; for so many have who are not yet exercised nor brought into that condition wherein spiritual consolations are either proper or needful unto them. The Spirit is promised as a comforter unto believers, as engaged in the profession of the gospel, and meeting with conflicts inward and outward on the account thereof. The first promise of the Holy Ghost as a comforter was made to the disciples, when their hearts were filled with sorrow on the departure of Christ; and this is the measure of all others, John xvi. 6, 7. And this is evident both from the nature of the thing itself, and from all the promises which are given concerning him to this end and purpose. And it will be wholly in vain at any time to apply spiritual consolations unto any other sort of persons. All men who have any interest in Christian religion, when they fall into troubles and distresses, be they of what sort they will, are ready to inquire after the things that may relieve and refresh them. And whereas there are many things in the word suited unto the relief and consolation of the distressed, they are apt to apply them unto themselves; and others also are ready to comply with them in the same charitable office, as they suppose. But no true spiritual consolation was ever administered by the word unto any but exercised believers, however the minds of men may be for the present a little relieved, and their affections refreshed, by the things that are spoken unto them out of the word: for the word is the instrument of the Holy Ghost, nor hath it any efficacy but as he is pleased to use it and apply it; and he useth it unto this end, and unto no other, as being promised as a Spirit of consolation, only to sanctified believers. And, therefore, when persons fall under spiritual convictions and trouble of mind or conscience upon the account of sin and guilt, it is not our first work to tender consolation unto them, whereby many in that condition are deluded, but to lead them on to believing, that, "being justified by faith, they may have peace with God;" which is their proper relief. And in that state God is abundantly willing that they should receive "strong consolation," even as many as "flee for refuge to the hope that is set before them."

(4.) The Spirit of God is promised and received as to gifts for the edification of the church. This is that which is intended, Acts ii. 38, 39. And his whole work herein we shall consider in its proper place. The rule and measure of the communication of the Spirit for regeneration is election; the rule and measure of the communication of the Spirit for sanctification is regeneration; and the rule and measure of his communication as a Spirit of consolation is sanctification, with the afflictions, temptations, and troubles of them that are sanctified. What, then, is the rule and measure of his communication as a Spirit of edification? I answer, Profession of the truth of the gospel and its worship, with a call unto the benefiting of others, 1 Cor. xii. 7. And here two rules must be observed:— [1.] That he carries not his gifts for edification out of the pale of the church, or profession of the truth and worship of the gospel. [2.] That he useth a sovereign and not a certain rule in this communication, 1 Cor. xii. 11, so as that he is not wanting unto any true professors, in proportion to their calls and opportunities.

Secondly, Whereas the Spirit of sanctification is promised only unto them that are regenerate and do believe, may we, in our prayers and supplications for him, plead these qualifications as arguments and motives for the farther communications of him unto us? Ans. 1. We cannot properly plead any qualification in ourselves, as though God were obliged, with respect unto them, to give a man increase of grace ex congruo, much less ex condigno. When we have done all, we are unprofitable servants. As we begin, so we must proceed with God, merely on the account of sovereign grace. 2. We may plead the faithfulness and righteousness of God as engaged in his promises. We ought to pray that he would "not forsake the work of his own hands;" that "he who hath begun the good work in us would perfect it until the day of Jesus Christ;" that with respect unto his covenant and promises he would preserve that new creature, that divine nature, which he hath formed and implanted in us.

3. Upon a sense of the weakness of any grace, we may humbly profess our sincerity therein, and pray for its increase. So cried the poor man with tears, "Lord, I believe; help thou mine unbelief," Mark ix. 24. And the apostles in their prayer, "Lord, increase our faith," Luke xvii. 5, owned the faith they had, and prayed for its increase by fresh supplies of the Holy Spirit. Again, Thirdly, May believers in trouble pray for the Spirit of consolation with respect unto their troubles, it being unto such that he is promised? Ans. 1. They may do so directly, and ought so to do; yea, when they do it not it is a sign they turn aside unto broken cisterns, that will yield them no relief. 2. Troubles are of two sorts, — spiritual and temporal. Spiritual troubles are so either, (1.) Subjectively, such as are all inward darknesses, and distresses on the account of sin; or, (2.) Objectively, such as are all persecutions for the name of Christ and the gospel. It is principally with respect unto these that the Spirit is promised as a comforter, and with regard unto them are we principally to pray for him as so promised. 3. In those outward troubles which are common unto believers with other men, as the death of relations, loss of estate or liberty, they may and ought to pray for the Spirit as a comforter, that the consolations of God,

administered by him, may outbalance their outward troubles, and keep up their hearts unto other duties.

Fourthly, May all sincere professors of the gospel pray for the Spirit with respect unto his gifts for the edification of others, seeing unto such he is promised for that end? Ans. 1. They may do so, but with the ensuing limitations:— (1.) They must do it with express submission to the sovereignty of the Spirit himself, who "divideth to every man as he will." (2.) With respect unto that station and condition wherein they are placed in the church by the providence and call of God. Private persons have no warrant to pray for ministerial gifts, such as should carry them out of their stations, without a divine direction going before them. (3.) That their end be good and right, to use them in their respective places unto edification. So ought parents and masters of families, and all members of churches, to pray for those gifts of the Spirit whereby they may fill up the duties of their places and relations.

From the consideration of this order of the dispensation of the Spirit we may be directed how to pray for him, which we are both commanded and encouraged to do, Luke xi. 13: for we are to pray for him with respect unto those ends and effects for which he is promised; and these are those which are before expressed, with all those particular instances which may be reduced unto them. We might, therefore, hence give direction in some inquiries, which, indeed, deserve a larger discussion if our present design would admit of it. One only I shall instance in:—

May a person who is yet unregenerate pray for the Spirit of regeneration to effect that work in him; for whereas, as such, he is promised only unto the elect, such a person, not knowing his election, seems to have no foundation to make such a request upon? Ans. 1. Election is no qualification on our part, which we may consider or plead in our supplications, but only the secret purpose on the part of God of what himself will do, and is known unto us only by its effects. 2. Persons convinced of sin and of a state of sin may and ought to pray that God, by the effectual communication of his Spirit unto them, would deliver them from that condition. This is one way whereby we "flee from the wrath to come." 3. The especial object of their supplications herein is sovereign grace, goodness, and mercy, as declared in and by Jesus Christ. Such persons cannot, indeed, plead any especial promise as made unto them; but they may plead for the grace and mercy declared in the promises, as indefinitely proposed unto sinners. It may be they can proceed no farther in their expectations but unto that of the prophet, "Who knoweth if God will come and give a blessing?" Joel ii. 14, yet is this a sufficient ground and encouragement to keep them waiting at the "throne of grace." So Paul, after he had received his vision from heaven, continued in great distress of mind, praying until he received the Holy Ghost, Acts ix. 11, 17. 4. Persons under such convictions have really sometimes the seeds of regeneration communicated unto them; and then, as they ought so they will continue in their supplications for the increase and manifestation of it.

It is evident that by these observations the foregoing objection is utterly removed out of the way, and that no disadvantage ariseth unto the doctrine of the free and effectual grace of God by confining this work of sanctification and holiness unto believers only. None are sanctified, none are made holy, but those who truly and savingly believe in God through Jesus Christ; which I shall now farther confirm:—

1. "Without faith it is impossible to please God," Heb. xi. 6. The faith discoursed of by the apostle is that whereby the fathers "received the promises, walked with God, and obtained the inheritance," — the faith of Abraham; that is, true, saving, justifying faith. This faith constitutes all them in whom it is true believers, and without it it is impossible to please God. Now, holiness, wherever it is, pleaseth God; and therefore without faith it is impossible we should have any interest in it. "This is the will of God, even our sanctification," 1 Thess. iv. 3; and walking therein we please God, verse 7. All that pleaseth God in us is our holiness, or some part of it, and it principally consists in an opposition unto all that displeaseth him. That which he commands pleaseth him, and that which he forbids displeaseth him; and our holiness consists in a compliance with the one and an opposition unto the other. Wherefore, that any others but believers should have any thing which really belongs unto this holiness, the apostle declares it to be impossible. Some would except against this sense of the words from the ensuing reason which the apostle gives of his assertion, which contains the nature of the faith intended: "For he that cometh unto God must believe that he is, and that he is a rewarder of them that diligently seek him;" for "this is that," they say, "which the light of nature directs unto, and therefore there is no other faith necessarily required that a man may please God, but only that which is included in the right use and exercise of natural reason." But this exception will no way evade the force of this testimony; for the apostle discourseth concerning such a coming unto God, and such a belief in him, as is guided, directed, and ingenerated in us, by the promises which it rests upon and is resolved into. Now these promises, all and every one of them, include Jesus Christ, with a respect unto him and his grace; and, therefore, the faith intended is that which is in God through Christ, as revealed and exhibited in the promises, and this coming unto God is a fruit and effect thereof.

2. Our Lord Jesus Christ affirms that men are sanctified by the faith that is in him: Acts xxvi 18, "That they may receive forgiveness of sins, and an inheritance among them that are sanctified by faith that is in me." If there were any other way or means whereby men might be sanctified or made holy, he would not have confined it unto the "faith that is in him;" at least, there is no other way to attain that holiness which may bring them unto the heavenly inheritance, or make them meet for it, Col. i. 12, which alone we inquire after. And, indeed, there can be no greater contempt cast on the Lord Jesus, and on the duty of believing in him, whereunto he makes this one of his principal motives, than to imagine that without faith in him anyone can be made holy.

3. Faith is the instrumental cause of our sanctification; so that where it is not, no holiness can be wrought in us. "God purifieth our hearts by faith," Acts xv. 9, and not otherwise; and where the heart is not purified, there is no holiness. All the duties in the world will not denominate him holy whose heart is not purified; nor will any such duties be holy themselves, seeing unto the unclean all things are unclean. All the obedience that is accepted with God is the "obedience of faith," Rom. i. 5; thence it springs, and therewith is it animated. So is it expressed, 1 Pet. i. 20–22, "You who by Christ do believe in God, and have purified your souls in obeying the truth through the Spirit." It is from faith in God through Jesus Christ, acting itself in obedience unto the gospel, that we purify or cleanse our souls; which is our sanctification. See Col. ii. 12–14, iii. 7–11.

4. All grace is originally intrusted in and with Jesus Christ. The image of God being lost in Adam, whatever was prepared or is used for the renovation of it in our natures and persons, wherein gospel holiness doth consist, was to be treasured up in him as the second Adam, by whom many are to be made alive who died in the first. It pleased the Father that "in him should all fullness dwell," — as the fullness of the Godhead, in and for his own divine personal subsistence, so the fullness of all grace for supplies unto us, that "of his fullness we might receive grace for grace." He is made the head unto the whole new creation, not only of power and rule, but of life and influence. God hath given him for a "covenant to the people," and communicates nothing that belongs properly to the covenant of grace, as our sanctification and holiness do, unto any, but in and through him. And we receive nothing by him but by virtue of relation unto him, or especial interest in him, or union with him. Where there is an especial communication, there must be an especial relation whereon it doth depend and whence it doth proceed; as the relation of the members unto the head is the cause and means why vital spirits are thence derived unto them. We must be in Christ as the branch is in the vine, or we can derive nothing from him: John xv. 4, "As the branch cannot bear fruit of itself, except it abide in the vine; no more can ye, except ye abide in me." Whatever any way belongeth unto holiness is our fruit, and nothing else is fruit but what belongeth thereunto. Now this our Saviour affirms that we can bring forth nothing of, unless we are in him and do abide in him. Now, our being in Christ and abiding in him is by faith, without which we can derive nothing from him, and consequently never be partakers of holiness in the least degree. But these things must be afterward spoken unto more at large. It is, therefore, undeniably evident that believers only are sanctified and holy; all others are unclean, nor is any thing they do holy, or so esteemed of God.

And the due consideration hereof discovers many pernicious mistakes that are about this matter, both notional and practical; for, — 1. There are some who would carry holiness beyond the bounds of an especial relation unto Christ, or would carry that relation beyond the only bond of it, which is faith; for they would have it to be no more than moral honesty or virtue, and so cannot with any modesty deny it unto those heathens who endeavoured after them according to the light of nature. And what need, then, is there of Jesus Christ? I can and do commend moral virtues and honesty as much as any man ought to do, and am sure enough there is no grace where they are not; yet to make any thing to be our holiness that is not derived from Jesus Christ, I know not what I do more abhor. An imagination hereof dethrones Christ from his glory, and overthrows the whole gospel. But we have a sort of men who plead that heathens may be eternally saved, so large and indulgent is their charity, and in the meantime endeavour, by all means possible, to destroy, temporally at least, all those Christians who stoop not to a compliance with all their imaginations. 2. Others there are who proceed much farther, and yet do but deceive themselves in the issue. Notions they have of good and evil by the light of nature, Rom. ii. 14, 15. As they come with men into the world, and grow up with them as they come to the exercise of their reason, so they are not stifled without offering violence to the principles of nature by the power of sin; as it comes to pass in many, Eph. iv. 19; 1 Tim. iv. 2; Rom. i. 31. These notions, therefore, are in many improved in process of time by convictions from the law, and great effects are produced hereby; for when the soul is once effectually convinced of sin, righteousness, and judgment, it cannot but endeavour after a deliverance from the one and an attainment of the other, that so it may be well with it at the last day. And here lie the springs or foundations of all the moral differences that we see amongst mankind. Some give themselves up unto all abominations, lasciviousness, uncleanness, drunkenness, frauds, oppressions, blasphemies, persecutions, as having no bounds fixed unto their lusts but what are given them by their own impotency or dread of human laws. Others endeavour to be sober, temperate, just, honest and upright in their dealings, with a sedulous performance of religious duties. This difference ariseth from the different power and efficacy of legal convictions upon the minds of men. And these convictions are in many variously improved, according to the light they receive in the means of knowledge which they do enjoy, or the errors and superstitions which they are misguided unto; for on this latter account do they grow up in some into penances, vows, uncommanded abstinences, and various self-macerations, with other painful and costly duties. Where the light they receive is, in the general, according unto truth, there it will engage men into reformation of life, a multiplication of duties, abstinence from sin, profession, zeal, and a cordial engagement into one way or other in religion. Such persons may have good hopes themselves that they are holy; they may appear to the world so to be, and be accepted in the church of God as such; and yet really be utter strangers from true gospel holiness. And the reason is, because they have missed it in the foundation; and not having, in the first place, obtained an interest in Christ, have built their house on the sand, whence it will fall in the time of trouble. If it be said that all those who come up unto the duties mentioned are to be esteemed believers, if therewith they make profession of the true faith of the gospel, I willingly grant it; but if it be said that necessarily they are so indeed, and in the sight of God, and therefore are also sanctified and holy, I must say the contrary[; it] is expressly denied in the gospel, and especial instances given thereof.

Wherefore let them wisely consider these things who have any conviction of the necessity of holiness. It may be they have done much in the pursuit of it, and have laboured in the duties that materially belong unto it. Many things they have done, and many things forborne, upon the account of it, and still continue so to do. It may be they think that for all the world they would not be found among the number of unholy persons at the last day. This may be the condition of some, perhaps of many, who are yet but young, and but newly engaged into these ways upon their convictions. It may be so with them who for many days and years have been so following after a righteousness in a way of duty. But yet they meet with these two evils in their way:— 1. That duties of obedience seldom or never prove more easy, familiar, or pleasant unto them than they did at first, but rather are more grievous and burdensome everyday. 2. That they never come up unto a satisfaction in what they do, but still find that there is somewhat wanting. These make all they do burdensome and unpleasant unto them, which at length will betray them into backsliding and apostasy. But yet there is somewhat worse behind; all they have done, or are ever able to do, on the bottom upon which they stand, will come to no account, but perish with them at the great day. Would we prevent all these fatal evils? would we engage in a real, thriving, everlasting holiness? — let our first business be to secure a relation unto Jesus Christ, without which nothing of it will ever be attained.

To close this discourse, I shall only from it obviate a putid calumny cast by the Papists, Quakers, and others of the same confederacy, against the grace of God, upon the doctrine of the free justification of a sinner, through the imputation of the righteousness of Christ: for with a shameless impudence they clamour on all by whom it is asserted, as those who maintain salvation to be attainable through a mere external imputation of righteousness; whilst those so saved are "unclean and unholy," as the Quakers, or "negligent of the duties of righteousness and obedience," as the Papists and others, slanderously report: for the frontless impudence of this calumny is sufficiently evident from hence, that as we assert sanctification and holiness to be peculiar only unto believing, justified persons, — that is, that faith and holiness are inseparable, habitually or actually, or in both regards, — so, in like manner, that all such persons are infallibly sanctified and made holy.

All believers, and only believers, being sanctified and made holy, what it is that is sanctified in them, or what is the proper seat and subject of this work, is, in the next place, to be declared; for it is not a mere external denomination, as things were called "holy" under the Old Testament, nor any transient act, nor any series or course of actions, that we plead about, but that which hath, as a real being and existence, so a constant abiding or residence in us. Hence, he that is holy is always so, whether he be in the actual exercise of the duties of holiness or no, though an omission of any of them in their proper season is contrary unto and an impeachment of holiness, as to its degrees. Now, this subject of sanctification is the entire nature or whole person of a believer. It is not any one faculty of the soul or affection of the mind or part of the body that is sanctified, but the whole soul and body, or the entire nature, of every believing person. And hereby is the work of sanctification really distinguished from any other mere common work which may represent it, or pretend unto it; for all such works are partial. Either they are in the mind only by light and notions of truth, or on the affections only in zeal and devotion, or on the mind and conscience in the convictions of sin and duty; but farther they proceed not. But true holiness consists in the renovation of our whole persons; which must be demonstrated.

1. That our entire nature was originally created in the image of God I have proved before, and it is by all acknowledged. Our whole souls, in the rectitude of all their faculties and powers, in order unto the life of God and his enjoyment, did bear his image. Nor was it confined unto the soul only; the body also, not as to its shape, figure, or natural use, but as an essential part of our nature, was interested in the image of God by a participation of original righteousness. Hence the whole person was a meet principle for the communication of this image of God unto others, by the means of natural propagation, which is an act of the entire person; for a person created and abiding in the image of God, begetting another in his own image and likeness, had, by virtue of the covenant of creation, begotten him in the image of God also, — that is, had communicated unto him a nature upright and pure.

2. By the entrance of sin, this image of God, so far as it was our righteousness and holiness before him, was utterly defaced and lost. This also I have sufficiently evidenced before. It did not depart from any one power, part, or faculty of our souls, but from our whole nature. Accordingly, the Scripture describes, — (1.) The depravation of our nature distinctly, in all the powers of it. In particular, the corruption that ensued on our minds, wills, and affections,

upon the loss of the image of God, I have before declared and vindicated. And, — (2.) In reference unto the first actings of all these faculties, in things moral and spiritual, the Scripture adds, that "all the thoughts and imaginations of our hearts are evil, and that continually," Gen. vi. 5. All the original first actings of the powers of our souls, in or about things rational and moral, are always evil; for "an evil tree cannot bring forth good fruit." That which is lame and distorted can act nothing that is straight and regular. Hence, — (3.) All the outward actions of persons in this state and condition are evil, unfruitful works of darkness. And not only so, but, (4.) The Scripture, in the description of the effects of this depravation of our nature, calls in the body and the members of it unto a partnership in all this obliquity and sin: the "members" of the body are "servants unto uncleanness and iniquity," Rom. vi. 19. And the engagement of them all in the course and actings of depraved nature is particularly declared by our apostle out of the psalmist, Rom. iii. 12–15, "They are all gone out of the way, they are together become unprofitable; there is none that doeth good, no, not one. Their throat is an open sepulchre; with their tongues they have used deceit; the poison of asps is under their lips: whose mouth is full of cursing and bitterness: their feet are swift to shed blood," in all ways of evil.

This being the state of our whole nature in its depravation, our sanctification, wherein alone its reparation in this life doth consist, must equally respect the whole. Some suppose that it is our affections only, in their deliverance from corrupt lusts and prejudices, with their direction unto heavenly objects, that are the subject of this work; for "the mind, or rational, intellectual power of the soul, is in itself," they say, "pure, noble, untainted, and needs no other aid but to be delivered from the prejudices and obstructions of its operations, which are cast upon it by the engagements and inclinations of corrupt affections, and a vicious course of conversation in the world, received by uninterrupted tradition from our fathers, from whence it is not able to extricate or deliver itself without the aid of grace." But they have placed their instance very unhappily; for, among all the things that belong unto our nature, there is not anyone which the Scripture so chargeth this depravation of it upon as the mind. This, in particular, is said to be "fleshly," to be "enmity against God," to be filled with "vanity, folly, and blindness," as we have at large before evinced. Nor is there any thing concerning which the work of sanctification and renovation is so expressly affirmed as it is concerning the mind. It is declared by the "renovation of our mind," Rom. xii. 2; or "being renewed in the spirit of our mind," Eph. iv. 23; that we "put on the new man, which is renewed in knowledge," Col. iii. 10; with other expressions of the like nature. It is therefore our entire nature that is the subject of evangelical holiness; for to manifest in particulars:—

1. Hence it is called the new man: Eph. iv. 24, "Put on the new man, which after God is created in righteousness and holiness." As the principle of sin and corrupted nature in us is called "The old man," for no other reason but that it possesseth all the active powers of the whole man, so that he neither doth nor can do any thing but what is influenced thereby; so this principle of holiness in us, the renovation of our natures, is called "The new man," because it possesseth the whole person with respect unto its proper operations and ends. And it extends itself as large as the old man, or the depravation of our natures, which takes in the whole person, soul and body, with all their faculties and powers.

2. The heart, in the Scripture, is taken for the whole soul, and all the faculties of it, as they are one common principle of all moral operations, as I have proved before; whatever, therefore, is wrought in and upon the heart, under this consideration, is wrought upon the whole soul. Now, this is not only said to be affected with this work of sanctification, or to have holiness wrought in it, but the principal description that is given us of this work consists in this, that therein and thereby a "new heart" is given unto us, or created in us, as it is expressed in the promise of the covenant. This, therefore, can be nothing but the possessing of all the powers and faculties of our souls with a new principle of holiness and obedience unto God.

3. There is especial mention made of the effecting of this work on our souls and bodies, with their powers and faculties distinctly. This I have already proved in the declaration of the work of our regeneration, or conversion to God; which is only preserved, cherished, improved, and carried on to its proper end, in our sanctification. The nature, also, of that spiritual light which is communicated unto our minds, of life unto our wills, of love unto our affections, hath been declared. Therefore doth it follow thence unavoidably, that the whole person is the subject of this work, and that holiness hath its residence in the whole soul entirely.

4. We need go no farther for the proof hereof than unto that prayer of the apostle for the Thessalonians which we insisted on at the beginning of this discourse: 1 Thess. v. 23, "The God of peace himself sanctify you ὁλοτελεῖς, throughout," — that is, "in your whole natures or persons, in all that you are and do, that you may not in this or that part, but be every whit clean and holy throughout." And to make this the more evident, that we may know what it is which he prays may be sanctified, and thereby preserved blameless to the coming of Christ, he distributes our whole nature into the two essential parts of soul and body. And in the former he considereth two things:— (1.) The spirit; (2.) The soul, peculiarly so called. And this distinction frequently occurs in the Scripture; wherein that by the "spirit" the mind or intellectual faculty is understood, and by the "soul" the affections, is generally acknowledged, and may evidently be proved. These, therefore, the apostle prays may be sanctified and preserved holy throughout and entirely,[1] and that by the infusion of a habit of holiness into them, with its preservation and improvement; whereof more afterward. But this is not all. Our bodies are an essential part of our natures, and by their union with our souls are we constituted individual persons. Now, we are the principles of all our operations as we are persons; every moral act we do is the act of the whole person. The body, therefore, is concerned in the good and evil of it. It became a subject of the depravation of our nature by concomitancy and participation, and is considered as one entire principle with the soul of communicating original defilement from parents unto children. Besides, it is now subject, in that corruption of its constitution which it is fallen under as a punishment of sin, unto many disorderly motions, that are incentives and provocations unto sin. Hence sin is said to "reign in our mortal bodies," and our "members to be servants unto unrighteousness," Rom. vi. 12, 19. Moreover, by its participation in the defilement and punishment of sin, the body is disposed and made obnoxious unto corruption and destruction; for death entered by sin, and no otherwise. On all these accounts, therefore, it is necessary, on the other hand, that the body should be interested in this work and privilege of sanctification and holiness; and so it is, — (1.) By

participation: for it is our persons that are sanctified and made holy ("Sanctify them throughout"); and although our souls are the first proper subject of the infused habit or principle of holiness, yet our bodies, as essential parts of our natures, are partakers thereof. (2.) By a peculiar influence of the grace of God upon them also, as far as they have any influence into moral operations; for the apostle tells us that "our bodies are members of Christ," 1 Cor. vi. 15, and so, consequently, have influences of grace from him as our head. (3.) In the work of sanctification the Holy Ghost comes and dwells in us; and hereon "our bodies are the temple of the Holy Ghost, which is in us;" and "the temple of God is holy," 1 Cor. iii. 16, 17, — although, I confess, this rather belongs unto the holiness of peculiar dedication unto God, whereof we shall treat afterward. And, [1.] Hereby are the parts and members of the body made instruments and "servants to righteousness unto holiness," Rom. vi. 19, — do become meet and fit for to be used in the acts and duties of holiness, as being made clean and sanctified unto God. [2.] Hereby are they disposed and prepared unto a blessed resurrection at the last day; which shall be wrought by the Spirit of Christ, which dwelt in them and sanctified them in this life, Rom. viii. 10, 11; Phil. iii. 20, 21; 2 Cor. iv. 14, 16, 17.

Our whole persons, therefore, and in them our whole natures, are the subject of this work, and true holiness invests the whole of it. Now, whether this universal investiture of our nature, in all the faculties and powers of it, by a new principle of holiness and obedience unto God, whereby it is renewed into his image, do belong unto that moral virtue which some so plead for as to substitute it in the room of gospel holiness, they may do well to consider who are the patrons of that cause; for if it do not, then doth not itself belong unto that holiness which the gospel teacheth, requireth, promiseth, and communicates, whatever else it be. And, moreover, it is practically worthy consideration that men deceive not themselves with a partial work in conviction only, or change of the affections also, instead of this evangelical sanctification. It is often and truly spoken unto, how men may have their minds enlightened, their affections wrought upon, and their lives much changed, and yet come short of real holiness. The best trial of this work is by its universality with respect unto its subject. If any thing remain unsanctified in us, sin may there set up its throne and maintain its sovereignty. But where this work is true and real, however weak and imperfect it may be as unto its degrees, yet it possesseth the whole person, and leaveth not the least hold unto sin, wherein it doth not continually combat and conflict with it. There is saving light in the mind, and life in the will, and love in the affections, and grace in the conscience, suited to its nature; there is nothing in us whereunto the power of holiness doth not reach according to its measure. Men may, therefore, if they please, deceive themselves by taking up with some notions in their minds, some devotions in their affections, or some good and virtuous deeds in their conversations, but holiness doth not consist therein.

And, lastly, men may hence see how vainly they excuse themselves in their sins, their passions, intemperances, and the like disorders of mind, from their constitutions and inclinations; for true sanctification reacheth unto the body also. It is true, grace doth not so change the natural constitution as to make him that was sickly to be healthy and strong, nor so as to make him who was melancholy to be sanguine, or the like; it altereth not the course of the blood, and the animal spirits, with the impressions they make on our minds. But consider these things morally, and as the whole person is a principle of spiritual and moral operations, and so it doth work such change and alteration on the whole person as to cure morally sinful distempers, as of passion, elation of mind, and intemperances, which men were before more than ordinarily inclined unto by their tempers and constitutions; yea, from the efficacy of it upon our whole persons, in the curing of such habitual inordinate and sinful distempers, lies the principal discovery of its truth and reality. Let no men, therefore, pretend that graçe and holiness do not change men's constitutions, thereby to excuse and palliate their disorderly passions before men, and to keep themselves from being humbled for them before God; for although it do not so naturally and physically, yet it doth so morally, so that the constitution itself shall be no more such a fomes and incentive unto disorderly passions as it hath been. If grace hath not cured that passion, pride, causeless anger, inveterate wrath, intemperance, which men's constitutions peculiarly incline unto, I know not, for my part, what it hath done, nor what a number of outward duties do signify. The Spirit and grace of Christ cause "the wolf to dwell with the lamb, and the leopard to lie down with the kid," Isa. xi. 6. It will change the most wild and savage nature into meekness, gentleness, and kindness; examples whereof have been multiplied in the world.

Footnotes:

1. "Fieri non potest ut sanctifcato Spiritu non sit sanctum etiam corpus, quo sanctificatus utitur Spiritus." — August. Lib. de Bono Viduitat.

Chapter IV - The defilement of sin, wherein it consists, with its purification

Purification the first proper notion of sanctification — Institution of baptism confirming the same apprehension — A spiritual defilement and pollution in sin — The nature of that defilement, or wherein it doth consist — Depravations of nature and acts with respect unto God's holiness, how and why called "filth" and "pollution" — Twofold pravity and defilement of sin — Its aggravations — We cannot purge it of ourselves, nor could it be done by the law, nor by any ways invented by men for that end.

These things being premised, we proceed to the consideration of sanctification itself, in a farther explication of the description before given; and the first thing we ascribe unto the Spirit of God herein, which constitutes the first part of it, is the purifying and cleansing of our nature from the pollution of sin. Purification is the first proper notion of internal real sanctification; and although, in order of time, it doth not precede the other acts and parts of this work, yet in order of nature it is first proposed and apprehended. To be unclean absolutely and to be holy are universally opposed. Not to be purged from sin is an expression of an unholy person, as to be cleansed is of him that is holy. And this purification, or the effecting of this work of cleansing, is ascribed unto all the causes and means of sanctification; as, — 1. Unto the Spirit, who is the principal efficient of the whole. Not that sanctification consists wholly herein, but firstly and necessarily it is required thereunto, Prov. xxx. 12; Ezek. xxxvi. 25, "I will sprinkle clean water upon you, and ye shall be clean: from all your filthiness, and from all your idols, will I cleanse you." That this sprinkling of clean water upon us is the communication of the Spirit unto us for the end designed, I have before evinced. It hath also been declared wherefore he is called "water," or compared thereunto. And the 27th verse shows expressly that it is the Spirit of God which is intended: "I will put my Spirit within you, and cause you to walk in my statutes." And that which he is thus in the first place promised for is the cleansing of us from the pollution of sin; which, in order of nature, is preposed unto his enabling us to walk in God's statutes, or to yield holy obedience unto him.

To the same purpose, among many others, is that promise, Isa. iv. 4, "When the Lord shall have washed away the filth of the daughters of Zion, and shall have purged the blood of Jerusalem from the midst thereof by the Spirit of judgment, and by the Spirit of burning." Upon what ground the Spirit is compared to fire, and thence here called a "Spirit of burning," hath been also declared. In brief, fire and water were the means whereby all things were purified and cleansed typically in the law, Num. xxxi. 23; and the Holy Spirit being the principal efficient cause of all spiritual cleansing is compared to them both (by which his work was signified), and called by their names. See Mal. iii. 2, 3. And "judgment" is frequently taken for holiness. "The Spirit of judgment," therefore, and the "Spirit of burning," is the Spirit of sanctification and purification. And he is here promised for the sanctification of the elect of God. And how shall he effect this work? He shall do it, in the first place, by "washing away their filth and purging away their blood;" — that is, all their spiritual, sinful defilements.

2. The application of the death and blood of Christ unto our souls, for our sanctification, by the Holy Ghost, is said to be for our cleansing and purging: Eph. v. 25, 26, "Christ loved the church, and gave himself for it; that he might sanctify and cleanse it with the washing of water by the word." He "gave himself for us, that he might redeem us from all iniquity, and purify unto himself a peculiar people, zealous of good works," Tit. ii. 14. "The blood of Jesus Christ cleanseth us from all sin," 1 John i. 7. "He loved us, and washed us from our sins in his own blood," Rev. i. 5. "The blood of Christ purgeth our conscience from dead works to serve the living God," Heb. ix. 14. Respect, I acknowledge, in some of these places, may be had unto the expiation of the guilt of sin by the blood of Christ as offered in sacrifice, for so "by himself he purged our sins," Heb. i. 3; but as they all suppose a defilement in sin, so the most of them respect its cleansing by the application of the virtue of the blood of Christ unto our souls and consciences in our sanctification. And, —

3. Moreover, where sanctification is enjoined us as our duty, it is prescribed under this notion of cleansing ourselves from sin: "Wash you, make you clean," Isa. i. 16. "O Jerusalem, wash thine heart from wickedness, that thou mayest be saved," Jer. iv. 14. "Having therefore these promises, let us cleanse ourselves from all filthiness of the flesh and spirit, perfecting holiness in the fear of God," 2 Cor. vii. 1. "Every man that hath this hope in him purifieth himself," 1 John iii. 3; Ps. cxix. 9; 2 Tim. ii. 21. And the like expressions of this duty occur in other places.

4. Answerable unto these promises and precepts, and in confirmation of them, we have the institution of the ordinance of baptism, the outward way and means of our initiation into the Lord Christ and the profession of the gospel, the great representation of the inward "washing of regeneration," Tit. iii. 5. Now this baptism, in the first place, expresseth the outward "putting away of the filth of the flesh," by external washing with material water, 1 Pet. iii. 21. And that which answers hereunto can be nothing but the inward purifying of our souls and consciences by the grace of the Spirit of God; that is, saith our apostle, the "putting off the body of the sins of the flesh," Col. ii. 11, which contains the whole defilement and corruption of sin: and this also was typed out unto us by all the legal purifications of old. Wherefore, we shall do three things in the explication of this first branch of our sanctification:— 1. Show that there is a spiritual pollution and defilement in sin; 2. Declare what it is, or wherein it doth consist; and, 3. Manifest how it is removed or washed away, and believers made holy thereby.

For the first, it needs not much to be insisted on. Our minds and their conceptions are in these things to be regulated by divine revelation and expressions. And in the whole representation made unto us in the Scripture of the nature of sin, of our concernment therein, of the respect of God towards us on the account thereof, of the way and means whereby we may be delivered from it, there is nothing so much inculcated as its being filthy, abominable, full of defilement and pollution; which is set forth both in plain expressions and various similitudes. On the account hereof is it said to be "abhorred of God, the abominable thing which his soul hateth, which he cannot behold, which he cannot but hate and detest;" and it is compared to "blood, wounds, sores, leprosy, scum, loathsome diseases." With respect hereunto is it so frequently declared that we must be "washed, purged, purified, cleansed," as in the testimonies before cited, before we can be accepted with him or be brought to the enjoyment of him. And the work of the Spirit of Christ in the application of his blood unto us for the taking away of sin is compared to the effects of "fire, water, soap, nitre," everything that hath a purifying, cleansing faculty in it. These things so frequently occur in the Scripture, and testimonies concerning them are so multiplied, that it is altogether needless to produce particular instances. This is evident and undeniable, that the Scripture, which regulates our conceptions about spiritual things, expressly declares all sin to be "uncleanness," and every sinner to be "defiled" thereby, and all unsanctified persons to be "wholly unclean;" and how far these expressions are metaphorical, or wherein the metaphor doth consist, must be afterward declared.

Besides, there is no notion of sin and holiness whereof believers have a more sensible, spiritual experience; for although they may not or do not comprehend the metaphysical notion or nature of this pollution and defilement of sin, yet they are sensible of the effects it produceth in their minds and consciences. They find that in sin which is attended with shame and self-abhorrency, and requires deep abasement of soul. They discern in it, or in themselves on the account of it, an unsuitableness unto the holiness of God, and an unfitness thereon for communion with him. Nothing do they more earnestly labour after in their prayers and supplications than a cleansing from it by the blood of Christ, nor are any promises more precious unto them than those which express their purification and purging from it; for these are they which, next unto their interest in the atonement made by the sacrifice of Christ, give them boldness in their approaches unto God. So our apostle fully expresseth it, Heb. x. 19–22: "Having therefore boldness to enter into the holiest by the blood of Jesus, by a new and living way, which he hath consecrated for us, through the veil, that is to say, his flesh; and having an high priest over the house of God; let us draw near with a true heart in full assurance of faith, having our hearts sprinkled from an evil conscience, and our bodies washed with pure water." The foundation of all our confidence in our access unto God, the right and title we have to approach unto him, is laid in the blood of Christ, the sacrifice he offered, the atonement he made, and the remission of sins which he obtained thereby: which effect of it he declares, verse 19, "Having boldness by the blood of Jesus." The way of our access is by pleading an interest in his death and suffering, whereby an admission and acceptance is consecrated for us: Verse 20, "By a new and living way, which he hath consecrated." And our encouragement to make use of this foundation and to engage in this way is taken from his discharge of the office of a high priest in our behalf: '"Having an high priest over the house of God, let us draw near."

But besides all this, when we come to an actual address unto God, that we may make use of the boldness given us in the full assurance of faith, it is moreover required that "our hearts be sprinkled, and our bodies washed;" — that is, that our whole persons be purified from the defilement of sin by the sanctification of the Spirit. And this experience of believers we cannot only oppose unto and plead against the stupidity of such persons by whom these things are derided, but conclude from it that those who are unacquainted with it, in some degree of sincerity, are wholly uninterested in that evangelical holiness which we inquire after. We need not, therefore, farther labour in the confirmation of that concerning which the testimonies of Scripture are so multiplied, and whereof we have such undoubted experience.

Secondly, The nature of this defilement of sin must be inquired into. 1. By some it is reckoned unto guilt; for whereas the inseparable effects of guilt are shame and fear, whereby it immediately evidenced itself in our first parents, and shame, in particular, is from this filth of sin, it may be esteemed an adjunct thereof. Hence sin was said to be "purged by sacrifices" when its guilt was expiated; and Christ is said to "purge our sins by himself," — that is, when he offered himself a sacrifice for us, chap. i. 3. And therefore it is granted, that so far as the filth of sin was taken away, not by actual purification, but by legal expiation, it is sin with its guilt that was intended. But the Scripture, as we have showed, intendeth more hereby, even such an internal, inherent defilement as is taken away by real actual sanctification, and no otherwise. 2. There are some especial sins which have a peculiar pollution and defilement attending them, and which thereon are usually called "uncleanness" in a peculiar manner. The ground hereof is in that of the apostle, 1 Cor. vi. 18: "Flee fornication. Every sin that a man doeth is without the body; but he that committeth fornication sinneth against his own body." All sins of that nature have a peculiar defilement and filth accompanying them. And holiness is sometimes mentioned in an opposition unto this especial pollution, 1 Thess. iv. 3. But yet this is not that which we inquire after, although it be included in it as one especial kind of it. That which we now consider always inseparably attends every sin as sin, as an adjunct or effect of it. It is the uncleanness of all sin, and not the sin of uncleanness, which we intend; and for the discovery of its proper nature we may observe, —

(1.) That the pollution of sin is that property of it whereby it is directly opposed unto the holiness of God, and which God expresseth his holiness to be contrary unto. Hence he is said to be "of purer eyes than to behold evil, or to look on iniquity," Hab. i. 13. It is a thing vile and loathsome unto the eyes of his holiness, Ps. v. 4–6. So, speaking concerning it, he useth that pathetical dehortation, "Oh, do not this abominable thing that I hate," Jer. xliv.

4. And with respect unto his own holiness it is that he sets it forth by the names of all things which are vile, filthy, loathsome, offensive, — everything that is abominable. It is so to him, as he is infinitely pure and holy in his own nature. And that consideration which ingenerates shame and self-abhorrency on the account of the defilement of sin is taken peculiarly from the holiness of God. Hence it is that persons are so often said to "blush," to be "ashamed," to be "filled with confusion of face," to be "vile," to be "abased in their own sight," under a sense and apprehension of this filth of sin.

(2.) The holiness of God is the infinite, absolute perfection and rectitude of his nature, as the eternal original cause and pattern of truth, uprightness, and rectitude in all. And this holiness doth God exert, as in all he doth, naturally and necessarily, so particularly in his law; which is therefore good, holy, and perfect, because it represents the holiness of God, which is impressed on it. God might not have made any creature nor given a law, which are free acts of his will; but on supposition he would do so, it was absolutely necessary from his own nature that this law of his should be holy. And, therefore, whatever is contrary unto or different from the law of God is so unto and from the holiness of God himself. Hence it follows, —

(3.) That this defilement and pollution of sin is that pravity, disorder, and shameful crookedness that is in it, with respect unto the holiness of God as expressed in the law. Sin is either original or actual. Original sin is the habitual inconformity of our natures unto the holiness of God expressed in the law of creation. Actual sin is our inconformity to God and his holiness expressed in the particular commands of the law. The nature of all sin, therefore, consists in its enmity, its inconformity to the rule. Now, this rule, which is the law, may be considered two ways, which give a twofold respect, or inseparable consequent or adjunct, unto every sin:—

[1.] As it expresseth the authority of God in its precepts and sanction. Hence guilt inseparably follows every sin, which is the respect it induceth on the sinner unto the law, upon the account of the authority of the Lawgiver. The act of sin passeth away, but this guilt abideth on the person, and must do so, until the law be satisfied, and the sinner thereon absolved. This naturally produceth fear, which is the first expression of a sense of guilt. So Adam expressed it upon his sin: "I heard thy voice, and I was afraid," Gen. iii. 10.

[2.] The law may be considered as it expresseth the holiness of God and his truth; which it was necessary, from the nature of God, that it should do. Hence there is in sin a peculiar inconformity to the holiness of God; which is the "macula," the "spot," "stain," and "filth" of it; which are inseparable from it whilst God is holy, unless it be purged and done away, as we shall show. And this is inseparably attended with shame; which is the expression of a sense of this filth of sin. So Adam upon his sin had his eyes open to see his nakedness, and was filled with shame. This is the order of these things:— God, who is the object of our obedience and sin, is considered as the supreme lawgiver. On his law he hath impressed his authority and his holiness. Sin, with respect unto his authority, is attended with guilt; and this, in the conscience of the sinner, produceth fear: as it respects the holiness of God, it is attended with filth or uncleanness; and this produceth shame. And the ultimate effects of it are, on the first account, "pœna sensus;" on the other, "pœna damni." This, therefore, is the spot, the stain, the pollution of sin, which is purged in our sanctification, — the perverse disorder and shameful crookedness that is in sin with respect unto the holiness of God.

And herein there is a real filthiness, but spiritual, which is compared with and opposed unto things materially and carnally so. "Not that which goeth into a man," meat of any sort, "defileth him," saith our Saviour, "but that which cometh out of the heart," — that is, spiritually, with respect unto God, his law and holiness. And as men are taught the guilt of sin by their own fear, which is the inseparable adjunct of it, so are they taught the filth of sin by their own shame, which unavoidably attends it. To instruct us herein is one end of the law and the gospel; for in the renovation of the law, which was added to the promise "because of transgressions," Gal. iii. 19, and in the institutions annexed unto it, God designed to instruct us farther in them both, with the ways whereby we may be freed from them. In the doctrine of the law, with the sanction and curse of it, and the institution of sacrifices to make atonement for sin, God declared the nature of guilt and its remedy. By the same law, and by the institution of sundry ordinances for purification and cleansing, as also by determining sundry ceremonial defilements, he makes known the nature of this filth and its remedy. To what end were so many meats and drinks, so many diseases and natural distempers, so many external fortuitous accidents, as touching the dead, and the like, made religiously unclean by the law? It was to no other but to teach us the nature of the spiritual defilement of sin. And to the same end, together with a demonstration of the relief and remedy thereof, were the ordinances of purification instituted; which, as they were outward and carnal, purged those uncleannesses, as they also were outward and carnal, made so by the law. But internal and spiritual things were taught and prefigured hereby, yea, wrought and effected, by virtue of their typical relation to Christ, as the apostle teacheth: Heb. ix. 13, 14, "If the blood of bulls and of goats, and the ashes of an heifer sprinkling the unclean, sanctifieth to the purifying of the flesh: how much more shall the blood of Christ purge your conscience from dead works to serve the living God?" And hence the whole work of sanctification is expressed by "opening a fountain for sin and for uncleanness;" that is, the purging of them away, Zech. xiii. 1. So is it in the gospel, where the blood of Christ is said to "purge" our sins with respect to guilt, and to "wash" our souls with respect to filth. Yea, so inseparable is this filth from sin, and shame from filth, that wherever abides a sense of sin, there is a sense of this filth with shame. The very heathen, who had only the workings of their minds and consciences for their guide, were never able to quit themselves from a sense of this pollution of sin; and thence proceeded all those ways of lustration, purgation, and cleansing, by washings, sacrifices, and mysterious ceremonious observances, which they had invented. It remains, therefore, only that we inquire a little into the reasons and causes why this pravity of sin and discrepancy from the holiness of God is such a defilement of our natures, and so inseparably attended with shame; for without the consideration hereof we can never understand the true nature of sanctification and holiness. And it will, also, then yet farther appear how openly they betray their prodigious ignorance of these things who pretend that all grace consists in the practice of moral virtues. And we may to this purpose observe, —

1. That the spiritual beauty and comeliness of the soul consists in its conformity unto God. Grace gives beauty. Hence it is said of the Lord Christ that he is "fairer," or more beautiful, "than the children of men," and that because "grace was poured into his lips," Ps. xlv. 2. And when the church is furnished or adorned with his graces, he affirms her to be "fair and comely," Cant. i. 5, vi. 4, vii. 6. Christ by washing of it takes away its "spots and wrinkles," rendering it beautiful, — that is, "holy and without blemish," Eph. v. 27. And this beauty originally consisted in the image of God in us, which contained the whole order, harmony, and symmetry of our natures, in all their faculties and actions, with respect unto God and our utmost end. That, therefore, which is contrary hereunto, as is all and every sin, hath a deformity in it, or brings spots, stains, and wrinkles on the soul. There is in sin all that is contrary to spiritual beauty and comeliness, to inward order and glory; and this is the filth and pollution of it.

2. Holiness and conformity to God is the honour of our souls. It is that alone which makes them truly noble; for all honour consists in an accession unto him who is the only spring and absolute possessor of all that is so, in whom alone is originally and perfectly all being and substance. Now, this we have alone by holiness, or that image of God wherein we are created. Whatever is contrary hereunto is base, vile, and unworthy. This is sin; which is, therefore,

the only base thing in nature. Hence it is said of some great sinners that they had "debased themselves to hell," Isa. lvii. 9. This belongs to the pollution of sin, — that it is base, vile, unworthy, dishonouring the soul, filling it with shame in itself and contempt from God; and there are no persons, who are not absolutely hardened, but are in their own minds and consciences sensible of this baseness of sin, as they are also of the deformity that is in it. When men's eyes are opened to see their nakedness, how vile and base they have made themselves by sin, they will have a sense of this pollution not easily to be expressed. And from hence it is that sin hath the properties and effects of uncleanness in the sight of God and in the conscience of the sinner:— God abhors, loathes it, accounts it an abominable thing, as that which is directly contrary to his holiness, which, as impressed on the law, is the rule of purity, integrity, spiritual beauty, and honour; and in the conscience of the sinner it is attended with shame, as a thing deformed, loathsome, vile, base, and dishonourable. See Jer. ii. 26.

In all in whom it is, I say, unless they are blind and obdurate, it fills them with shame. I speak not of such as are little or not at all spiritually sensible of sin or any of its properties, who fear not because of its guilt, nor are disquieted by its power, nor acquainted with its fomes or disposition to evil, and so not ashamed of its filth; much less of such as are given over to work all uncleanness with delight and greediness, wallowing in the pollution of it, like the sow in the mire, who not only do the things which God abhorreth, but also have pleasure in them that do them; but those I intend who have the least real conviction of the nature and tendency of sin, who are all, in one degree or other, ashamed of it as a filthy thing. And a casting off of outward shame, that is so from its object, or shame with respect unto the conscience and judgment of human kind, — as those do who "proclaim their sins as Sodom, and hide them not," — is the highest aggravation of sinning and contempt of God; and the casting out of inward shame, with respect unto the divine omniscience, is the highest evidence of a reprobate mind. But in all others, who have more light and spiritual sense, it produceth shame and self-abhorrency, which hath always a respect unto the holiness of God; as Job xlii. 5, 6. They see that in sin which is so vile, base, and filthy, and which renders them so, that, like unto men under a loathsome disease, they are not able to bear the sight of their own sores, Ps. xxxviii. 5. God detesteth, abhorreth, and turneth from sin as a loathsome thing, and man is filled with shame for it; it is, therefore, filthy. Yea, no tongue can express the sense which a believing soul hath of the uncleanness of sin with respect unto the holiness of God. And this may suffice to give a little prospect into the nature of this defilement of sin, which the Scripture so abundantly insisteth on, and which all believers are so sensible of.

This pravity or spiritual disorder with respect unto the holiness of God, which is the shameful defilement of sin, is twofold:— 1. That which is habitual in all the faculties of our souls by nature, as they are the principle of our spiritual and moral operations. They are all shamefully and loathsomely depraved, out of order, and no way correspondent unto the holiness of God. Hence by nature we are wholly unclean; — who can bring a clean thing out of that which is unclean? And this uncleanness is graphically expressed under the similitude of a wretched, polluted infant, Ezek. xvi. 3–5. 2. That which is actual in all the actings of our faculties as so defiled, and as far as they are so defiled; for, — (1.) Be any sin of what nature it will, there is a pollution attending it.

Hence the apostle adviseth us to "cleanse ourselves from all pollutions of the flesh and spirit," 2 Cor. vii. 1. The sins that are internal and spiritual, as pride, self-love, covetousness, unbelief, have a pollution attending them, as well as those which are fleshly and sensual. (2.) So far as any thing of this pravity or disorder mixeth itself with the best of our duties, it renders both us and them unclean: Isa. lxiv. 6, "We are all as an unclean thing, and all our righteousnesses are as filthy rags."

This uncleanness as it is habitual, respecting our natural defilement, is equal in and unto every one that is born into the world; we are by nature all alike polluted, and that to the utmost of what our nature is capable. But with respect unto actual sins it is not so; for in them it hath various degrees and aggravations, even as many as sin itself hath:— 1. The greater the sin is from its nature or circumstances, the greater is the defilement wherewith it is attended. Hence there is no sin expressed under such terms of filthiness and abhorrence as idolatry, which is the greatest of sins. See Ezek. xvi. 36, 37. Or, 2. There is an aggravation of it when the whole person is defiled, as it is in the case of fornication, before instanced in.

3. It is heightened by a continuance in sin, whereby an addition is made to its pollution every day, and which is called "wallowing in the mire," 2 Pet. ii. 22.

I have in this whole discourse but touched upon this consideration of sin, which the Scripture so frequently mentions and inculcates; for as all the first institutions of divine worship recorded therein had some respect hereunto, so the last rejection of obstinate sinners mentioned in it is, "He which is filthy," or unclean, "let him be filthy still," Rev. xxii. 11. Neither is there any notion of sin, whereby God would convey an apprehension of its nature and an abhorrency thereof unto our minds and consciences, so frequently insisted on as is this of its pollution. And in order to our use of it unto the discovery of the nature of holiness, we may yet observe these three [five?] things:—

1. Where this uncleanness abideth unpurged, there neither is nor can be any true holiness at all, Eph. iv. 22–24; for it is universally opposed unto it, — it is our unholiness. Where, therefore, it is absolute, and purified in no measure or degree, there is no work of sanctification, no holiness so much as begun; for in the purging hereof it makes its entrance upon the soul, and its effect therein is the first beginning of holiness in us. I acknowledge that it is not in any at once absolutely and perfectly taken away in this world; for the work of purging it is a continued act, commensurate unto the whole work of our sanctification: and, therefore, they who are truly sanctified and holy are yet deeply sensible of the remainder of it in themselves, do greatly bewail it, and earnestly endeavour after the removal of it. But there is an initial, real, sincere, and (as to all the faculties of the soul) universal purging of it, which belongs to the nature and essence of holiness, begun and carried on, though not absolutely perfected, in this life. And men who pretend unto a grace and holiness that should consist in moral virtue only, without a supposition of and respect unto the purification of this pollution of sin, do but deceive their own souls and others, so far as any are forsaken of God to give credit unto them. The virtues of men not purged from the uncleanness of their natures are an abomination to the Lord, Tit. i. 15.

2. Unless this uncleanness of sin be purged and washed away, we can never come unto the enjoyment of God: "Nothing that defileth shall in any wise enter into the new Jerusalem," Rev. xxi. 27. To suppose that an unpurified

sinner can be brought unto the blessed enjoyment of God, is to overthrow both the law and the gospel, and to say that Christ died in vain. It is, therefore, of the same importance with the everlasting salvation of our souls to have them purged from sin.

3. We are not able of ourselves, without the especial aid, assistance, and operation of the Spirit of God, in any measure or degree to free ourselves from this pollution, neither that which is natural and habitual nor that which is actual. It is true, it is frequently prescribed unto us as our duty, — we are commanded to "wash ourselves," to "cleanse ourselves from sin," to "purge ourselves" from all our iniquities, and the like, frequently; but to suppose that whatever God requireth of us that we have power of ourselves to do, is to make the cross and grace of Jesus Christ of none effect. Our duty is our duty, constituted unalterably by the law of God, whether we have power to perform it or no, seeing we had so at our first obligation by and unto the law, which God is not obliged to bend unto a conformity to our warpings, nor to suit unto our sinful weaknesses. Whatever, therefore, God worketh in us in a way of grace, he prescribeth unto us in a way of duty, and that because although he do it in us, yet he also doth it by us, so as that the same work is an act of his Spirit and of our wills as acted thereby. Of ourselves, therefore, we are not able, by any endeavours of our own, nor ways of our own finding out, to cleanse ourselves from the defilement of sin. "If I be wicked," saith Job, "why then labour I in vain? If I wash myself with snow water, and make my hands never so clean, yet shalt thou plunge me in the ditch, and mine own clothes shall make me to be abhorred," chap. ix. 29–31. There may be ways and means used whereby an appearance of washing and cleansing may be made; but when things come to be tried in the sight of God, all will be found filthy and unclean. In vain, saith the prophet, shalt thou take to thyself soap and much nitre, thou shalt not be purged, Jer. ii. 22. The most probable means of cleansing, and the most effectual in our judgment, however multiplied, shall fail in this case. Some speak much of "washing away their sins by the tears of repentance;" but repentance as prescribed in the Scripture is of another nature, and assigned unto another end. And for men's tears in this matter, they are but "soap and nitre," which, howsoever multiplied, will not produce the effect intended; and therefore doth God, in places of Scripture innumerable, take this to himself as the immediate effect of his Spirit and grace, — namely, to "cleanse us from our sins and our iniquities."

4. The institutions of the law for this end, to purge uncleanness, could not of themselves reach thereunto. They did, indeed, purify the unclean legally, and sanctified persons as to the "purifying of the flesh," Heb. ix. 13, so that they should not on their account be separated from their privileges in the congregation and the worship of God; but of themselves they could go no farther, chap. x. 1–4, only they did typify and signify that whereby sin was really cleansed. But the real stain is too deep to be taken away by any outward ordinances or institutions; and therefore God, as it were, rejecting them all, promiseth to open another fountain to that purpose, Zech. xiii. 1. Wherefore, —

5. There is a great emptiness and vanity in all those aids and reliefs which the papal church hath invented in this case. Sensible they are of the spot and stain that accompanies sin, of its pollution and defilement, which none can avoid whose consciences are not utterly hardened and blinded; but they are ignorant of the true and only means and remedy thereof. And, therefore, as in

the work of justification, being ignorant of the righteousness of God, and going about to establish their own righteousness, they submit not themselves to the righteousness of God, as the apostle spake of their predecessors; so in the work of sanctification, being ignorant of the ways of the working of the Spirit of grace and efficacy of the blood of Christ, they go about to set up their own imaginations, and submit not themselves unto a compliance with the grace of God. Thus, in the first place, they would (at least the most of them would) have the whole uncleanness of our natures to be washed away by baptism, "virtute operis operati." The ordinance being administered, without any more to do, or any previous qualifications of the person, internal or external, the filth of original sin is washed away; though it fell not out so with Simon Magus, who, notwithstanding he was baptized by Philip the evangelist, and that upon his visible profession and confession, yet continued "in the gall of bitterness and bond of iniquity," and was therefore certainly not cleansed from his sins. But there is a cleansing in profession and signification, and there is a cleansing in the reality of sanctification. The former doth accompany baptism when it is rightly administered. With respect hereunto are men said to be "purged from their old sins," — that is, to have made a profession, and have had a fair representation thereof in being made partakers of the outward sign of it, — 2 Pet. i. 9; as also to escape the "pollutions of the world" and the "lusts of the flesh," chap. ii. 18, 20. But all this may be, and yet sin not be really purged; for not only the "outward washing of regeneration" in the pledge of it, but the "internal renovation of the Holy Ghost," is required thereunto, Tit. iii. 5. But having thus shifted themselves of the filth of original sin, as easily as a man may put off his clothes when they are foul, they have found out many ways whereby the ensuing defilements that attend actual sins may be purged or done away. There is the sprinkling of holy water, confession to a priest, penances, in fasting and some other abstinences, that are supposed to be of wonderful virtue to this end and purpose. And I do acknowledge that the one art of confession is really the greatest invention to accommodate the inclinations of all flesh that ever this world was acquainted withal: for as nothing is so suited unto all the carnal interests of the priests, be they what they will, nor so secures them a veneration in the midst of their looseness and worthless conversation; so for the people, who, for the most part, have other business to do than long to trouble themselves about their sins, or find it uneasy to be conversant about their guilt and the consequences of it in their minds, it is such an expedite course of absolute exoneration, that they may be free for other sins or businesses, to deposit them wholly and safely with a priest, that nothing equal unto it could ever have been invented; — for the real way of dealing with God by Jesus Christ in these things, with endeavours of a participation in the sanctifying, cleansing work of the Holy Ghost, is long, and very irksome to flesh and blood, besides that it is intricate and foolish unto natural darkness and unbelief. But yet it so falls out that, after all these inventions, they can come to no perfect rest or satisfaction in their own minds. They cannot but find by experience that their sores sometimes break forth through all these sorry coverings, unto their annoyance; and their defilements yet fill them with shame, as well as the guilt of sin doth with fear. Wherefore they betake themselves to their sheet-anchor in this storm, — in the relief which they have provided in another world, when, let men find themselves never so much mistaken, they cannot complain of their disappointments. This is in their purgatory, whereunto they must trust at last for the cancelling of all their odd scores, and purging away that filth of sin which they have been unwilling to part withal in this world. But as this whole business of purgatory is a groundless fable, an invention set up in competition with and opposition unto the sanctification of the Spirit and cleansing virtue of the blood of Christ, as a matter of unspeakably more profit and secular advantage unto those who have its management committed unto them; so it is as great an encouragement unto unholiness and a continuance in sin for those who believe it, and at the same time love the pleasures of sin (which are the generality of their church), as ever was or can be found out or made use of: for, to come with a plain, downright dissuasure from holiness and encouragement unto sin is a design that would absolutely defeat itself, nor is capable of making impression on them who retain the notion of a difference between good and evil; but this side-wind, that at once pretends to relieve men from the filth of sin, and keeps them from the only ways and means whereby it may be cleansed, insensibly leads them into a quiet pursuit of their lusts, under an expectation of relief when all is past and done. Wherefore, setting aside such vain imaginations, we may inquire into the true causes and ways of our purification from the uncleanness of sin described, wherein the first part of our sanctification and the foundation of our holiness doth consist.

Chapter V - The filth of sin purged by the Spirit and the blood of Christ

Purification of the filth of sin the first part of sanctification — How it is effected — The work of the Spirit therein — Efficacy of the blood of Christ to that purpose — The blood of his sacrifice intended — How that blood cleanseth sin — Application unto it, and application of it by the Spirit — Wherein that application consists — Faith the instrumental cause of our purification, with the use of afflictions to the same purpose — Necessity of a due consideration of the pollution of sin — Considerations of the pollution and purification of sin practically improved — Various directions for a due application unto the blood of Christ for cleansing — Sundry degrees of shamelessness in sinning — Directions for the cleansing of sin continued — Thankfulness for the cleansing of sin, with other uses of the same consideration — Union with Christ, how consistent with the remainders of sin — From all that, differences between evangelical holiness and the old nature asserted.

Thirdly, The purging of the souls of them that believe from the defilements of sin is, in the Scripture, assigned unto several causes of different kinds; for the Holy Spirit, the blood of Christ, faith, and afflictions, are all said to cleanse us from our sins, but in several ways, and with distinct kinds of efficacy. The Holy Spirit is said to do it as the principal efficient cause; the blood of Christ as the meritorious procuring cause; faith and affliction as the instrumental causes, — the one direct and internal, the other external and occasional.

I. That we are purged and purified from sin by the Spirit of God communicated unto us hath been before in general confirmed by many testimonies of the holy Scriptures. And we may gather, also, from what hath been spoken, wherein this work of his doth consist; for, —

1. Whereas the spring and fountain of all the pollution of sin lies in the depravation of the faculties of our natures, which ensued on the loss of the image of God, he renews them again by his grace, Tit. iii. 5. Our want of due answering unto the holiness of God, as represented in the law, and exemplified in our hearts originally, is a principal part and universal cause of our whole pollution and defilement by sin; for when our eyes are opened to discern it, this is that which in the first place filleth us with shame and self-abhorrency, and that which makes us so unacceptable, yea, so loathsome to God. Who is there who considereth aright the vanity, darkness, and ignorance of his mind, the perverseness and stubbornness of his will, with the disorder, irregularity, and distemper of his affections, with respect unto things spiritual and heavenly, who is not ashamed of, who doth not abhor himself? This is that which hath given our nature its leprosy, and defiled it throughout. And I shall crave leave to say, that he who hath no experience of spiritual shame and self-abhorrency, upon the account of this inconformity of his nature and the faculties of his soul unto the holiness of God, is a great stranger unto this whole work of sanctification. Who is there that can recount the unsteadiness of his mind in holy meditation,

his low and unbecoming conceptions of God's excellencies, his proneness to foolish imaginations and vanities that profit not, his aversion to spirituality in duty and fixedness in communion with God, his proneness to things sensual and evil, all arising from the spiritual irregularity of divine purity and holiness, is sensible of his own vileness and baseness, and is ofttimes deeply affected with shame thereon? Now, this whole evil frame is cured by the effectual working of the Holy Ghost in the rectifying and renovation of our natures. He giveth a new understanding, a new heart, new affections, renewing the whole soul into the image of God, Eph. iv. 23, 24; Col. iii. 10. The way whereby he doth this hath been before so fully declared, in our opening of the doctrine of regeneration, that it need not be here repeated. Indeed, our original cleansing is therein, where mention is made of the "washing of regeneration," Tit. iii. 5. Therein is the image of God restored unto our souls. But we consider the same work now as it is the cause of our holiness. Look, then, how far our minds, our hearts, our affections, are renewed by the Holy Ghost, so far are we cleansed from our spiritual habitual pollution. Would we be cleansed from our sins, — that which is so frequently promised that we shall be, and so frequently prescribed as our duty to be, and without which we neither have not can have any thing of true holiness in us, — we must labour after and endeavour to grow in this renovation of our natures by the Holy Ghost. The more we have of saving light in our minds, of heavenly love in our wills and affections, of a constant readiness unto obedience in our hearts, the more pure are we, the more cleansed from the pollution of sin. The old principle of corrupted nature is unclean and defiling, shameful and loathsome; the new creature, the principal of grace implanted in the whole soul by the Holy Ghost, is pure and purifying, clean and holy.

2. The Holy Ghost doth purify and cleanse us by strengthening our souls by his grace unto all holy duties and against all actual sins. It is by actual sins that our natural and habitual pollution is increased. Hereby some make themselves base and vile as hell. But this also is prevented by the gracious actings of the Spirit. Having given us a principle of purity and holiness, he so acts it in duties of obedience and in opposition unto sin as that he preserves the soul free from defilements, or pure and holy, according to the tenor of the new covenant; that is, in such measure and to such a degree as universal sincerity doth require. But it may be yet said that indeed hereby he makes us pure, and prevents many future defilements, yet how is the soul freed from those it hath contracted before this work upon it, or those which it may and doth unavoidably afterward fall into; for as there is no man that doeth good and sinneth not, so there is none who is not more or less defiled with sin whilst he is in the body here in this world? The apostle answereth this objection or inquiry, 1 John i. 7–9, "If we say we have no sin, we deceive ourselves, and the truth is not in us." But if sin be in us we are defiled, and how shall we be cleansed? "God is just to forgive us our sins, and to cleanse us from all unrighteousness." But how may this be done, by what means may it be accomplished? "The blood of Jesus Christ his Son cleanseth us from all sin."

II. It is, therefore, the blood of Christ, in the second place, which is the meritorious procuring, and so the effective cause, that immediately purgeth us from our sins, by an especial application of it unto our souls by the Holy Ghost. And there is not any truth belonging unto the mystery of the gospel which is more plainly and evidently asserted, as hath in part been made to appear before:

"The blood of Jesus Christ cleanseth us from all sin," 1 John i. 7; "He hath washed us from our sins in his own blood," Rev. i. 5; "The blood of Christ purgeth our conscience from dead works, that we may serve the living God," Heb. ix. 14; "He gave himself for the church, that he might sanctify and cleanse it," Eph. v. 25, 26; to "purify to himself a peculiar people," Tit. ii. 14. Besides, whatever is spoken in the whole Scripture concerning purifying the unclean, the leprous, the defiled, by sacrifices or other instruments of the Old Testament, it is all instructive in and directive unto the purifying nature of the blood of Christ, from whence alone these institutions had their efficacy; and the virtue of it is promised under that notion, Zech. xiii. 1. And this the faith and experience of all believers doth confirm; for they are no imaginations of their own, but what, being built on the truth and promises of God, yield sensible [felt] spiritual relief and refreshment unto their souls. This they believe, this they pray for, and find the fruits and effects of it in themselves. It may be some of them do not, it may be few of them do, comprehend distinctly the way whereby and the manner how the blood of Christ, so long since shed and offered, should cleanse them now from their sins; but the thing itself they do believe as it is revealed, and find the use of it in all wherein they have to do with God. And I must say (let profane and ignorant persons, whilst they please, deride what they understand not, not are able to disprove) that the Holy Spirit of God, which leadeth believers in to all truth, and enableth them to pray according to the mind and will of God, doth guide them, in and by the working and experience of faith, to pray for those things the depths of whose mysteries they cannot comprehend. And he who well studieth the things which he is taught of the Spirit to ask of God, will find a door opened to much spiritual wisdom and knowledge; for (let the world rage on) in those prayers which believers are taught and enabled unto by the Holy Ghost helping of them as a Spirit of supplication, there are two things inexpressible:— First, the inward labouring and spiritual working of the sanctified heart and affections towards God; wherein consist those "groanings that cannot be uttered," Rom. viii. 26. God alone sees, and knows, and understands the fervent workings of the new creature, when acted by the Holy Ghost in supplications; and so it is added in the next words, verse 27, "And he that searcheth the hearts knoweth" τί τὸ φρόνημα τοῦ Πνεύματος, "what is the meaning of the Spirit," what it favours and inclines unto. It is not any distinct or separate acting of the Spirit by himself that is intended, but what and how he works in the hearts of believers as he is a Spirit of grace and supplication; and this is known only unto him who is the Searcher of hearts, and as he is so. And he knoweth what is the bent, frame, inclination, and acting of the inward man in prayer, from the power of the Spirit; which they themselves in whom they are wrought do not fathom or reach the depth of. This he doth in the subject of prayer, the hearts and minds of believers; the effects of his operation in them are inexpressible. Secondly, As to the object of prayer, or things prayed for, he doth in and by the word so represent and exhibit the truth, reality, subsistence, power, and efficacy of spiritual, mysterious things, unto the faith and affectations of believers, that they have a real and experimental sense of, do mix faith with, and are affected by, those things now made nigh, now realized unto them, which, it may be, they are not able doctrinally and distinctly to explain in their proper notions. And thus do we ofttimes see men low and weak in their notional apprehension of things, yet in their prayers led into communion with God in the highest and holiest mysteries of his grace, having an experience of the life and power of the things themselves in their own hearts and souls; and hereby do their faith, love, affiance, and adherence unto God, act and exercise themselves. So it is with them in this matter of the actual present purifying of the pollutions of sin by the blood of Jesus Christ, the way whereof we shall now briefly inquire into:—

1. Therefore, by the blood of Christ herein in intended the blood of his sacrifice, with the power, virtue, and efficacy thereof. And the blood of a sacrifice fell under a double consideration:— (1.) As it was offered unto God to make atonement and reconciliation; (2.) As it was sprinkled on other things for their purging and sanctification. Part of the blood in every propitiatory sacrifice was still to be sprinkled round about the altar, Lev. i. 11; and in the great sacrifice of expiation, some of the blood of the bullock was to be sprinkled before the mercy-seat seven times, chap. xvi. 14. This our apostle fully expresseth in a great and signal instance: Heb. ix. 19, 20, 22, "When Moses had spoken every precept to all the people according to the law, he took the blood of calves and of goats, with water, and scarlet wool, and hyssop, and sprinkled both the book and all the people, saying, This is the blood of the testament which God hath enjoined unto you. … And almost all things are by the law purged with blood." Wherefore, the blood of Christ, as it was the blood of his sacrifice, hath these two effects, and falls under this double consideration:— (1.) As he offered himself by the eternal Spirit unto God to make an atonement for sin, and procure eternal redemption; (2.) As it is sprinkled by the same Spirit on the consciences of believers, to purge them from dead works, as Heb. ix. 12–14. And hence it is called, with respect unto our sanctification, "The blood of sprinkling," chap. xii. 24; for we have the "sanctification of the Spirit unto obedience through the sprinkling of the blood of Jesus Christ," 1 Pet. i. 2.

2. The blood of Christ in his sacrifice is still always and continually in the same condition, of the same force and efficacy, as it was in that hour wherein it was shed. The blood of other sacrifices was always to be used immediately upon its effusion; for if it were cold and congealed it was of no use to be offered or to be sprinkled. Blood was appointed to make atonement, as the life or animal spirits were in it, Lev. xvii. 11. But the blood of the sacrifice of Christ is always hot and warm, having the same spirits of life and sanctification still moving in it. Hence the ζῶσα καὶ πρόσφατος, Heb. x. 20, — always living, and yet always as newly slain. Every one, therefore, who at any time hath an especial actual interest in the blood of Christ, as sacrificed, hath as real a purification from the defilement of sin as he had typically who stood by the priest and had blood or water sprinkled on him; for the Holy Ghost diligently declares that whatever was done legally, carnally, or typically, by any of the sacrifices of old at any time, as to the expiation or purification of sin, that was all done really and spiritually by that one sacrifice, — that is, the offering and sprinkling of the blood of Christ, — and abideth to be so done continually. To this purpose is the substance of our apostle's discourse in the ninth and tenth chapters of the Epistle to the Hebrews. And they had various sorts of sacrifices, wherein to this end the blood of them was sprinkled, they being propitiatory in their offering; as, — (1.) There was the תָּמִיד, or continual burntoffering of a lamb or kid for the whole congregation, morning and evening, whose blood was sprinkled as at other times. And hereby the habitual purification of the congregation, that they might be holy to the Lord, and their cleansing from the daily incursions of secret and unknown sins, was signified and carried on. (2.)

On the Sabbath-day this juge sacrificium was doubled morning and evening, denoting a peculiar and abounding communication of mercy and purging grace, through the administration of instituted ordinances, on that day. (3.) There was the great annual sacrifice at the feast of expiation, when, by the sacrifice of the sin-offering and the scape-goat, the whole congregation were purged from all their known and great sins, and recovered into a state of legal holiness; and other stated sacrifices there were. (4.) There were occasional sacrifices for every one, according as he found his condition to require; for those who were clean one day, yea, one hour, might by some miscarriage or surprisal be unclean the next. But there was a way continually ready for any man's purification, by his bringing his offering unto that purpose. Now, the blood of Christ must continually, and upon all occasions, answer unto all these, and accomplish spiritually what they did legally effect and typically represent. This our apostle asserts and proves, Heb. ix. 9–14. Thereby is the gradual carrying on of our sanctification habitually effected, which was signified by the continual daily sacrifice. From thence is especial cleansing virtue communicated unto us by the ordinances of the gospel, as is expressly affirmed, Eph. v. 25, 26, denoted by the doubling of the daily sacrifice on the Sabbath. By it we are purged from all our sins whatever, great or small, as was typified in the great sacrifice on the day of expiation. And unto him have we continual recourse upon all occasions of our spiritual defilements whatever. So was his blood, as to its purifying virtue, to answer and accomplish all legal institutions. Especially it doth so that of the "ashes of the red heifer," Num. xix., which was a standing ordinance, whereby every one who was any way defiled might immediately be cleansed; and he who would not make application thereunto was to be cut off from the people, verse 20. And it is no otherwise with respect unto the blood of Christ in our spiritual defilements; thence it is called "a fountain opened for sin and for uncleanness," Zech. xiii.

1. And he who neglects to make application thereunto shall perish in his uncleanness, and that eternally. Farther to clear this whole matter, two things are to be inquired into:— (1.) How the blood of Christ doth thus cleanse us from our sins, or what it is that is done thereby. (2.) How we come to be made partakers of the benefit thereof, or come to be interested therein. (1.) As to the first, it must be observed, what hath been declared before, that the uncleanness we treat of is not physical or corporeal, but moral and spiritual only. It is the inconformity of sin unto the holiness of God, as represented in the law, whence it is loathsome to God, and attended with shame in us. Now, wherever there is an interest obtained in the purifying virtue of the blood of Christ, it doth (by the will, law, and appointment of God) do these two things:— [1.] It takes away all loathsomeness in the sight of God, not from sin in the abstract, but from the sinner, so that he shall be as one absolutely washed and purified before him. See Isa. i. 16–18; Ps. li. 7; Eph. v. 25–27. [2.] It taketh away shame out of the conscience, and gives the soul boldness in the presence of God, Heb. x. 19–22. When these things are done then is sin purged, our souls are cleansed.

(2.) It may be inquired how we are to apply ourselves unto the blood of Christ for our purification, or how we may come continually to partake of the virtue of it, as it is sprinkled unto that purpose. Now, because what we do herein is wrought in us by the Spirit of God, my principal design being to declare his work in our sanctification, I shall at once declare both his work and our duty in the following instances:—

[1.] It is he who discovereth unto us, and spiritually convinceth us of, the pollution of sin, and of our defilement thereby. Something, indeed, of this kind will be wrought by the power of natural conscience, awakened and excited by ordinary outward means of conviction; for wherever there is a sense of guilt, there will be some kind of sense of filth, as fear and shame are inseparable. But this sense alone will never guide us to the blood of Christ for cleansing. Such a sight and conviction of it as may fill us with self-abhorrency and abasement, as may cause us to loathe ourselves for the abomination that is in it, is required of us; and this is the work of the Holy Ghost, belonging to that peculiar conviction of sin which is from him alone, John xvi. 8. I mean that self-abhorrency, shame, and confusion of face, with respect unto the filth of sin, which is so often mentioned in the Scripture as a gracious duty; as nothing is a higher aggravation of sin than for men to carry themselves with a carnal boldness with God and in his worship, whilst they are unpurged from their defilements. In a sense hereof the publican stood afar off, as one ashamed and destitute of any confidence for a nearer approach. So the holy men of old professed to God that they blushed, and were ashamed to lift up their faces unto him. Without this preparation, whereby we come to know the plague of our own hearts, the infection of our leprosy, the defilement of our souls, we shall never make application unto the blood of Christ for cleansing in a due manner. This, therefore, in the first place, is required of us as the first part of our duty and first work of the Holy Ghost herein.

[2.] The Holy Ghost proposeth, declareth, and presents unto us the only true remedy, the only means of purification. "When Ephraim saw his sickness, and Judah his wound, then went Ephraim to the Assyrian, and sent to king Jareb: yet could he not heal you, not cure you of your wound," Hos. v. 13. When men begin to discern their defilements, they are apt to think of many ways for their purging. What false ways have been invented to this purpose hath been before declared. And every one is ready to find out a way of his own; every one will apply his own soap and his own nitre. Though the only fountain for cleansing be nigh unto us, yet we cannot see it until the Holy Ghost open our eyes, as he did the eyes of Hagar; he it is who shows it unto us and leads us unto it. This is an eminent part of his office and work. The principal end of his sending, and consequently of his whole work, was to glorify the Son; as the end and work of the Son was to glorify the Father. And the great way whereby he glorifieth Christ is by showing such things unto us, John xvi. 14. And without his discovery we can know nothing of Christ, not of the things of Christ; for he is not sent in vain, to show us the things that we can see of ourselves. And what is more so of Christ than his blood, and its efficacy for the purging of our sins? We never, therefore, discern it spiritually and in a due manner but by him. To have a true spiritual sense of the defilement of sin, and a gracious view of the cleansing virtue of the blood of Christ, is an eminent effect of the Spirit of grace. Something like it there may be in the workings of an awakened natural conscience, with some beams of outward gospel light falling on it; but there is nothing in it of the work of the Spirit. This, therefore, secondly, we must endeavour after, if we intend to be cleansed by the blood of Christ.

[3.] It is he who worketh faith in us, whereby we are actually interested in the purifying virtue of the blood of Christ. By faith we receive Christ himself, and by faith do we receive all the benefits of his mediation, — that is, as they are tendered unto us in the promises of God. He is our propitiation through faith in his blood as offered; and he is our sanctification through faith in his blood as sprinkled. And particular acting of faith on the blood of Christ for the cleansing of the soul from sin is required of us. A renewed conscience is sensible of a pollution in every sin, and is not freed from the shame of it without a particular application unto the blood of Christ. It comes by faith to the fountain set open for sin and uncleanness, as the sick man to the pool of healing waters, and waiteth for a season to be cleansed in it. So David, on the defilement he had contracted by his great sins, addresseth himself unto God with that prayer, "Purge me with hyssop, and I shall be clean: wash me, and I shall be whiter than snow," Ps. li. 7. He alludeth unto the purging of leprous persons, the ordinance whereof is instituted, Lev. xiv. 2–7, or to that more general institution for the purification of all legal uncleanness by the water of separation, made of the ashes of the red heifer, Num. xix. 4–6, which our apostle hath respect unto, Heb. ix. 13, 14; for both these purifications were made by the sprinkling of blood or water with hyssop. It is plain, I say, that he alludeth unto these institutions; but it is as plain they are not the things which he intendeth: for there was not in the law any purging by hyssop for persons guilty of such sins as he lay under; and therefore he professeth, in the close of the psalm, that "sacrifice and burnt-offering God would not accept" in his case, Ps. li. 16. It was, therefore, that which was signified by those institutions which he made his application unto, — namely, really to the blood of Christ, by which he might be "justified from all things, from which he could not be justified by the law of Moses," Acts xiii. 39; and so likewise purified. In like manner do all believers make an actual application unto the blood of Christ for the purging away of their sins; which until it is done they have a "conscience of sins," — that is, condemning them for sin, and filling them with shame and fear, Heb. x. 1–3.

And this actual application by faith unto the blood of Christ for cleansing, the mystery whereof is scorned by many as a thing fanatical and unintelligible, consists in these four things:— 1st. A spiritual view and due consideration of the blood of Christ in his sacrifice, as proposed in the promises of the gospel for our cleansing and purification. "Look unto me," saith he, "and be ye saved," Isa. xlv. 22; which respects the whole work of our salvation, and all the means thereof. Our way of coming into our interest therein is by looking to him, — namely, as he is proposed unto us in the promise of the gospel: for as the serpent was lifted up by Moses in the wilderness, so was he in his sacrifice on the cross lifted up, John iii. 14; and so in the gospel is he represented unto us, Gal. iii. 1. And the means whereby they were healed in the wilderness was by looking unto the serpent that was lifted up. Herein, then, doth faith first act itself, by a spiritual view and due consideration of the blood of Christ, as proposed unto us in the gospel for the only means of our purification; and the more we abide in this contemplation, the more effectual will our success be in our application thereto. 2dly. Faith actually relieth on his blood for the real effecting of that great work and end for which it is proposed unto us; for God sets him forth as to be a propitiation through faith in his blood as offered, Rom. iii. 25, so to be our sanctification through faith in his blood as sprinkled. And the establishing of this especial faith in our souls is that which the apostle aims at in his excellent reasoning, Heb. ix. 13, 14; and his conclusion unto that purpose is so evident, that he encourageth us thereon to draw nigh in the full assurance of faith, chap. x. 22. 3dly. Faith worketh herein by fervent prayer, as it doth in its whole address unto God with respect unto his promises; because for all these things God will be sought unto by the house of Israel. By this means the soul brings itself nigh unto its own mercy. And this we are directed unto, Heb. iv. 15, 16. 4thly. An acquiescency in the truth and faithfulness of God for cleansing by the blood of Christ, whence we are freed from discouraging, perplexing shame, and have boldness in the presence of God.

[4.] The Holy Ghost actually communicates the cleansing, purifying virtue of the blood of Christ unto our souls and consciences, whereby we are freed from shame, and have boldness towards God; for the whole work of the application of the benefits of the mediation of Christ unto believers is his properly.

And these are the things which believers aim at and intend in all their fervent supplications for the purifying and cleansing of their souls by the sprinkling and washing of the blood of Christ, the faith and persuasion whereof give them peace and holy boldness in the presence of God, without which they can have nothing but shame and confusion of face in a sense of their own pollutions.

How the blood of Christ was the meritorious cause of our purification as it was offered, in that thereby he procured for us eternal redemption, with all that was conducing or needful thereunto, and how thereby he expiated our sins, belongs not unto this place to declare. Nor shall I insist upon the more mysterious way of communicating cleansing virtue unto us from the blood of Christ, by virtue of our union with him. What hath been spoken may suffice to give a little insight into that influence which the blood of Christ hath into this first part of our sanctification and holiness. And as for those who affirm that it no otherwise cleanseth us from our sins, but only because we, believing his doctrine, confirmed by his death and resurrection, do amend our lives, turning from sin unto righteousness and holiness, they renounce the mystery of the gospel, and all the proper efficacy of the blood of Christ.

III. Faith is the instrumental cause of our purification: "Purifying their hearts by faith," Acts xv. 9. The two unfailing evidences of sincere faith are, that within it purifieth the heart, and without it worketh by love. These are the touch-stones whereon faith may, yea, ought to be tried. We "purify our souls in obeying the truth through the Spirit," 1 Pet. i. 22; that is, by believing, which is our original obedience unto the truth. And hereby are our souls purified. "Unbelievers" and "unclean" are the same, Tit. i. 15; for they have nothing in them whereby they might be instrumentally cleansed. And we are purified by faith; because, —

1. Faith itself is the principal grace whereby our nature is restored unto the image of God, and so freed from our original defilement, Col. iii. 10; 1 John iii. 3. 2. It is by faith on our part whereby we receive the purifying virtue and influences of the blood of Christ; whereof we have before discoursed. Faith is the grace whereby we constantly adhere and cleave unto Christ, Deut. iv. 4; Josh. xxiii. 8; Acts xi. 22. And if the woman who touched his garment in faith obtained virtue from him to heal her issue of blood, shall not those who cleave unto him continually derive virtue from him for the healing of their spiritual defilements? 3. It is by the working of faith principally whereby those lusts and corruptions which are defiling are mortified, subdued, and gradually wrought out of our minds. All actual defilements spring from the remainders of defiling lusts, and their depraved workings in us, Heb. xii. 15; James i. 14. How faith

worketh to the correcting and subduing of them, by deriving supplies of the Spirit and grace to that end from Jesus Christ, as being the means of our abiding in them, whereon alone those supplies do depend, John xv. 3–5, as also by the acting of all other graces which are contrary to the polluting lusts of the flesh and destructive of them, is usually declared, and we must not too far enlarge on these things. 4. Faith takes in all the motives which are proposed unto us to stir us up unto our utmost endeavours and diligence, in the use of all means and ways, for the preventing of the defilements of sin, and for the cleansing of our minds and consciences from the relics of dead works. And these motives, which are great and many, may be reduced unto two heads:—(1.) A participation of the excellent promises of God at the present. The consideration hereof brings a singular enforcement on the souls of believers to endeavour after universal purity and holiness, 2 Cor. vii. 1. And, (2.) The future enjoyment of God in glory, whereunto we cannot attain without being purified from sin, 1 John iii. 2, 3. Now, these motives, which are the springs of our duty in this matter, are received and made efficacious by faith only.

IV. Purging from sin is likewise in the Scripture ascribed unto afflictions of all sorts. Hence they are called God's "furnace," and his "fining pot," Isa. xxxi. 9, xlviii. 10, whereby he taketh away the dross and filth of the vessels of his house. They are also called "fire" that trieth the ways and works of men, consuming their hay and stubble, and purifying their gold and silver, 1 Cor. iii. 12, 13. And this they do through an efficacy unto these ends communicated unto them in the design and by the Spirit of God; for by and in the cross of Christ they were cut off from the curse of the first covenant, whereunto all evil and trouble did belong, and implanted into the covenant of grace. The tree of the cross being cast into the waters of affliction hath rendered them wholesome and medicinal. And as, the Lord Christ being the head of the covenant, all the afflictions and persecutions that befall his members are originally his, Isa. lxiii. 9, Acts ix. 5, Col. i. 24; so they all tend to work us unto a conformity unto him in purity and holiness. And they work towards this blessed end of purifying the soul several ways; for, — 1. They have in them some token of God's displeasure against sin, which those who are exercised by them are led by the consideration of unto a fresh view of the vileness of it; for although afflictions are an effect of love, yet it is of love mixed with care to obviate and prevent distempers. Whatever they are else, they are always chastisements; and correction respects faults. And it is our safest course, in every affliction, to lodge the adequate cause of it in our own deserts, as the woman did, 1 Kings xvii. 18; and as God directs, Ps. lxxxix. 30–32, Lam. iii. 33. And this is one difference between his chastisements and those of the fathers of our flesh, that he doth it "not for his pleasure," Heb. xii. 9, 10. Now, a view of sin under suffering makes men loathe and abhor themselves for it, and to be ashamed of it; and this is the first step towards our purifying of ourselves by any ways appointed for it. Self-pleasing is sin in the highest degree of our pollution; and when we loathe ourselves for it, we are put into the way at least of seeking after a remedy.

2. Afflictions take off the beauty and allurements of all created good things and their comforts, by which the affections are solicited to commit folly and lewdness with them; that is, to embrace and cleave unto them inordinately, whence many defilements do ensue, Gal. vi. 14. This God designs them for, even to whither all the flowerings of this world in the minds of men, by

discovering their emptiness, vanity, and insufficiency to give relief. This intercepts the disorderly intercourse which is apt to be between them and our affections, whereby our minds are polluted; for there is a pollution attending the least inordinate actings of our mind and affections towards objects either in their own nature sinful, or such as may be rendered so by an excess in us towards them, whilst we are under the command of loving the Lord our God with all our minds, souls, and strength, and that always. 3. Afflictions take off the edge and put a deadness on those affections whereby the corrupt lusts of the mind and flesh, which are the spring and cause of all our defilements, do act themselves. They curb those vigorous and brisk affections which were always ready pressed for the service of lust, and which sometimes carry the soul into pursuit of sin, like the horse into battle, with madness and fury. There are no more such prepared channels for the fomes of concupiscence to empty itself into the conversation, nor such vehicles for the spirits of corrupted lusts and inclinations. God, I say, by afflictions brings a kind of death unto the world and the pleasures of it upon the desires and affections of the soul, which render them unserviceable unto the remainder of defiling lusts and corruptions. This in some, indeed, endures but for a season, as when, in sickness, wants, fears, distresses, losses, sorrows, there is a great appearance of mortification, when yet the strength of sin and the vigour of carnal affections do speedily revive upon the least outward relief. But with believers it is not so, but by all their chastisements they are really more and more delivered from the pollution of sin, and made partakers of God's holiness, 2 Cor. iv. 16–18. 4. God doth by them excite, stir up, and draw forth all the graces of the Spirit into a constant, diligent, and vigorous exercise; and therein the work of cleansing the soul from the pollution of sin is carried on. A time of affliction is the especial season for the peculiar exercise of all grace, for the soul can then no otherwise support or relieve itself; for it is cut short or taken off from other comforts and reliefs, every sweet thing being made bitter unto it. It must, therefore, live not only by faith, and love, and delight in God, but in some sense upon them; for if in their exercise supportment and comfort be not obtained, we can have none. Therefore doth such a soul find it necessary to be constantly abounding in the exercise of grace, that it may in any measure be able to support itself under its troubles or sufferings. Again, there is no other way whereby a man may have a sanctified use of afflictions, or a good issue out of them, but by the assiduous exercise of grace. This God calls for, this he designs, and without it afflictions have no other end but to make men miserable; and they will either have no deliverance from them, or such an one as shall tend to their farther misery and ruin.

And so have we taken a view of the first part of our sanctification and holiness; which I have the more largely insisted on, because the consideration of it is utterly neglected by them who frame us a holiness to consist only in the practice of moral virtue. And I do not know but what hath been delivered may be looked on as fanatical and enthusiastical; yet is there no other reason why it should be so, but only because it is taken from Scripture. Neither doth that so much insist on any consideration of sin and sanctification, as this of the pollution of the one and the purifying of it by the other. And to whom the words of the Holy Ghost are displeasing, we cannot in these things give any satisfaction; and yet I could easily demonstrate that they were well known to the ancient writers of the church; and, for the substance of them, were discerned and discussed by the schoolmen, in their manner. But where men hate the practice of holiness, it is to no purpose to teach them the nature of it.

But we may not pass over these things without some reflections upon ourselves, and some consideration of our concernment in them. And, first, hence we may take a view of our own state and condition by nature. It is useful for us all to be looking back into it, and it is necessary for them who are under it to be fully acquainted with it. Therein are we wholly defiled, polluted, and every way unclean. There is a spiritual leprosy spread all over our natures, which renders us loathsome to God, and puts us in a state of separation from him. They who were legally unclean were separated from the congregation, and therein from all the pledges of God's gracious presence, Num. v. 2. It is so virtually with all them who are spiritually defiled, under that pollution which is natural and universal; they are abhorred of God and separated from him, which was signified thereby. And the reason why so many laws, with so great severity and exactness, were given about the cleansing of a leprous person, and the judgement to be made thereon, was only to declare the certainty of the judgement of God, that no unclean person should approach unto him. Thus is it with all by nature; and whatever they do of themselves to be quit of it, it doth but hide and not cleanse it. Adam cured neither his nakedness nor the shame of it by his fig-leaves. Some have no other covering of their natural filth but outward ornaments of the flesh; which increase it, and indeed rather proclaim it than hide it. The greatest filth in the world is covered with the greatest bravery. See Isa. iii. 16–24. Whatever we do ourselves in answer unto our convictions is a covering, not a cleansing; and if we die in this condition, unwashed, uncleansed, unpurified, it is utterly impossible that ever we should be admitted into the blessed presence of the holy God, Rev. xxi. 27. Let no man deceive you, then, with vain words. It is not the doing of a few good works, it is not an outward profession of religion, that will give you an access with boldness and joy unto God. Shame will cover you when it will be too late. Unless you are washed by the Spirit of God and in the blood of Christ from the pollutions of your natures, you shall not inherit the kingdom of God, 1 Cor. vi. 9–11. Yea, you will be a horrid spectacle unto saints and angels, yea, to yourselves, unto one another, when the shame of your nakedness shall be made to appear, Isa. lxvi. 24. If, therefore, you would not perish, and that eternally; if you would not perish as base, defiled creatures, an abhorring unto all flesh, then when your pride, and your wealth, and your beauty, and your ornaments, and your duties, will stand you in no stead, — look out betimes after that only way of purifying and cleansing your souls which God hath ordained. But if you love your defilements; if you are proud of your pollutions; if you satisfy yourselves with your outward ornaments, whether moral, of gifts, duties, profession, conversation, or natural, of body, wealth, apparel, gold, and silver, — there is no remedy, you must perish for ever, and that under the consideration of the basest and vilest part of the creation.

Seeing this is the condition of all by nature, if any one now shall inquire and ask what they shall do, what course they shall take, that they may be cleansed according to the will of God, in answer hereunto I shall endeavour to direct defiled sinners, by sundry steps and degrees, in the way unto the cleansing fountain. There is a "fountain set open for sin and for uncleanness," Zech. xiii. 1. But it falleth out with many, as the wise man speaketh, "The labour of the foolish wearieth every one of them, because he knoweth not how to go to the city," Eccles. x. 15. Men weary themselves and pine away under their pollutions, because they cannot find the way; they know not how to go to the cleansing fountain. I shall, therefore, direct them from first to last, according to the best skill I have:—

1. Labour after an acquaintance with it, to know it in its nature and effects. Although the Scripture so abounds in the assertion and declaration of it, as we have showed, and believers find a sense of it in their experience, yet men in common take little notice of it. Somewhat they are affected with the guilt of sin, but little or not at all with its filth. So they can escape the righteousness of God, which they have provoked, they regard not their unanswerableness unto his holiness, whereby they are polluted. How few, indeed, do inquire into the pravity of their natures, that vileness which is come upon them by the loss of the image of God, or do take themselves to be much concerned therein! How few do consider aright that fomes and filthy spring which is continually bubbling up crooked, perverse, defiled imaginations in their hearts, and influencing their affections unto the lewdness of depraved concupiscence! Who meditates upon the holiness of God in a due manner, so as to ponder what we ourselves ought to be, how holy, how upright, how clean, if we intend to please him or enjoy him? With what appearances, what outsides of things, are most men satisfied! yea, how do they please themselves in the shades of their own darkness and ignorance of these things, when yet an unacquaintedness with this pollution of sin is unavoidably ruinous unto their souls! See the danger of it, Rev. iii. 16–18. Those who would be cleansed from it must first know it; and although we cannot do so aright without some convincing light of the Spirit of God, yet are there duties required of us in order thereunto; as, — (1.) To search the Scripture, and to consider seriously what it declareth concerning the condition of our nature after the loss of the image of God. Doth it not declare that it is shamefully naked, destitute of all beauty and comeliness, wholly polluted and defiled? And what is said of that nature which is common unto all is said of every one who is partaker of it. Every one is "gone aside," every one is become "altogether filthy," or stinking, Ps. liii. 3. This is the glass wherein every man ought to contemplate himself, and not in foolish, flattering reflections from his own proud imaginations; and he that will not hence learn his natural deformity shall live polluted and die accursed. (2.) He who hath received the testimony of the Scripture concerning his corrupted and polluted estate, if he will be at the pains to try and examine himself by the reasons and causes that are assigned thereof, will have a farther view of it. When men read, hear, or are instructed in what the Scripture teacheth concerning the defilement of sin, and give some assent to what is spoken, without an examination of their own state in particular, or bringing their souls unto that standard and measure, they will have very little advantage thereby. Multitudes learn that they are polluted by nature, which they cannot gainsay; but yet really find no such thing in themselves. But when men will bring their own souls to the glass of the perfect law, and consider how it is with them in respect of that image of God wherein they were at first created, what manner of persons they ought to be with respect unto the holiness of God, and what they are, — how vain are their imaginations, how disorderly are their affections, how perverse all the actings of their minds, — they will be ready to say, with the leprous man, "Unclean, unclean." But they are but few who will take the pains to search their own wounds, it being a matter of smart and trouble to corrupt and carnal affections.

Yet, (3.) Prayer for light and direction herein is required of all as a duty. For a man to know himself was of old esteemed the highest attainment of human wisdom. Some men will not so much as inquire into themselves, and some men dare not, and some neglect the doing of it from spiritual sloth, and other deceitful imaginations; but he that would ever be purged from his sins must thus far make bold with himself, and dare to be thus far wise. And in the use of the means before prescribed, considering his own darkness and the treacheries of his heart, he is to pray fervently that God by his Spirit would guide and assist him in his search after the pravity and defilement of his nature. Without this he will never make any great or useful discoveries. And yet the discerning hereof is the first evidence that a man hath received the least ray of supernatural light. The light of a natural conscience will convince men of, and reprove them for, actual sins as to their guilt, Rom. ii. 14, 15; but the mere light of nature is dark and confused about its own confusion. Some of the old philosophers discerned, in general, that our nature was disordered, and complained thereof; but as the principal reason of their complaints was because it would not throughout serve the end of their ambition, so of the causes and nature of it, with respect unto God and our eternal condition, they knew nothing of it at all. Nor is it discerned but by a supernatural light, proceeding immediately from the Spirit of God. If any, therefore, have a heart or wisdom to know their own pollution by sin, — without which they know nothing of themselves unto any purpose, — let them pray for that directing light of the Spirit of God, without which they can never attain to any useful knowledge of it.

2. Those who would indeed be purged from the pollution of sin must endeavour to be affected with it, suitably to the discovery which they have made of it. And as the proper effect of the guilt of sin is fear, so the proper effect of the filth of sin is shame. No man who hath read the Scriptures can be ignorant how frequently God calls on men to be ashamed and confounded in themselves for the pollutions and uncleannesses of their sin. So is it expressed in answer unto what he requires: "O my God, I am ashamed and blush to lift up my face to thee, my God, for our iniquities are increased over our head," Ezra ix. 6. And by another prophet: "We lie down in our shame, and our confusion covereth us: for we have sinned against the Lord our God," Jer. iii. 25. And many other such expressions are there of this affection of the mind with respect unto the pollution of sin. But we must observe that there is a twofold shame with respect unto it:— (1.) That which is legal, or the product of a mere legal conviction of sin. Such was that in Adam, immediately after his fall; and such is that which God so frequently calls open and profligate sinners unto, — a shame accompanied with dread and terror, and from which the sinner hath no relief, unless in such sorry evasions as our first parents made use of. And, (2.) There is a shame which is evangelical, arising from a mixed apprehension of the vileness of sin and the riches of God's grace in the pardon and purifying of it; for although this latter gives relief against all terrifying, discouraging effects of shame, yet it increaseth those which tend to genuine self-abasement and abhorrency. And this God still requires to abide in us, as that which tends to the advancement of his grace in our hearts. This is fully expressed by the prophet Ezekiel, chap. xvi. 60–63, "I will remember my covenant with thee in the days of thy youth, and I will establish unto thee an everlasting covenant. Then shalt thou remember thy ways, and be ashamed. And I will establish my covenant with thee; and thou shalt know that I am the Lord: that thou mayest remember,

and be confounded, and never open thy mouth any more because of thy shame, when I am pacified toward thee for all that thou hast done, saith the Lord God." There is a shame and confusion of face for sin that is a consequent, yea, an effect of God's renewing his covenant, and thereby giving in the full pardon of sin, as being pacified. And the apostle asks the Romans what fruit they had in those things whereof they were now ashamed, chap. vi. 21. Now, after the pardon of them they were yet ashamed, from the consideration of their filth and vileness. But it is a shame in the first sense that I here intend, as antecedent unto the first purification of our natures. This may be thought to be in all men; but it is plainly otherwise, and men are not at all ashamed of their sins, which they manifest in various degrees: for, —

(1.) Many are senseless and stupid. No instruction, nothing that befalls them, will fix any real shame upon them. Of some particular facts they may be ashamed, but for any thing in their natures, they slight and despise it. If they can but preserve themselves from the known guilt of such sins as are punishable amongst men, as to all other things they are secure. This is the condition of the generality of men living in sin in this world. They have no inward shame for any thing between God and their souls, especially not for the pravity and defilement of their natures, no, although they hear the doctrine of it never so frequently. What may outwardly befall them that is shameful, they are concerned in; but for their internal pollutions between God and their souls, they know none.

(2.) Some have such a boldness and confidence in their condition, as that which is well and pure enough: "There is a generation that are pure in their own eyes, yet are they not washed from their filthiness," Prov. xxx. 12. Although they were never sprinkled with the pure water of the covenant, or cleansed by the Holy Spirit; although their consciences were never purged from dead works by the blood of Christ, nor their hearts purified by faith, and so are no way "washed from their filthiness;" yet do they please themselves in their condition as "pure in their own eyes," and have not the least sense of any defilements. Such a generation were the Pharisees of old, who esteemed themselves as clean as their hands and cups, that they were continually washing, though within they were filled with all manner of defilements, Isa. lxv. 4, 5. And this generation is such as indeed despise all that is spoken about the pollution of sin and its purification, and deride it as enthusiastical, or a fulsome metaphor not to be understood.

(3.) Others proceed farther, and are so far from taking shame to themselves for what they are, or what they do, as that they openly boast of and glory in the most shameful sins that human nature can contract the guilt of. "They proclaim their sins," saith the prophet, "like Sodom," where all the people consented together in the perpetration of unnatural lusts. They are not at all ashamed, but glory in the things which, because they do not here, will hereafter fill them with confusion of face, Jer. vi. 15, viii. 12. And where once sin gets this confidence, wherein it completes a conquest over the law, the inbred light of nature, the convictions of the Spirit, and in a word God himself, then is it ripe for judgment. And yet is there a higher degree of shamelessness in sin; for, —

(4.) Some content not themselves with boasting in their own sins, but also they approve and delight in all those who give up themselves unto the like outrage in sinning with themselves. This the apostle expresseth as the highest degree of shameless sinning: Rom. i. 32, "Who knowing the judgment of God, that they which commit such things are worthy of death, not only do the same, but have pleasure in them that do them." When open profligate sinners do, as it were, make themselves up into societies, encouraging and approving one another in their abominable courses, so that no company pleaseth them but such as have obtained an impudence in sinning, then is the greatest defiance given unto the holiness and righteousness of God.

Now, such as these will never seek after cleansing; for why should they do so who are sensible of no spiritual pollution, nor have the least touch of shame with respect thereunto? It is necessary, therefore, unto the duty of purifying our souls that we be affected with shame for the spiritual defilements which our nature, under the loss of the image of God, is even rolled in; and where this is not, it will be but lost labour that is spent in the invitation of men to the cleansing fountain.

3. Let persons so affected be fully satisfied that they can never cleanse or purify themselves by any endeavours that are merely their own, or by any means of their own finding out. According unto men's convictions of the defilements of sin, so have and always will their endeavours be after purification, Hos. v. 13. And, indeed, it is the duty of believers to purify themselves more and more, in the exercise of all purifying graces, and the use of all means appointed of God for that purpose, 2 Cor. vii. 1; and their neglect thereof is the highest disadvantage, Ps. xxxviii. 5. But men in the state of nature, concerning whom we now treat, are no way able to cleanse their natures or purge themselves. He only who can restore, repair, and renew their natures unto the likeness of God, can cleanse them. But here many fall into mistakes; for when, by reason of their convictions, they can no longer satisfy and please themselves in the pollution of sin, they go about by vain attempts of their own to "purify their souls," Hos. v. 13; Jer. ii. 22; Job ix. 30, 31. Their own sorrow and repentance, and tears of contrition, and that sorry amendment of life they can attain unto, shall do this work for them; and every especial defiling act, or every renewed sense of it, shall have an especial act of duty for its cleansing! But though these things are good in themselves, yet there is required more wisdom to the right stating of them, as to their causes, respects, ends, and use, than they are furnished withal. Hence are they so frequently abused and turned into an effectual means not only of keeping men off and at a distance from Christ, but also from a due and acceptable performance of the very duties themselves pretended unto: for legal sorrow or repentance, or mere legal convictions, being trusted unto, will infallibly keep the soul from coming up unto that evangelical repentance which alone God accepts; and mere reformation of life rested in proves opposite to endeavours for the renovation of our natures. But let these duties be performed, however, in what manner you please, they are utterly insufficient of themselves to cleanse our natural defilements; nor will any seek duly for that which alone is effectual unto this purpose until they are fully convinced hereof. Let, therefore, sinners hear and know, whether they will or will not believe it, that as by nature they are wholly defiled and polluted with those abominations of sin which render them loathsome in the sight of God, so they have no power by any endeavours or duties of their own to cleanse themselves; but by all they do to this end, they do but farther plunge themselves into the ditch, and increase their own defilements. Yet are all those duties necessary in their proper place and unto their proper end.

4. It is, therefore, their duty to acquaint themselves with that only remedy in this case, that only means of cleansing, which God hath appointed, and which he makes effectual. One great end of the revelation of the will of God, from the foundation of the world, of his institutions and ordinances of worship, was, to direct the souls and consciences of men in and unto the way of their cleansing; which as it argues his infinite love and care, so the great importance of the matter itself. And one principal means which Satan from the beginning made use of to keep men in their apostacy from God, and to encourage them therein, was, by supplying them with innumerable ways of purification, suited to the imaginations of their dark, unbelieving, and superstitious minds. And in like manner, when he designed to draw men off from Christ and the gospel under the Papacy, he did it principally by the suggestion of such present and future purgatories of sin as might comply with their lusts and ignorance. Of so great importance is it, therefore, to be acquainted with the only true and real way and means hereof! And there are two considerations that are suited to excite the diligence of sinners in this inquiry: (1.) The weight that is laid on this matter by God himself. (2.) The difficulty of attaining an acquaintance with it. And, — (1.) As hath been observed, any one by considering, [1.] The legal institutions of old will see what weight God lays hereon. No sacrifice had any respect unto sin but there was somewhat peculiar in it that was for its cleansing; and there were sundry ceremonious ordinances which had no other end but only to purify from uncleannesses. [2.] Among all the promises of the Old Testament concerning the establishment of the new covenant and the grace thereof, which are many and precious, there are none more eminent than those which concern our cleansing from sin by the administration of the Spirit, through the blood of Christ; some of them have been mentioned before; — which also farther manifests the care that God hath taken for our instruction herein. [3.] There is nothing more pressed on us, nothing more frequently proposed unto us, in the gospel, than the necessity of our purification, and the only way of effecting it. If, therefore, either instructions, or promises, or precepts, or all concurring, may evidence the importance of a duty, then is this manifested to partake therein. And those who will prefer the guidance of carnal reason and vain tradition before these heavenly directions shall live in their ignorance and die in their sins. (2.) The difficulty of obtaining an acquaintance with it is to be duly considered. It is a part of the "mystery of the gospel," and such a part as is among those which the wisdom of the world or carnal reason esteemeth "foolishness." It is not easily admitted or received, that we can no otherwise be cleansed from our sins but by the sprinkling of that blood which was shed so long ago; yet this and no other way doth the Scripture propose unto us. To fancy that there is any cleansing from sin but by the blood of Christ is to overthrow the gospel. The doctrine hereof are persons, therefore, obliged to inquire after and come to the knowledge of, that, being satisfied with its truth, and that this is the only way of cleansing [from] sin, appointed and blessed by God himself, their minds may be exercised about it, and so be taken off from resting on those vain medicines and remedies, which (having nothing else to fix upon) their own hearts and others'; blind devotions would suggest unto them.

5. But now the great inquiry is, How a sinful, defiled soul may come to have an interest in, or be partaker of, the purifying virtue and efficacy of the blood of Christ? Ans. 1. The purifying virtue and force of the blood of Christ, with the administration of the Spirit for its application to make it effectual unto

our souls and consciences, is proposed and exhibited unto us in the promises of the covenant, 2 Pet. i. 4. This all the instances (which need not be recited) before produced do testify unto. 2. The only way to be made partaker of the good things presented in the promises is by faith. So Abraham is said to have "received the promises," Heb. xi. 17; and so are we also, and to receive Christ himself. Now, this is not from their being proposed unto us, but from our believing of that which is proposed, as it is expressed of Abraham, Rom. iv. 19–21, x. 6–9. The whole use, benefit, and advantage of the promises depend absolutely on our mixing them with faith; as the apostle declares, Heb. iv. 2. Where they are "mixed with faith," there they profit us — there we really receive the thing promised. Where they are not so mixed, they are of no use, but to aggravate our sins and unbelief. I know that by some men the whole nature and work of faith is derided; they say, "It is nothing but a strong fixing of the imagination upon what is said." However, we know that if a man promise us any thing seriously and solemnly which is absolutely in his power, we trust unto his word, or believe him, considering his wisdom, honesty, and ability. This, we know, is not a mere fixing of the imagination, but it is a real and useful confidence or trust. And whereas God hath given unto us great and precious promises, and that under several confirmations, especially that of his oath and covenant, if we do really believe their accomplishment, and that it shall be unto us according to his word, upon the account of his veracity, divine power, righteousness, and holiness, why shall this be esteemed "a fanatical fixing of the imagination?" If it be so, it was so in Abraham, our example, Rom. iv. 19–21. But this blasphemous figment, designed to the overthrow of the way of life and salvation by Jesus Christ, shall be elsewhere more fully examined. God, as was said, gives unto us great and precious promises, that by them we might be made partakers of the divine nature. These promises he requireth us to receive, and to mix them with faith, — that is, trusting to and resting on his divine power and veracity, ascribing unto him thereby the glory of them, to believe that the things promised unto us shall be accomplished; which is the means, by God's appointment, whereby we shall be really made partakers of them. Such was the faith of Abraham, so celebrated by our apostle; and such was all the true and saving faith that ever was in the world from the foundation of it. Wherefore, 3. This is the only way and means to obtain an interest in the cleansing virtue of the blood of Christ. God hath given this power and efficacy unto it by the covenant. In the promise of the gospel it is proposed and tendered unto us. Faith in that promise is that alone which gives us an interest in it, makes us partakers of it, and renders it actually effectual unto us; whereby we are really cleansed from sin. 4. There are two things which concur unto the efficacy of faith to this purpose:— (1.) The excellency of the grace or duty itself. Despise their ignorance who tell you this is but a deceitful fixing of the imagination; for they know not what they say. When men come to the real practice of this duty, they will find what it is to discard all other ways and pretences of cleansing; what it is sincerely and really to give unto God, against all difficulties and oppositions, the glory of his power, faithfulness, goodness, and grace; what it is to approve of the wisdom and love of God in finding out this way for us, and the infiniteness of his grace in providing it when we were lost and under the curse, and to be filled with a holy admiration of him on that account; — all which belong unto the faith mentioned, neither is it nor can be acted in a due manner without them. And when you understand these things, you will not think it so strange that God should appoint this way of believing only as the means to interest us in the purifying virtue of the blood of Christ. (2.) Hereby are we, as hath been shown, united unto Christ, from whom alone is our cleansing. He that declares another way must make another gospel.

6. Faith, in this case, will act itself in and by fervent prayer. When David had, by sin, brought himself into that condition wherein he stood in need of a new universal purification, how earnest is he in his supplications that God would again "purge and cleanse him!" Ps. li. And when any soul is really coming over to the way of God for his washing in the blood of Christ, he will not be more earnest and fervent in any supplication than in this. And herein and hereby doth Christ communicate of the purging efficacy of his blood unto us.

And these things may, in some measure, suffice for the direction and guidance of those who are yet wholly under the pollution of corrupted nature, how they may proceed to get themselves cleansed according to the mind of God. Not that this order or method is prescribed unto any; only, these are the heads of those things which, in one degree or other, are wrought in the souls of them whom Christ will and doth cleanse from their sins.

Secondly, Instruction, also, may be hence taken for them concerning whom our apostle says, "Such were some of you; but ye are washed, but ye are sanctified, but ye are justified in the name of the Lord Jesus, and by the Spirit of our God," 1 Cor. vi. 9–11; — such as are freed from the general pollution of nature "by the washing of regeneration and renewing of the Holy Ghost," Tit. iii. 5; —those, I mean, who have been made partakers of that cleansing, purifying work of the Holy Ghost which we have described. Several duties are incumbent on them with respect hereunto; as, —

1. Continual self-abasement, in the remembrance of that woful defiled state and condition from whence they have been delivered. This consideration is one of them which principally doth influence the minds of believers unto humility, and hideth pride from them; for what should creatures of such a base and defiled extraction have to boast of in themselves? It is usual, I confess, for vile men of the most contemptible beginnings, when they are greatly exalted in the world, to outgo others in pride and elation of mind, as they are behind them in the advantages of birth and education. But this is esteemed a vile thing amongst men, though it is but one potsherd of the earth boasting itself against another. But when believers shall consider what was their vile and polluted state with respect unto God, when first he had regard unto them, it will cause them to walk humbly in a deep sense of it, or I am sure it ought so to do. God calls his people to self-abasement, not only from what they are, but from what they were and whence they came. So he ordained that confession to be made by him that offered the first-fruits of his fields and possessions, "A Syrian ready to perish was my father;" or, "A Syrian" (that is, Laban) "was ready to destroy my father, a poor, helpless man, that went from one country to another for bread. How is it of sovereign mercy that I am now in this state and condition of plenty and peace!" Deut. xxvi. 1–5. And, in particular, God wonderfully binds upon them the sense of that defiled natural extraction whereof we speak, Ezek. xvi. 3–5. And when David, upon his great sin and his repentance, took in all humbling, self-abasing considerations, here he fixeth the head of them: Ps. li. 5, "Behold, I was shapen in iniquity; and in sin did my mother conceive me." His original natural defilement was that which, in the first place, influenced him unto self-abasement. So our apostle frequently calls the saints to a

remembrance of their former condition before they were purged, Eph. ii. 11–13; 1 Cor. vi. 9–11; and therewith are the minds of all true believers greatly affected and greatly humbled. When they consider what was their natural state and condition, — universally leprous and polluted, — with what remainders of it do still abide, it casts them on the earth, and causeth them to lay their mouths in the dust. Hence proceed their great and deep humiliations of themselves, and confessions of their own vileness in their prayers and supplications. Considering the holiness of God, with whom they have to do, unto whom they do approach, they are no way able to express what low thoughts and apprehensions they have of themselves. Even God himself doth teach them to use figurative expressions whereby to declare their own vileness by nature; which abound in the Scripture. It is true, all declarations hereof, in prayer and confession of sin, are derided and scorned by some, who seem to understand nothing of these things, yea, to glory that they do not. Whatever is spoken to express, as they are able, the deep sense any have of their natural defilement, with the remainder of it, their shame and self-abasement with respect unto the holiness of God, is reputed either as false and hypocritical, or that it containeth such things as for which men ought to be hanged. Such prodigious impudence in proclaiming a senselessness of the holiness of God and of the vileness of sin have we lived to see and hear of! But when we have to deal with God, who puts no trust in his servants, and chargeth his angels with folly, what shall we say? What lowliness becomes them "who dwell in houses of clay, whose foundation is in the dust, and who are crushed before the moth!"

2. That initial deliverance which believers have from their original pollution of sin is a matter and cause of everlasting thankfulness. When our Lord Jesus Christ cleansed the ten lepers, he manifests how much it was their duty to return unto him with their thankful acknowledgement, though nine of them failed therein, Luke xvii. 17. And when of old any one was cleansed from a carnal defilement, there was an offering enjoined him, to testify his gratitude. And, indeed, the consideration hereof is that which in an eminent manner influenceth the minds of believers in all their grateful ascriptions of glory, honour, and praise to Jesus Christ. "Unto him," say they, "that loved us, and washed us from our sins in his own blood, to him be glory and dominion for ever and ever," Rev. i. 5, 6. And there are three things which concur to this duty:— (1.) A due valuation of the causes and means of our purification, — namely, the sprinkling of the blood of Christ in the sanctification of the Spirit. As these alone have affected this great work, so they alone were able so to do. Had we not been washed in the blood of Christ, we must have lived and died in our pollutions, and have lain under them to eternity; for the fire of hell will never purge the defilements of sin, much less will the fictitious fire of purgatory cleanse any from them. How ought we then to prize, value, and admire, both the virtue or efficacy of the blood of Christ, and the love from whence it was given for us and is applied to us! And because this valuation and admiration are acts of faith, the very work itself, also, of cleansing our souls is carried on by them; for by the exercise of faith do we continually derive virtue from Christ to this purpose, as the woman did by touching of his garment for the stopping of her issue of blood. (2.) Inward joy and satisfaction in our freedom from that shame which deprived us of all boldness and confidence in God. This internal joy belongs unto the duty of thankfulness; for therein is God glorified when we are graciously sensible of the effects of his love and kindness

towards us. Every grace then glorifies God, and expresseth our thankfulness for his love, when a soul finds itself really affected with a sense of its being washed from all its loathsome defilements in the blood of Christ, and, being thereby freed from discouraging, oppressing shame, to have filial boldness in the presence of God. (3.) Acknowledgement in a way of actual praise. Again; we have declared not only that there is in our natural frame and spiritual constitution a discrepancy to the holiness of God, and consequently a universal defilement, but that there is, from its pravity and disorder, a pollution attending every actual sin, whether internal of the heart and mind only, or external in sin perpetrated, averse to holiness, and contrary to the carrying on of the work of sanctification in us. And sundry things believers, whose concernment alone this is, may learn from hence also; as —

1. How they ought to watch against sin and all the motions of it, though never so secret. They all of them defile the conscience. And it is an evidence of a gracious soul, to be watchful against sin on this account. Convictions will make men wary where they are prevalent, by continual representations of the danger and punishment of sin; and these are an allowable motive to believers themselves to abstain from it in all known instances. The consideration of the terror of the Lord, the use of threatenings both of the law and gospel, declare this to be our duty. Neither let any say that this is servile fear; that denomination is taken from the frame of our minds, and not from the object feared. When men so fear as thereon to be discouraged, and to incline unto a relinquishment of God, duty, and hope, that fear is servile, whatever be the object of it. And that fear which keeps from sin, and excites the soul to cleave more firmly to God, be the object of it what it will, is no servile fear, but a holy fear or due reverence unto God and his word. But this is the most genuinely gracious fear of sin, when we dread the defilement of it, and that contrariety which is in it to the holiness of God. This is a natural fruit of faith and love. And this consideration should always greatly possess our minds; — and the truth is, if it do not so, there is no assured preservative against sin; for together with an apprehension of that spiritual pollution wherewith sin is accompanied, thoughts of the holiness of God, of the care and concernment of the sanctifying Spirit, and of the blood of Christ, will continually abide in our minds, which are all efficaciously preservative against sin. I think that there is no more forcible argument unto watchfulness against all sin, unto believers, in the whole book of God, than that which is managed by our apostle, with especial respect unto one kind of sin, but may in proportion be extended unto all, 1 Cor. iii. 16, 17, vi. 15–19. Moreover, where this is not, where the soul hath no respect to the defilement of sin, but only considers how it may shift with the guilt of it, innumerable things will interpose, partly arising from the abuse of grace, partly from carnal hopes and foolish resolutions for after-times, as will set it at liberty from that watchful diligence in universal obedience which is required of us. The truth is, I do not believe that any one that is awed only with respect to the guilt of sin and its consequents doth keep up a firm integrity with regard to inward and outward actings of his heart and life in all things. But where the fear of the Lord and of sin is influenced by a deep apprehension of the holiness of the one, and the pollution that inseparably attends the other, there is the soul kept always upon its best guard and defence.

2. How we ought to walk humbly before the Lord all our days. Notwithstanding our utmost watchfulness and diligence against sin, there is yet "no man that liveth and sinneth not." Those who pretend unto a perfection here, as they manifest themselves to be utterly ignorant of God and themselves, and despise the blood of Christ, so for the most part they are left visibly and in the sight of men to confute their own pride and folly. But to what purpose is it to hide ourselves from ourselves, when we have to do with God? God knows, and our own souls know, that more or less we are defiled in all that we do. The best of our works and duties, brought into the presence of the holiness of God, are but as filthy rags; and man, even every man, of himself "drinketh in iniquity like water." Our own clothes are ready to defile us every day. Who can express the motions of lusts that are in the flesh; the irregular actings of affections, in their inordinate risings up to their objects; the folly of the imaginations of our hearts and minds, which, as far as they are not principled by grace, are only evil, and that continually; with the vanity of our words, yea, with a mixture of much corrupt communications; all which are defiling, and have defilements attending of them? I confess I know not that my heart and soul abhors any eruption of the diabolical pride of man like that whereby they reproach and scoff at the deepest humiliations and self-abasements which poor sinners can attain unto in their prayers, confessions, and supplications. Alas! that our nature should be capable of such a contempt of the holiness of God, such an ignorance of the infinite distance that is between him and us, and be so senseless of our own vileness, and of the abominable filth and pollution that is in every sin, as not to tremble at the despising of the lowest abasements of poor sinners before the holy God! "Behold, his soul which is lifted up is not upright in him; but the just shall live by his faith," Hab. ii. 4.

3. How we ought continually to endeavour after the wasting of sin in the root and principle of it. There is a root of sin in us, which springs up and defiles us. "Every man is tempted" (that is, chiefly and principally) "of his own lust, and seduced;" and then "when lust hath conceived, it bringeth forth sin." It is "the flesh that lusteth against the Spirit," and which bringeth forth corrupted and corrupting, polluted and polluting fruits. This principle of sin, of aversion from God, of inclination unto things sensual and present, however wounded, weakened, dethroned, impaired, yet still abides in all believers; and it is the foundation, the spring, the root, the next cause of all sin in us, which tempts, enticeth, draws aside, conceives, and brings forth. And this hath in us all more or less degrees of strength, power, and activity, according as it is more or less mortified by grace and the application of the virtue of the death of Christ unto our souls; and according to its strength and power, so it abounds in bringing forth the defiled acts of sin. Whilst this retains any considerable power in us, it is to no purpose to set ourselves merely to watch against the eruptions of actual sins in the frames of our hearts, in the thoughts of our minds, or outward actions. If we would preserve ourselves from multiplying our defilements, if we would continually be perfecting the work of holiness in the fear of the Lord, it is this we must set ourselves against. The tree must be made good if we expect good fruit; and the evil root must be digged up, or evil fruit will be brought forth; — that is, our main design should be, to crucify and destroy the body of the sins of the flesh that is in us, the remainders of the flesh or indwelling sin, by the ways and means which shall afterward be declared.

4. Hence also is manifest the necessity there is of continual applications to Jesus Christ for cleansing virtue from his Spirit, and the sprinkling of his blood on our consciences, in the efficacy of it, to purge them from dead works. We defile ourselves every day, and if we go not every day to the "fountain that is open for sin and for uncleanness," we shall quickly be all over leprous. Our consciences will be filled with dead works, so that we shall no way be able to serve the living God, unless they are daily purged out. How this is done hath been at large before declared. When a soul, filled with self-abasement under a sense of its own defilements, applies itself unto Christ by faith for cleansing, and that constantly and continually, with a fervency answering its sense and convictions, it is in its way and proper course. I am persuaded no true believer in the world is a stranger unto this duty; and the more any one abounds therein, the more genuine is his faith evidenced to be, and the more humble is his walk before the Lord.

But it may justly be inquired, after all that we have discoursed upon this subject concerning the defilement of sin, how, if it be so, believers can be united unto Jesus Christ, or be members of that mystical body whereof he is the head, or obtain fellowship with him; for whereas he is absolutely pure, holy, and perfect, how can he have union or communion with them who are in any thing defiled? There is no fellowship between righteousness and unrighteousness, no communion between light and darkness, and what can there be between Christ and those that are defiled with sin? and because he is "holy, harmless, and undefiled," he is said to be "separate from sinners."

Many things must be returned unto this objection, all concurring to take away the seeming difficulty that is in it; as, —

1. It must be granted that where men are wholly under the power of their original defilement, they neither have nor can have either union or communion with Christ. With respect unto such persons the rules before mentioned are universally true and certain. There is no more communion between them and Jesus Christ than is between light and darkness, as the apostle speaks expressly, 1 John i. 6. Whatever profession they may make of his name, whatever expectations they may unduly raise from him in their own minds, he will say unto them at the last day, "Depart from me, I never knew you." No person, therefore, whatever, who hath not been made partaker of the washing of regeneration and the renovation of the Holy Ghost, can possibly have any union with Christ. I do not speak this as though our purifying were in order of time and nature antecedent unto our union with Christ, for indeed it is an effect thereof; but it is such an effect as immediately and inseparably accompanieth it, so that where the one is not, there is not the other. The act whereby he unites us unto himself is the same with that whereby he cleanseth our natures.

2. Whatever our defilements are or may be, he is not defiled by them. They adhere only unto a capable subject, which Christ is not. He was capable to have the guilt of our sins imputed to him, but not the filth of one sin adhering to him. A member of a body may have a putrefied sore; the head may be troubled at it and grieved with it, yet is not defiled by it. Wherefore, where there is a radical, original cleansing by the Spirit of regeneration and holiness, whereby any one is meet for union and communion with Christ, however he may be affected with our partial pollutions, he is not defiled by them. He is able συμπαθῆσαι, "compati, condolere;" he suffers with us in his compassion; — but he is not liable συμμολύνεσθαι, to be defiled with us or for us. The visible mystical body

of Christ may be defiled by corrupt members, Heb. xii. 15; but the mystical body cannot be so, much less the head.

3. The design of Christ, when he takes believers into union with himself, is to purge and cleanse them absolutely and perfectly; and therefore the present remainders of some defilements are not absolutely inconsistent with that union. "He gave himself for the church, that he might sanctify and cleanse it with the washing of water by the word, that he might present it to himself a glorious church, not having spot, or wrinkle, or any such thing; but that it should be holy and without blemish," Eph. v. 25–27. This he aims at, and this he will, in his own way and in his own time, perfectly accomplish. But it is not done at once; it is a progressive work, that hath many degrees. God did never sanctify any soul at once, unless by death. The body must die by reason of sin. Every believer is truly and really sanctified at once, but none is perfectly sanctified at once. It is not, therefore, necessary unto union that we should be completely sanctified, though it is that we should be truly sanctified. Complete sanctification is a necessary effect of union in its proper time and season. See John xv. 1–5.

4. Where the work of sanctification and spiritual cleansing is really begun in any, there the whole person is, and is thence denominated, holy. As, therefore, Christ the head is holy, so are all the members holy according to their measure; for although there may be defilements adhering unto their actions, yet their persons are sanctified: so that no unholy person hath any communion with Christ, no member of his body is unholy, — that is, absolutely so, in such a state as thence to be denominated unholy.

5. Our union with Christ is immediately in and by the new creature in us, by the divine nature which is from the Spirit of holiness, and is pure and holy. Hereunto and hereby doth the Lord Christ communicate himself unto our souls and consciences, and hereby have we all our intercourse with him. Other adherences that have any defilement in them, and consequently are opposite unto this union, he daily worketh out by virtue hereof, Rom. viii. 10. The whole body of Christ, therefore, and all that belongs unto it, is holy, though those who are members of this body are in themselves oft-times polluted, but not in any thing which belongs to their union. The apostle describeth the twofold nature or principle that is in believers, the new nature by grace and the old of sin, as a double person, Rom. vii. 19, 20; and it is the former, the renewed (and not the latter, which he calls "I" also, but corrects as it were that expression, calling it "sin which dwelleth in him"), that is the subject of the union with Christ, the other being to be destroyed.

6. Where the means of purification are duly used, no defilement ensues, on any sin that believers fall into, which doth or can totally obstruct communion with God in Christ, according to the tenor of the covenant. There were many things under the Old Testament that did typically and legally defile men that were liable unto them; but for all of them were provided typical and legal purifications, which sanctified them as to the purifying of the flesh. Now, no man was absolutely cut off or separated from the people of God for being so defiled; but he that, being defiled, did not take care that he might be purified according to the law, he was to be cut off from among the people. It is in like manner in things spiritual and evangelical. There are many sins whereby believers are defiled; but there is a way of cleansing still open unto them. And it is not merely the incidence of a defilement, but the neglect of purification,

that is inconsistent with their state and interest in Christ. The rule of communion with God, and consequently of union with Christ, in its exercise, is expressed by David, Ps. xix. 12, 13, "Who can understand his errors? cleanse thou me from secret sins. Keep back thy servant also from presumptuous sins; let them not have dominion over me: then shall I be upright, and I shall be innocent from the great transgression." The design of psalmist is, to be preserved in such a state and condition as wherein he may be upright before God. To be upright before God is that which God requireth of us in the covenant, that we may be accepted of him and enjoy the promises thereof, Gen. xvii. 1. He that is so will be from that great transgression, or that abundance of sin which is inconsistent with the covenant love and favour of God. And hereunto three things are required:— (1.) A constant, humble acknowledgement of sin: "Who can understand his errors?" (2.) Daily cleansing from those defilements which the least and most secret sins are accompanied withal: "Cleanse thou me from secret sins." And, — (3.) A preservation from "presumptuous sins," or wilful sins committed with a high hand. Where these things are, there a man is upright, and hath the covenant-ground of his communion with God; and whilst believers are preserved within these bounds, though they are defiled by sin, yet is there not any thing therein inconsistent with their union with Christ.

7. Our blessed Head is not only pure and holy, but he is also gracious and merciful, and will not presently cut off a member of his body because it is sick or hath a sore upon it. He is himself passed through his course of temptations, and is now above the reach of them all. Doth he, therefore, reject and despise those that are tempted, that labour and suffer under their temptations? It is quite otherwise, so that, on the account of his own present state, his compassions do exceedingly abound towards all his that are tempted. It is no otherwise with him as to their sins and defilements. These he himself was absolutely free from in all his temptations and sufferings, but we are not; and he is so far from casting us away on that account, while we endeavour after purification, as that it draweth out his compassions towards us. In brief, he doth not unite us to himself because we are perfect, but that in his own way and time he may make us so; not because we are clean, but that he may cleanse us: for it is the blood of Jesus Christ, with whom we have fellowship, that cleanseth us from all our sins. Lastly, To wind up this discourse, there is hence sufficiently evidenced a comprehensive difference between a spiritual life unto God by evangelical holiness, and a life of moral virtue, though pretended unto God also. Unto the first, the original and continual purification of our nature and persons by the Spirit of God and blood of Christ is indispensably required. Where this work is not, there neither is nor can be any thing of that holiness which the gospel prescribes, and which we inquire after. Unless the purification and cleansing of sin belong necessarily unto the holiness of the new covenant, all that God hath taught us concerning it in the Old Testament and the New, by his institution of legal purifying ordinances; by his promises to wash, purify, and cleanse us; by his precepts to get ourselves cleansed by the means of our purification, namely, his Spirit and the blood of Christ; by his instruments and directions of us to make use of those means of our cleansing; by his declarations that believers are so washed and cleansed from all the defilements of their sins, — are things fanatical, enthusiastic notions, and unintelligible dreams. Until men can rise up to a confidence enabling them to own such horrible blasphemies, I desire to

know whether these things are required unto their morality? If they shall say they are so, they give us a new notion of morality, never yet heard of in the world; and we must expect until they have farther cleared it, there being little or no signification in the great swelling words of vanity which have hitherto been lavished about it. But if they do not belong thereunto, — then is their life of moral virtue (were it as real in them as it is with notorious vanity pretended) cast out from all consideration in a serious disquisition after evangelical holiness. And what hath been spoken may suffice to give us some light into the nature of this first act of our sanctification by the Spirit, which consists in the cleansing of our souls and consciences from the pollutions of sin, both original and actual.

Chapter VI - The positive work of the Spirit in the sanctification of believers

Differences in the acts of sanctification as to order — The manner of the communication of holiness by the Spirit — The rule and measure whereof is the revealed will of God, as the rule of its acceptance is the covenant of grace — The nature of holiness as inward — Righteousness habitual and actual — False notions of holiness removed — The nature of a spiritual habit — Applied unto holiness, with its rules and limitations — Proved and confirmed — Illustrated and practically improved — The properties of holiness as a spiritual habit declared — 1. Spiritual dispositions unto suitable acts; how expressed in the Scripture; with their effects — Contrary dispositions unto sin and holiness how consistent — 2. Power; the nature thereof; or what power is required in believers unto holy obedience; with its properties and effects in readiness and facility — Objections thereunto answered, and an inquiry on these principles after true holiness in ourselves directed — Gospel grace distinct from morality, and all other habits of the mind; proved by many arguments, especially its relation unto the mediation of Christ — The principal difference between evangelical holiness and all other habits of the mind, proved by the manner and way of its communication from the person of Christ as the head of the church, and the peculiar efficiency of the Spirit therein — Moral honesty not gospel holiness.

The distinction we make between the acts of the Holy Ghost in the work of sanctification concerneth more the order of teaching and instruction than any order of precedency that is between the acts themselves; for that which we have passed through concerning the cleansing of our natures and persons doth not, in order of time, go before those other acts which leave a real and positive effect upon the soul, which we now enter upon the description of, nor absolutely in order of nature: yea, much of the means whereby the Holy Ghost purifieth us consisteth in this other work of his which now lies before us; only we thus distinguish them and cast them into this order, as the Scripture also doth, for the guidance of our understanding in them, and furtherance of our apprehension of them.

We, therefore, now proceed unto that part of the work of the Holy Spirit whereby he communicates the great, permanent, positive effect of holiness unto the souls of believers, and whereby he guides and assists them in all the acts, works, and duties of holiness whatever; without which what we do is not so, nor doth any way belong thereunto. And this part of his work we shall reduce unto two heads, which we shall first propose, and afterward clear and vindicate.

And our first assertion is, That in the sanctification of believers, the Holy Ghost doth work in them, in their whole souls, their minds, wills, and affections, a gracious, supernatural habit, principle, and disposition of living unto God; wherein the substance or essence, the life and being, of holiness doth consist. This is that spirit which is born of the Spirit, that new creature, that new and divine nature which is wrought in them, and whereof they are made partakers. Herein consists that image of God whereunto our natures are repaired by the grace of our Lord Jesus Christ, whereby we are made conformable unto God, firmly and steadfastly adhering unto him through faith and love. That there is such a divine principle, such a gracious, supernatural habit, wrought in all them that are born again, hath been fully proved in our assertion and description of the work of regeneration. It is, therefore, acknowledged that the first supernatural infusion or communication of this principle of spiritual light and life, preparing, fitting, and enabling all the faculties of our souls unto the duties of holiness, according to the mind of God, doth belong unto the work of our first conversion. But the preservation, cherishing, and increase of it belong unto our sanctification, both its infusion and preservation being necessarily required unto holiness. Hereby is the tree made good, that the fruit of it may be good, and without which it will not so be. This is our new nature; which ariseth not from precedent actions of holiness, but is the root of them all. Habits acquired by a multitude of acts, whether in things moral or artificial, are not a new nature, nor can be so called, but a readiness for acting from use and custom. But this nature is from God, its parent; it is that in us which is born of God. And it is common unto or the same in all believers, as to its kind and being, though not as to degrees and exercise. It is that which we cannot learn, which cannot be taught us but by God only, as he teaches other creatures in whom he planteth a natural instinct. The beauty and glory hereof, as it is absolutely inexpressible, so have we spoken somewhat to it before. Conformity to God, likeness to Christ, compliance with the Holy Spirit, interest in the family of God, fellowship with angels, separation from darkness and the world, do all consist herein.

Secondly, The matter of our holiness consists in our actual obedience unto God, according to the tenor of the covenant of grace; for God promiseth to write his law in our hearts, that we may fear him and walk in his statutes. And concerning this, in general, we may observe two things:—

1. That there is a certain fixed rule and measure of this obedience, in a conformity and answerableness whereunto it doth consist. This is the revealed will of God in the Scripture, Mic. vi. 8. God's will, I say, as revealed unto us in the word, is the rule of our obedience. A rule it must have, which nothing else can pretend to be. The secret will or hidden purposes of God are not the rule of our obedience, Deut. xxix. 29, much less are our own imaginations, inclinations, or reason so; neither doth any thing, though never so specious, which we do in compliance with them, or by their direction, belong thereunto, Col. ii. 18–23. But the word of God is the adequate rule of all holy obedience:— (1.) It is so materially. All that is commanded in that word belongs unto our obedience, and nothing else doth so. Hence are we so strictly required neither to add unto it nor to diminish or take any thing from it, Deut. iv. 2, xii. 32; Josh. i. 7; Prov. xxx. 6; Rev. xxii. 18, 19. (2.) It is so formally; that is, we are not only to do what is commanded, all that is commanded, and nothing else, but whatever we do, we are to do it because it is commanded, or it is no part of our obedience or holiness, Deut. vi. 24, 25, xxix. 29; Ps. cxix. 9. I know there is an inbred light of nature as yet remaining in us, which gives great direction as to moral good and evil, commanding the one and forbidding the other, Rom. ii. 14, 15; but this light, however it may be made subservient and subordinate thereunto, is not the rule of gospel holiness as such, nor any part of

it. The law which God by his grace writes in our hearts answers unto the law that is written in the word that is given unto us; and as the first is the only principle, so the latter is the only rule, of our evangelical obedience. For this end hath God promised that his Spirit and his word shall always accompany one another, the one to quicken our souls, and the other to guide our lives, Isa. lix. 21. And the word of God may be considered as our rule in a threefold respect:— (1.) As it requires the image of God in us. The habitual rectitude of our nature with respect unto God and our living to him is enjoined us in the word, yea, and wrought in us thereby. The whole renovation of our nature, the whole principle of holiness before described, is nothing but the word changed into grace in our hearts; for we are born again by the incorruptible seed of the word of God. The Spirit worketh nothing in us but what the word first requireth of us. It is, therefore, the rule of the inward principle of spiritual life; and the growth thereof is nothing but its increase in conformity to that word. (2.) With respect unto all the actual frames, designs, and purposes of the heart. All the internal actings of our minds, all the volitions of the will, all the motions of our affections, are to be regulated by that word which requires us to love the Lord our God with all our minds, all our souls, and all our strength. Hereby is their regularity or irregularity to be tried. All that holiness which is in them consists in their conformity to the revealed will of God. (3.) With respect unto all our outward actions and duties, private and public, of piety, of righteousness, towards ourselves or others, Tit. ii. 12. This is the rule of our holiness. So far as what we are and what we do answer thereunto, so far are we holy, and no farther. Whatever acts of devotion or duties of morality may be performed without respect hereunto belong not to our sanctification.

2. As there is a rule of our performance of this obedience, so there is a rule of the acceptance of our obedience with God; and this is the tenor of the new covenant, Gen. xvii. 1. What answers hereunto is accepted, and what doth not so is rejected, both as to the universality of the whole and the sincerity that accompanies each particular duty in it. And these two things, universality and sincerity, answer now, as to some certain ends, the legal perfection at first required of us. In the estate of original righteousness, the rule of our acceptance with God in our obedience was the law and covenant of works; and this required that it should be absolutely perfect in parts and degrees, without the least intermixture of sin with our good, or interposition of it in the least instance, which was inconsistent with that covenant. But now, although we are renewed again by grace into the image of God really and truly (yet not absolutely nor perfectly, but only in part), we have yet remaining in us a contrary principle of ignorance and sin, which we must always conflict withal, Gal. v. 16, 17: wherefore God in the covenant of grace is pleased to accept of that holy obedience which is universal as to all parts, in all known instances of duty, and sincere as to the manner of their performance. What in particular is required hereunto is not our present work to declare; I only aim to fix in general the rule of the acceptance of this holy obedience. Now, the reason hereof is not that a lower and more imperfect kind of righteousness, holiness, and obedience, will answer all the ends of God and his glory now under the new covenant, than would have done so under the old. Nothing can be imagined more distant from the truth, or more dishonourable to the gospel, or that seems to have a nearer approach unto the making of Christ the minister of sin; for what would he be else, if he had procured that God would accept of a weak, imperfect obedience,

accompanied with many failings, infirmities, and sins, being in nothing complete, in the room and stead of that which was complete, perfect, and absolutely sinless, which he first required of us? Yea, God having determined to exalt and glorify the holy properties of his nature in a more eminent and glorious manner under the new covenant than the old, for which cause and end alone it is so exalted and preferred above it, it was necessary that there should be a righteousness and obedience required therein far more complete, eminent, and glorious than that required in the other. But the reason of this difference lies solely herein, that our evangelical obedience, which is accepted with God, according to the tenor of the new covenant, doth not hold the same place which our obedience should have had under the covenant of works; for therein it should have been our righteousness absolutely before God, that whereby we should have been justified in his sight, even the works of the law, and for which, in a due proportion of justice, we should have been eternally rewarded. But this place is now filled up by the righteousness and obedience of Christ, our mediator; which, being the obedience of the Son of God, is far more eminent and glorious, or tends more to the manifestation of the properties of God's nature, and therein to the exaltation of his glory, than all that we should have done had we abode steadfast in the covenant of works. "Whereunto, then," it may be some will say, "serves our holiness and obedience, and what is the necessity of them?" I must defer the answering of this inquiry unto its proper place, where I shall prove at large the necessity of this holiness, and demonstrate it from its proper principles and ends. In the meantime I say only, in general, that as God requireth it of us, so he hath appointed it as the only means whereby we may express our subjection to him, our dependence on him, our fruitfulness and thankfulness; the only way of our communion and intercourse with him, of using and improving the effects of his love, the benefits of the mediation of Christ, whereby we may glorify him in this world; and the only orderly way whereby we may be made meet for the inheritance of the saints in light: which is sufficient, in general, to manifest both its necessity and its use. These things being, then, in general premised, I shall comprise what I have farther to offer in the declaration and vindication of gospel sanctification and holiness in the two ensuing assertions:—

I. There is wrought and preserved in the minds and souls of all believers, by the Spirit of God, a supernatural principle or habit of grace and holiness, whereby they are made meet for and enabled to live unto God, and perform that obedience which he requireth and accepteth through Christ in the covenant of grace; essentially or specifically distinct from all natural habits, intellectual and moral, however or by what means soever acquired or improved.

II. There is an immediate work or effectual operation of the Holy Spirit by his grace required unto every act of holy obedience, whether internal only in faith and love, or external also; that is, unto all the holy actings of our understandings, wills, and affections, and unto all duties of obedience in our walking before God.

I. The first of these assertions I affirm not only to be true, but of so great weight and importance that our hope of life and salvation depends thereon; and it is the second great principle constituting our Christian profession. And there are four things that are to be confirmed concerning it:— 1. That there is such a habit or principle supernatural infused or created in believers by the Holy Ghost, and always abiding in them. 2. That, according to the nature of all habits, it inclines and disposeth the mind, will, and affections, unto acts of holiness suitable unto its own nature, and with regard unto its proper end, and to make us meet to live unto God. 3. [That] it doth not only incline and dispose the mind, but gives it power, and enables it to live unto God in all holy obedience. 4. That it differs specifically from all other habits, intellectual or moral, that by any means we may acquire or attain, or spiritual gifts that may be conferred on any persons whatever.

In the handling of these things, I shall manifest the difference that is between a spiritual, supernatural life of evangelical holiness and a course of moral virtue; which some, to the rejection of the grace of our Lord Jesus Christ, do endeavour to substitute in the room thereof. Such a spiritual, heavenly, supernatural life, so denominated from its nature, causes, acts, and ends, we must be partakers of in this world, if ever we mind to attain eternal life in another.

And herein we shall take what view we are able of the nature, glory, and beauty of holiness; and [I] do confess it is but little of them which I can comprehend. It is a matter, indeed, often spoken unto; but the essence and true nature of it are much hidden from the eyes of all living men. The sense of what the Scripture proposeth, what I believe, and what I desire an experience of, that I shall endeavour to declare. But as we are not in this life perfect in the duties of holiness, no more are we in the knowledge of its nature.

First, therefore, I say, it is a gracious, supernatural habit, or a principle of spiritual life. And with respect hereunto I shall briefly do these three things:— 1. Show what I mean by such a habit. 2. Prove that there is such a habit required unto holiness, yea, that the nature of holiness consists therein. 3. Declare in general the properties of it.

1. Our first inquiry is after the essence and form of holiness, that from which anyone is truly and really made and denominated holy; or what is the formal reason of that holiness which our nature is partaker of in this world. This must be something peculiar, something excellent and sacred, as that which constitutes the great and only difference that is between mankind, on their own part, in the sight of God, with respect unto eternity. Everyone that hath this holiness pleaseth God, is accepted with him, and shall come to the enjoyment of him; and everyone that hath it not is rejected of him, here and hereafter.

And this holiness, in the first place, doth not consist in any single acts of obedience unto God, though good in their own nature, and acceptable unto him; for such acts may be performed, yea, many of them, by unholy persons, with examples whereof the Scripture aboundeth. Cain's sacrifice and Ahab's repentance were signal single acts of obedience materially, yet no acts of holiness formally, nor did either make or denominate them holy. And our apostle tells us that men may "give all their goods to feed the poor, and their bodies to be burned, and yet be nothing," 1 Cor. xiii. 3; yet in single acts who can go farther? Such fruits may spring from seed that hath no root. Single acts may evidence holiness, as Abraham's obedience in sacrificing his son, but they constitute none holy; nor will a series, a course, a multiplication of acts and duties of obedience either constitute or denominate anyone so, Isa. i. 11–15. All the duties, a series and multiplication whereof are there rejected for want of holiness, were good in themselves, and appointed of God. Nor doth it consist in an habitual disposition of mind unto any outward duties of piety, devotion, or obedience, however obtained or acquired. Such habits there are, both intellectual and moral. Intellectual habits are arts and sciences. When men, by custom, usage, and frequent acts in the exercise of any science, art, or mystery, do get a ready facility in and unto all the parts and duties of it, they have an intellectual habit therein. It is so in things moral, as to virtues and vices. There are some seeds and sparks of moral virtue remaining in the ruins of depraved nature, as of justice, temperance, fortitude, and the like. Hence God calls on profligate sinners to remember and "show themselves men," or not to act contrary to the principles and light of nature, which are inseparable from us as we are men, Isa. xlvi. 8. These principles may be so excited in the exercise of natural light, and improved by education, instruction, and example, until persons, by an assiduous, diligent performance of the acts and duties of them, may attain such a readiness unto them and facility in them as is not by any outward means easily changed or diverted; and this is a moral habit. In like manner, in the duties of piety and religion, in acts of outward obedience unto God, men by the same means may so accustom themselves unto them as to have an habitual disposition unto their exercise. I doubt not but that it is so unto a high degree with many superstitious persons. But in all these things the acts do still precede the habits of the same nature and kind, which are produced by them and not otherwise. But this holiness is such a habit or principle as is antecedent unto all acts of the same kind, as we shall prove. There never was by any, nor ever can be, any act or duty of true holiness performed, where there was not in order of nature antecedently a habit of holiness in the persons by whom they were performed. Many acts and duties, for the substance of them good and approvable, may be performed without it, but no one that hath the proper form and nature of holiness can be so. And the reason is, because every act of true holiness must have something supernatural in it, from an internal renewed principle of grace; and that which hath not so, be it otherwise what it will, is no act or duty of true holiness.

And I call this principle of holiness a habit, not as though it were absolutely of the same kind with acquired habits, and would in all things answer to our conceptions and descriptions of them; but we only call it so because, in its effects and manner of operation, it agreeth in sundry things with acquired intellectual or moral habits. But it hath much more conformity unto a natural, unchangeable instinct than unto any acquired habit. Wherefore God chargeth it on men, that in their obedience unto him they did not answer that instinct which is in other creatures towards their lords and benefactors, Isa. i. 3, and which they cordially observe, Jer. viii. 7. But herein God "teacheth us more than the beasts of the earth, and maketh us wiser than the fowls of heaven," Job xxxv. 11.

This, therefore, is that which I intend, — a virtue, a power, a principle of spiritual life and grace, wrought, created, infused into our souls, and inlaid in all the faculties of them, constantly abiding and unchangeably residing in them, which is antecedent unto, and the next cause of, all acts of true holiness whatever. And this is that, as was said, wherein the nature of holiness doth consist, and from which, in those that are adult, the actual discharge of all duties and works of holiness is inseparable. This abideth always in and with all that are sanctified, whence they are always holy, and not only so when they are actually exercised in the duties of holiness. Hereby are they prepared, disposed, and enabled unto all duties of obedience, as we shall show immediately; and by the influence hereof into their acts and duties do they become holy, and no otherwise.

For the farther explanation of it, I shall only add three things:—

(1.) That this habit or principle, thus wrought and abiding in us, doth not, if I may so say, firm its own station, or abide and continue in us by its own natural efficacy, in adhering unto the faculties of our souls. Habits that are acquired by many actions have a natural efficacy to preserve themselves, until some opposition that is too hard for them prevail against them; which is frequently (though not easily) done. But this is preserved in us by the constant powerful actings and influence of the Holy Ghost. He which works it in us doth also preserve it in us. And the reason hereof is, because the spring of it is in our head, Christ Jesus, it being only an emanation of virtue and power from him unto us by the Holy Ghost. If this be not actually and always continued, whatever is in us would die and wither of itself. See Eph. iv. 15, 16; Col. iii. 3; John iv. 14. It is in us as the fructifying sap is in a branch of the vine or olive. It is there really and formally, and is the next cause of the fruit-bearing of the branch: but it doth not live and abide by itself, but by a continual emanation and communication from the root; let that be intercepted, and it quickly withers. So is it with this principle in us, with respect unto its root, Christ Jesus.

(2.) Though this principle or habit of holiness be of the same kind or nature in all believers, in all that are sanctified, yet there are in them very distinct degrees of it. In some it is more strong, lively, vigorous, and flourishing; in others, more weak, feeble, and inactive; and this in so great variety and on so many occasions as cannot here be spoken unto.

(3.) That although this habit and principle is not acquired by any or many acts of duty or obedience, yet is it, in a way of duty, preserved, increased, strengthened, and improved thereby. God hath appointed that we should live in the exercise of it; and in and by the multiplication of its acts and duties is it kept alive and stirred up, without which it will be weakened and decay.

2. This being what I intend as to the substance of it, we must, in the next place, show that there is such a spiritual habit or principle of spiritual life wrought in believers, wherein their holiness doth consist. Some few testimonies of many shall suffice as to its present confirmation.

The work of it is expressed, Deut. xxx. 6, "The Lord thy God will circumcise thine heart, to love the Lord thy God with all thine heart, and with all thy soul, that thou mayest live." The end of holiness is, that we may "live;" and the principal work of holiness is to "love the Lord our God with all our heart and soul;" and this is the effect of God's "circumcising our hearts," without which it will not be. Every act of love and fear, and consequently every duty of holiness whatever, is consequential unto God's circumcising of our hearts. But it should seem that this work of God is "only a removal of hinderances," and doth not express the collation of the principle which we assert. I answer, that although it were easy to demonstrate that this work of circumcising our hearts cannot be effected without an implantation of the principle pleaded for in them, yet it shall suffice at present to evince from hence that this effectual work of God upon our hearts is antecedently necessary unto all acts of holiness in us. But herewithal God writes his law in our hearts: Jer. xxxi. 33, "I will put my law in their inward parts, and write it in their hearts." The habit or principle which we have described is nothing but a transcript of the law of God implanted and abiding in our hearts, whereby we comply with and answer unto the whole will of God therein. This is holiness in the habit and principle of it. This is more fully expressed, Ezek. xxxvi. 26, 27, "A new heart will I give you, and a new spirit will I put within you, and cause you to walk in my statutes, and ye shall keep my judgments, and do them." The whole of all that actual obedience and all those duties of holiness which God requireth of us is contained in these expressions, "Ye shall walk in my statutes, and keep my judgments to do them." Antecedent hereunto, and as the principle and cause thereof, God gives a "new heart" and a "new spirit." This new heart is a heart with the law of God written in it, as before mentioned; and this new spirit is the habitual inclination of that heart unto the life of God, or all duties of obedience. And herein the whole of what we have asserted is confirmed, — namely, that antecedently unto all duties and acts of holiness whatever, and as the next cause of them, there is by the Holy Ghost a new spiritual principle or habit of grace communicated unto us and abiding in us, from whence we are made and denominated holy.

It is yet more expressly revealed and declared in the New Testament, John iii. 6. There is a work of the Spirit of God upon us in our regeneration; we are "born again of the Spirit." And there is the product of this work of the Spirit of God in us, that which is born in this new birth, and that is "spirit" also. It is something existing in us, that is of a spiritual nature and spiritual efficacy. It is something abiding in us, acting in a continual opposition against the flesh or sin, as Gal. v. 17, and unto all duties of obedience unto God. And until this spirit is formed in us, — that is, our whole souls have a furnishment of spiritual power and ability, — we cannot perform any one act that is spiritually good, nor any one act of vital obedience. This spirit, or spiritual nature, which is born of the Spirit, by which alone we are enabled to live to God, is that habit of grace or principle of holiness which we intend. And so also is it called a new creature: "If any man be in Christ he is a new creature," 2 Cor. v. 17. It is something that, by an almighty creating act of the power of God by his Spirit, hath the nature of a living creature, produced in the souls of all that are in Christ Jesus. And as it is called the "new creature," so it is also a "divine nature," 2 Pet. i. 4; and a nature is the principle of all operations. And this is what we plead for: The Spirit of God createth a new nature in us, which is the principle and next cause of all acts of the life of God. Where this is not, whatever else there may be, there is no evangelical holiness. This is that whereby we are enabled to live unto God, to fear him, to walk in his ways, and to yield obedience according to his mind and will. See Eph. iv. 23, 24; Col. iii. 10. This the Scripture plentifully testifieth unto; but withal I must add, that as to the proper nature or essence of it, no mind can apprehend it, no tongue can express it, none can perfectly understand its glory. Some few things may be added to illustrate it.

(1.) This is that whereby we have union with Jesus Christ, the head of the church. Originally and efficiently the Holy Spirit dwelling in him and us is the cause of this union; but formally this new principle of grace is so. It is that whereby we become "members of his flesh and of his bones," Eph. v. 30. As Eve was of Adam, — she was one with him, because she had the same nature with him, and that derived from him, which the apostle alludeth unto, — so are we of him, partakers of the same divine nature with him. Thus he that is "joined unto the Lord is one spirit," 1 Cor. vi. 17; that is, of one and the same spiritual nature with him, Heb. ii. 11, 14. How excellent is this grace, which gives us our interest in and continuity unto the body of Christ, and to his person as our head! It is the same grace, in the kind thereof, which is in the holy nature of Christ, and renders us one with him.

(2.) Our likeness and conformity unto God consists herein; for it is the reparation of his image in us, Eph. iv. 23, 24; Col. iii. 10. Something, I hope, I apprehend concerning this image of God in believers, and of their likeness unto him, how great a privilege it is, what honour, safety, and security depend thereon, what duties are required of us on the account thereof; but perfectly to conceive or express the nature and glory of it we cannot attain unto, but should learn to adore the grace whence it doth proceed and is bestowed on us, to admire the love of Christ and the efficacy of his mediation, whereby it is renewed in us; — but the thing itself is ineffable.

(3.) It is our life, our spiritual life, whereby we live to God. Life is the foundation and sum of all excellencies; without this we are dead in trespasses and sins; and how we are quickened by the Holy Ghost hath been declared. But this is the internal principle of life, whence all vital acts in the life of God do proceed. And whereas we know not well what is the true form and essence of life natural, only we find it, discern it, and judge of it by its effects, much less do we know the form and essence of life spiritual, which is far more excellent and glorious. This is that life which is "hid with Christ in God," Col. iii. 3; in which words the apostle draws a veil over it, as knowing that we are unable steadfastly to behold its glory and beauty.

But before I proceed unto a farther description of this principle of holiness in its effects, as before laid down, it may not be amiss practically to call over these general considerations of its nature; and our own concernment in this truth, which is no empty notion, will be therein declared. And, —

First, We may learn hence not to satisfy ourselves, or not to rest, in any acts or duties of obedience, in any good works, how good and useful soever in themselves, or howsoever multiplied by us, unless there be a vital principle of holiness in our hearts. A few honest actions, a few useful duties, do satisfy some persons that they are as holy as they should be, or as they need to be; and some men's religion hath consisted in the multiplying of outward duties, that they might be meritorious for themselves and others. But God expressly rejecteth not only such duties, but the greatest multitude of them, and their most frequent reiteration, if the heart be not antecedently purified and sanctified, if it be not possessed with the principle of grace and holiness insisted on, Isa. i. 11–15. Such acts and duties may be the effects of other causes, the fruits of other principles. Mere legal convictions will produce them, and put men upon a course of them. Fears, afflictions, terrors of conscience, dictates of reason, improved by education and confirmed by custom, will direct, yea, compel men unto their observance. But all is lost, men do but labour in the fire about them, if the soul be not prepared with this spiritual principle of habitual holiness, wrought in it immediately by the Holy Ghost. Yet we must here observe these two things:—

(1.) That so far as these duties, be they of morality or religion, of piety or divine worship, are good in themselves, they ought to be approved, and men encouraged in them. There are sundry ways whereby the best duties may be abused and misapplied, as when men rest in them, as if they were meritorious, or the matter of their justification before God; for this, as is known, is an effectual means to divert the souls of sinners from faith in Christ for life and salvation, Rom. ix. 31, 32, x. 3, 4. And there are reasons and causes that render them unacceptable before God, with respect unto the persons by whom they are performed; as when they are not done in faith, for which Cain's sacrifice was rejected; and when the heart is not previously sanctified and prepared with a spiritual principle of obedience. But yet on neither of these grounds or pretences can we or ought we to condemn or undervalue the duties themselves, which are good in their own nature, nor take off men from the performance of them; yea, it were greatly to be desired that we could see more of the fruits of moral virtues and duties of religious piety among unsanctified persons than we do. The world is not in a condition to spare the good acts of bad men. But this we may do, and as we are called we ought to do: When men are engaged in a course of duties and good works, on principles that will not abide and endure the trial, or for ends that will spoil and corrupt all they do, we may tell them (as our Saviour did the young man, who gave that great account of his diligence in all legal duties), "One thing is yet wanting unto you;" — "You want faith, or you want Christ, or you want a spiritual principle of evangelical holiness, without which all you do will be lost, and come to no account at the last day." The due assertion of grace never was nor ever can be an obstruction unto any duty of obedience. Indeed, when any will give up themselves unto those works or actings, under the name of duties and obedience unto God, which, although they may make a specious show and appearance in the world, yet are evil in themselves, or such as God requireth not of men, we may speak against them, deny them, and take men off from them. So persecution hath been looked on as a good work, men supposing they did God good service when they slew the disciples of Christ; and men giving their goods unto "pious uses," as they were called (indeed, impious abuses), to have others pray for their souls and expiate their sins, when they were gone out of this world. These and the like other innumerable pretended duties may be judged, condemned, exploded, without the least fear of deterring men from obedience.

(2.) That wherever there is this principle of holiness in the heart in those that are adult, there will be the fruits and effects of it in the life, in all duties of righteousness, godliness, and holiness; for the main work and end of this principle is, to enable us to comply with that "grace of God which teacheth us to deny all ungodliness and worldly lusts, and to live soberly, righteously, and godly in this present world," Tit. ii. 11, 12. That which we press for is the great direction of our Saviour, "Make the tree good, and the fruit will be so also." And there can be no more vile and sordid hypocrisy than for any to pretend unto inward, habitual sanctification, whilst their lives are barren in the fruits of righteousness and duties of obedience. Wherever this root is, there it will assuredly bear fruit.

Secondly, It will appear from hence whence it is that men propose and steer such various courses with respect unto holiness. All men who profess themselves to be Christians are agreed, in words at least, that holiness is absolutely necessary unto them that would be saved by Jesus Christ. To deny it is all one as openly to renounce the gospel. But when they should come to the practice of it, some take one false way, some another, and some actually despise and reject it. Now, all this ariseth from ignorance of the true nature of evangelical holiness on the one hand, and love of sin on the other. There is nothing wherein we are spiritually and eternally concerned that is more frequently insisted on than is the true nature of sanctification and holiness. But the thing itself, as hath been declared, is deep and mysterious, not to be understood without the aid of spiritual light in our minds. Hence some would have moral virtue to be holiness, which, as they suppose, they can understand by their own reason and practice in their own strength; and I heartily wish that we could see more of the fruits of it from them. But real moral virtue will hardly be abused into an opposition unto grace; the pretence of it will be so easily, and is so everyday. Some, on the other hand, place all holiness in superstitious devotions, in the strict observance of religious duties, which men, and not God, have appointed; and there is no end of their multiplication of them, nor measure of the strictness of some in them. The reason why men give up themselves unto such soul-deceiving imaginations is, their ignorance and hatred of that only true, real principle of evangelical holiness of which we have discoursed; for what the world knoweth not in these things it always hateth. And they cannot discern it clearly, or in its own light and evidence; for it must be spiritually discerned. This the natural man cannot do; and in that false light of corrupted reason wherein they discern and judge it, they esteem it foolishness or fancy, 1 Cor. ii. 14. There is not a more foolish and fanatical thing in the world, with many, than that internal, habitual holiness which we are in the consideration of; and hence are they led to despise and to hate it. But here the love of sin secretly takes place, and influenceth their minds. This universal change of the soul in all its principles of operation into the image and likeness of God, tending to the extirpation of all sins and vicious habits, is that which men fear and abhor. This makes them take up with morality and superstitious devotion, — any thing that will pacify a natural conscience, and please themselves or others with a reputation of religion. It is, therefore, highly incumbent on all that would not wilfully deceive their own souls unto their eternal ruin to inquire diligently into the true nature of evangelical holiness; and, above all, to take care that they miss it not in the foundation, in the true root and principle of it, wherein a mistake will be pernicious.

Thirdly, It is, moreover, evident from hence that it is a greater matter to be truly and really holy than most persons are aware of. We may learn eminently how great and excellent a work this of sanctification and holiness is from the causes of it. How emphatically doth our apostle ascribe it unto God, even the Father: 1 Thess. v. 23, "Even the God of peace himself sanctify you." It is so great a work as that it cannot be wrought by any but the God of peace himself. What is the immediate work of the Spirit therein, what the influence of the mediation and blood of Christ into it, hath been already in part declared, and we have yet much more to add in our account of it. And these things do sufficiently manifest how great, how excellent and glorious a work it is; for it doth not become divine and infinite wisdom to engage the immediate power and efficacy of such glorious causes and means for the producing of any ordinary or common effect. It must be somewhat, as of great importance unto the glory of God, so of an eminent nature in itself. And that little entrance which we have made into an inquiry after its nature manifests how great and excellent it is. Let us not, therefore, deceive ourselves with the shadows and appearances of things in a few duties of piety or righteousness; no, nor yet with many of them, if we find not this great work at least begun in us. It is sad to see what trifling there is in these things amongst men. None, indeed, is contented to be without a religion, and very few are willing to admit it in its power.

Fourthly, Have we received this principle of holiness and of spiritual life by the gracious operation of the Holy Ghost? — there are, among many others, three duties incumbent on us, whereof we ought to be as careful as of our souls. And the first is, carefully and diligently by all means to cherish and preserve it in our hearts. This sacred depositum of the new creature, of the divine nature, is intrusted with us to take care of, to cherish and improve. If we willingly, or through our neglect, suffer it to be wounded by temptations, weakened by corruptions, or not exercised in all known duties of obedience, our guilt is great, and our trouble will not be small. And then, secondly, it is equally incumbent on us to evince and manifest it by its fruits, in the mortification of corrupt lusts and affections, in all duties of holiness, righteousness, charity, and piety, in the world: for that God may be glorified hereby is one of the ends why he endues our natures with it; and without these visible fruits, we expose our entire profession of holiness to reproach. And in like manner is it required that we be thankful for what we have received.

3. As this principle of inherent grace or holiness hath the nature of a habit, so also hath it the properties thereof. And the first property of a habit is, that it inclines and disposeth the subject wherein it is unto acts of its own kind, or suitable unto it. It is directed unto a certain end, and inclines unto acts or actions which tend thereunto, and that with evenness and constancy. Yea, moral habits are nothing but strong and firm dispositions and inclinations unto moral acts and duties of their own kind, as righteousness, or temperance, or meekness. Such a disposition and inclination, therefore, there must be in this new spiritual nature, or principle of holiness, which we have described, wherewith the souls of believers are inlaid and furnished by the Holy Ghost in their sanctification; for, —

(1.) It hath a certain end, to enable us whereunto it is bestowed on us. Although it be a great work in itself, that wherein the renovation of the image of God in us doth consist, yet is it not wrought in any but with respect unto a farther end in this world; and this end is, that we may live to God. We are made like unto God, that we may live unto God. By the depravation of our natures we are "alienated from this life of God," this divine, spiritual life, Eph. iv. 18; we like it not, but we have an aversation unto it. Yea, we are under the power of a death that is universally opposed unto that life; for "to be carnally minded is death," Rom. viii. 6, — that is, it is so with respect unto the life of God, and all the acts that belong thereunto. And this life of God hath two parts:— [1.] The outward duties of it; [2.] The inward frame and actings of it. For the first, persons under the power of corrupted nature may perform them, and do so; but without delight, constancy, or permanency. The language of that principle whereby they are acted is, "Behold, what a weariness is it!" Mal. i. 13; and such hypocrites will not pray always. But as to the second, or the internal actings of faith and love, whereby all outward duties shall be quickened and animated, they are utter strangers unto them, utterly alienated from them. With respect unto this life of God, a life of spiritual obedience unto God, are our natures thus spiritually renewed, or furnished with this spiritual habit and principle of grace. It is wrought in us, that by virtue thereof we may "live to God:" without which we cannot do so in any one single act or duty whatever; for "they that are in the flesh cannot please God," Rom. viii. 8. Wherefore, the first property and inseparable adjunct of it is, that it inclineth and disposeth the soul wherein it is unto all acts and duties that belong to the life of God, or unto all the duties of holy obedience, so that it shall attend unto them, not from conviction or external impression only, but from an internal genuine principle, so inclining and disposing it thereunto. And these things may be illustrated by what is contrary unto them: There is in the state of nature a "carnal mind," which is the principle of all moral and spiritual operations in them in whom it is; and this carnal mind hath an enmity, or is "enmity against God," — "it is not subject unto the law of God, neither indeed can be," Rom. viii. 7; that is, the bent and inclination of it lies directly against spiritual things, or the mind and will of God in all things which concern a life of obedience unto himself. Now, as this principle of holiness is that which is introduced into our souls in opposition unto, and to the exclusion of, the carnal mind; so this disposition and inclination of it is opposite and contrary unto the enmity of the carnal mind, as tending always unto actions spiritually good, according to the mind of God.

(2.) This disposition of heart and soul, which I place as the first property or effect of the principle of holiness, before declared and explained, is in the Scripture called fear, love, delight, and by the names of such other affections as express a constant regard and inclination unto their objects: for these things do not denote the principle of holiness itself, which is seated in the mind, or understanding and will, whereas they are the names of affections only; but they signify the first way whereby that principle doth act itself, in a holy inclination of the heart unto spiritual obedience. So when the people of Israel had engaged themselves by solemn covenant to hear and do whatsoever God commanded, God adds concerning it, "O that there were such an heart in them, that they would fear me, and keep all my commandments always!" Deut. v. 29; that is, that the bent and inclination of their hearts were always unto obedience. It is that which is intended in the promise of the covenant: Jer. xxxii. 39, "I will give them one heart, that they may fear me;" which is the same with the "new spirit," Ezek. xi. 19. The new heart, as hath been declared, is the new nature, the new creature, the new, spiritual, supernatural principle of holiness. The first effect, the first fruit hereof is, the fear of God always, or a new spiritual bent and inclination of soul unto all the will and commands of God. And this new spirit, this fear of God, is still expressed as the inseparable consequent of the new heart, or the writing of the law of God in our hearts, which are the same. So it is called, "fearing the Lord and his goodness," Hos. iii. 5. In like manner it is expressed by "love;" which is the inclination of the soul unto all acts of obedience unto God and communion with him with delight and complacency. It is a regard unto God and his will, with a reverence due unto his nature, and a delight in him suited unto that covenantrelation wherein he stands unto us.

(3.) It is, moreover, expressed by being spiritually minded: "To be spiritually minded is life and peace," Rom. viii. 6; — that is, the bent and inclination of the mind unto spiritual things is that whereby we live to God and enjoy peace with him; it is "life and peace." By nature we savour only the things of the flesh, and "mind earthly things," Phil. iii. 19; our minds or hearts are set upon them, disposed towards them, ready for all things that lead us to the enjoyment of them and satisfaction in them. But hereby we mind the things that are above, or set our affections on them, Col. iii. 1, 2. By virtue hereof David professeth that his "soul followed hard after God," Ps. lxiii. 8, or inclined earnestly unto all those ways whereby he might live unto him, and come unto the enjoyment of him; like the earnestness which is in him who is in the pursuit of something continually in his eye, as our apostle expresseth it, Phil. iii. 13,

14. By the apostle Peter it is compared unto that natural inclination which is in those that are hungry unto food: 1 Pet. ii. 2, "As new-born babes, desire the sincere milk of the word, that ye may grow thereby;" which is a constant unalterable inclination.

This, therefore, is that which I intend:— Every nature hath its disposition unto actings suitable unto it. The principle of holiness is such a nature, a new or divine nature; wherever it is, it constantly inclines the soul unto duties and acts of holiness, it produceth a constant disposition unto them. And as by the principle itself the contrary principle of sin and flesh is impaired and subdued, so by this gracious disposition the inclination unto sin which is in us is weakened, impaired, and gradually taken away.

Wherefore, wherever this holiness is, it doth dispose or incline the whole soul unto acts and duties of holiness; and that, — (1.) Universally, or impartially; (2.) Constantly, or evenly; (3.) Permanently, unto the end. And where these things are not, no multiplication of duties will either make or denominate any person holy.

(1.) There is no duty of holiness whatever, but there is a disposition in a sanctified heart unto it. There is a respect unto all God's commands. Some of them may be more contrary unto our natural inclinations than others, some more cross unto our present secular interests, some attended with more difficulties and disadvantages than others, and some may be rendered very hazardous by the circumstances of times and seasons; but, however, if there be a gracious principle in our hearts, it will equally incline and dispose us unto every one of them in its proper place and season. And the reason hereof is, because it being a new nature, it equally inclines unto all that belongs unto it, as all acts of holy obedience do; for every nature hath an equal propensity unto all its natural operations, in their times and seasons. Hence our Saviour tried the rich young man, who gave an account of his duties and righteousness, with one that lay close unto his secular interests and worldly satisfactions. This immediately carried him off, and evidenced that all he had done besides was not from an internal principle of spiritual life. Any other principle or cause of duties and obedience will, upon solicitations, give way unto an habitual reserve of one thing or other that is contrary thereunto. It will admit either of the omission of some duties, or of the commission of some sin, or of the retaining of some lust. So Naaman, who vowed obedience, upon his conviction of the power of the God of Israel, would, nevertheless, upon the solicitation of his worldly interest, have a reserve to bow in the house of Rimmon. So omission of duties that are dangerous in a way of profession, or the reserve of some corrupt affections, love of the world, pride of life, will be admitted upon any other principle of obedience, and that habitually; for even those who have this real spiritual principle of holiness may be surprised into actual omission of duties, commission of sins, and a temporary indulgence unto corrupt affections. But habitually they cannot be so. An habitual reserve for any thing that is sinful or morally evil is eternally inconsistent with this principle of holiness. Light and darkness, fire and water, may as soon be reconciled in one. And hereby is it distinguished from all other principles, reasons, or causes, whereon men may perform any duties of obedience towards God.

(2.) It thus disposeth the heart unto duties of holiness constantly and evenly. He in whom it is feareth always, or is in the fear of the Lord all the day long. In all instances, on all occasions, it equally disposeth the mind unto acts of holy obedience. It is true that the actings of grace which proceed from it are in us sometimes more intense and vigorous than at other times. It is so, also, that we are ourselves sometimes more watchful and diligently intent on all occasions of acting grace, whether in solemn duties, or in our general course, or on particular occasions, than we are at some other times. Moreover, there are especial seasons wherein we meet with greater difficulties and obstructions from our lusts and temptations than ordinary, whereby this holy disposition is intercepted and impeded. But notwithstanding all these things, which are contrary unto it and obstructive of its operations, in itself and its own nature it doth constantly and evenly incline the soul, at all times and on all occasions, unto duties of holiness. Whatever falls out otherwise is accidental unto it. This disposition is like a stream that ariseth equally from a living fountain, as our Saviour expresseth it: John iv. 14, "A well of water springing up into everlasting life." As this stream passeth on in its course, it may meet with oppositions that may either stop it or divert it for a season; but its waters still press forward continually. Hereby doth the soul set God always before it, and walk continually as in his sight. Men may perform duties of obedience unto God, yea, many of them, yea, be engaged into a constant course of them, as to their outward performance, on other grounds, from other principles, and by virtue of other motives; but whatever they are, they are not a new nature in and unto the soul, and so do not dispose men constantly and evenly unto what they lead unto. Sometimes their impressions on the mind are strong and violent, there is no withstanding of them, but the duties they require must instantly be complied withal. So is it when convictions are excited by dangers or afflictions, strong desires, or the like. And again, they leave the soul unto its own formality and course, without the least impression from them towards any duties whatever. There is no cause, or principle, or reason of obedience, besides this one insisted on, that will evenly and constantly incline unto the acts of it. Men proceeding only upon the power of convictions are like those at sea, who sometimes meet with storms or vehement winds which fit them for their course, and would seem immediately to drive them, as it were, with violence into their port or harbour, but quickly after they have an utter calm, no breath of air stirs to help them forward; and then, it may be, after awhile another gust of wind befalls them, which they again suppose will despatch their voyage, but that also quickly fails them. Where this principle is, persons have a natural current, which carries them on quickly, evenly, and constantly; and although they may sometimes meet with storms, tempests, and cross winds, yet the stream, the current, which is natural, at length worketh its way, and holds on its course through all external occasional impediments.

(3.) It is also permanent herein, and abideth forever. It will never cease inclining and disposing the whole soul unto acts and duties of obedience, until it come unto the end of them all in the enjoyment of God. It is "living water," and whosoever drinketh of it shall never thirst anymore, that is, with a total indigence of supplies of grace, but it is "a well of water springing up into everlasting life," John iv. 14. It springs up, and that as always, without intermission, because it is living water, from which vital acts are inseparable, so permanently, without ceasing, it springs up into everlasting life, and faileth not until those in whom it is are safely lodged in the enjoyment of it. This is expressly promised in the covenant, "I will put my fear in their hearts, and they shall not depart from me," Jer. xxxii. 40. They shall never do so in whom is this fear, which is permanent and endless. It is true, that it is our duty, with all care and diligence, in the use of all means, to preserve, cherish, and improve both the principle itself and its actings in these holy dispositions; we are to "show all diligence unto the full assurance of hope unto the end," Heb. vi. 11; and in the use of means and the exercise of grace is it that it is infallibly kept and preserved, Isa. xl. 31; — and it is also true, that sometimes, in some persons, upon the fierce interposition of temptations, with the violent and deceitful working of lusts, the principle itself may seem for a season to be utterly stifled, and this property of it to be destroyed, as it seems to have been with David under his sad fall and decay; — yet such is the nature of it that it is immortal, everlasting, and which shall never absolutely die; such is the relation of it unto the covenant-faithfulness of God and mediation of Christ, as that it shall never utterly cease or be extinguished. It abideth, disposing and inclining the heart unto all duties of holy obedience, unto the grave; yea, ordinarily, and where its genuine work and tendency is not interrupted by cursed negligence or love of the world, it thrives and grows continually unto the end. Hence, some are not only fruitful, but fat and flourishing in their old age; and as the outward man decayeth, so in them the inward man is daily renewed in strength and power. But as unto all other principles of obedience whatever, as it is in their own nature to decay and wither, all their actings growing insensibly weaker and less efficacious, so, for the most part, either the increase of carnal wisdom, or the love of the world, or some powerful temptation, at one time or other, puts an utter end unto them, and they are of no use at all. Hence there is not a more secure generation of sinners in the world than those who have been acted by the power of conviction unto a course of obedience in the performance of many duties; and those of them who fall not openly to profaneness, or lasciviousness, or neglect of all duties of religion, do continue in their course from what they have been habituated unto, finding it compliant with their present circumstances and conditions in the world, as also having been preserved from such ways and practices as are inconsistent with their present course by the power of their former convictions. But the power of these principles, of conviction, education, impressions from afflictions, dangers, fears, all in one, die before men; and, if their eyes were open, they might see the end of them.

In this manner, therefore, doth the new, divine nature that is in believers dispose and incline them, impartially, evenly, and permanently, unto all acts and duties of holy obedience. One thing yet remains to be cleared, that there may be no mistake in this matter; and this is, that in those who are thus constantly inclined and disposed unto all the acts of a heavenly, spiritual life, there are yet remaining contrary dispositions and inclinations also. There are yet in them inclinations and dispositions to sin, proceeding from the remainders of a contrary habitual principle. This the Scripture calls the "flesh," "lust," the "sin that dwelleth in us," the "body of death;" being what yet remaineth in believers of that vicious, corrupted depravation of our nature, which came upon us by the loss of the image of God, disposing the whole soul unto all that is evil. This yet continueth in them, inclining them unto evil and all that is so, according to the power and efficacy that is remaining unto it in various degrees. Sundry things are here observable; as, — (1.) This is that which is singular in this life of God: There are in the same mind, will, and affections, namely, of a person regenerate, contrary habits and inclinations, continually opposing one another, and acting adversely about the same objects and ends. And this is not from any jarrings or disorder between the distinct faculties of the soul itself, — as in natural men there are adverse actings between their wills and affections on the one hand, bent unto sin, and the light of their minds and consciences on the other, prohibiting the committing of sin and condemning its commission, which disorder is discernible in the light of nature, and is sufficiently canvassed by the old philosophers, — but these contrary habits, inclinations, and actings, are in the same faculties. (2.) As this cannot be apprehended but by virtue of a previous conviction and acknowledgment both of the total corruption of our nature by the fall and the initial renovation of it by Jesus Christ, wherein these contrary habits and dispositions do consist; so it cannot be denied without an open rejecting of the gospel, and contradiction to the experience of all that do believe or know any thing of what it is to live to God. We intend no more but what the apostle so plainly asserts, Gal. v. 17, "The flesh lusteth against the spirit, and the spirit against the flesh;" that is, in the mind, will, and affections of believers: "and these are contrary the one to the other;" they are contrary principles, attended with contrary inclinations and actings: "so that ye cannot do the things that ye would." (3.) There cannot be contrary habits, merely natural or moral, in the same subject, with respect unto the same object, at the same time, at least they cannot be so in any high degree, so as to incline and act contrary one to another with urgency or efficacy: for violent inclinations unto sin, and a conscience fiercely condemning for sin, whereby sinners are sometimes torn and even distracted, are not contrary habits in the same subject; only conscience brings in from without the judgment of God against what the will and affections are bent upon.

But it is, as was said, otherwise in the contrary principles or habits of spirit and flesh, of grace and sin, with their adverse inclinations and actings; only they cannot be in the highest degree at the same time, nor be actually prevalent or predominant in the same instances, — that is, sin and grace cannot bear rule in the same heart at the same time, so as that it should be equally under the conduct of them both. Nor can they have in the same soul contrary inclinations equally efficacious; for then would they absolutely obstruct all sorts of operations whatever. Nor have they the same influence into particular actions, so as that they should not be justly denominated from one of them, either gracious or sinful. But by nature the vicious, depraved habit of sin, or the flesh, is wholly predominant and universally prevalent, constantly disposing and inclining the soul to sin. Hence "all the imaginations of men's hearts are evil, and that continually," and "they that are in the flesh cannot please God." There dwelleth no good thing in them, nor can they do any thing that is good; and the flesh is able generally to subdue the rebellions of light, convictions, and conscience, against it. But upon the introduction of the new principle of grace and holiness in our sanctification, this habit of sin is weakened, impaired, and so disenabled as that it cannot nor shall incline unto sin with that constancy and prevalency as formerly, nor press unto it ordinarily with the same urgency and violence. Hence in the Scripture it is said to be dethroned by grace, so as that it shall not reign or lord it over us, by hurrying us into the pursuit of its uncontrollable inclinations, Rom. vi. 12. Concerning these things the reader may consult my treatises of the "Remainder of Indwelling Sin," and the "Mortification of Sin in Believers."[2]

But so it is that this flesh, this principle of sin, however it may be dethroned, corrected, impaired, and disabled, yet is it never wholly and absolutely dispossessed and cast out of the soul in this life. There it will remain, and there it will work, seduce, and tempt, more or less, according as its remaining strength and advantages are. By reason hereof, and the opposition that hence ariseth against it, the principle of grace and holiness cannot, nor doth perfectly and absolutely, incline the heart and soul unto the life of God and the acts thereof, so as that they in whom it is should be sensible of no opposition made thereunto, or of no contrary motions and inclinations unto sin; for the flesh will lust against the spirit, as well as the spirit against the flesh, and these are contrary. This is the analogy that is between these two states: In the state of nature, the principle of sin, or the flesh, is predominant and bears rule in the soul; but there is a light remaining in the mind, and a judgment in the conscience, which, being heightened with instructions and convictions, do continually oppose it, and condemn sin both before and after its commission. In them that are regenerate, it is the principle of grace and holiness that is predominant and beareth rule; but there is in them still a principle of lust and sin, which rebels against the rule of grace, much in the proportion that light and convictions rebel against the rule of sin in the unregenerate: for as they hinder men from doing many evils which their ruling principle of sin strongly inclines them unto, and put them on many duties that it likes not, so do these on the other side in them that are regenerate; they hinder them from doing many good things which their ruling principle inclines unto, and carry them into many evils which it doth abhor.

But this belongs unto the principle of holiness inseparably and necessarily, that it inclineth and disposeth the soul wherein it is universally unto all acts of holy obedience. And these inclinations are predominant unto any other, and keep the soul pointed to holiness continually; this belongs unto its nature. And where there is a cessation or interruption in these inclinations, it is from the prevailing reaction of the principle of sin, it may be advantaged by outward temptations and incentives, which a holy soul will constantly contend against. Where this is not, there is no holiness. The performance of duties, whether of religious worship or of morality, how frequently, sedulously, and usefully soever, will denominate no man holy, unless his whole soul be disposed and possessed with prevalent inclinations unto all that is spiritually good, from the principle of the image of God renewed in him. Outward duties, of what sort soever, may be multiplied upon light and conviction, when they spring from no root of grace in the heart; and that which so riseth up will quickly wither, Matt. xiii. 20, 21. And this free, genuine, unforced inclination of the mind and soul, evenly and universally, unto all that is spiritually good, unto all acts and duties of holiness, with an inward labouring to break through and to be quit of all opposition, is the first fruit and most pregnant evidence of the renovation of our natures by the Holy Ghost.

It may be inquired, whence it is (if the habit or inherent principle of holiness do so constantly incline the soul unto all duties of holiness and obedience) that David prays that God would incline his heart unto his testimonies, Ps. cxix. 36; for it should seem from hence to be a new act of grace that is required thereunto, and that it doth not spring from the habit mentioned, which was then eminent in the psalmist.

Ans. 1. I shall show afterward that, notwithstanding all the power and efficacy of habitual grace, yet there is required a new act of the Holy Spirit by his grace unto its actual exercise in particular instances. 2. God inclines our hearts to duties and obedience principally by strengthening, increasing, and exciting the grace we have received, and which is inherent in us; but we neither have nor ever shall have, in this world, such a stock of spiritual strength as to do any thing as we ought without renewed co-operations of grace. 3. There is power accompanying this habit of grace, as well as propensity or inclinations. It doth not merely dispose the soul to holy obedience, but enables it unto the acts and duties of it. Our living unto God, our walking in his ways and statutes, keeping his judgments, — which things express our whole actual obedience, — are the effects of the new heart that is given unto us, whereby we are enabled unto them, Ezek. xxxvi. 26, 27. But this must be somewhat farther and distinctly declared; and, — (1.) I shall show that there is such a power of holy obedience in all that have the principle of holiness wrought in them by the sanctification of the Holy Spirit, which is inseparable from it; and, (2.) Show what that power is, or wherein it doth consist.

That by nature we have no power unto or for any thing that is spiritually good, or to any acts or duties of evangelical holiness, hath been sufficiently proved before: "When we were yet without strength, in due time Christ died for the ungodly," Rom. v. 6. Until we are made partakers of the benefits of the death of Christ, in and by his sanctifying grace, as we are "ungodly," so we are "without strength," or have no power to live to God. But, as was said, this hath been formerly fully and largely confirmed, in our declaration of the impotency of our nature by reason of its death in sin, and so need not here to be farther insisted on.

(1.) The present assertion which we are to prove is, That there is, in and by the grace of regeneration and sanctification, a power and ability given unto us of living unto God, or performing all the duties of acceptable obedience. This is the first act of that spiritual habit, arising out of it and inseparable from it. It is called "strength" or "power:" Isa. xl. 31, "They that wait upon the Lord shall renew their strength;" that is, for and unto obedience, or walking with God without weariness. Strength they have, and in their walking with God it is renewed or increased. By the same grace are we "strengthened with all might, according to the glorious power of God," Col. i. 11; or, "strengthened with might by his Spirit in the inner man," Eph. iii. 16; whereby "we can do all things through Christ which strengtheneth us," Phil. iv. 13. In our calling or conversion to God, "all things are given unto" us by his "divine power" which "pertain unto life and godliness," 2 Pet. i. 3, — everything that is needful to enable us unto a holy life. The habit and principle of grace that is wrought in believers gives them new power and spiritual strength unto all duties of obedience. The water of the Spirit therein is not only a "well of water" abiding in them, but it "springeth up into everlasting life," John iv. 14, or enables us continually to such gracious actings as have a tendency thereunto. There is a sufficiency in the grace of God bestowed on them that believe, to enable them unto the obedience required of them, — so God told our apostle, when he was ready to faint under his temptation, that "his grace was sufficient for him," 2 Cor. xii. 9, — or there is a power in all that are sanctified, whereby they are able to yield all holy obedience unto God. They are alive unto God, alive to righteousness and holiness. They have a principle of spiritual life; and where there is life, there is power in its kind and for its end. Whence there is in our sanctification not only a principle or inherent habit of grace bestowed on us, whereby we really and habitually, as to state and condition, differ from all unregenerate persons whatever, but there belongs moreover thereunto an active power, or an ability for and unto spiritual, holy obedience; which none are partakers of but those who are so sanctified. And unto this power there is a respect in all the commands or precepts of obedience that belong to the new covenant. The commands of each covenant respect the power given in and by it. Whatever God required or doth require of any, by virtue of the old covenant or the precepts thereof, it was on the account of and proportionate unto the strength given under and by that covenant. And that we have lost that strength by the entrance of sin exempts us not from the authority of the command; and thence it is that we are righteously obliged to do what we have no power to perform. So also the command of God under the new covenant, as to all that obedience which he requireth of us, respects that power which is given and communicated unto us thereby; and this is that power which belongs unto the new creature, the habit and principle of grace and holiness, which, as we have proved, is wrought by the Holy Ghost in all believers.

(2.) We may, therefore, inquire into the nature of this spiritual power, what it is, and wherein it doth consist. Now, this cannot be clearly understood without a due consideration of that impotency unto all spiritual good which is in us by nature, which it cures and takes away. This we have before at large declared, and thither the reader is referred. When we know what it is to be without power or strength in spiritual things, we may thence learn what it is to have them. To this purpose we may consider that there are three things or faculties in our souls which are the subject of all power or impotency in spiritual things, — namely, our understandings, wills, and affections. That our spiritual impotency ariseth from their depravation hath been proved before; and what power we have for holy, spiritual obedience, it must consist in some especial ability, communicated distinctly unto all these faculties. And our inquiry therefore is, what is this power in the mind, what in the will, and what in the affections. And, —

[1.] This power in the mind consists in a spiritual light and ability to discern spiritual things in a spiritual manner; which men in the state of nature are utterly devoid of, 1 Cor. ii. 13, 14. The Holy Spirit, in the first communication of the principle of spiritual life and holiness, "shines in our hearts, to give us the knowledge of the glory of God in the face of Jesus Christ," 2 Cor. iv. 6; yea, this strengthening of the mind by saving illumination is the most eminent act of our sanctification. Without this there is a veil with fear and bondage upon us, [so] that we cannot see in spiritual things. But "where the Spirit of the Lord is," where he comes with his sanctifying grace, "there is liberty;" and thereby "we all, with open face beholding as in a glass the glory of the Lord, are changed into the same image from glory to glory," 2 Cor. iii. 17, 18. See Eph. i. 17, 18.

Wherefore, all sanctified believers have an ability and power, in the renewed mind and understanding, to see, know, discern, and receive, spiritual things, the mysteries of the gospel, the mind of Christ, in a due and spiritual manner. It is true, they have not all of them this power and ability in the same degree; but every one of them hath a sufficiency of it, so as to discern what concerns themselves and their duties necessarily. Some of them seem, indeed, to be very low in knowledge, and, in comparison of others, very ignorant; for there are different degrees in these things, Eph. iv. 7. And some of them are kept in that condition by their own negligence and sloth; they do not use as they ought nor improve those means of growing in grace and in the knowledge of Jesus Christ which God prescribes unto them; as Heb. vi. 1–6. But everyone who is truly sanctified, and who thereby hath received the least degree of saving grace, hath light enough to understand the spiritual things of the gospel in a spiritual manner. When the mysteries of the gospel are preached unto believers, some of them may be so declared as that those of meaner capacities and abilities may not be able to comprehend aright the doctrine of them, — which yet is necessary to be so proposed, for the edification of those who are more grown in knowledge, — nevertheless there is not any, the meanest of them, but hath a spiritual insight into the things themselves intended, so far as they are necessary unto their faith and obedience in the condition wherein they are. This the Scripture gives such abundant testimony unto as to render it unquestionable; for "we have received the Spirit which is of God, that we may know the things that are freely given to us of God," 1 Cor. ii. 12. By virtue of what we have received, we know or discern spiritual things; so we "know the mind of Christ," verse 16. This is the substance of that double testimony,1 John ii. 20, 27. This abiding unction is no other but that habitual inherent grace which we plead for; and by it, as it is a holy light in our mind, we "know all things," it is the understanding that is given us to "know him that is true," chap. v. 20. Only it is their duty continually to endeavour the improvement and enlargement of the light they have, in the daily exercise of the spiritual power they have received, and in the use of means, Heb. v. 14. [2.] This power in the will consists in its liberty, freedom, and ability to consent unto, choose, and embrace, spiritual things. Believers have free will unto that which is spiritually good; for they are freed from that bondage and slavery unto sin which they were under in the state of nature. Whatever some dispute concerning the nature of free-will, that it consists in an indifferency unto good or evil, one thing or another, with a power of applying itself unto all its operations, whatever their objects be, as the Scripture knoweth nothing of it, so it is that which we cannot have; and if we could, it would be no advantage at all unto us, yea, we had much better be without it. Have it, indeed, we cannot; for a supposition of it includes a rejection of all our dependence on God, making all the springs of our actions to be absolutely and formally in ourselves. Neither, considering the prejudices, temptations, and corruptions that we are possessed and exercised with, would such a flexibility of will be of any use or advantage unto us, but would rather certainly give us up to the power of sin and Satan. All that the Scripture knows about free-will is, that in the state of nature, antecedent unto the converting, sanctifying work of the Spirit, all men whatever are in bondage unto sin, and that in all the faculties of their souls. They are "sold under sin;" are "not subject unto the law of God, neither indeed can be;" — can neither think, nor will, nor do, nor desire, nor love any thing that is spiritually good, according to the mind of God. But as unto what is evil, perverse, unclean, that they are free and open unto, — ready for, prone, and inclined, and every way able to do. On the other side, in those who are renewed by the Holy Ghost and sanctified, it acknowledgeth and teacheth a freedom of will, not in an indifferency and flexibility unto good and evil, but in a power and ability to like, love, choose, and cleave unto God and his will in all things. The will is now freed from its bondage unto sin, and, being enlarged by light and love, willeth and chooseth freely the things of God, having received spiritual power and ability so to do. It is the truth, — that is, faith in the gospel, the doctrine of the truth, — which is the means of this freedom; the "truth that makes us free," John viii. 32. And it is the Son of God by his Spirit who is the principal efficient cause of it: for "if the Son make us free, then are we free indeed," verse 36; and otherwise we are not, whatever we pretend. And this freedom unto spiritual good we have not of ourselves in the state of nature; for if we have, then are we free indeed, and there would be no need that the Son should make us free.

The difference, therefore, about free-will is reduced unto these heads:— 1st. Whether there be a power in man indifferently to determine himself his choice and all his actings, to this or that, good or evil, one thing or another, independently of the will, power, and providence of God, and his disposal of all future events? This, indeed, we deny, as that which is inconsistent with the prescience, authority, decrees, and dominion of God, and as that which would prove certainly ruinous and destructive to ourselves. 2dly. Whether there be in men unregenerate, not renewed by the Holy Ghost, a freedom, power, and ability unto that which is spiritually good, or to believe and obey according to the mind and will of God? This also we deny, as that which is contrary to innumerable testimonies of Scripture, and absolutely destructive of the grace of our Lord Jesus Christ. 3dly. Whether the freedom of will that is in believers do consist in an indifferency and freedom from any determination only, with a power equally ready for good or evil, according as the will shall determine itself? or whether it consist in a gracious freedom and ability to choose, will, and do that which is spiritually good, in opposition to the bondage and slavery unto sin wherein we were before detained? This last is that liberty and power of the will which we assert, with the Scripture, in persons that are sanctified. And a liberty this is every way consistent with all the operations of God, as the sovereign first cause of all things; every way compliant with and an effect of the special grace of God, and the operations of the Holy Ghost; a liberty whereby our obedience and salvation are secured, in answer to the promises of the covenant. And who that understands himself would change this real, useful, gracious free-will, given by Jesus Christ the Son of God, when he makes us free, and an effect of God's writing his law in our hearts, to cause us to walk in his statutes, — that property of the new heart whereby it is able to consent unto, choose, and embrace freely, the things of God, — for that fictitious, imaginary freedom, yea, for (if it were real) an indifferency unto all things, and an equal power unto everything, whether it be good or evil? I say, then, that by the habit of grace and holiness infused into us by the Spirit of sanctification, the will is freed, enlarged, and enabled to answer the commands of God for obedience, according to the tenor of the new covenant. This is that freedom, this is that power of the will, which the Scripture reveals and regards and which by all the promises and precepts of it we are obliged to use and exercise, and no other.

[3.] The affections, which naturally are the principal servants and instruments of sin, are hereby engaged unto God, Deut. xxx. 6.

And from what hath been thus far discoursed, the sense of our former assertion is evident, as also the nature of the principle of holiness insisted on. The Holy Ghost in our sanctification doth work, effect, and create in us a new, holy, spiritual, vital principle of grace, residing in all the faculties of our souls, according as their especial nature is capable thereof, after the manner of a permanent and prevalent habit, which he cherisheth, preserveth, increaseth, and strengtheneth continually, by effectual supplies of grace from Jesus Christ, disposing, inclining, and enabling the whole soul unto all ways, acts, and duties of holiness, whereby we live to God, opposing, resisting, and finally conquering, whatever is opposite and contrary thereunto. This belongs essentially unto evangelical holiness, yea, herein doth the nature of it formally and radically consist. This is that from whence believers are denominated holy, and without which none are so, nor can be so called.

The properties of this power are readiness and facility. Wherever it is, it renders the soul ready unto all duties of holy obedience, and renders all duties of holy obedience easy unto the soul.

(1.) It gives readiness by removing and taking away all those encumbrances which the mind is apt to be clogged with and hindered by from sin, the world, spiritual sloth, and unbelief. This is that which we are exhorted unto in a way of duty, Heb. xii. 1; Luke xii. 35; 1 Pet. i. 13, iv. 1; Eph. vi. 14. Herein is the spirit ready, though the flesh be weak, Mark xiv. 38. And those encumbrances which give an unreadiness unto obedience to God may be considered two ways:— [1.] As they are in their full power and efficacy in persons unregenerate, whence they are "unto every good work reprobate," Tit. i. 16. Hence proceed all those prevalent tergiversations against a compliance with the will of God and their own convictions which bear sway in such persons. "Yet a little slumber, a little sleep, a little folding of the hands to sleep," Prov. vi. 10. By these do men so often put off the calls of God, and perniciously procrastinate from time to time a full compliance with their convictions. And whatever particular duties such persons do perform, yet are their hearts and minds never prepared or ready for them, but the encumbrances mentioned do influence them into spiritual disorders in all that they do. [2.] These principles of sloth and unreadiness do ofttimes partially influence the minds of believers themselves unto great indispositions unto spiritual duties. So the spouse states her case, Cant. v. 2, 3. By reason of her circumstances in the world, she had an unreadiness for that converse and communion with Christ which she was called unto. And it is so not unfrequently with the best of men in this world. A spiritual unreadiness unto holy duties, arising from the power of sloth or the occasions of life, is no small part of their sin and trouble. Both these are removed by this spiritual power of the principle of life and holiness in believers. The total prevailing power of them, such as is in persons unregenerate, is broken by the first infusion of it into the soul, wherein it gives an habitual fitness and preparation of heart unto all duties of obedience unto God. And by various degrees it freeth believers from the remainders of the encumbrances which they have yet to conflict with. And this it doth three ways; as, — 1st. It weakeneth and taketh off the bent of the soul from earthly things, so as they shall not possess the mind as formerly, Col. iii. 2. How it doth this was declared before. And when this is done, the mind is greatly eased of its burden, and some way ready unto its duty. 2dly. It gives an insight into the beauty, the excellency, and glory of holiness, and all duties of obedience. This they see nothing of who, being unsanctified, are under the power of their natural darkness. They can see no beauty in holiness, no form nor comeliness why it should be desired; and it is no wonder if they are unfree to the duties of it, which they are but as it were compelled unto. But the spiritual light wherewith this principle of grace is accompanied discovers an excellency in holiness and the duties of it, and in the communion with God which we have thereby, so as greatly to incline the mind unto them and prepare it for them. 3dly. It causeth the affections to cleave and adhere unto them with delight. "How do I love thy law!" saith David; "my delight is in thy statutes; they are sweeter unto me than the honey-comb." Where these three things concur, — where the mind is freed from the powerful influences of carnal lusts and love of this world; where the beauty and excellency of holiness and the duties of obedience lie clear in the eyes of the soul; and where the affections cleave unto spiritual things as commanded, — then will be that readiness in obedience which we inquire after.

(2.) It gives facility or easiness in the performance of all duties of obedience. Whatever men do from a habit, they do with some kind of easiness. That is easy to them which they are accustomed unto, though hard and difficult in itself. And what is done from nature is done with facility. And the principle of grace, as we have showed, is a new nature, an infused habit with respect unto the life of God, or all duties of holy obedience. I grant there will be opposition unto them even in the mind and heart itself, from sin, and Satan, and temptations of all sorts; yea, and they may sometimes arise so high as either to defeat our purposes and intentions unto duties, or to clog us in them, to take off our chariot-wheels, and to make us drive heavily; but still it is in the nature of the principle of holiness to make the whole course of obedience and all the duties of it easy unto us, and to give us a facility in their performance: for, —

[1.] It introduceth a suitableness between our minds and the duties we are to perform. By it is the law written in our hearts; that is, there is an answerableness in them unto all that the law of God requires. In the state of nature, the great things of the law of God are a strange thing unto us, Hos. viii. 12; there is an enmity in our minds against them, Rom. viii. 7; there is no suitableness between our minds and them; — but this is taken away by the principle of grace. Thereby do the mind and duty answer one another, as the eye and a lightsome body. Hence the "commands of Christ are not grievous" unto them in whom it is, 1 John v. 3. They do not appear to contain any thing uncouth, unreasonable, burdensome, or any way unsuited to that new nature whereby the soul is influenced and acted. Hence "all the ways of wisdom are" unto believers, as they are in themselves, "pleasantness, and all her paths are peace," Prov. iii. 17.

The great notion of some in these days is about the suitableness of Christian religion unto reason; and to make good their assertion in the principal mysteries of it, because reason will not come to them, they bring them by violence unto their reason. But it is with respect unto this renewed principle that there is a suitableness in any of the things of God unto our minds and affections.

[2.] It keeps up the heart or whole person unto a frequency of all holy acts and duties; and frequency gives facility in every kind. It puts the soul upon reiterated actings of faith and love, or renewed holy thoughts and meditations. It is a spring that is continually bubbling up in them, on the frequent repetition of the daily duties of prayer, reading, holy discourse; as on closing with all opportunities and occasions of mercy, benignity, charity, and bounty amongst men. Hereby is the heart so accustomed unto the yoke of the Lord, and made so conversant in his ways, that it is natural and easy to it to bear them and to be engaged in them. And it will be found by experience that the more intermissions of duties of any sort we fall under, the more difficulty we shall find in the performance of them.

[3.] It engageth the assistance of Christ and his Spirit. It is the divine nature, the new creature, which the Lord Christ careth for; in and by its actings in all duties of obedience doth its life consist; therein, also, is it strengthened and improved. For this cause doth the Lord Christ continually come in by the supplies of his Spirit unto its assistance. And when the strength of Christ is engaged, then and there is his yoke easy and his burden light.

Some, perhaps, will say that they find not this facility or easiness in the course of obedience and in the duties of it. They meet with secret unwillingnesses in themselves, and great oppositions on other accounts; whence they are apt to be faint and weary, yea, are almost ready to give over. It is hard to them to pray continually, and not to faint; to stand in their watch night and day against the inroads of their spiritual adversaries; to keep themselves from the insinuations of the world, and up unto those sacrifices of charity and bounty that are so well-pleasing to God. Many weights and burdens are upon them in their course, many difficulties press them, and they are ready to be beset round about every moment. Wherefore they think that the principle of grace and holiness doth not give the facility and easiness mentioned, or that they were never made partakers of it.

I answer, — 1st. Let these persons examine themselves, and duly consider whence those obstructions and difficulties they complain of do arise. If they are from the inward inclinations of their souls, and unwillingness to bear the yoke of Christ, only they are kept up unto it by their convictions, which they cannot cast off, then is their condition to be bewailed. But if themselves are sensible and convinced that they arise from principles which, as far as they are within them, they hate and abhor, and long to be freed from, and, as they are from without, are such as they look on as enemies unto them, and do watch against them, then what they complain of is no more but what, in one degree or other, all that believe have experience of. And if their impediments do arise from what they know themselves to be opposite unto them, and [to] that principle whereby they are acted, then, notwithstanding this objection, it may be in the nature of the principle of holiness to give facility in all the duties of it.

2dly. Let inquiry be made whether they have been constant and assiduous in the performance of all those duties which they now complain that they find so much difficulty in. The principle of grace and holiness gives facility in all duties of obedience, but in the proper way and order. It first gives constancy and assiduity, and then easiness. If men comply not with its guidance and inclination in the former, it is in vain for them to expect the latter. If we are not constant in all acts of obedience, none of them will ever be easy unto us. Let not those who can omit proper and due seasons of meditation, prayer, hearing, charity, moderation in all things, patience, meekness, and the like, at their pleasure, on the least occasions, excuses, or diversions, ever think or hope to have the ways of obedience smooth, its paths pleasant, or its duties easy. Let him never think to attain any readiness, delight, or facility in any art or science, who is always beginning at it, touching upon it sometimes. As this is the way in all sorts of things, natural and spiritual, to be always learning, and never to come to the knowledge of the truth; so, in the practice of holy obedience, if men are, as it were, always beginning, one while performing, another intermitting the duties of it, fearing or being unwilling to engage into a constant, equal, assiduous discharge of them, they will be always striving, but never come unto any readiness or facility in them.

3dly. The difficulty and burdensomeness complained of may proceed from the interposition of perplexing temptations, which weary, disquiet, and distract the mind. This may be, and frequently is so; and yet our assertion is not impeached. We only say, that set aside extraordinary occasions and sinful neglects, this principle of grace and holiness doth give that suitableness to the mind unto all duties of obedience, that constancy in them, that love unto them, as make them both easy and pleasant.

By these things we may inquire after the habit or principle of holiness in our own minds, that we be not deceived by any thing that falsely pretendeth thereunto; as, —

First, Let us take heed that we deceive not ourselves, as though it would suffice unto gospel holiness that we have occasionally good purposes of leaving sin and living unto God, then when something urgeth upon us more than ordinary, with the effects which such purposes will produce. Afflictions, sicknesses, troubles, sense of great guilt, fear of death, and the like, do usually produce this frame; and although it is most remote from any pretence unto evangelical obedience, yet I could not but give a caution against it, because it is that whereby the generality of men in the world do delude themselves into eternal ruin. It is rare to find any that are so stubbornly profligate, but at one time or another they project and design, yea, promise and engage unto, a change of their course and amendment of their lives, doing sundry things, it may be, in the pursuit of those designs and purposes; for they will thereon abstain from their old sins, with whose haunt they are much perplexed, and betake themselves unto the performance of those duties from whence they expect most relief unto their consciences, and whose neglect doth most reflect upon them. Especially will they do so when the hand of God is upon them in afflictions and dangers, Ps. lxxviii. 34–37. And this produceth in them that kind of goodness which God says “is like the morning cloud or the early dew,” — things that make a fair appearance of something, but immediately vanish away, Hos. vi. 4. Certainly there need not much pains to convince any man how unspeakably this comes short of that evangelical holiness which is a fruit of the sanctification of the Spirit. It hath neither the root of it nor any fruit that doth so much as resemble it. But it is to be lamented that such multitudes of rational creatures, living under the means of light and grace, should so vainly and woefully delude their own souls. That which they aim at and intend is, to have that in them whereby they may be accepted with God. Now, not to insist on what will absolutely frustrate all the designs of such persons, — namely, their want of faith in Christ, and an interest in his righteousness thereby, which they are regardless of, — all that they project and design is as far beneath that holiness which God requireth of them, and which they think hereby to obtain, as the earth is beneath the heavens. All that they do in this kind is utterly lost; it will never be either a righteousness unto them or a holiness in them. But this deceit is frequently rebuked. God only by his grace can remove and take it away from the minds of men.

Secondly, And we may learn hence not to be imposed on by gifts, though never so useful, with a plausible profession thereon. These things go a great way in the world, and many deceive both themselves and others by them. Gifts are from the Holy Ghost in an especial manner, and therefore greatly to be esteemed. They are also frequently useful in and unto the church; for "the manifestation of the Spirit is given unto men to profit withal." And they put men on such duties as have a great show and appearance of holiness. By the help of them alone may men pray, and preach, and maintain spiritual communication among them with whom they do converse. And as circumstances may be ordered, they put sundry persons on a frequent performance of these duties, and so keep them up to an eminency in profession. But yet, when all is done, they are not holiness; nor are the duties performed in the strength of them alone duties of evangelical obedience, accepted of God in them by whom they are performed; and they may be where there is nothing of holiness at all. They are, indeed, not only consistent with holiness, but subservient unto it, and exceeding promoters of it, in souls that are really gracious; but they may be alone, without grace, and then are they apt to deceive the mind with a pretence of being and doing what they are not nor do. Let them be called to an account by the nature and properties of that habit and principle of grace which is in all true holiness, as before explained, and it will quickly appear how short they come thereof: for as their subject, where they have their residence, is the mind only, and not the will or affections, any farther but as they are influenced or restrained by light, so they do not renew or change the mind itself, so as to transform it into the image of God; neither do they give the soul a general inclination unto all acts and duties of obedience, but only a readiness for that duty which their exercise doth peculiarly consist in. Wherefore they answer no one property of true holiness; and we have not seldom seen discoveries made thereof.

Least of all can morality, or a course of moral duties, when it is alone, maintain any pretence hereunto. We have had attempts to prove that there is no specifical difference between common and saving grace, but that they are both of the same kind, differing only in degrees. But some, as though this ground were already gained, and needed no more contending about, do add, without any consideration of these "petty distinctions of common and saving grace," that "morality is grace and grace is morality, and nothing else." To be a gracious, holy man, according to the gospel, and to be a moral man, is all one with them; and as yet it is not declared whether there be any difference between evangelical holiness and philosophical morality. Wherefore I shall proceed to the fourth thing proposed, —

4. And this is farther to prove that this habit or gracious principle of holiness is specifically distinct from all other habits of the mind whatever, whether intellectual or moral, connate or acquired, as also from all that common grace and the effects of it whereof any persons not really sanctified may be made partakers.

The truth of this assertion is, indeed, sufficiently evident from the description we have given of this spiritual habit, its nature and properties; but whereas there are also other respects giving farther confirmation of the same truth, I shall call over the most important of them, after some few things have been premised: as, —

(1.) A habit, of what sort soever it be, qualifies the subject wherein it is, so that it may be denominated from it, and makes the actions proceeding from it to be suited unto it or to be of the same nature with it. As Aristotle says, "Virtue is a habit which maketh him that hath it good or virtuous, and his actions good."

Now, all moral habits are seated in the will. Intellectual habits are not immediately effective of good or evil, but as the will is influenced by them. These habits do incline, dispose, and enable the will to act according to their nature. And in all the acts of our wills, and so all external works which proceed from them, two things are considered:— first, The act itself, or the work done; and, secondly, The end for which it is done. And both these things are respected by the habit itself, though not immediately, yet by virtue of its acts. It is, moreover, necessary and natural that every act of the will, every work of a man, be for a certain end. Two things, therefore, are to be considered in all our obedience:— first, The duty itself we do; and, secondly, The end for which we do it. If any habit, therefore, do not incline and dispose the will unto the proper end of duty, as well as unto the duty itself, it is not of that kind from whence true gospel obedience doth proceed; for the end of every act of gospel obedience, — which is the glory of God in Jesus Christ, — is essential unto it. Let us, then, take all the habits of moral virtue, and we shall find that however they may incline and dispose the will unto such acts of virtue as materially are duties of obedience, yet they do it not with respect unto this end. If it be said that such moral habits do so incline the will unto duties of obedience with respect unto this end, then is there no need of the grace of Jesus Christ or the gospel to enable men to live unto God according to the tenor of the covenant of grace; which some seem to aim at.

(2.) Whereas it is the end that gives all our duties their special nature, this is twofold:—

[1.] The next; and, [2.] The ultimate; — or it is particular or universal. And these may be different in the same action. As a man may give alms to the poor, his next particular end may be to relieve and cherish them; this end is good, and so far the work or duty itself is good also. But the ultimate and general end of this action may be self, merit, reputation, praise, compensation for sin committed, and not the glory of God in Christ; which vitiates the whole. Now, moral habits, acquired by endeavours answerable unto our light and convictions, or the dictates of enlightened reason, with resolutions and perseverance, may incline and dispose the will unto actions and works that for the substance of them are duties, and are capable of having particular ends that are good; but a want of respect unto the general end allows them not to be any part of gospel obedience. And this is applicable unto all moral habits and duties whatever. But the difference asserted is farther manifested, —

(1.) From the especial fountain and spring of holiness, which constitutes its nature of another kind than any common grace or morality can pretend unto; and this is electing love, or God's purpose of election: Eph. i. 4, "He hath chosen us in Christ before the foundation of the world, that we should be holy and without blame before him in love." God chooseth us from eternity that we should be holy; that is, with a design and purpose to make us so. He sets some men apart in his eternal purpose, as those unto whom he will communicate holiness. It is, therefore, an especial work of God, in the pursuit of an especial and eternal purpose. This gives it its especial nature, and makes it, as was said, of another kind than any effect of common grace whatever. That is holiness which God works in men by his Spirit because he hath chosen them, and nothing else is so; for he "chooseth us unto salvation through sanctification of the Spirit," 2 Thess. ii. 13. Salvation is the end that God aimeth at in his choosing of us, in subordination unto his own glory; which is, and must be, the ultimate end of all his purposes and decrees, or of all the free acts of his wisdom and love. The means which he hath ordained whereby we shall be brought unto this salvation, so designed in his eternal purpose, is the "sanctification of the Spirit." Gospel holiness, therefore, is the effect of that sanctification of the Spirit, which God hath designed as the especial way and means on their part of bringing the elect unto salvation; and his choosing of them is the cause and reason why he doth so sanctify them by his Spirit. And where our sanctification is comprised under our vocation, because therein and thereby we are sanctified, by the sanctifying principle of holiness communicated unto us, it is not only reckoned as an effect and consequent of our predestination, but is so conjoined thereunto as to declare that none others are partakers of it but those that are predestinate, Rom. viii. 29, 30.

And this consideration is of itself sufficient to evince that this holiness whereof we treat differs essentially from all other habits of the mind and actions proceeding from them, as having an especial nature of its own. Whatever there may be in any men of virtue and piety, or whatever their endeavours may be, in ways of honesty and duty towards God and men, if the power and principle of it in them be not a fruit of electing love, of the Spirit of sanctification, given of God for this certain end, that we may attain the salvation whereunto we are chosen, it belongeth not unto this holiness. Wherefore, the apostle Peter, giving us in charge to use "all diligence," whereby we may make "our calling and election sure," — that is, unto our souls, and in our own minds, — prescribes as the means of it the exercise and increase of those graces which are its proper effects, 2 Pet. i. 5–7, 10. And the reason why we see so many glorious professions of faith and obedience utterly to fail as we do, is because the faith so professed was not "the faith of God's elect," Tit. i. 1; and the obedience of it was not the fruit of that Spirit of sanctification which God gives to man to make his purpose of election infallibly effectual, that so the "purpose of God which is according to election might stand," Rom. ix. 11, and "the election," or those elected, might obtain the grace and glory designed for them, chap. xi. 5, 7. And it is an evidence of much spiritual sloth in us, or that which is worse, namely, that our graces and obedience are not genuine and of the true heavenly race, if we endeavour not to satisfy ourselves that they are real effects of electing love.

If anyone shall inquire, how we may know whether the graces of holiness, which we hope are in us, and the duties that proceed from them, are fruits and effects of election, seeing such only are genuine and durable, I answer, it may be done three ways:—

[1.] By their growth and increase. This in ordinary cases, setting aside the seasons of prevalent temptations and desertions, is the best evidence hereof. Waters that proceed from a living fountain increase in their progress, because of the continual supplies which they have from their spring, when those which have only occasional beginnings, from showers of rain or the like, do continually decay until they are dried up. The graces that come from this eternal spring have continual supplies from it, so that, if they meet with no violent obstructions (as they may do sometimes for a season), they do constantly increase and thrive. And, therefore, no man can secure his spiritual comforts one moment under a sensible decay of grace; for such a decay is a very sufficient reason why he should call the truth of all his grace into question. Where the Spirit of sanctification is, as given in pursuit of the purpose of election, it is "a well of water springing up into everlasting life," John iv. 14. The quietness and satisfaction of professors under a decay of grace is a soul-ruining security, and hath nothing in it of spiritual peace.

[2.] We may discern it when we are much stirred up unto diligent acting and exercise of grace, out of a sense of that electing love from whence all grace doth proceed. It is the nature of that grace that is the fruit of election greatly to affect the heart and mind with a sense of the love that is therein: so the apostle says expressly that one grace exciteth and stirreth up another, from a sense of the love of God, which sets them all on work, Rom. v. 2–5. So God is said to "draw us with loving-kindness," because "he hath loved us with an everlasting love," Jer. xxxi. 3; that is, he gives us such a sense of his everlasting love as thereby to draw us after him in faith and obedience. Those principles of duties in us which are excited only by fear, awe, hope, and the jealous observances of an awakened conscience, will scarce at any time evince this heavenly extract unto a spiritual understanding. That grace which proceeds from especial love will carry along with it a holy quickening sense of it, and thereby be excited unto its due exercise. And we do what we can to famish and starve our graces, when we do not endeavour their supplies by faith on that spring of divine love from whence they proceed.

[3.] Seeing we are chosen in Christ, and predestinated to be like unto him, those graces of holiness have the most evident and legible characters of electing love upon them which are most effectual in working us unto a conformity to him. That grace is certainly from an eternal spring which makes us like unto Jesus Christ. Of this sort are meekness, humility, self-denial, contempt of the world, readiness to pass by wrongs, to forgive enemies, to love and do good unto all; which indeed are despised by the most, and duly regarded but by few. But I return.

(2.) The especial procuring cause of this holiness is the mediation of Christ. We are not, in this matter, concerned in any thing, let men call it what they please, virtue, or godliness, or holiness, that hath not an especial relation unto the Lord Christ and his mediation. Evangelical holiness is purchased for us by him, according to the tenor of the everlasting covenant, is promised unto us on his account, actually impetrated for us by his intercession, and communicated unto us by his Spirit. And hereby we do not only cast off all the moral virtues of the heathens from having the least concernment herein, but all the principles and duties of persons professing Christianity, who are not really and actually implanted into Christ, for he it is who "of God is made unto us sanctification," 1 Cor. i. 30; and this he is on several accounts, the heads whereof may be called over:—

[1.] He is made unto us of God sanctification with respect unto his sacerdotal office, because we are purified, purged, washed, and cleansed from our sins by his blood, in the oblation of it, and the application of it unto our souls, as hath been at large declared, Eph. v. 25–27; Tit. ii. 14, 1 John i. 7; Heb. ix. 14. All that we have taught before concerning the purification of our minds and consciences by the blood of Christ is peculiar unto gospel holiness, and distinguisheth it essentially from all common grace or moral virtues. And they do but deceive themselves who rest in a multitude of duties, it may be animated much with zeal, and set off with a profession of the most rigid mortification, whose hearts and consciences are not thus purged by the blood of Christ.

[2.] Because he prevails for the actual sanctification of our natures, in the communication of holiness unto us, by his intercession. His prayer, John xvii. 17, is the blessed spring of our holiness: "Sanctify them through thy truth; thy word is truth." There is not any thing of this grace wrought in us, bestowed on us, communicated unto us, preserved in us, but what is so in answer unto and compliance with the intercession of Christ. From his prayer for us is holiness begun in us: "Sanctify them," saith he, "by thy truth." Thence it is kept alive and preserved in us: "I have," saith he to Peter, "prayed for thee, that thy faith fail not." And through his intercession are we saved to the uttermost. Nothing belongs to this holiness but what, in the actual communication of it, is a peculiar fruit of Christ's intercession; what is not so, what men may be made partakers of upon any more general account, belongs not thereunto. And if we really design holiness, or intend to be holy, it is our duty constantly to improve the intercession of Christ for the increase of it; and this we may do by especial applications to him for that purpose. So the apostles prayed him to "increase their faith," Luke xvii. 5; and we may do so for the increase of our holiness. But the nature of this application unto Christ for the increase of holiness, by virtue of his intercession, is duly to be considered. We are not to pray unto him that he would intercede for us that we may be sanctified; for as he needs not our minding for the discharge of his office, so he intercedes not orally in heaven at all, and always doth so virtually, by his appearance in the presence of God, with the virtue of his oblation or sacrifice. But whereas the Lord Christ gives out no supplies of grace unto us but what he receiveth from the Father for that end by virtue of his intercession, we apply ourselves unto him under that consideration, — namely, as he who, upon his intercession with God for us, hath all stores of grace to give us supplies from. [3.] He is so, because the rule and measure of holiness unto us, the instrument of working it in us, is his word and doctrine, which he taught the church as the great prophet of it: "The law was given by Moses, but grace and truth came by Jesus Christ." The inbred dictates of the light and law of nature, in their greatest purity, are not the rule or measure of this holiness; much less are those rules and maxims which men deduce, partly right and partly wrong, from them of any such use. Nor is the written law itself so. It is the rule of original holiness, but not the adequate rule of that holiness whereunto we are restored by Christ. Neither are both these in conjunction, — the dictates of nature and the law written, — the instruments of working holiness in us. But it is the doctrine of the gospel which is the adequate rule and immediate instrument of it. My meaning is, that the word, the gospel, the doctrine of Christ, in the preceptive part of it, is so the rule of all our obedience and holiness as that all which it requireth belongeth thereunto, and nothing else but what it requireth doth so; and the formal reason of our holiness consists in conformity thereunto, under this consideration, that it is the word and doctrine of Christ. Nothing belongeth unto holiness materially but what the gospel requireth; and nothing is so in us formally but what we do because the gospel requireth it. And it is the instrument of it, because God maketh use of it alone as an external means for the communicating of it unto us, or the ingenerating of it in us. Principles of natural light, with the guidance of an awakened conscience, do direct unto, and exact the performance of, many material duties of obedience; the written law requireth of us all duties of original obedience; and God doth use these things variously for the preparing of our souls unto a right receiving of the gospel: but there are some graces, some duties, belonging unto evangelical holiness, which the law knows nothing of; such are the mortification of sin, godly sorrow, daily cleansing of our hearts and minds; — not to mention the more sublime and spiritual acts of communion with God by Christ, with all that faith and love which are required in us towards him; for although these things may be contained in the law radically, as it requires universal obedience unto God, yet are they not so formally. And it is not used as the means to beget faith and holiness in us; this is the effect of the gospel only. Hence it is said to be "the power of God unto salvation," Rom. i. 16, or that whereby God puts forth the greatness of his power unto that purpose; — "the word of his grace, which is able to build us up, and to give us an inheritance among all them which are sanctified," Acts xx. 32. It is that by whose preaching faith cometh, Rom. x. 17; and by the hearing whereof we receive the Spirit, Gal. iii. 2. It is that whereby we are begotten in Christ Jesus, 1 Cor. iv. 15; James i. 18; 1 Pet. i. 23–25. And all that is required of us, in the way of external obedience, is but that our conversation be such as becometh the gospel.

And this is a proper touchstone for our holiness, to try whether it be genuine, and of the right kind or no. If it be, it is nothing but the seed of the gospel quickened in our hearts, and bearing fruit in our lives. It is the delivery up of our souls into the mould of the doctrine of it, so as that our minds and the word should answer one another, as face doth unto face in water. And we may know whether it be so with us or no two ways; for, — 1st. If it be so, none of the commands of the gospel will be grievous unto us, but easy and pleasant. A principle suited unto them all, inclining unto them all, connatural unto them, as proceeding from them, being implanted in our minds and hearts, it renders the commands themselves so suited unto us, so useful, and the matter of them so desirable, that obedience is made pleasant thereby. Hence is that satisfaction of mind, with rest and joy, which believers have in gospel duties, yea, the most difficult of them; with that trouble and sorrow which ensue upon their neglect, omission, or their being deprived of opportunities for them. But in the strictest course of duties that proceedeth from any other principle, the precepts of the gospel, or at least some of them, on account of their spirituality or simplicity, are either esteemed grievous or despised. 2dly. None of the truths of the gospel will seem strange unto us. This makes up the evidence of a genuine principle of gospel holiness, when the commands of it are not grievous, nor the truths of it strange or uncouth: The mind so prepared receives every truth, as the eye doth every increase of light, naturally and pleasantly, until it come unto its proper measure. There is a measure of light which is suited unto our visive faculty; what exceeds it dazzles and amazes, rather than enlightens, but every degree of light which tends unto it is connatural and pleasant to the eye. So is it with the sanctified mind and spiritual truth. There is a measure of light issuing from spiritual truths that our minds are capable of: what is beyond this measure belongs to glory, and the gazing after it will rather dazzle than enlighten us; and such is the issue of overstrained speculations when the mind endeavours an excess as to its measure. But all light from truth which tends to the filling up of that measure is pleasant and natural to the sanctified mind. It sees wisdom, glory, beauty, and usefulness, in the most spiritual, sublime, and mysterious truths that are revealed in and by the word, labouring more and more to comprehend them, because of their excellency. For want hereof, we know how the truths of the gospel are by many despised, reproached, scorned, as those which are no less foolishness unto them to be believed than the precepts of it are grievous to be obeyed.

[4.] He is so as he is the exemplary cause of our holiness. The design of God in working grace and holiness in us is, that "we may be conformed unto the image of his Son, that he may be the firstborn among many brethren," Rom. viii. 29; and our design in the attaining of it is, first that we may be like him, and then that we may express or "show forth the virtues of him who hath called us out of darkness into his marvellous light," unto his glory and honour, 1 Pet. ii. 9. To this end is he proposed, in the purity of his natures, the holiness of his person, the glory of his graces, the innocency and usefulness of his conversation in the world, as the great idea and exemplar, which in all things we ought to conform ourselves unto. And as the nature of evangelical holiness consists herein, — namely, in a universal conformity unto him as he is the image of the invisible God, — so the proposal of his example unto us is an effectual means of ingenerating and increasing it in us.

It is by all confessed that examples are most effectual ways of instruction, and, if seasonably proposed, do secretly solicit the mind unto imitation, and almost unavoidably incline it thereunto. But when unto this power which examples have naturally and morally to instruct and affect our minds, things are peculiarly designed and instituted of God to be our examples, he requiring of us that from them we should learn both what to do and what to avoid, their force and efficacy is increased. This the apostle instructs us in at large, 1 Cor. x. 6–11. Now, both these concur in the example of holiness that is given us in the person of Christ; for, — 1st. He is not only in himself, morally considered, the most perfect, absolute, glorious pattern of all grace, holiness, virtue, obedience, to be chosen and preferred above all others, but he only is so; there is no other complete example of it. As for those examples of heroical virtue or stoical apathy which are boasted of among the heathens, it were an easy matter to find such flaws and tumours in them as would render them not only uncomely, but deformed and monstrous. And in the lives of the best of the saints there is declared what we ought expressly to avoid, as well as what we ought to follow; and in some things we are left at a loss whether it be safe to conform unto them or no, seeing we are to be followers of none any farther than they were so of Jesus Christ, and wherein they were so; neither, in what they were or did, were they absolutely our rule and example in itself, but only so far as therein they were conformable unto Christ: and the best of their graces, the highest of their attainments, and the most perfect of their duties, have their spots and imperfections; so that although they should have exceeded what we can attain unto, and are therefore meet to be proposed unto our imitation, yet do they come short of what we aim at, which is to be holy as God is holy. But in this our great exemplar, as there was never the least shadow of variableness from the perfection of holiness (for "he did no sin, neither was guile found in his mouth," yea, "in him was light, and no darkness at all"), so were all his graces, all his actings of them, all his duties, so absolute and complete, as that we ought to aim no higher, nor to propose any other pattern unto ourselves. And who is it that, aiming at any excellency, would not design the most absolute and perfect example? This, therefore, is to be found as unto holiness in Christ, and in him alone. And, 2dly. He is appointed of God for this purpose. One end why God sent his Son to take our nature upon him, and to converse in the world therein, was, that he might set us an example in our own nature, in one who was like unto us in all things, sin only excepted, of that renovation of his image in us, of that return unto him from sin and apostasy, of that holy obedience which he requireth of us. Such an example was needful, that we might never be at a loss about the will of God in his commands, having a glorious representation of it before our eyes; and this could be given us no otherwise but in our own nature. The angelical nature was not suited to set us an example of holiness and obedience, especially as to the exercise of such graces as we principally stand in need of in this world; for what examples could angels set unto us in themselves of patience in afflictions, of quietness in sufferings, seeing their nature is incapable of such things? Neither could we have had an example that was perfect and complete in our own nature, but only in one who was "holy, harmless, undefiled, and separate from sinners." To this end, therefore, among others, did God send his own Son to take our nature on him, and therein to represent unto us the perfect idea of that holiness and obedience which he requireth of us. It is evident, therefore, that these two considerations of an instructive example, that it hath a moral aptitude to incite the mind unto imitation, and that it is instituted of God unto that purpose, are both found eminently in this of Christ.

But there is yet more in this matter: for, — 1st. As God hath appointed the consideration of Christ as an especial ordinance unto the increase of holiness in us, so his holy obedience, as proposed unto us, hath a peculiar efficacy unto that purpose beyond all other instituted examples; for, — (1st.) We are often called to behold Christ, and to look upon him, or it is promised that we shall do so, Isa. xlv. 22; Zech. xii. 10. Now, this beholding of Christ, or looking on him, is the consideration of him by faith unto the ends for which he is exhibited, proposed, and set forth of God in the gospel and promises thereof. This, therefore, is an especial ordinance of God, and is by his Spirit made effectual. And these ends are two:— [1st.] Justification; [2dly.] Salvation, or deliverance from sin and punishment. "Look unto me," saith he, "and be ye saved." This was he on the cross, and is still so in the preaching of the gospel, wherein he is "evidently crucified before our eyes," Gal. iii. 1, lifted up as the brazen serpent in the wilderness, John iii. 14, 15, that we, looking on him by faith, as "bearing our sins in his own body on the tree," 1 Pet. ii. 24, and "receiving the atonement" made thereby, Rom. v. 11, may through faith in him be justified from all our sins, and saved from the wrath to come. But this we intend not; for, (2dly.) He is of God proposed unto us in the gospel as the great pattern and exemplar of holiness, so as that, by God's appointment, our beholding and looking on him, in the way mentioned, is a means of the increase and growth of it in us. So our apostle declares, 2 Cor. iii. 18, "We all, with open face beholding as in a glass the glory of the Lord, are changed into the same image from glory to glory, even as by the Spirit of the Lord." That which is proposed unto us is, the "glory of God," or the "glory of God in the face of Jesus Christ," chap. iv. 6; that is, God gloriously manifesting himself in the person of Christ. This are we said to "behold with open face." The veil of types and shadows being taken off and removed, faith doth now clearly and distinctly view and consider Jesus Christ as he is represented unto us in the glass of the gospel; that is, the evidences of the presence of God in him and with him, in his work, purity, and holiness. And the effect hereof is, that we are, through the operation of the Spirit of God, "changed into the same image," or made holy, and therein like unto him.

2dly. There is peculiar force and efficacy, by the way of motive, in the example of Christ, to incline us unto the imitation of him, that is not to be found in any other example, on any occasion whatever; because, (1st.) Whatever is proposed unto us, in what he was or what he did, as our pattern and example, he was it, and did it, not for his own sake, but out of free and mere love unto us. That pure nature of his, which we ought to be labouring after a conformity unto, 1 John iii. 3, and which he will at length bring us unto, Phil. iii. 21, he took it upon him, by an infinite condescension, merely out of love unto us, Heb. ii. 14, 15; Phil. ii. 5–8. And all the actings of grace in him, all the duties of obedience which he performed, all that glorious compliance with the will of God in his sufferings which he manifested, proceed all from his love unto us, John xvii. 19; Gal. ii. 20. These things being in themselves truly honourable and excellent, yea, being only so, the holiness and obedience which God requireth of us consisting in them, and being by the appointment of God proposed unto our imitation in the example of Jesus Christ, how must it needs influence and prevail on gracious souls to endeavour a conformity unto him therein, to be as he was, to do as he did, seeing he was what he was, and did what he did, merely out of love unto us, and for no other end! And, (2dly.) Everything which we are to imitate in Christ is other ways also beneficial unto us; for we are, in its place and way, even saved thereby. By his obedience we are made righteous, Rom. v. 19. There is no grace nor duty of Christ which he did perform, but we have the advantage and benefit of it. And this increaseth the efficacy of his example; for who would not strive to obtain those things in himself, of whose being in Christ he hath so great advantage?

In this regard also, therefore, is the Lord Christ made sanctification unto us, and is the cause of evangelical holiness in us; and certainly we are, the most of us, much to blame that we do not more abound in the use of this means unto the end mentioned. Did we abide more constantly in the beholding or contemplation of the person of Christ, of the glory and beauty of his holiness, as the pattern and great example proposed unto us, we should be more transformed into his image and likeness. But it is so fallen out that many who are called Christians delight to be talking of, and do much admire, the virtuous sayings and actions of the heathen, and are ready to make them the object of their imitation, whilst they have no thoughts of the grace that was in our Lord Jesus Christ, nor do endeavour after conformity thereunto; and the reason is, because the virtue which they seek after and desire is of the same kind with that which was in the heathen, and not that grace and holiness which was in Christ Jesus. And thence also it is that some, who, not out of love unto it, but to decry other important mysteries of the gospel thereby, do place all Christianity in the imitation of Christ, do yet indeed in their practice despise those qualities and duties wherein he principally manifested the glory of his grace. His meekness, patience, self-denial, quietness in bearing reproaches, contempt of the world, zeal for the glory of God, compassion to the souls of men, condescension to the weaknesses of all, they regard not. But there is no greater evidence that whatever we seem to have of any thing that is good in us is no part of evangelical holiness, than that it doth not render us conformable to Christ.

And we should always consider how we ought to act faith on Christ with respect unto this end. Let none be guilty practically of what some are falsely charged withal as to doctrine; — let none divide in the work of faith, and exercise themselves but in the one half of it. To believe in Christ for redemption, for justification, for sanctification, is but one half of the duty of faith; — it respects Christ only as he died and suffered for us, as he made atonement for our sins, peace with God, and reconciliation for us, as his righteousness is imputed unto us unto justification. Unto these ends, indeed, is he firstly and principally proposed unto us in the gospel, and with respect unto them are we exhorted to receive him and to believe in him; but this is not all that is required of us. Christ in the gospel is proposed unto us as our pattern and example of holiness; and as it is a cursed imagination that this was the whole end of his life and death, — namely, to exemplify and confirm the doctrine of holiness which he taught, — so to neglect his so being our example, in considering him by faith to that end, and labouring after conformity to him, is evil and pernicious. Wherefore let us be much in the contemplation of what he was, what he did, how in all instances of duties and trials he carried himself, until an image or idea of his perfect holiness is implanted in our minds, and we are made like unto him thereby.

[5.] That which principally differenceth evangelical holiness, with respect unto the Lord Christ, from all natural or moral habits or duties, and whereby he is made sanctification unto us, is, that from him, his person as our head, the principle of spiritual life and holiness in believers is derived; and by virtue of their union with him, real supplies of spiritual strength and grace, whereby their holiness is preserved, maintained, and increased, are constantly communicated unto them. On the stating and proof hereof the whole difference about grace and morality doth depend and will issue: for if that which men call morality be so derived from the Lord Christ by virtue of our union with him, it is evangelical grace; if it be not, it is either nothing or somewhat of another nature and kind, for grace it is not, nor holiness neither. And all that I have to prove herein is, that the Lord Jesus Christ is a head of influence, the spring or fountain of spiritual life, unto his church, — wherein I know myself to have the consent of the church of God in all ages; and I shall confine the proof of my assertion unto the ensuing positions, with their confirmation:—

1st. Whatever grace God promiseth unto any, bestoweth on them, or worketh in them, it is all so bestowed and wrought in, by, and through Jesus Christ, as the mediator or middle person between God and them. This the very notion and nature of his office of mediator, and his interposition therein between God and us, doth require. To affirm that any good thing, any grace, any virtue, is given unto us, or bestowed on us, or wrought in us by God, and not immediately through Christ; or that we believe in God, yield obedience unto him, or praise with glory, not directly by Christ, — is utterly to overthrow his mediation. Moses, indeed, is called a mediator between God and the people, Gal. iii. 19, as he was an internuntius, a messenger to declare the mind of God to them, and to return their answers unto God; but to limit the mediatory work of Christ unto such an interposition only is to leave him but one office, that of a prophet, and to destroy the principal uses and effects of his mediation towards the church. In like manner, because Moses is called λυτρωτής, a saviour or redeemer, Acts vii. 35, metaphorically, with respect unto his use and employment in that mighty work of the deliverance of the people out of Egypt, some will not allow that the Lord Christ is a redeemer in any other sense, subverting the whole gospel, with the faith and souls of men. But, in particular, what there is of this nature in the mediation of Christ, in his being the middle person between God and us, may be declared in the ensuing assertions:—

(1st.) God himself is the absolute infinite fountain, the supreme efficient cause, of all grace and holiness; for he alone is originally and essentially holy, as he only is good, and so the first cause of holiness and goodness to others. Hence he is called "The God of all grace," 1 Pet. v. 10; the author, possessor, and bestower of it. "He hath life in himself," and quickeneth whom he pleaseth, John v. 26; "With him is the fountain of life," Ps. xxxvi. 9; as hath been declared before. This, I suppose, needs no farther confirmation with them who really acknowledge any such thing as grace and holiness. These things, if any, are among those "perfect gifts" which are "from above," coming down "from the Father of lights, with whom is no variableness neither shadow of turning," James i. 17.

(2dly.) God from his own fullness communicates unto his creatures, either by the way of nature or by the way of grace. In our first creation God implanted his image on us, in uprightness and holiness, in and by the making or creation of our nature; and had we continued in that state, the same image of God should have been communicated by natural propagation. But since the fall and entrance of sin, God no more communicates holiness unto any by way of nature or natural propagation: for if he did so, there would be no necessity that everyone who is born must be born again before he enter into the kingdom of God, as our Saviour affirmeth there is, John iii. 3, for he might have grace and holiness from his first nativity; nor could it be said of believers that they are "born not of blood, nor of the will of the flesh, nor of the will of man, but of God," chap. i. 13, for grace might be propagated unto them by those natural means. It was the old Pelagian figment, that what we have by nature we have by grace, because God is the author of nature. So he was as it was pure, but it is our own as it is corrupt; and what we have thereby we have of ourselves, in contradiction to the grace of God. "That which is born of the flesh is flesh;" and we have nothing else by natural propagation.

(3dly.) God communicates nothing in a way of grace unto any but in and by the person of Christ, as the mediator and head of the church, John i. 18. In the old creation, all things were made by the eternal Word, the person of the Son, as the Wisdom of God, John i. 3; Col. i. 16. There was no immediate emanation of divine power from the person of the Father, for the production of all or any created beings, but in and by the person of the Son, their wisdom and power being one and the same as acted in him. And the supportation of all things in the course of divine providence is his immediate work also, whence he is said to "uphold all things by the word of his power," Heb. i. 3. And so it is in the new creation with respect unto his person as mediator. Therein was he the "image of the invisible God, the first-born of every creature, having the pre-eminence in all things; and he is before all things, and by him all things consist," Col. i. 15, 17, 18. In the raising of the whole new creation, which is by a new spiritual life and holiness communicated unto all the parts of it, the work is carried on immediately by the person of Christ the mediator; and none hath any share therein but what is received and derived from him. This is plainly asserted, Eph. ii. 10. So the apostle disposeth of this matter: "The head of every man is Christ, and the head of Christ is God," 1 Cor. xi. 3; which is so in respect of influence as well as of rule. As God doth not immediately govern the church, but in and by the person of Christ, whom he hath given to be head over all things thereunto, so neither doth he administer any grace or holiness unto any but in the same order; for "the head of every man is Christ, and the head of Christ is God."

(4thly.) God doth work real, effectual, sanctifying grace, spiritual strength and holiness, in believers, yea, that grace whereby they are enabled to believe and are made holy, and doth really sanctify them more and more, that they may be preserved "blameless to the coming of our Lord Jesus Christ." This hath been so fully confirmed in the whole of what hath been discoursed both concerning regeneration and sanctification as that it must not be here again insisted on.

Wherefore, all this grace, according unto the former assertion, is communicated unto us through and by Christ, and no otherwise.

2dly. Whatever is wrought in believers by the Spirit of Christ, it is in their union to the person of Christ, and by virtue thereof. That the Holy Spirit is the immediate efficient cause of all grace and holiness I have sufficiently proved already, unto them to whom any thing in this kind will be sufficient. Now, the end why the Holy Spirit is sent, and consequently of all that he doth as he is so sent, is to glorify Christ; and this he doth by receiving from Christ, and communicating thereof unto others, John xvi. 13–15. And there are two works of this kind which he hath to do and doth effect:— first, To unite us to Christ; and, secondly, To communicate all grace unto us from Christ, by virtue of that union.

(1st.) By him are we united unto Christ; — that is, his person, and not a light within us, as some think; nor the doctrine of the gospel, as others with an equal folly seem to imagine. It is by the doctrine and grace of the gospel that we are united, but it is the person of Christ whereunto we are united; for "he that is joined unto the Lord is one Spirit," 1 Cor. vi. 17, because by that one Spirit he is joined unto him; for "by one Spirit we are all baptized into one body," chap. xii. 13, — implanted into the body, and united unto the head. And therefore, "if we have not the Spirit of Christ, we are none of his," Rom. viii. 9. We are therefore his, — that is, united unto him, — by a participation of his Spirit. And hereby Christ himself is in us; for "Jesus Christ is in us, except we be reprobates," 2 Cor. xiii. 5; — that is, he is in us "by his Spirit that dwelleth in us," Rom. viii. 9, 11; 1 Cor. vi. 19. It may therefore be inquired, whether we receive the Spirit of the gospel from the person of Christ or no? And this is the inquiry which nothing but the extreme ignorance or impudence of some could render seasonable or tolerable, seeing formerly no Christian ever doubted of it, nor is he so now who doth disbelieve it. It is true, we receive him by the "preaching of the gospel," Gal. iii. 2; but it is no less true that we receive him immediately from the person of Christ. For no other reason is he called so frequently "The Spirit of Christ;" that is, the Spirit which he gives, sends, bestows, or communicates. He receives of the Father the "promise of the Holy Ghost," and sheddeth him forth, Acts ii. 33.

But it may be said, "That if hereby we are united unto Christ, — namely, by his Spirit, — then we must be holy and obedient before we so receive him, wherein our union doth consist; for certainly Christ doth not unite ungodly and impure sinners unto himself, which would be the greatest dishonour unto him imaginable. We must, therefore, be holy, obedient, and like unto Christ, before we can be united unto him, and so, consequently, before we receive his Spirit, if thereby we are united to him."

Ans. 1. If this be so, then indeed are we not beholden in the least unto the Spirit of Christ that we are holy, and obedient, and like to Christ; for he that hath the Spirit of Christ is united unto him, and he who is united to him hath his Spirit, and none else. Whatever, therefore is in any man of holiness, righteousness, or obedience, antecedent unto union with Christ, is no especial effect of his Spirit. Wherefore in this case we must purify ourselves without any application of the blood of Christ unto our souls, and we must sanctify ourselves without any especial work of the Spirit of God on our nature. Let them that can, satisfy themselves with these things. For my part, I have no esteem or valuation of that holiness, as holiness, which is not the immediate effect of the Spirit of sanctification in us.

2. It is granted that ordinarily the Lord Christ, by the dispensation of his word, by light and convictions thence ensuing, doth prepare the souls of men in some measure for the inhabitation of his Spirit. The way and manner hereof hath been fully before declared.

3. It is denied that, on this supposition, the Lord Christ doth unite impure or ungodly sinners unto himself, so as that they should be so united, and continue impure and ungodly: for in the same instant wherein anyone is united unto Christ, and by the same act whereby he is so united, he is really and habitually purified and sanctified; for where the Spirit of God is, there is liberty, and purity, and holiness. All acts and duties of holiness are in order of nature consequential hereunto, but the person is quickened, purified, and sanctified in its union.

Whereas, therefore, the Spirit of Christ, communicated from him for our union with him, is the cause and author of all grace and evangelical holiness in us, it is evident that we receive it directly from Christ himself; which gives it the difference from all other habits and acts pleaded for.

(2dly.) The second work of the Spirit is, to communicate all grace unto us from Christ by virtue of that union. I shall take it for granted, until all that hath been before discoursed about the work of the Holy Spirit in our regeneration and sanctification be disproved, that he is the author of all grace and holiness; and when that is disproved, we may part with our Bibles also, as books which do openly and palpably mislead us. And what he so works in us, he doth it in pursuit of his first communication unto us, whereby we are united unto Christ, even for the edification, preservation, and farther sanctification of the mystical body, making every member of it meet for the "inheritance of the saints in light." And in those supplies of grace which he so gives, acted by us in all duties of obedience, consists all the holiness which I desire any acquaintance withal or a participation of.

(3dly.) There is a mystical, spiritual body, whereof Christ is the head, and his church are the members of it. There is, therefore, a union between them in things spiritual, like unto that which is between the head and members of the body of a man in things natural. And this the Scripture, because of the weight and importance of it, with its singular use unto the faith of believers, doth frequently express. "God hath given him to be the head over all things to the church, which is his body, the fullness of him that filleth all in all," Eph. i. 22, 23. "For as the body is one, and hath many members, and all the members of that body, being many, are one body, so also is Christ," 1 Cor. xii. 12. "Christ is the head, from whom the whole body fitly joined together and compacted by that which every joint supplieth, according to the effectual working in the measure of every part, maketh increase of the body unto the edifying of itself in love," Eph. iv. 15, 16. And the same apostle speaks again to the same purpose, Col. ii. 19, "Not holding the Head, from which all the body by joints and bands having nourishment ministered, and knit together, increaseth with the increase of God." Now, it hath been always granted by all them who acknowledge the divine person of the Son of God, or the union of the human nature unto the divine in his person, that the Lord Jesus is the head of his church, in the double sense of that word; for he is the political head of it in a way of rule and government, and he is the really spiritual head, as unto vital influences of grace, unto all his members. The Romanists, indeed, cast some disturbance on the former, by interposing another immediate, ruling, governing head, between him and the catholic church; yet do they not deny but that the Lord Christ, in his own person, is the absolute, supreme king, head, and ruler of the church. And the latter the Socinians cannot grant; for denying his divine person, it is impossible to conceive how the human nature, subsisting alone by itself, should be such an immense fountain of grace as from whence there should be an emanation of it into all the members of the mystical body. But by all other Christians this hath hitherto been acknowledged; and, therefore, there is nothing belongs unto gospel grace or holiness but what is originally derived from the person of Christ, as he is the head of the church. And this is most evidently expressed in the places before alleged; for, 1 Cor. xii. 12, it is plainly affirmed that it is between Christ and the church as it is between the head and the members of the same natural body. Now, not only the whole body hath guidance and direction in the disposal of itself from the head, but every member in particular hath influences of life actually and strength from thence, without which it can neither act, nor move, nor discharge its place or duty in the body. "So also is Christ," saith the apostle. Not only hath the whole mystical body of the church guidance and direction from him, in his laws, rules, doctrine, and precepts, but spiritual life and motion also; and so hath every member thereof, — they all receive from him grace for holiness and obedience, without which they would be but withered and dead members in the body. But he hath told us that "because he liveth we shall live also," John xiv. 19: for the Father having given him to have "life in himself," chap. v. 26, whereon "he quickeneth" with spiritual life "whom he will," verse 21, from that fountain of spiritual life which is in him supplies of the same life are given unto the church; and, therefore, because he liveth we live also, — that is, a spiritual life here, without which we shall never live eternally hereafter. And, Eph. iv. 15, 16, the relation of believers unto Christ being stated exactly to answer the relation and union of the members of the body unto the head, it is expressly affirmed that as in the natural body there are supplies of nourishment and natural spirits communicated from the head unto the members, by the subserviency of all the parts of the body, designed unto that purpose, to the growth and increase of the whole in every part: so from Christ, the head of the church, which he is in his divine person as God and man, there is a supply of spiritual life, strength, and nourishment, made unto every member of the body, unto its increase, growth, and edification; for "we are members of his body, of his flesh, and of his bones," chap. v. 30, being made out of him as Eve was out of Adam, yet so continuing in him as to have all our supplies from him; "we in him, and he in us," as he speaks, John xiv. 20. And, Col. ii. 19, it is expressly affirmed that from him, the head, there is nourishment ministered unto the body, unto its increase with the increase of God. And what this spiritual nourishment, supplied unto the souls of believers for their increase and growth from Christ their head, can be, but the emanation from his person and communication with them of that grace which is the principle and spring of all holiness and duties of evangelical obedience, none has as yet undertaken to declare; and if any do deny it, they do what lies in them to destroy the life and overthrow the faith of the whole church of God. Yea, upon such a blasphemous imagination, that there could be an intercision for one moment of influences of spiritual life and grace from the person of Christ unto the church, the whole must be supposed to die and perish, and that eternally.

(4thly.) The whole of what we assert is plainly and evidently proposed in sundry instructive allusions, which are made use of to this purpose. The principal of them is that both laid down and declared by our Saviour himself: John xv. 1, 4, 5, "I am the true vine, and my Father is the husbandman. Abide in me, and I in you. As the branch cannot bear fruit of itself, except it abide in the vine; no more can ye, except ye abide in me. I am the vine, and ye are the branches: he that abideth in me, and I in him, the same bringeth forth much fruit: for without me" (or, severed from me, apart from me) "ye can do nothing." The natural in-being of the vine and branches in each other is known unto all, with the reason of it; and so is the way whereby the in-being of the branches in the vine is the cause and means of their fruitbearing. It is no otherwise but by the communication and derivation of that succus, — that is, juice and nourishment, — which alone is the preservative of vegetative life, and the next cause of fruit-bearing. In this juice and nourishment all fruit is virtually, yea, also, as to the first matter and substance of it; in and by the branch it is only formed into its proper kind and perfection. Let any thing be done to intercept this communication from the vine unto any branch, and it not only immediately loseth all its fruit-bearing power and virtue, but itself also withereth and dieth away. And there is a mutual acting of the vine and branches in this matter. Unto the vine itself it is natural from its own fullness to communicate nourishment unto the branches, — it doth it from the principle of its nature; and unto the branches it is also natural to draw and derive their nourishment from the vine. "Thus is it," saith the Lord Christ unto his disciples, "between me and you. 'I am the vine,' "saith he, "'and ye are the branches.' And there is a mutual in-being between us; I am in you, and ye are in me, by virtue of our union. That now which is expected from you is, that ye bring forth fruit; that is, that ye live in holiness and obedience, unto the glory of God. Unless ye do so ye are no true, real branches in me, whatever outward profession ye may make of your so being." But how shall this be effected? how shall they be able to bring forth fruit? This can be no otherwise done but by their abiding in Christ, and thereby continually deriving spiritual nourishment, — that is, grace and supplies of holiness, — from him; "for," saith he, χωρὶς ἐμοῦ, "separate," or apart, "from me, ye can do nothing of this kind." And that is, because nothing becomes fruit in the branch that was not nourishment from the vine.

Nothing is duty, nothing is obedience in believers, but what is grace from Christ communicated unto them. The preparation of all fructifying grace is in Christ, as the fruit of the branches is naturally in the vine. And the Lord Christ doth spiritually and voluntarily communicate of this grace unto all believers, as the vine communicates its juice unto the branches naturally; and it is in the new nature of believers to derive it from him by faith. This being done, it is in them turned into particular duties of holiness and obedience. Therefore, it is evident that there is nothing of evangelical holiness in any one person whatever but what is, in the virtue, power, and grace of it, derived immediately from Jesus Christ, by virtue of relation unto him and union with him; and it may be inquired whether this be so with moral virtue or no. The same is taught by our apostle under the similitude of an olive-tree and its branches, Rom. xi. 16–24; as also where he is affirmed to be a living stone, and believers to be built on him, as lively stones, into a spiritual house, 1 Pet. ii. 4, 5. Particular testimonies do so abound in this case as that I shall only name some few of them: John i. 14, 16, He is "full of grace and truth. And of his fullness have all we received, and grace for grace." It is of the person of Christ, or the "Word made flesh," the Son of God incarnate, that the Holy Ghost speaketh. He was made flesh, and dwelt among us, full of grace and truth. It is not the fullness of the Deity, as it dwelt in him personally, that is here intended, but that which was in him as he was made flesh, — that is, in his human nature, as inseparably united unto the divine; an all-fullness that he received by the good pleasure or voluntary disposal of the Father, Col. i. 19, and, therefore, belongeth not unto the essential fullness of the Godhead. And as to the nature of this fullness, it is said to consist in "grace and truth," that is, the perfection of holiness, — and knowledge of the whole mind, counsel, and mystery of the will of God. Of this fullness do we "receive grace for grace," — all the grace, in every kind, whereof we are made partakers in this world. That this fullness in Christ expresseth the inconceivable fullness of his human nature, by virtue of his indissolute personal union, with all graces in their perfection, wherein he received not the Spirit by measure, John iii. 34, is, as I suppose, by all Christians acknowledged; I am sure cannot be denied without the highest impiety and blasphemy. Hence, therefore, the Holy Ghost being witness, do we derive and receive all our grace, everyone according to his measure, Eph. iv. 7. Wherefore, grace is given unto the Lord Christ in an immeasurable perfection by virtue of his personal union, Col. ii. 9; and from him is it derived unto us by the gracious inhabitation of his Spirit in us, 1 Cor. vi. 19, Eph. iv. 7, according unto the degree of participation allotted unto us. This, in the substance of it, is contained in this testimony. There was and is in Jesus Christ a fullness and perfection of all grace; in us of ourselves, or by any thing that we have by nature or natural generation, by blood, or the flesh, or the will of man, John i. 13, there is none at all. Whatever we have is received and derived unto us from the fullness of Christ, which is an inexhaustible fountain thereof, by reason of his personal union.

To the same purpose is he said to be "our life," and "our life to be hid with him in God," Col. iii. 3, 4. Life is the principle of all power and operation. And the life here intended is that whereby we live to God, the life of grace and holiness; for the actings of it consist in the setting of our affections on heavenly things, and mortifying our members that are on the earth. This life Christ is. He is not so formally; for if he were, then it would not be our life, but his only. He is, therefore, so efficiently, as that he is the immediate cause and author of it, and that as he is now with God in glory. Hence it is said that we live, that is, this life of God, yet so as that we live not of ourselves, but "Christ liveth in us," Gal. ii. 20. And he doth no otherwise live in us but by the communication of vital principles and a power for vital acts; that is, grace and holiness from himself unto us. If he be our life, we have nothing that belongs thereunto, — that is, nothing of grace or holiness, — but what is derived unto us from him.

To conclude, we have all grace and holiness from Christ, or we have it of ourselves. The old Pelagian fiction, that we have them from Christ because we have them by yielding obedience unto his doctrine, makes ourselves the only spring and author of them, and on that account [it was] very justly condemned by the church of old, not only as false, but as blasphemous. Whatever, therefore, is not thus derived, thus conveyed unto us, belongs not unto our sanctification or holiness, nor is of the same nature or kind with it. Whatever ability of mind or will may be supposed in us; what application soever of means may be made for the exciting and exercise of that ability; whatever effects, in virtues, duties, all offices of humanity, and honesty, or religious observances, may be produced thereby from them, and wrought by us, — if it be not all derived from Christ as the head and principle of spiritual life unto us, it is a thing of another nature than evangelical holiness.

(3.) The immediate efficient cause of all gospel holiness is the Spirit of God. This we have sufficiently proved already. And although many cavils have been raised against the manner of his operation herein, yet none has been so hardy as openly to deny that this is indeed his work; for so to do is, upon the matter, expressly to renounce the gospel. Wherefore, we have in our foregoing discourses at large vindicated the manner of his operations herein, and proved that he doth not educe grace by moral applications unto the natural faculties of our minds, but that he creates grace in us by an immediate efficiency of almighty power. And what is so wrought and produced differeth essentially from any natural or moral habits of our minds, however acquired or improved.

(4.) This evangelical holiness is a fruit and effect of the covenant of grace. The promises of the covenant unto this purpose we have before, on other occasions, insisted on. In them doth God declare that he will cleanse and purify our natures, that he will write his law in our hearts, put his fear in our inward parts, and cause us to walk in his statutes; in which things our holiness doth consist. Whoever, therefore, hath any thing of it, he doth receive it in the accomplishment of these promises of the covenant: for there are not two ways whereby men may become holy, one by the sanctification of the Spirit according to the promise of the covenant, and the other by their own endeavours without it; though indeed Cassianus, with some of the semi-Pelagians, dreamed somewhat to that purpose. Wherefore, that which is thus a fruit and effect of the promise of the covenant hath an especial nature of its own, distinct from whatever hath not that relation unto the same covenant. No man can ever be made partaker of any the least degree of that grace or holiness which is promised in the covenant, unless it be by virtue and as a fruit of that covenant; for if they might do so, then were the covenant of God of none effect, for what it seems to promise in a peculiar manner may, on this supposition, be attained without it, which renders it an empty name. (5.) Herein consists the image of God, whereunto we are to be renewed. This I have proved before, and shall afterward have occasion to insist upon. Nothing less than the entire renovation of the image of God in our souls will constitute us evangelically holy. No series of obediential actings, no observance of religious duties, no attendance unto actions amongst men as morally virtuous and useful, how exact soever they may be, or how constant soever we may be unto them, will ever render us lovely or holy in the sight of God, unless they all proceed from the renovation of the image of God in us, or that habitual principle of spiritual life and power which renders us conformable unto him.

From what hath been thus briefly discoursed, we may take a prospect of that horrible mixture of ignorance and impudence wherewith some contend that the practice of moral virtue is all the holiness which is required of us in the gospel, neither understanding what they say nor whereof they do affirm. But yet this they do with so great a confidence as to despise and scoff at any thing else which is pleaded to belong thereunto. But this pretence, notwithstanding all the swelling words of vanity wherewith it is set off and vended, will easily be discovered to be weak and frivolous; for, —

1. The name or expression itself is foreign to the Scripture, not once used by the Holy Ghost to denote that obedience which God requireth of us in and according to the covenant of grace. Nor is there any sense of it agreed upon by them who so magisterially impose it on others: yea, there are many express contests about the signification of these words, and what it is that is intended by them, which those who contend about them are not ignorant of; and yet have they not endeavoured to reduce the sense they intend unto any expression used concerning the same matter in the gospel. But all men must needs submit unto it, that at least the main part, if not the whole of religion, consists in moral virtue, though it be altogether uncertain what they intend by the one or the other! These are they who scarce think any thing intelligible when declared in the words of the Scripture, which one hath openly traduced as a "ridiculous jargon." They like not, they seem to abhor, the speaking of spiritual things in the words which the Holy Ghost teacheth: the only reason whereof is, because they understand not the things themselves; and whilst they are "foolishness" unto any, it is no wonder the terms whereby they are declared seem also so to be. But such as have received the Spirit of Christ, and do know the mind of Christ (which profane scoffers are sufficiently remote from), do best receive the truth and apprehend it, when declared not in "the words which man's wisdom teacheth, but which are taught by the Holy Ghost." It is granted to be the wisdom and skill of men farther to explain and declare the truths that are taught in the gospel, by sound and wholesome words of their own; which yet all of them, as to their propriety and significancy, are to be tried and measured by the Scripture itself. But we have a new way of teaching spiritual things, sprung up among some, who, being ignorant of the whole mystery of the gospel, and therefore despising it, would debase all the glorious truths of it, and the declaration made of them, into dry, barren, sapless, philosophical notions and terms, and those the most common, obvious, and vulgar that ever obtained among the heathen of old. "Virtuous living," they tell us, "is the way to heaven;" but what this virtue is, or what is a life of virtue, they have added as little in the declaration of as any persons that ever made such a noise about them.

2. That ambiguous term moral hath, by usage, obtained a double signification, with respect unto an opposition unto other things, which either are not so or are more than so; for sometimes it is applied unto the worship of God, and so is opposed unto instituted. That religious worship which is prescribed in the decalogue or required by the law of creation is commonly called "moral," and that in opposition unto those rites and ordinances which are of a superadded, arbitrary institution. Again, it is opposed unto things that are more than merely moral, — namely, spiritual, theological, or divine. So the graces of

the Spirit, as faith, love, hope, in all their exercise, whatever they may have of morality in them, or however they may be exercised in and about moral things and duties, yet because of sundry respects wherein they exceed the sphere of morality, are called graces and duties, theological, spiritual, supernatural, evangelical, divine; in opposition unto all such habits of the mind and duties as, being required by the law of nature, and as they are so required, are merely moral. In neither sense can it with any tolerable congruity of speech be said that moral virtue is our holiness, especially the whole of it. But because the duties of holiness have, the most of them, a morality in them, as moral is opposed to instituted, some would have them have nothing also in them, as moral is opposed to supernatural and theological. But that the principle and acts of holiness are of another special nature hath been sufficiently now declared.

3. It is, as was before intimated, somewhat uncertain what the great pleaders for moral virtue do intend by it. Many seem to design no more but that honesty and integrity of life which was found among some of the heathens in their virtuous lives and actions; and, indeed, it were heartily to be wished that we might see more of it amongst some that are called Christians, for many things they did were materially good and useful unto mankind. But let it be supposed to be never so exact, and the course of it most diligently attended unto, I defy it as to its being the holiness required of us in the gospel, according unto the terms of the covenant of grace; and that because it hath none of those qualifications which we have proved essentially to belong thereunto. And I defy all the men in the world to prove that this moral virtue is the sum of our obedience to God, whilst the gospel is owned for a declaration of his will and our duty. It is true, all the duties of this moral virtue are required of us, but in the exercise of every one of them there is more required of us than belongs unto their morality, — as, namely, that they be done in faith and love to God through Jesus Christ; and many things are required of us as necessary parts of our obedience which belong not thereunto at all.

4. Some give us such a description of morality as that "it should be of the same extent with the light and law of nature, or the dictates of it as rectified and declared unto us in the Scripture;" and this, I confess, requires of us the obedience which is due towards God by the law of our creation, and according to the covenant of works materially and formally. But what is this unto evangelical holiness and obedience? Why, it is alleged that "religion before the entrance of sin and under the gospel is one and the same; and therefore there is no difference between the duties of obedience required in the one and the other." And it is true that they are so far the same as that they have the same Author, the same object, the same end; and so also had the religion under the law, which was, therefore, so far the same with them; but that they are the same as to all the acts of our obedience and the manner of their performance is a vain imagination. Is there no alteration made in religion by the interposition of the person of Christ to be incarnate, and his mediation? no augmentation of the object of faith? no change in the abolishing of the old covenant and the establishment of the new, the covenant between God and man being that which gives the especial form and kind unto religion, the measure and denomination of it? no alteration in the principles, aids, assistances, and whole nature of our obedience unto God? The whole mystery of godliness must be renounced if we intend to give way unto such imaginations. Be it so, then, that this moral virtue and the practice of it do contain and express all that obedience, materially

considered, which was required by the law of nature in the covenant of works, yet I deny it to be our holiness or evangelical obedience; and that, as for many other reasons, so principally because it hath not that respect unto Jesus Christ which our sanctification hath.

5. If it be said that by this moral virtue they intend no exclusion of Jesus Christ, but include a respect unto him, I desire only to ask whether they design by it such a habit of mind, and such acts thence proceeding, as have the properties before described, as to their causes, rise, effects, use, and relation unto Christ and the covenant, such as are expressly and plainly in the Scripture assigned unto evangelical holiness? Is this moral virtue that which God hath predestinated or chosen us unto before the foundation of the world? Is it that which he worketh in us in the pursuit of electing love? Is it that which gives us a new heart, with the law of God written in it? Is it a principle of spiritual life, disposing, inclining, enabling us to live to God, according to the gospel, produced in us by the effectual operation of the Holy Ghost, not educed out of the natural powers of our own souls by the mere application of external means? Is it that which is purchased and procured for us by Jesus Christ, and the increase whereof in us he continueth to intercede for? Is it the image of God in us, and doth our conformity unto the Lord Christ consist therein? If it be so, if moral virtue answer all these properties and adjuncts of holiness, then the whole contest in this matter is, whether the Holy Spirit or these men be wisest, and know best how to express the things of God rationally and significantly. But if the moral virtue they speak of be unconcerned in these things, if none of them belongs unto it, if it may and doth consist without it, it will appear at length to be no more, as to our acceptance before God, than what one of the greatest moralists in the world complained that he found it when he was dying, — "a mere empty name." But this fulsome Pelagian figment of a holiness, or evangelical righteousness, whose principle should be natural reason, and whose rule is the law of nature as explained in the Scripture, whose use and end is acceptation with God and justification before him, — whereby those who plead for it, the most of them, seem to understand no more but outward acts of honesty, nor do practice so much, — being absolutely opposite unto and destructive of the grace of our Lord Jesus Christ, being the mere doctrine of the Quakers, by whom it is better and more intelligibly expressed than by some new patrons of it amongst us, will not, in the examination of it, create any great trouble unto such as look upon the Scripture to be a revelation of the mind of God in these things.

Footnotes:

2. See vol. vi. of his works. — Ed.

Chapter VII - Of the acts and duties of holiness

Actual inherent righteousness in duties of holiness and obedience explained — The work of the Holy Spirit with respect thereunto — Distribution of the positive duties of holiness — Internal duties of holiness — External duties and their difference — Effectual operation of the Holy Spirit necessary unto every act of holiness — Dependence on providence with respect unto things natural, and on grace with respect unto things supernatural, compared — Arguments to prove the necessity of actual grace unto every duty of holiness — Contrary designs and expressions of the Scripture and some men about duties of holiness.

II. The second part of the work of the Spirit of God in our sanctification respects the acts and duties of holy obedience; for what we have before treated of chiefly concerns the principle of it as habitually resident in our souls, and that both as unto its first infusion into us, as also its preservation and increase in us. But we are not endued with such a principle or power to act it at our pleasure, or as we see good, but God, moreover, "worketh in us both to will and to do of his good pleasure." And all these acts and duties of holiness or gospel obedience are of two sorts, or may be referred unto two heads:— First, Such as have the will of God in positive commands for their object, which they respect in duties internal and external, wherein we do what God requireth. Secondly, Such as respect divine prohibitions, which consist in the actings of grace or holiness in an opposition unto or the mortification of sin. And what is the work of the Holy Spirit, what is the aid which he affords us, in both these sorts of duties, must be declared:—

1. The acts and duties of the first sort, respecting positive divine commands, fall under a double distinction; for they are in their own nature either, (1.) Internal only, or, (2.) External also. There may be internal acts of holiness that have no external effects; but no external acts or duties are any part of holiness which are only so and no more: for it is required thereunto that they be quickened and sanctified by internal actings of grace. Two persons may, therefore, at the same time, perform the same commanded duties, and in the same outward manner, yet may it be the duty of evangelical holiness in the one and not in the other; as it was with Cain and Abel, with the other apostles and Judas: for if faith and love be not acted in either of them, what they do is duty but equivocally, properly it is not so.

(1.) By the duties of holiness that are internal only, I intend all acts of faith, love, trust, hope, fear, reverence, delight, that have God for their immediate object, but go not forth nor exert themselves in any external duties. And in these doth our spiritual life unto God principally consist; for they are as the first acts of life, which principally evidence the strength or decays of it. And from these we may take the best measure of our spiritual health and interest in holiness; for we may abound in outward duties, and yet our hearts be very much alienated from the life of God: yea, sometimes men may endeavour to make up what is wanting with them by a multitude of outward duties, and so have "a name to live" when they are "dead," wherein the true nature of hypocrisy and superstition doth consist, Isa. i. 11–15. But when the internal actings of faith, — fear, trust, and love, — abound and are constant in us, they evidence a vigorous and healthy condition of soul.

(2.) Duties that are external, also, are of two sorts, or are distinguished with respect unto their objects and ends; for, — [1.] God himself is the object and end of some of them, as of prayer and praises, whether private or more solemn. And of this nature are all those which are commonly called "duties of the first table;" all such as belong unto the sanctification of the name of God in his worship. [2.] Some respect men of all sorts in their various capacities, and our various relations unto them, or have men for their object, but God for their end. And among these, also, I include those which principally regard ourselves, or our own persons. The whole of what we intend is summarily expressed by our apostle, Tit. ii. 12.

Concerning all these acts and duties, whether internal only or external also, whether their proper object be God, ourselves, or other men, so far as they are acts of holiness and are accepted with God, they proceed from a peculiar operation of the Holy Spirit in us. And herein, to make our intention the more evident, we may distinctly observe, —

(1.) That there is in the minds, wills, and affections of all believers, a meetness, fitness, readiness, and habitual disposition unto the performance of all acts of obedience towards God, all duties of piety, charity, and righteousness, that are required of them; and hereby are they internally and habitually distinguished from them that are not so. That it is so with them, and whence it comes to be so, we have before declared. This power and disposition is wrought and preserved in them by the Holy Ghost.

(2.) No believer can of himself act, — that is, actually exert or exercise, — this principle or power of a spiritual life, in any one instance of any duty, internal or external, towards God or men, so as that it shall be an act of holiness, or a duty accepted with God. He cannot, I say, do so of himself, by virtue of any power habitually inherent in him. We are not in this world intrusted with any such spiritual ability from God, as without farther actual aid and assistance to do any thing that is good. Therefore, —

(3.) That which at present I design to prove is, That the actual aid, assistance, and internal operation of the Spirit of God is necessary, required, and granted, unto the producing of every holy act of our minds, wills, and affections, in every duty whatever; or, That notwithstanding the power or ability which believers have received in or by habitual grace, they still stand in need of actual grace, in, for, and unto every single gracious, holy act or duty towards God. And this I shall now a little farther explain, and then confirm.

As it is in our natural lives with respect unto God's providence, so it is in our spiritual lives with respect unto his grace. He hath in the works of nature endowed us with a vital principle, or an act of the quickening soul upon the body, which is quickened thereby. By virtue hereof we are enabled unto all vital acts, whether natural and necessary or voluntary, according to the constitution of our being, which is intellectual. "God breathed into man the breath of life; and man became a living soul," Gen. ii. 7. Giving him a principle of life, he was fitted for and enabled unto all the proper acts of that life; for a principle of life is an ability and disposition unto acts of life. But yet, whosoever is thus made a living soul, whosoever is endued with this principle of life, he is not able originally, without any motion or acting from God as the first cause, or independently of him, to exert or put forth any vital act. That which hath not this principle, as a dead carcass, hath no meetness unto vital actions, nor is capable either of motion or alteration, but as it receives impressions from an outward principle of force or an inward principle of corruption. But he in whom it is hath a fitness, readiness, and habitual power for all vital actions, yet so as without the concurrence of God in his energetical providence, moving and acting of him, he can do nothing; for "in God we live, and move, and have our being," Acts xvii. 28. And if anyone could of himself perform an action without any concourse of divine operation, he must himself be absolutely the first and only cause of that action, — that is, the creator of a new being.

It is so as unto our spiritual life. We are, by the grace of God through Jesus Christ, furnished with a principle of it, in the way and for the ends before described. Hereby are we enabled and disposed to live unto God, in the exercise of spiritually vital acts, or the performance of duties of holiness. And he who hath not this principle of spiritual life is spiritually dead, as we have at large before manifested, and can do nothing at all that is spiritually good. He may be moved unto, and, as it were, compelled by the power of convictions, to do many things that are materially so; but that which is on all considerations spiritually good and accepted with God, he can do nothing of. The inquiry is, what believers themselves, who have received this principle of spiritual life and are habitually sanctified, can do as to actual duties by virtue thereof, without a new immediate assistance and working of the Holy Spirit in them; and I say, they can no more do any thing that is spiritually good, without the particular concurrence and assistance of the grace of God unto every act thereof, than a man can naturally act, or move, or do any thing in an absolute independency of God, his power and providence. And this proportion between the works of God's providence and of his grace the apostle expresseth, Eph. ii. 10, "We are his workmanship, created in Christ Jesus unto good works, which God hath before ordained that we should walk in them." God at the beginning made all things by a creating power, producing them out of nothing, and left them not merely to themselves and their own powers when so created, but he upholds, supports, sustains, and preserves them in the principles of their being and operations, acting powerfully in and by them, after their several kinds. Without his supportment of their being, by an actual incessant emanation of divine power, the whole fabric of nature would dissolve into confusion and nothing; and without his influence into and concurrence with their ability for operation by the same power, all things would be dead and deformed, and not one act of nature be exerted. So also is it in this work of the new creation of all things by Jesus Christ. "We are God's workmanship;" he hath formed and fashioned us for himself, by the renovation of his image in us. Hereby are we fitted for good works and the fruits of righteousness, which he appointed as the way of our living unto him. This new creature, this divine nature in us, he supporteth and preserveth, so as that without his continual influential power, it would perish and come to nothing. But this is not all; he doth moreover act it, and effectually concur to every singular duty, by new supplies of actual grace. So, then, that which we are to prove is, that there is an actual operation of the Holy Ghost in us, necessary unto every act and duty of holiness whatever, without which none either will or can be produced or performed by us; which is the second part of his work in our sanctification. And there are several ways whereby this is confirmed unto us:—

[1.] The Scripture declares that we ourselves cannot, in and by ourselves, — that is, by virtue of any strength or power that we have received, — do any thing that is spiritually good. So our Saviour tells his apostles when they were sanctified believers, and in them all that are so, "Without me ye can do nothing," John xv. 5; — χωρὶς ἐμοῦ, so "without me;" seorsim a me, so "separated from me," as a branch may be from the vine. If a branch be so separated from the root and body of the vine as that it receives not continual supplies of nourishment from them, if their influence into it be by any means intercepted, it proceeds not in its growth, it brings forth no fruit, but is immediately under decay. It is so, saith our Saviour, with believers in respect unto him. Unless they have continual, uninterrupted influences of grace and spiritually vital nourishment from him, they can do nothing. "Without me," expresseth a denial of all the spiritual aid that we have from Christ. On supposition hereof "we can do nothing," — that is, by our own power, or by virtue of any habit or principle of grace we have received; for when we have received it, what we can do thereby without farther actual assistance, we can do of ourselves. "Ye can do nothing," that is, which appertains to fruit-bearing unto God. In things natural and civil we can do somewhat, and in things sinful too much; we need no aid or assistance for any such purpose; — but in fruit-bearing unto God we can do nothing. Now, every act of faith and love, every motion of our minds or affections towards God, is a part of our fruit-bearing; and so, unquestionably, are all external works and duties of holiness and obedience. Wherefore, our Saviour himself being judge, believers, who are really sanctified and made partakers of habitual grace, yet cannot of themselves, without new actual aid and assistance of grace from him, do any thing that is spiritually good or acceptable with God.

Our apostle confirmeth the same truth, 2 Cor. iii. 4, 5, "And such trust have we through Christ to God-ward: not that we are sufficient of ourselves to think any thing as of ourselves; but our sufficiency is of God." It is a great and eminent grace which he declareth that he was acting, — namely, trust in God through Christ in the discharge of his ministry, and for the blessed success thereof; but he had no sooner expressed it than he seems to be jealous lest he should appear to have assumed something to himself in this work, or the trust he had for its success. This no man was ever more cautious against; and indeed it was incumbent on him so to be, because he was appointed to be the principal minister and preacher of the grace of Jesus Christ. Therefore, I say, he adds a caution against any such apprehensions, and openly renounceth any such power, ability, or sufficiency in himself, as that by virtue thereof he could act so excellent a grace or perform so great a duty: "Not that we are sufficient of ourselves." And in this matter he hath not only, in places innumerable, asserted the necessity and efficacy of grace, with our impotency without it, but in his own instance he hath made such a distinction between what was of himself and what of grace, with such an open disclaimer of any interest of his own in what was spiritually good, distinct from grace, as should be sufficient with all sober persons to determine all differences in this case. See 1 Cor. xv. 10, Gal. ii. 20, and this place. I assume no such thing to myself, I ascribe no such thing unto any other, as that I or they should have in ourselves a sufficiency unto any such purpose; for our apostle knew nothing of any sufficiency that needed any other thing to make it effectual. And he doth not exclude such a sufficiency in ourselves with respect unto eminent actings of grace and greater duties, but with respect unto every good thought, or whatever may have a tendency unto any spiritual duty. We cannot conceive, we cannot engage in the beginning of, any duty by our own sufficiency; for it is the beginning of duties which the apostle expresseth by "thinking," our thoughts and projections being naturally the first thing that belongs unto our actions. And this he doth as it were on purpose to obviate that Pelagian fiction, that the beginning of good was from ourselves, but we had the help of grace to perfect it. "But what then? if we have no such sufficiency, to what purpose should we set about the thinking or doing of any thing that is good? Who will be so unwise as to attempt that which he hath no strength to accomplish? And doth not the apostle hereby deny that he himself had performed any holy duties, or acted any grace, or done any thing that was good, seeing he had no sufficiency of himself so to do?" To obviate this cavil, he confines this denial of a sufficiency unto "ourselves;" we have it not of ourselves. "But," saith he, "our sufficiency is of God," — that is, we have it by actual supplies of grace, necessary unto every duty. And how God communicates this sufficiency, and how we receive it, he declares, 2 Cor. ix. 8, "God is able to make all grace abound toward you; that ye, always having all sufficiency in all things, may abound to every good work." God manifests the abounding of grace towards us when he works an effective sufficiency in us; which he doth so as to enable us to abound in good works or duties of holiness. These are those supplies of grace which God gives us unto all our duties, as he had promised unto him in his own case, chap. xii. 9. And this is the first demonstration of the truth proposed unto consideration, — namely, the testimonies given in the Scripture that believers themselves cannot of themselves perform any acts or duties of holiness, any thing that is spiritually good. Therefore, these things are effects of grace, and must be wrought in us by the Holy Ghost, who is the immediate author of all divine operations.

[2.] All actings of grace, all good duties, are actually ascribed unto the operation of the Holy Ghost. The particular testimonies hereunto are so multiplied in the Scripture as that it is not convenient nor indeed possible to call them over distinctly; some of them, in a way of instance, may be insisted on, and reduced unto three heads:—

1st. There are many places wherein we are said to be led, guided, acted by the Spirit, to live in the Spirit, to walk after the Spirit, to do things by the Spirit, that dwelleth in us: for nothing in general can be intended in these expressions but the actings of the Holy Spirit of God upon our souls; in a compliance wherewith, as acting when we are acted by him, our obedience unto God according to the gospel doth consist: Gal. v. 16, "Walk in the Spirit." To walk in the Spirit is to walk in obedience unto God, according to the supplies of grace which the Holy Ghost administers unto us; for so it is added, that "we shall not then fulfil the lusts of the flesh," — that is, we shall be kept up unto holy obedience and the avoidance of sin. So are we said to be "led of the Spirit," verse 18, being acted by him, and not by the vicious, depraved principles of our corrupted nature. Rom. viii. 4, "Walk not after the flesh, but after the Spirit." To walk after the flesh is to have the principle of indwelling sin acting itself in us unto the production and perpetration of actual sins. Wherefore, to walk after the Spirit is to have the Spirit acting in us, to the effecting of all gracious acts and duties. And this is given unto us in command, that we neglect not his motions in us, but comply with them in a way of diligence and duty: see verses 14, 15. So are we enjoined to attend unto particular duties through "the Holy Ghost which dwelleth in us," 2 Tim. i. 14; that is, through his assistance, without which we can do nothing.

2dly. As we are said to be led and acted by him, so he is declared to be the author of all gracious actings in us: Gal. v. 22, 23, "The fruit of the Spirit is love, joy, peace, long-suffering, gentleness, goodness, faith, meekness, temperance." All these things are wrought and brought forth in us by the Spirit, for they are his fruits. And not only the habit of them, but all their actings, in all their exercise, are from him. Every act of faith is faith, and every act of love is love, and consequently no act of them is of ourselves, but every one of them is a fruit of the Spirit of God. So in another place he adds a universal affirmative, comprehending all instances of particular graces and their exercise: Eph. v. 9, "The fruit of the Spirit is in all goodness and righteousness and truth." Unto these three heads all actings of grace, all duties of obedience, all parts of holiness, may be reduced. And it is through the supplies of the Spirit that he trusteth for a good issue of his obedience, Phil. i. 19. So is it expressly in the promise of the covenant, Ezek. xxxvi. 27, "I will put my Spirit within you, and cause you to walk in my statutes, and ye shall keep my judgments, and do them."

This is the whole that God requireth of us, and it is all wrought in us by his Spirit. So also, chap. xi. 19, 20; Jer. xxxii. 39, 40. All the obedience and holiness that God requires of us in the covenant, all duties and actings of grace, are promised to be wrought in us by the Spirit, after we are assured that of ourselves we can do nothing.

3dly. Particular graces and their exercise are assigned unto his acting and working in us: Gal. v. 5, "We through the Spirit wait for the hope of righteousness by faith." The hope of the righteousness of faith is the thing hoped for thereby. All that we look for or expect in this world or hereafter is by the righteousness of faith. Our quiet waiting for this is an especial gospel grace and duty. This we do not of ourselves, but "through the Spirit:" We "worship God in the Spirit," Phil. iii. 3; love the brethren "in the Spirit," Col. i. 8; we "purify our souls in obeying the truth through the Spirit unto unfeigned love of the brethren," 1 Pet. i. 22. See Eph. i. 17; Acts ix. 31; Rom. v. 5, viii. 15, 23, 26; 1 Thess. i. 6; Rom. xiv. 17, xv. 13, 16. Of faith it is said expressly that it is "not of ourselves; it is the gift of God," Eph. ii. 8.

[3.] There are testimonies that are express unto the position as before laid down: Phil. ii. 13, "It is God who worketh in you both to will and to do of his good pleasure." The things thus wrought are all things that appertain unto our obedience and salvation, as is evident from the connection of the words with verse 12, "Work out your salvation with fear and trembling." Hereunto two things are required:— 1st. Power for such operations, or for all the duties of holiness and obedience that are required of us. That this we are endued withal, that this is wrought in us, bestowed upon us, by the Holy Ghost, hath been before abundantly confirmed. But when this is done for us, is there aught else yet remaining to be done? Yea, 2dly. There is the actual exercise of the grace we have received. How may this be exercised? All the whole work of grace consists in the internal acts of our wills, and external operations in duties suitable thereunto. This, therefore, is incumbent on us, this we are to look unto in ourselves, it is our duty so to do, — namely, to stir up and exercise the grace we have received in and unto its proper operations. But it is so our duty as that of ourselves we cannot perform it. It is God who worketh effectually in us all those gracious acts of our wills, and all holy operations in a way of duty. Every act of our wills, so far as it is gracious and holy, is the act of the Spirit of God efficiently; he "worketh in us to will," or the very act of willing. To say he doth only persuade us, or excite and stir up our wills by his grace, to put forth their own acts, is to say he doth not do what the apostle affirms him to do; for if the gracious actings of our wills be so our own as not to be his, he doth not work in us to will, but only persuadeth us so to do. But the same apostle utterly excludeth this pretence: 1 Cor. xv. 10, "I laboured abundantly; yet not I, but the grace of God which was with me." He had a necessity incumbent on him of declaring the great labour he had undergone, and the pains he had taken in "preaching of the gospel;" but yet immediately, lest anyone should apprehend that he ascribed any thing to himself, any gracious, holy actings in those labours, he adds his usual epanorthosis, "Not I;" — "Let me not be mistaken; it was not I, by any power of mine, by any thing in me, but it was all wrought in me by the free grace of the Spirit of God." "Not I, but grace," is the apostle's assertion. Suppose now that God by his grace doth no more but aid, assist, and excite the will in its actings, that he doth not effectually work all the gracious actings of our souls in all our duties, the proposition would hold on the other hand, "Not grace, but I," seeing the principal relation of the effect is unto the next and immediate cause, and thence hath it its denomination. And as he worketh them "to will" in us, so also "to do," — that is, effectually to perform those duties whereunto the gracious actings of our wills are required.

And what hath been spoken may suffice to prove that the Holy Spirit, as the author of our sanctification, worketh also in us all gracious acts of faith, love, and obedience, wherein the first part of our actual holiness and righteousness doth consist. And the truth thus confirmed may be farther improved unto our instruction and edification.

(1.) It is easily hence discernible how contrary are the designs and expressions of the Scripture and the notions of some men among us. There is not any thing that is good in us, nothing that is done well by us in the way of obedience, but the Scripture expressly and frequently assigns it unto the immediate operations of the Holy Spirit in us. It doth so in general as to all gracious actings whatever; and not content therewith, it proposeth every grace and every holy duty, distinctly affirming the Holy Ghost to be the immediate author of them. And when it comes to make mention of us, it positively, indeed, prescribes our duty to us, but as plainly lets us know that we have no power in or from ourselves to perform it. But some men speak, and preach, and write, utterly to another purpose. The freedom, liberty, power and ability of our own wills; the light, guidance, and direction of our own minds or reasons; and from all, our own performance of all the duties of faith and obedience, — are the subjects of their discourses, and that in opposition unto what is ascribed in the Scriptures unto the immediate operations of the Holy Ghost. They are all for grace: "Not I, but grace; not I, but Christ; without him we can do nothing." These are all for our wills: "Not grace, but our wills do all." It is not more plainly affirmed in the Scripture that God created heaven and earth, that he sustains and preserves all things by his power, than that he creates grace in the hearts of believers, preserves it, acts it, and makes it effectual, working all our works for us and all our duties in us. But evasions must be found out, — strange, forced, uncouth senses must be put upon plain, frequently-repeated expressions, — to secure the honour of our wills, and to take care that all the good we do may not be assigned to the grace of God. To this purpose distinctions are coined, evasions invented, and such an explanation is given of all divine operations as renders them useless and insignificant. Yea, it is almost grown, if not criminal, yet weak and ridiculous, in the judgment of some, that any should assign those works and operations to the Spirit of God which the Scripture doth, in the very words that the Scripture useth. To lessen the corruption and depravation of our nature by sin; to extol the integrity and power of our reason; to maintain the freedom and ability of our wills in and unto things spiritually good; to resolve the conversion of men unto God into their natural good dispositions, inclinations, and the right use of their reason; to render holiness to be only a probity of life or honesty of conversation, upon rational motives and considerations, — are the things that men are now almost wearied with the repetition of. Scarce a person that hath confidence to commence for reputation in the world, but immediately he furnisheth himself with some new tinkling ornaments for these old Pelagian figments. But whoever shall take an impartial view of the design and constant doctrine of the Scripture in this matter will not be easily carried away with the plausible pretences of men exalting their own wills and abilities, in opposition to the Spirit and grace of God by Jesus Christ.

(2.) From what hath been discoursed, a farther discovery is made of the nature of gospel obedience, of all the acts of our souls therein, and of the duties that belong thereunto. It is commonly granted that there is a great difference between the acts and duties that are truly gracious, and those which are called by the same name that are not so, as in any duties of faith, of prayer, of charity. But this difference is supposed generally to be in the adjuncts of those duties, in some properties of them, but not in the kind, nature, or substance of the acts of our minds in them. Nay, it is commonly said that whereas wicked men are said to believe, and do many things gladly in a way of obedience, what they so do is, for the substance of the acts they perform, the same with those of them who are truly regenerated and sanctified; they may differ in their principle and end, but as to their substance or essence they are the same. But there is no small mistake herein. All gracious actings of our minds and souls, whether internal only, in faith, love, or delight, or whether they go out unto external duties required in the gospel, being wrought in us by the immediate efficacy of the Spirit of grace, differ in their kind, in their essence and substance of the acts themselves, from whatever is not so wrought or effected in us; for whatever may be done by anyone, in any acting of common grace or performance of any duty of obedience, being educed out of the power of the natural faculties of men, excited by convictions, as directed and enforced by reasons and exhortations, or assisted by common aids, of what nature soever, they are natural as to their kind, and they have no other substance or being but what is so. But that which is wrought in us by the especial grace of the Holy Ghost, in the way mentioned, is supernatural, as being not educed out of the powers of our natural faculties, but an immediate effect of the almighty supernatural efficacy of the grace of God. And, therefore, the sole reason why God accepts and rewards duties of obedience in them that are sanctified, and regardeth not those which for the outward matter and manner of performance are the same with them (as unto

Abel and his offering he had respect, but he had no respect unto Cain and his offering, Gen. iv. 4, 5), is not taken from the state and condition of the persons that perform them only, though that also has an influence thereinto, but from the nature of the acts and duties themselves also. He never accepts and rejects duties of the same kind absolutely with respect unto the persons that do perform them. The duties themselves are of a different kind. Those which he accepts are supernatural effects of his own Spirit in us, whereon he rewardeth and crowneth the fruits of his own grace; and as for what he rejects, whatever appearance it may have of a compliance with the outward command, it hath nothing in it that is supernaturally gracious, and so is not of the same kind with what he doth accept.

Chapter VIII - Mortification of sin, the nature and causes of it

Mortification of sin, the second part of sanctification — Frequently prescribed and enjoined as a duty — What the name signifies, with the reason thereof; as also that of crucifying sin — The nature of the mortification of sin explained — Indwelling sin, in its principle, operations, and effects, the object of mortification — Contrariety between sin and grace — Mortification a part-taking with the whole interest of grace against sin — How sin is mortified, and why the subduing of it is so called — Directions for the right discharge of this duty — Nature of it unknown to many — The Holy Spirit the author and cause of mortification in us — The manner of the operation of the Spirit in the mortification of sin — Particular means of the mortification of sin — Duties necessary unto the mortification of sin, directed unto by the Holy Ghost — Mistakes and errors of persons failing in this matter — How spiritual duties are to be managed, that sin may be mortified — Influence of the virtue of the death of Christ, as applied by the Holy Spirit, into the mortification of sin.

2. There is yet another part or effect of our sanctification by the Holy Ghost, which consisteth in and is called mortification of sin. As what we have already insisted on concerneth the improvement and practice of the principle of grace, wherewithal believers are endued; so what we now propose concerneth the weakening, impairing, and destroying of the contrary principle of sin, in its root and fruits, in its principle and actings. And whereas the Spirit of God is everywhere said to sanctify us, we ourselves are commanded and said constantly to mortify our sins: for sanctification expresseth grace communicated and received in general; mortification, grace as so received, improved, and acted unto a certain end. And I shall be brief in the handling of it, because I have formerly published a small discourse on the same subject.[3] And there are two things that I shall speak unto:— First, The nature of the duty itself; Secondly, The manner how it is wrought in us by the Holy Ghost, which I principally intend.

It is known that this duty is frequently enjoined and prescribed unto us: Col. iii. 5, "Mortify therefore your members which are upon the earth; fornication, uncleanness, inordinate affection, evil concupiscence, and covetousness, which is idolatry." Ἐν τῷ φεύγειν, may be supplied. "'Mortify your members which are upon the earth,' — that is, your carnal, earthly affections; avoiding (or 'by avoiding') 'fornication,'" etc.: and so a distinction is made between carnal affections and their fruits. Or, the special sins mentioned are instances of these carnal affections: "Mortify your carnal affections," — namely, fornication and the like; wherein there is a metonymy of the effect for the cause. And they are called "our members," — (1.) Because, as the whole principle of sin, and course of sinning which proceedeth from it, is called the "body of sin," Rom. vi. 6, or the "body of the sins of the flesh," Col. ii. 11, with respect thereunto these particular lusts are here called the members of that body, "Mortify your members;" for that he intends not the parts or members of our natural bodies, as though they were to be destroyed, as they seem to imagine who place mortification in outward afflictions and macerations of the body, he adds, τὰ ἐπὶ τῆς γῆς, "that are on the earth," — that is, earthly, carnal, and sensual. (2.) These affections and lusts, the old man, — that is, our depraved nature, — useth naturally and readily, as the body doth its members; and, which adds efficacy unto the allusion, by them it draws the very members of the body into a compliance with it and the service of it, against which we are cautioned by our apostle: Rom. vi. 12, "Let not sin therefore reign in your mortal bodies" (that is, our natural bodies), "that ye should obey it in the lusts thereof;" — which exhortation he pursues, verse 19, "As ye have yielded your members servants to uncleanness and to iniquity unto iniquity; even so now yield your members servants to righteousness unto holiness;" which some neglecting, do take "the members of Christ," — that is, of their own bodies, which are the members of Christ, — and make them the "members of an harlot," 1 Cor. vi. 15. And many other commands there are to the same purpose, which will afterward occur.

And concerning this great duty we may consider three things:— (1.) The name of it, whereby it is expressed; (2.) The nature of it, wherein it consists; (3.) The means and way whereby it is effected and wrought.

(1.) For the name, it is two ways expressed, and both of them metaphorical:— [1.] By νεκροῦν and θανατοῦν, which we render "to mortify ourselves." The first is used, Col. iii. 5, νεκρώσατε, which is "mortify," — that is, extinguish and destroy all that force and vigour of corrupted nature which inclines to earthly, carnal things, opposite unto that spiritual, heavenly life and its actings which we have in and from Christ, as was before declared. Νεκρόω is eneco, morte macto, — "to kill," "to affect with or destroy by death." But yet this word is used by our apostle not absolutely to destroy and to kill, so as that that which is so mortified or killed should no more have any being, but that it should be rendered useless as unto what its strength and vigour would produce. So he expresseth the effects of it in the passive word, Οὐ κατενόησε τὸ ἑαυτοῦ σῶμα ἤδη νεκερωμένον, Rom. iv. 19; — "He considered not his own body now dead," "now mortified." The body of Abraham was not then absolutely dead, only the natural force and vigour of it was exceedingly abated. And so he seems to mollify this expression, Heb. xi. 12, Ἀφ' ἑνὸς ἐγεννήθησαν, καὶ ταῦτα νενεκρωμένου, which we well render, "Of one, and him as good as dead," ταῦτα intimating a respect unto the thing treated of. So that νεκροῦν, "to mortify," signifies a continued act, in taking away the power and force of any thing until it come to be νενεκρωμένον, "dead," unto some certain ends or purposes, as we shall see it is in the mortification of sin. Rom. viii. 13, "If ye through the Spirit do mortify the deeds of the body, ye shall live," — θανατοῦτε, another word to the same purpose. It signifies, as the other doth, "to put to death;" but it is used in the present tense, to denote that it is a work which must be always doing: "If ye do mortify," — that is, "If ye are always and constantly employed in that work." And what the apostle here calls τὰς πράξεις τοῦ σώματος, "the deeds of the body," he therein expresseth the effect for the cause metonymically; for he intends τὴν σάρκα σὺν τοῖς παθήμασι καὶ ταῖς ἐπιθυμίαις, as he expresseth the same thing, Gal. v. 24, "The flesh with the affections and lusts," whence all the corrupt deeds wherein the body is instrumental do arise.

[2.] The same duty with relation unto the death of Christ, as the meritorious, efficient, and exemplary cause, is expressed by crucifying: Rom. vi. 6, "Our old man is crucified with him." Gal. ii. 20, "I am crucified with Christ." Chap. v. 24, "They that are Christ's have crucified the flesh with the affections and lusts." Chap. vi. 14, By the Lord Jesus Christ "the world is crucified unto me, and I unto the world." Now, as perhaps there may be something intimated herein of the manner of mortification of sin, which is gradually carried on unto its final destruction, as a man dies on the cross, yet that which is principally intended is the relation of this work and duty to the death of Christ, whence we and our sins are said to be crucified with him, because we and they are so by virtue of his death. And herein do we "always bear about in the body" τὴν νέκρωσιν, "the dying of the Lord Jesus," 2 Cor. iv. 10, representing the manner of it, and expressing its efficacy.

(2.) Thus is this duty expressed, whose nature, in the next place, we shall more particularly inquire into, and declare in the ensuing observations:—

[1.] Mortification of sin is a duty always incumbent on us in the whole course of our obedience. This the command testifieth, which represents it as an always present duty. When it is no longer a duty to grow in grace, it is so not to mortify sin. No man under heaven can at any time say that he is exempted from this command, nor on any pretence; and he who ceaseth from this duty lets go all endeavours after holiness. And as for those who pretend unto an absolute perfection, they are of all persons living the most impudent, nor do they ever in this matter open their mouths but they give themselves the lie; for, —

[2.] This duty being always incumbent on us, argues undeniably the abiding in us of a principle of sin whilst we are in the flesh, which, with its fruits, is that which is to be mortified. This the Scripture calleth the "sin that dwelleth in us," the "evil that is present with us," the "law in our members," "evil concupiscence," "lust," the "flesh," and the like. And thereunto are the properties and actings of folly, deceit, tempting, seducing, rebelling, warring, captivating, ascribed. This is not a place to dispute the truth of this assertion, which cannot, with any reputation of modesty, be denied by any who own the Scripture or pretend to an acquaintance with themselves. But yet, through the craft of Satan, with the pride and darkness of the minds of men, it is so fallen out that the want of a true understanding hereof is the occasion of most of those pernicious errors wherewith the church of God is at present pestered, and which practically keep men off from being seriously troubled for their sins, or seeking out for relief by Jesus Christ. Thus, one hath not feared of late openly to profess that he knows of no deceit or evil in his own heart, though a wiser than he hath informed us that "he that trusteth in his own heart is a fool," Prov. xxviii. 26.

[3.] Indwelling sin, which is the object of this duty of mortification, falls under a threefold consideration:— 1st. Of its root and principle; 2dly. Of its disposition and operations; 3dly. Of its effects. These in the Scripture are frequently distinguished, though mostly under metaphorical expressions. So are they mentioned together distinctly, Rom. vi. 6, "Our old man is crucified with Christ, that the body of sin might be destroyed, that henceforth we should not serve sin." 1st. The root or principle of sin, which by nature possesseth all the faculties of the soul, and as a depraved habit inclines unto all that is evil, is the "old man," so called in opposition unto the "new man," which "after God is created in righteousness and true holiness." 2dly. There is the inclination, actual disposition, and operations of this principle or habit, which is called the body of sin, with the members of it; for under these expressions sin is proposed as in procinctu, in a readiness to act itself, and inclining unto all that is evil. And this also is expressed by "The flesh with the affections and lusts," Gal. v. 24; "Deceitful lusts," Eph. iv. 22, "The old man is corrupt, according to the deceitful lusts;" "The wills of the flesh and of the mind," chap. ii. 3. 3dly. There are the effects, fruits, and products of these things, which are actual sins; whereby, as the apostle speaks, we serve sin, as bringing forth the fruits of it: "That henceforth we should not serve sin," Rom. vi. 6. And these fruits are of two sorts:— (1st.) Internal, in the figments and imaginations of the heart; which is the first way whereby the lusts of the old man do act themselves. And, therefore, of those that are under the power or dominion of sin, it is said that "every figment or imagination of their hearts is evil continually," Gen. vi. 5; for they have no other principle whereby they are acted but that of sin, and therefore all the figments of their hearts must be necessarily evil. And with respect hereunto our Saviour affirms that all actual sins "proceed out of the heart," Matt. xv. 19, because there is their root, and there are they first formed and framed. (2dly.) External, in actual sins, such as those enumerated by our apostle, Col. iii. 5; Gal. v. 19–21. All these things together make up the complete object of this duty of mortification. The old man, the body of death, with its members, and the works of the flesh, or the habit, operations, and effects of sin, are all of them intended and to be respected herein.

[4.] This principle, and its operations and effects, are opposed and directly contrary unto the principle, operations, and fruits of holiness, as wrought in us by the Spirit of God, which we have before described. 1st. They are opposed in their principle; for "the flesh lusteth against the Spirit, and the Spirit against the flesh, and these are contrary the one to the other," Gal. v. 17. These are those two adverse principles which maintain such a conflict in the souls of believers whilst they are in this world, and which is so graphically described by our apostle, Rom. vii. So the old and new man are opposed and contrary. 2dly. In their actings. The lusting of the flesh and the lusting or desires of the Spirit, walking after the flesh and walking after the Spirit, living after the flesh and living in the Spirit, are opposed also. This is the opposition that is between the body of sin with its members and the life of grace: "Who walk not after the flesh, but after the Spirit," Rom. viii. 1, 4, 5. "We are debtors, not to the flesh, to live after the flesh. For if ye live after the flesh, ye shall die: but if ye through the Spirit do mortify the deeds of the body, ye shall live," verses 12, 13. By this "walking after the flesh" I understand not, at least not principally, the committing of actual sins, but a compliance with the principle or habit of sin prevailing in depraved, unsanctified nature, allowing it a predominancy in the heart and affections. It is when men are disposed to act according to the inclinations, lustings, motions, wills, and desires of it; or it is to bend that way habitually, in our course and conversation, which the flesh inclines and leads unto. This principle doth not, indeed, equally bring forth actual sins in all, but hath various degrees of its efficacy, as it is advantaged by temptations, controlled by light, or hampered by convictions. Hence all that are under the power of sin are not equally vicious and sinful; but after the flesh goes the bent of the soul and the generality of its actings. To "walk after the Spirit" consists in our being given up to his rule and conduct, or walking according to the dispositions and inclinations of the Spirit, that which is born of the Spirit,— namely, a principle of grace implanted in us by the Holy Ghost; which hath been at large insisted on before. And, 3dly. The external fruits and effects of these two principles are contrary also, as our apostle expressly and at large declares, Gal. v. 19–24; for whereas, in the enumeration of the "works of the flesh," he reckons up actual sins, as adultery, fornication, and the like, in the account he gives of the "fruits of the Spirit," he insists on habitual graces, as love, joy, peace. He expresseth them both metaphorically. In the former he hath respect unto the vicious habits of those actual sins, and in the latter unto the actual effects and duties of those habitual graces. [5.] There being this universal contrariety, opposition, contending, and warfare, between grace and sin, the Spirit and the flesh, in their inward principles, powers, operations, and outward effects, the work and duty of mortification consists in a constant taking part with grace, in its principle, actings, and fruits, against the principle, actings, and fruits of sin; for the residence of these contrary principles being in, and their actings being by, the same faculties of the soul, as the one is increased, strengthened, and improved, the other must of necessity be weakened and decay. Wherefore, the mortification of sin must consist in these three things:— 1st. The cherishing and improving of the principle of grace and holiness which is implanted in us by the Holy Ghost, by all the ways and means which God hath appointed thereunto; which we have spoken unto before. This is that which alone can undermine and ruin the power of sin, without which all attempts to weaken it are vain and fruitless. Let men take never so much pains to mortify, crucify, or subdue their sins, unless they endeavour in the first place to weaken and impair its strength by the increase of grace and growing therein, they will labour in the fire, where their work will be consumed. 2dly. In frequent actings of the principle of grace in all duties, internal and external; for where the inclinations, motions, and actings of the Spirit, in all acts, duties, and fruits of holy obedience, are vigorous, and kept in constant exercise, the contrary motions and actings of the flesh are defeated. 3dly. In a due application of the principle, power, and actings of grace, by way of opposition unto the principle, power, and actings of sin. As the whole of grace is opposed unto the whole of sin, so there is no particular lust whereby sin can act its power, but there is a particular grace ready to make effectual opposition unto it, whereby it is mortified. And in this application of grace, in its actings in opposition unto all the actings of sin, consists the mystery of this great duty of mortification. And where men, being ignorant hereof, have yet fallen under a conviction of the power of sin, and been perplexed therewith, they have found out foolish ways innumerable for its mortification, wickedly opposing external, natural, bodily force and exercise, unto an internal, moral, depraved principle, which is no way concerned therein. But hereof we must treat more afterward under the third head, concerning the manner how this work is to be carried on or this duty performed.

[6.] This duty of weakening sin by the growth and improvement of grace, and the opposition which is made unto sin in all its actings thereby, is called mortification, killing, or putting to death, on sundry accounts:— First and principally, from that life which, because of its power, efficacy, and operation, is ascribed unto indwelling sin. The state of the soul by reason of it is a state of death; but whereas power and operations are the proper adjuncts or effects of life, for their sakes life is ascribed unto sin, on whose account sinners are dead. Wherefore this corrupt principle of sin in our depraved nature, having a constant, powerful inclination and working actually towards all evil, it is said metaphorically to live, or to have a life of its own. Therefore is the opposition that is made unto it for its ruin and destruction called mortification or killing, being its deprivation of that strength and efficacy whereby and wherein it is said to live. Secondly, It may be so called because of the violence of that contest which the soul is put unto in this duty. All other duties that we are called unto in the course of our obedience may be performed in a more easy, gentle, and plain manner. Though it is our work and duty to conflict with all sorts of temptations, yea, to wrestle with "principalities and powers, and spiritual wickednesses in high places," yet in this which we have with ourselves, which is wholly within us and from us, there is more of warring, fighting, captivating, wounding, crying out for help and assistance, a deep sense of such a violence as is used in taking away the life of a mortal enemy, than in any thing else we are called unto. And, thirdly, the end aimed at in this duty is destruction, as it is of all killing. Sin, as was said, hath a life, and that such a life as whereby it not only lives, but rules and reigns in all that are not born of God. By the entrance of grace into the soul it loseth its dominion, but not its being, — its rule, but not its life. The utter ruin, destruction, and gradual annihilation of all the remainders of this cursed life of sin is our design and aim in this work and duty; which is, therefore, called mortification. The design of this duty, wherever it is in sincerity, is to leave sin neither being, nor life, nor operation.

And some directions, as our manner is, may be taken from what we have discoursed concerning the nature of this duty, directive of our own practices. And, —

First, It is evident, from what hath been discoursed, that it is a work which hath a gradual progress, in the proceed whereof we must continually be exercised; and this respects, in the first place, the principle of sin itself. Everyday, and in every duty, an especial eye is to be had unto the abolition and destruction of this principle. It will no otherwise die but by being gradually and constantly weakened; spare it, and it heals its wounds, and recovers strength. Hence many who have attained to a great degree in the mortification of sin do by their negligence suffer it, in some instance or other, so to take head again that they never recover their former state whilst they live.

And this is the reason why we have so many withering professors among us, decayed in their graces, fruitless in their lives, and every way conformed to the world. There are some, indeed, who, being under the power of that blindness and darkness which is a principal part of the depravation of our nature, do neither see nor discern the inward secret actings and motions of sin, its deceit and restlessness, its mixing itself one way or other in all our duties, with the defilement and guilt wherewith these things are accompanied; who judge that God scarce takes notice of any thing but outward actions, and it may be not much of them neither, so as to be displeased with them, unless they are very foul indeed, which yet he is easily entreated to pass by and excuse; who judge this duty superfluous, despising both the confession and mortification of sin, in this root and principle of it. But those who have received most grace and power from above against it are of all others the most sensible of its power and guilt, and of the necessity of applying themselves continually unto its destruction.

Secondly, With respect unto its inclinations and operations, wherein it variously exerts its power, in all particular instances, we are continually to watch against it and to subdue it. And this concerns us in all that we are and do, — in our duties, in our calling, in our conversation with others, in our retirements, in the frames of our spirits, in our straits, in our mercies, in the use of our enjoyments, in our temptations. If we are negligent unto any occasion, we shall suffer by it. This is our enemy, and this is the war we are engaged in. Every mistake, every neglect, is perilous. And, —

Thirdly, The end of this duty, with respect unto us, expressed by the apostle, is, that henceforth we should not serve sin, Rom. vi. 6; which refers unto the perpetration of actual sins, the bringing forth of the actual fruits of the flesh, internal or external also. In whomsoever the old man is not crucified with Christ, let him think what he will of himself, he is a servant of sin. If he have not received virtue from the death of Christ, if he be not wrought unto a conformity to him therein, whatever else he may do or attain, however he may in any thing, in many things, change his course and reform his life, he serves sin, and not God. Our great design ought to be, that we should no longer serve sin; which the apostle in the ensuing verses gives us many reasons for. It is, indeed, the worst service that a rational creature is capable of, and will have the most doleful end. What, therefore, is the only way and means whereby we may attain this end, — namely, that although sin will abide in us, yet that we may not serve it, which will secure us from its danger? This is that mortification of it which we insist upon, and no other. If we expect to be freed from the service of sin by its own giving over to press its dominion upon us, or by any composition with it, or any other way but by being always killing or destroying of it, we do but deceive our own souls.

And, indeed, it is to be feared that the nature of this duty is not sufficiently understood or not sufficiently considered. Men look upon it as an easy task, and as that which will be carried on with a little diligence and ordinary attendance. But do we think it is for nothing that the Holy Ghost expresseth the duty of opposing sin, and weakening its power by mortification, killing, or putting to death? Is there not somewhat peculiar herein, beyond any other act or duty of our lives? Certainly there is intimated a great contest of sin for the preservation of its life. Everything will do its utmost to preserve its life and being. So will sin do also; and if it be not constantly pursued with diligence and holy violence, it will escape our assaults. Let no man think to kill sin with few, easy, or gentle strokes. He who hath once smitten a serpent, if he follow not on his blow until he be slain, may repent that ever he began the quarrel. And so will he who undertakes to deal with sin, and pursues it not constantly to death. Sin will after awhile revive, and the man must die. It is a great and fatal mistake if we suppose this work will admit of any remissness or intermission. Again, the principle to be slain is in ourselves, and so possessed of our faculties as that it is called ourselves. It cannot be killed without a sense of pain and trouble. Hence it is compared to the cutting off of right hands, and the plucking out of right eyes. Lusts that pretend to be useful to the state and condition of men, that are pleasant and satisfactory to the flesh, will not be mortified without such a violence as the whole soul shall be deeply sensible of. And sundry other things might be insisted on to manifest how men deceive themselves, if they suppose this duty of mortification is that which they may carry on in a negligent, careless course and manner. Is there no danger in this warfare? no watchfulness, no diligence required of us? Is it so easy a thing to kill an enemy who hath so many advantages of force and fraud? Wherefore, if we take care of our souls, we are to attend unto this duty with that care, diligence, watchfulness, and earnest contention of spirit, which the nature of it doth require.

And, moreover, there is no less fatal mistake where we make the object of this duty to be only some particular lusts, or the fruits of them in actual sins, as was before observed. This is the way with many. They will make head against some sins, which on one account or other they find themselves most concerned in; but if they will observe their course, they shall find with how little success they do it. For the most part, sin gets ground upon them, and they continually groan under the power of its victories; and the reason is, because they mistake their business. Contests against particular sins are only to comply with light and convictions. Mortification, with a design for holiness, respects the body of sin, the root and all its branches. The first will miscarry, and the latter will be successful. And herein consists the difference between that mortification which men are put upon by convictions from the law, which always proves fruitless, and that wherein we are acted by the spirit of the gospel. The first respects only particular sins, as the guilt of them reflects upon conscience; the latter, the whole interest of sin, as opposed to the renovation of the image of God in us.

(3.) That which remains farther to be demonstrated is, that the Holy Spirit is the author of this work in us, so that although it is our duty, it is his grace and strength whereby it is performed; as also the manner how it is wrought by him, which is principally intended:— [1.] For the first, we have the truth of it asserted, chap. viii. 13, "If ye through the Spirit do mortify the deeds of the flesh." It is we that are to mortify the deeds of the flesh. It is our duty, but of ourselves we cannot do it; it must be done in or by the Spirit. Whether we take "the Spirit" here for the person of the Holy Ghost, as the context seems to require, or take it for the gracious principle of spiritual life in the renovation of our nature, — not the Spirit himself, but that which is "born of the Spirit," — it is all one as to our purpose; the work is taken from our own natural power or ability, and resolved into the grace of the Spirit.

And, that we go no farther for the proof of our assertion, it may suffice to observe, that the confirmation of it is the principal design of the apostle, from the second verse of that chapter unto the end of the thirteenth. That the power and reign of sin, its interest and prevalency in the minds of believers, are weakened, impaired, and finally destroyed (so as that all the pernicious consequences of it shall be avoided) by the Holy Ghost, and that these things could no otherwise be effected, he both affirms and proves at large. In the foregoing chapter, from the seventh verse unto the end, he declares the nature, properties, and efficacy of indwelling sin, as the remainders of it do still abide in believers. And whereas a twofold conclusion might be made from the description he gives of the power and actings of this sin, or a double question arise, unto the great disconsolation of believers, he doth in this chapter remove them both, manifesting that there was no cause for such conclusions or exceptions from any thing by him delivered. The first of these is, "That if such, if this be the power and prevalency of indwelling sin, if it so obstruct us in our doing that which is good, and impetuously incline us unto evil, what will become of us in the end, how shall we answer for all the sin and guilt which we have contracted thereby? We must, we shall, therefore, perish under the guilt of it." And the second conclusion which is apt to arise from the same consideration is, "That seeing the power and prevalency of sin is so great, and that we in ourselves are no way able to make resistance unto it, much less to overcome it, it cannot be but that at length it will absolutely prevail against us, and bring us under its dominion, unto our everlasting ruin." Both these conclusions the apostle obviates in this chapter, or removes them if laid as objections against what he had delivered. And this he doth, —

1st. By a taçit concession that they will both of them be found true towards all who live and die under the law, without an interest in Jesus Christ; for, affirming that "there is no condemnation to them which are in Christ Jesus," he grants that those who are not so cannot avoid it. Such is the guilt of this sin, and such are the fruits of it, in all in whomsoever it abides, that it makes them obnoxious unto condemnation. But, —

2dly. There is a deliverance from this condemnation and from all liableness thereunto, by free justification in the blood of Christ, Rom. viii. 1. For those who have an interest in him, and are made partakers thereof, although sin may grieve them, trouble and perplex them, and, by its deceit and violence, cause them to contract much guilt in their surprisals, yet they need not despond or be utterly cast down; there is a stable ground of consolation provided for them, in that "there is no condemnation to them which are in Christ Jesus."

3dly. That none may abuse this consolation of the gospel to countenance themselves unto a continuance in the service of sin, he gives a limitation of the subjects unto whom it doth belong, — namely, all them, and only them, who walk not after the flesh, but after the Spirit, verse 1. As for those who give up themselves unto the conduct of this principle of indwelling sin, who comply with its motions and inclinations, being acted wholly by its power, let them neither flatter nor deceive themselves; there is nothing in Christ nor the gospel to free them from condemnation. It is they only who give up themselves to the conduct of the Spirit of sanctification and holiness that have an interest in this privilege.

4thly. As to the other conclusion, taken from the consideration of the power and prevalency of this principle of sin, he prevents or removes it by a full discovery how and by what means that power of it shall be so broken, its strength abated, its prevalency disappointed, and itself destroyed, as that we need not fear the consequents of it before mentioned, but rather may secure ourselves that we shall be the death thereof, and not that the death of our souls. Now this is, saith he, "by the law" or power "of the Spirit of life which is in Christ Jesus," verse 2. And thereon he proceeds to declare, that it is by the effectual working of this Spirit in us alone that we are enabled to overcome this spiritual adversary. This being sufficiently evident, it remaineth only that we declare, —

[2.] The way and manner how he produceth this effect of his grace.

1st. The foundation of all mortification of sin is from the inhabitation of the Spirit in us. He dwells in the persons of believers as in his temple, and so he prepares it for himself. Those defilements or pollutions which render the souls of men unmeet habitations for the Spirit of God do all of them consist in sin inherent-and its effects. These, therefore, he will remove and subdue, that he may dwell in us suitably unto his holiness: verse 11, "If the Spirit of him that raised up Jesus from the dead dwell in you, he that raised up Christ from the dead shall also quicken your mortal bodies by his Spirit that dwelleth in you."

Our "mortal bodies" are our bodies as obnoxious unto death by reason of sin, as verse 10; and the "quickening" of these mortal bodies is their being freed from the principle of sin, or death and its power, by a contrary principle of life and righteousness. It is the freeing of us from being "in the flesh," that we may be "in the Spirit," verse 9. And by what means is this effected? It is by "the Spirit of him that raised up Jesus from the dead," verse 11, — that is, of the Father; which also is called the "Spirit of God," and the "Spirit of Christ," verse 9, for he is equally the Spirit of the Father and the Son. And he is described by this periphrasis, both because there is a similitude between that work, as to its greatness and power, which God wrought in Christ when he raised him from the dead, and what he worketh in believers in their sanctification, Eph. i. 19, 20, and because this work is wrought in us by virtue of the resurrection of Christ. But under what especial consideration doth he effect this work of mortifying sin in us? It is as he dwelleth in us. God doth it "by his Spirit that dwelleth in us," Rom. viii. 11. As it is a work of grace, it is said to be wrought by the Spirit; and as it is our duty, we are said to work it "through the Spirit," verse 13. And let men pretend what they please, if they have not the Spirit of Christ dwelling in them, they have not mortified any sin, but do yet walk after the flesh, and, continuing so to do, shall die.

Moreover, as this is the only spring of mortification in us as it is a grace, so the consideration of it is the principal motive unto it as it is a duty. So our apostle pressing unto it doth it by this argument: "Know ye not that your body is the temple of the Holy Ghost which is in you, which ye have of God?" 1 Cor. vi. 19. To which we may add that weighty caution which he gives us to the same purpose: chap. iii. 16, 17, "Know ye not that ye are the temple of God, and that the Spirit of God dwelleth in you? If any man defile the temple of God, him shall God destroy; for the temple of God is holy, which temple ye are."

Whereas, therefore, in every duty two things are principally considered, — first, The life and spring of it, as it is wrought in us by grace; secondly, The principal reason for it and motive unto it, as it is to be performed in ourselves by the way of duty; both these, as to this matter of mortifications, do centre in this inhabitation of the Spirit. For, — (1st.) It is he who mortifies and subdues our corruptions, who quickens us unto life, holiness, and obedience, as he "dwelleth in us," that he may make and prepare a habitation meet for himself. And, (2dly.) The principal reason and motive which we have to attend unto it with all care and diligence as a duty is, that we may thereby preserve his dwelling-place so as becometh his grace and holiness. And, indeed, whereas (as our Saviour tells us) they are things which arise from and come out of the heart that defile us, there is no greater nor more forcible motive to contend against all the defiling actings of sin, which is our mortification, than this, that by the neglect hereof the temple of the Spirit will be defiled, which we are commanded to watch against, under the severe commination of being destroyed for our neglect therein.

If it be said, that "whereas we do acknowledge that there are still remainders of this sin in us, and they are accompanied with their defilements, how can it be supposed that the Holy Ghost will dwell in us, or in anyone that is not perfectly holy?" I answer, — (1st.) That the great matter which the Spirit of God considereth in his opposition unto sin, and that of sin to his work, is dominion and rule. This the apostle makes evident, Rom. vi. 12–14. Who or what shall have the principal conduct of the mind and soul (chap. viii. 7–9) is the matter in question. Where sin hath the rule, there the Holy Ghost will never dwell. He enters into no soul as his habitation, but at the same instant he dethrones sin, spoils it of its dominion, and takes the rule of the soul into the hand of his own grace. Where he hath effected this work, and brought his adversary into subjection, there he will dwell, though sometimes his habitation be troubled by his subdued enemy. (2dly.) The souls and minds of them who are really sanctified have continually such a sprinkling with the blood of Christ, and are so continually purified by virtue from his sacrifice and oblation, as that they are never unmeet habitations for the Holy Spirit of God.

2dly. The manner of the actual operation of the Spirit of God in effecting this work, or how he mortifies sin, or enables us to mortify it, is to be considered; and an acquaintance herewith dependeth on the knowledge of the sin that is to be mortified, which we have before described. It is the vicious, corrupt habit and inclination unto sin, which is in us by nature, that is the principal object of this duty; or, "the old man, which is corrupt according to the deceitful lusts." When this is weakened in us as to its power and efficacy, when its strength is abated and its prevalency destroyed, then is this duty in its proper discharge, and mortification carried on in the soul.

Now, this the Holy Ghost doth, —

(1st.) By implanting in our minds and all their faculties a contrary habit and principle, with contrary inclinations, dispositions, and actings, — namely, a principle of spiritual life and holiness, bringing forth the fruits thereof. By means hereof is this work effected; for sin will no otherwise die but by being killed and slain. And whereas this is gradually to be done, it must be by warring and conflict. There must be something in us that is contrary unto it, which, opposing it, conflicting with it, doth insensibly and by degrees (for it dies not at once) work out its ruin and destruction. As in a chronical distemper, the disease continually combats and conflicts with the powers of nature, until, having insensibly improved them, it prevails unto its dissolution, so is it in this matter. These adverse principles, with their contrariety, opposition; and conflict, the apostle expressly asserts and describes, as also their contrary fruits and actings, with the issue of the whole, Gal. v. 16–25. The contrary principles are the flesh and Spirit; and their contrary actings are in lusting and warring one against the other: Verse 16, "Walk in the Spirit, and ye shall not fulfil the lust of the flesh." Not to fulfil the lusts of the flesh is to mortify it; for it neither will nor can be kept alive if its lusts be not fulfilled. And he gives a fuller account hereof, verse 17, "For the flesh lusteth against the Spirit, and the Spirit against the flesh: and these are contrary the one to the other." If by the "Spirit," the Spirit of God himself be intended, yet he "lusteth" not in us but by virtue of that spirit which is born of him; that is, the new nature, or holy principle of obedience which he worketh in us. And the way of their mutual opposition unto one another the apostle describes at large in the following verses, by instancing in the contrary effects of the one and the other. But the issue of the whole is, verse 24, "They that are Christ's have crucified the flesh with the affections and lusts." They have "crucified" it; that is, fastened it unto that cross where at length it may expire. And this is the way of it, — namely, the actings of the Spirit against it, and the fruits produced thereby. Hence he shuts up his discourse with that exhortation, "If we live in the Spirit, let us walk in the Spirit;" that is, "If we are endowed with this spiritual principle of life, which is to live in the Spirit, then let us act, work, and improve that spiritual principle unto the ruin and mortification of sin."

This, therefore, is the first way whereby the Spirit of God mortifieth sin in us; and in a compliance with it, under his conduct, do we regularly carry on this work and duty, — that is, we mortify sin by cherishing the principle of holiness and sanctification in our souls, labouring to increase and strengthen it by growing in grace, and by a constancy and frequency in acting of it in all duties, on all occasions, abounding in the fruits of it. Growing, thriving, and improving in universal holiness, is the great way of the mortification of sin. The more vigorous the principle of holiness is in us, the more weak, infirm, and dying will be that of sin. The more frequent and lively are the actings of grace, the feebler and seldomer will be the actings of sin. The more we abound in the "fruits of the Spirit," the less shall we be concerned in the "works of the flesh." And we do but deceive ourselves if we think sin will be mortified on any other terms. Men when they are galled in their consciences and disquieted in their minds with any sin or temptation thereunto, wherein their lusts or corruptions are either influenced by Satan, or entangled by objects, occasions, and opportunities, do set themselves ofttimes in good earnest to oppose and subdue it, by all the ways and means they can think upon. But all they do is in vain; and so they find it at last, unto their cost and sorrow. The reason is, because they neglect this course, without which never any one sin was truly mortified in the world, nor ever will so be. The course I intend is that of labouring universally to improve a principle of holiness, not in this or that way, but in all instances of holy obedience. This is that which will ruin sin, and without it nothing else will contribute any thing thereunto. Bring a man unto the law, urge him with the purity of its doctrines, the authority of its commands, the severity of its threatenings, the dreadful consequences of its transgression; suppose him convinced hereby of the evil and danger of sin, of the necessity of its mortification and destruction, will he be able hereon to discharge this duty, so as that sin may die and his soul may live? The apostle assures us of the contrary, Rom. vii. 7–9. The whole effect of the application of the law in its power unto indwelling sin is but to irritate, provoke, and increase its guilt. And what other probable way besides this unto this end can anyone fix upon?

(2dly.) The Holy Ghost carrieth on this work in us as a grace, and enableth us unto it as our duty, by those actual supplies and assistances of grace which he continually communicates unto us; for the same divine operations, the same supplies of grace, which are necessary unto the positive acts and duties of holiness, are necessary also unto this end, that sin in the actual motions and lustings of it may be mortified. So the apostle issues his long account of the conflict between sin and the soul of a believer, and his complaint thereon, with that good word, "I thank God through Jesus Christ our Lord," verse 25, — namely, who supplies me with gracious assistance against the power of sin. Temptation is successful only by sin, James i. 14. And it was with respect unto an especial temptation that the Lord Christ gives that answer unto the apostle, "My grace is sufficient for thee," 2 Cor. xii. 9. It is the actual supply of the Spirit of Christ that doth enable us to withstand our temptations and subdue our corruptions. This is the ἐπιχορηγία τοῦ Πνεύματος, Phil. i. 19, — an "additional supply," as occasion requireth, beyond our constant daily provision; or χάρις εἰς εὔχαιρον βοήθειαν, Heb. iv. 16, — grace given in to help seasonably, upon our cry made for it. Of the nature of these supplies we have discoursed before. I shall now only observe, that in the life of faith and dependence on Christ, the expectation and derivation of these supplies of grace and spiritual strength is one principal part of our duty. These things are not empty notions, as some imagine. If Christ be a head of influence unto us as well as of rule, as the head natural is to the body; if he be our life, if our life be in him, and we have nothing but what we do receive from him; if he give unto us supplies of his Spirit and increases of grace; and if it be our duty by faith to look for all these things from him, and that be the means of receiving them, — which things are all expressly and frequently affirmed in the Scripture; — then is this expectation and derivation of spiritual strength continually from him the way we are to take for the actual mortification of sin. And, therefore, if we would be found in a successful discharge of this duty, it is required of us, — [1st.] That we endeavour diligently, in the whole course of our lives, after these continual supplies of grace, — that is, that we wait for them in all those ways and means whereby they are communicated; for although the Lord Christ giveth them out freely and bountifully, yet our diligence in duty will give the measure of receiving them. If we are negligent in prayer, meditation, reading, hearing of the word, and other ordinances of divine worship, we have no ground to expect any great supplies to this end. And, [2dly.] That we live and abound in the actual exercise of all those graces which are most directly opposite unto those peculiar lusts or corruptions that we are most exercised withal or obnoxious unto; for sin and grace do try their interest and prevalency in particular instances. If, therefore, any are more than ordinarily subject unto the power of any corruption, — as passion, inordinate affections, love of the world, distrust of God, — unless they be constant in the exercise of those graces which are diametrically opposed unto them, they will continually suffer under the power of sin.

(3dly.) It is the Holy Spirit which directs us unto, and helps us in, the performance of those duties, which are appointed of God unto this end, that they may be means of the mortification of sin. Unto the right use of those duties (for such there are), two things are required:— [1st.] That we know them aright in their nature and use, as also that they are appointed of God unto this end; and then, [2dly.] That we perform them in a due manner. And both these we must have from the Spirit of God. He is given to believers "to lead them into all truth;" he teacheth and instructs them by the word, not only what duties are incumbent on them, but also how to perform them, and with respect unto what ends:—

[1st.] It is required that we know them aright, in their nature, use, and ends. For want hereof, or through the neglect of looking after it, all sorts of men have wandered after foolish imaginations about this work, either as to the nature of the work itself, or as to the means whereby it may be effected; for it being a grace and duty of the gospel, thence only is it truly to be learned, and that by the teachings of the Spirit of God. And it may not be amiss to give some instances of the darkness of men's minds and their mistakes herein.

First, A general apprehension that somewhat of this nature is necessary, arising from the observation of the disorder of our passions, and the exorbitancy of the lives of most in the world, is suited even to the light of nature, and was from thence variously improved by the philosophers of old. To this purpose did they give many instructions about denying and subduing the disorderly affections of the mind, conquering passions, moderating desires, and the like. But whilst their discoveries of sin rose no higher than the actual disorder they found in the affections and passions of the mind, — whilst they knew nothing of the depravation of the mind itself, and had nothing to oppose unto what they did discover but moral considerations, and those most of them notoriously influenced by vainglory and applause, — they never attained unto any thing of the same kind with the due mortification of sin.

Secondly, We may look into the Papacy, and take a view of the great appearance of this duty which is therein, and we shall find it all disappointed; because they are not led unto nor taught the duties whereby it may be brought about by the Spirit of God. They have, by the light of the Scripture, a far clearer discovery of the nature and power of sin than had the philosophers of old. The commandment, also, being variously brought and applied unto their consciences, they may be, and doubtless are and have been, many of them, made deeply sensible of the actings and tendency of indwelling sin. Hereon ensues a terror of death and eternal judgment. Things being so stated, persons who were not profligate nor had their consciences seared could not refrain from contriving ways and means how sin might be mortified and destroyed. But whereas they had lost a true apprehension of the only way whereby this might be effected, they betook themselves unto innumerable false ones of their own. This was the spring of all the austerities, disciplines, fastings, self-macerations, and the like, which are exercised or in use among them: for although they are now in practice turned mostly to the benefit of the priests, and an indulgence unto sin in the penitents, yet they were invented and set on foot at first with a design to use them as engines for the mortification of sin; and they have a great appearance in the flesh unto that end and purpose. But yet, when all was done, they found by experience that they were insufficient hereunto: sin was not destroyed, nor conscience pacified by them. This made them betake themselves to purgatory. Here they have hopes all will be set right when they are gone out of this world; from whence none could come back to complain of their disappointments. These things are not spoken to condemn even external severities and austerities, in fastings, watchings, and abstinences, in their proper place. Our nature is apt to run into extremes. Because we see the vanity of the Papists in placing mortification of sin in an outward shadow and appearance of it, in that bodily exercise which profiteth not, we are apt to think that all things of that nature are utterly needless, and cannot be subordinate unto spiritual ends. But the truth·is, I shall much suspect their internal mortification (pretend what they will) who always pamper the flesh, indulge to their sensual appetite, conform to the world, and lead their lives in idleness and pleasures; yea, it is high time that professors, by joint consent, should retrench that course of life, in fullness of diet, bravery of apparel, expense of time in vain conversation, which many are fallen into. But these outward austerities of themselves, I say, will never effect the end aimed at; for as to the most of them, they being such as God never appointed unto any such end or purpose, but being the fruit of men's own contrivances and inventions, let them be insisted on and pursued unto the most imaginable extremities, being not blessed of God thereunto, they will not contribute the least towards the mortification of sin. Neither is there either virtue or efficacy in the residue of them, but as they are subordinated unto other spiritual duties. So Hierom gives us an honest instance in himself, telling us that whilst he lived in his horrid wilderness in Judea, and lodged in his cave, his mind would be in the sports and revels at Rome!

Thirdly, The like may be said of the Quakers amongst ourselves. That which first recommended them was an appearance of mortification; which it may be also some of them really intended, though it is evident they never understood the nature of it: for in the height of their outward appearances, as they came short of the sorry weeds, begging habits, macerated countenances, and severe looks, of many monks in the Roman church, and dervises among the Mohammedans; so they were so far from restraining or mortifying their real inclinations, as that they seemed to excite and provoke themselves to exceed all others in clamours, railings, evilspeakings, reproaches, calumnies, and malicious treating of those who dissented from them, without the least discovery of a heart filled with kindness and benignity unto mankind, or love unto any but themselves; in which frame and state of things sin is as secure from mortification as in the practice of open lusts and debaucheries. But supposing that they made a real industrious attempt for the mortification of sin, what success have they had, what have they attained unto? Some of them have very wisely slipped over the whole work and duty of it into a pleasing dream of perfection; and generally, finding the fruitlessness of their attempt, and that indeed sin will not be mortified by the power of their light within, nor by their resolutions, nor by any of their austere outward appearances, nor peculiar habits or looks, which in this matter are openly pharisaical, they begin to give over their design: for who, among all that pretend to any reverence of God, do more openly indulge themselves unto covetousness, love of the world, emulation, strife, contentions among themselves, severe revenges against others, than they do, — not to mention the filth and uncleanness they begin mutually to charge one another withal? And so will all self-devised ways of mortification end. It is the Spirit of God alone who leads us into the exercise of those duties whereby it may be carried on.

[2dly.] It is required that the duties to be used unto this end be rightly performed, in faith, unto the glory of God. Without this a multiplication of duties is an increase of burden and bondage, and that is all. Now, that we can perform no duty in this way or manner without the especial assistance of the Holy Spirit hath been sufficiently before evinced. And the duties which are appointed of God in an especial manner unto this end are, prayer, meditation, watchfulness, abstinence, wisdom or circumspection with reference unto temptations and their prevalency. Not to go over these duties in particular, nor to show wherein their especial efficacy unto this end and purpose doth consist, I shall only give some general rules concerning the exercising of our souls in them, and some directions for their right performance:—

First, All these duties are to be designed and managed with an especial respect unto this end. It will not suffice that we are exercised in them in general, and with regard only unto this general end. We are to apply them unto this particular case, designing in and by them the mortification and ruin of sin, especially when, by its especial actings in us, it discovers itself in a peculiar manner unto us. No man who wisely considereth himself, his state and condition, his occasions and temptations, can be wholly ignorant of his especial corruptions and inclinations, whereby he is ready for halting, as the psalmist speaks. He that is so lives in the dark to himself, and walks at peradventures with God, not knowing how he walketh nor whither he goeth. David probably had respect hereunto when he said, "I have kept the ways of the Lord, and have not wickedly departed from my God. For all his judgments were before me, and

I did not put away his statutes from me. I was also upright before him, and I kept myself from mine iniquity," Ps. xviii. 21–23. He could have done nothing of all this, nor have preserved his integrity in walking with God, had he not known and kept a continual watch upon his own iniquity, or that working of sin in him which most peculiarly inclined and disposed him unto evil. Upon this discovery, we are to apply these duties in a particular manner to the weakening and ruin of the power of sin. As they are all useful and necessary, so the circumstances of our condition will direct us which of them in particular we ought to be most conversant in. Sometimes prayer and meditation claim this place, as when our danger ariseth solely from ourselves, and our own perverse inclinations, disorderly affections, or unruly passions; sometimes watchfulness and abstinence, when sin takes occasion from temptations, concerns, and businesses in the world; sometimes wisdom and circumspection, when the avoidance of temptations and opportunities for sin is in an especial manner required of us. These duties, I say, are to be managed with a peculiar design to oppose, defeat, and destroy the power of sin, into which they have a powerful influence, as designed of God unto that end; for, —

Secondly, All these duties, rightly improved, work two ways towards the end designed: first, Morally, and by way of impetration, — namely, of help and assistance; secondly, Really, by an immediate opposition unto sin and its power, whence assimilation unto holiness doth arise:—

(First.) These duties work morally and by way of impetration. I shall instance only in one of them, and that is prayer. There are two parts of prayer with respect unto sin and its power: first, Complaints; secondly, Petitions:—

[First.] Complaints. So is the title of Ps. cii., "A prayer of the afflicted, when he is overwhelmed, and poureth out his complaint before the Lord." So David expresseth himself, Ps. lv. 2, "Attend unto me, and hear me: I mourn in my complaint, and make a noise." His prayer was a doleful lamentation. And Ps. cxlii. 2, "I poured out my complaint before him; I showed before him my trouble." This is the first work of prayer with respect unto sin, its power and prevalency. The soul therein pours out its complaints unto God, and showeth before him the trouble it undergoes on the account thereof. And this it doth in an humble acknowledgment of its guilt, crying out of its deceit and violence; for all just and due complaint respecteth that which is grievous, and which is beyond the power of the complainer to relieve himself against. Of this sort there is nothing to be compared with the power of sin, as to believers.

This therefore is, and ought to be, the principal matter and subject of their complaints in prayer; yea, the very nature of the whole case is such as that the apostle could not give an account of it without great complaints, Rom. vii. 24. This part of prayer, indeed, is with profligate persons derided and scorned, but it is acceptable with God, and that wherein believers find ease and rest unto their souls; for, let the world scoff while it pleaseth, what is more acceptable unto God than for his children, out of pure love unto him and holiness, out of fervent desires to comply with his mind and will, and thereby to attain conformity unto Jesus Christ, to come with their complaints unto him of the distance they are kept from these things by the captivating power of sin, bewailing their frail condition, and humbly acknowledging all the evils they are liable unto upon the account thereof? Would any man have thought it possible, had not experience convinced him, that so much Luciferian pride and atheism should possess the minds of any who would be esteemed Christians as to scoff at and deride these things? that anyone should ever read the Bible, or once consider what he is, and with whom he hath to do, and be ignorant of this duty? But we have nothing to do with such persons, but to leave them to please themselves whilst they may with these fond and impious imaginations. They will come either in this world (which we hope and pray for), in their repentance, to know their folly, or in another. I say, these complaints of sin, poured out before the Lord, these cryings out of deceit and violence, are acceptable to God, and prevalent with him to give out aid and assistance. He owns believers as his children, and hath the bowels and compassion of a father towards them. Sin he knows to be their greatest enemy, and which fights directly against their souls. Will he, then, despise their complaints, and their bemoaning of themselves before him? will he not avenge them of that enemy, and that speedily? See Jer. xxxi. 18–20. Men who think they have no other enemies, none to complain of, but such as oppose them, or obstruct them, or oppress them, in their secular interests, advantages, and concerns, are strangers unto these things. Believers look on sin as their greatest adversary, and know that they suffer more from it than from all the world; suffer them, therefore, to make their complaints of it unto him who pities them, and who will relieve them and avenge them.

[Secondly.] Prayer is directly petitions to this purpose. It consists of petitions unto God for supplies of grace to conflict and conquer sin withal. I need not prove this. No man prays as he ought, no man joins in prayer with another who prays as he ought, but these petitions are a part of his prayer. Especially will they be so, and ought they so to be, when the mind is peculiarly engaged in the design of destroying sin. And these petitions or requests are, as far as they are gracious and effectual, wrought in us by the Holy Ghost, who therein "maketh intercession for us, according to the will of God;" and hereby doth he carry on this work of the mortification of sin, for his work it is. He makes us to put up prevalent requests unto God for such continual supplies of grace, whereby it may be constantly kept under, and at length destroyed.

And this is the first way whereby this duty hath an influence into mortification, — namely, morally and by way of impetration.

(Secondly.) This duty hath a real efficiency unto the same end. It doth itself (when rightly performed and duly attended unto) mightily prevail unto the weakening and destruction of sin; for in and by fervent prayer, especially when it is designed unto this end, the habit, frame, and inclinations of the soul unto universal holiness, with a detestation of all sin, are increased, cherished, and strengthened. The soul of a believer is never raised unto a higher intension of spirit in the pursuit of, love unto, and delight in holiness, nor is more conformed unto it or cast into the mould of it, than it is in prayer. And frequency in this duty is a principal means to fix and consolidate the mind in the form and likeness of it; and hence do believers ofttimes continue in and come off from prayer above all impressions from sin, as to inclinations and compliances. Would such a frame always continue, how happy were we! But abiding in the duty is the best way of reaching out after it. I say, therefore, that this duty is really efficient of the mortification of sin, because therein all the graces whereby it is opposed and weakened are excited, exercised, and improved unto that end, as also the detestation and abhorrency of sin is increased in us; and where this is not so, there are some secret flaws in the prayers of men, which it will be their wisdom to find out and heal.

(4thly.) The Holy Spirit carrieth on this work by applying in an especial manner the death of Christ unto us for that end. And this is another thing which, because the world understandeth not, it doth despise. But yet in whomsoever the death of Christ is not the death of sin, he shall die in his sins. To evidence this truth we may observe, — [1st.] In general, That the death of Christ hath an especial influence into the mortification of sin, without which it will not be mortified. This is plainly enough testified unto in the Scripture. By his cross, — that is, his death on the cross, — "we are crucified unto the world," Gal. vi. 14. "Our old man is crucified with him, that the body of sin might be destroyed," Rom. vi. 6; that is, sin is mortified in us by virtue of the death of Christ. [2dly.] In the death of Christ with respect unto sin there may be considered, — First, His oblation of himself; and, Secondly, The application thereof unto us. By the first it is that our sins are expiated as unto their guilt; but from the latter it is that they are actually subdued as to their power; for it is by an interest in, and a participation of the benefits of his death, which we call the application of it unto us. Hereon are we said to be "buried with him" and to "rise with him," whereof our baptism is a pledge, chap. vi. 3, 4; not in an outward representation, as some imagine, of being dipped into the water and taken up again (which were to make one sign the sign of another), but in a powerful participation of the virtue of the death and life of Christ, in a death unto sin and newness of life in holy obedience, which baptism is a pledge of, as it is a token of our initiation and implanting into him. So are we said to be "baptized into his death," or into the likeness of it, that is, in its power, verse 3. Thirdly, The old man is said to be crucified with Christ, or sin to be mortified by the death of Christ, as was in part before observed, on two accounts:—

(First.) Of conformity. Christ is the head, the beginning or idea, of the new creation, the first-born of every creature. Whatever God designeth unto us therein, he first exemplified in Jesus Christ; and we are "predestinated to be conformed to the image of his Son," Rom. viii. 29. Hereof the apostle gives us an express instance in the resurrection: "Christ the firstfruits; afterward they that are Christ's at his coming," 1 Cor. xv. 23. It is so in all things; all that is wrought in us, it is in resemblance and conformity unto Christ. Particularly, we are by grace "planted in the likeness of his death," Rom. vi. 5, being "made conformable unto his death," Phil. iii. 10; and so "dead with Christ," Col. ii. 20. Now, this conformity is not in our natural death, nor in our being put to death as he was; for it is that which we are made partakers of in this life, and that in a way of grace and mercy. But Christ died for sin, for our sin, which was the meritorious procuring cause thereof; and he lived again by the power of God. A likeness and conformity hereunto God will work in all believers. There is by nature a life of sin in them, as hath been declared. This life must be destroyed, sin must die in us; and we thereby become dead unto sin. And as he rose again, so are we to be quickened in and unto newness of life. In this death of sin consists that mortification which we treat about, and without which we cannot be conformed unto Christ in his death, which we are designed unto. And the same Spirit which wrought these things in Christ will, in the pursuit of his design, work that which answers unto them in all his members.

(Secondly.) In respect of efficacy. Virtue goeth forth from the death of Christ for the subduing and destruction of sin. It was not designed to be a dead, inactive, passive example, but it is accompanied with a power conforming and changing us into his own likeness. It is the ordinance of God unto that end;

which he therefore gives efficacy unto. It is by a fellowship or participation in his sufferings that we are "made conformable unto his death," Phil. iii. 10; — this κοινωνία τῶν παθημάτων is an interest in the benefit of his sufferings; we also are made partakers thereof. This makes us conformable to his death, in the death of sin in us. The death of Christ is designed to be the death of sin, let them who are dead in sin deride it whilst they please. If Christ had not died, sin had never died in any sinner unto eternity. Wherefore, that there is a virtue and efficacy in the death of Christ unto this purpose cannot be denied without a renunciation of all the benefits thereof. On the one hand, the Scripture tells us that he is "our life," our spiritual life, the spring, fountain, and cause of it; we have nothing, therefore, that belongs thereunto but what is derived from him. They cast themselves out of the verge of Christianity who suppose that the Lord Christ is no otherwise our life, or the author of life unto us, but as he hath revealed and taught the way of life unto us; he is our life as he is our head. And it would be a sorry head that should only teach the feet to go, and not communicate strength to the whole body so to do. And that we have real influences of life from Christ I have sufficiently proved before. Unto our spiritual life doth ensue the death of sin; for this, on the other hand, is peculiarly assigned unto his death in the testimonies before produced. This, therefore, is by virtue derived from Christ, — that is, in an especial manner from his death, as the Scripture testifies.

All the inquiry is, How the death of Christ is applied unto us, or, which is the same, How we apply ourselves to the death of Christ for this purpose. And I answer, we do it two ways:— [1st.] By faith. The way to derive virtue from Christ is by touching of him. So the diseased woman in the gospel touched but the hem of his garment, and virtue went forth from him to stay her bloody issue, Matt. ix. 20–22. It was not her touching him outwardly, but her faith, which she acted then and thereby, that derived virtue from him; for so our Saviour tells her in his answer, "Daughter, be of good comfort; thy faith hath made thee whole." But unto what end was this touching of his garment? It was only a pledge and token of the particular application of the healing power of Christ unto her soul, or her faith in him in particular for that end: for at the same time many thronged upon him in a press, so as his disciples marvelled he should ask who touched his clothes, Mark v. 30, 31; yet was not any of them advantaged but the poor sick woman. A great emblem it is of common profession on the one hand, and especial faith on the other. Multitudes press and throng about Christ in a profession of faith and obedience, and in the real performance of many duties, but no virtue goeth forth from Christ to heal them. But when anyone, though poor, though seemingly at a distance, gets but the least touch of him by especial faith, this soul is healed. This is our way with respect unto the mortification of sin. The Scripture assures us that there is virtue and efficacy in the death of Christ unto that end. The means whereby we derive this virtue from him is by touching of him, — that is, by acting faith on him in his death for the death of sin.

But how will this effect it? how will sin be mortified hereby? I say, How, by what power and virtue, were they healed in the wilderness who looked unto the brazen serpent? was it not because that was an ordinance of God, which by his almighty power he made effectual unto that purpose? The death of Christ being so as to the crucifying of sin, when it is looked on or applied unto by faith, shall not divine virtue and power go forth unto that end? The Scripture and experience of all believers give testimony unto the truth and reality thereof. Besides, faith itself, as acted on the death of Christ, hath a peculiar efficacy unto the subduing of sin: for, "beholding" him thereby "as in a glass, we are changed into the same image," 2 Cor. iii. 18; and that which we peculiarly behold, we are peculiarly transformed into the likeness of. And, moreover, it is the only means whereby we actually derive from Christ the benefits of our union with him. From thence we have all grace, or there is no such thing in the world; and the communication of it unto us is in and by the actual exercise of faith principally. So it being acted with respect unto his death, we have grace for the killing of sin, and thereby become dead with him, crucified with him, buried with him, as in the testimonies before produced. This is that which we call the application of the death of Christ unto us, or our application of ourselves to the death of Christ for the mortification of sin. And they by whom this means thereof is despised or neglected, who are ignorant of it or do blaspheme it, must live under the power of sin, unto what inventions soever they turn themselves for deliverance. According as we abide and abound herein will be our success. Those who are careless and remiss in the exercise of faith, by prayer and meditation, in the way described, will find that sin will keep its ground, and maintain so much power in them as shall issue in their perpetual trouble; and men who are much conversant with the death of Christ, — not in notions and lifeless speculations, not in natural or carnal affections, like those which are raised in weak persons by images and crucifixes, but by holy actings of faith with respect unto what is declared in the Scripture as to its power and efficacy, — will be implanted into the likeness of it, and experience the death of sin in them continually.

[2dly.] We do it by love. Christ as crucified is the great object of our love, or should so be; for he is therein unto sinners "altogether lovely." Hence one of the ancients cried out, Ὁ ἔρως ἐμὸς ἐσταύρωται; — "My love is crucified, and why do I stay behind?" In the death of Christ do his love, his grace, his condescension, most gloriously shine forth. We may, therefore, consider three things with respect unto this love:— first, The object of it; secondly, The means of the representation of that object unto our minds and affections; thirdly, The effects of it as to the case in hand.

First, The object of it is Christ himself, in his unsearchable grace, his unspeakable love, his infinite condescension, his patient suffering, and victorious power, in his death or dying for us. It is not his death absolutely, but himself, as all these graces conspicuously shine forth in his death, which is intended.

Secondly, And there are various ways whereby this may be represented unto our minds:— (First,) Men may do it unto themselves by their own imaginations. They may frame and fancy dolorous things unto themselves about it, which is the way of persons under deep and devout superstitions; but no love in sincerity will ever be ingenerated towards Jesus Christ hereby. (Secondly,) It may be done by others, in pathetical and tragical declarations of the outward part of Christ's sufferings. Herein some have a great faculty to work upon the natural affections of their auditors; and great passions, accompanied with tears and vows, may be so excited. But, for the most part, there is no more in this work than what the same persons do find in themselves, it may be, in the reading or hearing of a feigned story; for there is a sympathy in natural affections with the things that are their proper objects, though represented by false imaginations. (Thirdly,) It is done in the Papacy, and among some others, by images, in crucifixes and dolorous pictures, whereunto they pay great devotion, with an appearance of ardent affections; but none of these is such a due representation of this object as to ingenerate sincere love towards Christ crucified in any soul. Wherefore, (Fourthly,) This is done effectually only by the gospel, and in the dispensation of it according to the mind of God; for therein is "Jesus Christ evidently crucified before our eyes," Gal. iii. 1. And this it doth by proposing unto our faith the grace, the love, the patience, the condescension, the obedience, the end and design of Christ therein. So is Christ eyed by faith as the proper object of sincere love. And being so stated, —

Thirdly, The effects of it, as of all true love, are, first, Adherence; secondly, Assimilation:— (First,) Adherence. Love in the Scripture is frequently expressed by this effect; the soul of one did cleave, or was knit, unto another, as that of Jonathan to David, 1 Sam. xviii. 1. So it produceth a firm adherence unto Christ crucified, that makes a soul to be in some sense always present with Christ on the cross. And hence ensues, (Secondly,) Assimilation or conformity. None treat of the nature or effects of love but they assign this as one of them, that it begets a likeness between the mind loving and the object beloved. And so I am sure it is in this matter. A mind filled with the love of Christ as crucified, and represented in the manner and way before described, will be changed into his image and likeness by the effectual mortification of sin, through a derivation of power and grace from thence for that purpose.

(5thly.) The Holy Ghost carrieth on this work by constant discoveries unto and pressing on believers, on the one hand, the true nature and certain end of sin; and, on the other, the beauty, excellency, usefulness, and necessity of holiness, with the concerns of God, Christ, the gospel, and their own souls therein. A rational consideration of these things is all the ground and reason of mortification in the judgment of some men. But we have proved that there are other causes of it also; and now I add, that if we have no consideration of these things but what our own reason is of itself able to suggest unto us, it will never be prevalent unto any sincere or permanent attempt in the mortification of any sin whatever. Let men make the best of their reason they can, in the searching and consideration of the perverse nature and dreadful consequents of sin, of the perfect peace and future blessedness which attendeth the practice of holiness, they will find an obstinacy and stubbornness in their hearts not conquerable by any such reasonings or considerations. That conviction of sin and righteousness which is useful and prevalent unto that end and purpose is wrought in us by the Holy Ghost, John xvi. 8. Although he makes use of our minds, understandings, reasons, consciences, and the best of our consideration, in this matter, yet if he give not a peculiar efficacy and power unto all, the work will not be effectual. When he is pleased to make use of reasons and motives, taken from the nature and end of sin and holiness, unto the mortification of sin, they shall hold good, and bind the soul unto this duty, against all objections and temptations that would divert it whatever.

And thus I have briefly, and I confess weakly and obscurely, delineated the work of the Holy Ghost in the sanctification of them that do believe. Many things might have been more enlarged and particularly inquired into; what have been discoursed I judge sufficient to my present purpose. And I doubt not but that what hath been argued from plain Scripture and experience is sufficient, as to direct us in the practice of true evangelical holiness, so, with all sober persons, to cast out of all consideration that fulsome product of pride and ignorance, that all gospel holiness consists in the practice of moral virtues.

Footnotes:

3. See vol. vi. of his works. — Ed.

Book V

Chapter I - Necessity of holiness from the consideration of the nature of God

The necessity of evangelical holiness owned by all Christians — Doctrines falsely charged with an inconsistency with it — Though owned by all, yet practised by few, and disadvantageously pleaded for by many — The true nature of it briefly expressed — First argument for the necessity of holiness, from the nature of God; frequently proposed unto our consideration for that end — This argument cogent and unavoidable; pressed, with its limitation — Not the nature of God absolutely, but as he is in Christ, the foundation of this necessity, and a most effectual motive unto the same end — The nature and efficacy of that motive declared — The argument enforced from the consideration of our conformity unto God by holiness, with that communion and likeness with him which depend thereon, with our future everlasting enjoyment of him — True force of that consideration vindicated — Merit rejected, and also the substitution of morality in the room of gospel holiness — False accusations of the doctrine of grace discarded; and the neglect of the true means of promoting gospel obedience charged — The principal argument farther enforced, from the pre-eminence of our natures and persons by this conformity to God, and our accesses unto God thereby, in order unto our eternal enjoyment of him; as it also alone renders us useful in this world unto others — Two sorts of graces by whose exercise we grow into conformity with God: those that are assimilating, as faith and love; and those which are declarative of that assimilation, as goodness or benignity, and truth — An objection against the necessity of holiness, from the freedom and efficacy of grace, answered.

That wherewith I shall close this discourse is, the consideration of the necessity of that holiness which we have thus far described unto all persons who make profession of the gospel, with the reasons of that necessity and principal motives unto it. And for our encouragement in this part of our work, this necessity is such as that it is by all sorts of Christians allowed, pleaded for, and the thing itself pretended unto; for whereas the gospel is eminently ἀληθεία, or διδασκαλία ἡ κατ εὐσέβειαν, 1 Tim. vi. 3, Tit. i. 1, "The truth" or "doctrine which is according to godliness," or that which is designed and every way suited unto the attaining, furtherance, and practice of it, no men can with modesty refuse the trial of their doctrines by their tendency thereunto. But what is of that nature, or what is a hinderance thereunto, that many are not yet agreed about. The Socinians contend that the doctrine of the satisfaction of Christ doth overthrow the necessity of a holy life; the Papists say the same concerning the imputation of the righteousness of Christ unto our justification; the same charge is laid by others against the doctrine of the gratuitous election of God, the almighty efficacy of his grace in the conversion of sinners, and his faithfulness in the preservation of true believers in their state of grace unto the end. On the other hand, the Scripture doth so place the foundations of all true and real holiness in these things, that without the faith of them, and an influence on our minds from them, it will not allow any thing to be so called.

To examine the pretences of others concerning the suitableness of their doctrines unto the promotion of holiness is not my present business. It is well that it hath always maintained a conviction of its necessity, and carried it through all different persuasions in Christianity. In this one thing alone almost do all Christians agree; and yet, notwithstanding, the want of it is, if not the only yet the principal thing whereby the most who are so called are ruined. So ordinary a thing is it for men to agree for the necessity of holiness, and live in the neglect of it when they have so done! Conviction comes in at an easy rate, as it were whether men will or no; but practice will stand them in pains, cost, and trouble. Wherefore, unto the due handling of this matter, some few things must be premised; as, —

First, It is disadvantageous unto the interest of the gospel to have men plead for holiness with weak, incogent arguments, and such as are not taken out of the stores of its truth, and so really affect not the consciences of men; and it is pernicious to all the concerns of holiness itself to have that defended and pleaded for under its name and title which indeed is not so, but an usurper of its crown and dignity; which we shall afterward inquire into.

Secondly, It is uncomely and unworthy, to hear men contending for holiness as the whole of our religion, and, in the meantime, on all occasions, expressing in themselves a habit and frame of mind utterly inconsistent with what the Scripture so calls and so esteems. There is certainly no readier way, on sundry accounts, to unteach men all the principles of religion, all respect unto God and common honesty. And if some men did this only, as being at variance with themselves, without reflections on others, it might the more easily be borne; but to see or hear men proclaiming themselves, in their whole course, to be proud, revengeful, worldly, sensual, neglecters of holy duties, scoffers at religion and the power of it, pleading for a holy life against the doctrine and practice of those who walked unblamably before the Lord in all his ways, yea, upon whose breasts and foreheads was written, "Holiness unto the Lord," — such as were most of the first reformed divines, whom they reflect upon, — is a thing which all sober men do justly nauseate, and which God abhors. But the farther consideration hereof I shall at present omit, and pursue what I have proposed.

Thirdly, In my discourse concerning the necessity of holiness, with the grounds and reasons of it, and arguments for it, I shall confine myself unto these two things:—

1. That the reasons, arguments, and motives which I shall insist on, being such as are taken out of the Gospel or the Scripture, are not only consistent and compliant with the great doctrines of the grace of God in our free election, conversion, justification, and salvation by Jesus Christ, but such as naturally flow from them, [and] discover what is their true nature and tendency in this matter.

2. That I shall at present suppose all along what that holiness is which I do intend. Now, this is not that outward show and pretence of it which some plead for; not an attendance unto, or the observation of, some or all moral virtues only; not a readiness for some acts of piety and charity, from a superstitious, proud conceit of their being meritorious of grace or glory. But I intend that holiness which I have before described; which may be reduced to these three heads:— (1.) An internal change or renovation of our souls, our minds, wills, and affections, by grace; (2.) An universal compliance with the will of God in all duties of obedience and abstinence from sin, out of a principle of faith and love; (3.) A designation of all the actions of life unto the glory of God by Jesus Christ, according to the gospel. This is holiness; so to be and so to do is to be holy.

And I shall divide my arguments into two sorts:— 1. Such as prove the necessity of holiness as to the essence of it, — holiness in our hearts and natures; 2. Such as prove the necessity of holiness as to the degrees of it, — holiness in our lives and conversations.

I. First, then, The nature of God as revealed unto us, with our dependence on him, the obligation that is upon us to live unto him, with the nature of our blessedness in the enjoyment of him, do require indispensably that we should be holy. The holiness of God's nature is everywhere in the Scripture made the fundamental principle and reason of the necessity of holiness in us. Himself makes it the ground of his command for it: Lev. xi. 44, "I am the Lord your God: ye shall therefore sanctify yourselves, and ye shall be holy; for I am holy." So also chap. xix. 2, xx. 7. And to show the everlasting equity and force of this reason, it is transferred over to the gospel: 1 Pet. i. 15, 16, "As he which hath called you is holy, so be ye holy in all manner of conversation; because it is written, Be ye holy; for I am holy." God lets them know that his nature is such as that unless they are sanctified and holy, there can be no such intercourse between him and them as ought to be between a God and his people. So he declares the sense of this enforcement of that precept to be: Lev. xi. 45, "I brought you up out of the land of Egypt, to be your God: ye shall therefore be holy, for I am holy;" — "Without this the relation designed cannot be maintained, that I should be your God and ye should be my people." To this purpose belongs that description given us of his nature, Ps. v. 4–6, "Thou art not a God that hath pleasure in wickedness: neither shall evil dwell with thee. The foolish shall not stand in thy sight: thou hatest all workers of iniquity. Thou shalt destroy them that speak lying: the Lord will abhor the bloody and deceitful man;" — answerable unto that of the prophet, "Thou art of purer eyes than to behold evil, and canst not look on iniquity," Hab. i. 13. He is such a God, — that is, such is his nature, so pure, so holy, — that previous to the consideration of any free acts of his will, it is evident that he can take no pleasure in fools, liars, or workers of iniquity. Therefore Joshua tells the people, that if they continued in their sins they could not serve the Lord, "for he is an holy God," chap. xxiv. 19. All the service of unholy persons towards this God is utterly lost and cast away, because it is inconsistent with his own holiness to accept of it. And our apostle argues in the same manner, Heb. xii. 28, 29, "Let us have grace, whereby we may serve God acceptably with reverence and godly fear: for our God is a consuming fire." He lays his argument for the necessity of grace and holiness in the worship of God from the consideration of the holiness of his nature, which, as a consuming fire, will devour that which is unsuited unto it, inconsistent with it. There would be no end of pursuing this reason of the necessity of holiness in all places where it is proposed expressly in the Scripture. I shall only add, in general, that God of old strictly required that no unholy, no unclean, no defiling thing should be in the camp of his people, because of his presence among them, who is himself holy; and without an exact observance hereof he declares that he will depart and leave them.

If we had no other argument to prove the necessity of holiness, and that it is indispensably required of us, but only this, that the God whom we serve and worship is absolutely holy, that his being and nature is such as that he can have no delightful intercourse with any that are unholy, it were abundantly sufficient unto our purpose. He who resolveth not to be holy had best seek another god to worship and serve; with our God he will never find acceptance. And therefore the heathen, who gave up themselves unto all filthiness with delight and greediness, to stifle the notions of a divine Being, that they might not control them in their sins and pleasures, fancied such gods to themselves as were wicked and unclean, that they might freely conform unto them and serve them with satisfaction. And God himself lets us know that men of wicked and flagitious lives have some secret thoughts that he is not holy, but like themselves, Ps. l. 21; for if they had not, they could not avoid it but they must either think of leaving him or their sins.

But we must yet farther observe some things to evidence the force of this argument; as, —

First, That unto us, in our present state and condition, the holiness of God as absolutely considered, merely as an infinite eternal property of the divine nature, is not the immediate ground of and motive unto holiness; but it is the holiness of God as manifested and revealed unto us in Christ Jesus. Under the first consideration, we who are sinners can make no conclusion from it but that of Joshua, "He is a holy God, a jealous God; he will not forgive your iniquities, nor spare." This we may learn, indeed, from thence, that nothing which is unholy can possibly subsist before him or find acceptance with him. But a motive and encouragement unto any holiness that is not absolutely perfect no creature can take from the consideration thereof; and we do not, we ought not to urge any such argument for the necessity of holiness as cannot be answered and complied with by the grace of God as to the substance, though we come short in the degrees of it. My meaning is, that no argument can be rationally and usefully pleaded for the necessity of holiness which doth not contain in itself an encouraging motive unto it. To declare it, necessary for us and at the same time impossible unto us, is not to promote its interest. They understand neither the holiness of God nor man who suppose that they are absolutely and immediately suited unto one another, or that, under that notion of it, we can take any encouraging motive unto our duty herein. Nay, no creature is capable of such a perfection in holiness as absolutely to answer the infinite purity of the divine nature, without a covenant condescension, Job iv. 18, xv. 15. But it is the holiness of God as he is in Christ, and as in Christ represented unto us, that gives us both the necessity and motive unto ours.

Wherefore, God, in dealing with his people of old in this matter, did not propose unto them to this end the absolute perfection of his own nature, but his being holy as he dwelt among them and was their God, — that is, in covenant; both which had respect unto Jesus Christ. In him all the glorious perfections of

God are so represented unto us as we may not thence only learn our duty, but also be encouraged unto it; for, —

1. All the properties of God as so represented unto us are more conspicuous, resplendent, alluring, and attractive, than as absolutely considered. I know not what light into and knowledge of the divine perfections Adam had in his state of innocency, when God had declared himself only in the works of nature, — sufficient, no doubt, it was to guide him in his love and obedience, or that life which he was to live unto him; — but I know that now all our knowledge of God and his properties, unless it be that which we have in and by Jesus Christ, is insufficient to lead or conduct us in that life of faith and obedience which is necessary unto us. He, therefore, gives us the "light of the knowledge of his glory in the face of Jesus Christ," 2 Cor. iv. 6, — that is, clear manifestations of his glorious excellencies. The light of the knowledge hereof is a clear, useful, saving perception and understanding of them. And this is not only directive unto holiness, but also effective of it; for thus "beholding the glory of the Lord," we are "changed into the same image from glory to glory," chap. iii. 18.

2. In particular, the fiery holiness of God is represented unto us in Christ, so as that although it loses nothing of declaring the indispensable necessity of holiness in all that draw nigh to him, yet under such a contemperation with goodness, grace, love, mercy, condescension, as may invite and encourage us to endeavour after a conformity thereunto.

3. Together with a representation of the holiness of God in Christ, there is a revelation made of what holiness in us he doth require and will accept. As was observed before, the consideration of it absolutely neither requires nor admits of any but that which is absolutely perfect; and where there is anyone failing, the whole of what we do is condemned, James ii. 10. This, therefore, can only perplex and torture the soul of a sinner, by pressing on him at the same time the necessity and impossibility of holiness, Isa. xxxiii. 14. But now, as God is in Christ, through his interposition and mediation he accepts of such a holiness in us as we are capable of, and which no man hath any discouragement from endeavouring to attain.

4. There is in and by Christ declared and administered a spiritual power of grace, which shall work this holiness in us, or that conformity unto the holiness of God which he doth require. From this fountain, therefore, we draw immediately, as the reasons of the necessity, so prevalent motives unto holiness in our souls. Hence some things may be inferenced; as, —

(1.) That the mediation of Christ, and in particular his satisfaction, is so far from being a hinderance of or a discouragement unto holiness, as some blasphemously pretend, that the great fundamental reason of it in us, — namely, the holiness of God himself, — can have no influence upon us without the supposition of it and faith in it. Unless faith be built hereon, no sinner upon a view of God's holiness, as absolutely considered, can have any other thoughts but those of Cain, "My sin is great; it cannot be pardoned. God is a holy God; I cannot serve him, and therefore will depart out of his presence." But the holiness of God as manifested in Jesus Christ, including a supposition of satisfaction made unto what is required by its absolute purity, and a condescension thereon to accept in him that holiness of truth and sincerity which we are capable of, doth equally maintain the indispensable necessity of it and encourage us unto it. And we may see what contrary conclusions will be made on these different considerations of it. Those who view it only in the first way can come to no other issue in their thoughts but that which they express in the prophet, Isa. xxxiii. 14, "Who among us shall dwell with the devouring fire? who among us shall dwell with everlasting burnings?" God's fiery holiness serves, towards them, unto no other end but to fill them with terror and despair. But other inferences are natural from the consideration of the same holiness in the latter way. "Our God," saith the apostle, "is a consuming fire." What then? what follows as our duty thereon? "Let us have grace, whereby we may serve him acceptably with reverence and godly fear," Heb. xii. 28, 29. There is no such forcible reason for, no such powerful motive unto, our adherence unto him in holy obedience. Such different conclusions will men make from these different considerations of the holiness of God, when once they come to be serious and in good earnest about them!

(2.) It follows from hence, also, that our holiness under the new covenant, although it has the same general nature and one principal end with that which was required in the covenant of works, yet as it hath an especial spring and fountain which that had not, and relates unto sundry causes which the other had no concernment in, so it is not of the same especial use therewith. The immediate end and use of that holiness in us was, to answer the holiness of God absolutely as expressed in the law; whereon we should have been justified. This is now done for us by Christ alone, and the holiness which God requireth of us respects only those ends which God hath proposed unto us in compliance with his own holiness as he will glorify it in Jesus Christ; which must be afterward declared.

Secondly, We may consider in what particular instances the force of this argument is conveyed unto us, or what are the especial reasons why we ought to be holy because God is so; and they are three:—

1. Because herein consists all that conformity unto God whereof in this world we are capable; which is our privilege, pre-eminence, glory, and honour. We were originally created in the image and likeness of God. Herein consisted the privilege, pre-eminence, order, and blessedness of our first state. And that, for the substance of it, it was no other but our holiness is by all confessed. Wherefore, without this conformity unto God, without the impress of his image and likeness upon us, we do not, we cannot, stand in that relation unto God which was designed us in our creation. This we lost by the entrance of sin. And if there be not a way for us to acquire it again, if we do not so, we shall always come short of the glory of God and of the end of our creation. Now, this is done in and by holiness alone, for therein consists the renovation of the image of God in us, as our apostle expressly declares, Eph. iv. 22–24, with Col. iii. 10. It is, therefore, to no purpose for any man to expect an interest in God, or any thing that will prove eternally to his advantage, who doth not endeavour after conformity unto him; for such a man despiseth all the glory that God designed unto himself in our creation, and all that was eminent and peculiarly bestowed upon ourselves.

He, therefore, whose design is not to be like unto God, according to his measure and the capacity of a creature, always misseth both of his end, his rule, and his way. Our Saviour would have his disciples to do all things so as that they may be the "children of their Father which is in heaven," Matt. v. 45; that is, like him, representing him, as children do their father. And the truth is, if this necessity of conformity unto God be once out of our view and consideration, we are easily turned aside by the meanest temptation we meet withal. In brief, without that likeness and conformity unto God which consists in holiness, as we do under his eye bear the image of his great adversary the devil, so we can have no especial interest in him, nor hath he any in us.

2. The force of the argument ariseth from the respect it bears unto our actual intercourse and communion with God. This we are called unto; and this, in all our duties of obedience, we must endeavour to attain. If there be not in them a real intercourse between God and our souls, they are all but uncertain beatings of the air. When we are accepted in them, when God is glorified by them, then have we in them this intercourse and communion with God. Now, whereas God is holy, if we are not in our measure holy, according to his mind, this cannot be; for God neither accepts of any duties from unholy persons nor is he glorified by them, and therefore as unto these ends doth he expressly reject and condemn them. It is a good duty to preach the word; but "unto the wicked God saith, What hast thou to do to declare my statutes, or that thou shouldest take my covenant in thy mouth? seeing thou hatest instruction, and castest my words behind thee," Ps. l. 16, 17, — "seeing thou art unholy." To pray is a good duty; but unto them that are not "washed" and made "clean," and "put not away the evil of their doings from before his eyes," saith God, "When ye spread forth your hands, I will hide mine eyes from you; yea, when ye make many prayers, I will not hear," Isa. i. 15, 16. And the like may be said of all other duties whatever.

It is certain, therefore, that whereas God is holy, if we are not so, all the duties which we design or intend to perform towards him are everlastingly lost, as unto their proper ends; for there is no intercourse or communion between light and darkness: "God is light, and in him is no darkness at all;" and "if we say that we have fellowship with him, and walk in darkness," as all unholy persons do, "we lie, and do not the truth: but if we walk in the light, as he is in the light, we have fellowship one with another; and truly our fellowship is with the Father, and with his Son Jesus Christ," 1 John i. 5–8. Now, what man that shall consider this, unless he be infatuated, would, for the love of any one sin, or out of conformity to the world, or any other thing, whereby the essence and truth of holiness is impeached, utterly lose and forfeit all the benefit and fruit of all those duties wherein perhaps he hath laboured, and which he hath, it may be, been at no small charge withal? But yet this is the condition of all men who come short in any thing that is essentially necessary unto universal holiness. All they do, all they suffer, all the pains they take, in and about religious duties, all their compliance with convictions, and what they do therein, within doors and without, is all lost, as unto the great ends of the glory of God and their own eternal blessedness, as sure as God is holy.

3. It ariseth from a respect unto our future everlasting enjoyment of him. This is our utmost end, which if we come short of (life itself is the greatest loss), better ten thousand times we had never been; for without it a continuance in everlasting miseries is inseparable from our state and condition. Now, this is never attainable by any unholy person. "Follow holiness," saith our apostle, "without which no man shall see the Lord;" for it is the "pure in heart" only that "shall see God," Matt. v. 8. It is hereby that we are "made meet for the inheritance of the saints in light," Col. i. 12. Neither can we attain it before we are thus made meet for it. No unclean thing, nothing that defileth or is defiled, shall ever be brought into the glorious presence of this holy God. There is no

imagination wherewith mankind is besotted more foolish, none so pernicious, as this, that persons not purified, not sanctified, not made holy, in this life, should afterward be taken into that state of blessedness which consists in the enjoyment of God. There can be no thought more reproachful to his glory, nor more inconsistent with the nature of the things themselves; for neither can such persons enjoy him, nor would God himself be a reward unto them. They can have nothing whereby they should adhere unto him as their chiefest good, nor can they see any thing in him that should give them rest or satisfaction; nor can there be any medium whereby God should communicate himself unto them, supposing them to continue thus unholy, as all must do who depart out of this life in that condition. Holiness, indeed, is perfected in heaven, but the beginning of it is invariably and unalterably confined to this world; and where this fails, no hand shall be put unto that work unto eternity. All unholy persons, therefore, who feed and refresh themselves with hopes of heaven and eternity do it merely on false notions of God and blessedness, whereby they deceive themselves. Heaven is a place where as well they would not be as they cannot be; in itself it is neither desired by them nor fit for them. "He that hath this hope" indeed, that he shall see God, "purifieth himself, even as he is pure," 1 John iii. 2, 3. There is, therefore, a manifold necessity of holiness impressed on us from the consideration of the nature of that God whom we serve and hope to enjoy, which is holy.

I cannot pass over this consideration without making some especial improvement of it. We have seen how all our concernment and interest in God, both here and hereafter, do depend on our being holy. They invented a very effectual means for the prejudicing, yea, indeed, a fatal engine for the ruin, of true holiness in the world, who built it on no other bottom, nor pressed it on any other motive, but that the acts and fruits of it were meritorious in the sight of God; for whether this be believed and complied withal or not, true holiness is ruined if no other more effectual reason be substituted in its room. Reject this motive, and there is no need of it; which I am persuaded hath really taken place in many, who, being taught that good deeds are not meritorious, have concluded them useless. Comply with it, and you destroy the nature of true holiness, and turn all the pretended duties of it into fruits and effects of spiritual pride and blind superstition. But we see the necessity of it with respect unto God hath other foundations, suited unto and consistent with the grace, and love, and mercy of the gospel. And we shall fully show in our progress, that there is not one motive unto it, that is of any real force or efficacy, but perfectly complies with the whole doctrine of the free, undeserved grace of God towards us by Jesus Christ; nor is there any of them which gives the least countenance unto any thing of worth in ourselves, as from ourselves, or that should take us off from an absolute and universal dependence on Christ for life and salvation. But yet such they are as render it as necessary unto us to be holy, — that is, to be sanctified, — as to be justified. He that thinks to please God and to come to the enjoyment of him without holiness makes him an unholy God, putting the highest indignity and dishonour imaginable upon him. God deliver poor sinners from this deceit! There is no remedy; you must leave your sins or your God. You may as easily reconcile heaven and hell, the one remaining heaven and the other hell, as easily take away all difference between light and darkness, good and evil, as procure acceptance for unholy persons with our God. Some live without God in the world; whether they have any notion of his being or no is not material. They live without any regard unto him, either as unto his present rule over them or his future disposal of them. It is no wonder if holiness, both name and thing, be universally despised by these persons, their design being to serve their lusts to the utmost, and immerse themselves in the pleasures of the world, without once taking God into their thoughts; they can do no otherwise. But for men who live under some constant sense of God and an eternal accountableness unto him, and thereon do many things he requires, and abstain from many sins that their inclinations and opportunities would suggest and prompt them unto, not to endeavour after that universal holiness which alone will be accepted with him, is a deplorable folly. Such men seem to worship an idol all their days; for he that doth not endeavour to be like unto God doth contrarily wickedly think that God is like unto himself. It is true, our interest in God is not built upon our holiness; but it is as true that we have none without it. Were this principle once well fixed in the minds of men, that without holiness no man shall see God, and that enforced from the consideration of the nature of God himself, it could not but influence them unto a greater diligence about it than the most seem to be engaged in.

There is, indeed, amongst us a great plea for morality, or for moral virtue; — I wish it be more out of love to virtue itself and a conviction of its usefulness than out of a design to cast contempt on the grace of our Lord Jesus Christ and the gospel, as it is declared by the faithful dispensers of it. However, we are bound to believe the best of all men. Where we see those who so plead for moral virtue to be in their own persons, and in their lives, modest, sober, humble, patient, self-denying, charitable, useful towards all, we are obliged to believe that their pleas for moral virtue proceed from a love and liking of it; but where men are proud, furious, worldly, revengeful, profane, intemperate, covetous, ambitious, I cannot so well understand their declamations about virtue. Only, I would for the present inquire what it is that they intend by their morality. Is it the renovation of the image of God in us by grace? is it our conformity from thence unto him in his holiness? is it our being holy in all manner of holiness, because God is holy? is it the acting of our souls in all duties of obedience, from a principle of faith and love, according to the will of God, whereby we have communion with him here and are led towards the enjoyment of him? If these are the things which they intend, what is the matter with them? Why are they so afraid of the words and expressions of the Scripture? Why will they not speak of the things of God in words that the Holy Ghost teacheth? Men never dislike the words of. God but when they dislike the things of God. Is it because these expressions are not intelligible, — people do not know what they mean, but this of moral virtue they understand well enough? We appeal to the experience of all that truly fear God in the world unto the contrary. There is none of them but the Scripture expressions of the causes, nature, work, and effects of holiness, do convey a clear, experimental apprehension of them unto their minds; whereas, by their "moral virtue," neither themselves nor any else do know what they intend, since they do or must reject the common received notion of it, for honesty amongst men. If, therefore, they intend that holiness hereby which is required of us in the Scripture, and that particularly on the account of the holiness of that God whom we serve, they fall into a high contempt of the wisdom of God, in despising of those notices and expressions of it which, being used by the Holy Ghost, are suited unto the spiritual light and understanding of believers; substituting their own arbitrary, doubtful, uncertain sentiments and words in their room and place. But if it be something else which they intend (as, indeed, evidently it is, nor doth any man understand more in the design than sobriety and usefulness in the world, things singularly good in their proper place), then it is no otherwise to be looked on but as a design of Satan to undermine the true holiness of the gospel, and to substitute a deceitful and deceiving cloud or shadow in the room of it. And, moreover, what we have already discoursed doth abundantly evince the folly and falsehood of those clamorous accusations, wherein the most important truths of the gospel are charged as inconsistent with and as repugnant unto holiness. "The doctrine," say the Socinians, "of the satisfaction of Christ, ruins all care and endeavours after a holy life; for when men do believe that Christ hath satisfied the justice of God for their sins, they will be inclined to be careless about them, yea, to live in them." But as this supposition doth transform believers into monsters of ingratitude and folly, so it is built on no other foundation than this, that if Christ take away the guilt of sin, there is no reason in the nature of these things, nor mentioned in the Scripture, why we should need to be holy, and keep ourselves from the power, filth, and dominion of sin, or any way glorify God in this world; which is an inference weak, false, and ridiculous. The Papists, and others with them, lay the same charge on the doctrine of justification through the imputation of the righteousness of Christ unto us. And it is wonderful to consider with what virulent railing this charge is managed by the Papists, so with what scorn and scoffing, with what stories and tales, some amongst ourselves endeavour to expose this sacred truth to contempt, as though all those by whom it is believed must consequently be negligent of holiness and good works. Now, although I deny not but that such men may find a great strength of connection between these things in their own minds, seeing there is a principle in the corrupt heart of men to "turn the grace of God into lasciviousness;" yet (as shall in due time be proved) this sacred truth is, both doctrinally and practically, the great constraining principle unto holiness and fruitfulness in obedience. For the present, I shall return no other answer unto those objections, but that the objectors are wholly mistaken in our thoughts and apprehensions concerning that God whom we serve. God in Christ, whom we worship, hath so revealed his own holiness unto us, and what is necessary for us on the account thereof, as that we know it to be a foolish, wicked, and blasphemous thing for anyone to think to please him, to be accepted with him, to come to the enjoyment of him, without that holiness which he requireth, and from his own nature cannot but require. That the grace, or mercy, or love of this God, who is our God, should encourage those who indeed know him unto sin, or countenance them in a neglect of holy obedience to him, is a monstrous imagination. There are, as I shall show afterward, other invincible reasons for it, and motives unto it; but the owning of this one consideration alone by them who believe the grace of the gospel is sufficient to secure them from the reproach of this objection.

Moreover, from what hath been discoursed, we may all charge ourselves with blame for our sloth and negligence in this matter. It is to be feared that we have none of us endeavoured as we ought to grow up into this image and likeness of God. And although, for the main of our duty herein, our hearts may not condemn us, yet there are, no doubt, sundry things that belong unto it wherein we have all failed. Our likeness unto God, that wherein we bear his image, is our holiness, as hath been declared. Wherever there is the holiness of truth before described, in the essence of it, there is a radical conformity and likeness unto God. In the first communication of it unto us through the promises of the gospel, we are "made partakers τῆς[1] θείας φύσεως, of the divine nature," 2 Pet. i. 4, — such a new spiritual nature as represents that of God himself. Being begotten by him, we are made partakers of his nature. But though all children do partake of the nature of their parents, yet they may be, and some of them are, very deformed, and bear very little of their likeness. So is it in this matter. We may have the image of God in our hearts, and yet come short of that likeness unto him, in its degrees and improvement, which we ought to aim at. And this happens two ways:— (1.) When our graces are weak, withering, and unthrifty; for in their flourishing and fruit-bearing is our likeness unto God evidenced, and in them doth the glory of God in this world consist. (2.) When, by the power of our corruptions or our temptations, we contract a deformity, something that hath the likeness of the old crooked serpent. Where either of these befall us, that our graces are low and thriftless, [or] that our corruptions are high and active, frequently discovering themselves, there, though the image of God may be in us, there is not much of his likeness upon us, and we come short of our duty in this great and fundamental duty of our faith and profession. So far as it is thus with us, may we not, ought we not, greatly to blame ourselves? Why are we so slow, so negligent, in the pursuit of our principal interest and happiness? Why do we suffer everything, why do we suffer any thing, to divert our minds from, or retard our endeavours in, this design? Wherefore, that I may contribute something to the awakening of our diligence herein, I shall add some few motives unto it and some directions for it, that herein we may be found "perfecting holiness in the fear of God;" which is the only way whereby we may be like unto him in this world:—

First, In our likeness unto God consists the excellency and preeminence of our nature above that of all other creatures in the world, and of our persons above those of other men who are not partakers of his image. For, —

1. With reference unto other things, this is the highest excellency that a created nature is capable of. Other things had external impressions of the greatness, power, and goodness of God upon them; man alone, in this lower world, was capable of the image of God in him. The perfection, the glory, the pre-eminence of our nature, in the first creation, was expressed only by this, that we were made in the image and likeness of God, Gen. i. 26, 27. This gave us a pre-eminence above all other creatures, and hence a dominion over them ensued; for although God made a distinct grant of it unto us, that we might the better understand and be thankful for our privilege, yet was it a necessary consequence of his image in us. And this is that which James respects, where he tells us that πᾶσα φύσις, "every nature," the nature of all things in their several kinds, δαμάζεται τῇ φύσει τῇ ἀνθρωπίνῃ, "is tamed," that is, subjected to the nature of man, chap. iii. 7. He renders כָּבַשׁ, Gen. i. 28, by δαμάζω, which the LXX. render κατακυριεύω, "subdue it." But being not contented to be like God, that is, in holiness and righteousness, we would be as God in wisdom and sovereignty; and not attaining what we aimed at, we lost what we had, chap. iii. 5, 6. Being in "honour we continued not, but became like the beasts that perish," Ps. xlix. 12. We were first like God, and then like beasts, 2 Pet. ii. 12. By the loss of the image of God, our nature lost its preeminence, and we were reduced into order amongst perishing beasts; for notwithstanding some feeble relics of this image yet abiding with us, we have really, with respect unto our

proper end, in our lapsed condition, more of the bestial nature in us than of the divine. Wherefore, the restoration of this image in us by the grace of Jesus Christ, Eph. iv. 24, Col. iii. 10, is the recovery of that pre-eminence and privilege of our nature which we had foolishly lost. Hereby there is an impression again made upon our nature of the authority of God, which gives us a pre-eminence above other creatures and a rule over them; yea, that whole dominion which mankind scrambles for with craft and violence over the residue of the creation depends on this renovation of the image of God in some of them. Not that I judge that men's right and title to their portion and interests in this world doth depend on their own personal grace or holiness; but that if God had not designed to renew his image in our nature by Jesus Christ, and, as the foundation thereof, to take our nature into union with himself in the person of his Son, and thereby to gather up all things unto a new head in him, and to make him the first-born of the creation, the head and heir of all, he would not have continued any thing of right or title therein. It was upon the promise and the establishment of the new covenant that this right was restored unto us. So it is expressed in the renovation of the covenant with Noah and his children: Gen. ix. 1, 2, "God blessed Noah and his sons, and said unto them, Be fruitful, and multiply, and replenish the earth. And the fear of you and the dread of you shall be upon every beast of the earth, and upon every fowl of the air, and upon all that moveth upon the earth, and upon all the fishes of the sea; into your hand are they delivered;" which is an express renovation of the grant made unto us at our first creation, chap. i. 28, the right whereunto we had lost in our loss of the image of God. And, therefore, in that service wherein the creature is continued unto mankind, it is made "subject to vanity" and put into "bondage;" in which state, though it groan and look out, as it were, for deliverance, it must continue until God hath accomplished the whole design of the "glorious liberty of his children," Rom. viii. 20, 21. Whatever they may pride themselves in, their parts or enjoyments, however they may sport themselves in the use or abuse of other creatures, if this image of God be not renewed in them, they have really no great preeminence above the things which perish under their hands, 2 Pet. ii. 12. God having exalted our natures, by union with himself in the person of his Son, requires of us to preserve its dignity above others.

2. Again, this is that which gives privilege and pre-eminence unto the persons of some above others. "The righteous," saith the wise man, "is more excellent than his neighbour," Prov. xii. 26. It is seldom that this is so upon the account of civil wisdom, wealth, greatness, or power. There is nothing can establish this general rule but their conformity and likeness to God. Hence are such persons called "the saints in the earth," and "the excellent," Ps. xvi.

3. Both the terms, קְדוֹשִׁים and אַדִּירִים, do first belong properly to God. He above [all] is absolutely קָדוֹשׁ, or "holy," and he is אַדִּיר, Ps. viii. 9. Unto men they are ascribed upon their likeness unto him in holiness. This makes them the "saints and excellent in the earth;" which gives them a pre-eminence of office and authority in some above others. And this dignity of office reflects a dignity of person on them who are vested in it, and communicates a pre-eminence unto them; for their office and authority is from God, which gives both it and them a real privilege and honour above others. But that which is originally in and from persons themselves is solely from the renovation of the image of God in them, and is heightened and increased according to the degrees they attain in the participation of it. The more holy, the more honourable. Hence, wicked men in

the Scripture are said to be vile: אָדָם לִבְנֵי זֻלּוּת, Ps. xii. 8, "quisquiliæ hominum," — "trifling vilenesses;" and the righteous are said to be "precious" and valuable. And hence it is that there hath ofttimes an awe been put on the spirits of vile and outrageous sinners from the appearances of God in holy persons. And, indeed, at all times, where men do eminently bear a conformity to God in holiness, wicked men, exasperated by their secular interests, prejudices, and an unconquerable adherence to their lusts, may oppose, revile, reproach, and persecute them; but secretly, in their hearts, they have an awe, from the likeness of God in them, whence they will sometimes dread them, sometimes flatter them, and sometimes wish that they were not, even as they deal with God himself. Why do we weary ourselves about other things? Why do we "spend our labour in vain, and our strength for that which is not bread?" Such will all endeavours after any other excellency at length appear.

Herein lies the whole of that dignity which our nature was made for, and is capable of. Sin is the sole debasement of it, — that alone whereby we render ourselves base and contemptible. Men's self-pleasing in the ways and fruits of it, or in worldly advantages, and their mutual applauses of one another, will suddenly vanish into smoke. It is holiness alone that is honourable, and that because there is in it the image and representation of God. I think we are satisfied that the dignity of professors above others doth not consist in worldly or secular advantages, for they are very few who have them: "Not many wise men after the flesh, not many mighty, not many noble, are called," 1 Cor. i. 26. Nor doth it consist in spiritual gifts. Many who have excelled us, not only in the degree of them, but in the kind also, who have had extraordinary gifts of the Spirit, shall be shut out of heaven with the worst of the world: Matt. vii. 22, 23, "Many will say to me in that day, Lord, Lord, have we not prophesied in thy name? and in thy name have cast out devils? and in thy name wrought δυνάμεις πολλάς, many miraculous works?" — which is more than any of us can say; — yet Christ will "profess unto them, 'I never knew you: depart from me, ye that work iniquity,' ye unholy persons." Nor is it in profession itself. Many make it in rigid austerities, renunciation of the world, and outward works of charity, beyond the most of us, and yet perish in their superstitions. Nor is it in the purity of worship, without such mixtures of human inventions as others defile the service of God withal; for multitudes may be made partakers thereof in the "great house" of God, and yet be "vessels of wood and stone," who, being not "purged from sin," are not "vessels unto honour, sanctified, and meet for the Master's use," 2 Tim. ii. 20, 21. It consists, therefore, alone in that likeness unto God which we have in and by holiness, with what doth attend it and is inseparable from it. Where this is not, no other thing will exempt us from the common herd of perishing mankind.

Secondly, According unto our growth and improvement in this likeness unto God are our accesses and approaches towards glory. We are drawing everyday towards our natural end, whether we will or no; and if we do not therewithal draw nearer towards our supernatural end in glory, we are most miserable. Now, men do but deceive themselves if they suppose that they are approaching towards glory in time, if they are not at the same time making nearer unto it in grace. It is some representation of future glory, that therein we shall be ἰσάγγελοι, Luke xx. 36, like or "equal unto the angels." But that respects one particular only of that state. It is a far more excellent description of it that we shall be like unto God: "When he shall appear, we shall be like him;

for we shall see him as he is," John iii. 2. Our glory, as subjectively considered, will be our likeness unto God, according to the capacity of creatures. And it is the highest folly for any to think that they shall love that hereafter which now they hate; that that will be their glory which they now abhor. Such sottish contradictions are the minds of men filled withal! There is nothing in this world which they more despise than to be like unto God, and they hate everyone that is so; yet pretend a desire and expectation of that estate wherein they shall be so, which is a being so forever! But this will be our glory, to "behold the face of God in righteousness," and to be "satisfied with his likeness," Ps. xvii. 15. How, then, shall we make approaches towards this glory spiritually, which at least may answer the approaches we make towards our end naturally, seeing not to do so is folly and intolerable negligence? We have no other way but thriving and growing in that likeness of God which we have here in holiness. Hereby alone are we "changed into the image of God from glory to glory," 2 Cor. iii. 18, — from one glorious degree of grace unto another, until one great change shall issue all grace and holiness in eternal glory. And in our desires for heaven, if they are regular, we consider not so much our freedom from trouble as from sin; nor is our aim in the first place so much at complete happiness as perfect holiness. And they who desire heaven as that which would only ease them of their troubles, and not as that which will perfectly free them of sin, will fall into a state wherein sin and trouble shall be eternally inseparable. As, therefore, we would continually tend towards our rest and blessedness, as we would have assured and evident pledges of it in our own souls, as we would have foretastes of it and an experimental acquaintance with it, (as who would not know as much as is possible of his eternal blessedness?) this is the design which we ought to pursue. It is to be feared that the most of us know not how much of glory may be in present grace, nor how much of heaven may be attained in holiness on the earth. We have a generation amongst us that would fain be boasting of perfection, whilst in their minds they are evidently under the power of darkness, — corrupt in their affections and worldly in their lives. But our duty it is to be always "perfecting holiness in the fear of God." This, pursued in a due manner, is continually transforming the soul into the likeness of God. Much of the glory of heaven may dwell in a simple cottage, and poor persons, even under rags, may be very like unto God.

Thirdly, It is from our likeness and conformity unto God alone that we are or may be useful in the world, in a due manner and order. I shall have occasion to speak more unto this afterward, and shall therefore here only touch upon it, with respect unto one concernment or circumstance. God is the great preserver and benefactor of the whole creation; "he is good, and doeth good;" he is the sole cause and fountain of all good that in any kind any creature is made partaker of. And there is no property of God more celebrated in the Scripture than this of his goodness, and his giving out of the fruits of it to all his creatures. And he is so only good, that there is nothing so in any sense but by a participation of it, and a likeness unto him therein. They, therefore, who are like unto God, and they only, are useful in this world. There is, indeed, or at least there hath been, much good, useful good, done by others, on various convictions and for various ends; but there is one flaw or other in all they do. Either superstition, or vain-glory, or selfishness, or merit, or one thing or other, gets into all the good that is done by unholy persons, and brings death into the pot; so that although it may be of some use in particulars, unto individual persons, in some seasons, it is of none unto the general good of the whole. He that bears the likeness of God, and in all that he doth acts from that principle, he alone is truly useful, represents God in what he doth, and spoils it not by false ends of his own. If, therefore, we would keep up the privilege and pre-eminence of our nature and persons; if we would make due and daily accessions towards glory and blessedness; if we would be of any real use in this world, — our great endeavour ought to be to grow up more and more into this likeness of God, which consists in our holiness.

It will, therefore, or it may, be justly here inquired, how or what we may do that we may thrive and grow up more and more into this likeness unto God. To remit other considerations unto their proper place, at present I answer, that there are some graces of holiness that are effectually assimilating, and others that are declarative and expressive of this likeness of God in us:—

First, Those of the first sort, which have a peculiar efficacy to promote the likeness of God in our souls, are faith and love, in whose constant exercise we ought to abide and abound if we intend to grow in likeness and conformity to God:—

1. Faith is a part of our holiness as it is a grace of the sanctifying Spirit, and it is a principle of holiness as it purifies the heart and is effectual by love. The more faith is in its due and proper exercise, the more holy we shall be, and consequently the more like unto God. This were a large theme; I shall confine it unto one instance. The glorious properties of God, as we have showed before, are manifested and revealed in Jesus Christ; "in his face do they shine forth." The only way whereby we behold them, whereby we have an intuition into them, is by faith. In Christ are the glorious excellencies of God represented unto us, and by faith do we behold them. And what is the effect hereof? "We are changed into the same image" and likeness "from glory to glory," 2 Cor. iii. 18. This is the great mystery of growing in holiness and thriving in the image of God, which the world being ignorant of have laboured in vain by other means to satisfy their notions and convictions. But this is the great way and means of it, appointed and blessed of God unto that purpose, — namely, constantly by faith, in a way of believing the revelation made in the gospel, to view, behold, and contemplate on the excellencies of God, his goodness, holiness, righteousness, love, and grace, as manifested in Jesus Christ, and that so as to make use of, and apply unto ourselves and our condition, the effects and fruits of them, according to the promise of the gospel. This is the great arcanum of growing up into the likeness of God, without which, however men may multiply duties in a compliance with their convictions, they will have never the more conformity to God; and all professors who come short in this matter do or may know, that it ariseth from their want of a constant exercise of faith on God in Christ. If, therefore, we have a real design of being yet more like unto God, — which is our privilege, safety, glory, blessedness, — this is the way we must take for its accomplishment. Abound in actings of faith, and we shall thrive in holiness; and they are but acts of presumption, under the name of faith, which do not infallibly produce this effect.

2. Love hath the same tendency and efficacy; I mean, the love of God. He that would be like unto God must be sure to love him, or all other endeavours to that purpose will be in vain; and he that loves God sincerely will be like him. Under the Old Testament, none in his general course so like unto God as David, called, therefore, "The man after God's own heart;" and none ever made greater

expressions of love unto him, which occur continually in the Psalms. And let men take what pains they can in acts and duties of obedience, if they proceed not from a principle of divine love, their likeness unto God will not be increased by them. All love, in general, hath an assimilating efficacy; it casts the mind into the mould of the thing beloved. So love of this world makes men earthly minded; their minds and affections grow earthly, carnal, and sensual. But of all kinds, divine love is most effectual to this purpose, as having the best, the most noble, proper, and attractive object. It is our adherence unto God with delight, for what he is in himself, as manifested in Jesus Christ. By it we cleave unto God, and so keep near him, and thereby derive transforming virtue from him. Every approach unto God by ardent love and delight is transfiguring. And it acts itself continually by, — (1.) Contemplation; (2.) Admiration; and, (3.) Delight in obedience.

(1.) Love acts itself by contemplation. It is in the nature of it to be meditating and contemplating on the excellencies of God in Christ; yea, this is the life of it, and where this is not, there is no love. A heart filled with the love of God will night and day be exercising itself in and with thoughts of God's glorious excellencies, rejoicing in them. This the psalmist exhorts us unto: Ps. xxx. 4, "Sing unto the Lord, O ye saints of his, and give thanks at the remembrance of his holiness." And love will do the same with respect unto all his other properties. See to this purpose Ps. lxiii. throughout. And this will further our likeness unto him. Our minds by it will be changed into the image of what we contemplate, and we shall endeavour that our lives be conformed thereunto.

(2.) It works by admiration also. This is the voice of love, "How great is his goodness! how great is his beauty!" Zech. ix. 17. The soul being, as it were, ravished with that view which it hath of the glorious excellencies of God in Christ, hath no way to express its affections but by admiration. "How great is his goodness! how great is his beauty!" And this beauty of God is that sweetness and holy symmetry of glory (if I may be allowed to speak so improperly) in all the perfections of God, being all in a sweet correspondency exalted in Christ, which is the proper object of our love. To see infinite holiness, purity, and righteousness, with infinite love, goodness, grace, and mercy, all equally glorified in and towards the same things and persons, one glimpse whereof is not to be attained in the world out of Christ, is that beauty of God which attracts the love of a believing soul, and fills it with a holy admiration of him. And this also is a most effectual furtherance of our conformity unto him, which without these steps we shall labour in vain after.

(3.) Again, love gives delight in obedience and all the duties of it. The common instance of Jacob is known, of whom it is said that his seven years' service seemed short and easy to him, for the love he bare to Rachel. He did that with delight which he would not afterward undergo for the greatest wages. But we have a greater instance. Our Lord Jesus Christ says concerning all the obedience that was required of him, "Thy law, O God, is in my heart; I delight to do thy will." And yet we know how terrible to nature were the things he did and suffered in obedience to that law. But his unspeakable love to God and the souls of men rendered it all his delight. Hence follow intension and frequency in all the duties of it. And where these two are, intension of mind and spirit, with a frequency of holy duties, both proceeding from delight, there holiness will thrive; and consequently we shall do so in our conformity to God. In brief, love and likeness unto God are inseparable, and proportionate unto one another; and without this no duties of obedience are any part of his image.

Secondly, There are graces which are declarative of this assimilation, or which evidence and manifest our likeness unto God. I shall instance only in two of them, —

1. And the first is such as I shall give many names unto it in its description, as the Scripture doth also; but the thing intended is one and the same. This is goodness, kindness, benignity, love, with readiness to do good, to forgive, to help and relieve, and this towards all men, on all occasions. And this also is to be considered in opposition unto an evil habit of mind exerting itself in many vices, which yet agree in the same general nature: such are anger, wrath, envy, malice, revenge, frowardness, selfishness; all which are directly opposite to the grace of holiness at present instanced in and pleaded for. And this, I fear, is not so considered as it ought to be; for if it were, it would not be so common a thing as, it may be, it is, for men to plead highly for the imitation of God, and almost in all they do give us a full representation of the devil: for as this universal benignity and love to all is the greatest representation of the nature of God on earth, so is fierceness, envy, wrath, and revenge, of that of the devil. Would we, then, be like unto our heavenly Father, would we manifest that we are so unto his glory, would we represent him in and unto the world, it must be by this frame of spirit, and actings constantly suited thereunto. This our blessed Saviour instructs us in and unto, Matt. v. 44, 45. A man, I say, thus good, his nature being cured and rectified by grace, thence useful and helpful, free from guile, envy and selfishness, pride and elation of mind, is the best representation we can have of God on the earth, since the human nature of Christ was removed from us.

This, therefore, we are to labour after if we intend to be like God, or to manifest his glory in our persons and lives unto the world. And no small part of our holiness consists herein. Many lusts, corruptions, and distempered passions, are to be subdued by grace, if we design to be eminent. Strong bents and inclinations of mind to comply with innumerable provocations and exasperations that will befall us must be corrected and discarded; many duties [must] be constantly attended unto, and sundry graces kept up to their exercise. The whole drove of temptations, all whose force consists in a pretence of care for self, must be scattered or resisted. And hence it is that in the Scripture a good man, a merciful man, a useful, liberal man, is frequently spoken of, by way of eminency and distinction, as one whom God hath an especial regard unto, and concerning whom there are peculiar promises. When men live to themselves, and are satisfied that they do no hurt, though they do no good; are secure, selfish, wrathful, angry, peevish, or have their kindness confined to their relations, or are otherwise little useful but in what they are pressed unto, and therein come off with difficulty in their own minds; who esteem all lost that is done for the relief of others, and the greatest part of wisdom to be cautious, and disbelieve the necessities of men; in a word, that make self and its concernments the end of their lives; — whatever otherwise their profession be, or their diligence in religious duties, they do very little either represent or glorify God in the world. If we, therefore, design to be holy, let us constantly, in our families, towards our relations, in churches, in our conversation in the world, and dealings with all men; towards our enemies and persecutors, the worst of them, so far as they are ours only; towards all mankind as we have opportunity, — labour after conformity unto God, and to express our likeness unto him, in this philanthropy, goodness, benignity, condescension, readiness to forgive, to help and relieve; without which we neither are nor can be the children of our Father which is in heaven.

Especially is this frame of heart, and actings suitable thereunto, required of us with respect unto the saints of God, unto believers. Even God himself, whom we are bound to imitate, and a conformity unto whom we are pressing after, doth exercise his benignity and kindness in a peculiar manner towards them: 1 Tim. iv. 10, "He is the saviour of all men," but "specially of those that believe." There is a speciality in the exercise of his saving goodness towards believers. And in answer hereunto, we are likewise commanded to "do good unto all men," but "especially unto them who are of the household of faith," Gal. vi. 10. Although we are obliged to the exercise of the goodness before described unto all men whatever, as we have opportunity, yet we are allowed, yea, we are enjoined, a peculiar regard herein unto the household of faith. And if this were more in exercise, if we esteemed ourselves (notwithstanding the provocations and exasperations which we meet withal, or suppose we do so, when perhaps none are given us or intended us) obliged to express this benignity, kindness, goodness, forbearance, and love towards all believers in an especial manner, it would prevent or remove many of those scandalous offences and animosities that are among us. If in common we do love them that love us, and do good to them that do good to us, and delight in them who are of our company and go the same way with us, it may advance us in the condition of Pharisees and publicans, for they did so also. But if among believers we will take this course, love them only, delight in them only, be open and free in all effects of genuine kindness towards them who go our way, or are of our party, or are kind and friendly to us, or that never gave us provocations really nor in our own surmises, we are so far and therein worse than either Pharisees or publicans. We are to endeavour conformity and likeness unto God, not only as he is the God of nature, and is good unto all the works of his hands, but as he is our heavenly Father, and is good, kind, benign, merciful, in an especial manner, unto the whole family of his children, however differenced among themselves, or indeed unkind or provoking unto him. I confess, when I see men apt to retain a sense of old provocations and differences; ready to receive impressions of new ones, or ready for apprehensions of such, where there are none; incredulous of the sincerity of others who profess a readiness for love and peace; to take things in the worst sense; to be morose and severe towards this or that sort of believers, unready to help them, scarce desiring their prosperity, or it may be their safety, — I cannot but look upon it as a very great stain to their profession, whatever else it be: and by this rule would I have my own ways examined.

2. Truth is another grace, another part of holiness, of the same import and nature. Truth is used in the Scripture for uprightness and integrity, — "Thou requirest truth in the inward parts," Ps. li. 6, — and frequently for the doctrine of truth, as of God revealed and by us believed. But that which I intend is only what is enjoined us by the apostle, — namely, in all things to "speak the truth in love," Eph. iv. 15. Our apostasy from God was eminently from him as the God of truth; by an opposition to which attribute we sought to dethrone him from his glory. We would not believe that his word was truth. And sin entered into the world by and with a long train of lies; and ever since, the whole world,

and everything in it, is filled with them; which represents him and his nature who is the father of lies and liars. Hereby doth it visibly and openly continue in its apostasy from the God of truth. I could willingly stay to manifest how the whole world is corrupted, depraved, and sullied by lies of all sorts, but I must not divert thereunto. Wherefore, truth and sincerity in words, — for that at present I must confine myself unto, — is an effect of the renovation of the image of God in us, and a representation of him to the world. No duty is more frequently pressed upon us: "Put away false speaking;" "Lie not one to another;" "Speak the truth in love." And the consideration hereof is exceeding necessary unto all those who by their course of life are engaged in trading; and that both because of the disreputation which by the evil practices of some, of many (that I say not of the most), is cast upon that course of life, and also because failures in truth are apt a thousand ways to insinuate themselves into the practices of such persons, yea, when they are not aware thereof. "It is naught, it is naught, saith the buyer, but when he goeth away he boasteth;" and "It is good, it is good, saith the seller, but when he hath sold it he boasteth," or is well pleased with the advantage which he hath made by his words. But these things have the image of Satan upon them, and are most opposite to the God of truth. Another occasion must be taken farther to press this necessary duty; only at present, I do but intimate that where truth is not universally observed, according to the utmost watchfulness of sincerity and love, there all other marks and tokens of the image of God in any persons are not only sullied but defaced, and the representation of Satan is most prevalent. And these things I could not but add, as naturally consequential unto that first principal argument for the necessity of holiness which we have proposed and insisted on.

Having despatched this first argument, and added unto it some especial improvements with respect unto its influence into our practice, it remains only that we free it from one objection, which it seems exposed unto. Now, this ariseth from the consideration of the infinite grace, mercy, and love of God, as they are proposed in the dispensation of the word; for it may be said unto us, and like enough it will, considering the frame of men's minds in the days wherein we live, "Do not you yourselves, who thus press unto holiness, and the necessity of it, from the consideration of the nature of God, preach unto us every day the greatness of his mercy towards all sorts of sinners, his readiness to receive them, his willingness to pardon them, and that freely in Christ, without the consideration of any worth, merit, or righteousness of their own? And do you not herein invite all sorts of sinners, the worst and the greatest, to come unto him by Christ, that they may be pardoned and accepted? Whence, then, can arise any argument for the necessity of holiness from the consideration of the nature of this God, whose inestimable treasures of grace, and the freedom of whose love and mercy towards sinners, no tongue, as you say, can express?"

Ans. 1. This objection is very natural unto carnal and unbelieving minds, and therefore we shall meet with it at every turn. There is nothing seems more reasonable unto them than that we may live in sin because grace hath abounded. If men must yet be holy, they can see no need nor use of grace; and they cannot see that God is gracious to any purpose, if notwithstanding men may perish because they are not holy. But this objection is raised, rejected, and condemned by our apostle, in whose judgment we may acquiesce, Rom. vi. 1; and in the same place he subjoins the reasons why, notwithstanding the superabounding grace of God in Christ, there is an indispensable necessity that all believers should be holy.

2. God himself hath obviated this objection. He proclaims his name, Exod. xxxiv. 6, 7, "The Lord, The Lord God, merciful and gracious, long-suffering, and abundant in goodness and truth, keeping mercy for thousands, forgiving iniquity and transgression and sin." Had he stood here, and neither in this nor in any other place of Scripture farther declared his nature and unchangeable purposes concerning sinners, some colour might have been laid on this objection. But he adds immediately, "and that will by no means clear the guilty," — that is, as it is explained in places of Scripture innumerable, such as go on in their sins, without regard unto obedience and holiness springing from the atonement made for their guilty souls in the blood of Christ.

3. We do, we ought to declare the rich and free love, grace, mercy, and bounty of God unto sinners in and by Jesus Christ. And woe unto us if we should not be found in that work all our days, and thereby encourage all sorts of sinners to come unto him for the free pardon of their sins, "without money or price," without merit or desert on their part! for this is the gospel. But notwithstanding all this grace and condescension, we declare that he doth not dethrone himself, nor deny himself, nor change his nature, nor become unholy, that we may be saved. He is God still, naturally and essentially holy, — holy as he is in Christ, reconciling the sinful world unto himself, — and therefore indispensably requires that those whom he pardons, receives, accepts into his love and communion with himself, should be holy also. And these things are not only consistent but inseparable. Without the consideration of this grace in God, we can have no encouragement to be holy; and without the necessity of holiness in us, that grace can neither be glorified nor useful.

Footnotes:

1. Though most translations give the definite article, it does not exist in the Greek text. Owen seems to hit the true meaning of the phrase in the remark appended to the quotation, when he refers it, not to the divine nature, but to one resembling or corresponding to it. — Ed.

Chapter II - Eternal election a cause of and motive unto holiness

Other arguments for the necessity of holiness, from God's eternal election — The argument from thence explained, improved, vindicated.

We have seen, upon the whole matter, what conclusions (as unto our own duty) we ought to draw from that revelation of the nature of God in Christ which is made unto us, and our relation unto him. If we are not thereby prevailed on always, in all instances of obedience, to endeavour to be holy universally, in all manner of holy conversation, we neither can enjoy his favour here nor be brought unto the enjoyment of him in glory hereafter.

That consideration which usually we take of God next after his nature and the properties of it, is of the eternal free acts of his will, or his decrees and purposes; and we shall now inquire what respect they have unto holiness in us, what arguments and motives may be taken from them to evince the necessity of it unto us and to press us thereunto, especially from the decree of election, which in an especial manner is by some traduced as no friend to this design. I say, then, that, —

II. It is the eternal and immutable purpose of God, that all who are his in a peculiar manner, all whom he designs to bring unto blessedness in the everlasting enjoyment of himself, shall antecedently thereunto be made holy. This purpose of his God hath declared unto us, that we may take no wrong measures of our estate and condition, nor build hopes or expectations of future glory on sandy foundations that will fail us. Whatever we are else, in parts, abilities, profession, moral honesty, usefulness unto others, reputation in the church, if we are not personally, spiritually, evangelically holy, we have no interest in that purpose or decree of God whereby any persons are designed unto salvation and glory. And this we shall briefly confirm:— Eph. i. 4, "He hath chosen us in Christ before the foundation of the world, that we should be holy and without blame before him in love." But is this that which firstly and principally we are ordained unto, and that for its own sake, — namely, holiness and unblamableness in the obedience of love? No; we are firstly "ordained to eternal life," Acts xiii. 48; we are "from the beginning chosen to salvation," 2 Thess. ii. 13. That which God, in the first place, intends as his end in the decree of election is our eternal salvation, to the "praise of the glory of his grace," Eph. i. 5, 6, 11. How, then, is he said to "choose us that we should be holy?" in what sense is our holiness proposed as the design of God in election? It is as the indispensable means for the attaining of the end of salvation and glory. "I do," saith God, "choose these poor lost sinners to be mine in an especial manner, to save them by my Son, and bring them, through his mediation, unto eternal glory. But in order hereunto, I do purpose and decree that they shall be holy and unblamable in the obedience of love; without which, as a means, none shall ever attain that end." Wherefore, the expectation and hope of any man for life and immortality and glory, without previous holiness, can be built on no other foundation but this, that God will rescind his eternal decrees and change his purposes, — that is, cease to be God, — merely to comply with them in their sins! And who knows not what will be the end of such a cursed hope and expectation? The contrary is seconded by that of the apostle, Rom. viii. 30, "Whom he did predestinate, them he also called." Wherever predestination unto glory goes before concerning any person, there effectual vocation unto faith and holiness infallibly ensues; and where these never were, the other never was. So 2 Thess. ii. 13, "God hath from the beginning chosen you to salvation through sanctification of the Spirit." Chosen we are unto salvation by the free, sovereign grace of God. But how may this salvation be actually obtained? how may we be brought into the actual possession of it? Through the sanctification of the Spirit, and no otherwise. Whom God doth not sanctify and make holy by his Spirit, he never chose unto salvation from the beginning. The counsels of God, therefore, concerning us do not depend on our holiness; but upon our holiness our future happiness depends in the counsels of God.

Hence we may see wherein lies the force of the argument for the necessity of holiness from God's decree of election; and it consists in these two things:—

First, That such is the nature of the unalterable decree of God in this matter, that no person living can ever attain the end of glory and happiness without the means of grace and holiness; the same eternal purpose respecteth both. I shall afterward show how the infallible and indissolvable connection of these things is established by the law of God. Our present argument is from hence, that it is fixed by God's eternal decree. He hath ordained none to salvation, but he hath ordained them antecedently to be holy. Not the least infant that goes out of this world shall come to eternal rest unless it be sanctified, and so made habitually and radically holy. He chooseth none to salvation but through the sanctification of the Spirit. As, therefore, whatever else we have or may seem to have, it is contrary to the nature of God that we should come to the enjoyment of him if we are not holy, so it is contrary to his eternal and unchangeable decree also.

Secondly, It ariseth from hence, that we can have no evidence of our interest in God's decree of election, whereby we are designed unto life and glory, without holiness effectually wrought in us. Wherefore, as our life depends upon it, so do all our comforts. To this purpose speaks our apostle, 2 Tim. ii. 19, "The foundation of God standeth sure, having this seal, The Lord knoweth them that are his." It is the decree of election which he intends, and he proposeth it as that alone which will give security against apostasy in a time of great temptations and trials; as our Saviour doth likewise, Matt. xxiv. 24. Everything else will fail but what is an especial fruit and effect of this decree. What, therefore, is incumbent on us with respect thereunto, that we may know we have an interest in this single security against final apostasy? Saith the apostle, "Let every one that nameth the name of Christ depart from iniquity." There is no other way to come unto an evidence thereof but by a departure from all iniquity, by universal holiness. So the apostle Peter directs us to "give all diligence to make our election sure," 2 Pet. i. 10. Sure it is in itself from all eternity, — "The foundation of God standeth sure," — but our duty it is to make it sure and certain unto ourselves; and this is a thing of the highest importance and concernment unto us, whence we are required to give all diligence unto that end. How, then, may this be done or effected? This he declares in the foregoing verses, and it is only by finding in ourselves and duly exercising that train of gospel grace and duties which he there enumerates, verses 5–9.

It is evident, therefore, and necessary from God's decree of election, that if we intend either eternal glory hereafter or any consolation or assurance here, we must endeavour to be "holy and without blame before him in love;" for whomsoever God purposeth to save, he purposeth first to sanctify. Neither have we any ground to suppose that we are built on that foundation of God which standeth sure, unless we depart from all iniquity. What farther motives may be taken from the especial nature of this decree shall be considered when we have removed one objection out of our way.

Some there are who apprehend that these things are quite otherwise; for they say that a supposition of God's decree of personal election is a discouragement unto all endeavours for holiness, and an effectual obstruction thereof in the lives of men. And under this pretence chiefly is the doctrine concerning it blasphemed and evil spoken of; for say they, "If God have freely from eternity chosen men unto salvation, what need is there that they should be holy? They may live securely in the pursuit of their lusts, and be sure not to fail of heaven at the last; for God's decree cannot be frustrated, nor his will resisted. And if men be not elected, whatever they endeavour in the ways of holy obedience, it will be utterly lost; for eternally saved they cannot, they shall not be. This, therefore, is so far from being a conviction of the necessity of holiness and a motive unto it as that indeed it renders it unnecessary and useless; yea, defeats the power and efficacy of all other arguments for it and motives unto it."

Now, this objection, if not for the sake of those who make use of it as a cavil against the truth, yet of those who may feel the force of it in the way of a temptation, must be removed out of our way. To this end I answer two things:—

1. In general, That this persuasion is not of Him that calleth us. This way of arguing is not taught in the Scripture, nor can thence be learned. The doctrine of God's free electing love and grace is fully declared therein; and withal it is proposed as the fountain of all holiness, and made a great motive thereunto. Is it not safer, now, for us to adhere to the plain testimonies of Scripture, confirmed by the experience of the generality of believers, captivating our understandings to the obedience of faith, than hearken unto such perverse cavils as would possess our minds with a dislike of God and his ways? Those who hate gospel holiness, or would substitute something else in the room of it, will never want exceptions against all its concernments. A holiness they lay claim unto and plead an interest in; for, as I said formerly, a confession in general of the necessity hereof is almost the only thing wherein all that are called Christians do agree: but such a holiness they would have as doth not spring from eternal, divine election, as is not wrought in us originally by the almighty efficacy of grace in our conversion, as is not promoted by free justification through the imputation of the righteousness of Christ. Now, this is such a holiness as the Scripture knoweth nothing of, unless it be to reject and condemn it. Wherefore, this objection proceeding only from the craft of Satan, opposing the ways and methods of God's grace when he dareth not openly oppose the thing itself, it is safer for a believer to rest quietly in the clear Scripture revelation than to attend unto such proud, perverse, and froward cavillings.

2. In particular, We are not only obliged to believe all divine revelations, but also in the way, order, and method wherein, by the will of God, they are proposed unto us, and which is required by the nature of the things themselves. For instance, the belief of eternal life is required in the gospel; but yet no man is obliged to believe that he shall be eternally saved whilst he lives in his sins, but rather the contrary. On this supposition, which is plain and evident, I shall, in the ensuing propositions, utterly cast this objection out of consideration:— (1.) The decree of election, considered absolutely in itself, without respect unto its effects, is no part of God's revealed will; that is, it is not revealed that this or that man is or is not elected. This, therefore, can be made neither argument nor objection about any thing wherein faith or obedience is concerned: for we know it not, we cannot know it, it is not our duty to know it; the knowledge of it is not proposed as of any use unto us, yea, it is our sin to inquire into it. It may seem to some to be like the tree of knowledge of good and evil unto Eve, — good for food, pleasant to the eyes, and much to be desired to make one wise, as all secret, forbidden things seem to carnal minds; but men can gather no fruit from it but death. See Deut. xxix. 29. Whatever exceptions, therefore, are laid against this decree as it is in itself, whatever inferences are made on supposition of this or that man's being or not being elected, they are all unjust and unreasonable, yea, proud contending with God, who hath appointed another way for the discovery hereof, as we shall see afterward.

(2.) God sends the gospel to men in pursuit of his decree of election, and in order unto its effectual accomplishment. I dispute not what other end it hath or may have, in its indefinite proposal unto all; but this is the first, regulating, principal end of it. Wherefore, in the preaching of it, our apostle affirms that he "endured all things for the elect's sakes, that they might obtain the salvation which is in Christ Jesus with eternal glory," 2 Tim. ii. 10. So God beforehand commanded him to stay and preach the gospel at Corinth, because "he had much people in that city," — namely, in his purpose of grace, Acts xviii. 10. See chap. ii. 47, xiii. 48.

(3.) Wherever this gospel comes, it proposeth life and salvation by Jesus Christ unto all that shall believe, repent, and yield obedience unto him. It plainly makes known unto men their duty, and plainly proposeth unto them their reward. In this state of things, no man, without the highest pride and utmost effect of unbelief, can oppose the secret decree of God unto our known duty. Saith such an one, "I will neither repent, nor believe, nor obey, unless I may first know whether I am elected or no; for all at last will depend thereon." If this be the resolution of any man, he may go about his other occasions; the gospel hath nothing to say or offer unto him. If he will admit of it on no other terms, but that he may set up his own will, and wisdom, and methods, in opposition unto and exclusion of those of God, he must, for aught I know, take his own course, whereof he may repent when it is too late.

(4.) The sole way of God's appointment whereby we may come to an apprehension of an interest in election is by the fruits of it in our own souls; nor is it lawful for us to inquire into it or after it any other way. The obligation which the gospel puts upon us to believe any thing respects the order of the things themselves to be believed, and the order of our obedience, as was before observed. For instance, when it is declared that Christ died for sinners, no man is immediately obliged to believe that Christ died for him in particular, but only that he died to save sinners, to procure a way of salvation for them, among whom he finds himself to be. Hereon the gospel requires of men faith and obedience; this are they obliged to comply withal. Until this be done, no man is under an obligation to believe that Christ died for him in particular. So is it in this matter of election. A man is obliged to believe the doctrine of it, upon the first promulgation of the gospel, because it is therein plainly declared; but as for his own personal election, he cannot believe it, nor is obliged to believe it, any otherwise but as God reveals it by its effects. No man ought, no man can justly question his own election, doubt of it, or disbelieve it, until he be in such a condition as wherein it is impossible that the effects of election should ever be wrought in him, if such a condition there be in this world; for as a man whilst he is unholy can have no evidence that he is elected, so he can have none that he is not elected, whilst it is possible that ever he may be holy. Wherefore, whether men are elected or no is not that which God calls any immediately to be conversant about. Faith, obedience, holiness, are the inseparable fruits, effects, and consequents of election, as hath been proved before. See Eph. i. 4; 2 Thess. ii. 13; Tit. i. 1; Acts xiii. 48. In whomsoever these things are wrought, he is obliged, according to the method of God and the gospel, to believe his own election. And any believer may have the same assurance of it as he hath of his calling, sanctification, or justification; for these things are inseparable. And by the exercise of grace are we obliged to secure our interest in election, 2 Pet. i. 5–10. But as for those who are as yet unbelievers and unholy, they can draw no conclusion that they are not elected but from this supposition, that they are in a state and condition wherein it is impossible that ever they should have either grace or holiness; which cannot be supposed concerning any man but him that knows himself to have sinned against the Holy Ghost.

Wherefore, all the supposed strength of the objection mentioned lieth only in the pride of men's minds and wills, refusing to submit themselves unto the order and method of God in the dispensation of his grace and his prescription of their duty, where we must leave it.

To return unto our designed discourse: The doctrine of God's eternal election is everywhere in the Scripture proposed for the encouragement and consolation of believers, and to further them in their course of obedience and holiness. See Eph. i. 3–12; Rom. viii. 28–34. As unto men's present concernment therein, it is infallibly assured unto them by its effects; and being so, it is filled with motives unto holiness, as we shall now farther declare in particular.

First, The sovereign and ever-to-be-adored grace and love of God herein is a powerful motive hereunto; for we have no way to express our resentment[2] of this grace, our acknowledgment of it, our thankfulness for it, but by a holy, fruitful course of obedience, nor doth God on the account hereof require any thing else of us. Let us, therefore, inquire what sense of obligation this puts upon us, that God from all eternity, out of his mere sovereign grace, not moved by any thing in ourselves, should first choose us unto life and salvation by Jesus Christ, decreeing immutably to save us out of the perishing multitude of mankind, from whom we neither then did, in his eye or consideration, nor by any thing in ourselves ever would, differ in the least. What impression doth this make upon our souls? What conclusion as to our practice and obedience do we hence educe? Why, saith one, "If God have thus chosen me, I may then live in sin as I please; all will be well and safe in the latter end, which is all I need care for." But this is the language of a devil, and not of a man. Suggestions, possibly, of this nature, by the craft of Satan, in conjunction with the deceitfulness of sin, may be injected into the minds of believers, (as what may not so be?) but he that shall foment, embrace, and act practically according to this inference, is such a monster of impiety and presumptuous ingratitude as hell itself cannot parallel in many instances. I shall use some boldness in this matter. He that doth not understand, who is not sensible, that an apprehension by faith of God's electing love in Christ hath a natural, immediate, powerful influence, upon the souls of believers, unto the love of God and holy obedience, is utterly unacquainted with the nature of faith, and its whole work and actings towards God in the hearts of them that believe. Is it possible that anyone who knows these things can suppose that those in whom they are in sincerity and power can be such stupid, impious, and ungrateful monsters, so devoid of all holy ingenuity and filial affections towards God, as, merely out of despite unto him, to cast poison into the spring of all their own mercies? Many have I known complain that they could not arrive at a comfortable persuasion of their own election; never any who [complained,] when they had received it in a due way and manner, that it proved a snare unto them, that it tended to ingenerate looseness of life, unholiness, or a contempt of God in them. Besides, in the Scripture it is still proposed and made use of unto other ends. And those who know any thing of the nature of faith or of the love of God, any thing of intercourse or communion with him by Jesus Christ, any thing of thankfulness, obedience, or holiness, will not be easily persuaded but that God's electing love and grace is a mighty constraining motive unto the due exercise of them all.

God himself knoweth this to be so, and therefore he maketh the consideration of his electing love, as free and undeserved, his principal argument to stir up the people unto holy obedience, Deut. vii. 6–8, 11. And a supposition hereof lies at the bottom of that blessed exhortation of our apostle, Col. iii. 12, 13, "Put on therefore, as the elect of God, holy and beloved, bowels of mercies, kindness, humbleness of mind, meekness, long-suffering; forbearing one another, and forgiving one another." These things, which are so great a part of our holiness, become the elect of God; these are required of them on the account of their interest in electing love and grace. Men may frame a holiness to themselves, and be stirred up unto it by motives of their own (as there is a religion in the world that runs in a parallel line by that of evangelical truth, but toucheth it not, nor will do so to eternity); but that which the gospel requires is promoted on the grounds and by the motives that are peculiar unto it, whereof this of God's free electing love and grace is among the principal. Farther to confirm this truth, I shall instance in some especial graces, duties, and parts of holiness, that this consideration is suited to promote:—

1. Humility in all things is a necessary consequent of a due consideration of this decree of God; for what were we when he thus set his heart upon us, to choose us, and to do us good forever? — poor, lost, undone creatures, that lay perishing under the guilt of our apostasy from him. What did he see in us to move him so to choose us? — nothing but sin and misery. What did he foresee that we would do of ourselves more than others, if he wrought not in us by his effectual grace? — nothing but a continuance in sin and rebellion against him, and that forever. How should the thoughts hereof keep our souls in all humility and continual self-abasement! for what have we in or from ourselves on the account whereof we should be lifted up? Wherefore, as the elect of God, let us put on humility in all things; and let me add, that there is no grace whereby at

this day we may more glorify God and the gospel, now the world is sinking into ruin under the weight of its own pride.

The spirits of men, the looks of men, the tongues of men, the lives of men, are lifted up by their pride unto their destruction. The good Lord keep professors from a share in the pride of these days! Spiritual pride in foolish self-exalting opinions, and the pride of life in the fashions of the world, are the poison of this age.

2. Submission to the sovereign will and pleasure of God, in the disposal of all our concerns in this world. That this is an excellent fruit of faith, an eminent part of holiness, or duty of obedience, is acknowledged; and never was it more signally called for than it is at this day.

He that cannot live in an actual resignation of himself and all his concerns unto the sovereign pleasure of God, can neither glorify him in any thing nor have one hour's solid peace in his own mind. This public calamities, this private dangers and losses, this the uncertainty of all things here below, call for at present in an especial manner. God hath taken all pretences of security from the earth, by what some men feel and some men fear. None knows how soon it may be his portion to be brought unto the utmost extremity of earthly calamities. There is none so old, none so young, none so wise, none so rich, as thence to expect relief from such things? Where, then, shall we in this condition cast anchor? whither shall we betake ourselves for quietness and repose? It is no way to be obtained but in a resignation of ourselves and all our concernments into the sovereign pleasure of God; and what greater motive can we have thereunto than this? The first act of divine sovereign pleasure concerning us was the choosing of us from all eternity unto all holiness and happiness. This was done when we were not, when we had no contrivances of our own. And shall we not now put all our temporary concerns into the same hand? Can the same fountain send out sweet and bitter water? — can the same sovereign pleasure of God be the free only cause of all our blessedness, and can it do that which is really evil unto us? Our souls, our persons, were secure and blessedly provided for, as to grace and glory, in the sovereign will of God; and what a prodigious impiety is it not to trust all other things in the same hand, to be disposed of freely and absolutely! If we will not forego our interest in mere, absolute, free, sovereign grace, for ten thousand worlds (as no believer will), how ready should we be to resign up thereunto that little portion which we have in this world among perishing things!

3. Love, kindness, compassion, forbearance towards all believers, all the saints of God, however differenced among themselves, are made indispensably necessary unto us, and pressed on us from the same consideration. And herein also doth no small part of our holiness consist. To this purpose is the exhortation of the apostle before mentioned, Col. iii. 12, 13; for if God have chosen them from all eternity, and made them the objects of his love and grace, as he hath done so concerning all sincere believers, do we not think it necessary, doth not God require of us, that we should love them also? How dare any of us entertain unkind, severe thoughts? how dare we maintain animosities and enmities against any of them whom God hath eternally chosen to grace and glory? Such things, it may be, upon provocations and surprisals, and clashings of secular interests, have fallen out, and will fall out amongst us; but they are all opposite and contrary unto that influence which the consideration of God's electing love ought to have upon us. The apostle's rule is, that, as unto our

communion in love, we ought to receive him whom God hath received, and because God hath received him; against which no other thing can be laid in bar, Rom. xiv. 1, 3. And the rule is no less certain, yea, is subject to less exceptions, that we ought to choose, embrace, and love all those, whoever they be, whom God hath chosen and loved from eternity. There is no greater evidence of low, weak, selfish Christians, than to prescribe any other rules or bounds unto their spiritual, evangelical affections than the decree of God's election, as manifesting itself in its effects. "I endure all things," saith our apostle, not for the Jews or Gentiles, not for the weak or strong in the faith, not for those of this or that way, but, "for the elect's sake." This should regulate our love, and mightily stir it up unto all actings of kindness, mercy, compassion, forbearance, and forgiveness.

4. Contempt of the world, and all that belongs unto it, will hence also be ingenerated in us. Did God set his heart upon some from eternity? Did he choose them to be his own peculiar [people], to distinguish them as his from all the residue of mankind? Doth he design to give them the highest, greatest, best fruits and effects of his love, and to glorify himself in their praises forever? What, then, will he do for them? Will he make them all kings or emperors in the world? or, at least, will he have them to be rich, and noble, and honourable among men, that it may be known and proclaimed, "Thus shall it be done to the man whom the King of heaven delighteth to honour;" however, that they should be kept from straits, and difficulties, and trials, from poverty, and shame, and reproach in the world? Alas! none of these things were in the least in the heart of God concerning them. They deserve not to be named on the same day, as we use to speak, with the least of those things which God hath chosen his unto. Were there any real, substantial good in them on their own account, he would not have cast them out of the counsels of his love. But, on the contrary, "Ye see your calling, brethren" (which is the infallible fruit and consequent of election), "how that not many wise men after the flesh, not many mighty, not many noble, are called:" but God hath chosen the poor of the world, the base and the contemptible, for the most part; yea, he hath designed the generality of his elect to a poor, low, and afflicted condition in this world. And shall we set our hearts on those things that God hath so manifestly put an under-valuation upon, in comparison of the least concernment of grace and holiness? Wherefore, let them that are poor and despised in the world learn to be satisfied with their state and condition. Had God seen it to have been good for you to have been otherwise, he would not have passed it by when he was acting eternal love towards you. And let them that are rich not set their hearts upon uncertain riches. Alas! they are things which God had no regard unto when he prepared grace and glory for his own. Let the remembrance hereof suit your esteem and valuation of them. Do but think with yourselves that these are not the things that God had any regard unto when he chose us unto grace and glory, and it will abate of your care about them, cool your love towards them, and take off your hearts from them; which is your holiness.

Secondly, Electing love is a motive and encouragement unto holiness, because of the enabling supplies of grace which we may and ought thence to expect by Jesus Christ. The difficulties we meet withal in a course of holiness are great and many. Here Satan, the world, and sin, do put forth and try their utmost strength. Ofttimes the best are foiled, ofttimes discouraged, sometimes weary and ready to give over; it requires a good spiritual courage to take a prospect of the lions, serpents, and snares that lie in the way of a constant persevering course in gospel obedience. Hereon our knees are ready to grow feeble, and our hands to hang down. It is no small relief herein, no small encouragement to continue in our progress, that the fountain of electing grace will never fail us, but continually give out supplies of spiritual strength and refreshment. Hence may we take heart and courage to rise again when we have been foiled, to abide when the shock of temptation is violent, and to persevere in those duties which are most wearisome to the flesh. And they are unacquainted with a course of holy obedience who know not how needful this consideration is unto a comfortable continuance therein.

Thirdly, It hath the same tendency and effect in the assurance we have from thence, that notwithstanding all the oppositions we meet withal, we shall not utterly and finally miscarry. God's "election" will at last "obtain," Rom. xi. 7; and "his foundation standeth sure," 2 Tim. ii. 19. His purpose, which is "according unto election," is unchangeable; and, therefore, the final perseverance and salvation of those concerned in it are everlastingly secured. This is the design of the apostle's discourse, Rom. viii, from verse 28 unto the end. Because of the immutability of God's eternal purpose in our predestination, and his effectual operations in the pursuit and for the execution thereof, the elect of God shall infallibly be carried through all, even the most dreadful oppositions that are made against them, and be at length safely landed in glory. And there is no greater encouragement to grow and persist in holiness than what is administered by this assurance of a blessed end and issue of it.

Those who have had experience of that spiritual slumber and sloth which unbelief will cast us under; of those weaknesses, discouragements, and despondencies, which uncertainties, doubts, fears, and perplexities of what will be the issue of things at last with them, do cast upon the souls of men; how duties are discouraged, spiritual endeavours and diligence are impaired, delight in God weakened, and love cooled by them, — will be able to make a right judgment of the truth of this assertion. Some think that this apprehension of the immutability of God's purpose of election, and the infallibility of the salvation of believers on that account, tend only to carelessness and security in sin; and that to be always in fear, dread, and uncertainty of the end, is the only means to make us watchful unto duties of holiness. It is very sad that any man should so far proclaim his inexperience and unacquaintedness with the nature of gospel grace, the genius and inclination of the new creature, and the proper workings of faith, as to be able thus to argue, without a check put upon him by himself and from his own experience. It is true, were there no difference between faith and presumption; no difference between the spirit of liberty under the covenant of grace and that of bondage under the old covenant; no spirit of adoption given unto believers; no genuine filial delight in and adherence unto God ingenerated in them thereby, — there might be something in this objection. But if the nature of faith and of the new creature, the operations of the one and disposition of the other, are such as they are declared to be in the gospel, and as believers have experience of them in their own hearts, men do but bewray their ignorance, whilst they contend that the assurance of God's unchangeable love in Christ, flowing from the immutability of his counsel in election, doth any way impeach, or doth not effectually promote, the industry of believers in all duties of obedience.

Suppose a man that is on his journey knoweth himself to be in the right way, and that, passing on therein, he shall certainly and infallibly come to his journey's end, especially if he will a little quicken his speed as occasion shall require, will you say that this is enough to make such a man careless and negligent, and that it would be much more to his advantage to be lost and bewildered in uncertain paths and ways, not knowing whither he goes, nor whether he shall ever arrive at his journey's end? Common experience declares the contrary, as also how momentary and useless are those violent fits and gusts of endeavours which proceed from fear and uncertainty, both in things spiritual and temporal, or civil. Whilst men are under the power of actual impressions from such fears, they will convert to God, yea, they will "momento turbinis," and perfect holiness in an instant; but so soon as that impression wears off (as it will do on every occasion, and upon none at all), such persons are as dead and cold towards God as the lead or iron, which ran but now in a fiery stream, is when the heat is departed from it. It is that soul alone, ordinarily, which hath a comfortable assurance of God's eternal, immutable, electing love, and thence of the blessed end of its own course of obedience, who goeth on constantly and evenly in a course of holiness, quickening his course and doubling his speed, as he hath occasion from trials or opportunities. And this is the very design of our apostle to explain and confirm, Heb. vi., from the tenth verse unto the end of the chapter, as is declared elsewhere.

It appears, from what hath been discoursed, that the electing love of God is a powerful constraining motive unto holiness, and that which proves invincibly the necessity of it in all who intend the eternal enjoyment of God. But it will be said, "That if it be supposed or granted that those who are actually believers, and have a sense of their interest herein, may make the use of it that is pleaded; yet as for those who are unconverted, or are otherwise uncertain of their spiritual state and condition, nothing can be so discouraging unto them as this doctrine of eternal election. Can they make any other conclusion from it but that, if they are not elected, all care and pains in and about duties of obedience are vain; if they are, they are needless?" The removal of this objection shall put a close unto our discourse on this subject; and I answer, —

1. That we have showed already that this doctrine is revealed and proposed in the Scripture principally to acquaint believers with their privilege, safety, and fountain of their comforts. Having, therefore, proved its usefulness unto them, I have discharged all that is absolutely needful to my present purpose. But I shall show, moreover, that it hath its proper benefit and advantage towards others also. For, —

2. Suppose the doctrine of personal election be preached unto men, together with the other sacred truths of the gospel, two conclusions, it is possible, may by sundry persons be made from it:— (1.) That whereas this is a matter of great and eternal moment unto our souls, and there is no way to secure our interest in it but by the possession of its fruits and effects, which are saving faith and holiness, we will, we must, it is our duty, to use our utmost endeavours, by attaining of them and growth in them, to make our election sure; and herein, if we be sincere and diligent, we shall not fail. Others may conclude, (2.) That if it be so indeed, that those who shall be saved are chosen thereunto before the foundation of the world, then it is to no purpose to go about to believe or obey, seeing all things must fall out at last according as they were fore-ordained. Now, I ask, which of these conclusions is (I will not say

most suited unto the mind and will of God, with that subjection of soul and conscience which we owe to his sovereign wisdom and authority, but whether of them is) the most rational, and most suitable to the principles of sober love of ourselves and care of our immortal condition? Nothing is more certain than that the latter resolution will be infallibly destructive (if pursued) of all the everlasting concernments of our souls; death and eternal condemnation are the unavoidable issues of it. No man giving himself up to the conduct of that conclusion shall ever come to the enjoyment of God. But in the other way, it is possible, at least, that a man may be found to be the object of God's electing love, and so be saved. But why do I say it is possible? There is nothing more infallibly certain than that he who pursues sincerely and diligently the ways of faith and obedience, — which are, as we have often said, the fruits of election, — shall obtain in the end everlasting blessedness, and, ordinarily, shall have in this world a comfortable evidence of his own personal election. This, therefore, on all accounts, and towards all sorts of persons, is an invincible argument for the necessity of holiness, and a mighty motive thereunto: for it is unavoidable, that if there be such a thing as personal election, and that the fruits of it are sanctification, faith, and obedience, it is utterly impossible, that without holiness anyone should see God; the reason of which consequence is apparent unto all.

Footnotes:

2. Resentment once denoted a lively sense of good or favour conferred, as well as irritation under wrong or injustice. It is obviously used in the former meaning in this passage. — Ed.

Chapter III - Holiness necessary from the commands of God

Necessity of holiness proved from the commands of God in the law and the gospel.

III. We have evinced the necessity of holiness from the nature and the decrees of God; our next argument shall be taken from his word or commands, as the nature and order of these things do require. And in this case it is needless to produce instances of God's commands that we should be holy; it is the concurrent voice of the law and gospel. Our apostle sums up the whole matter, 1 Thess. iv. 1–3, "We exhort you, that as ye have received of us how ye ought to walk and to please God, so ye would abound more and more. For ye know what commandments we gave you by the Lord Jesus. For this is the will of God, even your sanctification," or holiness; whereunto he adds one especial instance. This is that which the commandments of Christ require, yea, this is the sum of the whole commanding will of God. The substance of the law is, "Be ye holy; for I the Lord your God am holy," Lev. xix. 2; the same with what it is referred unto by our Saviour, Matt. xxii. 37–39. And whereas holiness may be reduced unto two heads, — 1. The renovation of the image of God in us; 2. Universal actual obedience, — they are the sum of the preceptive part of the gospel, Eph. iv. 22–24; Tit. ii. 11, 12. Hereof, therefore, there needeth no farther confirmation by especial testimonies.

Our inquiry must be, what force there is in this argument, or whence we do conclude unto a necessity of holiness from the commands of God. To this end the nature and proper adjuncts of these commands are to be considered, — that is, we are to get our minds and consciences affected with them, so as to endeavour after holiness on their account, or with respect unto them: for whatever we may do which seems to have the matter of holiness in it, if we do it not with respect unto God's command, it hath not the nature of holiness in it; for our holiness is our conformity and obedience to the will of God, and it is a respect unto a command which makes any thing to be obedience, or gives it the formal nature thereof. Wherefore, as God rejects that from any place in his fear, worship, or service, which is resolved only into the doctrines or precepts of men, Isa. xxix. 13, 14; so for men to pretend unto I know not what freedom, light, and readiness unto all holiness, from a principle within, without respect unto the commands of God without, as given in his word, is to make themselves their own god, and to despise obedience unto him who is over all, God blessed forever. Then are we the servants of God, then are we the disciples of Christ, when we do what is commanded us, and because it is commanded us. And what we are not influenced unto by the authority of God in his commands, we are not principled for by the Spirit of God administered in the promises. Whatever good any man doth in any kind, if the reason why he doth it be not God's command, it belongs neither to holiness nor obedience. Our inquiry, therefore, is after those things in the commands of God which put such an indispensable obligation upon us unto holiness, as that whatever we may be or may have without it will be of no use or advantage unto us, as unto eternal blessedness or the enjoyment of him.

But to make our way more clear and safe, one thing must yet be premised unto these considerations; and this is, that God's commands for holiness may be considered two ways:—

1. As they belong unto and are parts of the covenant of works; 2. As they belong and are inseparably annexed unto the covenant of grace. In both respects they are materially and formally the same; that is, the same things are required in them, and the same person requires them, and so their obligation is joint and equal. Not only the commands of the new covenant do oblige us unto holiness, but those of the old also, as to the matter and substance of them. But there is a great difference in the manner and ends of these commands as considered so distinctly. For, —

1. The commands of God, as under the old covenant, do so require universal holiness of us, in all acts, duties, and degrees of them, that upon the least failure, in substance, circumstance, or degree, they allow of nothing else we do, but determine us transgressors of the whole law; for, with respect unto them, "whosoever shall keep the whole law, and yet offend in one point, he is guilty of all," James ii. 10. Now, I acknowledge that although there ariseth from hence an obligation unto holiness to them who are under that covenant, and such a necessity of it as that without it they must certainly perish, yet no argument of the nature with those which I insist upon can hence be taken to press us unto it: for no arguments are forcible unto this purpose but such as include encouragements in them unto what they urge; but that this consideration of the command knoweth nothing of, seeing a compliance with it is, in our lapsed condition, absolutely impossible, and for the things that are so, we can have no endeavours. And hence it is that no man influenced only by the commands of the law, or first covenant, absolutely considered, whatever in particular he might be forced or compelled unto, did ever sincerely aim or endeavour after universal holiness.

Men may be subdued by the power of the law, and compelled to habituate themselves unto a strict course of duty, and being advantaged therein by a sedate natural constitution, desire of applause, self-righteousness, or superstition, may make a great appearance of holiness; but if the principle of what they do be only the commands of the law, they never tread one true step in the paths of it.

2. The end why these commands require all the duties of holiness of us is, that they may be our righteousness before God, or that we may be justified thereby: for "Moses describeth the righteousness which is of the law, That the man which doeth those things shall live by them," Rom. x. 5; that is, it requires of us all duties of obedience unto this end, that we may have justification and eternal life by them. But neither on this account can any such argument be taken as those we inquire into; for by the deeds of the law no man can be justified: "If thou, Lord, shouldest mark iniquities, O Lord, who shall stand?" Ps. cxxx. 3. So prays David, "Enter not into judgment with thy servant; for in thy sight shall no man living be justified," Ps. cxliii. 2; Rom. iii. 20; Gal. ii. 16. And if none can attain the end of the command, as in this sense they cannot, what argument can we take from thence to prevail with them unto obedience? Whosoever, therefore, presseth men unto holiness merely on the commands of

the law, and for the ends of it, doth but put them upon tormenting disquietments and deceive their souls. However, men are indispensably obliged hereby, and those must eternally perish for want of what the law so requires who do not or will not by faith comply with the only remedy and provision that God hath made in this case. And for this reason we are necessitated to deny a possibility of salvation unto all to whom the gospel is not preached, as well as unto those by whom it is refused; for they are left unto this law, whose precepts they cannot answer, and whose end they cannot attain.

It is otherwise on both these accounts with the commands of God for holiness under the new covenant, or in the gospel; for, —

1. Although God in them requireth universal holiness of us, yet he doth not do it in that strict and rigorous way as by the law, so as that if we fail in any thing, either as to the matter or manner of its performance, in the substance of it or as to the degrees of its perfection, that thereon both that and all we do besides should be rejected. But he doth it with a contemperation of grace and mercy, so as that if there be a universal sincerity, in a respect unto all his commands, he both pardoneth many sins, and accepts of what we do, though it come short of legal perfection; both on the account of the mediation of Christ. Yet this hindereth not but that the law or command of the gospel doth still require universal holiness of us, and perfection therein, which we are to do our utmost endeavour to comply withal, though we have a relief provided in sincerity on the one hand and mercy on the other; for the commands of the gospel do still declare what God approves and what he doth condemn, — which is no less than all holiness on the one hand and all sin on the other, — as exactly and extensively as under the law: for this the very nature of God requireth, and the gospel is not the ministry of sin, so as to give an allowance or indulgence unto the least, although in it pardon be provided for a multitude of sins by Jesus Christ. The obligation on us unto holiness is equal unto what it was under the law, though a relief be provided where unavoidably we come short of it. There is, therefore, nothing more certain than that there is no relaxation given us as unto any duty of holiness by the gospel, nor any indulgence unto the least sin. But yet, upon the supposition of the acceptance of sincerity, and a perfection of parts instead of degrees, with the mercy provided for our failings and sins, there is an argument to be taken from the command of it unto an indispensable necessity of holiness, including in it the highest encouragement to endeavour after it; for, together with the command, there is also grace administered, enabling us unto that obedience which God will accept. Nothing, therefore, can void or evacuate the power of this command and argument from it but a stubborn contempt of God, arising from the love of sin.

2. The commands of the gospel do not require holiness and the duties of righteousness of us to the same end as the commands of the law did, — namely, that thereby we might be justified in the sight of God; for whereas God now accepts from us a holiness short of that which the law required, if he did it still for the same end, it would reflect dishonour upon his own righteousness and the holiness of the gospel. For, —

(1.) If God can accept of a righteousness unto justification inferior unto or short of what he required by the law, how great severity must it be thought in him to bind his creatures unto such an exact obedience and righteousness at first as he could and might have dispensed withal! If he doth accept of sincere obedience now unto our justification, why did he not do so before, but obliged mankind unto absolute perfection according to the law, for coming short wherein they all perished? Or shall we say that God hath changed his mind in this matter, and that he doth not stand so much now on rigid and perfect obedience for our justification as he did formerly? Where, then, is the glory of his immutability, of his essential holiness, of the absolute rectitude of his nature and will? Besides, —

(2.) What shall become of the honour and holiness of the gospel on this supposition? Must it not be looked on as a doctrine less holy than that of the law? for whereas the law required absolute, perfect, sinless holiness unto our justification, the gospel admits of that to the same end, on this supposition, which is every way imperfect, and consistent with a multitude of sins and failings? What can be spoken more to the derogation of it? Nay, would not this indeed make "Christ the minister of sin," which our apostle rejects with so much detestation, Gal. ii. 17? for to say that he hath merited that our imperfect obedience, attended with many and great sins ("for there is no man that liveth and sinneth not"), should be accepted unto our justification, instead of the perfect and sinless obedience required under the law, is plainly to make him the minister of sin, or one that hath acquired some liberty for sin beyond whatever the law allowed. And thus, upon the whole matter, both Christ and the gospel, in whom and whereby God unquestionably designed to declare the holiness and righteousness of his own nature much more gloriously than ever he had done any other way, should be the great means to darken and obscure them; for in and by them, on this supposition, God must be thought (and is declared) to accept of a righteousness unto our justification unspeakably inferior unto what he required before.

It must be granted, therefore, that the end of gospel commands, requiring the obedience of holiness in us, is not that thereby or thereon we should be justified. God hath therein provided another righteousness for that end, which fully, perfectly, absolutely answers all that the law requires, and on some considerations is far more glorious than what the law either did or could require. And hereby hath he exalted more than ever the honour of his own holiness and righteousness, whereof the external instrument is the gospel; which is also, therefore, most holy. Now, this is no other but the righteousness of Christ imputed unto us; for "he is the end of the law for righteousness unto them that do believe," Rom. x. 4. But God hath now appointed other ends unto our holiness, and so unto his command of it, under the gospel, all of them consistent with the nature of that obedience which he will accept of us, and such as we may attain through the power of grace; and so all of them offering new encouragements, as well as enforcements, unto our endeavours after it. But because these ends will be the subject of most of our ensuing arguments, I shall not here insist upon them. I shall only add two things in general:— [1.] That God hath no design for his own glory in us or by us, in this world or unto eternity, — that there is no especial communion that we can have with him by Jesus Christ, nor any capacity for us to enjoy him, — but holiness is necessary unto it, as a means unto its end. [2.] These present ends of it under the gospel are such as that God doth no less indispensably require it of us now than he did when our justification was proposed as the end of it. They are such, in brief, as God upon the account of them judgeth meet to command us to be holy in all manner of holiness; which what obligation and necessity it puts upon us so to be, we are now to inquire:—

First, The first thing considerable in the command of God to this purpose is the authority wherewith it is accompanied. It is indispensably necessary that we should be holy on the account of the authority of God's command. Authority, wherever it is just and exerted in a due and equal manner, carrieth along with it an obligation unto obedience. Take this away, and you will fill the whole world with disorder. If the authority of parents, masters, and magistrates, did not oblige children, servants, and subjects unto obedience, the world could not abide one moment out of hellish confusion. God himself maketh use of this argument in general, to convince men of the necessity of obedience: "A son honoureth his father, and a servant his master: if then I be a father, where is mine honour? and if I be a master, where is my fear? saith the Lord of hosts unto you, O priests, that despise my name," Mal. i. 6; — "If in all particular relations, where there is any thing of superiority, which hath the least parcel of authority accompanying of it, obedience is expected and exacted, is it not due to me, who have all the authority of all sovereign relations in me towards you?" And there are two things that enforce the obligation from the command on this consideration, jus imperandi and vis exsequendi, both comprised in that of the apostle James iv. 12, "There is one lawgiver, who is able to save and to destroy:"—

1. He who commands us to be holy is our sovereign lawgiver, he that hath absolute power to prescribe unto us what laws he pleaseth. When commands come from them who have authority, and yet are themselves also under authority, there may be some secret abatement of the power of the command. Men may think either to appeal from them, or one way or other subduct themselves from under their power. But when the power immediately commanding is sovereign and absolute, there is no room for tergiversation. The command of God proceeds from the absolute power of a sovereign legislator. And where it is not complied withal, the whole authority of God, and therein God himself, is despised. So God in many places calleth sinning against his commands, the "despising of him," Num. xi. 20, 1 Sam. ii. 30; the "despising of his name," Mal. i. 6; the "despising of his commandment," and that in his saints themselves, 2 Sam. xii. 9.

Being, then, under the command of God to be holy, not to endeavour always and in all things so to be is to despise God, to reject his sovereign authority over us, and to live in defiance of him. This state, I suppose, there are few who would be willing to be found in. To be constant despisers of God and rebels against his authority is a charge that men are not ready to own, and do suppose that those who are so indeed are in a very ill condition. But this, and no better, is the state of every one who is not holy, who doth not follow after holiness. Yet so it is, propose unto men the true nature of evangelical holiness; press them to the duties wherein the exercise of it doth consist; convince them with evidence as clear as the light at noonday that such and such sins, such and such courses, wherein they live and walk, are absolutely inconsistent with it and irreconcilable unto it, — yet, for the most part, it is but little they will heed you, and less they will do to answer your exhortations. Tell the same persons that they are rebels against God, despisers of him, that they have utterly broken the yoke and cast off his authority, and they will defy you, and perhaps revile you. But yet these things are inseparable. God having given his command unto men to be holy, declared his sovereign will and pleasure therein, if we are not so accordingly, we are not one jot better than the persons described. Here, then, in the first place, we found the necessity of holiness on the command of God. The authority wherewith it is accompanied makes it necessary; yea, from hence if we endeavour not to thrive in it, if we watch not diligently against everything that is contrary unto it, we are therein and so far despisers of God and his name, as in the places before cited.

This, therefore, evidenceth unto the consciences of men that the obligation unto holiness is indispensable. And it would be well if we always carried this formal consideration of the commandment in our minds. Nothing is more prevalent with us unto watchfulness in holiness, as nothing doth more effectually render what we do to be obedience, properly so called. Forgetfulness hereof, or not heeding it as we ought, is the great reason of our loose and careless walking, of our defect in making a progress in grace and holiness. No man is safe a moment whose mind by any means is dispossessed of a sense of the sovereign authority of God in his commands, nor can any thing secure such a soul from being pierced and entered into by various temptations. This, therefore, are we to carry about with us wherever we go and whatever we do, to keep our souls and consciences under the power of it, in all opportunities of duties, and on all occasions of sin. Had men always, in their ways, trades, shops, affairs, families, studies, closets, this written on their hearts, they would have "Holiness to the Lord" on their breasts and foreheads also.

2. The apostle tells us, that as God in his commands is a sovereign lawgiver, so he is able to kill and keep alive; that is, his commanding authority is accompanied with such a power as that whereby he is able absolutely and eternally to reward the obedient, and to return unto the disobedient a meet recompense of punishment; for although I would not exclude other considerations, yet I think this of eternal rewards and punishments to be principally here intended.

But, (1.) Supposing it to have respect unto things temporal also, it carries along with it the greater enforcement. God commands us to be holy. Things are in that state and condition in the world as that if we endeavour to answer his will in a due manner, designing to "perfect holiness in the fear of God," we shall meet with much opposition, many difficulties, and at length, perhaps, it may cost us our lives; multitudes have made profession of it at no cheaper rate. But let us not mistake in this matter: he who commands us to be holy is the only sovereign Lord of life and death, that hath alone the disposal of them both, and consequently of all things that are subservient and conducing unto the one or the other. It is he alone who can kill in a way of punishment, and he alone can keep alive in a way of merciful preservation. This power of our Lawgiver the holy companions of Daniel committed themselves unto, and preserved themselves by the consideration of, when with the terror of death they were commanded to forsake the way of holiness, Dan. iii. 16–18. And with respect unto it, our Lord Jesus Christ tells us that "he who would save his life," — namely, by a sinful neglect of the command, — "shall lose it." This, therefore, is also to be considered: The power of him who commands us to be holy is such as that he is able to carry us through all difficulties and dangers which we may incur upon the account of our being so. Now, whereas the fear of man is one principal cause or means of our failing in holiness and obedience, either by sudden surprisals or violent temptations, and the next hereunto is the consideration of other things esteemed good or evil in this world, the faith and sense hereof will bear us up above them, deliver us from them, and carry us through them.

Be of good courage, all ye that trust in the Lord; you may, you ought, without fear or dauntedness of spirit, to engage into the pursuit of universal holiness. He who hath commanded it, who hath required it of you, will bear you out in it. Nothing that is truly evil or finally disadvantageous shall befall you on that account: for let the world rage whilst it pleaseth, and threaten to fill all things with blood and confusion, "to God the Lord belong the issues from death;" he alone can "kill" and "make alive." There is, therefore, no small enforcement unto holiness from the consideration of the command, with respect unto the power of the commander, relating unto things in this world.

(2.) But I suppose it is a power of eternal rewards and punishments that is principally here intended. The "killing" here is that mentioned by our Saviour, and opposed to all temporal evils, and death itself: Matt. x. 28, "Fear not them who can kill the body, but are not able to kill the soul: but rather fear him who is able to destroy both soul and body in hell." And this "keeping alive" is a deliverance from the wrath to come in everlasting life. And this is that which gives an unavoidable efficacy to the command. Every command of a superior doth tacitly include a reward and punishment to be intended; for a declaration is made of what is pleasing and what is displeasing unto him that gives the command, and therein is there a virtual promise and threatening. But unto all solemn laws rewards and punishments are expressly annexed.

But there are two reasons why, for the most part, they do but little influence the minds of men who are inclined unto their transgression :— [1.] The first is, that the rewards and punishments declared are such as men think they do justly prefer their own satisfaction in the transgression of the laws before them. It is so with all good men with respect unto laws made contrary to the laws of God; and wise men also may do so with respect unto useless laws, with trifling penalties; and evil men will do so with respect unto the highest temporal punishments, when they are greedily set on the satisfaction of their lusts. Hence I say it is, in the first place, that the minds of men are so little influenced with those rewards and punishments that are annexed unto human laws. And, [2.] A secret apprehension that the commanders or makers of the laws neither will nor are able to execute those penalties in case of their transgression, evacuates all the force of them. Much they ascribe to their negligence, that they will not take care to see the sanction of their laws executed; more to their ignorance, that they shall not be able to find out their transgressions; and somewhat in sundry cases to their power, that they cannot punish nor reward though they would. And for these reasons are the minds of men little influenced by human laws beyond their own honest inclinations and interest. But things are quite otherwise with respect unto the law and commands of God that we should be holy. The rewards and punishments, called by the apostle "killing" and "keeping alive," being eternal, in the highest capacities of blessedness or misery, cannot be balanced by any consideration of this present world without the highest folly and villainy unto ourselves; nor can there be any reserve on the account of mutability, indifferency, ignorance, impotency, or any other pretence that they shall not be executed. Wherefore, the commands of God, which we are in the consideration of, are accompanied with promises and threatenings, of eternal blessedness on the one hand or of misery on the other; and these will certainly befall us, according as we shall be found holy or unholy. All the properties of the nature of God are immutably engaged in this matter, and hence ensues an indispensable necessity of our being holy. God commands that we should be so; but what if we are not so? Why, as sure as God is holy and powerful, we shall eternally perish, for with the threatening of that condition is his command accompanied in case of disobedience. What if we do comply with the command and become holy? Upon the same ground of assurance we shall be brought into everlasting felicity. And this is greatly to be considered in the authority of the commandment. Some, perhaps, will say, that to yield holy obedience unto God with respect unto rewards and punishments is servile, and becomes not the free spirit of the children of God. But these are vain imaginations; the bondage of our own spirits may make everything we do servile. But a due respect unto God's promises and threatenings is a principal part of our liberty. And thus doth the necessity of holiness, which we are engaged in the demonstration of, depend on the command of God, because of that authority from whence it doth proceed and wherewith it is accompanied. It is, therefore, certainly our duty, if we would be found walking in a course of obedience and in the practice of holiness, to keep a sense hereof constantly fixed on our minds. This is that which, in the first place, God intends in that great injunction of obedience, Gen. xvii. 1, "I am the Almighty God; walk before me, and be thou perfect." The way to walk uprightly, to be sincere or perfect in obedience, is always to consider that he who requires it of us is God Almighty, accompanied with all the authority and power before mentioned, and under whose eye we are continually. And, in particular, we may apply this unto persons and occasions:—

[1.] As to persons. Let them, in an especial manner, have a continual regard hereunto, who on any account are great, or high, or noble in the world, and that because their especial temptation is to be lifted up unto a forgetfulness or regardlessness of this authority of God. The prophet [Jeremiah] distributes incorrigible sinners into two sorts, and gives the different grounds of their impenitency respectively. The first are the poor; and it is their folly, stupidity, and sensual lusts, that keep them off from attending to the command: chap. v. 3, 4, "They have refused to receive correction: they have made their faces harder than a rock; they have refused to return. Therefore I said, Surely these are poor; they are sottish: for they know not the way of the Lord, nor the judgment of their God." There is a sort of poor incorrigible sinners, whose impenitency ariseth much out of their ignorance, blindness, and folly, which they please themselves in, although they differ but little from the beasts that perish; and such do we abound withal, who will take no pains for, who will admit of no means of, instruction. But there is another sort of sinners to whom the prophet makes his application, and discovers the ground of their incorrigible impenitency also: "I will get me to the great men, and will speak unto them; for they have known the way of the Lord, and the judgment of their God," verse 5. Great men, by reason of their education and other advantages, do attain unto a knowledge of the will of God, or at least may be thought so to have done, and would be esteemed to excel therein. They, therefore, are not likely to be obstinate in sin merely from stupid ignorance and folly. "No," saith the prophet, "they take another course; 'they have altogether broken the yoke, and burst the bonds.' " They are like a company of rude beasts of the field, which, having broken their yokes and cords, do run up and down the fields, treading down the corn, breaking up the fences, pushing with the horn, and trampling down all before them. This is the course of men, in the pursuit of their lusts, when they have "broken the yoke of the Lord." And this the prophet declares to be the especial evil of great men, the rich, the mighty, the honourable in the world. Now, this "breaking of the yoke" is the neglecting and despising of the authority of God in the command. Seeing, therefore, that this is the especial temptation of that sort of persons, and things innumerable there are of all sorts that concur to render that temptation prevalent upon them, let all those who are of that condition, and have the least sincere desire after holiness, watch diligently, as they love and value their souls, to keep always and in all things a due sense of the authority of God in his commands upon their minds and consciences. When you are in the height of your greatness, in the fullness of your enjoyments, in the most urgent of your avocations by the things or societies of the world, and those who belong to it, when the variety of public appearances and attendancies are about you, when you are uppermost in the words of others, and it may be in your own thoughts, remember Him who is over all, and consider that you are subject and obnoxious unto his authority, equally with the poorest creature on the earth. Remember that it is your especial temptation to do otherwise. And if you do yet abhor those who by this means are come to be sons of Belial, or such as have altogether broken the yoke, and run up and down the world in the pursuit of their lusts, saying, "Our lips are our own, and who is lord over us?" be you watchful against the least beginnings or entrances of it in yourselves.

[2.] In general, let us all endeavour to carry a constant regard unto the authority of God in his commands into all those seasons, places, societies, occasions, wherein we are apt to be surprised in any sin or a neglect of duty. And I may reduce this instruction or point it unto three heads or occasions, — namely, secrecy, businesses, and societies. 1st. Carry this along with you into your secret retirements and enjoyments. Neglect hereof is the next cause of those secret actual provoking sins which the world swarms with. When no eye sees but the eye of God, men think themselves secure. Hereby have many been surprised into folly, which hath proved the beginning of a total apostasy. An awe upon the heart from the authority of God in the command will equally secure us in all places and on all occasions. 2dly. Let us carry it into our businesses, and the exercise of our trades or callings. Most men in these things are very apt to be intent on present occasions, and having a certain end before them, do habituate themselves into the ways of its attainment; and whilst they are so engaged, many things occur which are apt to divert them from the rule of holiness. Whenever, therefore, you enter into your occasions, wherein you may suppose that temptations will arise, call to mind the greatness, power, and authority over you of Him who hath commanded you in all things to be holy. Upon every entrance of a surprisal, make your retreat unto such thoughts, which will prove your relief. 3dly. Carry it with you into your companies and societies; for many have frequent occasions of engaging in such societies, as wherein the least forgetfulness of the sovereign authority of God will betray them unto profuseness in vanity and corrupt communication, until they do with delight and hear with pleasure such things as wherewith the Holy Spirit of God is grieved, their own consciences are defiled, and the honour of profession is cast to the ground.

Secondly, The command of God that we should be holy is not to be considered only as an effect of power and authority, which we must submit unto, but as a fruit of infinite wisdom and goodness also, which it is our highest advantage and interest to comply withal. And this introduceth a peculiar necessity of holiness, from the consideration of what is equal, reasonable, ingenuous; the contrary whereunto is foolish, perverse, ungrateful, every way unbecoming rational creatures. Where nothing can be discerned in commands but mere authority, will, and pleasure, they are looked on as merely respecting the good of them that command, and not at all theirs who are to obey, which disheartens and weakens the principle of obedience. Now, though God, because his dominion over us is sovereign and absolute, might have justly left unto us no other reason or motive of our obedience, and, it may be, did so deal with the church of old, as to some particular, temporary, ceremonial institutions; yet he doth not, nor ever did so, as to the main of their obedience. But as he proposeth his law as an effect of infinite wisdom, love, and goodness, so he declares and pleads that all his commands are just and equal in themselves, good and useful unto us, and that our compliance with them is our present as well as it will be our future happiness. And that this is so, that the command of God requiring that we should be holy, as a fruit of wisdom and goodness, is equal and advantageous unto ourselves, appears from all the considerations of it:—

1. Look upon it formally, as a law prescribed unto us, and it is so, because the obedience in holiness which it requires is proportioned unto the strength and power which we have to obey, which declares it equal unto us, and an effect of infinite wisdom and goodness in God. The command, as we showed before, may be considered either as it belonged unto the old covenant, or as it is annexed unto, and so is a part of, the new. In the first way, as it belonged unto the old covenant, the strength of grace which we had originally from God under the law of creation was sufficient to enable us unto all that holy obedience which was required therein, and our not doing so was from wilful rebellion, and not from any impotency or weakness in us. We fell not from our first estate for want of power to obey, but by the neglect of the exercise of that power which we had. God made us upright, but we sought out many inventions. And in the latter way, as it belongs to the covenant of grace, there is, by virtue of that covenant, a supply of spiritual strength given in by the promise unto all them who are taken into it, enabling them to answer the commands for holiness, according to the rule of the acceptance of their obedience, before laid down. No man who is instated in the covenant of grace comes short or fails of the performance of that obedience which is required and accepted in that covenant merely for want of power and spiritual strength; for God therein, according to his divine power, gives unto us "all things that pertain unto life and godliness, through the knowledge of him that hath called us to glory and virtue," 2 Pet. i. 3. It is true, this grace or strength is administered unto them by certain ways and means, which if they attend not unto they will come short of it. But this I say, in the careful, diligent, sedulous use of those means appointed, none who belong to the covenant of grace shall ever fail of that power and ability which shall render the commands of the gospel easy and not grievous unto them, and whereby they may so fulfil them as infallibly to be accepted. This the Scripture is plain in, where Christ himself tells us that "his yoke is easy, and his burden light," Matt. xi. 30; and his holy apostle, that "his commandments are not grievous," 1 John v. 3: for if they should exceed all the strength which we

either have or he is pleased to give unto us, they would be like the Jewish ceremonies, — a yoke which we could not bear, and a law not only grievous but unprofitable. But, on the contrary, our apostle expressly affirms (and so may we) that "he could do all things," — that is, in the way and manner, and unto the end for which they are required in the gospel, — "through Christ that strengthened him. Some would confound these things, and cast all into disorder. They would have men that are under the old covenant to have a power and spiritual strength to fulfil the commands of the new; which God hath never spoken of nor declared, and which, indeed, is contrary to the whole design of his grace. They would have men who have broken the old covenant, and forfeited all their strength and ability which they had by it for obedience, and who are not initiated in the new covenant, yet to have a power of their own to fulfil the command of the one or the other; which God neither giveth nor is obliged to give. Nor is it necessary to prove that the command is equal and holy; for, as was observed, God giveth us no command for holiness and obedience but in, with, and by virtue of some covenant. And there is no more required to prove them to be just and equal, but that they are easy unto them who walk with God in that covenant whereunto they do belong, and that that performance of them shall be accepted which they have power for. If any will sinfully cast away their covenant interest and privilege, as we all did that of our original creation, we must thank ourselves if we have not power to answer its commands. Nor doth it belong unto the equity of the commands of the new covenant that those who are not yet made partakers of it by grace should have power to fulfil them. Nay, if they had so, and should do so accordingly (were any such thing possible), it would not avail them: for being supposed not as yet to belong unto the new covenant, they must belong unto the old; and the performance of the commands of the new covenant, in the way and manner which are required therein, would not avail them who are really under the rule and law of the old, which admits of nothing short of absolute perfection. But "what the law speaks, it speaks unto them that are under the law;" and what the gospel speaks, it speaks unto them "who are not under the law, but under grace." And the formal transition of men from one of these states unto another is by an act of God's grace, wherein themselves are merely passive, as hath elsewhere been demonstrated. See Col. i. 13.

This is that which I do intend: God at first made a covenant with mankind, the first covenant, the covenant of works. Herein he gave them commands for holy obedience. These commands were not only possible unto them, both for matter and manner, by virtue of that strength and power which was concreated with them, but easy and pleasant, every way suited unto their good and satisfaction in that state and condition. This rendered their obedience equal, just, reasonable, and aggravated their sin with the guilt of the most horrible folly and ingratitude. When by the fall this covenant was broken, we lost therewith all power and ability to comply with its commands in holy obedience. Hereupon the "law" continued "holy, and the commandment holy, and just, and good," as our apostle speaks, Rom. vii. 12; for what should make it otherwise, seeing there was no change in it by sin, nor did God require more or harder things of us than before? But to us it became impossible, for we had lost the strength by which alone we were enabled to observe it; and so "the commandment, which was ordained to life, we find to be unto death," verse 10. Towards all, therefore, that remain in that state we say, "The commandment is still just and holy, but it is neither easy nor possible." Hereon God brings in the covenant of grace by Christ, and renews therein the commands for holy obedience, as was before declared. And here it is that men trouble themselves and others about the power, ability, and free-will that men have as yet under the first covenant, and the impotence that ensued on the transgression of it to fulfil the condition of the new covenant, and yield the obedience required in it; for this is the place where men make their great contests about the power of free-will and the possibility of God's command. Let them but grant that it is the mere work of God's sovereign and almighty grace effectually to instate men in the new covenant, and we shall contend with them or against them, that by virtue thereof they have such spiritual strength and grace administered unto them as render all the commands of it to be not only possible but easy also, yea, pleasant, and every way suited unto the principle of a holy life, wherewith they are endued. And this we make an argument for the necessity of holiness. The argument we have under consideration is that whereby we prove the necessity of holiness with respect unto God's command requiring it, because it is a fruit of infinite wisdom and goodness. It is so in an especial manner as it belongs unto the new covenant. And, therefore, by our disobedience or living in sin, unto the contempt of God's authority we add that of his wisdom and goodness also. Now, that it is so a fruit of them appears, in the first place, from hence, that it is proportioned unto the strength and ability which we have to obey. Hence obedience in holiness becomes equal, easy, and pleasant unto all believers who sincerely attend unto it; and this fully evinceth the necessity of it, from the folly and ingratitude of the contrary. That these things, and in them the force of the present argument, may the better be apprehended, I shall dispose them into the ensuing observations:—

(1.) We do not say that anyone hath this power and ability in himself or from himself. God hath not in the new covenant brought down his command to the power of man, but by his grace he raiseth the power of man unto his command. The former were only a compliance with the sin of our nature, which God abhors; the latter is the exaltation of his own grace, which he aimeth at. It is not men's strength in and of themselves, the power of nature, but the grace which is administered in the covenant, that we intend. For men to trust unto themselves herein, as though they could do any thing of themselves, is a renunciation of all the aids of grace, without which we can do nothing. We can have no power from Christ unless we live in a persuasion that we have none of our own. Our whole spiritual life is a life of faith; and that is a life of dependence on Christ for what we have not of ourselves. This is that which ruins the attempt of many for holiness, and renders what they do (though it be like unto the acts and duties of it) not at all to belong unto it; for what we do in our own strength is no part of holiness, as is evident from the preceding description of it. Neither doth the Scripture abound in any thing more than in testifying that the power and ability we have to fulfil the commands of God, as given in the new covenant, is not our own, nor from ourselves, but merely from the grace of God administered in that covenant: as John xv. 5; Phil. ii. 13; 2 Cor. iii. 5. It will be said, then, "Where lies the difference? Because it is the mere work of grace to instate us in the covenant, you conclude that we have no power of our own to that purpose. And if when we are in covenant, all our strength and power is still from grace, we are, as to any ability of our own to fulfil the command of God, as remote from it as ever." I answer, The first work of grace is merely upon us. Hereby the image of God is renewed, our hearts are changed, and a principle of spiritual life is bestowed on us. But this latter work of grace is in us and by us. And the strength or ability which we have thereby is as truly our own as Adam's was his which he had in the state of innocency; for he had his immediately from God, and so have we ours, though in a different way.

(2.) There is no such provision of spiritual strength for any man, enabling him to comply with the command of God for holiness, as to countenance him in the least carnal security, or the least neglect of the diligent use of all those means which God hath appointed for the communication thereof unto us, with the preservation and increase of it. God, who hath determined graciously to give us supplies thereof, hath also declared that we are obliged unto our utmost diligence for the participation of them, and unto their due exercise when received. This innumerable commands and injunctions give testimony unto, but especially is the whole method of God's grace and our duty herein declared by the apostle Peter, 2 Epist. i. 3–11; which discourse I have opened and improved elsewhere.[3] The sum is, That God creating in us a new spiritual nature, and therewithal giving unto us "all things pertaining unto life and godliness," or a gracious ability for the duties of a holy, godly, spiritual life, we are obliged to use all means, in the continual exercise of all grace, which will ascertain unto us our eternal election, with our effectual vocation, whereon we shall obtain an assured, joyful entrance into the kingdom of glory.

(3.) This administration of grace and spiritual strength is not equally effectual at all times. There are seasons wherein, to correct our negligences in giving place to our corruptions and temptations, or on other grounds, to discover unto us our own frailty and impotency, with other holy ends of his own, God is pleased to withhold the powerful influences of his grace, and to leave us unto ourselves. In such instances we shall assuredly come short of answering the command for universal holiness, one way or other. See Ps. xxx. 6, 7. But I speak of ordinary cases, and to prevent that slothfulness and tergiversation unto this duty of complying with all the commands of God for holiness which we are so obnoxious unto. (4.) We do not say that there is in the covenant of grace spiritual strength administered, so as that by virtue thereof we should yield sinless and absolutely perfect obedience unto God, or to render any one duty so absolutely perfect. If any such there are, or ever were, who maintain such an imputation of the righteousness of Christ unto us as should render our own personal obedience unnecessary, they do overthrow the truth and holiness of the gospel. And to say that we have such supplies of internal strength as to render the imputation of the righteousness of Christ unto our justification unnecessary, is to overthrow the grace of the gospel and the new covenant itself. But this alone we say, There is grace administered by the promises of the gospel, enabling us to perform the obedience of it in that way and manner which God will accept. And herein there are various degrees, whereof we ought constantly to aim at the most complete, and so to be "perfecting holiness in the fear of God." And where we signally come short of the best rules and examples, it is principally from our neglect of those supplies of grace which are tendered in the promises.

(5.) There is a twofold gracious power necessary to render the command for holiness and obedience thereunto easy and pleasant: —

[1.] That which is habitually resident in the hearts and souls of believers, whereby they are constantly inclined and disposed unto all fruits of holiness. This the Scripture calls our "life," a new principle of life, without which we are dead in trespasses and sins. Where this is not, whatever arguments you constrain and press men withal to be holy, you do, as it were, but offer violence unto them, endeavouring to force them against the fixed bent and inclination of their minds. By them all you do but set up a dam against a stream of water, which will not be permanent, nor turn the course of the stream contrary to its natural inclination. Unto such the command for holiness must needs be grievous and difficult. But such a disposition and inclination, or a principle so inclining and disposing us unto duties of holiness, we have not in or of ourselves by nature, nor is it to be raised out of its ruins; for the "carnal mind" (which is in us all) "is enmity against God," which carrieth in it an aversation unto everything that is required of us in a way of obedience, as hath been proved at large. And yet without this habitual principle, we can never in a due manner comply with any one command of God that we should be holy. Want hereof is that which renders obedience so grievous and burdensome unto many. They endure it for a season, and at length either violently or insensibly cast off its yoke. Light and conviction have compelled them to take it on themselves, and to attend unto the performance of those duties which they dare not omit; — but having no principle enabling or inclining them unto it, all they do, though they do much, and continue long therein, is against the grain with them; they find it difficult, uneasy, and wearisome. Wherein they can by any pretence countenance themselves in a neglect of any part of it, or bribe their consciences into a compliance with what is contrary unto it, they fail not to deliver themselves from their burden. And, for the most part, either insensibly, by multiplied instances of the neglect of duties of obedience, or by some great temptation before they leave the world, they utterly leave all the ways of holiness and respect unto the commands of God, or if they continue in any, it is unto external acts of morality, which pass with approbation in the world; the inward and spiritual part of obedience they utterly renounce. The reason hereof, I say, is, because having no principle within, enabling them unto a compliance with the commands of God with delight and satisfaction, they grow grievous and intolerable unto them. So unto many, on the same ground, the worship of God is very burdensome, unless it be borne for them by external additions and ornaments.

[2.] There is an actual assistance of effectual grace required hereunto. We are not put into such condition by the covenant as that we should be able to do any thing of ourselves without actual divine assistance. This were to set us free from our dependence on God, and to make us gods unto ourselves. The root still bears us, and the springs of our spiritual life are in another. And where both these are, there the command is equal, not only in itself but unto us, and obedience unto it as easy as just.

(6.) And both these sorts of grace are administered in the new covenant, suited unto the holy obedience it requires:—

[1.] For the first, it is that which God so frequently, so expressly promiseth, where he says that "he will take away the heart of stone, and give us a heart of flesh;" that "he will write his laws in our hearts, and put his fear in our inward parts;" that we shall "fear him," and "never depart from him;" that he will "circumcise our hearts" to "know" and "love" him; — which promises, and the nature of the grace contained in them, I have before at large explained. It is sufficient unto our present purpose that in and by these promises we are made partakers of the divine nature, and are therein endowed with a constant, habitual disposition and inclination unto all acts and duties of holiness; for our power followeth our love and inclinations, as impotency is a consequent of their defect.

And here we may stay a little to confirm our principal assertion. Upon the supply of this grace, which gives both strength for and a constant inclination unto holy obedience, the command for it becomes equal and just, meet and easy to be complied withal: for none can refuse a compliance with it in any instance, but their so doing is contrary unto that disposition and inclination of the new nature which God hath implanted in themselves; so that for them to sin is not only contrary to the law without them, to the light of their minds and warning of their consciences, but it is also unto that which is their own inclination and disposition, which hath sensibly in such cases a force and violence put upon it by the power of corruptions and temptations. Wherefore, although the command for holiness may and doth seem grievous and burdensome unto unregenerate persons, as we have observed, because it is against the habitual bent and inclination of their whole souls, yet neither is it nor can it be so unto them who cannot neglect it or act any thing against it, but that therein, also, they must crucify and offer violence unto the inclinations of the new creature in them, which are their own; for in all things "the spirit lusteth against the flesh," Gal. v. 17, and the disposition of the new creature is habitually against sin and for holiness. And this gives a mighty constraining power unto the command, when it is evident in our own minds and consciences that it requires nothing of us but what we do or may find an inclination or disposition in our own hearts unto. And by this consideration we may take in the power of it upon our souls, which is too frequently disregarded. Let us but, upon the proposal of it unto us, consider what our minds and hearts say to it, what answer they return, and we shall quickly discern how equal and just the command is; for I cannot persuade myself that any believer can be so captivated at any time, under the power of temptations, corruptions, or prejudices, but that (if he will but take counsel with his own soul, upon the consideration of the command for obedience and holiness, and ask himself what he would have) he will have a plain and sincere answer, "That, indeed, I would do and have the good proposed, this holiness, this duty of obedience." Not only will conscience answer, that he must not do the evil whereunto temptation leadeth, for if he do, evil will ensue thereon; but the new nature, and his mind and spirit, will say, "This good I would do; I delight in it; it is best for me, most suited unto me." And so it joins all the strength and interest it hath in the soul with the command. See to this purpose the arguing of our apostle, Rom. vii. 20–22. It is true, there is a natural light in conscience, complying with the command in its proposal, and urging obedience thereunto, which doth not make it easy to us, but, where it is alone, increaseth its burden and our bondage; for it doth only give in its suffrage unto the sanction of the command, and add to the severity wherewith it is attended. But that compliance with the command which is from a principle of grace is quite of another nature, and greatly facilitates obedience. And we may distinguish between that compliance with the command which is from the natural light of conscience, which genders unto bondage, and that which, being from a renewed principle of grace, gives liberty and ease in obedience: for the first respects principally the consequent of obedience or disobedience, the good or evil that will ensue upon them, Rom. ii. 14, 15; set aside this consideration, and it hath no more to say; — but the latter respects the command itself, which it embraceth, delighteth in, and judgeth good and holy, with the duties themselves required, which are natural and suited thereunto. [2.] Grace of the latter sort, also, actual grace for every holy act and duty, is administered unto us according to the promise of the gospel. So God told Paul that "his grace was sufficient for him." And "he worketh in us both to will and to do of his good pleasure," Phil. ii. 13, so as that we "may do all things" through him that enables us; the nature of which grace also hath been before discoursed of. Now, although this actual working of grace be not in the power of the wills of men, to make use of or refuse as they see good, but its administration depends merely on the grace and faithfulness of God, yet this I must say, that where it is sought in a due manner by faith and prayer, it is never so restrained from any believer but that it shall be effectual in him, unto the whole of that obedience which is required of him, and as it will be accepted from him.

If, then, this be the condition of the command of holiness, how just and equal must it needs be confessed to be! and therefore how highly reasonable is it that we should comply with it, and how great is their sin and folly by whom it is neglected! It is true, we are absolutely obliged unto obedience by the mere authority of God who commands, but he not only allows us to take in, but directs us to seek after, those other considerations of it which may give it force and efficacy upon our souls and consciences. And among these, none is more efficacious towards gracious, ingenuous souls than this of the contemperation of the duties commanded unto spiritual aids of strength promised unto us; for what cloak or pretence of dislike or neglect is here left unto any? Wherefore not only the authority of God in giving a command, but the infinite wisdom and goodness of God in giving such a command, so just, equal, and gentle, fall upon us therein, to oblige us to holy obedience. To neglect or despise this command is to neglect or despise God in that way which he hath chosen to manifest all the holy properties of his nature.

2. The command is equal, and so to be esteemed from the matter of it, or the things that it doth require. Things they are that are neither great nor grievous, much less perverse, useless, or evil, Mic. vi. 6–8. There is nothing in the holiness which the command requires but what is good to him in whom it is, and useful to all others concerned in him or what he doth. What they are the apostle mentions in his exhortation unto them, Phil. iv. 8. They are "things true," and "honest," and "just," and "pure," and "lovely," and "of good report." And what evil is there in any of these things, that we should decline the command that requires them? The more we abound in them, the better it will be for our relations, our families, our neighbours, the whole nation, and the world, but best of all for ourselves. "Godliness is profitable unto all things," 1 Tim. iv. 8. "These things are good and profitable unto men," Tit. iii. 8, — good to them that do them, and good to those towards whom they are done. But both these things, — namely, the usefulness of holiness unto ourselves and others, — must be spoken unto distinctly afterward, and are, therefore, transmitted unto their proper place.

Therefore, as it was before observed, it is incumbent on us, in the first place, to endeavour after holiness and the improvement of it, with respect unto the command of God that we should be holy, and because of it, and that especially under the consideration of it which we have insisted on. I know not what vain imaginations have seemed to possess the minds of some, that they have no need of respect unto the command, nor to the promises and threatenings of it, but to obey merely from the power and guidance of an inward principle; nay, some have supposed that a respect unto the command would vitiate our obedience, rendering it legal and servile! But I hope that darkness which hindered men from discerning the harmony and compliance which is between the principle of grace in us and the authority of the command upon us is much taken away from all sincere professors. It is a respect unto the command which gives the formal nature of obedience unto what we do; and without a due regard unto it there is nothing of holiness in us. Some would make the light of nature to be their rule; some, in what they do, look no farther for their measure than what carries the reputation of common honesty among men. He that would be holy indeed must always mind the command of God, with that reverence and those affections which become him to whom God speaks immediately. And that it may be effectual towards us we may consider, —

(1.) How God hath multiplied his commands unto this purpose, to testify not only his own infinite care of us and love unto us, but also our eternal concernment in what he requires. He doth not give out unto us a single command that we should be holy (which yet were sufficient to oblige us forever), but he gives his commands unto that purpose, "line upon line, line upon line, precept upon precept, precept upon precept." He that shall but look over the Bible, and see almost every page of it filled with commands, or directions, or instructions for holiness, cannot but conclude that the mind and will of God is very much in this matter, and that our concernment therein is inexpressible. Nor doth God content himself to multiply commands in general that we should be holy, so as that if we have regard unto him they may never be out of our remembrance, but there is not any particular duty or instance of holiness but he hath given us especial commands for that also. No man can instance in the least duty that belongs directly unto it, but it falls under some especial command of God. We are not only, then, under the command of God in general, and that often reiterated unto us, in an awful reverence whereof we ought to walk, but, upon all occasions, whatever we have to do or avoid in following after holiness is represented unto us in especial commands to that purpose; and they are all of them a fruit of the love and care of God towards us. Is it not, then, our duty always to consider these commands, to bind them unto our hearts, and our hearts to them, that nothing may separate them? O that they might always dwell in our minds, to influence them unto an inward constant watch against the first disorders of our souls, that are unsuited to the inward holiness God requires, — abide with us in our closets, and all our occasions for our good!

(2.) We may do well to consider what various enforcements God is pleased to give unto those multiplied commands. He doth not remit us merely to their authority, but he applieth all other ways and means whereby they may be made effectual. Hence are they accompanied with exhortations, entreaties, reasonings, expostulations, promises, threatenings; all made use of to fasten the command upon our minds and consciences. God knows how slow and backward we are to receive due impressions from his authority, and he knows by what ways and means the principles of our internal faculties are apt to be wrought upon, and therefore applies these engines to fix the power of the command upon us. Were these things to be treated of severally, it is manifest how great a part of the Scripture were to be transcribed. I shall, therefore, only take a little notice of the re-enforcement of the command for holiness by those especial promises which are given unto it. I do not intend now the promises of the gospel in general, wherein, in its own way and place, we are interested by holiness, but such peculiar promises as God enforceth the command by. It is not for nothing that it is said that "godliness hath the promise of the life that now is, and of that which is to come," 1 Tim. iv. 8. There is in all the promises an especial respect unto it; and it gives them in whom it is an especial interest in all the promises.

This is, as it were, the text which our Saviour preached his first sermon upon; for all the blessings which he pronounceth consist in giving particular instances of some parts of holiness, annexing an especial promise unto each of them. "Blessed," saith he, "are the pure in heart." Heart purity is the spring and life of all holiness. And why are such persons blessed? Why, saith he, "they shall see God." He appropriates the promise of the eternal enjoyment of God unto this qualification of purity of heart. So also it hath the promise of this life, and that in things temporal and spiritual. In things temporal, we may take out from amongst many that especial instance given us by the psalmist, "Blessed is he that considereth the poor." Wisely to consider the poor in their distress, so as to relieve them according to our ability, is a great act and duty of holiness. "He that doeth this," saith the psalmist, "he is a blessed man." Whence doth that blessedness arise, and wherein doth it consist? It doth so in a participation of those especial promises which God hath annexed unto this duty even in this life: "The Lord will deliver him in time of trouble. The Lord will preserve him, and keep him alive; and he shall be blessed upon the earth: and thou wilt not deliver him unto the will of his enemies. The Lord will strengthen him upon the bed of languishing: thou wilt make all his bed in his sickness," Ps. xli. 1–3. Many especial promises in the most important concerns of this life are given unto the right discharge of this one duty; for godliness hath the promise of this life. And other instances might be multiplied unto the same purpose. It is so also with respect unto things spiritual. So the apostle Peter, having repeated a long chain of graces, whose exercise he presenteth unto us, adds for an encouragement, "If ye do these things ye shall never fall," 2 Pet. i. 10. The promise of permanency in obedience, with an absolute preservation from all such fallings into sin as are inconsistent with the covenant of grace, is affixed unto our diligence in holiness. And who knows not how the Scripture abounds in instances of this nature? That which we conclude from hence is, that together with the command of God requiring us to be holy, we should consider the promises wherewith it is accompanied (among other things) as an encouragement unto the cheerful performance of that obedience which the command itself makes necessary.

Wherefore the force of this argument is evident and exposed unto all. God hath in this matter positively declared his will, interposing his sovereign authority, commanding us to be holy, and that on the penalty of his utmost displeasure; and he hath therewithal given us redoubled assurance (as in a case wherein we are very apt to deceive ourselves) that, be we else what we will or can be, without sincere holiness he will neither own us nor have any thing to do with us. Be our gifts, parts, abilities, places, dignities, usefulness in the world, profession, outward duties, what they will, unless we are sincerely holy (which we may not be and yet be eminent in all these things), we are not, we cannot, we shall not be, accepted with God.

And the Holy Ghost is careful to obviate a deceit in this matter which he foresaw would be apt to put itself on the minds of men; for whereas the foundation of our salvation in ourselves, and the hinge whereon the whole weight of it doth turn, is our faith, men might be apt to think that if they have faith, it will be well enough with them, although they are not holy. Therefore, because this plea and pretence of faith is great, and apt to impose on the minds of men, who would willingly retain their lusts with a hope and expectation of heaven, we are plainly told in the Scripture that that faith which is without holiness, without works, without fruits, which can be so, or is possible that it should be so, is vain, [is] not that faith which will save our souls, but equivocally so called, that may perish forever with those in whom it is.

Footnotes:

3. He has had frequent occasion to refer to this passage, but see more especially book iv. chap. ii., on page 395 of this volume. — Ed.

Chapter IV - Necessity of holiness from God's sending Jesus Christ

The necessity of holiness proved from the design of God in sending Jesus Christ, with the ends of his mediation.

IV. We have yet other considerations and arguments to plead unto the same purpose with them foregoing; for one principal end of the design of God in sending his Son into the world was, to recover us into a state of holiness, which we had lost: "For this purpose the Son of God was manifested, that he might destroy the works of the devil," 1 John iii. 8. The manifestation of the Son of God was his incarnation, 1 Tim. iii. 16, in order to the work which he had to accomplish in our nature; and this was, in general, the destruction of the works of the devil; and among these, the principal was the infecting of our nature and persons with a principle of sin and enmity against God, which was the effect of his temptation. And this is not done but by the introduction of a principle of holiness and obedience. The image of God in us was defaced by sin. The renovation or restoration hereof was one principal design of Christ in his coming. Unless this be done, there is no new world, no new creatures, no restoration of all things, — no one end of the mediation of Christ fully accomplished. And whereas his great and ultimate design was to bring us unto the enjoyment of God, unto his eternal glory, this cannot be before, by grace and holiness, we are "made meet for that inheritance of the saints in light." But we shall consider this matter a little more distinctly. The exercise of the mediation of Christ is confined unto the limits of his threefold office. Whatever he doth for the church, he doth it as a priest, or as a king, or as a prophet. Now, as these offices agree in all the general ends of his mediation, so they differ in their acts and immediate objects: for their acts, it is plain, — sacerdotal, regal, and prophetical acts and duties, — are of different natures, as the offices themselves are unto which they appertain; and for their objects, the proper immediate object of the priestly office is God himself, as is evident both from the nature of the office and its proper acts. For as to the nature of the office, "every priest taken from among men is ordained for men in things pertaining to God, that he may offer both gifts and sacrifices for sins," Heb. v. 1. A priest is one who is appointed to deal with God in the behalf of them for whom he executes his office. And the acts of the priestly office of Christ are two, oblation and intercession, of both which God is the immediate object. He offered himself unto God, and with him he makes intercession. But the immediate object of Christ's kingly and prophetical offices are men or the church. As a priest, he acts with God in our name and on our behalf; as a king and prophet, he acts towards us in the name and authority of God.

This being premised, we may consider how each of these offices of Christ hath an influence into holiness, and makes it necessary unto us:—

First, For the priestly office of Christ, all the proper acts of it do immediately respect God himself, as hath been declared; and, therefore, he doth not by any sacerdotal act immediately and efficiently work holiness in us. But the effects of these priestly acts, that is, his oblation and intercession, are of two sorts:— 1. Immediate, such as respect God himself; as atonement, reconciliation, satisfaction. In these consist the first and fundamental end of the mediation of Christ. Without a supposition of these all other things are rendered useless. We can neither be sanctified nor saved by him unless sin be first expiated and God atoned. But they are not of our present consideration. 2. The mediate effects of Christ's sacerdotal actings respect us, and are also of two sorts:— (1.) Moral, as our justification and pardon of sin. (2.) Real, in our sanctification and holiness. And hereunto, as God doth design them, so he effecteth holiness in all believers by virtue of the oblation and intercession of Jesus Christ. Wherefore, although the immediate actings of that office respect God alone as their proper object, yet the virtue and efficacy of them extend themselves unto our sanctification and holiness.

Tit. ii. 14, "He gave himself for us, that he might redeem us from all iniquity, and purify unto himself a peculiar people, zealous of good works." His "giving himself for us" is the common expression for his offering himself a sacrifice to God as a priest, Eph. v. 2. And this he did not only that he might "redeem us from all iniquity," from the guilt of our sins, and punishment due unto them, which are regarded in redemption, but also that he might "purify us to himself," sanctify us, or make us holy and fruitful, or "zealous of good works." His blood, as through the eternal Spirit he offered himself unto God, "purgeth our conscience from dead works to serve the living God," Heb. ix. 14. There is a purging of sin which consists in the legal expiation of it, in making atonement; but the purging of a sinner, or of the conscience, is by real efficiency, in sanctification, which is declared to be one end of the oblation of Christ, chap. i. 3. So where he is said to "wash us from our sins in his own blood," — namely, as shed and offered for us, — Rev. i. 5, it is not only the expiation of guilt, but the purification of filth, that is intended.

The way and manner how holiness is communicated unto us by virtue of the death and oblation of Christ, I have showed before at large, and shall not, therefore, here again insist upon it. I shall only observe, that holiness being one especial end for which Christ "gave himself for us," or "offered himself unto God" for us, without a participation thereof it is impossible that we should have the least evidence of an interest in his oblation as to any other end of it; and as for those who are never made holy, Christ never died or offered himself for them. I cannot understand what advantage it is unto religion to affirm that the most of them for whom Christ died as a priest, or offered himself as an oblation to God, shall have no benefit thereby as to grace or glory, and incomparably the most of them without any especial fault of their own, as never hearing of him. Neither can I find in the Scripture a double design of Christ in giving himself for mankind; — towards some, that they may be redeemed from all iniquity, and purified to be his peculiar ones; towards others, that they may yet be left under the guilt and power of their sins. And it evacuates the force of the motive unto the necessity of holiness from the consideration of the oblation of Christ, when men are taught that Christ offered himself a sacrifice for them who are never made holy. Wherefore, I say, no unholy person can have any certain evidence that he hath an interest in the oblation of Christ, seeing he gave himself to purify them for whom he was offered.

The intercession of Christ, which is his second sacerdotal act, hath also the same end, and is effectual to the same purpose. It is true, he doth intercede with God for the pardon of sin by virtue of his oblation, — whence he is said to be our advocate with God, to comfort us in case of surprisals by sin,1 John ii. 1, 2, — but this is not all he designeth therein; he intercedes also for grace and supplies of the Spirit, that we may be made and kept holy. See John xvii. 15, 17.

Secondly, As to the prophetical office of Christ, the church or men alone are its immediate object, and of all the acts and duties of it. He is therein God's legate and ambassador, his apostle and messenger unto us. Whatever he doth as a prophet, he doth it with us and towards us in the name of God. And there are two parts or works of Christ in this office relating only to the doctrine he taught:— 1. The revelation of God in his name and love, in the mystery of his grace, and goodness, and truth, by his promises, that we may believe in him. 2. The revelation of God in his will and commands, that we may obey him. For the first, wherein, indeed, his prophetical office was principally exercised, see John i. 18, iii. 2, xvii. 6. The revelation of the preceptive will of God made by Jesus Christ may be considered two ways:— (1.) As he was peculiarly sent to the house of Israel, the "minister of the circumcision for the truth of the promises of God unto the fathers," Rom. xv. 8. (2.) With respect unto the whole church of all ages.

(1.) The first, which took up much of his personal ministry in the flesh, consisted in the declarations, exposition, and vindication, that he gave unto the church of all divine precepts for obedience which had been given before. God had from the beginning, and in an especial manner at the promulgation of the law on Sinai, and by the ensuing expositions of it by the prophets, given excellent precepts for holiness and obedience; but the people unto whom they were given being carnal, they were not able to bear the spiritual light and sense of them, which was, therefore, greatly veiled under the Old Testament. Not only the promises, but the precepts also of the law, were then but obscurely apprehended. Besides, the church being grown corrupt, they were solemn expositions of God's commands received amongst them, whose sole design was to accommodate them unto the lusts and sins of men, or to exempt men, if not totally yet in many instances, from an obligation unto obedience to them. Our blessed Saviour applies himself, in the discharge of his prophetical office, with respect unto the end of the command, which is our holy obedience, unto both these, in the declaration of its excellency and efficacy.

And, — [1.] He declares the inward spiritual nature of the law, with its respect unto the most secret frames of our hearts and minds, with the least disorder or irregularity of our passions and affections. And then, — [2.] He declares the true sense of its commands, their nature, signification, and extent, vindicating them from all the corrupt and false glosses which then passed current in the church, whereby there was an abatement made of their efficacy and an indulgence granted unto the lusts of men. Thus they had, by their traditional interpretation, restrained the sixth commandment, "Thou shalt not kill," unto actual murder; and the seventh, "Thou shalt not commit adultery," unto actual uncleanness; — as some now would restrain the second commandment unto the making of images and worshipping them, excluding the primary intent of the precept, restraining all means and manners of worship unto divine institution. How, in his doctrine, he took off these corruptions we may see, Matt. v. 21, 22, 27, 28.

Thus he restored the law to its pristine crown, as the Jews have a tradition that it shall be done in the days of the Messiah. Herein did the Lord Christ place the beginning of his prophetical office and ministry, Matt. v., vi., vii. He opened, unveiled, explained, and vindicated, the preceptive part of the will of God before revealed, to the end that by a compliance therewith we should be holy. The full revelation of the mind and will of God, in the perfection and spirituality of the command, was reserved for Christ in the discharge of his office; and he gave it unto us that we might have a perfect and complete rule of holiness. This, therefore, was the immediate end of this work or duty of the office of Christ; and when we answer it not, we reject that great prophet which God hath sent; to which excision is so severely threatened.

(2.) The second part of this office, or of the discharge of it with respect unto the church of all ages, which takes in the ministry of the apostles, as divinely inspired by him, consisted in the revelation of those duties of holiness, which although they had a general foundation in the law, and the equity of them was therein established, yet could they never have been known to be duties in their especial nature, incumbent on us and necessary unto us, but by his teachings and instructions. Hence are they called old and new commandments in distinct senses. Such are faith in God through himself, brotherly love, denial of ourselves in taking up the cross, doing good for evil, with some others of the same kind; and how great a part of evangelical holiness consists in these things is known. Besides, he also teacheth us all those ordinances of worship wherein our obedience unto him belongs unto our holiness also, whereby it is enlarged and promoted. This, I say, is the nature and end of the prophetical office of Christ, wherein he acts towards us from God and in his name, as to the declaration of the will of God in his commands; and it is our holiness which is his only end and design therein. So it is summarily represented, Tit. ii. 11, 12.

There are three things considerable in the doctrine of obedience that Christ teacheth:— [1.] That it reacheth the heart itself, with all its inmost and secret actings, and that in the first place. The practice of most goes no farther but unto outward acts; the teachings of many go no farther, or at best unto the moderation of affections; but he, in the first place, requires the renovation of our whole souls, in all their faculties, motions, and actings, into the image of God, John iii. 3, 5; Eph. iv. 22–24. [2.] It is extensive. There is nothing in any kind pleasing to God, conformable to his mind, or compliant with his will, but he requires it; nothing crooked, or perverse, or displeasing to God, but it is forbidden by him. It is, therefore, a perfect rule of holiness and obedience. [3.] Clearness, perspicuity, and evidence of divine truth and authority in all.

[1.] Hereby, I say, the doctrine of Christ for universal obedience, in all the duties of it, comes to be absolute, every way complete and perfect. And it is a notable effect of the atheistical pride of men, that, pretending to design obedience (at least in moral duties) unto God, they betake themselves unto other rules and directions, as either more plain, or full, or efficacious, than those of the gospel, which are the teachings of Christ himself, as the great prophet and apostle sent of God to instruct us in our duty. Some go to the light of nature and the use of right reason (that is, their own) as their guide; and some add the additional documents of the philosophers. They think a saying of

Epictetus, or Seneca, or Arrianus, being wittily suited to their fancies and affections, to have more life and power in it than any precept of the gospel. The reason why these things are more pleasing unto them than the commands and instructions of Christ is because, proceeding from the spring of natural light, they are suited to the workings of natural fancy and understanding; but those of Christ, proceeding from the fountain of eternal spiritual light, are not comprehended in their beauty and excellency without a principle of the same light in us, guiding our understandings and influencing our affections. Hence, take any precept, general or particular, about moral duties, that is materially the same in the writings of philosophers and in the doctrine of the gospel, not a few prefer it as delivered in the first way before the latter. Such a contempt have men risen unto of Jesus Christ, the wisdom of God and the great prophet of the church! When he entered upon his office, the "voice came from the excellent glory, This is my beloved Son, hear him." This succeeded into the room of all those terrible appearances and dreadful preparations which God made use of in the giving of the law; for he gave the law by the ministry of angels, who being mere creatures, he manifested the dread of his own presence among them, to give authority unto their ministrations. But when he came to reveal his will under the gospel, it being to be done by him "in whom dwelleth all the fullness of the Godhead bodily," and who was intrusted himself with all divine power, he did no more but indigitate or declare which was the person, and give us a command in general to hear him. And this he did with respect unto what he had fixed before as a fundamental ordinance of heaven, — namely, that when he should raise up and send the great prophet of the church, whosoever would not hear him should be cut off from the people. A compliance, therefore, with this command, in hearing the voice of Christ, is the foundation of all holiness and gospel obedience. And if men will be moved neither with the wisdom, nor authority, nor goodness of God, in giving us this command and direction for our good; nor with the consideration of the endowments and faithfulness of Jesus Christ, the Son of God, in the discharge of his prophetical office; nor from the remembrance that it is he, and not Epictetus, or Seneca, or Plato, to whom at the last day they must give their account, so as to take him alone for their guide in all obedience unto God and duty among themselves, — they will find, when it is too late, that they have been mistaken in their choice.

Let us suppose, if you please, at present, for the sake of them who would have it so, that all our obedience consists in morality, or the duties of it, — which is the opinion of (as one well calls them) our "modern heathens," — from whence or whom shall we learn it, or to whom shall we go for teaching and instruction about it? Certainly, where the instruction or system of precepts is most plain, full, perfect, and free from mistakes; where the manner of teaching is most powerful and efficacious; and where the authority of the teacher is greatest and most unquestionable, — there we ought to apply ourselves to learn and be guided. In all these respects we may say of Christ, as Job said of God, "Who teacheth like him?" Job xxxvi. 22. Then, probably, shall we be taught of God, when we are taught by him. The commands and precepts of duties themselves which are given us by the light of nature, however improved by the wits and reasons of contemplative men, are many ways defective. For, —

1st. The utmost imaginations of men never reached unto that wherein the life and soul of holiness doth consist, — namely, the renovation of our lapsed nature into the image and likeness of God. Without this, whatever precepts are given about the moderation of affections and duties of moral holiness, they are lifeless, and will prove useless. And hence it is that by all those documents which were given by philosophers of old, the nature of no one individual person was ever renewed, what change soever was wrought on their conversation. But that this is plainly and directly required in the doctrine of obedience taught by Jesus Christ as the great prophet of the church, I have sufficiently proved in this whole discourse.

2dly. Very few of the precepts of it are certain, so as that we may take them for an undoubted and infallible rule. There are some general commands, I acknowledge, so clear in the light of nature as that no question can be made but that what is required in them is our duty to perform; such are they, that God is to be loved, that others are not to be injured, that everyone's right is to be rendered unto him, whereunto all reasonable creatures do assent at their first proposal; — and where any are found to live in an open neglect, or seem to be ignorant of them, their degeneracy into bestiality is open, and their sentiments not at all to be regarded. But go a little farther, and you will find all the great moralists at endless, uncertain disputes about the nature of virtue in general, about the offices and duties of it, about the rule and measure of their practice. In these disputes did most of them consume their lives, without any great endeavours to express their own notions in their conversations. And from the same reason in part it is, I suppose, that our present moralists seem to care for nothing but the name; virtue itself is grown to be a strange and uncouth thing. But what is commanded us by Jesus Christ, there is no room for the least hesitation whether it be an infallible rule for us to attend unto or no. Every precept of his about the meanest duty is equally certain, and [as] infallibly declarative of the nature and necessity of that duty, as those of the greatest, and that have most evidence from the light of nature. If once it appear that Christ requires any thing of us by his word, that he hath taught us any thing as the prophet of the church, there is no doubt remains with us whether it be our duty or no.

3dly. The whole rule of duties given by the most improved light of nature, setting aside those that are purely evangelical, which some despise, is obscure and partial. There are sundry moral duties, which I instanced in before, which the light of nature, as it remains in the lapsed, depraved condition of it, never extended itself to the discovery of. And this obscurity is evident from the differences that are about its precepts and directions. But now as the revelation made by Christ, and his commands therein, are commensurate unto universal obedience and gives bounds unto it, so that there is no duty of it but what he hath commanded, and it is sufficient to discharge the most specious pleas and pretences of any thing to be a duty towards God or man, by showing that it is not required by him, so his commands and directions are plain and evidently perspicuous. I dare challenge the greatest and most learned moralist in the world to give an instance of any one duty of morality, confirmed by the rules and directions of the highest and most contemplative moralist, that I will not show and evince is more plainly and clearly required by the Lord Christ in the gospel, and pressed on us by far more effectual motives than any they are acquainted withal. It is, therefore, the highest folly as well as wickedness for men to design, plead, or pretend the learning duties of obedience from others rather than from Christ, the prophet of the church.

[2.] The manner of teaching, as to power and efficacy, is also considerable unto this end. And concerning this also we may say, "Who teacheth like him?" There was such eminency in his personal ministry, whilst he was on the earth, as filled all men with admiration. Hence it is said that "he taught as one having authority, and not as the scribes," Matt. vii. 29; and another while "they wondered at the gracious words which proceeded out of his mouth," Luke iv. 22; and the very officers that were sent to apprehend him for preaching came away astonished, saying, "Never man spake like this man," John vii. 46. It is true, it was not the design of God that multitudes of that hardened generation should be converted by his personal ministry, John xii. 37–40, as having another to fulfil in them, by them, and upon them; yet it is evident from the gospel that there was θεῖον τί, a divine power and glory accompanying his ministerial instructions. Yet this is not that which I intend, but his continued and present teaching of the church by his word and Spirit. He gives such power and efficacy unto it as that by its effects everyday it demonstrates itself to be from God, being accompanied with the evidence and demonstration of a spiritual power put forth in it. This the experiences, consciences, and lives of multitudes, bear witness unto continually. They do, and will to eternity, attest what power his word hath had to enlighten their minds, to subdue their lusts, to change and renew their hearts, to relieve and comfort them in their temptations and distresses, with the like effects of grace and power.

What is in the manner of teaching by the greatest moralist, and what are the effects of it? Enticing words, smoothness and elegancy of speech, composed into snares for the affections and delight unto the fancy, are the grace, ornament, and life of the way or manner of their teaching. And hereof evanid satisfaction, temporary resolutions for a kind of compliance with the things spoken, with, it may be, some few perishing endeavours after some change of life, are the best effects of all such discourses. And so easy and gentle is their operation on the minds of men, that commonly they are delighted in by the most profligate and obstinate sinners; as is the preaching of them who act in the same spirit and from the same principles.

[3.] Whereas the last thing considerable in those whose instructions we should choose to give up ourselves unto is their authority, that must be left without farther plea to the consciences of all men, whether they have the higher esteem of the authority of Christ the Son of God, or of those others whom they do admire; and let them freely take their choice, so they will ingenuously acknowledge what they do.

Whereas, therefore, the great end of the prophetical office of Christ, in the revelation he made of the will of God in the Scriptures, in his personal ministry, and in the dispensation of his word and Spirit continued in the church, is our holiness and obedience unto God, I could not but remark upon the atheism, pride, and folly of those "modern heathens," who really, or in pretence, betake themselves to the light of nature and philosophical maxims for their guidance and direction, rather than to him who is designed of God to be the great teacher of the church. I deny not but that in the ancient moralists there are found many excellent documents concerning virtue and vice; but yet, having been, it may be, more conversant in their writings than most of those who pretend so highly unto their veneration, I fear not to affirm that as their sayings may be of use for illustration of the truth, which is infallibly learned another way, so take them alone, [and] they will sooner delight the minds and fancies of men than benefit or profit them as to the true ends of morality or virtue.

Thirdly, This, also, is one great end of the kingly power of Christ; for as such doth he subdue our enemies and preserve our souls from ruin. And those are our adversaries which fight against our spiritual condition and safety; such principally are our lusts, our sins, and our temptations, wherewith they are accompanied. These doth our Lord Christ subdue by his kingly power, quickening and strengthening in us, by his aids and supplies of grace, all principles of holy obedience. In brief, the work of Christ as a king may be reduced unto these heads:— 1. To make his subjects free; 2. To preserve them in safety, delivering their souls from deceit and violence; 3. In giving them prosperity, and increasing their wealth; 4. In establishing assured peace for them; 5. In giving them love among themselves; 6. In placing the interest and welfare of his kingdom in all their affections; 7. In eternally rewarding their obedience. And all these he doth principally by working grace and holiness in them, as might be easily demonstrated. I suppose none question but that the principal work of Christ towards us as our head and king is in making and preserving of us holy; I shall not, therefore, farther insist thereon.

It remains that we improve these considerations unto the confirmation of our present argument concerning the necessity of holiness.

And, first, it is hence evident how vain and fond a thing it is for any persons continuing in an unholy condition to imagine that they have any interest in Christ, or shall have any benefit by him. This is the great deceit whereby Satan, that enemy of the common salvation, hath ruined the generality of mankind who profess the Christian religion. The gospel openly declares a way of life and salvation by Jesus Christ This is thus far admitted by all who are called Christians, that they will allow of no other way for the same end unto competition with it; for I speak not of them who, being profligate and hardened in sins, are regardless of all future concernments, but I intend only such as in general have a desire to escape the damnation of hell, and to attain immortality and glory. And this they at least profess to do by Jesus Christ, as supposing that the things to this purpose mentioned in the gospel do belong unto them as well as unto others, because they also are Christians. But they consider not that there are certain ways and means whereby the virtue and benefit of all that the Lord Christ hath done for us are conveyed to the souls of men, whereby they are made partakers of them. Without these we have no concernment in what Christ hath done or declared in the gospel. If we expect to be saved by Christ, it must be by what he doth and hath done for us, as a priest, a prophet, and a king. But one of the principal ends of what he doth in all these is to make us holy; and if these be not effected in us, we can have no eternal benefit by any thing that Christ hath done or continueth to do as the mediator of the church.

Hence the miserable condition of the generality of those who are called Christians, who live in sin, and yet hope to be saved by the gospel, is greatly to be bewailed. They contract to themselves the guilt of the two greatest evils that any reasonable creatures are liable unto in this world; for, — 1. They woefully deceive and ruin their own souls. Their whole profession of the gospel is but a crying, "Peace, peace," when sudden destruction lies at the door. They "deny the Lord that bought them, and bring upon themselves swift destruction." They are bought and vindicated into the knowledge and profession of the truth, but in their works they deny him whom in words they own, — "whose damnation slumbereth not." For men to live in covetousness, sensuality, pride, ambition, pleasures, hatred of the power of godliness, and yet to hope for salvation by the gospel, is the most infallible way to hasten and secure their own eternal ruin. And, 2. They cast the greatest dishonour on Christ and the gospel that any persons are capable of casting on them. Those by whom the Lord Christ is rejected as a seducer and the gospel as a fable do not more (I may say, not so much) dishonour the one and the other than those do who, professing to own them both, yet continue to live and walk in an unholy condition: for as to the open enemies of Christ, they are judged and condemned already, and none have occasion to think the worse of him or the gospel for their opposition unto them; but for those others who profess to own them, they endeavour to represent the Lord Christ as a minister of sin, as one who hath procured indulgence unto men to live in their lusts and in rebellion against God, and the gospel as a doctrine of licentiousness and wickedness. What else can anyone learn from them concerning the one or the other? The whole language of their profession is, that Christ is such a Saviour, and the gospel such a law and rule, as that men loving sin and living in sin may be saved by them. This is that which hath reflected all kind of dishonour on Christian religion, and put a stop unto its progress in the world. These are they of whom our apostle makes his bitter complaint: Phil. iii. 18, 19, "Many walk, of whom I have told you often, and now tell you even weeping, that they are the enemies of the cross of Christ; whose end is destruction, whose god is their belly, and whose glory is in their shame, who mind earthly things." How many that are called Christians doth this character suit in these days! Whatever they think of themselves, they are "enemies of the cross of Christ," and do "tread under their feet the blood of the covenant."

Secondly, Let more serious professors be most serious in this matter. The apostle having given assurance of the certain salvation of all true believers, from the immutable purpose of God, presently adds, "Let every one that nameth the name of Christ depart from iniquity," 2 Tim. ii. 19; plainly intimating that without holiness, without a universal departure from iniquity, we cannot have the least evidence that we are interested in that assured condition. You name the name of Christ, profess an interest in him, and expect salvation by him; which way will you apply yourselves unto him? From which of his offices do you expect advantage? is it from his sacerdotal? Hath his blood purged your consciences from dead works that you should serve the living God? Are you cleansed, and sanctified, and made holy thereby? Are you redeemed out of the world by it, and from your vain conversation therein, after the customs and traditions of men? Are you by it dedicated unto God, and made his peculiar ones? If you find not these effects of the blood-shedding of Christ in and upon your souls and consciences, in vain will you expect those others of atonement, peace, and reconciliation with God, of mercy, pardon, justification, and salvation, which you look for. The priestly office of Christ hath its whole effects towards all on whom it hath any effect. Despisers of its fruits in holiness shall never have the least interest in its fruits in righteousness.

Is it from his actings as the great prophet of the church that you expect help and relief?

Have you effectually learned of him "to deny all ungodliness and worldly lusts, and to live soberly, righteously, and godly, in this present world?" Hath he taught you to be humble, to be meek, to be patient, to "hate the garment spotted with the flesh?" Hath he instructed you unto sincerity in all your ways, dealings, and whole conversation among men? Above all, hath he taught you, have you learned of him, to purify and cleanse your hearts by faith, to subdue your inward spiritual and fleshly lusts, to endeavour after a universal conformity unto his image and likeness? Do you find his doctrine effectual unto these ends? and are your hearts and minds cast into the mould of it? If it be so, your interest in him by his prophetical office is secured unto you. But if you say that you hear his voice in his word read and preached; that you have learned many mysteries and have attained much light or knowledge thereby, at least that you know the substance of the doctrine he hath taught so as that you can discourse of it; yea, and that you do many things or perform many duties according unto it; but cannot say that the effects before inquired after are wrought in you by his word and Spirit, — you lose the second expectation of an interest in Christ as mediator, or any advantage thereby.

Will you betake yourselves to the kingly office of Christ? and have you expectations on him by virtue thereof? You may do well to examine how he ruleth in you and over you. Hath he subdued your lusts, those enemies of his kingdom which fight against your souls? Hath he strengthened, aided, supported, assisted you by his grace, unto all holy obedience? And have you given up yourselves to be ruled by his word and Spirit, to obey him in all things, and to intrust all your temporal and eternal concernments unto his care, faithfulness, and power? If it be so, you have cause to rejoice, as those who have an assured concern in the blessed things of his kingdom. But if your proud, rebellious lusts do yet bear sway in you; if sin have dominion over you; if you continue to "fulfil the lusts of the flesh and of the mind;" if you walk after the fashions of this world, and not as obedient subjects of that kingdom of his which is not of this world, — deceive not yourselves any longer, Christ will be of no advantage unto you.

In these things lie the sum of our present argument. If the Lord Christ act no otherwise for our good but in and by his blessed offices of priest, prophet, and king; and if the immediate effect of the grace of Christ acting in all these offices towards us be our holiness and sanctification, — those in whom that effect is not wrought and produced have neither ground nor reason to promise themselves an interest in Christ, or any advantage by his mediation. For men to "name the name of Christ," to profess themselves Christians, or his disciples, to avow an expectation of mercy, pardon, life and salvation by him, and in the meantime to be in themselves worldly, proud, ambitious, envious, revengeful, haters of good men, covetous, living in divers lusts and pleasures, is a scandal and shame unto Christian religion, and unavoidably destructive to their own souls.

Chapter V - Necessity of holiness from our condition in this world

Necessity of holiness farther argued from our own state and condition in this world; with what is required of us with respect unto our giving glory to Jesus Christ.

V. Another argument for the necessity of holiness may be taken from the consideration of ourselves, and our present state and condition; for it is hereby alone that the vicious distemper of our nature is or can be cured. That our nature is fearfully and universally depraved by the entrance of sin, I have before declared and sufficiently confirmed, and I do not now consider it as to the disability of living unto God, or enmity unto him, which is come upon us thereby, nor yet as to the future punishment which it renders us obnoxious unto; but it is the present misery that is upon us by it, unless it be cured, which I intend. For the mind of man being possessed with darkness, vanity, folly, and instability; the will under the power of spiritual death, stubborn and obstinate; and all the affections carnal, sensual, and selfish; the whole soul being hurried off from God, and so out of its way, is perpetually filled with confusion and perplexing disorder. It is not unlike that description which Job gives of the grave: "A land of darkness, and of the shadow of death, without any order, and where the light is as darkness," chap. x. 21, 22. When Solomon set himself to search out the causes of all the vanity and vexation that is in the world, of all the troubles that the life of man is filled withal, he affirms that this was the sum of his discovery, "God made men upright, but they have found out many inventions," Eccles. vii. 29; that is, cast themselves into endless entanglements and confusions. What is sin in its guilt, is punishment in its power, yea, the greatest that men are liable unto in this world. Hence, God for the guilt of some sins penally gives many up to the power of others, Rom. i. 24, 26, 28; 2 Thess. ii. 11, 12. And this he doth, not only to secure and aggravate their condemnation at the last day, but to give them in this world a recompense of their folly in themselves; for there is no greater misery nor slavery than to be under the power of sin.

This proves the original depravation of our nature: The whole soul, filled with darkness, disorder, and confusion, being brought under the power of various lusts and passions, captivating the mind and will unto their interests, in the vilest drudgeries of servitude and bondage, no sooner doth the mind begin to act any thing suitably unto the small remainders of light in it, but it is immediately controlled by impetuous lusts and affections, which darken its directions and silence its commands. Hence is the common saying not so common as what is signified by it, —

"Video meliora proboque,
Deteriora sequor."
[Ovid. Metam., lib. vii. 20.]

Hence the whole soul is filled with fierce contradictions and conflicts, Vanity, instability, folly, sensual, irrational appetites, inordinate desires, self-disquieting and torturing passions, act continually in our depraved natures. See the account hereof, Rom. iii. 10–18. How full is the world of disorder, confusion, oppression, rapine, uncleanness, violence, and the like dreadful miseries! Alas! they are but a weak and imperfect representation of the evils that are in the minds of men by nature; for as they all proceed from thence, as our Saviour declares, Matt. xv. 18, 19, so the thousandth part of what is conceived therein is never brought forth and acted: "From whence come wars and fightings among you? come they not hence, even of your lusts that war in your members? Ye lust, and have not: ye kill, and desire to have, and cannot obtain: ye fight and war, yet ye have not," James iv. 1, 2. All evils proceed from the impetuous lusts of the minds of men; which, when they are acted unto the utmost, are as unsatisfied as they were at their first setting out. Hence the prophet Isaiah tells us that wicked men, under the power and disorder of depraved nature, are like "the troubled sea, when it cannot rest, whose waters cast up mire and dirt," and have "no peace," chap. lvii. 20, 21. The heart is in continual motion, is restless in its figments and imaginations, as the waters of the sea when it is stormy and troubled; and they are all evil, "only evil continually," Gen. vi. 5. Herein doth it "cast up mire and dirt." And those who seem to have the greatest advantages above others, in power and opportunity to give satisfaction unto their lusts, do but increase their own disquietness and miseries, Ps. lxix. 14: for as these things are evil in themselves and unto others, so they are penal unto those in whom they are, especially in whom they abound and reign; and if their breasts were opened, it would appear, by the confusion and horror they live in, that they are on the very confines of hell.

Hence is the life of man full of vanity, trouble, disappointments, vexations, and endless self-dissatisfactions; which those who were wise among the heathens saw, complained of, and attempted in vain reliefs against. All these things proceed from the depravation of our nature, and the disorder that is come upon us by sin; and as, if they are not cured and healed, they will assuredly issue in everlasting misery, so they are woeful and calamitous at present. True peace, rest, and tranquillity of mind, are strangers unto such souls. Alas! what are the perishing profits, pleasures, and satisfactions by them, which this world can afford? How unable is the mind of man to find out rest and peace in them or from them! They quickly satiate and suffocate in their enjoyment, and become to have no relish in their varieties, which only heighten present vanity, and treasure up provision for future vexation. We have, therefore, no greater interest in the world than to inquire how this disorder may be cured, and a stop put to this fountain of all abominations. What we intend will be cleared in the ensuing observations:—

1. It is true that some are naturally of a more sedate and quiet temper and disposition than others are. They fall not into such outrages and excesses of outward sins as others do; nay, their minds are not capable of such turbulent passions and affections as the most are possessed withal. These comparatively are peaceable, and useful to their relations and others. But yet their minds and hearts are full of darkness and disorder: for so it is with all by nature (as we have proved), who have not an almighty effectual cure wrought upon them; and the less troublesome waves they have on the surface, the more mire and dirt ofttimes they have at the bottom.

2. Education, convictions, afflictions, illuminations, hope of a righteousness of their own, love of reputation, engagements into the society of good men, resolutions for secular ends, with other means of the like kind, do often put great restraints upon the actings and ebullitions of the evil imaginations and turbulent affections of the minds of men; yea, the frame of the mind and the course of the life may be much changed by them, how, wherein, and how far, is not our present business to declare.

3. Notwithstanding all that may be effected by these means, or any other of like nature, the disease is uncured, the soul continues still in its disorder and in all inward confusion; for our original order, harmony, and rectitude, consisted in the powers and inclinations of our minds, wills, and affections, unto regular actings towards God as our end and reward. Hence proceeded all that order and peace which were in all their faculties and their actings. Whilst we continued in due order towards God, it was impossible that we should be otherwise in ourselves; but being by sin fallen off from God, having lost our conformity and likeness unto him, we fell into all the confusion and disorder before described. Wherefore, —

4. The only cure and remedy of this evil condition is by holiness; for it must be, and can be no otherwise, but by the renovation of the image of God in us, for from the loss hereof doth all the evil mentioned spring and arise. By this are our souls in some measure restored unto their primitive order and rectitude; and without this, attempts for inward peace, real tranquillity of mind, with due order in our affections, will be in vain attempted. It is the holy soul, the sanctified mind alone, that is composed into an orderly tendency towards the enjoyment of God. That which we aim at is what we are directed unto by our apostle, Eph. iv. 22–24. Our deliverance from the power of corrupt and deceitful lusts, which are the spring and cause of all the confusion mentioned, is by the renovation of the image of God in us, and no otherwise; and hence, unto all persons not in love with their lusts and ruin, ariseth a cogent argument and motive unto holiness. But sundry things may be objected hereunto; as, —

First, "That we do admit and maintain that in all sanctified persons there are yet certain remainders of our original depravation and disorder; that sin still abideth in believers; yea, that it works powerfully and effectually in them, leading them captive unto the law of sin. Hence ensue great and mighty wars and conflicts in the souls of regenerate persons that are truly sanctified. Herein they suffer so far as to groan, complain, and cry out for deliverance. 'The flesh lusteth against the spirit, and the spirit against the flesh; and these are contrary.' Wherefore, it doth not appear that this holiness doth so heal and cure the sinful distempers of our minds. On the other side, men supposed as yet under the power of sin, who have not that grace and holiness in the renovation of the image of God which is pleaded for, seem to have more peace and quietness in their minds. They have not that inward conflict which others complain of, nor those groans for deliverance; yea, they find satisfaction in their lusts and pleasures, relieving themselves by them against any thing that occasioneth their trouble."

Ans. 1. [As] for that peace and order which is pretended to be in the minds of men under the power of sin, and not sanctified, it is like that which is in hell and the kingdom of darkness. Satan is not divided against himself, nor is there such a confusion and disorder in his kingdom as to destroy it, but it hath a consistency from the common end of all that is in it; which is, an opposition unto God and all that is good. Such a peace and order there may be in an unsanctified mind. There being no active principle in it for God and that which is spiritually good, all works one way, and all its troubled streams have the same course. But yet they continually "cast up mire and dirt." There is only that peace in such minds which the "strong man armed," that is, Satan, keeps his goods in, until a stronger than he comes to bind him. And if anyone think that peace and order to be sufficient for him, wherein his mind in all its faculties acts uniformly against God, or for self, sin, and the world, without any opposition or contradiction, he may find as much in hell when he comes there.

2. There is a difference between a confusion and a rebellion. Where confusion is in a state, all rule or government is dissolved, and everything is let loose unto the utmost disorder and evil; but where the rule is firm and stable, there may be rebellions that may give some parts and places disturbance and damage, but yet the whole state is not disordered thereby. So is it in the condition of a sanctified soul on account of the remainders of sin; there may be rebellion in it, but there is no confusion. Grace keeps the rule in the mind and heart firm and stable, so that there is peace and assurance unto the whole state of the person, though lusts and corruptions will be rebelling and warring against it. The divine order, therefore, of the soul consisting in the rule of grace, subordinating all to God in Christ, is never overthrown by the rebellion of sin at any time, be it never so vigorous or prevalent. But in the state of unsanctified persons, though there be no rebellion, yet is there nothing but confusion. Sin hath the rule and dominion in them; and however men may be pleased with it for a season, yet is it nothing but a perfect disorder, because it is a continual opposition to God. It is a tyranny that overthrows all law, and rule, and order, with respect unto our last and chiefest end.

3. The soul of a believer hath such satisfaction in this conflict as that its peace is not ordinarily disturbed, and is never quite overthrown by it. Such a person knows sin to be his enemy, knows its design, with the aids and assistances which are prepared for him against its deceit and violence; and, considering the nature and end of this contest, is satisfied with it. Yea, the greatest hardships that sin can reduce a believer unto do but put him to the exercise of those graces and duties wherein he receiveth great spiritual satisfaction. Such are repentance, humiliation, godly sorrow, self-abasement and abhorrency, with fervent outcries for deliverance. Now, although these things seem to have that which is grievous and dolorous prevailing in them, yet the graces of the Spirit of God being acted in them, they are so suited unto the nature of the new creature, and so belong unto the spiritual order of the soul, that it finds secret satisfaction in them all. But the trouble others meet withal in their own hearts and minds on the account of sin is from the severe reflections of their consciences only; and they receive them no otherwise but as certain presages and predictions of future and eternal misery.

4. A sanctified person is secured of success in this conflict, which keeps blessed peace and order in his soul during its continuance. There is a twofold success against the rebellious actings of the remainders of indwelling sin:—(1.) In particular instances; (2.) In the whole cause. And in both these have we sufficient assurance of success, if we be not wanting unto ourselves.

(1.) For suppose the contest be considered with respect unto any particular lust and corruption, and that in conjunction with some powerful temptation, we have sufficient and blessed assurance, that, abiding in the diligent use of the ways and means assigned unto us, and the improvement of the assistance provided in the covenant of grace, we shall not so fail of actual success as that lust should conceive, bring forth, and finish sin, James i. 15. But if we be wanting unto ourselves, negligent in our known duties and principal concerns, it is no wonder if we are sometimes cast into disorder, and foiled by the power of sin. But, — (2.) As to the general success in the whole cause, — namely, that sin shall not utterly deface the image of God in us, nor absolutely or finally ruin our souls, which is its end and tendency, — we have the covenant faithfulness of God (which will not fail us) for our security, Rom. vi. 14.

Wherefore, notwithstanding this opposition and all that is ascribed unto it, there is peace and order preserved by the power of holiness in a sanctified mind and soul.

Secondly, But it will be farther objected, "That many professors who pretend highly unto sanctification and holiness, and whom you judge to be partakers of them, are yet peevish, froward, morose, unquiet in their minds, among their relations and in the world; yea, much outward vanity and disorder (which you make tokens of the internal confusion of the minds of men and of the power of sin) do either proceed from them or are carried on by them. And where, then, is the advantage pretended, that should render holiness so indispensably necessary unto us?"

Ans. If there are any such, the more shame for them, and they must bear their own judgment. These things are diametrically opposite to the work of holiness and the "fruit of the Spirit," Gal. v. 22; and, therefore, I say, — 1. That many, it may be, are esteemed holy and sanctified, who indeed are not so. Though I will judge no man in particular, yet I had rather pass this judgment on any man, that he hath no grace, than that, on the other hand, grace doth not change our nature and renew the image of God in us. 2. Many who are really holy may have the double disadvantage, first, to be under such circumstances as will frequently draw out their natural infirmities, and then to have them greatened and heightened in the apprehension of them with whom they have to do; which was actually the case of David all his days, and of Hannah, 1 Sam. i. 6, 7. I would be far from giving countenance unto the sinful distempers of any, but yet I doubt not but that the infirmities of many are represented, by envy and hatred of profession, unto an undeserved disadvantage. 3. Wherever there is the seed of grace and holiness, there an entrance is made on the cure of all those sinful distempers, yea, not only of the corrupt lusts of the flesh, that are absolutely evil and vicious in their whole nature, but even of those natural infirmities and distempers of peevishness, moroseness, inclination to anger and passion, unsteadiness in resolution, which lust is apt to possess, and use unto evil and disorderly ends. And I am pressing the necessity of holiness, — that is, of the increase and growth of it, — that this work may be carried on to perfection, and that so, through the power of the grace of the gospel, that great promise may be accomplished which is recorded, Isa. xi. 6–9.,And as, when a wandering, juggling impostor, who pretended to judge of men's lives and manners by their physiognomy, beholding Socrates, pronounced him, from his countenance, a person of a flagitious, sensual life, the people derided his folly, who knew his sober, virtuous conversation, but Socrates excused him, affirming that such he had been had he not bridled his nature by philosophy; how much more truly may it be said of multitudes, that they had been eminent in nothing but untoward distempers of mind, had not their souls been rectified and cured by the power of grace and holiness!

I find there is no end of arguments that offer their service to the purpose in hand; I shall, therefore, waive many, and those of great importance, attended with an unavoidable cogency, and shut up this discourse with one which must not be omitted:— In our holiness consists the principal part of that revenue of glory and honour which the Lord Christ requireth and expecteth from his disciples in this world. That he doth require this indispensably of us is, I suppose, out of question amongst us, although the most who are called Christians live as if they had no other design but to cast all obloquies, reproach, and shame on him and his doctrine. But if we are indeed his disciples, he hath bought us with a price, and we are not our own, but his, and that to glorify him in soul and body, because they are his, 1 Cor. vi. 19, 20. He died for us, that we should not live unto ourselves, but unto him that so died for us, and by virtue of whose death we live, 2 Cor. v. 15; Rom. xiv. 7–9. "He gave himself for us, that he might redeem us from all iniquity, and purify unto himself a peculiar people, zealous of good works," Tit. ii. 14. But we need not to insist hereon. To deny that we ought to glorify and honour Christ in the world, is to renounce him and the gospel. The sole inquiry is, how we may do so, and what he requireth of us to that purpose?

Now, the sum of all that the Lord Christ expects from us in this world may be reduced unto these two heads:— 1. That we should live holily to him; 2. That we should suffer patiently for him. And in these things alone is he glorified by us. The first he expecteth at all times and in all things; the latter on particular occasions, as we are called by him thereunto. Where these things are, where this revenue of glory is paid in and returned unto him, he repents not of his purchase, nor of the invaluable price he hath paid for us, yea, says, "The lines are fallen unto me in pleasant places; yea, I have a goodly heritage;" which are the words of Christ concerning the church, which is his lot, and the "portion of his inheritance," Ps. xvi.

6. Now, amongst many others, we shall consider but one way whereby we glorify the Lord Christ by our holy obedience, and whence also it will appear how much we dishonour and reproach him when we come short thereof.

The Lord Christ, coming into the world as the mediator between God and man, wrought and accomplished a mighty work amongst us; and what he did may be referred to three heads:— 1. The life which he led; 2. The doctrine which he taught; and, 3. The death which he underwent. Concerning all these, there ever was a great contest in the world, and it is yet continued. And on the part of the world, it is managed under a double appearance: for some openly have traduced his life as unholy, his doctrine as foolish, and his death as justly deserved; which was the sense of the Pagan world and the apostate Judaical church of old, as it is of many at this day: others allow them to pass with some approbation, pretending to own what is taught in the gospel concerning them, but in fact and practice deny any such power and efficacy in them as is pretended, and without which they are of no virtue; which is the way of carnal gospellers, and all idolatrous, superstitious worshippers among Christians. And of late there is risen up amongst us a generation who esteem all that is spoken concerning him to be a mere fable. In opposition hereunto, the Lord Christ calls all his true disciples to bear witness and testimony unto the holiness of his life, the wisdom and purity of his doctrine, the efficacy of his death to expiate sin, to make atonement and peace with God, with the power of his whole mediation to renew the image of God in us, to restore us unto his favour, and to bring us unto the enjoyment of him. This he calls all his disciples to avow unto and express in the world; and by their so doing is he glorified (and no otherwise) in a peculiar manner. A testimony is to be given unto and against the world, that his life was most holy, his doctrine most heavenly and pure, his death most precious and efficacious; and, consequently, that he was sent of God unto his great work, and was accepted of him therein. Now, all this is no otherwise done but by obedience unto him in holiness, as it is visible and fruitful; for, —

1. We are obliged to profess that the life of Christ is our example. This, in the first place, are we called unto, and every Christian doth virtually make that profession. No man takes that holy name upon him, but the first thing he signifies thereby is, that he makes the life of Christ his pattern, which it is his duty to express in his own; and he who takes up Christianity on any other terms doth woefully deceive his own soul. How is it, then, that we may yield a revenue of glory herein? How may we bear testimony unto the holiness of his life against the blasphemies of the world and the unbelief of the most, who have no regard thereunto? Can this be any otherwise done but by holiness of heart and life, by conformity to God in our souls, and living unto God in fruitful obedience? Can men devise a more effectual expedient to cast reproach upon him than to live in sin, to follow divers lusts and pleasures, to prefer the world and present things before eternity, and, in the meantime, to profess that the life of Christ is their example, as all unholy professors and Christians do? Is not this to bear witness with the world against him, that indeed his life was unholy? Surely it is high time for such persons to leave the name of Christians or the life of sin. It is, therefore, in conformity alone to him, in the holiness we are pressing after, that we can give him any glory on the account of his life being our example.

2. We can give him no glory unless we bear testimony unto his doctrine that it is holy, heavenly, filled with divine wisdom and grace, as we make it our rule. And there is no other way whereby this may be done but by holy obedience, expressing the nature, end, and usefulness of it, Tit. ii. 11, 12. And, indeed, the holy obedience of believers, as hath been declared at large before, is a thing quite of another kind than any thing in the world which, by the rules, principles, and light of nature, we are directed unto or instructed in. It is spiritual, heavenly; mysterious, filled with principles and actings of the same kind with those whereby our communion with God in glory unto eternity shall be maintained. Now, although the life of evangelical holiness be, in its principle, form, and chief actings, secret and hidden, hid with Christ in God from the eyes of the world, so that the men thereof neither see, nor know, nor discern the spiritual life of a believer, in its being, form, and power; yet there are always such evident appearing fruits of it as are sufficient for their conviction that the rule of it, which is the doctrine of Christ alone, is holy, wise, and heavenly. And multitudes in all ages have been won over unto the obedience of the gospel, and faith in Christ Jesus, by the holy, fruitful, useful conversation of such as have expressed the power and purity of his doctrine in this kind.

3. The power and efficacy of the death of Christ, as for other ends, so to "purify us from all iniquity," and to "purge our conscience from dead works, that we may serve the living God," is herein also required. The world, indeed,

sometimes riseth unto that height of pride and contemptuous atheism as to despise all appearance and profession of purity; but the truth is, if we are not cleansed from our sins in the blood of Christ, if we are not thereby purified from iniquity, we are an abomination unto God, and shall be objects of his wrath forever. However, the Lord Christ requireth no more of his disciples in this matter, unto his glory, but that they profess that his blood cleanseth them from their sins, and evidence the truth of it by such ways and means as the gospel hath appointed unto that end. If their testimony herein unto the efficacy of his death be not received, be despised by the world, and so at present no apparent glory redound unto him thereby, he is satisfied with it, as knowing that the day is coming wherein he will call over these things again, when the rejecting of this testimony shall be an aggravation of condemnation unto the unbelieving world.

I suppose the evidence of this last argument is plain, and exposed unto all; it is briefly this: Without the holiness prescribed in the gospel, we give nothing of that glory unto Jesus Christ which he indispensably requireth. And if men will be so sottishly foolish as to expect the greatest benefits and advantages by the mediation of Christ, — namely, pardon of sin, salvation, life, and immortality, — whilst they neglect and refuse to give him any revenue of glory for all he hath done for them, we may bewail their folly, but cannot prevent their ruin. He saves us freely by his grace; but he requires that we should express a sense of it, in ascribing unto him the glory that is his due. And let no man think this is done in wordy expressions; it is no otherwise effected but by the power of a holy conversation, "showing forth the praises of him who hath called us out of darkness into his marvellous light." Nay, there is more in it also; if anyone profess himself to be a Christian, — that is, a disciple of Jesus Christ, to follow the example of his life, to obey his doctrine, to express the efficacy of his death, — and continue in an unholy life, he is a false traitor to him, and gives in his testimony on the side of the world against him and all that he hath done for us. And it is indeed the flagitious lives of professed Christians that have brought the life, doctrine, and person of our Lord Jesus Christ into contempt in the world. And I advise all that read or hear of these things diligently and carefully to study the gospel, that they may receive thence an evidence of the power, truth, glory, and beauty of Christ and his ways; for he that should consider the conversation of men for his guide will be hardly able to determine which he should choose, whether to be a Pagan, a Mohammedan, or a Christian. And shall such persons, by reason of whom the name of Christ is dishonoured and blasphemed continually, expect advantage by him or mercy from him? Will men think to live in sensuality, pride, ambition, covetousness, malice, revenge, hatred of all good men, and contempt of purity, and yet to enjoy life, immortality, and glory by Christ? Who can sufficiently bewail the dreadful effects of such a horrid infatuation? God teach us all duly to consider, that all the glory and honour of Jesus Christ in the world, with respect unto us, depends on our holiness, and not on any other thing either that we are, have, or may do! If, therefore, we have any love unto him, any spark of gratitude for his unspeakable love, grace, condescension, sufferings, with the eternal fruits of them, any care about or desire of his glory and honour in the world; if we would not be found the most hateful traitors at the last day unto his crown, honour, and dignity; if we have any expectation of grace from him or advantage by him here or hereafter, — let us labour to be "holy in all manner of conversation," that we may thereby adorn his doctrine, express his virtues and praises, and grow up into conformity and likeness unto him, who is the first-born and image of the invisible God.

Μόνῳ Θεῷ σωτῆρι δόξα!

www.ingramcontent.com/pod-product-compliance
Lightning Source LLC
Chambersburg PA
CBHW060321100426
42812CB00003B/837

* 9 7 8 1 7 7 3 5 6 4 0 2 9 *